Eschatology:

A History of the Global Future

Volume 5

Rochelle Ray

Spring Bud Media, 2025
1st edition
Paperback ISBN: 978-1-966579-07-6
Kindle ASIN: B0F1KS7MB9

*To God the Father,
God the Son Jesus Christ,
and God the Holy Spirit,
for developing this perfect, awesome,
magnificent, cosmic and eternal plan
and for pouring out on me,
more love than I can possibly receive*

To my sister and friends for their encouragement

*To my husband who provided this opportunity
for researching and for writing*

Eschatology: A History of the Global Future
Volume 5

A Biblical Chronology of Eschatology,
the Apocalypse, Last Things, and End of the Era Events:
What the Bible and the Prophets Said About the Era of the
Time of Jacob's Trouble,
Reestablishment of the Nation of Israel, Prophecies of Daniel,
John's Revelation,
Beasts, Seals, Trumpets, Bowls, Plagues, Battles, etc.
Ordered by Scripture, with Commentary

Book 1: Loss of the Perfection of the Original Creation, Era of the Time of Jacob's Trouble, Biblical Study Notes, God's Revelation and the Conflict of Revelation with Evolutionary Theory, This Cosmic Conflict's Beginning, The Author of Rebellion Against God the Creator, Deception of the First Woman and Rebellion of the First Man, God the Creator's First Covenant Agreements, Development and Growth of the Red Dragon / Serpent / Satan, Inc. and the Development of the Plan for Fully Establishing the Kingdom of Satan, Inc. / Kingdom of Man on Earth and in Heaven, The Problem of a Broken World and Broken Relationships, Corruption of the Human Lineage, Establishment of the Covenant Lineage, Plan for Redemption and Reclamation and Regeneration, Seasons to Mark Time, Fight Against Spiritual Force of Evil

Book 2: Major Prophecies of the Prophets of the Old Testament / Tanakh Concerning the Nation of Israel, Daniel's Four Beasts, Daniel's Seventy Sevens and the Seventieth Seven, Gospels' Presentation of Jesus Christ, Priest of the Order of Melchizedek, Two Messiahs or Two Visitations, Nation of Israel's Rejection of Jesus as Promised and Prophesied Messiah, Times of the Gentiles, Holy Spirit in the Book of Revelation, John's Book of Revelation, Jesus Christ's Message to the Angels of the Seven Churches, Other Messages Concerning This Historical Era

Book 3: God's Revelation for Our Generation, Jesus Christ's Revelation to John the Apostle, Responsibilities of the

Followers of the Lamb During the Era of the Time of Jacob's Trouble, Purpose for this Era, The Red Dragon and the Three Predominate Beast and the Three Women of Revelation, Allies of the Rebellion / Antichrist System / Unholy Trinity – Red Dragon and Beast of the Sea and Beast of the Earth

Book 4: Prophetic Importance of the Use of Specific Numbers, Problems with Rapture Theology, As It Was in the Days Before Noah, God's Plan for the Restoration of Nations and the Restoration of the Nation of Israel in Preparation for Jesus' Return, Sealing of the 144,000 Israelites and of the 144,000 Followers of the Lamb, Signs in the Heavens, Timeline Overview for the Era of the Time of Jacob's Trouble, Daniel's Seventieth Seven, First Half of the Era of the Time of Jacob's Trouble, Seven Seals, Seven Trumpets, Instructions of Three Angels, Events on the Temple Mount in Jerusalem Israel and the Resumption and Suspension of Animal Sacrifices

Book 5: Second Portion of the Era of the Time of Jacob's Trouble Begins, Red Dragon / Serpent / Satan, Inc. Hurled to Earth, War Against the People of Israel, Two Witnesses from Heaven, Abomination of Desolation Events, Activity of the Beast of the Sea and Beast of the Earth, Mark of the Beasts System, Miracles Performed Through the Followers of the Lamb / Jesus Christ

Book 6: Significance of Historical Events for the Second Portion of the Era of the Time of Jacob's Trouble and for the Finale for the Era of the Time of Jacob's Trouble, Ministry of the Two Witnesses, Third Heavenly Sign and Consecration of God's Temple in Heaven, Resumption of Animal Sacrifices, Israel's Rejection of Jesus Christ as the Promised and Prophesied Messiah, Flooding in the Land of Israel, People of Israel Recognize Jesus Christ as Promised and Prophesied Messiah, God Most High Remembers Israel and Fights on Israel's Side, Red Dragon / Serpent / Satan, Inc. Pursues the Followers of the Lamb, Three Nations Conquered, Assassination and Death of the Two Witnesses and the Commencement of the Events for the Finale for the Era of the Time of Jacob's Trouble – Final Seventy Five Days, Preparation for the Glorious Return of Jesus Christ, Preparation for the Destruction of the Allies of the Rebellion and the Full Establishment of the Kingdom of Heaven on Earth

Book 7: The Three Women of the Book of Revelation, Description of the Great Prostitute / Mystery Babylon the Great!, Description of the Scarlet Beast of Revelation 17, Relationship of the Great Prostitute / Mystery Babylon the Great! and the Scarlet Beast

Book 8: Scarlet Beast, The Abyss, Historical Development of the Scarlet Beast, Seven / Eight Pope Kings, Eighth King Beast, Relationships Between Prophetic Beasts and Heads and Horns

Book 9: Order of the Events for the Finale for the Era of the Time of Jacob's Trouble Required for the Destruction of the Allies of the Rebellion, Accomplishment of the Mystery of God and the Little Scroll, Sounding of the Seventh Trumpet / Pouring Out of the Seven Bowls of God Most High's Wrath / Seven Last Plagues, Complete Union of the Great Prostitute / Mystery Babylon the Great! with the Scarlet Beast, Judgment and Destruction of Mystery Babylon the Great!, Ten Horns / Ten Kings Given Power for One Hour, Gathering of the Armies of the Nations of the Earth to Make War Against the Nation of Israel and Jesus Christ, Fall Feasts as Prophecy Documenting the Return of Jesus Christ, Necessity of the Practice of the Sacrificial System

Book 10: Order of the Events for the Finale for the Era of the Time of Jacob's Trouble Required for the Destruction of the Allies of the Rebellion, Immediate Events that Accompany the Return of Jesus Christ, Harvest of the Earth, Resurrection of God's Holy People, Reunion of the Kingdom of Heaven with Earth, Jesus Christ Prepares for the Final Battle of this Age, The Day of the Lord / Day of Atonement / Yom Kippur, Events for the Day of the Lord, Siege of Jerusalem, Jesus Christ Defeats the Enemies of God Most High, Destruction of Mystery Babylon the Great!, Gathering of the Grapes, Beast of the Earth and Beast of the Sea Captured, Books Opened and Closed, Cleanup of the Dead, Everlasting Kingdom of Heaven Permeates the Earth, Rewards for God's Holy People

Table of Contents

Table of Contents 6

SECOND HALF OF THE ERA OF THE TIME OF JACOB'S TROUBLE BEGINS – PERIOD OF EXACTLY 1,260 DAYS / 42 MONTHS / 3 ½ YEARS   14

The Measurement of Time for the Era of the Time of Jacob's Trouble   14

Timespan for the second half of the era of the time of Jacob's Trouble: time, times and half a time / half of the seventieth seven / forty two months / one thousand two hundred sixty days – Daniel 7:25, 9:26b-27, 12:5-7, 12:11-12, Revelation 11:2-5, 12: 12:6, 12:14, 13:5-8, 13:11-12   15

Timespan for the finale for the era of the time of Jacob's Trouble that will follow the second half of the era of the time of Jacob's Trouble – Daniel 12:11-12   24

The second half of the era of the time of Jacob's Trouble, as the conclusion of six thousand years of waiting for the arrival of messiah / the Lamb / Jesus Christ to defeat the enemies of God Most High and of the kingdom of heaven, and bring lasting peace and freedom to the people of Israel and to the world   26

Events associated with the sounding of the first six of the seven trumpets   27

The General Order of Events for the Second Half of the Era of the Time of Jacob's Trouble   33

The Red Dragon / Serpent / Satan, Inc. Being Hurled to Earth   34

Jesus Christ's teaching on the expulsion of Satan and the rebellious angels from heaven, and the authority that the followers of the Lamb / Jesus Christ will have over the rebellious angels   50

The Roman Catholic Church's preparatory plan for receiving the 'stars' / rebellious / fallen angels as they physically land on earth   52

The Red Dragon / Serpent / Satan, Inc. Makes War with the People and Nation of Israel – Revelation 12   61

The Old Testament / Tanakh prophet Jeremiah's message of restoration of the people of Israel in the land of Israel, and the preparation of the nation of Israel for the arrival of their promised and prophesied messiah – Jeremiah 30:3-9, etc.   66

The instruction for the people of Israel on how to respond to this
  war – Matthew 24:15-25, Mark 13:14-23   69
The People of Israel Will Be Cared for by God – Hosea 2:14-15,
  Revelation 12:6, 12:13-14, etc.   74

The Representatives of the Two Different Kingdoms Will Converge Upon the Temple Mount and the Future Abomination of Desolation Event will Take Place – the two witnesses, Revelation 11:1-14 and the two beasts, Revelation 13   **77**

The Two Witnesses From Heaven – Revelation 11:1-14   **81**
  Moses (1526 to 1406 BC (fl. c. 1447 to 1406 BC))   84
    Moses' death – or Moses' ascension into heaven while alive? 86
    Moses as a humble man – Numbers 12:3   89
    Moses as the master of plagues – Exodus 7-8, Revelation 11:6 90
    Moses' unfinished work   91
      Moses' staff and the ark of the covenant   93
    The Law and the prophets: Moses and Elijah – Malachi 4:1-6   94
  Elijah (c. 900 to c. 848 BC (fl. 875 to c. 848 BC)) – prophet of Israel
       95
    The significance of rain and drought as a communication device
      of God Most High   104
  The possibility of the two witnesses being Enoch and Elijah   105
  The mission of the two witnesses / two olive branches – Zechariah
    4   106
  The importance of sending two witnesses   111
  The temple court in the possession of the Gentiles for forty two
    months – Revelation 11:2   114
  The opposition against the two witnesses – Revelation 11:1-14 117
  The supernatural authority and power of the two witnesses   123
  The assassination, death, resurrection and ascension of the two
    witnesses   126

Abomination of Desolation Events – Past and Future   **126**
  The purpose of the future abomination of desolation event   128
  Relocating the headquarters of the apostate baal / mystery /
    mythology religion, global governance, global economic
    structure and global theoterrorism, to the temple mount of
    God's holy city   132
  The requirement of a temple in Jerusalem as the site for the
    abomination of desolation   134
    God Most High's temple as a representation of the union of the
      relationship between God the Father, Jesus Christ the
      bridegroom and God's holy people the bride, and the
      traditional Jewish marriage protocol   136

The promise made in the Garden of Eden / garden of God / paradise to send the promised and prophesied messiah, and the red dragon / serpent / Satan, Inc.'s need to supply a facsimile candidate to fulfill that prophecy	137
Daniel's vision of the ram and the shaggy goat – Daniel 8	138
The future abomination of desolation event as described in Daniel's vision of the seventy 'sevens' – Daniel 9:20-27	146
Daniel's prayer life	149
The era of hate against God's holy people, truly begins	154
God Most High's provision for the followers of the lamb / Jesus Christ during the ministry of the two witnesses and the second half of the era of the time of Jacob's Trouble	157
The Old Testament / Tanakh prophet Daniel's description of prerecorded history prior to the first abomination of desolation event, and Daniel's description of the king that will exalt himself who will accomplish the future abomination of desolation event – Daniel 11	159
Historical details that provided context and foundation for the first abomination of desolation event, as prerecorded by Daniel – Daniel 11:1-35	167
Timeline from Darius the Mede in 530 BC to the Third Jewish Roman War / Third Jewish Revolt / Bar Kokhba (son of a star) revolt (132 – 136 AD)	170
Why was John the Baptist a prophet, and not a priest in the temple like his father Zechariah?	211
Jesus celebrated the feast of dedication / Hanukah	213
Various views for the interpretation of the 'second abomination of desolation' event	216
Inspirational / spiritual / allegorical interpretation	217
Idealist interpretation	217
Preterist interpretation	218
Preterist possibilities for the 'second abomination of desolation'	225
Timeline from the Hasmonean dynasty through the Bar Kokhba Revolt	231
Timeline from the Hasmonean dynasty through the reign of Herod the Great	232
Selected Members of Herod the Great's Family Tree	246
First generation	246
Second generation	246
Third generation	248
Fourth generation	251
Fifth generation	253
Timeline from after Herod the Great, to the First Jewish Roman War 66-73 AD	254

Herod Archelaus	254
Herod Antipas	255
Philip the tetrarch	256
Caligula / Gaius Julius Caesar Augustus Germanicus, his order to establish his statue in Jerusalem, and beyond	258
The possibility of the First Jewish Roman War of 66 to 73 AD as the fulfillment of Daniel 11 29-12:12, and the prophecy of Jesus Christ concerning the future abomination of desolation event	269
Timeline for the First Jewish Roman War 66 – 73 AD	273
Timeline:	275
The era of the Roman emperor Hadrian (fl. 117 to 138 AD) and the Third Jewish Roman War / Third Jewish Revolt / Bar Kokhba (son of a star) revolt (132 – 136 AD)	284
Historicist interpretation	286
Futurist / literal interpretation	290
The inspirational / spiritual / allegorical, idealist, and preterist problem of the establishment of the nationhood of Israel in 1948	294
The possibility of a historical past event as fulfilling the criteria of the prophecies concerning the future abomination of desolation event	296

The Future Abomination of Desolation Scheduled for the Era of the Time of Jacob's Trouble   **298**

The religious, political, economic, social and cultural requirements for the future abomination of desolation event	303
Temple must be present and the beast of the earth must have authority over temple to provide leadership for the future abomination of desolation event – Daniel 7:25, 8:24-25, 9:27, 11:42-43, 12:7, 12:11-12, Revelation 11:3, 12:6, 12:14, 13:5, 13:8-13).	321
The fully consecrated, functional and operational temple sacrificial system, halted	328
Set at the right time in history	330
Rebellion against God must be prevalent	332
Idolatry will prevail	334
People will expect signs, wonders and miracles as proof of the beast of the earth's divinity and sovereignty.	337
The sign of Jonah that Jesus Christ offered – Matthew 16:1-4, Luke 11:29-32	344
Government sponsored persecution of those who believe in Yahweh / the Lord - Daniel 8:20-26, 11:31-33, 12:1, Amos 8:1-	

12, Zephaniah 1:14-18, Matthew 24:21, Mark 13:17-19, Luke
21:23, Romans 2:5-11, Revelation 12: 347
God Most High cutting the days short, and Jesus Christ's
instruction for dealing with the onslaught of persecution
that will begin with the future abomination of desolation
event – Matthew 10:21-23a, 24:15-25, Mark 13:14-20, Luke
21:20-24, John 16:2-4 355
Timing and duration of the abomination of desolation events 360
The understanding of the Old Testament / Tanakh prophet
Daniel (fl. 605 to 530 BC) – a prophet of Judah, of the
marking of time by the future abomination of desolation
event, for further events 369
Paul's instruction concerning the approaching return of messiah
/ the Lamb / Jesus Christ 373
The purpose of the future abomination of desolation event 374
To separate people from God Most High 377
To destroy the people of God: the people of Israel and the
followers of the Lamb 379
Composite of the prophesied requirements for the future
abomination of desolation event – Daniel 7:25, 8:9-14, 8:23-
26, 9:26-27, 11:29-45, 12:1-12, Matthew 24:15-28, Mark
13:14-22, Revelation 13:11-18 382

**The Two Beasts of Revelation 13: The Beast of the Sea and the
Beast of the Earth – Revelation 13** **392**
The beast of the sea / false prophet / beast from the Abyss /
eighth king beast begins his forty two months reign of
supernatural power and authority – Revelation 13 392
The little horn / eleventh king / final horn on the shaggy goat /
prince who is to come / king that will exalt himself / beast of
the earth / final world ruler revealed, and begins sharing the
supernatural power and authority of the beast of the sea –
Revelation 13 401
The identity of the beast of the earth revealed with the future
abomination of desolation event and his activity at that
time 404
Temple sacrifice discontinued 417
The red dragon / serpent / Satan, Inc.'s magic, sorcery, occult
practices, illusion, dark arts, etc., used to support the
supernatural power and authority of the kingdom of Satan,
Inc. / kingdom of man – Revelation 16:12-16 422
The two beasts of Revelation 13 use of magic, sorcery, occult
practices, illusion, dark arts, etc. 429
The beast of the sea / false prophet / beast from the Abyss /
eighth king beast's use of magic, sorcery, occult practices,

illusion, dark arts, etc. - Revelation 13:1-7, 16:12-16, 18:23c 430

The beast of the earth's magic, sorcery, occult practices, illusion, dark arts, etc., signs and wonders – Daniel 8:23-25, 2 Thessalonians 2:9-11, Revelation 13:13-15, 16:12-16, 19:19-21 433

The beast of the earth animates the idol / image of the beast of the sea – Revelation 13:11-18 437

The technology available for making the idol / image of the beast of the sea effective in its task – gene editing, artificial intelligence (AI), implants / Internet of Bodies (IoB), ability to hack humans 441

Daniel's understanding of the methodology of the plan of the final horn on the shaggy goat and of the king that will exalt himself – Daniel 8:23-25, 11:36, 11:39c 445

John the Revelator's understanding of the methodology of the plan of the two beasts of Revelation 13 and the implications of bringing the idol / image of the beast of the sea 'to life' 446

Modern evolutionary theory's cosmology, omega point, noosphere (sphere of human cognitive process), etc., and its application within the idol / image of the beast of the sea 448

Nebuchadnezzar's compulsory worship of his own image of gold and the futility of worshiping an idol / image instead of worshiping God the Creator – Daniel 3 470

The biblical record's understanding of the futility of worshiping a created idol / image instead of worshiping the Creator 471

The Roman Catholic Church's recent prototypes of computer priests 478

The pervasive following of beast of the sea / false prophet / beast from the Abyss / eighth king beast will enjoy that will allow the idol / image of the beast of the sea to assume control of the inhabitants of the earth who worship it 478

The mark of the beasts system initiated – Revelation 13:14-18 479

Hippolytus of Rome's understanding of the significance of the mark of the beasts system 482

The mark of the beasts and the days before Noah – Matthew 24:38-39 490

The condition of the religious community that will foster the establishment of the mark of the beasts system 494

The Roman Catholic Church's catechism concerning the ten commandments that will allow for the worship of the idol / image of the beast of the sea, and the endorsement by the

global religious community of the worship of the idol / image of the beast of the sea   499
The political leader whose name is a number, '666' – Revelation 13:18   505
   Six hundred sixty six / χξς, or six hundred sixteen / χις? – Revelation 13:18   510
      The establishment of a new identity upon the recipients of the mark of the beasts   512
      The mark of the beasts system's attempt to redefine the personal identities of the inhabitants of the earth   516
The economic status of the world that will render the inhabitants of the earth susceptible to welcome the economic solution provided by the mark of the beasts system   518
   The financial component of the mark of the beasts system and its economy   519
The societal and cultural environment of idolatry, adultery, sexism and porn that will be present to aid in the ascent of the beast of the earth / final world ruler   523
   The societal culture of the transhumanist agenda of the oligarchy of the global elites   525
   The societal cultural environment of the global elites' theoterrorism movement   532
   The acceptance of magic, sorcery, occult practices, illusion, dark arts, etc.   534
   Sexual immorality and its acceptance in cultural norms   535
   Theft as an accepted practice   538
   The termination of the mark of the beasts system   538
The willingness to martyr God's holy people   539
The convergence of the rise of the Roman Catholic Church's global papal authority, the modern evolutionary theory birthed in the Royal Society of London, the United Nations' Agenda 2030 pursuit of the Omega Point of modern evolutionary theory's eschatology, the pursuit of establishing the Great Reset with the result of economically enriching the global elites, the implementation of the United Nations' Agenda 2030 global plan for global population reduction, etc.; with the mark of the beasts system   542
   United Nations Agenda 21 and Agenda 2030 as the formal plan for establishing global governance   545
   The World Economic Forum / WEF's plan for the implementation of the Great Reset   549

The importance of not receiving the mark of the beasts and the warning of the angel – Revelation 14:9-12, 16:2, 19:20, 20:4-5   551

The requirement of the willingness of the recipient, to receive the mark of the beasts – Revelation 14:9-12, 20:4-5   554

The ultimate reward for rejecting the mark of the beasts and its system – Revelation 20:4-6   558

The fragility of the mark of the beasts system   558

The shattering of the nation of Israel's covenant peace treaty agreement – Daniel 9:24-27   560

The beast of the sea / false prophet / beast from the Abyss / eighth king beast's traditional foundation for antisemitism   562

The Character of God is Unchanging and God's Promises Are Forever (Not Just for Sometimes)   **565**

The Miracles Performed Through the Followers of the Lamb / Jesus Christ   **574**

Greater things than what Jesus did   576

The power of the Holy Spirit poured out in these days   578

Further instruction on how to better access the power of the God of the kingdom of heaven   581

Second Half of the Era of the Time of Jacob's Trouble Begins – Period of Exactly 1,260 Days / 42 months / 3 ½ years

It was the Old Testament / Tanakh prophet Daniel (fl. 605 to 530 BC) - a prophet of Judah, who foretold that the era of the time of Jacob's Trouble would be seven years (Daniel 9:25-27).

And it was Daniel, along with John the Revelator, who foretold that the second half of the era of the time of Jacob's Trouble would be one thousand three hundred thirty five days (Daniel) / forty two months, plus an additional amount of time for the finale (John the Revelator) (Daniel 12:11-12, (1,260 days plus the time for the pouring out of God Most High's wrath / seven last plagues - Revelation (8:13), 11:2-3, (11:14), 12:6, (13:5), (16))

Both Daniel and John the Revelator identified that the heaviest activity on earth during the era of the time of Jacob's Trouble, will begin with the breaking of the covenant peace treaty agreement and the future abomination of desolation event. The future abomination of desolation event will mark the midpoint of the seven years designated for the era of the time of Jacob's Trouble.

The Measurement of Time for the Era of the Time of Jacob's Trouble

One of the details documented repeatedly concerning the era of the time of Jacob's Trouble, was the amount of time that God Most High allotted for the scheduled events to occur in.

The Old Testament / Tanakh prophet Daniel (fl. 605 to 530 BC) - a prophet of Judah, and John the Revelator (c. 6 to c. 100 AD) whose last book was also recorded as the last book of the Bible, repeatedly documented that time was marked for these events in days and months and years, but not in decades or centuries or millennia. No other era documented within the biblical record was marked with the same kind of precision.

The first event to mark this final era in human history prior to the kingdom of heaven being fully established on earth, was the first great sign of Revelation 12:1-2 that was fulfilled on September 23, 2027.

The second event to mark the beginning of the seven years of the era of the time of Jacob's Trouble was the signing of the Abraham Accords / the covenant peace treaty, on September 15, 2020.

The next event that will mark the midpoint in the era of the time of Jacob's Trouble will be the future abomination of desolation event that was scheduled to take place roughly three and a half years after the covenant peace treaty was signed.

The next event that will mark time, will be the assassination, death, resurrection and ascension of the two witnesses that will take place exactly one thousand two hundred sixty days after their arrival on earth.

And the final events that will mark kingdom change will be the arrival of messiah / the Lamb / Jesus Christ to resurrect the dead and the living, to defeat the enemies of God Most High and of the kingdom of heaven, and to fully establish the kingdom of heaven on earth.

All the scheduled events for the era of the time of Jacob's Trouble will fit someplace on this framework of time. But there are so many threads of events, and so many events that will interact with other simultaneously unfolding events interwoven into still other events, that it will be important to understand the anchor points, and then to understand the interactions of the dynamics of the various participants.

Timespan for the second half of the era of the time of Jacob's Trouble: time, times and half a time / half of the seventieth seven / forty two months / one thousand two hundred sixty days – Daniel 7:25, 9:26b-27, 12:5-7, 12:11-12, Revelation 11:2-5, 12: 12:6, 12:14, 13:5-8, 13:11-12

According to the angel Gabriel (Daniel 9:24-27), the ministry of the Anointed One / messiah / Jesus Christ was allotted a full seven years, the sixty ninth seven. But the Anointed One / messiah / Jesus Christ was 'cut off from finishing the sixty ninth 'seven.' The stoning of Stephen the martyr took place in the autumn that would have concluded the sixty ninth seven of Jesus Christ's full term of ministry (Acts 7).

It appears as if the red dragon / serpent / Satan, Inc. and the allies of the rebellion will pick up where Jesus Christ's ministry left off attempting to finish the second half of the three and a half years that was denied to Jesus Christ during his earthly ministry. Daniel's prophecy of the seventy sevens, set the time limit on the power and authority that the two beasts of Revelation 13 will exercise. And that time limit will be the second half of the seventieth 'seven.'

Or it may be that because Jesus Christ was allotted three and a half of the seven years of the sixty ninth seven, that God Most High has allotted the red dragon / serpent / Satan, Inc. the same amount of time for the attempt to fully establish the kingdom of Satan, Inc. / kingdom of man on earth, during the seventieth seven.

Time, times and half a time

The Old Testament / Tanakh prophet Daniel (fl. 605 to 530 BC) - a prophet of Judah documented that the time scheduled for the second half of the era of the time of Jacob's Trouble, when God's holy people will experience the tyrannical rule of the little horn / eleventh king / king that will exalt himself, would be for a time, times and half a time.

'He (little horn / eleventh king) will speak pompous words against God Most High, and against the saints of God Most High. He will persecute the saints and will intend to change the times and the law. The saints will be given into his hand for <u>a time and times and half a time</u>.' Daniel 7:25 translated

Then I, Daniel, looked. And there in front of me were two others. One stood on this bank of the river, and one stood on that bank of the river. One said to the man clothed in linen who was above the water of the river, 'How long will it be until the fulfillment of these wonders?'

I heard the man clothed in linen who was above the water of the river, and when he held up his right and left hands to heaven, he swore by the one who lives forever, 'It will be for <u>a time, times and half a time</u>. And it will be when the power of the holy people has been completely shattered. Then all these things will be finished.' Daniel 12:5-7 translated

In the context of the record of Daniel and later according to John the Revelator, 'time, times and half a time' was measured as three and a half years.

Jesus Christ was traditionally known as the man clothed in linen in the biblical record. The man clothed in linen was recognized as a special messenger of God Most High, even before Jesus came to live with humanity in the flesh (4 BC to 30 AD). It was the man clothed in linen who told Daniel the purpose of the events of the era of the time of Jacob's Trouble.

The purpose of the era of the time of Jacob's Trouble, especially the second half, will be to break the power that is over the 'holy people' / the people of Israel. The power over the 'holy people' / the people of Israel was defined in other places as the power that prevents the people of Israel from accepting both Jesus Christ as the resurrected messiah and the power that prevents Israel from seeking and understanding the relationship that they were intended to have with God Most High. When the people of Israel finally acknowledge Jesus Christ as their messiah, then this purpose will have been accomplished. Then and only then, will all things concerning the return of Jesus Christ and the full establishment of the kingdom of heaven on earth be able to be completed.

The second half of the era of the time of Jacob's Trouble has a definite focus, to bring the holy people / the people of Israel to the place where they will recognize Jesus Christ as messiah. God Most High anticipated that this process will take drastic global events and three and a half years to complete. But all that this process entails will be necessary to forge the people of Israel into the holy priests that God Most High promised Moses that they would become.

Time measured as 'time, times and half a time,' was used in relationship to the people of Israel and the duration of time until they will come to an understanding of the true identity of Jesus Christ as their promised and prophesied messiah (Daniel 7:25, 12:7, Revelation 12:14).

Half of the seventieth seven
After the sixty two weeks, messiah will be cut off, and will have nothing.

The people of the prince / ruler who is to come, will destroy the city and the sanctuary.

And the end of it shall come with a flood. War will continue until the end and desolations are determined.

The prince / ruler will confirm a covenant with many, for one 'seven' / 'week.' But <u>in the middle of the 'seven' / 'week,' the prince / ruler will bring an end to the sacrifice and offering</u>. On the wing (of the temple), the prince / ruler will establish abominations that will cause desolation, even until the consumption which has been determined is poured out on the desolate / the one who destroys. Daniel 9:26-27 translated

Daniel defined the ruler who is to come as arriving on the global stage halfway through the seven years of the era of the time of Jacob's Trouble, which set the time for the first half of the era of the time of Jacob's Trouble, until the future abomination of desolation event, to be three and a half years. But the halfway point also designated the second half that follows, to also be three and a half years.

Time measured on the scale of the seventy sevens, referred to the ministry of messiah the Lamb / Jesus Christ to the people of Israel, and to the facsimile messiah / ruler who is to come / beast of the earth, as they convince the people of Israel of the true identity of the promised and prophesied messiah, in the preparation of the people of Israel's progression toward becoming the holy nation of priests for God Most High, along with the preparation of the city / Jerusalem and the sanctuary / temple mount.

Forty two months
In addition to Daniel's accounting of time for the era of the time of Jacob's Trouble, John the Revelator (c. 6 to c. 100 AD) also was provided with time spans for events during the same era.

When an idea or piece of information is repeated multiple times in the biblical record, it has the effect of emphasizing that portion of the message. The fact that the time periods were repeated on multiple scales of days, months and years, etc., and in multiple contexts, also

communicated that the events were carefully planned by God Most High.

Included in John the Revelator's instructions for measuring the future temple: 'But leave out the courtyard outside the temple, and do not measure it because it has been given up to the Gentiles, and they will trample the holy city for forty two months.' Revelation 11:2 translated

John the Revelator was given an instruction to measure the new temple that will be built during the era of the time of Jacob's Trouble. But John was instructed to not measure the outer court. In fact, John seems to have forgotten to even provide the measurements of the future temple at all. Instead of providing the measurements, John revealed information regarding the timeline for the era of the time of Jacob's Trouble.

The forty two months that the temple court will be under the control of the Gentiles who will not respect the Jewish religious practices and the Law as it was given to Moses and to the people of Israel, was a reference to the forty two month term of power and authority of the two beasts of Revelation 13, that will begin with the future abomination of desolation event when they will have desecrated the temple mount.

Forty two months was also noted as the time period for the term of supernatural power and authority that the two beasts of Revelation 13 will have beginning with the future abomination of desolation event, to attempt to firmly establish their global governance.

The beast of the sea was given a mouth speaking great things and blasphemy. And to it was given authority to act for <u>forty two months</u>. It opened its mouth to speak blasphemies against God, to blaspheme the name of God, and the tabernacle of God, those who dwell in heaven.

The beast of the sea was given the power to make war with the saints and to overcome them. And the beast was given authority over every tribe and people and tongue and nation.

All inhabitants of the earth will worship the beast — all whose names have not been written in the book of life belonging to the Lamb who was slain, that began to be written from the creation of the world. Revelation 13:5-8 translated

For forty two months, the beast of the sea / false prophet / beast from the Abyss / eighth king beast will open his mouth to blaspheme God Most High, to slander God's name, to slander heaven / God's dwelling place, and to slander the people of God who live in heaven. Blaspheme can only be accomplished by those who know that Jesus Christ is the promised and prophesied messiah, and then deny it. Therefore, the beast of the sea will not be Jewish because the people of Israel have a veil over their hearts and minds concerning Jesus Christ. The people of Israel have not been able to recognize the sovereignty and divinity of Jesus Christ and therefore were not recognized by John the Revelator as blasphemers.

The current pope, Francis, has already declared that Jesus was not divine, that Jesus did not finish what he was sent to accomplish and so Jesus failed. Francis' declarations concerning Jesus Christ were blasphemies.

During the era of the time of Jacob's Trouble, the people of Israel will have their veil of understanding removed, reverse their rejection of Jesus Christ as Lord and recognize the sovereignty and divinity of Jesus Christ.

When Jesus Christ came the first time, it was the leaders of the Sanhedrin / religious court of the people of Israel, who rejected the sovereignty and divinity of Jesus Christ. And it was the Gentiles that received and believed in Jesus Christ as the path for salvation.

When Jesus Christ arrives this time, it will all be reversed. It will be the leaders within the Christian church that will reject his sovereignty and divinity. And it will be the people of Israel who will receive and believe in Jesus Christ as the promised and prophesied messiah.

As the beast of the sea / false prophet, he will have forty two months, for fully redefining theology and establishing a new definition for how to enter heaven without the necessity of recognizing Jesus Christ as Lord. And having created a theological void that Jesus Christ once occupied, the beast of the sea will offer himself as a substitute focus for worship. (Revelation 13)

Those who continue to insist that God Most High exists, is the greater power, and is sovereign and divine, will be targeted to be conquered / reeducated / destroyed. Those who continue to believe in God Most High and have their names written in the book of life belonging to the Lamb / Jesus Christ will not worship the beast of the sea / false prophet / eighth king beast. They will not bow down to him. They will not kiss his ring. They will not fall under the beast of the sea / false prophet's sway. But the inhabitants of the earth will find themselves under the supernatural authority of the beast of the sea / false prophet, forced to live by the law that the two beasts of Revelation 13 will establish.

It was God Most High that established that the two beasts of Revelation 13 will have only forty two months. The forty two months term of supernatural power and authority will begin with the future abomination of desolation event. And it will end when the two witnesses that will be assassinated by the beast from the Abyss, will be resurrected, proving that their supernatural power and authority is insufficient in comparison to the power of the kingdom of heaven to provide authentic resurrection.

The point to be made here is that as the beast of the sea / false prophet, he has **only** forty two months for the institution of the compulsory worship system. The Dark Ages / Middle Ages / medieval period led by the influence of the Roman Catholic Church lasted approximately a thousand years. The crusades began in 1096 AD and lingered into the 15th century. The Inquisitions began in 1184 and continued for centuries. The Protestant Reformation wars / European wars of religion began in 1517 AD and continued until around 1712 AD, with an estimated six million to seventeen million lives.

But the two beasts of Revelation 13 will have only forty two months to attempt to complete their coup attempt against God Most High. During the forty two months of the reign of the two beasts of Revelation 13, there will be hundreds of millions of people who will become their victims. For the benefit of the survival of humanity, it will *be essential that their reign of terror will only be allowed forty two months.*

I saw another beast rising out of the earth. And the beast of the earth had two horns like a lamb, and it was speaking like a dragon. The beast of the earth *exercises all the authority of the first beast*, on behalf of the first beast. The beast of the earth causes the earth and those dwelling in it, to worship the first beast of whom had its fatal wound healed. Revelation 13:11-12 translated

The second beast of Revelation 13 / beast of the earth, will share in the forty two months of supernatural power and authority.

Because the beast of the sea and the beast of the earth will share a co-regency, the terms of their reign must coincide together.

Time measured on the scale of the <u>forty two months</u>, referred to the term of supernatural power and authority that the two beasts of Revelation 13 will be allotted to attempt to fully establish the kingdom of Satan, Inc. / kingdom of man on earth.

1,260 days

Also, in the description of the two witnesses and the instructions to measure the temple mount, John the Revelator included the period of time that people of Israel will be cared for in the wilderness, and the period of time that the two witnesses will prophesy.

And the woman fled into the wilderness where she has a place there that has been prepared by God, so that there, they should nourish her for <u>one thousand two hundred sixty days</u>. Revelation 12:6 translated

The one thousand two hundred sixty days, coincided with a time, times and half a time.

And two wings of the great eagle were given to the woman so that she could fly into the wilderness, into her place, where she is nourished there for <u>a time and times and half a time</u>, away from the face of the serpent. Revelation 12:14

But leave out the courtyard outside the temple, and do not measure it because it has been given up to the Gentiles, and they will trample the holy city for <u>forty two months</u>. And I will appoint my two witnesses, and they will prophesy <u>one thousand two hundred and sixty days</u>, clothed in sackcloth. Revelation 11:3-5 translated

When the people of Israel rejected God Most High's plan for them to immediately enter into the Promised Land following their exodus from Egypt, God Most High 'exiled' them to the wilderness for forty years until the next generation was prepared to take the land.

When the people of Israel rejected God Most High's plan for them to be totally devoted to God Most High, and they embraced the gods of the other nations, the baal / mystery / mythology religion gods; and they rejected the observance of the Jubilee Years; God Most High sent the people of Israel into exile through the Assyrians and Babylonians for seventy years.

When the people of Israel rejected Jesus Christ as their messiah, God Most High gave them forty years to repent before sending the people of Israel into the exile that was labeled 'the diaspora.' In 70 AD, the nation of Israel ceased to exist and the people of Israel were 'scattered to the wind' until May 14, 1948 when the nation of Israel was reestablished in a single day.

During the era of the time of Jacob's Trouble, it will be necessary for the people of Israel to again experience a form of exile in order to forge them into the people that God Most High can receive the full blessing of God Most High and into the people that God Most High will be able to use for sharing the blessing of God Most High with the nations of the world as the nation of priests for God Most High. This future 'exile' will last for the duration of the second half of the era of the time of Jacob's Trouble. The people of Israel who had been living in Jerusalem and the surrounding area will be cared for by God Most High during this time as refugees for one thousand two hundred sixty days / three and a half years / forty two months.

In order for the people of Israel to return to God Most High and to receive the plan of God Most High with Jesus Christ as messiah, the people of Israel will again experience a kind of exile in the wilderness. And again, their theological leader will be Moses. This time when the people of Israel leave the wilderness to enter into the

Promised Land, they will never again be exiled, nor leave the Promised Land, nor be separated from God Most High.

Lament over Jerusalem

Before messiah / the Lamb / Jesus Christ was crucified, Jesus Christ mourned and said, 'Jerusalem, Jerusalem, you who kill the prophets and stone those who have been sent to you. How often I longed to gather your children together, like a hen gathers her chicks under her wings. And you were not willing. Look, your house is left desolate! I say to you, you will not see me again from now until you say, 'Blessed is the one who comes in the name of the Lord." Matthew 23:37-39 translated (Luke 13:34)

During the second half of the era of the time of Jacob's Trouble, it will be as if the people of Israel will finally arrive at that place where they will be willing to be gathered as chicks to abide under the wings of God Most High.

Time measured on the scale of the <u>1,260 days</u>, *referred to the courtship period between God Most High and the people of Israel, that has been scheduled to take place during the second half of the era of the time of Jacob's Trouble.*

The two witnesses will be returning to minister primarily to the people of Israel, during the same 1,260 days.

The followers of the Lamb / Jesus Christ have already heard and received the message of the kingdom of heaven. The inhabitants of the earth have already decided to reject the sovereignty and divinity of Jesus Christ. Only the people of Israel will be changing their minds concerning the identity of Jesus Christ, and the two witnesses will be instrumental in that work.

Timespan for the finale for the era of the time of Jacob's Trouble that will follow the second half of the era of the time of Jacob's Trouble – Daniel 12:11-12

In addition to the multiple points of documentation for the time period designated as the second half of the era of the time of Jacob's Trouble, Daniel provided the time period for the finale for the era of the time of Jacob's Trouble.

'From the time the daily sacrifice is taken away, and the abomination of desolation is set up, there will be one thousand two hundred ninety days.'

'Blessed is the one who waits and arrives at the one thousand three hundred thirty five days.' Daniel 12:11-12 translated

Daniel was told that for the second half of the era of the time of Jacob's Trouble, and for the finale for the era of the time of Jacob's Trouble, that time was to be marked beginning with the future abomination of desolation event and the abolishment of the daily sacrifice.

But in Daniel's message there were two more additional time markers that were included; the second endpoint will be located one thousand two hundred ninety days after the future abomination of desolation event, and the third endpoint will be located one thousand three hundred thirty five days after the future abomination of desolation event. Both endpoints marked the conclusion of different significant events.

Daniel's vision clearly demarcated three deadlines for the various activities of the second half of Jacob's Trouble. But Daniel did not include the details of what must be completed for the middle deadline in this record.

Following the one thousand two hundred sixty days of the ministry of the two witnesses, there will be many events that must still be accomplished (Revelation 11:14); the seventh trumpet / pouring out of the seven bowls of God Most High's wrath / seven last plagues (Revelation 16), the harvest of the earth (Revelation 14:14-16), the gathering of the armies of the world, the battle that will take place with the siege of Jerusalem, etc.

The end point when the full establishment of the kingdom of heaven on earth will be accomplished, was designated by the endpoint of the one thousand three hundred thirty five days marked in time counting from the future abomination of desolation event.

But there was no further clarity concerning what the one thousand two hundred ninety days will mark the end of.

Between the death of the two witnesses / end of the reign of the two beasts of Revelation 13, and the one thousand three hundred thirty five days that mark the full conclusion of the end of the era of the time of Jacob's Trouble, there will be only seventy five days. One thousand three hundred thirty five days after the date of the future abomination of desolation event, the fulfillment of the full realization of the full establishment of the kingdom of heaven on earth will be accomplished, and the Thousand Years Reign of Jesus Christ will have begun.

The second half of the era of the time of Jacob's Trouble, as the conclusion of six thousand years of waiting for the arrival of messiah / the Lamb / Jesus Christ to defeat the enemies of God Most High and of the kingdom of heaven, and bring lasting peace and freedom to the people of Israel and to the world

With all childbirths, at the end of the period of labor, there is relief.

The era of the time of Jacob's Trouble will be an era when the people of Israel will discover that the plan of the red dragon / serpent / Satan, Inc., the two beasts of Revelation 13, the global religious community, and the global governance system, was to once again enslave the people of Israel, like the Pharaoh of Egypt had before, like the nations surrounding Israel had after they returned from exile, and like the nations of the world have since the time of the diaspora of 70 AD.

But at the end of the era of the time of Jacob's Trouble, the Lord's promise was that the Lord will break the yoke of slavery off their necks and tear off their bonds. The Lord's promise to the people of Israel was that they will never again be threatened with slavery.

However, there is a condition for receiving the insurance of God Most High's freedom. The people of Israel must serve the Lord their God and 'messiah, the son of David their king.' *In order to serve the Lord their God and* 'messiah, the son of David their king,' *they must first recognize Jesus Christ the descendant of David, as their messiah.*

Officially, the people of Israel rejected God Most High's choice for messiah / Jesus Christ, during the first century AD. During the era of the time of Jacob's Trouble, the people of Israel will this time reject the red dragon / serpent / Satan, Inc.'s choice for 'messiah.'

Ultimately, it will be Jesus Christ who will eventually assume the throne of David when he returns at the end of the era of the time of Jacob's Trouble. It will be Jesus Christ who also invites the followers of the Lamb / Jesus Christ, both Jews and Gentiles, to share the throne with him.

Events associated with the sounding of the first six of the seven trumpets

Events scheduled to take place with the sounding of the first six of the seven trumpets

Event	When the event will take place	Biblical reference	Additional notes
Sign of Revelation 15:1 in the heavens. Consecration service in heaven will begin. The worshipers will begin to collect in heaven and collect until the mark of the beast system has ended with the sounding of the seventh trumpet.	The sign in the heavens of Revelation 15:1 will take place around the same time as the future abomination of desolation event. Because the worshipers in heaven are those who have been victorious over the beast, its image, the number of its name, the consecration service will	Revelation 15:1-4 worship led by the people of Israel and the followers of the Lamb who had been victorious over the beast, its image, the number of its name.	April 8, 2024 was the pinnacle of the sign in the heavens when the seven planets will all be on the other side of the sun from the earth and there will be a solar eclipse over the United States.

	begin and end around the 1,263 ½ days following the future abomination of desolation event and the season of the two witnesses.		
Silence in heaven for ½ hour, seven trumpets distributed, prayers of God's people mixed with the incense smoke from the altar - hurled to earth, thunder, lightning and an earthquake	*After the seventh seal was opened*	*Revelation 8:1-5*	
First angel will sound the first trumpet. Hail and fire mixed with blood, will be hurled to earth. Third of earth will be burned up, third of trees will be burned up, all green grass will be burned up.	*After the ½ hour silence in heaven*	*Revelation 8:7*	
Second angel will sound the second trumpet. Huge mountain like something, on fire, will be thrown into the sea. Third of the sea will turn to blood, third of living sea		*Revelation 8:8-9*	

creatures will die, third of the ships will be destroyed.			
Third angel will sound the third trumpet. A great blazing star named Wormwood, will fall from the sky on a third of the rivers and on the springs of water, third of the waters will turn bitter, and many people will die.		Revelation 8:10-11	
Fourth angel will sound the fourth trumpet. A third of the sun will be struck, with a third of the moon and a third of the stars becoming dark. A third of the day and a third of the night will be without light.		Revelation 8:12	
The eagle flying in midair will announce the three woes that correspond to the last three trumpet blasts.	Between the sounding of the fourth and fifth trumpets.	Revelation 8:13	
Fifth angel will sound the fifth trumpet. Scorpion locusts will be released from the Abyss. The plague of boils will last		Revelation 9:1-12	Instead of seeking God Most High for relief, people will seek death and long to

five months as **woe #1**.			die (Revelation 9:6).
Sixth angel will sound the sixth trumpet. Part 1: four angels released under the Euphrates River will lead the two hundred million army released to kill a third of humanity.		Revelation 9:13-21	People did not repent and so the process continues (Revelation 9:20-21).
The announcement will be made that the mystery of the seven thunders will be sealed up to be released with the sounding of the seventh trumpet. Declaration that there will be no more delay. The declaration that there will be no more delay, served as an indication that the message of the seven thunders is related to the question of 'How long will it be?' that was asked with the opening of the fifth seal. With the opening of the fifth seal, the answer to 'How long will it	After the seven thunders have spoken, provisions will be made for the little scroll. While the time of the sealing and unsealing of the little scroll was not disclosed, the mystery of the seven thunders will be disclosed after the conclusion of the events of the second woe, that will correspond with the assassination, death, resurrection and ascension of the two	Revelation 10:4-10	The accomplishment of the mystery of God Most High will be completed after the events associated with the sounding of the sixth trumpet / woe #2, have transpired; and before the sounding of the seventh trumpet / woe #3 commence.

be?' was answered with the distribution of white robes and the instruction to 'wait a little longer' (Revelation 6:10-11). The answer given at the time of the sounding of the seventh trumpet will be, 'There will be no more delay' (Revelation 10:6).	witnesses, and just before the sounding of the seventh trumpet.		
Three angels will announce: 1. The hour of judgment has come. 2. Babylon the Great is fallen. 3. Do not receive the mark of the beast.	While John the Revelator listed the announcements after recording the sounding of the first six trumpets, the announcements of warnings should be made prior to the sounding of the trumpets, in order to have effect.	Revelation 14:6-13	Blessed are the dead who die in the Lord from now on. They are seen worshiping during the consecration service in heaven Revelation 15.
Sixth trumpet / woe #2 – part 2 Linked with the conclusion of the events associated with the sounding of the sixth trumpet / woe #2, was the conclusion of the term of ministry for the	1,263 ½ days after the abomination of desolation event and the arrival of the two witnesses.	Revelation 11:1-14	Woe #2 will end. Woe #3 will begin.

two witnesses; the conclusion of the one thousand two hundred sixty days.			
Mystery of God will be accomplished.		Revelation 10:7	
Second announcement of kingdom change. The consecration service in heaven will conclude. Declaration will be made that it is time for rewarding God Most High's people and for destroying those who destroy the earth.	Around the time of the sounding of the seventh trumpet.	Revelation 11:15-19	The mystery of God Most High will be accomplished as announced to the prophets. The events of the little scroll and the seven thunders, will be connected with the conclusion of the consecration service.
God's temple in heaven will be opened and the ark of the covenant will be seen.	After the sounding of the seventh trumpet	Revelation 11:19	
Flashes of lightning, rumblings, peals of thunder, an earthquake and a severe hailstorm.	After the sounding of the seventh trumpet	Revelation 11:19	
The opened fifth seal contained the question of 'How long it will be?'		Revelation 6:9-11 Revelation 10:4-10	

The answer was the distribution of white robes and the instruction to 'Wait a little longer.' At this point, the 'wait time' will have expired.			

The General Order of Events for the Second Half of the Era of the Time of Jacob's Trouble

Throughout the Old Testament / Tanakh Daniel's account of events, John the Revelator's account of events, and the rest of the biblical record, events concerning eschatology / the era of the time of Jacob's Trouble, were not reported in chronological order ... except for when chronological order was confirmed.

Understanding that the scheduled events for the era of the time of Jacob's Trouble is not a simple timeline, but more closely resembles a spiderweb of time, a woven tapestry of time, a complex set of interactions placed in the context of time; will aid in understanding the actual timing of events.

The participants in the events will be interactive, like a play, or a sports game. To focus on the activity of only one actor or player, without understanding the interaction of the other actors or players, would not supply a sufficient understanding of the dynamics that will take place.

God Most High supplied the playbook. But the playbook remains only words on a page until the events are experienced.

With that understanding, the second half of the era of the time of Jacob's Trouble will begin with:

- *the red dragon / serpent / Satan, Inc. being hurled to earth;*

- the red dragon / serpent / Satan, Inc. beginning the final offensive against the people of Israel and the followers of the Lamb / Jesus Christ;
- the people of Israel being cared for by God and two wings of a great eagle,
- the two witnesses arriving from heaven;
- the two beasts of Revelation 13 making themselves known, breaking the covenant peace treaty agreement between the nation of Israel and other nations;
- the future abomination of desolation event taking place on the temple mount, with the erection and animation of the idol / image of the beast of the sea, the institution of the mark of the beasts system, and the cessation of the temple sacrificial system;
- the scheduled events associated with the sounding of the first six trumpets;
- the commencement of the consecration service of God's temple in heaven;

These events will be so closely linked that they will begin almost simultaneously, within days or weeks of each other.

The Red Dragon / Serpent / Satan, Inc. Being Hurled to Earth

The first book of Enoch and the biblical record documented that there have been multiple times in human history when groups of rebellious angels have already been judged, sentenced and incarcerated (e.g., first book of Enoch 6, Job 4:18, 2 Peter 2:4, Jude 1:6).

And the biblical record documented that there will be a time in the future when all rebellious angels will be released from their current incarcerations and will be judged again along with all other currently nonincarcerated rebellious angels. And then all rebellious angels will be incarcerated in the fiery lake. (Matthew 25:41, 1 Corinthians 6:3, Revelation 20:1-3, 20:7-10).

The biblical record also documented that the era of the time of Jacob's Trouble will experience rebellious angels being released from their incarceration temporarily, to participate in the scheduled events of the era of the time of Jacob's Trouble (Revelation 9).

In addition, the biblical record documented that during the era of the time of Jacob's Trouble, the rebellious angels still residing in heaven, will be ejected from heaven, exiled from heaven, and hurled to earth.

Even though John the Revelator recorded the rebellious angels associated with the activities associated with the sounding of the seven trumpets, first (Revelation 8, 9), the actual expulsion of the rebellious angels began with the first and second heavenly signs that John the Revelator documented in the description of the red dragon / serpent / Satan, Inc. (Revelation 12).

And another sign was seen in heaven: behold a great red dragon having seven heads and ten horns, and upon his heads were seven royal crowns (diademata / διαδηματα). The tail of the dragon drags a third of the stars of heaven, and he cast them to the earth. And the dragon stands before the woman that is about to bring forth (her child), so that when she should bring forth her child. the red dragon might devour the child. Revelation 12:3-4 translated

And there was war in heaven. Michael and his angels warred against the dragon and the dragon with his angels, warred (back). And the dragon and his angels did not have strength. There was no longer any place found for them in heaven. And the dragon, the ancient great serpent, who is called the devil and Satan, was thrown out. Satan is the deceiver of the whole inhabited world. Satan was thrown down to the earth and his angels were thrown down with him. Revelation 12:7-9 translated

And when the dragon saw that he had been thrown down to the earth, the dragon pursued the woman who had brought forth the male (child). Revelation 12:13 translated

In preparation for the second half of the era of the time of Jacob's Trouble, the rebellious angels still residing in heaven, must be ejected from heaven. John the Revelator's description of the sounding of the seven trumpets depicted that the expulsion of the rebellious angels may take months to complete.

The first noted event for this era of an angel being expelled from heaven will occur with the sounding of the

third trumpet. This rebellious angel was named Wormwood and will fall from the sky. Wormwood will be responsible for turning a third of the rivers and springs of water bitter and for poisoning to death many people. (Revelation 8:10)

The next notable event of a rebellious angel exiting heaven will take place with the sounding of the fifth trumpet / woe #1. This unnamed rebellious angel will be the angel who will be given the key to the shaft of the Abyss. Yet another rebellious angel, the angel of the Abyss / king of the Abyss / Abaddon (Hebrew) / Apollyon (Greek) / Destroyer (English), apparently is currently incarcerated in the Abyss and must be released at the designated time. (Revelation 9:1-12)

The next noted event of the activity of the rebellious angels, was recorded with the sixth trumpet / woe #2; part 1. But this time the four angels are located under the Euphrates River and have been bound for centuries or millenniums. For the purposes of the events that take place during the era of the time of Jacob's Trouble, they do not originate from having lived in heaven recently. They have already been expelled and incarcerated under the Euphrates River, prior to the era of the time of Jacob's Trouble. (Revelation 9:13-15)

Jesus Christ also taught that the prince of this world is coming. The prince of this world was another title for Satan who stole dominion over the earth when he deceived and enticed the first woman and first man to eat the fruit of the tree of the knowledge of good and evil (Genesis 3).

Jesus said to his disciples: 'You heard me say, 'I am going away and I am coming back to you.'
I have told you now before it happens, so that when it does happen you will believe. I will not speak with you much longer, for the prince of this world is coming. The prince of this world has no hold on me, but the world must learn that I love the Father and that I do exactly what my Father has commanded me.' John 14:28-31

The prince of this world was active in influencing the crucifixion of Jesus Christ.

And then after Jesus Christ rose from the dead, the tradition of the early church held that Jesus Christ descended into hell. Hell was designated as the abode for *those who found the confines of the kingdom of heaven and God Most High's law for the kingdom of heaven, too restrictive and offensive. But when Jesus Christ descended into hell, hell and death could not hold Jesus Christ, so Jesus Christ rose from death.*

The common human understanding of the term 'death' has been defined as something that is marked with a physical body no longer breathing or without brain activity, a certificate of death, a casket or cremation, a funeral service and a final resting place. But for God Most High, 'death' is defined as separation from God Most High. Death as a separation from God Most High, also includes an eternal life, just not in the presence of God Most High. What is in question concerning death then becomes, 'Which address does one choose for eternal life?'

There is an eternal destination for those who do not desire to meet heaven's requirements for entrance into the kingdom of heaven, for those that do not desire that the kingdom of heaven becomes their eternal address. For them, the eternal alternative to living life in the kingdom of heaven, is known by several names including Satan's abode. However, Satan does not currently dwell there. Currently, according to the biblical record, there is a portion of heaven that Satan continues to access, complete with the ability to hold audience with God Most High and with Jesus Christ (Job 1:6-12, Matthew 4:1-11, Mark 1:9-13, Luke 4:1-13, etc.).

When everyone originally lived in the Garden of Eden / garden of God / paradise, the first man and first woman were given dominion over the earth (Genesis 1:26-30, 2:15-20). But when the first man and first woman ate the fruit of the forbidden tree, they transferred dominion of the earth to the serpent / Satan; and they changed the hierarchical order of power and authority, elevating the position of the serpent / Satan and demoting their own position as humanity. This act also impacted the relationship that God the Creator held with the first man and first woman. And the activity of the serpent / Satan, threatened all order that God the Creator had established. (See Hebrews 2:5-18, etc.)

God the Creator's solution was to make a covenant with the serpent / Satan that there would be a time when the earth and humanity would be redeemed from the serpent / Satan's dominion. God the Creator promised that dominion of the earth would be purchased back from Satan and returned to humanity through a perfect human who would be able to resist Satan's temptation to rule the earth on Satan's terms with Satan as the divine and sovereign ruler / prince of this world.

It is Satan's determination that this transaction to return dominion over the earth to humanity, should not be completed. And this is the source of the cosmic conflict that resulted in the current war in heaven between the rebellious angels and Michael's loyal angels.

Because of the serpent / Satan's deception and theft of the dominion over the earth, and because of humanity's rebellion against the created order, God the Creator could no longer live in a face to face relationship with the first man and first woman. The first man and first woman were exiled from the Garden of Eden / garden of God / paradise – temporarily until the promised and prophesied messiah exiles the adherents to the red dragon / serpent / Satan, Inc. from earth and fully establishes the kingdom of heaven once again on earth.

But the question remained of where and how to exile Satan and his adherents.

Knowing that Satan and Satan's adherents have determined that God the Creator's perfect kingdom of heaven be marked for destruction, God the Creator also needed to develop a plan for where to house Satan and Satan's adherents for eternity, where they could no longer harm earth and humanity. The solution became a multipronged approach for separation from the God that included: sheol / grave, the sea, Gehenna / Valley of Hinnom / burning trash heap, hell / Hades, Tartarus / torture of Hades, the Abyss / bottomless pit, outer darkness with weeping and gnashing of teeth, lake of fire of burning sulfur / second death, etc.

The rebellious angels / red dragon / serpent / Satan, Inc. have determined that the only way to avoid God Most

High's plan for their separation and incarceration, was to also seize dominion over heaven itself, to unseat God Most High from the throne of heaven, and to prevent the promised and prophesied messiah / the Lamb / Jesus Christ from assuming his throne on earth as the King of kings and Lord of lords. Taking dominion over heaven, and especially taking dominion over the throne of God Most High, is the only solution that the red dragon / serpent / Satan, Inc. has for a defense against the future judgment and incarceration that God Most High promised for all members of the red dragon / serpent / Satan, Inc. and adherents to the kingdom of Satan, Inc. / kingdom of man.

This cosmic and ancient quest to determine which kingdom is stronger and will prevail, will ultimately determine which kingdom's plan for eternity will be imposed upon the earth, upon heaven and upon the cosmos.

Hence, war broke out in heaven.

... And war on earth will follow. (Revelation 12, etc.)

As Jesus Christ was preparing for his crucifixion, Jesus came to the region of Caesarea Philippi / the foot of Mount Hermon, to pose to the disciples the question of 'Who do you say that I am?' (Matthew 16:13-20). According to Enoch, Mount Hermon was the mountain where the two hundred angels held a conference to establish their pack to mate with humanity and produce Nephilim offspring as an act of rebellion against God, God's creation of humanity, and the superior status over the heavenly beings / angels that humanity was created to possess. Mount Hermon was known as the mountain of oath. Mount Hermon had become the world's headquarters for the worship of the god Pan and the pantheon of other baal / mystery / mythology religion deities. Mount Hermon was also thought to be the location for the gates of hell.

When Jesus posed the question at the base of Mount Hermon to Peter and Peter answered, 'You are the Messiah, the Son of the living God,' Jesus' response was '...And I tell you that on this rock I will build my church, and the gates of Hades will not overcome it...' It was a statement that was intended to confirm Peter's understanding of Jesus Christ's right to *rule as the promised and prophesied messiah, and at the same time it was intended to taunt any who were listening connected to the realm of Hades. It was a statement to those who dwell in the spiritual world to notify them of Jesus Christ's superiority even over the powers of the domain of Hades / hell. And it was a statement to the rebellious angels who were determined to see Jesus Christ killed, to 'get on with it.'*

When Jesus Christ was crucified and descended into hell, it was an intrusion of perfection into the domain of evil, in a similar way that Satan brought evil into the domain of the perfection of heaven.

Jesus Christ's excursion into hell was also the opportunity for Death and Hades to hold Jesus Christ, to exert power over Jesus Christ in a final attempt to cause Jesus Christ to become a servant of the kingdom of Satan, Inc. / kingdom of man. Descending into hell was a test of Jesus Christ to see if there were any transgressions within Jesus Christ, of God Most High's standard of perfection (feast of unleavened bread). Because in the rules of this ancient cosmic contest between God Most High and the red dragon / serpent / Satan, Inc., any transgression would have caused Jesus Christ to be required to experience death / separation from God Most High and to have been subjected to the authority of Death, Hades and the red dragon / serpent / Satan, Inc. When Jesus Christ was able to escape Death and Hades, he proved that the 'prince of this world' *has no hold upon him, which made Jesus Christ eligible to defeat and incarcerate the* prince of this world.

In the mind of God Most High, the prince of this world *has already been defeated. And yet, the* prince of this world *continues to not capitulate to God Most High's superiority, authority, or sovereignty. The* prince of this world *will continue to hold access to heaven, and to hell, until Satan and his angels are fully expelled from heaven.*

God Most High determined that the time for the expulsion of the rebellious angels from heaven, would be during the era of the time of Jacob's Trouble.

During the era of the time of Jacob's Trouble, the red dragon / serpent / Satan, Inc., the rebellious angels that still maintain access to heaven, will be expelled. And they will not just be asked to leave. They will be hurled / thrown to earth. The implication was that they will be hurled / thrown to earth with a bit of vitriol from those who expel them.

The actual event of Satan and his angels being hurled to earth has been described in other places within the biblical record as resembling 'stars falling to earth,' implying that those who live during the era of the time of Jacob's Trouble will be able to physically observe the coming of the 'prince of this world' and his companions as they make their transition into what they inaccurately hope will be their enduring dwelling on earth.

And when they have been expelled, they will know that their time is short on earth, for achieving their mission of assuming total global and cosmic domination. During the era of the time of Jacob's Trouble, their window of opportunity for attempting to fully establish the kingdom of Satan, Inc. / kingdom of man, will be closing quickly. In fact, their window of opportunity will be closing so quickly that it will be measured in days and months and a few short years, not even a decade.

The red dragon / serpent / Satan, Inc. and their adherents have had six thousand years to prepare for this moment in history. In order to provide any facsimile of a successful attempt to fully establish the kingdom of Satan, Inc. / kingdom of man on earth, it is imperative that Satan and his angels be fully present on earth, fully focused on the activities that take place on earth, without the distraction that comes from also having residence in heaven.

When Jesus predicted his death, he said, 'Now is the time for judgment on this world. Now the prince of this world will be driven out. And I, when I am lifted up from the earth, will draw all people to myself.' John 12:31-32

When Jesus died on the cross and rose again, it provided all that was needed in heaven to establish provisions legally and physically, for casting Satan and the other rebellious angels, from heaven. The question that we who live on earth ask is, 'When does the red dragon / serpent / Satan Inc. actually leave heaven?'

The kingdom of heaven's standard has consistently been that once God Most High has declared a thing, that thing has been set and has been acknowledged to be completed even before the event takes place.

However, the biblical record did not give enough information to determine with absolute certainty the 'when' of the red dragon / serpent / Satan, Inc.'s complete exodus from heaven. But John the Revelator did document that the consecration service of God's temple in heaven will begin with the fulfillment of the third heavenly sign (Revelation 15). Consecration is that act of separating the sacred from the common, the act of devoting or dedicating someone or something to the full service and worship of God Most High. And consecration usually happens when the effects of the consecration can be maintained, in this case after the rebellious angels have been cast out of heaven.

Jesus Christ provided this description for the era of the time of Jacob's Trouble, to John the Revelator.

And the dragon, the ancient great serpent, who is called the devil and Satan, was thrown out. Satan is the deceiver of the whole inhabited world. Satan was thrown down to the earth and his angels were thrown down with him.

And I heard a great voice in heaven saying, 'Now has come the salvation and the power, and the kingdom of our God and the authority of the Christ of God, because the accuser of our brothers has been thrown down, the one who is accusing them day and night before our God. And they (our brothers) have overcome the accuser by reason of the blood of the Lamb, and by reason of the word of their testimony, and because they have not loved their life unto death.'

'Because of this, rejoice Oh heavens and those dwelling there!'

'Woe to the earth and the sea because the devil has come down to you, having great fury, knowing that he has a short time.'

And when the dragon saw that he had been thrown down to the earth, the dragon pursued the woman *(Israel)* who had brought forth the male child *(messiah / Jesus Christ)*. Revelation 12:9-13 translated

Jesus Christ provided John the Revelator the vision for what the outcome of the war in heaven will be, almost two thousand years before the war began. Michael the

archangel and Michael's angels will prevail against the great dragon / red dragon / serpent / Satan, Inc. and will hurl Satan to earth along with Satan's angels.

The vision that Jesus Christ gave to John the Revelator of Satan coming to earth described Satan being hurled down. Satan will not float to earth gently on a cloud. Satan will not softly and safely land on earth as if carried by a parachute. There will not be first class travel accommodations for Satan and his angels as they make their journey from heaven. Satan will not accidentally slip and fall out of heaven.

Satan will be hurled with violent force from heaven.

Even though the previous portions of the vision described in the book of Revelation were loaded with descriptions of violence, God Most High's activity and the Lamb / Jesus Christ's activity will be metered and restrained before this event. Up to this point in the scheduled events of the era of the time of Jacob's Trouble, God Most High and the Lamb / Jesus Christ relax their control upon world dynamics, providing the opportunity for the red dragon / serpent / Satan, Inc.'s plan to attempt to be fully manifested, complete with the violence that is inherent within their plan, and essential for God Most High's plan of causing all of humanity to choose their kingdom.

Satan has been identified as 'the accuser... who accuses... before our God, day and night...' (Revelation12:10b). When the kingdom of heaven will be fully established on earth, there will be no more opportunity given to Satan to continue his practice of accusing humanity before God Most High. Satan's job in heaven will come to an end. Consequently, there will be no reason to continue to allow Satan access to heaven.

The expulsion of Satan and his angels from heaven will allow the full effect of the perfect blood of Jesus Christ that was shed on the cross to wash away the effects of Satan's accusations against the followers of the Lamb / Jesus Christ. But Satan's expulsion from heaven, while boosting Satan's power on earth, will also allow the power of God the Father, the Lamb / Jesus Christ and the Holy Spirit to be undistracted, more focused, more powerful in accomplishing the goals of the kingdom of heaven on behalf of the followers of the Lamb / Jesus Christ and God Most High's strategy for connecting with the people of Israel in order to remove their veil that covers their understanding of Jesus Christ, and to allow them to perceive the deep things of God Most High.

The mere testimony of the followers of the Lamb / Jesus Christ will cause the followers of the Lamb / Jesus Christ to be triumphant to the challenges of the red dragon / serpent / Satan, Inc. and the kingdom of Satan, Inc. / kingdom of man. Some will face death and die. Others will face death and be delivered from death, just as it was during the time of the apostles recorded by Jesus Christ's apostle Luke, in the book of Acts.

The events for the second half of the era of the time of Jacob's Trouble require that Satan and his angels be expelled from heaven because:
1. The presence of Satan and his angels needs to be eliminated from heaven in order for heaven to experience the consecration of heaven described in Revelation 15 that precedes the pouring out of the seven bowls / seven last plagues upon the earth that contain the wrath of God.
2. Satan and his angels need to be expelled from heaven as an act of forcing the attention of Satan and his angels to focus their attention to matters on earth. The red dragon / serpent / Satan, Inc. needs to not be able to claim that the competition was not fair, that the attempt to fully establish the kingdom of Satan, Inc. / kingdom of man on earth was not given an optimal opportunity.
3. Satan and his angels leaving the comfort of living in heaven will cause stress that is associated with a change of this kind of magnitude. In order for the truth of the nature of the kingdom of Satan, Inc. / kingdom of man

to be realized, the rebellious angel's need to be jolted and motivated into displaying to the people of the world and especially the people of Israel, the true character of the kingdom of Satan, Inc. / kingdom of man. The people of the world and especially the people of Israel need to be able to make an informed decision concerning which kingdom they will choose to invest in; the kingdom of Satan, Inc. / kingdom of man where wrath is the norm and honest peace is the exception, or the kingdom of heaven with the Lamb / Jesus Christ as king and priest where wrath is the exception and honest peace is the norm.

4. After the expulsion of Satan and his angels from heaven, the nature of the activity during the era of the time of Jacob's Trouble that takes place in heaven and on earth will change. Prior to the expulsion of Satan and his angels from heaven, the nature of the activities described in John's Revelation will have acted in a manner of having been more of a release of the red dragon / serpent / Satan, Inc. to be allowed to attempt to fully establish the kingdom of Satan, Inc. / kingdom of man, than to be activities of God Most High demonstrating God's wrath. For example, the sounding of the sixth trumpet / woe #2 which has two parts with the first part being the release of the two hundred million cavalry and the four angels held under the Euphrates River, will clearly be a result of the activity of the red dragon / serpent / Satan, Inc. God Most High's part in the activity of the sixth trumpet / woe #2 will be for the four horns of the altar to order their release. But following the full expulsion of Satan and his angels from heaven, the nature of the activity on earth will change. On earth the change in the nature of the kingdom of heaven's activity will be initiated with the future abomination of desolation and

will be responses to the offensive activity of the kingdom of Satan, Inc. / kingdom of man. With the future abomination of desolation event, the kingdom of heaven will become more active in the activities on earth, with the kingdom of heaven contributing a much greater response and defense of the people of Israel and the followers of the Lamb / Jesus Christ. Following the rebellious angels' release of their best offensive military that currently is bound, following the announcement from heaven of victory, and the future abomination of desolation will take place. Following the scheduled future abomination of desolation event, the second part of the sixth trumpet / woe #2 will begin with the coming of the two witnesses from heaven which is clearly the direct activity of the kingdom of heaven, with God Most High providing a more direct participation instead of merely granting release or permission to act. It will be with the advent of the two witnesses from heaven that the mighty works of God Most High will be displayed through the work of the two witnesses. The two witnesses will be authorized by heaven to control rain and drought, and to bring or stop plagues. Following the sixth trumpet / woe #2; part 2 events, the rest of the scheduled events will continue to crescendo with the events of the seventh trumpet / woe #3 / seven bowls / seven last plagues, where God's wrath is actually poured out upon the earth, along with the harvesting of the earth and the culmination of the residual of all the other yet unconcluded events of the seven seals and seven trumpets. The seventh trumpet / woe #3 / seven bowls / seven last plagues will be entirely the activity of God's angels, as a wrathful response to the activity of the red dragon / serpent / Satan, Inc. and their adherents.

If God Most High were to have dispersed the fulness of God's wrath before Satan and his angels were expelled from heaven, the consequence would have the same kind of catastrophic effect of causing a minor explosion within an airplane in flight. Waiting until Satan and his angels have been hurled to earth before focusing God's wrath upon God Most High's enemies will be much more effective in both bringing about the destruction of the kingdom of Satan, Inc. / kingdom of man and in bringing about the environment on earth that will be necessary for the full establishment of the kingdom of heaven on earth.

5. Satan and his angels need to relocate to earth in order for the red dragon / serpent / Satan, Inc. to better focus on the activity of attempting to fully establish the kingdom of Satan, Inc. / kingdom of man on earth. Along with the two beasts of Revelation 13, Satan himself and his angels will dramatically make their presence known on earth.

There are elements of the current church community that have already convened and tackled the problem of how the apostate church will present / spin the occurrence of Satan and his angels on earth. The pope and the Roman Catholic Church have already held conferences at the Vatican campuses in preparation for the advent of Satan and his angels coming to earth and have determined how they will explain them to the people of the world. The focus on astrobiology of the Roman Catholic Church will enable them to offer an academic and scientism explanation for the existence and presence of Satan, Satan's angels and also demons. Satan, Satan's angels and the demons will be presented as aliens who possess hidden and special knowledge that they desire to share with humanity in exchange for the world receiving them. This strategy of sharing hidden / secret knowledge has worked in the past in the enticement of the first woman and first man to eat the fruit of the tree of the knowledge of good and evil by the first man and first woman in the Garden of Eden / garden of God / paradise exchanged dominion of the earth for this 'secret' knowledge. In the antediluvian / preflood world, it was the practice to trade hidden / secret knowledge in exchange for women to breed Nephilim. The religion of Gnosticism was based on the exchange of hidden / secret knowledge / mysteries from the spiritual realm.

During the era of the time of Jacob's Trouble, the red dragon / serpent / Satan, Inc. will use their ancient practice of trading 'so called hidden / secret knowledge' once again in the manipulative conspiracy of taking dominion of the earth, to a new and higher level.

6. Satan and his angels need to dwell on earth also as a proof to humanity that the rebellious angels / gods exist. The actual observable presence of Satan and his angels on earth will add validity to the existence of Satan and his angels for any who had previously doubted that they existed. Their presence will make it easier for the people of the world to believe in their power and in the power of the red dragon / serpent / Satan, Inc. to fully establish the kingdom of Satan, Inc. / kingdom of man on earth.

While Satan and his angels are currently veiled from human eyes and general physical experience, there is reason to doubt their existence. Doubting the existence of the rebellious angels / gods translates into the rebellious angels / gods also having limited power to accomplish their goals. It will be necessary during the era of the time of Jacob's Trouble for Satan and his angels to fully reveal themselves to their adherents to garner the *power that they will need to realistically attempt to establish the kingdom of Satan, Inc. / kingdom of man on earth.*

7. *In the chronology of the events of the era of the time of Jacob's Trouble, a main focus of the red dragon / serpent / Satan, Inc. will be pursuing the people of Israel. The kingdom of Satan, Inc. / kingdom of man will declare war upon the people of Israel. The red dragon / serpent / Satan, Inc. will be more effective at making war with the people of Israel, if Satan and his angels are actually dwelling amongst the inhabitants of the earth.*

When the dragon saw that he had been thrown down to the earth, the dragon pursued the woman who had brought forth the male child. And two wings of the great eagle were given to the woman so that she could fly into the wilderness, into her place, where she is nourished there for a time and times and half a time, away from the face of the serpent. Revelation 12:13-14 translated

John the Revelator recorded that it will be after Satan and his angels are hurled to earth that the red dragon / serpent / Satan, Inc. will pursue the woman / the people of Israel who has given birth to the male child / Jesus Christ. The time that the people of Israel will be pursued will be for a time, times and half a time / one thousand two hundred sixty days / forty two months / three and a half years.

The taunt that the people of Jacob were to offer:
'How you have fallen from heaven, O Lucifer, son of the morning! How you are cut down to the ground. You who weakened the nations!'

'For you have said in your heart, 'I will ascend into heaven!'
"I will exalt my throne above the stars of God."
"I will sit on the mount of the congregation *(Mount Zaphon / the most sacred mountain of the Canaanites).*"
"On the farthest sides of the north, I will ascend above the heights of the clouds."
"I will be like the Most High."
'Yet you will be brought down to the lowest depths of the Pit.'

'Those who see you will gaze at you and consider you, saying: 'Is this the man who made the earth tremble, who shook kingdoms, who made the world a wilderness, and who destroyed its cities, who did not open the house of his prisoners?" Isaiah 14:12-17 translated

The taunt continued in Isaiah 14.

The Hebrew word that was referred to as the morning star was translated into Greek as 'Phosphorus' and into Latin as 'Lucifer.' The morning star was also equated with the planet Venus with its morning appearances. Venus is the most brilliant of the planets and is not seen during the night.

To refer to Satan as the morning star was God Most High's recognition of the goals of Satan's heart, to be the brightest of all the heavenly bodies, the morning star. Approximately two thousand seven hundred years ago, Isaiah recorded God Most High's vision of the event of Satan being cast to earth, along with the later event of Satan being defeated and destined to enter the realm of the dead and the depths of the pit. Within Isaiah's prophecy of Isaiah 14 was a short span of time between the event where Satan and his angels will be cast down to earth, to the event where Satan will be defeated and brought to the depths of the pit where nations will stare and ponder Satan's fate.

Jesus Christ's teaching on the expulsion of Satan and the rebellious angels from heaven, and the authority that the followers of the Lamb / Jesus Christ will have over the rebellious angels

During his earthly ministry, Jesus Christ taught about the expulsion of Satan from heaven.

Jesus replied, 'I saw Satan fall like lightning from heaven. I have given you *(the disciples / followers of the Lamb / Jesus Christ)* authority to trample on snakes and scorpions and to overcome all the power of the enemy; nothing will harm you.' Luke 10:18-19

It is interesting that Jesus connected the two seemingly unrelated thoughts:
- I saw Satan fall like lightning from heaven.
- I have given you authority to trample on snakes and scorpions and to overcome all the power of the enemy. Nothing will harm you.

The fact that Jesus connected the two thoughts, hinted that this may be a message especially directed to

those who live during the era of the time of Jacob's Trouble when the red dragon / serpent / Satan, Inc. will fall from heaven.

The red dragon / Satan was also defined as the ancient serpent. From the beginning of human history, the snake has been the representative of all that is incorporated into the red dragon / serpent / Satan, Inc. (Revelation 12:9).

During the era of the time of Jacob's Trouble, the locust scorpions will rise from the Abyss when the angel takes the key held in heaven and opens the shaft of the Abyss, as documented in the sounding of the fifth trumpet / woe #2 (Revelation 9:1-12).

For Jesus Christ to give authority during the era of the time of Jacob's Trouble 'to trample on snakes and scorpions and to overcome all the power of the enemy...' indicated that those who are followers of the Lamb / Jesus Christ, will experience the same kind of power that Jesus Christ experiences and is authorized to share, to overcome the challenges that the red dragon / serpent / Satan, Inc. presents during this era; just as Jesus Christ possessed this kind of power when Jesus Christ overcame his time with death and Hades following his crucifixion.

It is vital for the followers of the Lamb / Jesus Christ to note that while the rebellious angels will be exiting heaven to focus their destructive power on the inhabitants of the earth, Jesus Christ has promised that as the rebellious angels exit heaven, the greater authority has been given to the followers of the Lamb / Jesus Christ to overcome all the power of the enemy!

There were also other passages in the biblical record that indicated that during the era of the time of Jacob's Trouble, while the red dragon / serpent / Satan, Inc. will be 'released' upon the earth and exhibiting a magnified presence and power, God Most High will also exhibit a magnified presence and activity on the events taking place on earth. God Most High will rise to the challenge of displaying God's mighty acts and God Most High's glory that is superior to the power and might that the red *dragon / serpent / Satan, Inc. has accumulated and will temporarily possess.*

(For another depiction of how God Most High acts in doing battle with a spiritual enemy, reference the experience of Egypt with the ten plagues, a battle between God Most High and the gods of Egypt.)

The Roman Catholic Church's preparatory plan for receiving the 'stars' / rebellious / fallen angels as they physically land on earth

Jewish tradition has always defined demons as the dead spirits of the Nephilim that are not allowed access to heaven and not able to enter hell.

But angels are different from demons. It was rebellious angels mating with human women, that produced the Nephilim that became demons when the Nephilim died.

The term 'angel' means 'messenger' and includes all forms of heavenly hosts; cherubim, seraphim, etc. Currently, their first abode is heaven. Angels were associated with stars throughout the biblical record. And historically, specific angels were associated with specific stars.

When the rebellious angels will be finally and completely expelled from heaven, their only option will be to descend to earth. With an incursion of rebellious angels making their presence known on earth, the global religious community will need to offer an explanation for the 'stars' / rebellious angels, falling to earth.

The Roman Catholic Church and the Vatican have already laid the foundation for their approach for providing an explanation for the arrival of the rebellious angels on earth as they are expelled from heaven, and for the demonic activity that will be reinvigorated as the rebellious angels relocate to earth.

In May 2008, Father Jose Gabriel Funes, an Argentinean Jesuit who oversees the Vatican's astronomy program, made a series of startling statements about how extraterrestrial life is likely to be more ethically evolved than humanity, and should be welcomed as brothers. The 'extraterrestrials' will be viewed by the Vatican as intelligent and free from the original sin that plagues humanity. Therefore, the extraterrestrials / rebellious angels will be viewed as possessing a fuller friendship relationship with their creator than humanity can possess with God Most High.

In November 2009, the Vatican sponsored the first conference on astrobiology / life from beyond the earth, organized by the Pontifical Academy of Sciences and the Vatican Observatory. Father Jose Gabriel Funes explained, 'Although astrobiology is an emerging field and still a developing subject, the questions of life's origins and of whether life exists elsewhere in the universe are very interesting and deserve serious consideration. These questions offer many philosophical and theological implications.'

Funes also said there is no clash between believing in Catholic doctrine and believing in the possibility of alien life. 'To say it with St Francis, if we can consider some earthly creatures as 'brothers' or 'sisters,' why could we not speak of a 'brother alien'? He would also belong to the creation.'

For Funes, there is no problem with acknowledging that the universe has been created, and at the same time participate in questioning the origins of life to entertain modern evolutionary theory as life's source.

Paul Davies, a theoretical physicist and cosmologist from Arizona State University added: 'The real threat would come from the discovery of extraterrestrial intelligence, because if there are beings elsewhere in the universe, then Christians, they're in this horrible bind. They believe that God became incarnate in the form of Jesus Christ in order to save humankind, not dolphins or chimpanzees or little green men on other planets.'

When the rebellious angels have been fully exiled from heaven to earth, the Vatican Observatory and the Vatican decided that they will encourage humanity to receive the extraterrestrials / rebellious angels, as educators, leaders and rulers for humanity. It will be a cultural understanding reminiscent of the time of Enoch during the antediluvian / preflood era (first book of Enoch).

The extraterrestrials / rebellious angels will also be presented as objects worthy of worship. But the biblical record documented that angels loyal to God Most High and to the kingdom of heaven, refuse to be worshiped (Matthew

4:9-10, Luke 4:7-8, Romans 1:25, Colossians 2:18, Revelation 19:10, 22:8-9, etc.).

According to the early followers of the Lamb / Jesus Christ, history was clear that Jesus Christ came to provide redemption to humanity, and humanity alone. The rebellious angels and demons / 'aliens' are not and will not be offered redemption in God Most High's plan of redemption, reclamation and regeneration. The biblical record did not allow for humanity or for God Most High to forget that the rebellious angels are responsible for necessitating the scheduled events of the era of the time of Jacob's Trouble in the process of redeeming and reclaiming earth's dominion from the red dragon / serpent / Satan, Inc.

The biblical record taught this: To which of the angels did God ever say, 'Sit at my right hand until I make your enemies a footstool for your feet?' Are not all angels ministering spirits sent to serve those who will inherit salvation? Hebrews 1:13-14

For surely it is not angels that Jesus helps, but Abraham's descendants. Hebrews 2:16

For if God did not spare angels when they sinned, but sent them to hell, putting them in chains of darkness to be held for judgment... 2 Peter 2:4

The Vatican Observatory was first established in Rome Italy. The Gregorian Tower / Tower of Winds was completed in 1580 and is located next to Saint Peter's Basilica. Under the authority of the Society of Jesus / Jesuits, the observatory was relocated to the top of the Church of Saint Ignatius in Rome. In 1870 with the unification of Italy, the observatory was administered by the Italian government. In 1891, Leo XIII refounded the Specola Vaticana / Vatican Observatory on the walls at the edge of the Vatican. Pius XI (fl. 1922 to 1939) relocated the Vatican Observatory to Castel Gandolfo Italy, the pope's summer villa, sixteen miles southeast of Rome. In 1961, the Vatican Observatory Research Group (VORG) established offices at the Steward Observatory of the University of Arizona in Tucson. In 1984, the University of Arizona and the Vatican selected Mount Graham as the site for a complex of eighteen telescopes. In 1993, the VORG completed construction of the Vatican Advanced Technology Telescope on Mount Graham, near Safford Arizona.

Mount Graham in Arizona is considered by the Native Americans as one of three holiest sites. Native Americans understand that these sacred places are portals to the spirit world. For the Arizona Apache, Mount Graham is also known as Dzil Nchaa Si An / Big Seated Mountain and was mentioned in the sacred songs which have been handed down through the oral tradition, for many generations. Mount Graham is understood to be where the Ga'an / guardian spirits of the Apache, live.

While the Apache opposed the construction of the Vatican Observatory complex on Mount Graham, the Roman Catholic Church labeled their opposition as 'part of a Jewish conspiracy' from Jewish lawyers of the American Civil Liberties Union who attempted to undermine and destroy the Roman Catholic Church. While the controversy between the Apache and the Roman Catholic Church continues, the connection between the choice of this site location for the Vatican Observatory complex, and the Apache's tradition that this mountain is a portal site, cannot be lost.

Early in his papacy, Francis said, 'If, for example, tomorrow an expedition of Martians came, and some of them came to us, here… Martians, right? Green, with that long nose and big ears, just like children paint them…. And one says, 'But I want to be baptized!' What would happen?'

'When the Lord shows us the way, who are we to say, 'No, Lord, it is not prudent! No, let's do it this way'… Who are we to close doors? In the early church, even today, there is the ministry of the ostiary [usher]. And what did the ostiary do? He opened the door, received the people, allowed them to pass. But it was never the ministry of the closed door, never.'

Francis anticipates that under his leadership, humanity will receive and revere extraterrestrial life / rebellious angels, and come to understand that the extraterrestrials / rebellious angels will provide superior knowledge to humanity. Francis' theology holds that the extraterrestrials / rebellious angels will be sent as messengers of God Most High, not as adversaries to God Most High.

Baptism is the spiritual and physical act of cleansing for the purpose of meeting God Most High, and of becoming presentable for entrance into heaven. Water baptism is the symbolic act of the death of the physical and spiritual impurities and the rising to new life, new eternal life. It would be wholly inappropriate to ever offer any of heaven's various forms of baptism to the very creatures that have necessitated the need for baptism originally. It would also be wholly inappropriate to defy God Most High's action of expelling the rebellious angels to earthy by baptizing them as a promise to reenter the very kingdom of heaven that they have been violently expelled from.

Francis, the hierarchy of the Vatican and the Vatican Observatory, will consider the extraterrestrials / rebellious angels as being free from original sin. Baptism will not be necessary for them.

In order to substitute the Vatican's version of scientism for authentic science, the Vatican must also discredit, minimize, dismiss, and terminate any authority and authenticity that the biblical record presented. 'The Bible is not a scientific book. If we look for scientific responses to our questions in the Bible, we are making a mistake.' Funes.

If the biblical record has been successfully discredited and its authority dismissed, then the resurrection of messiah / the Lamb / Jesus Christ must also be placed in the category of allegory and unproven. If the resurrection of messiah / the Lamb / Jesus Christ is successfully fabulized, then there can be no expectation of his return to defeat the enemies of God Most High and of the kingdom of heaven. If messiah / the Lamb / Jesus Christ does not return to fully establish the kingdom of heaven on earth, then the Garden of Eden / garden of God / paradise living conditions cannot be established. And if regeneration of the earth were not able to reestablish Garden of Eden living conditions, then the argument could be made that there is no reason to believe that God the Creator created humanity to begin with and has no claim to have authority over humanity or over the earth; leaving dominion over the earth to be able to be claimed by others. And it is the serpent / Satan who continues to make the claim that the red dragon / serpent / Satan, Inc. is the only lawful and truthful owner of dominion over the earth.

Humanity is left to decide which is the greater authority, God Most High and the kingdom of heaven, or the hierarchy of the Vatican? Is the greater authority the biblical record that has been six thousand years in the making, or the scientism developed through the Vatican Observatory, the Jesuits and the hierarchy of the Roman Catholic Church?

Prior to the future abomination of desolation event, the earth and humanity will have already experienced the fifth trumpet's five months of the locust scorpions torture and possibly the sixth trumpet's four Euphrates River bound angels as they will have led their two hundred million horse and rider cavalry to destroy humanity. Along with the expulsion of rebellious angels falling to earth, these events will provide the global religious community with the 'evidence' that they need to further grab power, for the purpose of fully establishing the kingdom of Satan, Inc. / kingdom of man on earth. The inhabitants of the earth will be primed and ready for a solution to the spiritual and religious activity that will be globally experienced.

The beast of the sea / false prophet / eighth king beast and the global religious community will use the hurling of the rebellious angels to earth as further evidence for the need of a 'messiah' who will be a leader that will provide global rule. The timing will be optimum for the introduction of the beast of the earth to be coronated as 'king of kings,' 'son of god,' and divine himself. The people of the world will implore the two beasts of Revelation 13 to contain and control the rebellious angels and demons / aliens, and to be the broker for the trading of hidden / secret knowledge obtained from the rebellious angels and demons / aliens. And with the amount of death that will have taken place, there will be global chaos within the governmental structures of the nations, cities, and municipalities, so that the inhabitants of the earth will also seek out a leader who can bring a new kind of order to the world without the idea of law that is under the authority of God Most High.

While this is the portrait that the biblical record depicted, those who have invested in establishing the global governance system have painted an almost exact duplicate of the same portrait with the advancement of the need for an 'Omega Point' where the world will be brought to a level of chaos so that humanity will globally capitulate to the institution of global governance.

Feudalism was and is a system where the law applies to those who are governed, but the law does not apply to those who provide the governance. When the rule of law is not applied to every individual equally, the result is that only the greater power structures or entities that are a threat to the existing ruling body are able to hold the ruling body in check. In practice, Feudalism was a failed system of the Dark Ages / Middle Ages / medieval period. But a form of feudalism will be revived as the model for the global governance system that will be imposed during the era of the time of Jacob's Trouble. The new form of feudalism was also known as communism, Marxism, socialism, fascism, progressivism, etc. All forms provided an oligarchy of rulers whose tyrannical rule was considered to be better than forms of governments where the people were able to make self-determining decisions concerning their rule.

With the arrival of the rebellious angels and demons / aliens to live entirely on earth when their access to heaven has been entirely revoked, the rebellious angels will work to increase the sense of lawlessness. Not only will the elite ruling class live against the law, but the rebellious angels and demons will also be given special privilege to destroy life without accountability. Both the ruling elite and the rebellious angels and demons will expound on the benefits of living in rebellion against God Most High and against God's law.

Toward the end of the era of the time of Jacob's Trouble, the destruction that the rebellious angels and demons / aliens will employ, will fully replace the growth and life that is the foundation for the kingdom of heaven.

With the active and present leadership of the rebellious angels and demons, rebellion against God Most High will reach its apex. It will eventually seem as if there is no one or nothing that will be able to stop the fierceness and terribleness of their activity. Jesus' comment to the disciples to describe this era of time was, 'If those days had not been shortened, no one would have survived. But because of the elect, the days will be shortened.' Matthew 24:22 translated. *The 'elect,' are those who have chosen to be followers of the Lamb / Jesus Christ.*

While the emphasis on giving a 'scientific' explanation for events, will be the focus of the Roman Catholic Church and the global religious community, in reality, there is no authentic 'scientific' explanation that can exist in conjunction with the elimination of the sovereign and divine God Most High and of God's mighty activity. The scientism / pseudo-scientific explanation that the global religious community will offer, will deny that God created the world and the universe / cosmos. The fact that the nature of true science is also a creation of God the Creator, will be rejected in the presentation to the inhabitants of the earth. And the inhabitants of the earth will accept the global religious community's redefinition of science, along with modern evolutionary theory and the rebranding of extraterrestrials / rebellious angels as superior and more knowledgeable beings, worthy of reverence and worship.

Using the institution and the authority of the traditional, organized, and established 'church,' the red dragon / serpent / Satan, Inc. will use the global religious community to continue to deny the divinity of Jesus Christ, Jesus Christ's resurrection from the dead, Jesus Christ's ascension into heaven, and Jesus Christ's scheduled return, and instead understand the biblical Jesus Christ as the myth. And the global religious community will present the myth of the baal / mystery / mythology religion as the 'reality.' The majority of the people of the world will accept the redefined presentation of 'science' merely because they will acquiesce to the recognized authority that is assumed to be inherent within the 'church' as God's instrument.

There are also other organizations that have embraced the concept of portals into the supernatural realm.

The European Organization for Nuclear Research / Conseil européen pour la recherche nucléaire / CERN is based in a suburb of Geneva on the Franco-Swiss border and has twenty three member states. Even Israel has been granted full membership. As an official United Nations Observer, CERN is connected to the mission of the United Nations. One of the goals of CERN is to use the large Hadron Collider for opening portals to other dimensions. Another goal is to identify the 'God particle' which scientists fear may trigger a catastrophic vacuum decay which would cause space and time to collapse.' The town in France where CERN is partially situated is called 'Saint Genus Pouilly.' The name 'Pouilly' comes from the Latin 'Appolliacum' and is so named possibly because of a connection in Roman times to a temple that existed there in honor of Apollo, because it was believed to be a gateway to the underworld. Also on the CERN location is a statue of the dancing Hindu god Shiva / Hindu god of both creation and destruction, a gift from the nation of India. Even the CERN logo seems to sport '666.' While the CERN organization would stress the scientific nature of the research conducted there, the connection to eschatological aspects of religion must be acknowledged.

There are other organizations that also seek to discover connections into other worlds and to prepare the people of the world mentally and emotionally for receiving what may be found from those other worlds.

But the biblical record has the longest history of recognizing and defining what will be experienced when beings from 'other worlds' fully enter into the realm of the earth. And it is the biblical record that has defined those beings as rebellious angels and demons.

The Red Dragon / Serpent / Satan, Inc. Makes War with the People and Nation of Israel – Revelation 12

The first purpose of the era of the time of Jacob's Trouble, will bring the people of Israel to the realization that God Most High already provided the promised and prophesied messiah to them, in the form of Jesus Christ. To convince the people of Israel of their need to accept Jesus Christ as their promised and prophesied messiah, the people of Israel must be challenged to wrestle with their theology. And the entity that will provide the people of Israel with that challenge will be the red dragon / serpent / Satan, Inc.

And the dragon stands before the woman that is about to bring forth (her child), so that when she should bring forth her child, the red dragon might devour the child. Revelation 12:4b translated

When the dragon saw that he had been thrown down to the earth, the dragon *(serpent / Satan)* pursued the woman *(Israel)* who had brought forth the male child *(messiah / Jesus Christ)*. And two wings of the great eagle were given to the woman so that she could fly into the wilderness, into her place, where she is nourished there for a time and times and half a time, away from the face of the serpent. Revelation 12:13-14 translated

The history of this prophecy began with the birth of the male child / Jesus Christ. Although this prophecy was given almost one hundred years <u>after</u> the birth of Jesus Christ, the imagery here was clearly connected with the birth of Jesus Christ.

King Herod was king over Israel when Jesus was born. King Herod was not Jewish through his genetics. Herod's heritage was Idumean, a descendant of Esau the brother of Jacob. Esau was not included in the messianic lineage. The Idumeans and the Israelites shared a deadly rivalry. Herod's family converted to Judaism in order to rule over Israel as a Roman empire appointee. Because of his heritage, Herod's seat upon the throne of Israel was tenuous and illegitimate in the eyes of God Most High. First, the throne of Israel truly belonged to a descendant of David who was in the messianic lineage, as established by God Most High. Second, Herod's ability to relate to the people of Israel was fragile. When Herod heard that the

Israelite messiah was born, Herod perceived this child as a true threat to his throne.

Viewing Jesus' birth as a threat, Herod attempted to assassinate the infant. Failing to capture and destroy the infant, Herod pursued the other infant boys in Bethlehem through what became known as the 'slaughter of the innocents' (Matthew 2:16-18). Herod working as an agent of the red dragon / serpent / Satan, Inc. provided the first defeat for the kingdom of Satan, Inc. / kingdom of man in the direct attempts to 'devour the child.'

Jesus Christ's crucifixion was the second direct attempt by the red dragon / serpent / Satan, Inc. to devour the male child. Unfortunately for the red dragon / serpent / Satan, Inc., even though the death of Jesus Christ was accomplished through crucifixion (a cursed death that should have rendered Jesus unacceptable for God Most High to ever receive Jesus again), God resurrected Jesus as the firstfruits of resurrection. It was the second failed direct attempt to 'devour the child' that was thwarted. Following the crucifixion, death, resurrection and ascension of Jesus Christ, the persecution of the followers of the Way / Christians, began.

During the era of the time of Jacob's Trouble, there will be another direct attempt to 'devour the child.' The ruler who is to come / beast of the earth will be instrumental in providing an environment for the people of Israel to feel safe (Daniel 9:27). But it will be a ruse for the red dragon / serpent / Satan, Inc. to lie in wait for an opportunity to devour the people of Israel.

One of the historical strategies of the red dragon / serpent / Satan, Inc. has been to destroy the mother with the expectation that without the mother, the child cannot be born. If the nation of Israel were to no longer exist, then the people of Israel would not come to the realization that Jesus Christ is the promised and prophesied messiah, rendering the people of Israel ineligible to become the nation of priests for God Most High, and negating the possibility of Jesus Christ to be accepted by the people of Israel. This circumstance would render God Most High's covenant with the people of Israel, void.

So while God Most High will be allowing the people of Israel to wrestle with their choice of who they will receive as their promised and prophesied messiah, Jesus Christ or the beast of the earth, the red dragon / serpent / Satan, Inc. will be actively involved in war with the people of Israel.

This will not be a kind war. It will not be a regional war. It will not be a conventional war.

This time the entities at war will actively include members of the red dragon / serpent / Satan, Inc. that will come with their fury from the sting of being exiled from heaven - after access to heaven has been available to them for six thousand years.

There was war in heaven. Michael and his angels warred against the dragon and the dragon with his angels, warred (back). And the dragon and his angels did not have strength. There was no longer any place found for them in heaven. And the dragon, the ancient great serpent, who is called the devil and Satan, was thrown out. Satan is the deceiver of the whole inhabited world. Satan was thrown down to the earth and his angels were thrown down with him. Revelation 12:7-9 translated

It will be a war of rage because of the expulsion of the rebellious angels from heaven. And that rage will be flung to the earth.

It will be a war of revenge by the red dragon / serpent / Satan, Inc. for the six thousand years that the people dedicated to God Most High, have thwarted the attempts of the red dragon / serpent / Satan, Inc. to fully establish an everlasting dominion over the earth. The red dragon / serpent / Satan, Inc. considers the people of Israel as the first people to be blamed for this failure.

So, the first object of vengeance will be the people of Israel / 'the woman who had given birth to the male child.'

This will be a war involving the cosmos. Hence the inclusion of various plagues that will affect the earth and its waters.

The red dragon / serpent / Satan, Inc. will utilize their limited powers over creation, to attempt to destroy the people of Israel, in the same manner that God the Creator utilized the deluge / flood of Noah's time to destroy

the 'creation' of the red dragon / serpent / Satan, Inc. (Nephilim, chimera and rebellious humanity).

The serpent cast out of his mouth, a river of water after the woman, so that the serpent might cause her to be carried away by a flood.

And the earth helped the woman, and opened its mouth and swallowed up the river, which the dragon had cast out of his mouth. Revelation 12:15-16 translated

With unimaginable fury, Satan and the rebellious angels will focus their attention on the biggest threat to the full establishment of the kingdom of Satan, Inc. / kingdom of man; the people that God Most High covenanted with approximately four thousand years ago. They are the people that God Most High has loved dearly. It will be important for the red dragon / serpent / Satan, Inc. to inflict vitriol upon them in the attempt to injure the heart of God Most High.

When the red dragon / serpent / Satan, Inc. has decided that the direct attempt to annihilate the people of Israel has failed, the red dragon / serpent / Satan, Inc. will pursue those who have a connection with the people of Israel, the Gentile followers of the Lamb / Jesus Christ.

And the dragon was angry with the woman, and went to make war with the rest of her children who are keeping the commandments of God and holding the testimony of Jesus. Revelation 12:17 translated

After being unsuccessful in destroying the apple of God Most High's eye (Deuteronomy 32:10, Zechariah 2:8), the red dragon / serpent / Satan, Inc. will pursue the rest of the people that have been nestled in the heart of God.

During this cosmic war, the people and nation of Israel will experience its greatest vulnerability in all its history.

First the nation of Israel will be vulnerable because it rejected its greatest ally, messiah / the Lamb / Jesus Christ, around 30 AD. When the nation of Israel rejected Jesus Christ, the nation of Israel effectively placed their greatest ally in the category of enemy, rendering the aid that Jesus Christ offers to the nation of Israel to be somewhat ineffectual.

Second the nation of Israel will be vulnerable because Israel will have a false sense of security through its established covenant peace treaty agreement with other nations. One of Adolph Hitler's greatest tactics was to establish peace treaties with nations just prior to attacking the Nazi enemies.

Third the nation of Israel will be vulnerable because Israel will have a trusting relationship with the apostate church, even though the apostate church is antisemitic. The evidence for this dynamic will be the establishment of the idol / image of the beast of the sea, a Christian religious leader, on the temple mount (Revelation 13:14-18). And the people of Israel will have a trusting relationship with the nations that are supportive of the apostate church.

While the red dragon / serpent / Satan, Inc. will view the vulnerability of the people of Israel as a great advantage for the kingdom of Satan, Inc. / kingdom of man, it will be the vulnerability of the people of Israel that will render the people of Israel to be willing to receive God Most High's intervention. This will be the greatest opportunity in the history of Israel for God Most High to display the immeasurable love that God Most High holds for the people and nation of Israel. God Most High has a protection plan for Israel, out of the serpent's reach. And when the hearts of the people of Israel have become soft again, they will seek to reestablish the whole and holy relationship with God Most High. And this time, they will accept the promised and prophesied messiah that God Most High will send to them.

two wings of the great eagle were given to the woman so that she could fly into the wilderness, into her place, where she is nourished there for a time and times and half a time, away from the face of the serpent. Revelation 12:14 translated

Some say that the great eagle represented the United States and the aid that the United States will provide to the people and the nation of Israel. Currently the United States hosts almost half of the world's population of the people of Israel and so this is a very real possibility for the fulfillment of the great eagle refuge prophecy.

John the Revelator identified that the great eagle had two wings. The two wings of the great eagle may represent the wings of an eagle torn off the lion that was the first beast of Daniel's vision of the four beasts / four kingdoms (Daniel 7:4). But it was John who recognized that the great eagle has two wings, and John recognized that this eagle will be great.

Possibilities for the fulfillment of the prophecy of the two wings of a great eagle do include the eagle as the United States. It is also possible that the two wings may represent the United States providing protection of the people of Israel, in two locations, possibly nestling the people of Israel within the United States, and protecting the people of Israel who live in the land of Israel. Or there may be another route for God Most High's fulfillment of the two wings of a great eagle.

Other nations have the eagle as their emblem as well, including Hitler's Nazi Germany. This prophecy will need to be realized in order to accurately understand its full meaning.

The Old Testament / Tanakh prophet Jeremiah's message of restoration of the people of Israel in the land of Israel, and the preparation of the nation of Israel for the arrival of their promised and prophesied messiah – Jeremiah 30:3-9, etc.

'The days are coming,' says the Lord, 'when I will bring back my people Israel and Judah from captivity, and will cause them to return to the land that I gave their fathers to possess.'

These are the words that the Lord spoke concerning Israel and Judah. This is what the Lord said, 'A voice of trembling, we have heard a voice of fear, and not of peace. Ask now and see whether a man is ever in labor with child.' So why do I see every man with his hands on his loins, in labor like a woman, and all their faces turned pale?'

'Alas, that day is great and there is no other day like it. It will be a time of trouble for Jacob. But out of it, Jacob will be saved.'

'For it will come to pass in that day,' says the Lord of hosts, 'that I will break the yoke off of Jacob's neck. And your bonds will burst, and no longer will they be enslaved by foreigners.'

'Instead, they will serve the Lord their God, and David their king, whom I will raise up, for them.' Jeremiah 30:3-9 translated

The king of the united kingdom of Israel, David (1040 - 970 BC), lived long before the prophet Jeremiah prophesied (628 - 585 BC). In the Targum (ancient Aramaic

paraphrase), the term 'David their king' *was translated to read* 'Messiah, the son of David their king.' *In Jeremiah 23:5-6, the Lord gave a more in-depth description of the plan to raise up messiah. Jeremiah used the term of* 'David their king' *whom God would raise up for them after the life of Jeremiah, as a reference for the promised and prophesied messiah, describing Jesus Christ.*

The term 'in that day' *frequently referred to the* 'day' *that messiah will come to rule the world. Combined with the reference to* messiah, the son of David *who will rule the people of Israel in the land of Israel, and with the description of the era of Jacob's Trouble, Jeremiah's message was truly directed to the people living during the era of the time of Jacob's Trouble.*

Jeremiah's message began with the restoration of Israel and Judah out of captivity. The nations of Israel and Judah were depicted as being reestablished back to the land that God had promised Abram / Abraham, Isaac, Jacob / Israel, Moses, the people of Israel, David, etc.; to the land of Israel.

God's promise to Jeremiah to restore Israel also included a promise to restore Israel with a restoration that would be marked with freedom from oppression. Instead of being ruled over in hegemony as the nation of Israel experienced under the Greek and Roman empires, the nation of Israel would rule itself.

When God restored Israel after the seventy years of exile around 516 BC, Israel did not experience freedom from oppression. Even after the Israelites returned from exile, they were not restored in the manner that Jeremiah described here. After returning from exile, the people of Israel remained under the control of others; of the Greeks, Ptolemies / Syrians, Seleucids / Egyptians, and finally of the Romans at the time of Jesus' first coming.

It was not until the nation of Israel was established in 1948 that the nation of Israel experienced its own sovereignty and the military presence to establish its position as a sovereign nation on the world palette of nations.

Therefore, there was no previous time in Israel's history for Jeremiah's prophecy to have been fulfilled ... until May 14, 1948. Jeremiah's prophecy was entirely directed to be a message to those living after 1948, after the nation of Israel was restored.

Jeremiah's description of this era of the time of Jacob's Trouble depicted an intensity and involvement of conflict that will be unprecedented in all human history. It will be a time when people will cry not out of fear, but out of terror. It will be like a terrible nightmare with no hope of waking up to end the night terror. People who have experienced Post Traumatic Stress have similar terror experiences.

When a woman is in labor to deliver a child, she must remain focused on the work at hand. It is an all-consuming time of just focusing on the muscles in her body working to push the child through the birth canal. But this era will be one where even men / all men, will grab their stomachs like a woman in labor and experience that kind of sensation where they are so focused that it demands everything in them to concentrate on the events around them. They will seek to hold themselves together and grab their stomachs in the same way that a woman in labor holds herself. The distress will also show in their deathly pale faces.

The Lord's declaration concerning this era depicted men clutching their stomachs as if they were experiencing childbirth and connected that experience to the woman who gave birth to the male child that the dragon was ready to devour the moment he was born of Revelation 12. Revelation 12:13 read, And when the dragon saw that he had been thrown down to the earth, the dragon pursued the woman who had brought forth the male child. *The woman who gave birth to the male child was a prophetic image of the nation of Israel that brought messiah / Jesus Christ to the world. But at the time that the nation of Israel experienced the first arrival of Jesus, the nation of Israel officially rejected the child. The era of the time of Jacob's Trouble will be the second opportunity for the people of Israel to accept their promised and prophesied messiah. But they will need to experience* 'labor pains' *in order to come to the place where they will be willing and able to accept their promised and prophesied messiah this time.*

The instruction for the people of Israel on how to respond to this war – Matthew 24:15-25, Mark 13:14-23

Jesus Christ provided instruction for the people of Israel, on how to respond to this unique cosmic war.

'Therefore, when you see the abomination of desolation, spoken of by Daniel the prophet, standing in the holy place – let the reader understand – then let those who are in Judea, flee to the mountains. Do not let the one on the housetop come down to take anything out of the house. Do not let the one in the field return back to take his cloak. It will be dreadful to those who are pregnant and nursing infants in those days. Pray that your flight is not in the winter nor on a Sabbath. For then there will be great tribulation, such unequaled from the beginning of the world until now, and never to be equaled again.'

'If those days had not been shortened, no one would have survived. But because of the elect, the days will be shortened.'

'If anyone says to you, 'Behold, here is the messiah!' Or 'Here he is!' Do not believe it. False messiahs and false prophets, will arise; and they will provide great signs and wonders to intentionally mislead, if possible, even the elect.'

'Behold, I have foretold you, ahead of time.' Matthew 24:15-25 translated

'When you see the abomination of the desolation which was spoken of by Daniel the prophet, standing where it should not be – let the one reading understand – then those in Judea should flee to the mountains. Do not let the one on the housetop come down or go in to take anything out of his house. The one in the field should not return to the things behind, to retrieve his clothing.'

'How dreadful it will be for pregnant women and nursing mothers in those days! Pray that this will not take place in winter. For those days will be tribulation such as never has been equaled from the beginning of creation, when God Created the world, until now – and never will be again.'

'If the Lord had not shortened the days, none of humanity would have been saved. But because of the elect whom God chose, God has shortened the days.'

'If anyone says, 'Look, here is the messiah!' or 'Look, there he is!' Do not believe it. False messiahs and false prophets will appear, and will provide signs and wonders to deceive the elect, if that is possible.'

'You however, need to be on your guard. I have told you everything ahead of time.' Mark 13:14-23 translated

The gospel writers described Jesus as throwing in this phrase, 'let the reader understand' and then Jesus assumed that the reader would understand without giving the details that the reader needs to understand.

One possibility for including the phrase may have been to communicate that Matthew, Mark, and / or Jesus, assumes and expects that the reader will be familiar with the message of the prophet Daniel. They may have assumed that the message of Daniel would have been thoroughly presented to the reader and digested through an exhaustive study of the scriptures which would have been practiced at least by some, within the culture of the people of Israel.

Another possibility for including the phrase may have been to communicate that during the time of the fulfillment of the prophecy, the reader will have contemporary and experiential context to connect with the prophecy so that a complete understanding of the message would be achieved at the time that the prophecy fulfillment would be experienced.

Early during the First Jewish Roman War / First Jewish Revolt of 66 – 73 AD, there was an incident when armies surrounded Jerusalem for nine days.

Prior to the Roman siege of 70 AD, there was this unique siege of Jerusalem by Cestius Gallus of Syria that lasted for nine days. Gallus marched into Judea with a force of over thirty thousand in September 66 AD, in an attempt to restore order at the outset of the Great Jewish Revolt. Gallus reached Mount Scopus in Jerusalem and penetrated the outer city, but was unable to take the temple mount. After a siege of nine days, with no definitive explanation, Gallus and his army, left. The Christians living in Jerusalem at the time, remembered Jesus' words, 'When you see the armies surrounding Jerusalem… flee!' Consequently, the followers of Jesus Christ left town. The early Christians escaped to Pella and missed the horrific blood bath that followed under the siege by the Roman General Titus.

Daniel (fl. 605 to 530 BC) - a prophet of Judah, provided a description of the first abomination of desolation event that took place in the month of Kislev 167 BC. It was a vision of the work of Antiochus IV Epiphanes.

'He will muster his forces and they will defile the sanctuary fortress. Then they will take away the daily sacrifices, in the place of the abomination of desolation.' Daniel 11:31 translated

Dainel provided other details concerning the future abomination of desolation in other chapters as well. But the first abomination of desolation that Daniel documented, acted as a typology for the future abomination of desolation event. The evidence that the two abomination of desolation events are related, was the fact that Daniel's description of the abomination of desolation event, was included within Daniel's historical list of the kings of the north and the kings of the south and the king that will exalt himself.

The list of the kings of the north and the kings of the south covered history that was completed during the four hundred years of silence prior to the arrival of Jesus Christ for his earthly ministry.

Daniel's gap between the accounting of the kings of the north and kings of the south, and the king that will exalt himself, was where the description of the abomination of desolation fit in, connecting the two eras of time in Daniel's description.

Just as the previous abomination of desolation event was marked by war in and around Jerusalem, this future abomination of desolation event will be marked by war. Instead of the Seleucid Antiochus IV Epiphanes of Syria (167 BC), or the events of the First Jewish Roman War / First Jewish Revolt of 66 - 73 AD; the war surrounding this future abomination of desolation will be extensively supernaturally empowered by the red dragon / serpent / Satan, Inc. Only with the supernatural empowerment of the red dragon / serpent / Satan, Inc. will this war be able to reach the massive intensity to be able to be described as the 'great distress, unequaled from the beginning of the world until now and never to be equaled again.'

The intensity of this future war will be so great that God Most High will not just aid those who work for God Most High's will to be done, but God Most High be forced to intercede using superior extraordinary power, power that nothing on earth will be able to resource. The world has not yet experienced days when if God did not intervene and shorten the days, no one would survive.

Multiple possibilities exist for the meaning of the phrase 'but for the sake of the elect those days will be shortened.' Some of the possibilities include:

- shortening the lifespan of humanity. Previously, God Most High decided to shorten the human lifespan with the deluge / flood. God Most High said that the Holy Spirit would not contend with humanity forever, so the lifespan was shortened from a thousand years to a hundred and twenty years (Genesis 6:3).
- the darkness that will come with the sounding of the fourth trumpet when a third of the sun will be struck, a third of the moon, and a third of the stars, so that a third of them turned dark. A third of the day was without light, and also a third of the night (Revelation 8:12).
- shortening the days through the pouring out of the fifth bowl / fifth last plague which will be poured out on the throne of the beast / the red dragon / serpent / Satan, Inc., plunging the beast's kingdom into darkness (Revelation 16:10).
- shortening the days in the same manner that the day was lengthened for Joshua as the people of Israel battled the Amorites (Joshua 10:12-14).
- shortening the days by having the return of messiah / the Lamb / Jesus Christ scheduled ahead of the timeline determined by the kingdom of Satan, Inc. / kingdom of man for the full establishment of global governance on earth. Or
- yet another manner in which God Most High will shorten the days that has not yet been revealed to us.

Prior to the first abomination of desolation, Antiochus IV Epiphanes had militarily traveled through the land of Israel on his way to Egypt. It was on his return home that Antiochus IV Epiphanes stopped to plunder the wealth of the temple of Israel, which incited the people of Israel to revolt, and Antiochus to respond with a policy of extermination of the people of Israel, and the destruction of the national religion.

During the siege of Jerusalem and the destruction of the 'second temple' in 70 AD, the Roman General Titus was able to kill over a million Jewish people and enslave around ninety seven thousand. In 70 AD, this was a substantial portion of the world's Jewish population that was eliminated.

If the current Israeli Knesset and Sanhedrin during the era of the time of Jacob's Trouble will be able to establish a greater level of Mosaic Law, then the Sabbath Day will not allow travel and less freedom of travel would make escape difficult. On the seventeenth of Tammuz / July 19, 2018 the Knesset voted that Israel would be a Jewish state which meant that more elements of Mosaic Law will be honored including the Mosaic Law to refrain from travel on the Sabbath.

To survive the red dragon / serpent / Satan, Inc.'s war with the people of Israel, the people of Israel and the followers of the Lamb / Jesus Christ, living in Jerusalem must again leave Jerusalem immediately when they witness the armies encamped around Jerusalem. There will be no time to go home or to pack a suitcase. There will not even be time to pick up a coat. Just as it was for the first abomination of desolation event of 167 BC and for the First Jewish Roman War / First Jewish Revolt of 66 - 73 AD, those who heed this warning will leave town immediately. Those who do not heed the warning will be slaughtered.

Note that these phrases 'but for the sake of the elect...' and 'to deceive even the elect...' indicated that 'the elect' will be present to experience and witness global events. Those phrases also indicated that the elect will experience a certain level of protection as well as challenge.

The People of Israel Will Be Cared for by God – Hosea 2:14-15, Revelation 12:6, 12:13-14, etc.

God Most High's promise concerning the people of Israel: 'Therefore I am now going to allure her. I will lead her into the desert and speak tenderly to her. There I will give her back her vineyards, and will make the Valley of Achor / Valley of trouble, a door of hope. There she will sing as in the day she came up out of Egypt.' Hosea 2:14-15

While the red dragon / serpent / Satan, Inc. will be at war with the people of Israel, God Most High will take the opportunity to woo the people of Israel back.

The Old Testament / Tanakh prophet Hosea (fl. 750 to 715 BC) - of Israel, was not the only prophet to document God Most High's enduring love for the people and nation of Israel, and God Most High's insistence upon preserving the people and nation of Israel. Although two thirds of the people of Israel will be killed during the era of the time of Jacob's Trouble, the one third that will remain / the remnant, will be tried by fire, refined and loyal to God Most High, returning that love that God Most High so lavishes upon God's holy people.

There will be something special that takes place between the people of Israel and God Most High while the people of Israel are in the desert, averting the full effects of the war of the red dragon / serpent / Satan, Inc. against them. Only in the desert will the people of Israel be free from their daily distractions in order to be able to focus on reestablishing their right and full relationship with God Most High.

When the people of Israel left Egypt, after the spies had made their report concerning the giants of the land of Canaan / the Promised Land, the response of the people of Israel was to step away from God Most High's plan for them to take and reside in the Promised Land. God Most High's response was to lead the people of Israel in the wilderness for forty years, until the next generation was ready to enter and reside in the Promised Land.

It is in the desert / the wilderness that God Most High was able to shape and form God Most High's people so that they were equipped for achieving God Most High's work. It will again be in the desert that the people of Israel will be able to hear God Most High as God speaks tenderly to her.

The woman fled into the wilderness where she has a place there that has been prepared by God, so that there, they should nourish her for one thousand two hundred sixty days. Revelation 12:6 translated

This time as the people of Israel flee, they will again flee to the desert, to a place already prepared for her. This may be the area of Petra / Seir where King David eluded Saul. Or their protective refuge may be in some other desert, or their refuge may come from another nation that is supportive of the people and nation of Israel.

While there are some who would place the one thousand two hundred sixty days of refugee status for the people of Israel, on the calendar to take place during the first part of the era of the time of Jacob's Trouble, that would be improbable because the covenant peace treaty agreement will be honored during the first half of the era of the time of Jacob's Trouble.

Also, it is the red dragon / serpent / Satan, Inc. that will be an active participant in this cosmic portion of the war against the people of Israel, led by the expelled and exiled Satan and his angels who have been hurled to earth. At the beginning of the seven year covenant peace treaty agreement, the rebellious angels still have occupancy within heaven itself.

It will be the future abomination of desolation event that will be simultaneously a breaking of the covenant peace treaty agreement with Israel and a declaration of war against the people and the nation of Israel.

There is also the matter of the temple needing to be rebuilt during the first half of the era of the time of Jacob's Trouble in order for there to be a site for the future abomination of desolation to take place. Building a temple while at war would be a monumental task, especially if the people of Israel were refugees hiding out south of Jerusalem.

The evidence of the biblical record supported that the one thousand two hundred sixty days of refugee status

will take place after the era of the future abomination of desolation and that the future abomination of desolation will be a time for the people of Israel to heed Jesus Christ's words of warning from Matthew 24:15-28 and Mark 13:14-20 to leave town.

When the dragon saw that he had been thrown down to the earth, the dragon pursued the woman *(Israel)* who had brought forth the male child *(messiah / Jesus Christ)*. And two wings of the great eagle were given to the woman so that she could fly into the wilderness, into her place, where she is nourished there for a time and times and half a time, away from the face of the serpent. Revelation 12:13-14 translated

John the Revelator recorded God Most High's plan for providing for the people of Israel, twice within the description of the red dragon / serpent / Satan, Inc.! In case it was missed the first time, the preservation of the remnant of the people of Israel is important to God Most High!

In addition to the desert providing a kind of 'hiding place' for the people of Israel, there will be aid given to Israel as represented by the two wings of a great eagle.

The eagle may represent a nation that is represented by an eagle or God Most High may have some other interpretation of the eagle, waiting for this time.

This will not be the first time that God Most High has provided eagle wing's protection for the people of Israel. As the people of Israel were exiting from Egypt as they were pursued by the Egyptians, in 1446 BC, God Most High provided the escape route for the people of Israel through the Red Sea. The Red Sea path was salvation for the people of Israel, but was utter and complete destruction for the Egyptian military. At the conclusion of the Red Sea experience, God Most High spoke to the people of Israel and said, 'You yourselves have seen what I did to Egypt, and how I carried you on eagles' wings and brought you to myself.' Exodus 19:4

The Representatives of the Two Different Kingdoms Will Converge Upon the Temple Mount and the Future Abomination of Desolation Event will Take Place – the two witnesses, Revelation 11:1-14 and the two beasts, Revelation 13

In every major conflict, there is one event that defines the point when hostilities have reached a point where war has been declared and the various sides in the conflict have committed themselves to the destruction of their enemies. Usually, the event of the declaration of war, is defined as when the first shots were fired.

There have been many points throughout human history when the hostilities of this cosmic conflict have flared and could potentially have been identified as points when fully engaged war could have been declared: the moment when God the Creator addressed the serpent / Satan, the first man and first woman for their rebellion; the moment when God the Creator determined that it was time for the deluge / flood; the moment when the Egyptians attempted to thwart the people of Israel from worshiping God Most High and the Egyptians attempted to annihilate the people of Israel while they were camped by the Red Sea; the moment when Haman attempted to annihilate the people of Israel living in exile in Persia; the moment when messiah / the Lamb / Jesus Christ was crucified; etc.

But the biblical record was clear that none of those conflict points throughout human history, match the heightened hostilities that exist during the era of the time of Jacob's Trouble (Jeremiah 30:7) (time of great distress: Daniel 12:1, Zephaniah 1:14-18, Matthew 24:21, Mark 13:17-19, Luke 21:23, Romans 2:5-11).

In past history, God Most High has sent a leader here, a leader there; a prophet here, a prophet there. And the kingdom of Satan, Inc. / kingdom of man has generally sent one person at a time to represent its kingdom.

But during the era of the time of Jacob's Trouble, both kingdoms will be sending in teams of two leaders to provide leadership in the pursuit of the respective kingdoms' interests.

  To understand the events that will take place during the second half of the era of the time of Jacob's Trouble, it is essential to understand the different teams that represent the two kingdoms; the kingdom of Satan, Inc. / kingdom of man and the kingdom of heaven. At the time of the future abomination of desolation event, both kingdoms will have two representatives. All four of the main representatives of the two kingdoms in conflict, will converge upon the temple mount around the time of the future abomination of desolation event.

  Working on behalf of the kingdom of heaven will be the two witnesses who will return from heaven, Moses and Elijah. Moses and Elijah will witness on the temple mount for one thousand two hundred sixty days. The two witnesses will be empowered by the Holy Spirit. The mission of the two witnesses will be to invite people to repent and turn to God Most High, accepting Jesus Christ as the promised and prophesied messiah. (Revelation 11:1-14)

  Working on behalf of the kingdom of Satan, Inc. / kingdom of man will be the two beasts of Revelation 13. These two beasts will be empowered by the red dragon / serpent / Satan, Inc. The mission of the two beasts / two men, will be to fully establish the kingdom of Satan, Inc. / kingdom of man through the full establishment and implementation of the global religious community, the global governance system, the global economic structure and the global cultural theoterrorism movement. The two beasts will manipulate the inhabitants of the earth into accepting the kingdom of Satan, Inc. / kingdom of man as the ultimate authority for the world. A portion of their strategy will be to attempt to eliminate the image of God the Creator that was pressed into all of humanity, so that the inhabitants of the earth will no longer be acceptable as potential citizens for the kingdom of heaven. Together, the men, with the assistance of their supporting institutions and their supernatural endowment, will become beasts. The two men who will fill the position of the two beasts of Revelation 13, are currently living on earth.

  Both teams will be given one thousand two hundred sixty days / forty two months to work (one thousand two hundred sixty days for the two witnesses, Revelation 11:3: forty two months for the two beasts of Revelation 13, Revelation 13:5). The fact that both teams are limited to the same amount of specified time was evidence that the two teams will work consecutively.

The work of the two witnesses will end with the murder of the two witnesses when the beast that comes from the Abyss attacks them, overpowers them, and kills them (Revelation 11:7). Only after the two witnesses have been assassinated, resurrected and ascend into heaven, can the final set of events proceed; the sounding of the seventh trumpet, the pouring out of the seven bowls of God Most High's wrath / seven last plagues, the harvest of the earth, the final battle of this age, the gathering of the grapes, etc.

It is within the theology of the people of Israel that their messiah will be preceded by a forerunner, an 'Elijah.' The red dragon / serpent / Satan, Inc. must imitate the prophecy as described in the biblical record.

The Lord communicated through the prophet Malachi, 'I will send my messenger, who will prepare the way before me. Then suddenly the Lord you are seeking will come to his temple. The messenger of the covenant, whom you desire, will come,' says the Lord Almighty.' Malachi 3:1

'Behold, I will send you Elijah the prophet, before the coming of the great and dreadful day of the Lord. And he will turn the hearts of the fathers to their children, and the hearts of children to their fathers. Otherwise, I will come and strike the earth with a curse.' Malachi 4:5-6 translated

At the Passover Seder meal, it has been a tradition to set an extra place setting for the expected Elijah and to even check at the door to see if Elijah has come.

The red dragon / serpent / Satan, Inc. understands that any candidate that would be presented to assume the role of ruler of the earth, also needs a forerunner. But the forerunner for the beast of the earth will be a counterfeit Elijah, a false prophet, a pseudo fulfillment for the position that God Most High has reserved for the true forerunner Elijah, who must arrive prior to the coming of messiah.

The beast of the earth will also be a counterfeit candidate for the role of messiah, a pseudo fulfillment for the position that God Most High has reserved for the true messiah / the Lamb / Jesus Christ.

There has also been much speculation concerning the identity of the forerunner for God Most High's promised and prophesied messiah. For those who do not believe that Elijah will personally return, a host of other candidates have been considered as the forerunner. One of the most popular candidates for the role is the current Israeli Prime Minister Benjamin Netanyahu.

But the biblical record has defined the true forerunner for messiah to be the actual Elijah who was taken into heaven around 842 BC, and who will return to earth and minister for exactly one thousand two hundred sixty days before finally being assassinated (Malachi 3:1, 4:5-6, Revelation 11:1-14).

For those who believe that Jesus Christ is God Most High's messiah, it is difficult to mentally envelope the idea that the people of Israel would consider either Benjamin Netanyahu or others, or even one of the two beasts of Revelation 13 as potentially filling the position of forerunner to the coming messiah, a position that always in Jewish tradition has been designated to be filled personally by Elijah the prophet.

What has been definitively documented by the prophets of the Old Testament / Tanakh and John the Revelator was that both kingdoms will have their teams arriving on the temple mount around the time of the future abomination of desolation event (Daniel 8:11-14, 9:27, Revelation 11:1-14, 13).

And both teams will have the foundation for their support systems in place for the future abomination of desolation event. God Most High will have as a support system the followers of the Lamb / Jesus Christ. And the kingdom of Satan, Inc. / kingdom of man will have developed the global religious community, the global governance system, the global economic structure and the global cultural theoterrorism movement.

The Two Witnesses From Heaven – Revelation 11:1-14

Just before Jesus Christ came for his earthly ministry, there was one unique witness / prophet of God Most High, sent to prepare the way: John the Baptist (Matthew 3:1-12, 11:11-12, 17:9-13, Mark 1:1-8, Luke 1:5-25, 1:57-66, 3:1-20, Luke 7:18-35, John 1:15-42).

Just before Jesus Christ returns, there will be two witnesses / prophets of God Most High, to prepare the way for the work that he will do in fully establishing the kingdom of heaven on earth. The two witnesses were once prophets for the people and nation of Israel, taken to heaven at the conclusion of their original work.

But when these two witnesses return, they will not be received as they were in the past. Jesus said that if the people of Israel did not listen to Moses and the Prophets, they will not be convinced of God Most High's divinity and sovereignty, even if someone rises from the dead (Luke 16:31). This was a statement that may have been a veiled foretelling of how the people of Israel will receive the two witnesses when they return.

I will appoint my two witnesses, and they will prophesy one thousand two hundred and sixty days, clothed in sackcloth. These are the two olive trees and the two lampstands standing before the Lord of the earth. If anyone should desire to harm them, fire comes out of their mouths and devours their enemies. And if anyone should desire to harm them, it is necessary for them to be killed in this manner. They have the power to shut heaven, so that no rain falls in the days of their prophecy. They have power over the waters, to turn them into blood; and to strike the earth with every plague, as often as they might desire.

When they have completed their testimony, the beast that ascends out of the Abyss will make war against them, and overcome them, and kill them. And their dead bodies will lie in the street of the great city which spiritually is called Sodom and Egypt, where also their Lord was crucified. And those from the peoples, multitudes, languages, and nations, will gaze upon their bodies for three and a half days, and will not allow their bodies to be put into a tomb. And the inhabitants of the earth will rejoice over them. They will celebrate and send gifts to one another, because these two prophets tormented the inhabitants of the earth.

But after the three and a half days, the breath of life from God entered into them, and they stood upon their feet. Great fear fell upon those who saw them. And they heard a great voice out of heaven saying to them, 'Come up here.' And they went up to heaven in a cloud; and their enemies saw them. In that same hour, there was a great earthquake and a tenth of the city fell. And in the earthquake, seven thousand men of names / well known men (global leaders) were killed. The rest became terrified and gave glory to the God of heaven.

The second woe has passed. Behold the third woe is coming quickly. Revelation 11:3-14 translated

The possibilities for the identities of the two witnesses that will be sent from heaven are; Enoch, Moses, and Elijah.

According to the biblical record, Enoch and Elijah were both taken to heaven without dying. Moses' death was prerecorded in the biblical record, by Moses himself as if he expected to die and so he recorded it. But there was also presented in the biblical record the idea that Moses was taken to heaven without dying.

Before Jesus was crucified, he went up on a mountain and chatted with Moses and Elijah, who were residing in heaven, but dropped in for a visit. The three of them shone with glory. This experience was possibly the greatest evidence that Moses has not yet experienced death. (Matthew 17:1-13, Mark 9:2-13, Luke 9:28-36)

... Jesus led them up a high mountain by themselves. There Jesus was transfigured before them. Jesus' face shone like the sun, and his clothes became as white as the light. Just then there appeared before them Moses and Elijah, talking with Jesus. Matthew 17:1-3

The mountain was referred to in the biblical record as the 'mountain of transfiguration.' *There is dispute about which mountain in Israel was the actual mountain of transfiguration.*

The biblical record also documented that it is appointed unto every person to die once (Hebrews 9:27).

It is appointed unto every person to die once... Hebrews 9:27a

But there have been exceptions to this rule in the past. Various people have died, risen from death, and then died again later. Some who have experienced death twice were:

- *the son of the widow in Zarephath Phoenicia (Elijah's work - 1 Kings 17:17-24),*

- the Shunammite woman's son (Elisha's work – 2 Kings 4:18-37),
- the man who came to life when his body touched Elisha's bones / tomb (2 Kings 13:20-21),
- the widow of Nain's son (Jesus Christ's work – Luke 7:11-17),
- Jairus' daughter (Jesus Christ's work – Luke 8:49-56),
- Lazarus (Jesus Christ's work – John 11:1-44, 12:1-2, 12:9-11),
- those whose graves were opened at the time that Jesus Christ was crucified, died and was resurrected (Matthew 27:52-53),
- Tabitha / Dorcus (Peter's work – Acts 9:36-43),
- Eutychus (Paul's work – Acts 20:7-12).

These people were risen from death and then experienced their earthly deaths for a second time.

In the biblical record there are only three prophets who have not died:
1. Enoch who walked with God and was no more because he was taken out of the antediluvian / preflood world (Genesis 5:24, Hebrews 11:5),
2. Moses who was taken as he viewed the Promised Land that he was forbidden to enter (Deuteronomy 34 and Josephus Antiquities of the Jews IV:48-49), and
3. Elijah who was taken to heaven in a fiery chariot (2 Kings 2:11).

Each person is appointed to die once. But, these three prophets live in heaven without having experienced death ...
    ... yet. ...

Any two of these prophets could be the two witnesses described in Revelation 11:1-14.

Malachi documented that one of the two witnesses will definitely be Elijah (Malachi 4:5). The Jewish tradition also maintains that the promised and prophesied messiah will have a forerunner who will be Elijah. This is why the

Jewish celebration of Passover sets an empty place for Elijah at the Passover feast table in constant anticipation that this will be the year that Elijah joins them.

Because Elijah has been associated with Passover, the people of Israel also believe that when Elijah appears, it will be during the season of Passover.

The other witness who will return, has generally been considered to be Moses because it was Moses carried the Law of God Most High to the people of Israel and Moses was God's instrument to bring the plagues to Egypt during the Exodus. Because one of these two witnesses will be the instrument to bring plagues to Israel during the second half of the era of the time of Jacob's Trouble, Moses became the best candidate as one of the two witnesses.

Moses was considered to represent the Law given by God Most High. Elijah was recognized to be the greatest prophet of Israel. With Moses and Elijah, both the Law and the prophets would be represented to the people of Israel.

The people of Israel are most familiar with Moses and Elijah.

For these reasons, Moses and Elijah would be the most appropriate choices as leaders that would be most effective in communicating with and for the people of Israel.

Moses (1526 to 1406 BC (fl. c. 1447 to 1406 BC))
Why would Moses be one of the two witnesses?

Moses was the greatest leader the people of Israel ever had.

Moses was trained from infancy, in the best that Egypt had to offer. And at that time, Egypt was the superpower of the world, with the greatest technology, greatest education, greatest military advancements and strategies, etc. Moses was one of the best educated in the world because of the education he received next to the Pharaoh's own son, with Egypt's position as the greatest superpower in the world at the time. (Acts 7:21-22)

Moses was provided with the power to perform signs and wonders as the work of God Most High (Exodus, Acts 7:36). And then Moses led the people of Israel out of Egypt, at the age of eighty, defeating the Egyptian military without a single Israelite going to war, and taking the spoils of war with them when they left.

Moses was known as the people of Israel's greatest teacher.

Moses was a family man. Moses was a man of character.

For forty years before the people of Israel entered the Promised Land, Moses kept the people of Israel together in the wilderness. Moses successfully led the people of Israel, against those who opposed Moses' leadership among the people of Israel, and against the other peoples who were opposed to the people of Israel becoming the nation of Israel. Moses will be the right man to lead the people of Israel again. (Acts 7, 2 Timothy 3:8 (3:1-9), etc.)

For many people of Israel even today, the only books that they recognize as being valid are the five books Moses wrote, the Torah / the Pentateuch. Moses was the historian who documented for the people of Israel, a synopsis of the first two thousand five hundred years of human history.

Moses' connection with God Most High was supremely unique. Moses was able to experience glory when Moses was in the presence of the Lord, and it showed on his physical being. Moses met with God on the mountain. Moses was the representative for the people of Israel when they received the Law. Moses provided the conduit for God Most High to give the Law to the people of Israel. The Law defined what sin consisted of, and God Most High's plan for curing sin. (John 1:45, Romans 5:13-15)

Moses was provided with the blueprint for the tabernacle / temples that were constructed to demonstrate God's redemption, reclamation and regeneration plan; and how humanity would be able to establish right relationships with God Most High. Moses was provided with the instructions for the required feast that dramatically foretold the work of the promised and *prophesied messiah, in reestablishing humanity's right relationship with God Most High.*

For all these reasons, Moses was recognized as the greatest leader in all of Israel's history. Moses continues to be recognized as an authentic leader among the people of Israel. (John 1:45, 9:28-29, Acts 7:20-40, etc.)

Because the people of Israel recognize Moses' authority, God Most High has planned for Moses to return to the very nation of people that Moses led over three thousand four hundred years ago. Back then, Moses wore a veil to cover the glory that shone on his face. When Moses returns, it will be to unveil for the people of Israel, the message that Jesus Christ is their promised and prophesied messiah and Lord, that humanity crucified messiah / the Lamb / Jesus Christ, and that God the Holy Spirit raised messiah / the Lamb / Jesus Christ from the dead.

Until the time when God Most High removes the veil that covers this truth from the nation of the people of Israel, the biblical message will be discovered by only individuals.

Therefore, since we have such hope, we use great boldness of speech — unlike Moses, who put a veil over his face so that the children of Israel could not look steadily at the end of what was passing away. But their minds were blinded. For until this day the same veil remains unlifted in the reading of the Old Testament, because the veil is taken away in Christ. But even to this day, when Moses is read, a veil lies on their heart. Nevertheless, when one turns to the Lord, the veil is taken away. 2 Corinthians 3:12-16

Moses' death - or Moses' ascension into heaven while alive?

According to whoever finished the book of Deuteronomy, the Lord 'buried' Moses. If the Lord 'buried' Moses and yet the body cannot be found, then where is the evidence that Moses died?

Moses the servant of the Lord died there in Moab, as the Lord had said. The Lord buried Moses in Moab, in the valley opposite Beth Peor, but to this day no one knows where his grave is. Deuteronomy 34:5

The author of the book of Deuteronomy was undisputedly Moses. This record of Moses' death was also attributed to the pen of Moses, written prior to his 'death.'

It was assumed that Moses wrote about his own death, under the assumption that because God Most High was going to deny Moses entrance into the Promised Land, that Moses would die. But the presumption that Moses would die was not actual proof that Moses did die.

> ... the archangel Michael, when he was disputing with the devil about the body of Moses... Jude 1:9

While Jude attributed the archangel Michael as having disputed with the devil about the body of Moses, there was not an indication that offered assurance that the body of Moses was dead at the time. The focus of the discussion here as read in context, was upon the interaction between Michael and Satan.

The mere fact that the devil was in dispute over the body of Moses was itself a statement that the end of Moses' earthly life was unique.

> Moses was taken in the cloud, was hidden by the cloud, and was sanctified by the cloud. Babylonian Talmud Yoma 4a

Although the Babylonian Talmud is not the biblical record, it did relay the understanding of Jewish tradition. Josephus also presented Moses as having not died, but as having ascended into heaven.

> When Moses was to ascend, a cloud descended and lay before him... And the cloud covered Moses and carried him up. Pesikta Rabbati 20:4

This was more extrabiblical material that represented Jewish tradition.

The Jewish tradition of the scene as Moses prepared to leave the people of Israel as the people of Israel prepared to enter the Promised Land, was remembered from around 1406 BC to the era of the life of Josephus around 70 AD.

> 48. When Moses had spoken thus, at the end of his life, and had foretold what would befall to every one of their tribes afterward, with the addition of a blessing to them, the multitude fell into tears; insomuch that even the women, by beating their breasts, made manifest the deep concern they had when he was about to die. The children also lamented still more, as not able to contain their grief; and thereby declared that even at their age they were sensible of his virtue, and mighty deeds. And truly there seemed to be a strife between the

young and the old, who should most grieve for him. The old grieved, because they knew what a careful protector they were to be deprived of; and so lamented their future state: but the young grieved, not only for that, but also because it so happened, that they were to be left by him before they had well tasted of his virtue. Now one may make a guess at the excess of this sorrow and lamentation of the multitude, from what happened to the Legislator himself. For although he was always persuaded that he ought not to be cast down at the approach of death; since the undergoing it was agreeable to the will of God, and the law of nature; yet what the people did, so overbore him, that he wept himself. Now as he went thence to the place where he was to vanish out of their sight, they all followed after him, weeping. But Moses beckoned with his hand to those that were remote from him; and bid them stay behind in quiet: while he exhorted those that were near to him, that they would not render his departure so lamentable. Whereupon they thought they ought to grant him that favour, to let him depart according as he himself desired: so they restrained themselves, though weeping still towards one another. All those who accompanied him were, the Senate (seventy elders / future Sanhedrin); and Eleazar the High Priest; and Joshua their Commander. Now as soon as they were come to the mountain called *Abarim*, (which is a very high mountain situate over against Jericho; and one that affords to such as are upon it a prospect of the greatest part of the excellent land of Canaan) he dismissed the Senate. And as he was going to embrace Eleazar and Joshua, and was still discoursing with them, a cloud stood over him on the sudden, and he disappeared, in a certain valley: although he wrote in the Holy Books that he died: which was done out of fear lest they should venture to say, that because of his extraordinary virtue he went to God.

49. Now Moses lived in all one hundred and twenty years; a third part of which time, abating one month, he was the people's Ruler. And he died on the last month of the year, which is called by the Macedonians *Dystrus*; but by us *Adar*: on the first day of the month. He was one that exceeded all men that ever were, in understanding, and made the best use of what that understanding suggested to him. He had a very graceful way of speaking, and addressing himself to the multitude: and as to his other qualifications, he had such a full command of his passions, as if he hardly had any such in his soul; and only knew them by their names; as rather perceiving them in other men, than in himself. He was also such a General of an army as is seldom seen; as well as such a Prophet as was never known: and this to such a degree, that whatsoever he pronounced, you would think you heard the voice of God himself. So the people mourned for him thirty days. Nor did ever any grief so deeply affect the Hebrews as did this upon the death of Moses. Nor were those that had experienced his conduct the only persons that desired him; but those also that perused the laws he left behind him had a strong desire after him; and by them gathered the extraordinary virtue he was master of. And this shall

suffice for the declaration of the manner of the death of Moses.
Josephus *Antiquities of the Jews* Book IV.48-49

Moses as a humble man – Numbers 12:3
Now Moses was a very humble man, more humble than anyone else on the face of the earth. Numbers 12:3

The humility of Moses served Moses well throughout his lifetime. There were a variety of sources that share the Jewish understanding as to how Moses became humble and how his humility was an asset for Moses in accomplishing great things. As the leader of the people of Israel while God was attempting to humble the people of Israel in preparation for accomplishing God's purposes in the Promised Land, Moses' humility served as a model.

In contrast to Moses' humility was Pharaoh's enormous arrogance. Even after the staff – snake demonstration, the ten massively devastating and invasive plagues visited upon Egypt, the pillar of stone / cloud that protected the people of Israel from Pharaoh's army, and the parting of the Red Sea, Pharaoh's arrogance still caused Pharaoh to believe that he was a god himself, greater than the God of the people of Israel. Pharaoh's arrogance led to his own destruction and the destruction of the Egyptian world superpower empire.

Moses has had massive experience in standing up to the arrogance of the major world leader of the time. This will make Moses the most qualified in addressing the massive arrogance of the king that will exalt himself / beast of the earth / final world ruler. The biblical record portrayed the fantastic contrast between the king that will exalt himself / beast of the earth / final world ruler's arrogance and Moses' renown humility.

Moses' experience in the past, causes awe when it is realized that Moses' experience in representing God Most High against Pharaoh was merely on the job training that was preparation for Moses' future work of facing the world's most arrogant world leader of all time, the king that will exalt himself / beast of the earth / final world ruler. Imagine that in 1447 - 1446 BC, God Most High was training the leader who would be needed during the era of the time of Jacob's Trouble.

Humility verses arrogance.

The Lord verses the gods of Egypt. God Most High verses the red dragon / serpent / Satan, Inc.

Notice that the entire biblical record was about making the case for God Most High's sovereignty and documenting that the Lord has this conflict won.

For Moses, the fact that God Most High's sovereignty and divinity is greater than anything that the red dragon / serpent / Satan, Inc. has to offer, is merely a footnote in Moses' understanding and body of knowledge.

The Old Testament / Tanakh prophet Malachi (fl. 440 to 430 BC) - of Judah stressed the contrast between the strategies of arrogance and humility. And Malachi documented which strategy would be destroyed.

'For behold, the day is coming, burning like an oven, when all the proud, and yes, all who are sinful, will be stubble. And the day which is coming, will burn them up. It will leave them neither root nor branch.' says the Lord Almighty.

'But for you who fear my name, the sun of righteousness will rise with healing in his wings. And you will go out and frolic like well-fed calves.'

'Then you will trample the wicked for they will be ashes under the soles of your feet, on the day that I do this,' says the Lord Almighty.

'Remember the Law of Moses my servant. I commanded him in Horeb, for all Israel, with the laws and judgments.'

'Behold, I will send you Elijah the prophet, before the coming of the great and dreadful day of the Lord. And he will turn the hearts of the fathers to their children, and the hearts of children to their fathers. Otherwise, I will come and strike the earth with a curse.' Malachi 4:1-6 translated

Moses as the master of plagues – Exodus 7-8, Revelation 11:6

The two witnesses will be masters of plagues and weather control.

They have power over the waters, to turn them into blood; and to strike the earth with every plague, as often as they might desire. Revelation 11:6 translated

They have power to shut up the heavens so that it will not rain during the time they are prophesying. And they have power to turn the waters into blood and to strike the earth with every kind of plague as often as they want. Revelation 11:6 NIV

Multiple prophets in the history of the people of Israel, were equipped to master plagues and to control rain

and drought. But Moses remains the one prophet of Israel, who best mastered the oversight of God Most High's plagues (Exodus 7-11).

During the era of the time of Jacob's Trouble, there will be plagues that will be brought upon earth with the sounding of the first four trumpets (Revelation 8). There will be plagues brought upon the inhabitants of the earth by the scorpion locusts from the Abyss and the two hundred million calvary from under the Euphrates River, with the sounding of the fifth and sixth trumpets / woe #1 and #2 (Revelation 9).
During the finale for the era of the time of Jacob's Trouble, there will be the plagues that will come upon the earth and upon the inhabitants of the earth with the pouring out of the seven bowls of God Most High's wrath / seven last plagues (Revelation 16).
In between the plagues of the first six trumpets and the plagues of the seven bowls of God Most High's wrath / seven last plagues, there will be the plagues brought under the authority of the two witnesses (Revelation 11:6).

Moses' experience with the plagues that God Most High brought against the gods of the Egyptians (~1447 to 1446 BC), provided Moses with the kind of experience that will be needed by the two witnesses as they minister on the temple mount.
Also on the temple mount, attempting to reign over the earth, will be the beast of the earth and the lifelike idol / image beast of the sea. They will all have the ability and power to kill people, but not each other, until the two witnesses have ministered for their one thousand two hundred sixty days.

Moses' unfinished work
After God used Moses in Egypt for the awesome staff - snake demonstration, after the ten plagues that devastated Egypt, after convincing three million obstinate people of Israel to put lamb's blood on their doorposts in order to miraculously avoid the plague of death upon the

firstborn, after leading three million people out of Egypt in a single night, after being used in the parting of the Red Sea as an escape route for the people of Israel when they were pursued by the Egyptian Pharaoh and the entire Egyptian army, after receiving the Law on God's holy mountain and meeting with God face to face in two forty day conferences in the presence of the entire nation of Israel; the Lord made this promise to Moses. 'Before all your people I will do wonders never before done in any nation in all the world.'

This was a personal and private covenant that God Most High made with Moses alone.

The Lord said: 'I am making a covenant with you. Before all your people I will do wonders never before done in any nation in all the world. The people you live among will see how awesome is the work that I, the Lord, will do for you...' Exodus 34:10

This message was given directly to Moses, not to the people of Israel. The Lord made a personal covenant with Moses to do wonders that have not been experienced by humanity throughout human history.

The great wonders recorded in the biblical record, that Moses provided leadership for, all occurred before this covenant. The people of the world heard about what God had done. Even Rahab, forty years later, in Jericho remembered the God of the Israelites and honored their God.

*But this message was given to Moses **after** Moses had been used to display the Lord's mighty acts, and after Moses had met with God Most High on the mountain.*

Which means that the Lord has promised that even greater wonders are yet to be performed and Moses has been promised to lead them. God Most High was clear that there is more for Moses to do yet in the world. Moses needs to be present on earth for Yahweh's / the Lord's fulfillment to be satisfied.

God Most High even designated the audience that Moses will play for. Before all your people you live among...

When the people of Israel left Egypt, they followed Moses because he was the best and only option they had. But they never really accepted the God of Moses with their hearts. Because they did not believe fully in God Most High so they did things like build a golden calf, rejected God's plan to defeat the enemies of God living in the Promised Land, repeatedly attempted to return to Egypt, grumbled about the living conditions, etc. God Most High needed to wait for forty years and the next generation to mature, in order to finish the relocation process from Egypt to the Promised Land. The people of Israel who left Egypt had not even circumcised their sons, an act of disbelief and rejection. Moses has become accustomed to stiff-necked and obstinate people.

But the biblical record documented that this time when Yahweh / the Lord provides even greater wonders through Moses' leadership, there will be a better reception. This time the people will recognize how awesome is the work that the Lord does through Moses.

If Moses is one of the two witnesses who arrives at the temple during the era of the time of Jacob's Trouble, this will be the second time recorded for Moses to travel into the Promised Land of Israel. The first time that Moses set foot in the Promised Land of Israel was during the transfiguration with Jesus, and that was very temporary.

This time, Moses will finally have the opportunity to enter into the Promised Land, and to live there for three and a half years.

Moses' staff and the ark of the covenant

While Moses led the people of Israel out of Egypt, Moses had a staff that was instrumental in Moses' accomplishments.

And then at the mountain conference with Moses, Yahweh / the Lord instructed Moses on how to construct the ark of the covenant.

The staff of Moses and the ark of the covenant were essential in Moses' leading the people of Israel.

The biblical record was unclear concerning whether the ark of the covenant, or Moses' staff, will be available to Moses during the era of the time of Jacob's Trouble. If Moses will have access to the ark of the covenant, will the *other contents of the ark of the covenant be important for the era of the time of Jacob's Trouble?*

Currently, there is no official knowledge of the location of the ark of the covenant.

The Law and the prophets: Moses and Elijah – Malachi 4:1-6

Jesus acknowledged that the people of Israel held Moses in high authority, and noted that the religious leaders of Israel even twisted the Law of Moses to justify their rejection of Jesus as the promised and prophesied messiah.

'But do not think I will accuse you before the Father. Instead, your accuser is Moses, on whom your hopes are set. If you believed Moses, you would believe me, for Moses wrote about me. But since you do not believe what Moses wrote, how are you going to believe what I say?' John 5:45-47

Jesus' acknowledgement of the authority of Moses, was also an acknowledgement that even though the leaders of the people of Israel rejected the Law provided through Moses, what Moses wrote about the promised and prophesied messiah remained an authoritative.

What Moses wrote about the promised and prophesied messiah included the prophecy inherent within the required feasts. Jesus Christ fulfilled the spring feasts with his earthly ministry, crucifixion, death, resurrection and ascension. But Jesus Christ has yet to fulfill the prophesy inherent within the fall feasts. It would be appropriate for Moses to personally reiterate this prophecy prior to the return of Jesus Christ.

The people of Israel have been historically led by the 'Law and the prophets.'

Moses represented the Law. Elijah represented the prophets.

'Remember the Law of Moses my servant. I commanded him in Horeb, for all Israel, with the laws and judgments.'

'Behold, I will send you Elijah the prophet, before the coming of the great and dreadful day of the Lord. And he will turn the hearts of the fathers to their children, and the hearts of children to their fathers. Otherwise, I will come and strike the earth with a curse.' Malachi 4:4-6

The understanding of the prophecy provided through the prophet Malachi, was that the Moses and Elijah are packaged together for the people of Israel.

The full mission of messiah / the Lamb / Jesus Christ is to fulfill all that was required of him, that was documented by the Law and the prophets (2 Kings 17:13, Daniel 9:10, Zechariah 7:12, Matthew 5:17, 7:12, 11:12-13, 22:40, Luke 16:16, 24:44, John 1:45, Acts 13:15, 24:14, 28:23, Romans 3:21, etc.).

Elijah (c. 900 to c. 848 BC (fl. 875 to c. 848 BC)) – prophet of Israel

There were multiple reasons for why Elijah was considered to be one of the greatest prophets of the nation of Israel (northern kingdom).

- *Elijah was able to effectively pray for rain and drought.*
- *Elijah's prayer and work caused supplies to last throughout drought.*
- *Elijah was demonstrated the ability to bring a dead person to life, and to perform miracles.*
- *Elijah called down fire from heaven multiple times.*
- *Elijah was taken alive into heaven with a chariot of fire.*
- *Etc.*

This is the account of the widow of Zarephath and her son who became ill.

Sometime later the son of the woman who owned the house became ill. He grew worse and worse, and finally stopped breathing. She said to Elijah, 'What do you have against me, man of God? Did you come to remind me of my sin and kill my son?'

'Give me your son,' Elijah replied. He took him from her arms, carried him to the upper room where he was staying, and laid him on his bed. Then he cried out to the Lord, 'O Lord my God, have you brought tragedy also upon this widow I am staying with, by causing her son to die?'

Then Elijah stretched himself out on the boy three times and cried to the Lord, 'O Lord my God, let this boy's life return to him!'

The Lord heard Elijah's cry, and the boy's life returned to him, and he lived.

Elijah picked up the child and carried him down from the room into the house. He gave him to his mother and said, 'Look, your son is alive!'

Then the woman said to Elijah, 'Now I know that you are a man of God and that the word of the Lord from your mouth is the truth.' 1 Kings 17:17-24

Elijah raised the woman's son from the dead.

This was the first biblical account of God raising the dead and it was provided to a non-Israelite whose mother had provided lodging and food for Elijah, the prophet of Israel.

Elijah was able to be used for the performing of many miracles in the past. Elijah will be the second witness, performing miracles during the era of the time of Jacob's Trouble.

When Ahaziah the son of Ahab and the king of the northern ten tribes of Israel, had an accident in his home, he sent messengers to consult Baal-Zebub, the god of Ekron, to find out if he would recover from his injury. But the messengers were intercepted by Elijah the Tishbite who had actually been instructed by God Most High, to tell Ahaziah that because he had sought to consult with Baal-Zebub, Ahaziah would die.

Ahaziah sent a captain and fifty men to Elijah, to remove Elijah from the top of the hill he was sitting on. The called to him, 'Man of God, the king says, 'Come down!'' But Elijah answered the captain, 'If I am a man of God, may fire come down from heaven and consume you and your fifty men!' Then fire fell from heaven and consumed the captain and his men. 2 Kings 1:9-10

When Ahaziah sent another captain with another fifty men, the whole scenario was repeated (2 Kings 1:11-12).

So, the king sent a third captain with another fifty men. This captain instead of demanding that Elijah as a man of God honor the king's command, fell on his knees before Elijah. He begged, 'Man of God, please have respect for my life and the lives of these fifty men, your servants!...' *(2 Kings 1:13-14).*

Elijah was able to call down fire in the past. Elijah will be the second witness, also demonstrating bringing fire down from heaven during the era of the time of Jacob's Trouble.

As they (Elijah and Elisha) were walking along and talking together, suddenly a chariot of fire and horses of fire appeared and separated the two of them, and Elijah went up to heaven in a whirlwind. 2 Kings 2:11

Elijah was taken to heaven in the presence of Elisha. As Elijah ascended into heaven, the cloak of Elijah fell upon Elisha as a sign to validate Elisha's tenure as prophet of God Most High.

Elijah was a man just like us. Elijah prayed earnestly that it would not rain and it did not rain on the land for three and a half years. Again, he prayed and the heavens gave rain, and the earth produced its crops. James 5:17-18

It was important to James that we know that Elijah was a man just like us. It was important to God Most High that it be humanity that wins the victory over the red dragon / serpent / Satan, Inc. and the kingdom of Satan, Inc. / kingdom of man. It must be humanity that rules in the kingdom of heaven.

To accomplish the defeat of the kingdom of Satan, Inc. / kingdom of man, during the second half of the era of the time of Jacob's Trouble, the fully human Elijah will be provided with the responsibility for controlling rain and drought. Elijah is already practiced in praying to stop and start rain.

'I will send my messenger, who will prepare the way before me. Then suddenly the Lord you are seeking will come to his temple; the messenger of the covenant, whom you desire, will come,' says the Lord Almighty? Malachi 3:1

The fact that 'the messenger must be sent to prepare the way before the Lord Almighty to come to the temple' presupposes a number of requirements. First, there must be a temple. Second, it must be the time in human history when the people of Israel must be readied to be prepared for the scheduled return of the Lord. Third, there must be preparation made in order for the Lord to return to us, and preparation means change. Fourth, the goal of the messenger of the covenant will be to prepare the people of Israel for the return of the Lord.

The people who are citizens of the kingdom of heaven will become remarkably different in their character from the adherents and allies of the rebellion, the kingdom of Satan, Inc. / kingdom of man.

The people of Israel will become people who will be seeking the arrival of the promised and prophesied messiah, the one whom they desire.

The inhabitants of the earth will remain as people who are not seeking the messenger of the covenant and do not desire to see him come. They will not acknowledge or recognize the lordship and the divinity of the promised and prophesied messiah.

The cultural dynamic that Malachi described was reminiscent of what Jesus Christ described as a separation of the sheep and the goats, wheat and the weeds / tares, etc. Elijah will be assigned to do the prep work for Jesus Christ's harvesting of the wheat and gathering of the grapes (Revelation 14:14-20).

'For behold, the day is coming, burning like an oven, when all the proud, and yes, all who are sinful, will be stubble. And the day which is coming, will burn them up. It will leave them neither root nor branch.' says the Lord Almighty.

'But for you who fear my name, the sun of righteousness will rise with healing in his wings. And you will go out and frolic like well-fed calves.'

'Then you will trample the wicked for they will be ashes under the soles of your feet, on the day that I do this,' says the Lord Almighty.

'Remember the Law of Moses my servant. I commanded him in Horeb, for all Israel, with the laws and judgments.'

'Behold, I will send you Elijah the prophet, before the coming of the great and dreadful day of the Lord. And he will turn the hearts of the fathers to their children, and the hearts of children to their fathers. Otherwise, I will come and strike the earth with a curse.' Malachi 4:1-6 translated

Malachi's prophecy connected Moses and Elijah with the some of the scheduled events and the battle that the Lord will take part in, during the era of the time of Jacob's Trouble.

As with everything that the Lord does, there is a purpose. The Lord does not exercise the Lord's activity in vain. The purpose of Elijah's work during the second half of the era of the time of Jacob's Trouble will include turning

the hearts of family members so that they will become close (Also Luke 1:17, Acts 28:27, Romans 2:29, Hebrews 4:12, etc.).

Predestination theology does not have an allowance for an individual's or a nation's choice concerning eternal things. But Malachi's theology does. If everything were already determined, there would be no need to experience the era of the time of Jacob's Trouble because there would be no purpose to it. God Most High would have already decided the end result; and with predestination theology, the torture of the era of the time of Jacob's Trouble would be a mere formality, vengeful; God Most High's repaying what God Most High has promised through the millennia, the 'sins of the parents visited upon the children.'

Instead, Malachi was clear that God Most High has a purpose during the era of the time of Jacob's Trouble. Not everything has been decided. In the kingdom of heaven, an individual is not predestined. In the kingdom of heaven, the heart is sought after. Unlike the slavery that characterizes the kingdom of Satan, Inc. / kingdom of man, in the kingdom of heaven, compulsion is not allowed. In the kingdom of heaven, the decision of the heart is respected.

There will be remarkable differences between the citizens of the kingdom of heaven and the adherents / allies of the kingdom of Satan, Inc. / kingdom of man. In the kingdom of Satan, Inc. / kingdom of man, one of those differences will be that the hearts of parents and children will be marked by conflict.

Notice the purpose for Elijah's coming; to turn the hearts of the parents to their children, and the hearts of the children to their parents. Turning hearts is always the work of the Holy Spirit. If Elijah's coming will be an era when hearts are turned, then it was also implied that there will be a new outpouring of the Holy Spirit and the Holy Spirit's activity that will come with Elijah when Elijah returns.

When Moses and the seventy elders of Israel ascended the mountain to receive the Law from God Most High after the Israelite exodus from Egypt, it was addressed as the first season of Pentecost. When the men and women disciples gathered in the upper room to await *the coming of the Holy Spirit, it was on the Day of Pentecost that the Holy Spirit was poured out to them and given to all followers of Jesus Christ. When Elijah returns, it may be Elijah's turn to be the person through which the Holy Spirit is again poured out upon people.*

Malachi was written just prior to the four hundred years of silence / the absence of prophets of God Most High providing messages to Israel, that preceded the coming of Jesus Christ.

Those familiar with the Old Testament will recognize that when the beast of the earth declares himself as a pseudo messiah, that the beast of the earth cannot be the actual promised and prophesied messiah because Elijah will not be a forerunner for the beast of the earth, but a simultaneous contender.

Instead, the beast of the sea / false prophet will act as the biblically required forerunner for the beast of the earth.

The fact that Elijah and the beast of the earth will be enemies of each other should be a signal to the people of Israel that the beast of the earth will be an imposter for the true messiah of God. Additional proof that the beast of the earth will be an imposter messiah, will be the beast of the earth's pursuit of God's holy people including the people of Israel.

John the Baptist was the forerunner for Jesus' first coming. Jesus taught that John the Baptist fulfilled the position of forerunner like Elijah.

'This is the one about whom it is written: "I will send my messenger ahead of you, who will prepare your way before you.' I tell you the truth: Among those born of women there has not risen anyone greater than John the Baptist; yet he who is least in the kingdom of heaven is greater than he. From the days of John the Baptist until now, the kingdom of heaven has been forcefully advancing and forceful men lay hold of it. For the Prophets and the Law prophesied until John. And if you are willing to accept it, he is the Elijah who was to come. The one who has ears, let that one hear.' Matthew 11:10-15

But for the second coming of Jesus Christ, there will be two witnesses, two forerunners. Before Jesus Christ's second coming, the original Elijah will be with us, again.

Also note that the two witnesses will have a ministry of forty two months / three and a half years, similar to the ministry length of John the Baptist and the ministry length of Jesus Christ during his earthly ministry.

Jesus replied, 'To be sure, Elijah comes and will restore all things. But I tell you, Elijah has already come, and they did not recognize him, but have done to him everything they wished. In the same way the Son of Man is going to suffer at their hands.'
Then the disciples understood that he was talking to them about John the Baptist. Matthew 17:11-13

John the Baptist was beheaded near the beginning of Jesus' ministry by Herod Antipas (fl. 4 BC to 39 AD), son of Herod the Great. But John the Baptist acted as a prototype of the future activity of Elijah.

John the Baptist wore sackcloth and ashes. The two witnesses will also be dressed in sackcloth and ashes.

John the Baptist was one crying in the wilderness, 'make way for the coming of the Lord.' *Elijah's message will be very similar to John the Baptist's message.*

Jesus replied, 'To be sure, Elijah does come first, and restores all things. Why then is it written that the Son of Man must suffer much and be rejected? But I tell you, Elijah has come, and they have done to him everything they wished, just as it is written about him.' Mark 9:12-13

When Jesus said that when Elijah comes, he 'restores all things,' we are left to wonder what 'all things' consists of that Elijah will restore. Elijah's work sounds promising in the midst of a world whose dynamics will be described as being in chaos and destruction.

The fact that both Matthew and Mark recorded this conversation elevated this conversation with heightened importance. It also indicated that the mission of Elijah and the other witness, will accomplish all that God Most High will send them to accomplish.

The two witnesses will be clothed in sackcloth, material made of coarse camel or goat hair, attire used for mourning. Sackcloth was also a garment that displayed humility in the presence of authority (1 Kings 20:31-32, Daniel 9:3).

This statement that Elijah must restore all things, implied that Elijah will be able to accomplish more than what the mere historical prophets of old were able to accomplish. When Elijah came the first time, he was able to thwart the activity of King Ahab and Queen Jezebel, but not able to restore the northern kingdom of Israel. To be able to restore all things implied that the restoration of the kingdom of heaven on earth will be what they will take part in restoring along with the coming of Jesus Christ as Lord to defeat the enemies of the kingdom of heaven. The act of restoring all things will require extraordinary power and authority at a level not previously experienced.

Elijah was originally pursued politically by King Ahab and Queen Jezebel of the northern kingdom of Israel / northern ten tribes. Jezebel was the daughter of the king of Tyre, Ethbaal I. Jezebel was totally effective in promoting the worship of the baal and Asherah deities, originally modeled her life after Semiramis, with Ahab acting after the model of Nimrod. Together Ahaz and Jezebel were effective in making the gods of the baal / mystery / mythology religion, the accepted gods for the ten northern tribes of the nation of Israel, on a national scale. To further this goal, Jezebel authorized the slaughter of the prophets of the Lord at an unprecedented level.

Jezebel orchestrated the acquisition of Naboth's vineyard for her husband Ahab, through her conspiracy and the arranged testimony of false witnesses within the political government system of the area (1 Kings 21).

Jezebel also put a contract out on for the head of Elijah, wanted dead, not alive.

What Elijah encountered with Ahab and Jezebel has prepared Elijah and qualified him for the future work that he must accomplish in addressing the two beasts of Revelation 13. During the era of the time of Jacob's Trouble, Elijah may even be expected to repeat the Mount Carmel altar challenge at a new and higher level.

Is anyone among you in trouble? Let them pray. Is anyone happy? Let them sing songs of praise. Is anyone among you sick? Let them call the elders of the church to pray over them and anoint them with oil in the name of the Lord. And the prayer offered in faith will

make the sick person well; the Lord will raise them up. If they have sinned, they will be forgiven. Therefore, confess your sins to each other and pray for each other so that you may be healed. The prayer of a righteous person is powerful and effective.
Elijah was a human being, even as we are. He prayed earnestly that it would not rain, and it did not rain on the land for three and a half years. Again he prayed, and the heavens gave rain, and the earth produced its crops. James 5:13-17

Elijah has experience effectively praying for rain to be stopped. The duration of the stopped rain during the time of Ahaz and Jezebel was three and a half years, the same length of time that Elijah has been scheduled to witness to the people of Israel and to the world during the second half of the era of the time of Jacob's Trouble.

The connection of Elijah to the message of encouragement provided by James, was another example that supported the promise of the miracles that will be accomplished by the followers of the Lamb / Jesus Christ during the era of the time of Jacob's Trouble.

Side note:
It was an established Jewish tenet that before the promised and prophesied messiah comes, there must be the forerunner to announce messiah's impending arrival. The forerunner traditionally was interpreted to be Elijah. Every year in the celebration of the Passover feast, the people of Israel set a place at the table for welcoming the prophet Elijah when he returns.

When Jesus came the first time, John the Baptist acted as the forerunner for Jesus Christ. This second coming of Jesus Christ, the forerunner will be the actual Elijah in person.

Currently, there is a segment of the people of Israel who believe that the prime minister of Israel is supposed to bring messiah and that the prime minister has been ignoring this duty. It may be that the prime minister of Israel will be mistaken by the people of Israel as the required the forerunner.

The significance of rain and drought as a communication device of God Most High

During the era of the time of Jacob's Trouble, the two witnesses will be responsible for bringing additional plagues, drought and rain.

The prophet Moses was known for the plagues that God Most High used in battling the gods of Egypt (Exodus 7-13).

But Elijah was the prophet who called for drought and for rain (1 Kings 17-18).

God Most High will be using drought and rain to reinforce the message of the two witnesses, similar to God Most High's use of drought and rain for the northern ten tribes of Israel during the reign of Ahab and Jezebel.

When Ahab and Jezebel, monarchs over the northern kingdom of Israel, greatly offended God Most High, Elijah was sent to them. Elijah carried a message from God Most High.

Now Elijah the Tishbite, from Tishbe in Gilead, said to Ahab, 'As the Lord, the God of Israel, lives, whom I serve, there will be neither dew nor rain in the next few years except at my word.' 1 Kings 17:1 *(1 Kings 17:7, 17:14, 18:1-2, 18:41-45)*

Elijah was a human being, even as we are. He prayed earnestly that it would not rain, and it did not rain on the land for three and a half years. Again he prayed, and the heavens gave rain, and the earth produced its crops. James 5:17-18

Elisha who inherited Elijah's ministry, also was able to influence drought and rain (2 Kings 3:16-18).

Through the prophet Ezekiel, God Most High declared that false prophets will not be included within the kingdom of heaven.

'My hand will be against the prophets who see false visions and utter lying divinations. They will not belong to the council of my people or be listed in the records of Israel, nor will they enter the land of Israel. Then you will know that I am the Sovereign Lord.'

'Because they lead my people astray, saying, 'Peace,' when there is no peace, and because, when a flimsy wall is built, they cover it with whitewash, therefore tell those who cover it with whitewash that it is going to fall. Rain will come in torrents, and I will send hailstones hurtling down, and violent winds will burst forth.' Ezekiel 13:9-11 *(Ezekiel 13:13)*

During the era of the time of Jacob's Trouble, drought and rain will be under the control of the two witnesses. It will be a response to prove that God Most High is the one who ultimately is in control of climate changes, in a society that has been taught that humanity controls climate change.

They have the power to shut heaven, so that no rain falls in the days of their prophecy. They have power over the waters, to turn them into blood; and to strike the earth with every plague, as often as they might desire. Revelation 11:6 translated

Near the conclusion of the era of the time of Jacob's Trouble, the fully consecrated, functional and operational temple sacrificial system will be reactivated. And around that time, the remnant of the people of Israel will recognize Jesus Christ as the promised and prophesied messiah. Once the remnant of the people of Israel have accepted Jesus Christ as the promised and prophesied messiah, there will no longer be any need for the temple sacrificial system because God Most High will hear their prayers directly. And just a few months later, messiah / the Lamb / Jesus Christ will return to defeat the enemies of the people and nation of Israel.

But during the second half of the era of the time of Jacob's Trouble, there was a special message for the people of Israel, recorded in 1 Kings in the dedication prayer for Solomon's temple.

'When the heavens are shut up and there is no rain because your people have sinned against you, and when they pray toward this place and give praise to your name and turn from their sin because you have afflicted them, then hear from heaven and forgive the sin of your servants, your people Israel. Teach them the right way to live, and send rain on the land you gave your people for an inheritance.' 1 Kings 8:35-36 *(2 Chronicles 6:26-27, 7:13-15)*

The possibility of the two witnesses being Enoch and Elijah

Enoch was documented to be the first person in human history, to not die.

After he became the father of Methuselah, Enoch walked faithfully with God 300 years and had other sons and daughters. Altogether, Enoch lived a total of 365 years. Enoch walked faithfully with God; then he was no more, because God took him away. Genesis 5:22-24

...Daniel meant the last week (the seventieth 'seven') which is to be at the end of the whole world of which week the two prophets Enoch and Elias will take up the half. For they will preach 1,260 days clothed in sackcloth, proclaiming repentance to the people and to all the nations. Hippolytus of Rome: *Treatise on Christ and Antichrist*, 43

Hippolytus of Rome was a disciple of Irenaeus who was a disciple of Polycarp who was a disciple of John the Revelator. Hippolytus of Rome believed the two witnesses that would fulfill the prophecy of Revelation 11 to be Enoch and Elijah. Enoch would be a representative from the antediluvian / preflood world and Elijah would be a representative from the postdiluvian / postflood world.

Because one biblical account portrayed Moses as dying instead of being taken into heaven, there is still the question of which two out of the three possibilities; Enoch, Moses, or Elijah, will God send?

For Hippolytus of Rome, the two witnesses will be Enoch and Elias / Elijah. But for a significant portion of biblical scholars, the interpretation has been that the two witnesses will be Moses and Elijah.

What Hippolytus of Rome pointed out that was sometimes been overlooked, was that the two witnesses will be urging the people of all the nations to turn away from the baal / mystery / mythology religion alternative provided by the kingdom of Satan, Inc. / kingdom of man, and turn toward the redemptive faith system provided by God Most High through Jesus Christ as messiah.

The mission of the two witnesses / two olive branches – Zechariah 4

The symbol that represents the modern nation of Israel is the picture of the lampstand / menorah with the two olive branches on the sides. This imagery was taken from Zechariah's vision.

Zerubbabel the son of Shealtiel was tasked with rebuilding the temple when the time of the exile was completed of the northern ten tribes of Israel and the southern kingdom of Judah. Apparently, Zerubbabel also received the word of the Lord, like a prophet would. But there was no book of Zerubbabel. It was Zechariah who recorded the word of the Lord provided to Zerubbabel.

The lampstand in Zechariah's vision was the Anointed One / messiach ben David / messiah son of David / the Lamb that was to come. The two olive branches depicted the two witnesses that will come to the people of Israel during the era of the time of Jacob's Trouble.

'...'I see a solid gold lampstand with a bowl at the top and seven lights on it, with seven channels to the lights. Also, there are two olive trees by it, one on the right of the bowl and the other on its left.' Zechariah 4:2b-3

'This is the word of the Lord to Zerubbabel (of the royal house of David): 'Not by might nor by power, but by my Spirit,' says the Lord Almighty.' Zechariah 4:6

Concerning the two olive trees: 'These are the two who are anointed to serve the Lord of all the earth.' Zechariah 4:14

The phrase 'not by might nor by power,' *was a way of saying that military supremacy and governmental political agreement will not be the methods used for achieving God Most High's desired results. The fact that the Lord Almighty foregoes the military supremacy and governmental politics to accomplish results provided a clue for how the nature of the Lord Almighty's work will manifest itself during the era of the time of Jacob's Trouble. The Lord Almighty displayed* 'might' *and* 'power' *through words inspired by the Holy Spirit. The sword was not the Lord Almighty's tool of choice. Communication was the Lord Almighty's best used tool. The Lord Almighty spoke to those who would listen.*

When we watch the news on television and hear of wars and rumors of wars, the Lord Almighty may have used the wars and rumors of wars to speak, but only to focus attention upon the Lord's greater message. Wars and rumors of wars are never the heart of the message of the Lord, merely the outcome of the symptom of spiritual deafness on the part of at least one of the parties involved. The Lord Almighty was, is and always will be at work first through the Holy Spirit speaking to the hearts and minds of God's holy people.

War, how to make war, how to make weapons of war, and wars themselves have always been the first tool of the red dragon / serpent / Satan, Inc. And this fact was inherently impressed within the promise made to the first woman in the Garden of Eden when God Most High said that in sorrow women would bring their children into the world. Later, the details of the teaching of the red dragon / serpent / Satan, Inc. on how to make war, how to make weapons of war, and of wars themselves was recorded by Enoch in the first book of Enoch and reiterated in the messages of the prophets.

But as massively destructively powerful that war and military might is, the Holy Spirit was always presented as being even mightier, more powerful, and more effective than any military might or political arrangement that the red dragon / serpent / Satan, Inc. can contrive.

For those living during the era of the time of Jacob's Trouble, the Lord Almighty's message through Zerubbabel and through Zechariah was that to understand what the Lord Almighty will be doing, one must understand the methods by which the Lord Almighty acts.

The Holy Spirit was likened to holy oil, holy oil from olive trees, throughout the biblical record. Olive trees produced olives that were pressed for their oil three times. Only the first pressing of the olives produced the most pure oil and was used for the tabernacle / temple to anoint and to light the tabernacle / temple menorah.

When the Lord Almighty referred to the two witnesses as olive trees, it was a statement that defined the purpose and activity of the two witnesses. They are to bring anointing to God's purposes during the second half of the era of the time of Jacob's Trouble, to bring light to the tabernacle / temple, and to bring the glory and light of the Lord Almighty's message to the world.

The Lord Almighty's message / God's word was not just a single word. God's word said, 'Let there be light.' And there was light. God's word was the plan of God for all of creation. God's word was also documented in the biblical record. God's word is Jesus Christ who is the light of the world (John 1). God's word / Jesus Christ was also a living human being who also happens to be divine / God. God's word will be written upon the true rider of the second white horse described in the book of Revelation who will come to fulfill God's word. God's word will also proceed from the mouth of Jesus Christ as the double edged sword that will be used to defeat the enemies of God. God's word will provide the order that God began on the week of creation and that continues to infuse life into our world.

It was the word of the Lord Almighty that the red dragon / serpent / Satan, Inc. has worked for six thousand years to interrupt with the kingdom of chaos. It will be God's word that will ultimately defeat the armies of the world that will be under the influence of the red dragon / serpent / Satan, Inc. as they unite against Jerusalem for the final battle of this age.

God's word is powerful enough to completely renovate the human heart of those who have chosen to be followers of the Lamb / Jesus Christ. It is not by might, nor by power, but by the Spirit of the Lord using God's word that the world will experience the change that is needed to bring the full kingdom of heaven / Garden of Eden / paradise back to the earth for us to dwell in.

The two witnesses will be sent to bring just a portion of God's word to the world during the second half of the era of the time of Jacob's Trouble. They will speak of God and God's word. They will not be able to be killed because of the fire that comes out of their mouths as they defend themselves. The two witnesses will not be able to be destroyed by the might and power of humanity. It will require the red dragon / serpent / Satan, Inc. in the form of the beast of the Abyss, to finally kill them at the end of their scheduled one thousand two hundred sixty days of witnessing.

The two olive trees standing by the gold lampstand were a vision of the two witnesses sent from heaven for this time and was why the two olive trees stand together with the gold lampstand in this vision. The two olive trees provide the oil / the presence of the Holy Spirit, in order to allow the light of the menorah / lampstand to shine. In this vision, the mission of the two witnesses was presented as *providing the fuel for the light, to share the message of God's word with the people of the world, to use words to tell of the true light, the lampstand, the truly Anointed One, Jesus Christ.*

During the second half of the era of the time of Jacob's Trouble, the message of the red dragon / serpent / Satan, Inc. will be about the greatness, the glory, the worthiness of the beast of the earth to rule the world with the global religious community and the global governance system, and to fully establish the kingdom of Satan, Inc. / kingdom of man on earth.

But the message of the two witnesses during the same era of time, the second half of the era of the time of Jacob's Trouble, will be that the true glory, the true light of the world was, is and always will be, messiah / the Lamb / Jesus Christ.

When studying the layout of the tabernacle and the temple, there was a process that a penitent person was required to follow that included cleansing, placing one's sin upon the sacrificial animal, offering the sacrificial animal that carried the sin to the Lord Almighty which allowed the sin to be taken away, entering the tabernacle / temple itself in the act of drawing near to God Most High, etc. Once inside the tabernacle / temples, there was the menorah on one side and the table of showbread on the other. The entire layout of God Most High's redemption, reclamation and regeneration plan was laid out in the tabernacle / temple experience.

God Most High's redemption, reclamation and regeneration plan applied to the human being first, and then on another level, to the earth and heaven and the cosmos. So, when the two olive branches / two witnesses come to highlight the light of the world, it will mean that human history has arrived at that place on the tabernacle / temples map, where the cosmos is close to fully reestablishing relationship with God Most High as represented by the Holy of Holies.

To share in partaking of the showbread, there must be a relationship built between God and the one partaking of the showbread.

To experience the presence of the light of the world / menorah, will require the ordering of both space and time.

When the two witnesses arrive on the temple mount, one of their purposes will be to establish that it is Jesus Christ who will be the actual final world ruler, who will rule not by might, nor by power, but by the Holy Spirit. They will fuel the lampstand.

The other purpose of their message will be to foster the reestablishment of the nation of Israel with God Most High and also with Jesus Christ. They will be sent to bring light, to allow humanity to see, that it is the Lord Almighty that provides sustenance, daily bread, and life to the world.

The fact that the two witnesses represented the oil of the menorah and Jesus Christ is the menorah in this imagery, would mean that on a historical timeline, when the two witnesses arrive, the world is rapidly approaching the era when what is left for the world to experience is the worship of God Most High at its fullest level, as represented by actually entering of the Holy of Holies.

The work of Moses and Elijah will be completed as the two olive trees prepare the people of Israel and the people of the world for the coming of the gold lampstand / Jesus Christ, and for the arrival of the fully established kingdom of heaven on earth.

Together the two witnesses will fulfill the plan of the Lord Almighty by describing for the world what is the true light of the world / Jesus Christ, and by bringing the message that reflects the bread that sustains life.

And do this, understanding the present time: The hour has already come for you to wake up from your slumber, because our salvation is nearer now than when we first believed. The night is nearly over. The day is almost here.

So let us put aside the deeds of darkness and put on the armor of light. Romans 13:11-12

The importance of sending two witnesses

One witness is not enough to convict anyone accused of any crime or offense they may have committed. A matter must be established by the testimony of two or three witnesses. Deuteronomy 19:15

Having two witnesses for validation was a tradition that originated from the God of the Israelites. This condition can be applied to both the conviction of a crime and also to the validity of a precept, idea, or theory.

God decided that a man and a woman should be a team together on the sixth day of creation. The Law of Moses required two witnesses to give testimony in order for the evidence to be declared valid. Jesus Christ sent the disciples out in teams of two.

Because the people of Israel have rejected Jesus Christ as their promised and prophesied messiah, they rejected the old covenant / Old Testament / first witness that defined their promised and prophesied messiah through the Law and the prophets, and they rejected the new covenant / New Testament / second witness that was established through grace by Jesus Christ.

Because the people of Israel rejected the covenant of grace, they remain bound by the old covenant of the Mosaic Law. Their relationship with God Most High must still depend upon the fulfillment of Mosaic Law, until they recognize that messiah / the Lamb / Jesus Christ has fulfilled Mosaic Law on their behalf.

Therefore, it is necessary that God will send to Israel, not one, but two witnesses from heaven.

In the case of the two witnesses from heaven, if a third witness is needed, it will be the Holy Spirit witnessing to human spirits.

But for the deluded and stiff necked people of Israel to recognize Jesus Christ as their promised and prophesied messiah, it will require the testimony of two witnesses, plagues, drought and rain, and the miraculous power of the Holy Spirit. This process will require the full one thousand two hundred sixty days for its completion.

I will appoint my two witnesses, and they will prophesy one thousand two hundred and sixty days, clothed in sackcloth. These are the two olive trees and the two lampstands standing before the Lord of the earth. If anyone should desire to harm them, fire comes out of their mouths and devours their enemies. And if anyone should desire to harm them, it is necessary for them to be killed in this manner.

They have the power to shut heaven, so that no rain falls in the days of their prophecy. They have power over the waters, to turn them into blood; and to strike the earth with every plague, as often as they might desire. Revelation 11:3-6 translated

When the plagues were visited upon Egypt prior to the Israelites' exodus from Egypt, the Egyptians remained unconvinced and as a result Egypt lost its wealth, its military, and its superpower status in the world.
This time, it will be the apostate church / global religious community and the global governance system that will remain unconvinced. As a result, at the conclusion of the one thousand two hundred sixty days, they will lose their wealth, their militaries, and their superpower status in the world. (Revelation 17, 18, 19)
Notice that these two witnesses will be dressed in sackcloth, not fancy clothes, which will cause the elites of the world to refrain from giving them respect. They will also have power to prevent rain and bring plagues which will also not endear them to the global elites. In fact, the pseudo-scientific / scientism community that has negated the creative power of the Creator God in opting for an evolutionary theory explanation for the basis of life on earth, will attribute the mighty acts of God Most High through the two witnesses as a result of things like 'climate change,' 'overpopulation,' 'the need for the ruling classes' leadership in the distribution of resources,' etc.
But how will the pseudo-scientific / scientism community be able to fully explain the fact that this kind of power is directed through these two witnesses, mere men? How will the pseudo-scientific / scientism community be able to fully explain that these two men will exercise their own protection through fire that comes out of their mouths to consume their enemies? How will the pseudo-scientific / scientism community be able to fully explain why they cannot kill the two witnesses for one thousand two hundred sixty days?

In supplying two witnesses, God Most High will be fulfilling the requirement of Mosaic Law to the people of Israel, who have already rejected the personal witness of messiah / the Lamb / Jesus Christ and the witness of the Holy Spirit.

In supplying Moses and Elijah, God Most High supplies two witnesses that the people of Israel might still be able to hear.

The temple court in the possession of the Gentiles for forty two months – Revelation 11:2

In John's revelation concerning the two witnesses, John was instructed to measure the temple, the altar, and the worshipers.

A measuring rod like a staff was given to me. (I was told,) 'Rise and measure the temple of God, and the altar, and those worshiping in it. But leave out the courtyard outside the temple, and do not measure it because it has been given up to the Gentiles, and they will trample the holy city for forty two months.' Revelation 11:2 translated

The measurement for the temple's outer court was especially excluded because it was not considered holy / consecrated to God Most High. The fact that the temple court was recognized as being under the control of the Gentiles, may be a factor for the two witnesses to be wearing sackcloth.

In Jesus' description of the temple mount prior to his return, Jesus said: 'Jerusalem will be trampled on by the Gentiles until the times of the Gentiles are fulfilled.' Luke 21:24b

When Jesus Christ was condemned by the leaders of the people of Israel, he was then given to the Gentiles to conduct his crucifixion. The imagery of the dynamics that provide context for the future third temple, indicated that the temple was also in the context of being under the control of the Gentiles. This may have been the reason that event though John the Revelator was instructed to measure the temple and its worshipers, those measurements were not recorded.

In addition, John the Revelator documented that the holy city / Jerusalem Israel, would be trampled on by the Gentiles for forty two months. Forty two months was a reference to the term of the supernatural power and authority that the two beasts of Revelation 13 will share. John the Revelator recognized that the outer courts of the temple and the holy city / Jerusalem were under the authority of the two beasts of Revelation 13.

During the era of the time of Jacob's Trouble, the third temple will be built. Provisions for the building of the third temple may even be included in the confirmation of the seven year covenant peace treaty agreement.

Currently, the people of Israel have limited access to the temple mount. When the second temple was destroyed in 70 AD, the temple mount technically became under the authority of the Roman empire. Following the Roman empire's domination of the temple mount, it was under the authority of various Islamic sects. Since 1187, the temple mount has been governed by some form of the Waqf. Currently, the Jordanian Waqf governs the temple mount and assigned the nation of Israel to maintain security and operate activities on the temple mount. In addition, to being under the control of the Gentiles, there are also two Islamic mosques located on the temple mount.

Some have questioned whether the two Islamic mosques would need to be demolished for a temple to be built on the temple mount with a fully consecrated, functional and operational temple sacrificial system. John the Revelator's description of the situation on the temple mount with the outer court being under the governance of the Gentiles, supported the possibility that the mosques will remain on the temple mount during the era of the time of Jacob's Trouble.

John the Revelator's description of the two witnesses required that a temple of some kind would be established on the temple mount prior to the arrival of the two witnesses. The two witnesses will come to a functional temple that will conduct evening and morning daily sacrifices.

The Gentiles that will hold authority over the outer court of the temple and the city of Jerusalem, will be the two beasts of Revelation 13. It will be the future abomination of desolation event that will cause the temple to become unclean, unholy and unconsecrated, which will mean the temple will become unable to be effective as a part of the people of Israel's full and effective worship of

God. And so, the evening and morning daily sacrifices will be discontinued.

The Gentiles will have discontinued the evening and morning sacrifices of the third temple for only one thousand one hundred fifty days (Daniel). But the Gentiles will hold control over the temple mount and the city of Jerusalem for the full one thousand two hundred sixty days that the two witnesses are present.

There will be one hundred ten days in between the reestablishment of the temple sacrifice, and the release of the city of Jerusalem from the authority of the two beasts of Revelation 13.

Notice that from Jesus Christ's perspective, the temple and Jerusalem will not have been taken as if they were acquired by military defeat or a world political agreement. From the perspective of Jesus Christ, the author of the book of Revelation, the city of Jerusalem will be <u>given</u> to the Gentiles.

At the time of Jesus Christ's crucifixion, the religious leaders of the people of Israel represented Judaism, and the state religion of the Roman government that held hegemony over the nation of Israel was a form of the baal / mystery / mythology religion. The nation of Israel conducted their worship in the temple, with the permission of the Roman empire. And it required the cooperation of both the religious leaders of the people of Israel and the Roman authorities, to accomplish the crucifixion of messiah / the Lamb / Jesus Christ.

The same dynamic will be in effect during the term of ministry of the two witnesses. The beast that will represent the people of Israel and Judaism / beast of the earth, will act under the authority of the beast of the sea that represents Gentiles, and the scarlet beast that represents apostate Christianity. The two beasts will create an amalgamated religion from their Christian and Jewish foundations that propelled them into global leadership positions.

Consequently, the two witnesses will be immersed into a sea of unimaginable hostility against God Most

High. The two witnesses will effectively preach for one thousand two hundred sixty days to an absolutely hostile Gentile audience. And yet the two witnesses will successfully prepare the hearts and minds of the remnant of the people of Israel, to recognize Jesus Christ as the promised and prophesied messiah, and to reject the beast of the earth as false.

When the temple mount is returned to the authority of God's holy people, the times of the Gentiles will come to a close. The focus will turn to God Most High's fulfillment of the covenant promise that God Most High established with Abram / Abraham, Isaac, and Jacob / Israel concerning their descendants receiving a place of honor and responsibility in the fully established kingdom of heaven on earth.

The opposition against the two witnesses – Revelation 11:1-14

The Lord said: 'Do not touch my anointed ones; do my prophets no harm.' 1 Chronicles 16:22

This message from the Old Testament / Tanakh, given almost three thousand years ago, went unheeded by the people of Israel. The people of Israel have continually killed the prophets.

Isaiah of Jerusalem was sawn in two by Manasseh (according to the *Martyrdom of Isaiah*) and buried near the Pool of Siloam. Jewish tradition sited Isaiah's prayer as the impetus for the miraculous powers of the waters of the Pool of Siloam (John 9).

Jeremiah of Anathoth was stoned to death and was buried at Tahpanhes in Egypt. Later his body was moved to Alexandria, spread out in a circle around the city as a protection against poisonous snakes, asps, plagues, and crocodiles.

Ezekiel was killed while in exile in Babylon, possibly after refusing to worship idols.

Amos was tortured by Amaziah, the priest of Bethel (Amos 7:10) and then killed by the priest's son.

Zechariah of Jerusalem, son of the priest Jehoiada who had shown kindness to King Joash (2 Chronicles 24:20-

22) *was stoned to death by order of King Joash in the courtyard, near the altar of the temple. After the death of Zechariah, the priests of the temple where no longer able to experience the presence and visions of the angels, nor use the Ephod / breastplate of the high priest, used inside the Holy of Holies for obtaining answers from the Lord.*

Jesus Christ acknowledged that the people of Jerusalem had a nasty habit of killing the prophets and stoning those sent by God Most High (Luke 13:34).

Jesus Christ, the greatest of all prophets, was crucified.

The deacon Stephen would later be stoned as the first martyr of those who were followers of the Lamb / Jesus Christ, about three and a half years after the death and resurrection of Jesus Christ (Acts 6-7). In Luke's record of Stephen's sermon prior to the stoning of Stephen, Stephen stated, 'You stiff-necked people! Your hearts and ears are still uncircumcised. You are just like your ancestors: You always resist the Holy Spirit! Was there ever a prophet your ancestors did not persecute? They even killed those who predicted the coming of the Righteous One. And now you have betrayed and murdered him – you who have received the law that was given through angels but have not obeyed it! Acts 7:51-53 *With fury and gnashed teeth they stoned Stephen.*

During the second half of the era of the time of Jacob's Trouble, the two witnesses who will definitely be prophets of God Most High sent to us specifically for this era, will also be people who will be targeted for destruction by those who oppose God Most High.

The description given by Jesus Christ to John the Revelator, of the work of these two witnesses, was labeled for us as being two parts of the same verse. The two witnesses, although having come from two different eras of time and having not worked together on earth, will come as a team, each bringing their own skills, abilities, and talents.

These men have power to shut up the sky so that it will not rain during the time they are prophesying… Revelation 11:6a NIV

Throughout the ancient world, cultures have traditionally given credit to the kings, queens, and

pharaohs of the nations for being responsible for controlling the natural elements of sunshine and rain / climate change. The distribution of food, especially in the times of famine, have been the responsibility of the kings, queens, and pharaohs of the nations. Traditionally, if a king, queen, or pharaoh did not provide for the people, their reign would be cut short. This dynamic also made the account of Joseph's plan for setting aside provisions in Egypt for the upcoming world famine, into a God event.

The opposition to Moses was incubated when Moses led the war of God Most High against the gods of Egypt, the baal / mystery / mythology gods, with the ten plagues. In the conclusion of that war, Egypt lost their wealth, their military and their superpower status.

The opposition to Elijah was incubated from the heart of Queen Jezebel and King Ahab of the ten tribes of Israel / northern kingdom. King Ahab and Queen Jezebel had instituted political power over the religious community, a crossing of boundaries of the political community into the realm of religious authority. 'Church and state' were no longer separate and equal authorities to provide checks and balances between church and state. In the conclusion of the war between God Most High and the monarchs of the ten northern tribes of Israel, the baal / mystery / mythology religion lost its priests, Ahab and Jezebel lost their lives and their wealth, and their descendants were killed.

During the era of the time of Jacob's Trouble, the two witnesses will again encounter fierce opposition. They have already been equipped to deal with opposition, with their experiences thousands of years ago.

The opposition of the kingdom of Satan, Inc. / kingdom of man against the two witnesses will include the opposition of the global religious community.

Ahab and Jezebel used religion to enhance their political clout to steal land, destroy the prophets of God Most High, revamp the usage of the Lord's religious places and build up 'high places' / altars to the god baal and goddess Asherah.

During the era of the time of Jacob's Trouble, the global religious community will proclaim that true and authentic peace comes through rebellion against the rules and law of God Most High and the kingdom of heaven, and the adoption of the hybridized religion presented by the two beasts of Revelation 13.

In the rules and law of God Most High, each individual person was created to be a treasure, and to own their own land, and to have an unobstructed relationship with God Most High.

But the global religious community will insist that the value of a human being must be assessed by what that person contributes ... to the elites, and to the society that the elites desire to govern.

The two witnesses will arrive in sackcloth, not Giorgio Armoni. Their message will be that it is the person inside that is the true treasure, and that true treasure cannot be falsely valued, or stripped away. Every person is a creation of God the Creator, and bears God the Creator's image.

The opposition of the kingdom of Satan, Inc. / kingdom of man against the two witnesses, will also include the opposition of the global governance system.

The two beasts of Revelation 13 will persuade the inhabitants of the earth that the control of rain and drought, food and food distribution, are under the control of the two beasts; and that global governance should ration it all. Rain and drought, more than any other force, effect the source of food for people. By controlling food and food distribution, people can be controlled. Already, the world leaders view the solution to 'climate change' as being the depopulation of the earth and legislation that controls the food consumption of those who remain living.

During the era of the time of Jacob's Trouble, the rain and drought brought with this witness, will be explained away by the pseudo-scientific / scientism community and global governance system as having been the result of humanly created and humanly controllable 'climate change.'

But the reality will be that the control of rain and drought will be under the authority of the two witnesses. God Most High will again use the rain and drought to counter the effects of the global governance system's attempts to control people.

Jesus taught us to pray, 'Our Father, … Give us this day our daily bread…' During the era of the time of Jacob's Trouble, it will be God the Father who ultimately will remain in control of the production of 'daily bread.' And the mission of God the Father has consistently been to preserve and grow life.

The opposition of the kingdom of Satan, Inc. / kingdom of man against the two witnesses, will also include the opposition of the global economic structure.

During the era of the time of Jacob's Trouble, the global governance system will be active in 'eliminating poverty' (Agenda 2030) through the enhancement of the global economic structure. Under the guise of eliminating poverty, the global governance system and global economic structure, will publicly present their plan as stealing from the rich in order to give to the poor.

While Robin Hoodian economics has been taught as a great legend that brings good to humanity, their version of stealing from the rich to give to the poor will result in everyone just becoming poorer. With Robin Hood, the stealing was accomplished against the elite ruling class and accomplished loosely by the middle class, with the poor as the beneficiaries. But during the era of the time of Jacob's Trouble, with the deception of the people of the world by the elite ruling class, the stealing will be accomplished against both the upper and middle classes, and accomplished by the elite ruling class, with only the elite ruling class as the beneficiary and all other classes now designated as the 'poor' and destitute, with their dependence upon the global governance system for sustenance. (Envision a modern version of the system of feudalism that reigned during the Dark Ages / Middle Ages / medieval period.)

The opposition of the kingdom of Satan, Inc. / kingdom of man against the two witnesses, will also include the opposition of the global cultural theoterrorism movement.

… and they have power to turn the waters into blood and to strike the earth with every kind of plague as often as they want. Revelation 11:6b

Because the two witnesses will have the power to turn the waters into blood and bring plagues, one witness is believed to be Moses who also turned water into blood and brought plagues to Egypt / the enemies of the God of the Israelites.

When Jacob / Israel brought his family into Egypt under the leadership of Jacob's son Joseph, the Egyptian pharaoh had respect for the God of Abraham, Isaac, and Jacob, and heeded the message of God Most High concerning the worldwide famine that was about to come. But in the four hundred thirty years that followed, the hearts of the pharaohs no longer respected the God of Abraham, Isaac, and Jacob. The pharaohs during the time of Moses sought to genocide the people of Israel and later to enslave them, even denying them the opportunity to worship God Most High.

While Moses dealt with the political power of Egypt, the plagues sent to Egypt were first a dramatic demonstration of God Most High's power over the religious community. It was the priests of the baal / mystery / mythology religion and their power over the people of Egypt, that were the first to be affected by the plagues. The result of the plagues of Egypt upon Pharaoh and his reign were secondary. It was not until the plague of the firstborn, the tenth plague upon Egypt, that Pharaoh finally relented and allowed the people of Israel to leave Egypt. On the way out of town, the Israelites were given the spoils of Egypt, draining the Egyptian economy. But it was the pressure of the Egyptians that urged the military to pursue the people of Israel to the Red Sea in an effort to annihilate the defenseless people of Israel.

And during the era of the time of Jacob's Trouble, the inhabitants of the earth will oppose the message of the two witnesses, concerning God Most High, concerning

messiah / the Lamb / Jesus Christ, concerning the kingdom of heaven.

But the two witnesses will have the supernatural authority and power to protect themselves against the global cultural theoterrorism movement.

If anyone should desire to harm them, fire comes out of their mouths and devours their enemies. And if anyone should desire to harm them, it is necessary for them to be killed in this manner. Revelation 11:5 translated

The supernatural authority and power of the two witnesses

John the Revelator documented the forty two month term of supernatural power and authority that the two beasts of Revelation 13 will share.

And John the Revelator also documented the one thousand two hundred sixty days of supernatural authority and power that the two witnesses will share (Revelation 11:1-14).

But added to John the Revelator's documentation, would be the authority and power that Moses and Elijah held the first time they lived on earth. As the greatest leader and greatest prophet in all the nation of Israel's history, accomplished some awesome fetes, and provided some tremendous miracles.

When they return, they will need to achieve some even greater accomplishments.

When Jesus Christ came for his earthly ministry, Jesus Christ provided even greater miracles than the prophets.

When Jesus, Peter, James, and John the brother of James came to the home of the synagogue ruler, Jesus saw a commotion, with people crying and wailing loudly. Jesus went in and said to them, 'Why all this commotion and wailing? The child is not dead but asleep.' But they laughed at him. Mark 5:38-40

Jesus took her by the hand and said to the little girl, 'Talitha koum!' which means, 'Little girl, I say to you, get up!'

Immediately the girl stood up and walked around.

The little girl was twelve years old. Mark 5:41-43

For Jesus to fulfill the prophecy to be qualified to be the promised and prophesied messiah, and to be the Son of God Most High, Jesus needed to perform miracles that

were similar to all the miracles of all the prophets before him. Jesus needed to be greater than all the other prophets.

In Jesus' lifetime, Jesus made the lame to walk, the blind to see. Jesus fed multitudes, multiple times. And Jesus needed to raise people from the dead as Elijah had done. The raising of Lazarus from the dead after four days was the other resurrection that Jesus accomplished (John 11).

Jesus Christ was rejected by the leadership of the nation of Israel. In order for the two witnesses to be able to be heard, they will need to provide miracles that will be even greater than the miracles Jesus Christ did during his earthly ministry.

Jesus also promised that the followers of the Lamb / Jesus Christ, will do greater things than what Jesus has already done while living with us on earth. The two witnesses will be two of the many who will do greater things. This promise was also extended to the followers of the Lamb / Jesus Christ.

It is reasonable to expect that the two witnesses will again be active in providing miracles on behalf of God Most High during their stay on the temple mount.

Jesus taught in the Synagogue and they took offense at him. Jesus said to them, 'Only in his hometown, among his relatives and in his own house is a prophet without honor.'
Jesus could not do any miracles there, except lay his hands on a few sick people and heal them. And he was amazed at their lack of faith. Mark 6:1-6

Jesus Christ performed many miracles. But the intended purpose of the miracles of God Most High is not for manipulation.

In contrast to the supernatural miracles of God Most High, given as a gift to those who have gifted God Most High with their trust, the supernatural magic that belongs to the kingdom of Satan, Inc. / kingdom of man is truly focused upon manipulating people through manipulating their faith.

Magic is designed to convince the audience of a lie. Magic is trading an illusion for truth. Magic is used for trading your trust, your property, your belief in something or someone; for something that either does not exist or is not true and real. Magicians will perform magic in exchange for their own personal reward. Magic originates from the power of the red dragon / serpent / Satan, Inc. and is performed for the benefit of the kingdom of Satan, Inc. / kingdom of man and their adherents.

True miracles originate from God Most High, the God of truth which includes the Holy Spirit of Truth. Miracles are a gift, undeserved and given without expectation of anything in return, not even faith, even though they cannot be accomplished without faith in God Most High. For the environment to exist in which miracles can happen, faith must come first. Miracles are not intended to convince someone to believe. Miracles are simply proof of God Most High's presence. Miracles are the reward of faith.

When Jesus attended the grave of Lazarus, Jesus questioned Mary, Martha, and the disciples about what they believed. Their belief that God Most High could raise someone from death and will raise all who believe in God Most High from death, came before Jesus called Lazarus from the tomb. Of course, afterward their faith was increased. But God Most High begins with the faith system that we have as the foundation for God's miracles. (John 11:1-44)

Where there is no faith, Jesus Christ refrained from providing miracles. Where there is no faith, God Most High will also refrain from providing miracles.

The two witnesses from heaven have a faith that comes from living thousands of years in close connection with the God of the universe in heaven. They will provide God Most High's miracles. And those who will be the recipients of God Most High's miracles through them will be influenced by the kind of faith that they possess at that time and in that place.

This statement by Jesus Christ implied that the qualifier for receiving miracles will not be based on one's genetic heritage, but rather based on one's level of faith in God Most High.

The assassination, death, resurrection and ascension of the two witnesses
When they have completed their testimony, the beast that ascends out of the Abyss will make war against them, and overcome them, and kill them. And their dead bodies will lie in the street of the great city which spiritually is called Sodom and Egypt, where also their Lord was crucified. And those from the peoples, multitudes, languages, and nations, will gaze upon their bodies for three and a half days, and will not allow their bodies to be put into a tomb. And the inhabitants of the earth will rejoice over them. They will celebrate and send gifts to one another, because these two prophets tormented the inhabitants of the earth.

But after the three and a half days, the breath of life from God entered into them, and they stood upon their feet. Great fear fell upon those who saw them. And they heard a great voice out of heaven saying to them, 'Come up here.' And they went up to heaven in a cloud; and their enemies saw them. In that same hour, there was a great earthquake and a tenth of the city fell. And in the earthquake, seven thousand men of names / well known men (global leaders) were killed. The rest became terrified and gave glory to the God of heaven.
Revelation 11:7-13 translated

The beast from the Abyss was identified as the beast of the sea / false prophet / eight king beast in John the Revelator's description of the eighth king beast atop the scarlet beast (Revelation 17:8).

The seven thousand men of names / well known men, referenced global leaders from the list of the global elite.

Abomination of Desolation Events – Past and Future

In the biblical record, two abomination of desolation events were prophesied. In between Daniel receiving the main vision (536 BC) (Daniel 11 -12) that described the abomination of desolation events and the era of the life of Jesus Christ (~4 BC - 30 / 33 AD), the first abomination of desolation event took place in 167 BC led by the king of the Seleucid / Syrian empire, Antiochus IV Epiphanes.

As Jesus instructed his disciples just prior to his death in what was titled the Olivet Discourse, Jesus gave further description of the future abomination of desolation event that will take place during the era of the time of

Jacob's Trouble, and referenced the first abomination of desolation event as a template for the future abomination of desolation event.

Matthew recorded Jesus' instructions in Matthew 24. Mark's record was recorded in Mark 13.

The visions of Daniel and the instructions of messiah / the Lamb / Jesus Christ, are the foundation for the description of the abomination of desolation events. Other biblical sources add to understanding the abomination of desolation events. But Daniel and messiah / the Lamb / Jesus Christ have provided the greatest amount of substance for understanding.

The future abomination of desolation event will be the most important event of the era of the time of Jacob's Trouble for setting time and for anchoring the calendar of events that God Most High has established for this era. The future abomination of desolation event will be a kind of coronation of the little horn / eleventh king / final horn on the shaggy goat / prince who is to come / king that will exalt himself / beast of the earth / final world ruler, that will be recognized worldwide.

- little horn / eleventh king - Daniel 7:8, 7:25
- final horn on the shaggy goat - Daniel 8:11-14, 8:23-26
- ruler who is to come - Daniel 9:26b-27
- king that will exalt himself - Daniel 11:31-32
- Daniel 12:6-7, 12:11-12

The future abomination of desolation event will act to 'synch the watches' for all that will happen after the future abomination of desolation. It has been scheduled in heaven that from the time of the future abomination of desolation event, until the beginning of God's wrath being poured out upon the earth through the seventh trumpet / woe #3 / seven bowls / seven last plagues, that the red dragon / serpent / Satan, Inc. will be allowed to have his two representatives, the two beasts of Revelation 13, to be given the opportunity to rule over the earth. This future abomination of desolation event will officially inaugurate the final phase of the red dragon / serpent / Satan, Inc.'s final attempt to fully establish the kingdom of Satan, Inc. / kingdom of man on earth.

The two beasts of Revelation 13, along with the supernatural spiritual force of the red dragon / serpent / Satan, Inc. will comprise the unholy trinity (Revelation 12-13). God Most High has set a time limit on how long the unholy trinity will have to reign. They will be allowed one thousand two hundred sixty days / forty two months / three and a half years, with some residue of power leaching into the final seventy five days (Daniel 12:11-12). Their reign of one thousand two hundred sixty days will begin with the future abomination of desolation event. Their forty two month reign will end at the same time that God Most High's two witnesses are killed by the red dragon / serpent / Satan, Inc. (Revelation 11:1-14).

The purpose of the future abomination of desolation event

To understand the future abomination of desolation event, it is vital to understand the need for the future abomination of desolation event.

When Jesus entered into our world as fully human, along with being fully divine, Jesus Christ's ministry lasted three and a half years before it was cut off, severing the second half of the allotted time that it would have taken for Jesus Christ to have prepared the people of the nation of Israel for priesthood. While there were many people of Israel who became followers of Jesus, who believed that Jesus Christ was the promised messiah, the religious leaders and the elite of the people of Israel rejected Jesus Christ as messiah.

The first abomination of desolation event (167 BC), although it took place almost two hundred years before the coming of Jesus, was essential in setting the cultural, political, and religious environment that was required for Jesus Christ to minister, to be crucified, to be resurrected, and to ascend into heaven.

The future abomination of desolation event will also set the cultural, political, and religious environment that will be required for Jesus Christ to return, to defeat the armies of the world, to forge the people of Israel into a nation of priests, and to fully establish the kingdom of heaven on earth.

Both Daniel and messiah / the Lamb / Jesus Christ have presented the first abomination of desolation and the coming future abomination of desolation as intertwined. Not only did the first abomination of desolation event set the pattern for how the future abomination of desolation event will take place, but the first abomination of desolation event impacted the people of Israel to bring them to the place where they needed to decide on a very personal level, how far they would travel away from God Most High and whether or not they would return to God Most High.

There were also other ways in which the first and future abomination of desolation events were comparable.

The first abomination of desolation event of 167 BC primarily effected the people of Israel and the nation of Israel. But the future abomination of desolation event that will mark the midway point of the seven years of the era of the time of Jacob's Trouble, will affect every person in the world. With the future abomination of desolation event, global governance will have been established, attempting to change all governmental structures, regulating areas of life that have never been regulated before, and impacting the people of the world in drastic ways. The events of the era of the time of Jacob's Trouble will be a time when everyone will be forced to consider what they think, feel, and believe about God Most High, and more importantly what they think, feel, and believe about Jesus as God Most High's promised and prophesied messiah.

The future abomination of desolation event will be crucial as the last attempt of this era for the red dragon / serpent / Satan, Inc. to fully establish the kingdom of Satan, Inc. / kingdom of man on earth. There will be several dynamics that will result from the entire process of implementing the future abomination of desolation event and from God Most High's response to the future abomination of desolation event. But the main result of the future abomination of desolation event will be to introduce the little horn / eleventh king / final horn on the shaggy goat / prince who is to come / king that will exalt himself / beast of the earth / final world ruler to the world as the leader of the global governance system, and as candidate for the one who <u>the red dragon / serpent / Satan, Inc. has designated</u> to fulfill the role of God Most High's promised and prophesied messiah. The future abomination of desolation event will act for the beast of the earth as an attempt to establish himself above God Most High and coronate himself as King of kings / Lord of lords / Supreme and Sovereign Ruler / contender for the throne of heaven / a solution to substitute for Jesus whom the adherents of the red dragon / serpent / Satan, Inc. continue to tag as a failure in accomplishing what he was supposed to do.

    From the perspective of the red dragon / serpent / Satan, Inc., the purpose of the seven years of the era of the time of Jacob's Trouble will be to give the red dragon / serpent / Satan, Inc. a truly authentic opportunity to attempt to fully establish the kingdom of Satan, Inc. / kingdom of man on earth. If the red dragon / serpent / Satan, Inc. were to be successful in accomplishing this goal, it would be definitive proof that the baal / mystery / mythology religion is superior to authentic Christianity. It would also be definitive proof that God Most High can be displaced from his throne and that the position of God Most High is not determined by the God who created the heavens and the earth, but rather by the being that can amass the greatest amount of cosmic, spiritual, and physical power. This message of the red dragon / serpent / Satan, Inc. has throughout human history been provided through the various flavors of the baal / mystery / mythology religion. Included in this message has been the declaration that the gods of the universe / rebellious angels, fight amongst each other and that the most powerful god / rebellious angel, wins the right to occupy the highest position, at least until that powerful god / rebellious angel is also dethroned by the next most powerful god.

    But God Most High's kingdom of heaven standard for defining who will be qualified to sit upon the throne of the heavens and the earth has been intrinsically lodged with the One who is the author of love and peace, and who has the ability to create: to create life, to sustain life, to redeem life. God Most High's kingdom economy operates on love, where God Most High's deep and unconditional love is actually greater than power.

Power without love can only be destructive. Power with love can only bring life.

This historical ultimate cosmic battle will determine which is greater; a kingdom that operates with power that is devoid of love as its economy, or a kingdom that through love can create life, sustain life, redeem life, and infuse life with love?

The biblical record established that power devoid of love can only destroy. But the magnitude of God Most High's love is greater than all power that is devoid of love.

The conflict between the two different kingdoms, the two different principles concerning life and death, and the two different economies, has been active since the Garden of Eden / garden of God / paradise incident when the serpent induced the first woman and first man to defy the will of God Most High and to eat the fruit of the tree of the knowledge of good and evil. Because the nature of evil is to defy God Most High, to eliminate God Most High and God's influence, and because God Most High has been defined as love, then the nature of evil is to exert power that is devoid of love and to eradicate love. Because the nature of good is to place oneself into the will of God Most High, to embrace God Most High and God's influence; and because God Most High has been defined as the powerful creator of the universe; then the nature of good is to experience love that is inherently powered by God Most High.

Power devoid of love can only be destructive.

Love that is fueled by the power of God Most High can only bring life, redemption, regeneration, reconciliation, eternal life after death, the tree of life, etc.

Authentic Christianity and the faith system of ancient Judaism, with God Most High as its cornerstone / foundation stone, is a redemptive system that offers every individual person the opportunity for reestablishing a right relationship with God Most High and for relinquishing the grasp that the red dragon / serpent / Satan, Inc. holds over each and every individual.

The second half of the era of the time of Jacob's Trouble will be the time when the question will be dramatically proposed to every individual, 'Which king and kingdom are you going to be loyal to?' There are only two possible answers. There have only ever been two possible answers. Each person must choose their king. The future abomination of desolation will serve to clarify and to present this question in a way in which every individual will be required, compelled, forced, bound, obligated, etc., to provide their own personal answer.

Relocating the headquarters of the apostate baal / mystery / mythology religion, global governance, global economic structure and global theoterrorism, to the temple mount of God's holy city

There is one more dynamic of the future abomination of desolation event that must be recognized in order to understand this cosmic conflict. The future abomination of desolation event will have the effect of 'planting the flag' and claiming territory for the kingdom of Satan, Inc. / kingdom of man.

In this case, claiming the territory of God Most High's temple mount, the place where Abraham sacrificed Isaac four thousand years ago, the place where the first temple was constructed three thousand years ago, the place where messiah / the Lamb / Jesus Christ was sacrificed two thousand years ago, and the place where messiah / the Lamb / Jesus Christ is scheduled to return to in less than one thousand three hundred thirty five days, will be the kingdom of Satan, Inc. / kingdom of man's final act of defiance against the kingdom of heaven.

The day that the prince who is to come / king that will exalt himself / beast of the earth / final world ruler will declare himself to be divine, sovereign and superior to God Most High, in the future abomination of desolation event, he will also 'bring to life' the idol / image of the beast of the sea / false prophet / beast from the Abyss / eighth king beast that will be located on the temple mount in Jerusalem.

In the act of establishing the idol / image of the beast of the sea on the temple mount, and bringing the idol / image to life, the beast of the earth will believe that he has successfully claimed the temple mount for the kingdom of Satan, Inc. / kingdom of man. The transfer of the baal / mystery / mythology religion from Babylon / tower of Babel empire, to Pergamum, to Rome, to Jerusalem Israel, will have been completed.

The entire future abomination of desolation event will be the attempt to effectively move the center of worship of the Roman Catholic Church (that was intended to be the representation of the kingdom of heaven on earth), to Jerusalem Israel (God's holy city).

And in bringing the idol / image of the beast of the sea to life, and establishing the mark of the beasts global system, the two beasts of Revelation 13, will have integrated global religion, global governance, global economy and global social cultural structure, into a single system.

The future abomination of desolation event, with all its parts, will effectively be the kingdom of Satan, Inc. / kingdom of man's final declaration of war against the kingdom of heaven and the God who created all life, all aspects of life, and all things.

The beast of the sea / false prophet / beast from the Abyss / eighth king beast will be the leader of the 'church' that has now become infiltrated and consumed by the baal / mystery / mythology religion of the red dragon / serpent Satan, Inc. But the beast of the sea / false prophet / beast from the Abyss / eighth king beast will also be the leader of the 'empire' that was birthed by the Roman empire and has carried the cause of the Roman empire to expand into the world through colonies, for the purpose of taking over the world and establishing global governance. 'Catholic' means 'universal.' In addition, the beast of the sea / false prophet / eighth king beast will covenant with the merchants of the earth to manage trade and controlling economy for the purpose of dominating the peoples, multitudes, nations and languages. And the beast of the sea

/ false prophet / beast from the Abyss / eighth king beast will lead people's hearts to honor the gods of the kingdom of Satan, Inc. / kingdom of man through activity that defies and attacks every aspect of the Law and rules of the kingdom of heaven, through his influence in the social cultural movement of theoterrorism.

So, when the idol / image of the beast of the sea / false prophet / beast from the Abyss / eighth king beast will be erected on the temple mount and seemingly brought to life, it will not just symbolize a new era of terror against humanity, it will also be the greatest defiance of the God of the kingdom of heaven in all of human history. It will be the ultimate act of cosmic war.

The future abomination of desolation event, will place the kingdoms of this world represented by Babylon / tower of Babel empire, Pergamum, and the Roman empire, at war with the kingdom of heaven represented by God's holy city Jerusalem Israel.

The requirement of a temple in Jerusalem as the site for the abomination of desolation

In order to have an abomination of desolation event, there must be a temple for the abomination of desolation event to take place in. The term 'abomination of desolation' actually refers to 'an abomination that will cause the temple to become desolate' (Daniel 9:27, 11:31, 12:11, Matthew 24:15, Mark 13:14) 'Abomination' is a term referring to the introduction of an idol or idolatry into the holy place. 'Desolate' refers to the state of the relationship with God Most High that the temple experiences following the abomination of desolation events; unfit and unconsecrated for the process of offering sacrifices to God Most High, or for communicating with God Most High.

Prior to the future abomination of desolation event that will take place during the era of the time of Jacob's Trouble, there must be a temple constructed in order for the people of Israel to be able to have a fully consecrated, functional and operational temple sacrificial system, and to fully worship God Most High. After the sacrificial system will be established in the future temple, it will be the act of abomination that will desolate the temple and effectively cause the temple to become unfit for the continuance of the evening and morning sacrifice, along with the other forms of sacrifice that are crucial for the people of Israel who practice Judaism.

People who have rejected Jesus Christ as their promised and prophesied messiah, do not have the benefit of living under the law of grace ushered in through Jesus Christ. They remain under the restriction of the Mosaic Law which requires sacrifice in order for their personal sins to be forgiven and the sins of the nation of Israel to be forgiven. Without the forgiveness of sins, there can be no restoration of an individual or a nation to a right relationship with God Most High. People that are not living with a belief in Jesus Christ as Lord, remain confined to their hope of obtaining a right relationship with God through the temple sacrificial system. This is the reason why a temple and a fully consecrated, functional and operational temple sacrificial system are so very crucial for the people of Israel who have rejected Jesus Christ as their promised and prophesied messiah.

The first temple was built by Solomon in 966-960 BC and destroyed in 586 BC by the Babylonians, three hundred seventy four years later in 586 BC. The second temple was built in 559-516 BC and was destroyed in 70 AD by the Romans, five hundred eighty five years later.

The future temple will be dubbed the 'third temple.' The 'third temple' must be built in order for the future abomination of desolation event to take place. Therefore the third temple must be built either prior to the beginning of the future abomination of desolation event or during the first half of the era of the time of Jacob's Trouble. The temple must be in place in time for the midpoint of the seven year confirmation of the covenant peace treaty when the future abomination of desolation event has been scheduled. The confirmation of the covenant peace treaty will probably include provisions for the building of the third temple.

Following an eight day consecration service, the future third temple will provide a period of time when the people of Israel will be able to offer animal sacrifices for the forgiveness of their sin and for the forgiveness of their nation as is required for having a right relationship with God Most High according to the law given to Moses.

The temple sacrificial system was designed to cover both individual sin and the sins of the nation of Israel. In the temple, there were also the daily evening and morning sacrifices to God Most High, along with the required sacrifices of the feast holy days / holidays.

The people of Israel who do not recognize Jesus as their promised and prophesied messiah, are still waiting for God Most High to send to them their messiah. Currently, the people of Israel expect that Prime Minister Benjamin Netanyahu will be instrumental in the building of the third temple and that Bibi will be the one to make provisions for bringing the messiah to the people of Israel. The red dragon / serpent / Satan, Inc.'s candidate for messiah cannot arrive unless messiah has a temple to arrive to.

God Most High's temple as a representation of the union of the relationship between God the Father, Jesus Christ the bridegroom and God's holy people the bride, and the traditional Jewish marriage protocol

As a side note, according to the Jewish tradition, the wedding ceremony takes place under the chuppah / wedding canopy as a symbol that God's canopy of blessing is held over the marriage and over the couple being married. The entire Jewish marriage ceremony is the story of God Most High's redemptive love, with Jesus Christ as the bridegroom. The marriage covenant includes acts that demonstrate the groom's love and the groom making provisions for the bride. The groom represents Jesus Christ's and God Most High's love and provisions for God's people. The bride represents those who believe in God Most High's redemption, reclamation and regeneration plan. The Jewish marriage begins with the betrothal process involving the fathers, the groom, and the bride who must accept the arrangement willingly, drinking from the first *cup as a sign that the covenant agreement is acceptable to her. Every portion of the marriage process is an essential piece of the story that corresponds to the redemptive plan of God Most High. The groom who must remove himself after the betrothal contract has been made, goes to prepare rooms in his father's house for the couple, rooms that must meet the groom's father's satisfaction before the groom will be allowed to return to the bride in order to claim her. The arrival of the groom to claim his bride is announced with the sound of trumpets and may take place at any time of the day or night. Each detail of the traditional Jewish marriage ceremony demonstrates the relationship that Jesus Christ has with his bride / the followers of the Lamb.*

The actual wedding ceremony takes place under the chuppah / wedding canopy, which symbolizes God Most High's canopy of blessing that is held over the marriage. The couple concludes the ceremony with the groom and the bride drinking from the cup of marriage. After the partaking of the cup of marriage, the glass is wrapped in cloth and crushed by the husband as a reminder that the people of Israel will not be complete until the temple is rebuilt and the promised and prophesied messiah comes.

The promise made in the Garden of Eden / garden of God / paradise to send the promised and prophesied messiah, and the red dragon / serpent / Satan, Inc.'s need to supply a facsimile candidate to fulfill that prophecy

In the Garden of Eden / garden of God / paradise, when the first man / Adam sinned, God Most High's response was to promise to send a messiah that would not have a biological father. The messiah would be born of only a woman, the seed of a woman (Genesis 3:15).

Joseph, the husband of Mary had the legitimate genealogy for being an heir to the throne of David (Matthew 1). But Joseph's genealogy included Jehoiachin who had been so evil that God discontinued his lineage for further consideration in the messianic lineage. Jehoiachin, the ancestor of Joseph, was another reason why Joseph could not be the biological father of Jesus.

Mary the mother of Jesus also had the legitimate genealogy for being an heir to the throne of David, through David's son Nathan (Luke 3). It was because Mary was a woman and her genealogy met the required criteria that God Most High had established, that Mary became the biological parent for the promised and prophesied messiah / Jesus Christ.

When Nimrod developed the tower of Babel empire, Nimrod's genealogy, Nimrod's life mission, and Nimrod's prowess, served as an attempt to place Nimrod as the man who would fulfill the prophesy made in the Garden of Eden.

During the life of Jesus, the red dragon / serpent / Satan, Inc. provided King Herod for the position as leader for the people of Israel. King Herod the Great was an Edomite / Idumean who converted to Judaism and married an Israelite in order to gain a level of legitimacy for occupying the throne as King of Israel.

The red dragon / serpent / Satan, Inc. will again offer their own candidate to fill this position of sitting on the throne of David. Their candidate may be an Israelite through genealogy. Or their candidate may be someone who does not have a connection with Judaism. But somehow, in the mind of the red dragon / serpent / Satan, Inc. organization, their candidate should be eligible for seizing the throne of David and ruling the nation of Israel.

Daniel's vision of the ram and the shaggy goat – Daniel 8
In order to understand the full dynamics and the type of activities that will comprise the future abomination of desolation event, it is important to understand the dynamics and the type of activities that have comprised the previous abomination of desolation event, along with the messages that God Most High has provided that described the various abomination of desolation events.

The first person in the biblical record to describe the nature of abomination of desolation events in great detail was Daniel. Daniel 8, 9, 10, 11 and 12 contained the visions given to Daniel that conveyed the greatest amount of *information concerning the abomination of desolation events.*

But the order of the chapters of the book of Daniel were not given to us in the chronological order that the visions were given to Daniel and Nebuchadnezzar. And the visions recorded in Daniel were also not given to us in the chronological order that they are to be fulfilled.

Added to the lack of chronological orderliness in Daniel's record and the lack of chronological orderliness in the timing of the fulfillments of the prophecies, was the element that the visions themselves sometimes acted as one description for multiple events as well as multiple descriptions of the same event. For example, the ram and the shaggy goat that represented the Medo – Persian and the Greek empires, addressed the same empires as the Nebuchadnezzar's vision of the man's arms and torso.

The 'disordering' of the chronology of the book of Daniel along with the 'overlap' in the visions, set the precedent that allowed for John the Revelator's visions to be interpreted as not having been recorded in the chronological order that they will be fulfilled in. To view the book of Revelation, or any of the prophecies of any of the prophets that were reported in the biblical record, as strictly chronological descriptions of visions, can only offer a very incomplete representation of the message of God Most High's plan.

Time / chronology was created by God the Creator, for the purpose of aiding humanity in understanding God's plan. God the Creator is not confined by time. Humanity is.

The 'disordering' of the chronology of the book of Daniel and the 'overlap' in the visions served to provide a focus upon the details of the events, from multiple perspectives, which aids in understanding God Most High's message in giving the visions. The 'disordering' of the chronology of the book of Daniel and the 'overlap' in the visions also acts as a communicative device that focuses the attention of each vision beyond just a mere telling of the events, to the motives of the actors and the purposes of the actions.

Included here is a timeline which identified when each chapter of the book of Daniel was written and who the predominant ruler of the time was during those times. This listing ordered Daniel's record chronologically according to when each vision was recorded.

- 605 to 603 BC: *Daniel 1*; 3rd year of the rule of Jehoiakim king of Judah to the 1st year of the reign of Nebuchadnezzar king of Babylon
- 603 BC: *Daniel 2*; 2nd year of the reign of Nebuchadnezzar king of Babylon
- 602 to 652 BC: *Daniel 3? and 4?*; 2nd year of the reign of Nebuchadnezzar king of Babylon to the death of Nebuchadnezzar and the reign of Evil-Merodach / Amel-Marduk, son of Nebuchadnezzar
- 553 BC: *Daniel 7*; Belshazzar, either the grandson or great grandson of Nebuchadnezzar, assumed the throne of Babylon.
- 551 BC: *Daniel 8*; 3rd year of the reign of Belshazzar
- 539 BC: *Daniel 5, 9 and 6?*; 1st year of the reign of Darius king of the Medes and Cyrus king of the Persians
- 536 BC: *Daniel 10-12*; 3rd year of the reign of Cyrus king of the Persians
- 516 to 515 BC: The second temple was built in Jerusalem
- 336 to 323 BC: Reign of Alexander the Great of Macedon, emperor of the Greek empire
- 167 BC: The Seleucid / Syrian king Antiochus IV Epiphanes committed the abomination of desolation in the temple in Jerusalem (After Alexander the Great died, his empire was divided among four of his generals into four empires. The Seleucid / Syrian empire was one of the four empires that rose from Alexander the Great's empire and it was the empire that spawned Antiochus IV Epiphanes.)
- 164 BC: Temple was reconsecrated and the sacrificial system restored. The first feast of dedication / Hanukah was celebrated.

In Daniel's vision, after the discussion of the image of the ram / Medes and Persians rising to power, was the image of the shaggy goat / Greece.

As I was thinking about this (the ram's rise to power), suddenly a goat with a prominent horn between its eyes came from the west, crossing the whole earth without touching the ground. It came toward the two-horned ram I had seen standing beside the canal and charged at it with great rage. I saw it attack the ram furiously, striking the ram and shattering its two horns. The ram was powerless to stand against it; the goat knocked it to the ground and trampled on it, and none could rescue the ram from the power of the shaggy goat. The goat became very great, but at the height of its power the large horn was broken off, and in its place four prominent horns grew up toward the four winds of heaven.

Daniel documented in his description, the transition that was made between Alexander the Great / large horn with his four generals / four prominent horns who succeeded him, and the coming final horn on the shaggy goat.

Out of one of the four horns came another horn, which started small but grew in power to the south and to the east and toward the Beautiful Land. It grew until it reached the host of the heavens, and it threw some of the starry host down to the earth and trampled on them. It set itself up to be as great as the commander of the army of the Lord. It took away the daily sacrifice from the Lord, and his sanctuary was thrown down. Because of rebellion, the Lord's people and the daily sacrifice were given over to it. It prospered in everything it did, and truth was thrown to the ground. Daniel 8:5-12

Rams are male sheep. Sheep are considered to be desirable sacrifices in the Mosaic sacrificial system. Goats are associated with undesirability in the Mosaic sacrificial system. Goats were used for the sacrifice of the annual fall feast of Yom Kippur / Day of Atonement where the goat named Azazel was thrown off a cliff, symbolically representing the future event when the rebellious angel Azazel / Satan will be cast into the fiery lake when he joins the two beasts of Revelation 13. The connection of the imagery of the ram and the goat to the use of the goat sacrifice during Yom Kippur / Day of Atonement and to the future disposition of Satan scheduled to take place at the end of the Thousand Years Reign of Jesus Christ, indicated that this vision cannot be contained in a single period of time measured in increments of human lifetimes. The connection of the final little horn that grows from the ancient history of the Greek empire under Alexander the Great, indicated that this vision represented God Most High's work throughout human history, and it will not be the work of an individual or an empire.

Daniel received this vision in the third year of the reign of King Belshazzar of the Babylonians, even before the Medes and the Persians / ram with two horns, entered the storyline for the fulfillment of this prophecy. This vision was given before the handwriting on the wall event, before the Medes conquered Babylon in a single night. The third year of the reign of King Belshazzar was approximately 551 BC.

The vision of the ram and the events that it represented, took place during Daniel's lifetime and Daniel's experience. Daniel served as a high official in the court of King Cyrus, king of the Persians and the Medes. But the vision of the shaggy goat / kingdom of Greece, and the events that it represented and still represents, began taking place after the end of Daniel's life and will effectively continue into the era of the time of Jacob's Trouble / 'the distant future.'

The ram with two horns represented the Medes and the Persians, and the goat with its large horn coming from the west represented the Greek empire under the leadership of Alexander the Great. Daniel's vision of the goat's attack of the ram gave a strikingly accurate description of the Greek empire as it conquered the Medes and the Persians. (Greco Persian Wars, 499 to 449 BC)

The large horn of the shaggy goat represented Alexander the Great and the Greek empire. The large horn of the shaggy goat was broken off, a prophecy of the abruptness of the end of the reign of Alexander the Great. The four prominent horns that came from the large horn represented the four generals and their empires that eventually divided the Greek empire, following the death of Alexander the Great. From the perspective of Jerusalem being a 'center point,' the four generals established their four empires to the north, south, east, and west of Jerusalem, in four directions, as if expanding from the four winds of heaven.

Daniel's vision presented the ancient empires of the world; the Greek, Seleucid / Syrian, Ptolemaic / Egyptian, Antipatrid, and Lysimachus empires, as somehow having provided the 'seed' for the final horn on the shaggy goat.

But notice that out of the four prominent horns on the shaggy goat, came another little horn, which started small but grew in power to the south and to the east and toward the Beautiful Land / the land of Israel. This little horn grew until it reached the host of the heavens, and it threw some of the starry host / rebellious angels down to the earth and trampled on them...

It was here in Daniel's record that there was a gap of time to allow the little horn to grow. This little horn grew out of one of the four prominent horns / four empires that followed Alexander the Great's Greek empire. The time gap between the four prominent horns / four empires, and the rising of the little horn, was not defined.

Note that the leadership of both abomination of desolation events will be people represented by horns that originated from the shaggy goat: Antiochus IV Epiphanes from the Seleucid / Syrian empire (167 BC), and the final horn on the shaggy goat for the future abomination of desolation event.

What was not defined in this vision was the direct relationship of the final horn to the four prominent horns. The four prominent horns became four substantial empires. But the little horn was presented with an image that instead of rising like an empire, the little horn will rise as a man that garners enough power to create his own empire.

The final horn on the shaggy goat will also possess the power and authority to throw some of the starry host down to the earth and trample on them. And he will set himself up to be as great as the commander of the army of the Lord.

There will only be one time in all human history when the starry host / rebellious angels will be thrown to earth and be trampled upon, during the era of the time of Jacob's Trouble (Daniel 8:10-11, Revelation 12:7-9).

The note that the little horn will set himself up to be as great as the commander of the army of the Lord, coincided with Daniel's other vision of the final horn on the shaggy goat where he will destroy God's holy people. (Daniel 8:9-12, 8:24c, see also Revelation 12).

The responsibility for leading in the destruction of God's holy people was assigned to the beast of the earth through the installment of the idol / image of the beast of the sea on the temple mount, and the initialization of the mark of the beasts system (Revelation 13:11-18).

Daniel's vision documented that the final horn on the shaggy goat will have the authority to take away the daily sacrifice from the Lord and to throw don his sanctuary. Because of rebellion, God's people and the daily sacrifice were given to the final horn on the shaggy goat. (Daniel 8:11-12, Revelation 13:14-17)

In order for the final horn on the shaggy goat (or the beast of the earth) to have authority over the activities of the temple / daily sacrifice, the final horn on the shaggy goat must have authority over the Jewish temple system. (Note that the beast of the sea / eighth king beast will be sourced from the city with the seven hills (Revelation 17:9-11).)

The most important aspect of the message of Daniel's vision of the final horn on the shaggy goat was described as his activity of discontinuing the temple sacrifice and cutting off the access of the people of Israel to God Most High, along with the consequences both to the people of Israel and to the people of Israel's relationship with God Most High.

But without accessing God Most High through the temple fully consecrated, functional and operational temple sacrificial system, the people of Israel will be forced to seek a new method for accessing God Most High, bringing them closer to discovering Jesus Christ as their promised and prophesied messiah.

And because it will be the final horn on the shaggy goat / beast of the earth who will be the one to cut off access to God Most High, and who will make war against what should be his own people, the people of Israel will recognize that he is _NOT_ their promised and prophesied messiah, causing them to look elsewhere for their messiah.

The person who discontinued the temple sacrifice and cut off the access of the people of Israel to God through the first abomination of desolation event, was the king of the Seleucid / Syrian empire, Antiochus IV Epiphanes in 167 BC. Antiochus IV Epiphanes, ruler of the Seleucid / Syrian empire, who was represented by one of the four prominent horns that rose out of the broken large horn. Antiochus IV Epiphanes was the leader of a truly vast empire. It was Antiochus IV Epiphanes that set the template that provided the original description for what an abomination of desolation event consists of. But the cultural theology of the people of Israel prior to that event, that established the foundation that allowed the first abomination of desolation event to take place.

The Old Testament / Tankah prophet Malachi (fl. 440 to 430 BC) - of Judah, wrote the last prophetic book of the Old Testament around 433 to 430 BC. At that time, the rebellion of the people of Israel against God Most High resulted in the people of Israel rejecting the messages from prophets. God Most High's response to the people of Israel rejecting the messages from prophets, resulted in the next four hundred years of silence when God Most High quit sending prophets to the people of Israel.

It was the rebellion of the people of Israel and the corruption of the priesthood that allowed the people of Israel to become vulnerable to the destruction and desecration of the temple that was brought to the people of Israel through the king of the Seleucid / Syrian empire, Antiochus IV Epiphanes. It was the corruption of the priesthood and of the sacrificial system that was a result of the rebellion of the people of Israel against God Most High, that Jesus ultimately addressed during the days prior to his crucifixion, Jesus turned over the tables of the money changers in the temple.

The same form of rebellion against God Most High that existed during the four hundred years of silence / Intertestamental period, will be prevalent during the time *when the final horn on the shaggy goat will ascend to power during the era of the time of Jacob's Trouble. And the final horn on the shaggy goat will be the leader of the rebellion of the world, against God Most High. It will be as the leader of rebellion that the final horn on the shaggy goat will squash resistance to his ascension.*

The future abomination of desolation event as described in Daniel's vision of the seventy 'sevens' – Daniel 9:20-27

Daniel was provided with the vision of seventy 'sevens' as a method of God Most High for marking time for major events of the redemption, reclamation and regeneration plan. The future abomination of desolation event was highlighted as one of those major events in the process of bringing this plan to fruition.

Seventy weeks are determined for your people, for your holy city, to finish the transgression – to make an end of sins, and to make reconciliation for iniquity and to bring in everlasting righteousness; and to seal up vision and prophecy, and to anoint the Most Holy.

Therefore, know and understand, that from the going forth of the command to restore and build Jerusalem, until messiah the prince, there will be seven weeks, and sixty two weeks.

The street and the wall will be built, but in troublesome times.

After the sixty two weeks, messiah will be cut off, and will have nothing.

The people of the prince / ruler who is to come, will destroy the city and the sanctuary.

And the end of it shall come with a flood. War will continue until the end and desolations are determined.

The prince / ruler will confirm a covenant with many, for one 'seven' / 'week.' But in the middle of the 'seven' / 'week,' the prince / ruler will bring an end to the sacrifice and offering. On the wing (of the temple), the prince / ruler will establish abominations that will cause desolation, even until the consumption which has been determined is poured out on the desolate / the one who destroys. Daniel 9:24-27 translated

Daniel 9 was God Most High's message to Daniel that documented the time for the future abomination of desolation event. This message provided great overall insight of the event, and its impact upon the people of Israel.

John the Revelator provided more of the details that will take place at the actual event.

It was the seventy 'sevens' that identified the connection between the people of Israel's rejection and death of the Anointed One, and the destruction of the temple and city of Jerusalem that took place forty years after Jesus Christ's death. And the fact that Jesus Christ's crucifixion, death, resurrection and ascension into heaven took place precisely as Daniel's seventy 'sevens' predicted, served to authenticate the rest of Daniel's message.

Within Daniel's message of the seventy 'sevens' there was a notice of multiple abomination of desolation events that have been determined. The first abomination of desolation event took place in 167 BC. The future abomination of desolation event is yet to take place at the midway point of the seven years of the era of the time of Jacob's Trouble.

- It was during the period of the sixty two 'sevens' that the first abomination of desolation event took place. It would be 70 AD when the first ruler came who destroyed the city of Jerusalem and the sanctuary / temple.
- 'The <u>end</u> will come like a flood' was a reference to the future abomination of desolation event that will take place during the era of the time of Jacob's Trouble. The <u>'end'</u> was a reference to the end of this age, prior to the second coming of Jesus Christ, prior to the Thousand Years Reign of Jesus Christ, and prior to the full establishment of the kingdom of heaven on earth. The reference to the swiftness of the flood indicated the swiftness that events will take place during the future abomination of desolation event and the other events that the future abomination of desolation event will initiate. The attempt will be made again, to destroy the city of Jerusalem and the sanctuary / temple. In addition, the red dragon / serpent / Satan, Inc. was prophesied to actually provide a flood (Revelation 12:15-16).

It was the seventy 'sevens' that also linked the relationship of the abomination of desolation events as preliminary activity for the preparation of the arrival of the incarnate Jesus Christ for his earthly ministry, and for the return of Jesus Christ to defeat the ruler who is to come and to fully establish the kingdom of heaven on earth.

The first abomination of desolation event took place in 167 BC, only one hundred sixty three years before the birth of Jesus Christ and served to establish the political, social, cultural, and religious environment that was necessary in order for the work of Jesus Christ to be accomplished in the nation of Israel. While one hundred sixty three years may seem distant to the arrival of the incarnate Jesus, when one hundred sixty three years is compared with the six thousand years of human history, then one hundred sixty three years is a quite short span of time. The events of the first abomination of desolation functioned to prepare the political, social, cultural, and religious environment for the arrival of the incarnate Jesus. During this time, the Hellenization under the Greek empire provided a common language to be spoken between nations and cultures, in time for taking the message of Jesus Christ into the world. The Roman road was developed in time for taking the message of Jesus Christ throughout the Roman empire. Etc. This kind of preparation required one hundred sixty three years.

The future abomination of desolation event has been scheduled to take place approximately three and a half years before Jesus Christ returns. The future abomination of desolation event will again prepare the political, social, cultural, and religious environment that will be needed in order for the work of Jesus Christ to be accomplished in the hearts of the people of Israel and throughout the world, in order for the kingdom of heaven to be able to be fully established on earth.

Daniel and Jesus Christ (Matthew 24, Mark 13, and Luke 21) recognized that there would be more than one abomination of desolation event. But in the Daniel 9:26

presentation, the abomination of desolation events were presented almost as one event.

Because Daniel presented the abomination of desolation events as a kind of package, it is more informative to view the abomination of desolation events from the end point looking backward instead of from the first abomination of desolation looking forward. Much of God Most High's message was told ahead of time so that we will be able to recognize God Most High's work.

Rather than view the first abomination of desolation event as a crescendo toward the future abomination of desolation event, it may be helpful to view the future abomination of desolation event scheduled to take place during the era of the time of Jacob's Trouble as the version that is complete, incorporating the previous abomination of desolation event details, and combining the rest of the details for what the future abomination of desolation event will seek to aspire to be.

The first abomination of desolation event, although ultimately used for God Most High's purposes, displayed to the red dragon / serpent / Satan, Inc. those areas where he fell short in the goal of fully establishing the kingdom of Satan, Inc. / kingdom of man on earth.

The first abomination of desolation event acted as a dress rehearsal for the drama that the red dragon / serpent / Satan, Inc. has planned for the final show. But the seventy 'sevens' identified the future abomination of desolation event as being more dramatic, impactful and far reaching, than the first abomination of desolation event.

Daniel's prayer life

Daniel's prayer life greatly influenced Daniel so that Daniel was ready to hear the messages that God Most High desired to communicate to Daniel. Daniel was already so dedicated to God Most High, that Daniel had received numerous other communications before receiving this message from God concerning the future history of Israel, the coming of messiah, and especially the events that will take place during the era of the time of Jacob's Trouble.

The message contained in Daniel chapters 10, 11 and 12, were the direct result of Daniel's most dedicated prayer.

Daniel had been taken into exile as a teenager from the southern kingdom of Judah, when Nebuchadnezzar II (fl. 605 to 562 BC) was the king of the Babylonian empire. Daniel and Daniel's three friends, distinguished themselves in the court of Nebuchadnezzar II. Daniel chapters 1 through 4, detailed Daniel's life in the court of Nebuchadnezzar II.

Following the reign of Nebuchadnezzar II, there were a series of other kings who reigned for terms that lasted a few months to almost six years. Nabonidus (fl. 556 to 539 BC), was possibly the son-in-law of Nebuchadnezzar II. Nabonidus had seized power in a coup and in the process had angered the priests and commoners of Babylon, when Nabonidus neglected Babylon's chief deity Marduk and elevated the moon god Sin. Consequently, Nabonidus needed to invest time in putting down unrest. In Nabonidus' spare time, he was leading excavations for archaeological work, which meant that Nabonidus needed to leave the responsibility for ruling the Babylonian empire, to Nabonidus' son Belshazzar. It was Belshazzar who received the handwriting on the wall message (Daniel 5).

Cyrus the Great / Cyrus the Elder / Cyrus II of Persia (600 to 530 BC), was the founder of the Achaemenid / Persian empire, first by conquering the Median empire and the Lydian empire, and in October 539, conquering the Neo-Babylonian / Second Babylonian / Chaldean empire. Cyrus respected the customs and religions of the lands that he conquered, establishing a successful government administration.

During Daniel's life under both the Babylonian and Medo-Persian empires, Daniel held high positions within the governments, counseling the kings and leaders of both empires. The rest of the book of Daniel recorded the level of authority that Daniel held over the course of Daniel's life which spanned over eighty years. Daniel also recorded through the book of Daniel, the impact that his prayer life had upon Daniel personally and also upon Daniel as a person of great authority.

The message of Daniel 9 through 12, became one of the most important records concerning the prophecy concerning the future history of the people of the nation of Israel, in preparation for both the first coming of messiah (Daniel 9 and Daniel 11:1-35), and the second coming of messiah (Daniel 11:36-12:13). After two thousand five hundred years, Daniel will have the opportunity to meet us, the people who will have lived to see the fulfillment of the prophecies that Daniel was given, when the resurrection of God's holy people takes place with the return of the promised and prophesied messiah.

It must be noted that all of Daniel's messages from God Most High were communicated because Daniel's dedicated prayer life qualified Daniel to receive the messages from God Most High. In Daniel 10, Daniel described his prayer life that led to receiving the understanding of the message concerning 'a great war.' In the third year of Cyrus king of Persia, for three weeks, Daniel mourned over his knowledge of the coming great war. Daniel ate nothing fancy, no meat or wine. And Daniel did not even bathe. This was not just Sunday morning prayer, offered in the short few minutes bracketed within the rest of the liturgy that fills an hour of worship. This was prayer that Daniel lived. And it required the best portion of the first month of the Hebrew religious calendar, Nisan. The month of Nisan is the same month during which the first three required spring feasts of Passover, unleavened bread and firstfruits, are celebrated. In the spiritual realm, there would have been an additional heightened awareness during this month. For Daniel, the practice of prayer had consumed his life.

On the twenty fourth day of the first month, Daniel and his entourage, had taken his prayer practice to the banks of the Tigris River, a river in the Euphrates River system. There Daniel saw 'a man dressed in linen, with a belt of fine gold from Uphaz around his waist. His body was like topaz, his face like lightning, his eyes like flaming torches, his arms and legs like the gleam of burnished bronze, and his voice like the sound of a multitude.' Daniel 10:5-6 *Daniel's description of this man, was very much like the description of Jesus Christ that John the Revelator identified (Revelation 1). The image and scene were so powerful that Daniel was overwhelmed and fell on his face to the ground.*

Another spiritual being touched Daniel and communicated the message that Daniel recorded. The angel explained to Daniel that Daniel's prayer had been heard the first day that Daniel had prayed, three weeks earlier. But the prince of the Persian kingdom / angel who had authority over the region of Persia, had resisted the angel from coming for twenty one days. Only when the messenger angel was assisted by one of the chief princes, Michael (one of the highest of the heavenly hosts), was the messenger angel able to get through to deliver the message. And after delivering the message to Daniel, the angel needed to address the angel of Greece / angel who had authority over the region of Greece.

Daniel remained overwhelmed, unable to speak, until the messenger angel gave him strength.

The message contained in Daniel 11 and 12 told of the future king that will exalt himself, and the details that will accompany the coming 'great war.' But the message was of such a great importance, that Daniel's prayer life in receiving the message required an entire chapter, Daniel 10, to describe just how that message came to be communicated.

Daniel's prayer life throughout the book of Daniel, provided instruction about the nature of prayer and how it works. Understanding the interaction of the spiritual realm with the physical realm, assists in understanding the deeper dynamics of the future abomination of desolation event, an event that will take place in the temple in Jerusalem which is the location that both kingdoms seek to claim as fully belonging to their respective kingdoms.

1. *Prayer is communication with the spiritual world. And in that spiritual world, there is unseen warfare that takes place there.*

John the Revelator noted the importance of the prayers of God's holy people being used by God Most High throughout the era of the time of Jacob's Trouble (Revelation 8:3-5).

Paul said, 'Our struggle is not against flesh and blood, but against the rulers, against the authorities, against the powers of this dark world and against the spiritual forces of evil in the heavenly realms.' Ephesians 6:12

2. *Prayer can be hindered by unconfessed sin.*
   Isaiah recorded, 'Surely the arm of the Lord is not too short to save, nor is the Lord's ear too dull to hear. But your iniquities have separated you from your God. Your sins have hidden God's face from you, so that God will not hear.' Isaiah 59:1-2.
   David wrote in the psalm, 'Come and hear, all you who fear God. Let me tell you what God has done for me. I cried out to God with my mouth. If I had cherished sin in my heart, the Lord would not have listened. But God has surely listened and has heard my prayer. Praise be to God who has not rejected my prayer or withheld God's love from me!' Psalm 66:16-20. *In order for God Most High to hear prayer, sin must be confessed and given to God. Sin cannot be coddled and cherished in the heart and continued to be practiced in life.*

3. *One of the elements that caused Daniel's prayers to be so effective was Daniel's devotion and dedication to God and to God's people. Daniel cared, and Daniel cared deeply.*
   Proverbs 21:13 *said,* 'Whoever shuts their ears to the cry of the poor will also cry out and not be answered.'
   Daniel's prayer life was concerned with the issues that the people around him faced. In particular, Daniel was so concerned with the issues that would face those who will live through the era of the time of Jacob's Trouble, that it caused Daniel to fast for three weeks, and then to be overwhelmed so that Daniel fainted because of what Daniel foresaw for us.

4. *Daniel also prayed with the right motives.*
   James wrote, 'You do not have because you do not ask God. When you do ask, you do not receive, because you

ask with wrong motives, that you may spend what you receive on your pleasures. You adulterous people, don't you know that friendship with the world means enmity / hatred against God? Therefore, anyone who chooses to be a friend of the world becomes an enemy of God' James 4:2c-4.

God Most High is never motivated to aid in the rebellion against the kingdom of heaven and the people who make up the kingdom of heaven. The economy of the kingdom of heaven is diametrically opposed to the economy of the kingdom of Satan, Inc. / kingdom of man. God Most High does not aid in investing in the kingdom of Satan, Inc. / kingdom of man.

When Jesus taught how to pray, Jesus taught, 'And when you pray, do not be like the hypocrites, for they love to pray standing in the synagogues and on the street corners to be seen by others. Truly I tell you, they have received their reward in full. But when you pray, go into your room, close the door and pray to your Father who is unseen. Then your Father, who sees what is done in secret, will reward you. Matthew 6:5-6

This then is how you should pray: 'Our Father in heaven, your name is holy, may your kingdom come and your will be done, on earth as it is in heaven. Matthew 6:9-10.

When prayer is offered with right motives, it will always be heard. This is the confidence we have in approaching God, that if we ask anything according to God's will, God hears us. 1 John 5:14.

Prayer does not come naturally or easily to people. If it were easy, everyone would be doing it. But people like Daniel, who loved to seek God's face, dedicated themselves to hearing and receiving God Most High's message, and have recorded what God Most High said.

It was in this setting that Daniel devoted himself to receiving this message that will experience its fulfillment and climax during the era of the time of Jacob's Trouble. And then Daniel cared enough to record it for us.

The era of hate against God's holy people, truly begins

During the World War II (1938 to 1945) era, part of the magnitude of devastation was due to the division that was already inherent within the world culture on an individual level, between what is truly good and what is truly evil. During that era, people were willing to assail and assault other people and did not recognize that they were crossing boundaries and infringing upon what should belong to others.

Because they were willing to behave this way toward others on a personal level, they also shared a willingness to allow nations like Nazi Germany, Japan, Italy, etc. to infringe upon the rights and boundaries of others. In this environment, classes develop between the rich and poor, the elite and the common, the privileged and underprivileged, the superior and the inferior, and between those that insist upon ruling and those that are compelled to be ruled. This pattern of behavior becomes especially prominent when individuals and governments have decided to not take personal responsibility for their own actions and instead transfer the blame onto others.

For example, when Nazi Germany experienced financial challenges and needed additional resources, Nazi Germany would not provide and market a product or service. Instead, Nazi Germany would invade people's homes and businesses, and nations, and steal from people and businesses and nations. Their rationalization for raiding was that the people they raided deserved to be raided because of their inferiority.

This detachment of individuals and nations from an understanding of authentic good and authentic evil, meant that people and leaders that embraced authentic good, were challenged, harassed and persecuted by people and leaders that embraced authentic evil.

During World War II, Great Britain's Neville Chamberlain was willing to enter into an appeasement relationship with Nazi Germany. An appeasement strategy may have had benefit, if Nazi Germany had not been willing to make agreements that they never had any intention of fulfilling.

In contrast to Neville Chamberlain's leadership, was the leadership of Winston Churchill. Winston Churchill's strategy was to enhance that boundary between authentic good and authentic evil. Winston Churchill defined evil as evil, bad, undesirable, and abhorrent. For taking this stance, Winston Churchill was labeled a war monger and was rallied against by those who embraced authentic evil as acceptable and good.

But it was Winston Churchill's strength in leadership that was a vital element of the strategy for Allied success over the Nazi and fascist regimes, and their attempts to establish global governance.

Some presidents of the United States have made it a point to remove the bust of Winston Churchill from the oval office. Other presidents have made it a point to return his bust to its place. And their administrations have accordingly embraced and fostered either authentic evil or authentic good. Their administrations have accordingly fostered either advancements in global governance, or thwarted the growth of the movement toward global governance.

God Most High instructed that during this second half of the era of the time of Jacob's Trouble, the amount of pure evil will have reached its greatest level in all human history.

'Behold, the day of the Lord comes, cruel, with both wrath and fierce anger, to lay the land desolate. And the Lord will destroy the sinners from it.' Isaiah 13:9 translated

'And there will be a time of trouble such as was there never was since the establishment of this nation and that moment.' Daniel 12:1b translated

The nation of Israel will feel this culture of authentic evil more than anyone else. God said that in that time, 'The days are coming, declares the Lord, 'when I will bring my people Israel and Judah back from captivity and restore them to the land I gave their ancestors to possess,' says the Lord. Jeremiah 30:3

'How awful that day will be! No other will be like it. It will be a time of trouble for Jacob, but Jacob will be saved out of it.' Jeremiah 30:7

Jesus said about this era, 'You will begin to hear of wars and rumors of wars. Do not be alarmed. It is necessary for these things to take place. But the end is still to come. Nation will rise up against nation, and kingdom against kingdom. There will be famines and earthquakes in various places. All these are the beginning of birth pains.'

'Then they will deliver you to tribulation and will kill you and you will be hated by all the nations on account of my name. And then many will fall away, and they will betray one another, and will hate one another. And many false prophets will appear and will mislead many. Because of the increase in lawlessness, the love of many will grow cold. But the one who endures to the end will be saved. And this gospel of the kingdom, will be proclaimed in all the earth, as a testimony to all nations. And then the end will come.' Matthew 24:6-14 translated

In the context of the future abomination of desolation event, Jesus said, 'For then there will be great tribulation, such unequaled from the beginning of the world until now, and never to be equaled again.' Matthew 24:21 translated

'Immediately after the tribulation of those days, 'the sun will be darkened, and the moon will not give its light, and the stars will fall from the sky, and the powers of the heavens will be shaken." (Isaiah 13:10, 34:4) Matthew 24:29 translated

The biblical record provided more documentation that the era of the time of Jacob's Trouble will be marked with hatred, torture and death; and that the kingdom of Satan, Inc. / kingdom of man has made provision for the destruction of God's holy people (Revelation 8, 9, 11, 12, 13, 17, etc.). This will be an era marked by hatred against all God Most High's holy people, both from the people of Israel and from the followers of the Lamb / Jesus Christ.

God Most High's provision for the followers of the lamb / Jesus Christ during the ministry of the two witnesses and the second half of the era of the time of Jacob's Trouble

While the kingdom of Satan, Inc. / kingdom of man plotted the destruction of God's holy people to be intensified during the era of the time of Jacob's Trouble, God Most High has made provision both for the remnant of the people of Israel and for the followers of the Lamb / Jesus Christ.

Paul and Barnabas taught, 'God has not left himself without testimony. God has shown kindness by giving you rain from heaven and crops in their seasons. God provides you with plenty of food and fills your hearts with joy.' Acts 14:17 translated

God Most High's nature is never changing. The same God who created the universe, is the same God who so loved the world that God sent a member of the office of God, as a fully human being to be the perfect sacrifice in order to reclaim dominion over the earth and to provide humanity with everlasting life. Even the annual crops proclaim God Most High's provision for humanity.

Even though two thirds of the people of Israel will be killed during this era, the one third that will be the remnant of the people of Israel, will be refined as silver is refined and tested as gold is tested. They will be the people who will call on the name of God Most High. (Zechariah 13:8-9). What remains will be qualified to be priests for God Most High in the fully established kingdom of heaven on earth. (See also Revelation 7:1-17.)

Concerning the followers of the Lamb / Jesus Christ, Jesus Christ always taught that those who endure to the end will be saved (Matthew 24:13). Those who overcome receive eternal rewards (Revelation 2, 3). In the final battle of this age, those who are faithful followers of the Lamb, will be with the Lamb, and will prevail (Revelation 17:14).

God Most High established the pattern of the God Most High's provision for the people of Israel during the ten plagues that came upon Israel, especially the tenth plague / plague of the death of the first born, passing over the people of Israel whose homes were covered with the lambs' blood (Exodus 12). When messiah / the Lamb / Jesus Christ fulfilled the prophecy of the annual Passover feast, with his crucifixion, death and resurrection, Jesus Christ made it available to every believer in messiah (BC) and every follower of the Lamb (AD) to experience resurrection with Jesus Christ's return.

But most importantly for the followers of the Lamb / Jesus Christ, who live during the era of the time of Jacob's Trouble, God Most High will place a seal upon them. The sealing of God Most High will not provide total protection from the wrath of the kingdom of Satan, Inc. / kingdom of man. But it will provide protection that is total; and that promise was strewn throughout John the Revelator's record. (especially Revelation 9:4)

The prophet Joel also wrote about the dynamics of this era, and about the Lord's provisions for it (Joel 2).

The prophet Isaiah documented God Most High's instruction for God Most High's people at this time. And the instruction indicated that God Most High's wrath will again pass over God's people.

Go my people. Enter your rooms and shut the doors behind you. Hide yourselves for a little while until the wrath is past.

Look! The Lord is coming out of God's dwelling to punish the inhabitants of the earth for their iniquity. The earth will disclose her blood, and will no longer conceal those slain. Isaiah 26:20-21 translated

While the era of the time of Jacob's Trouble will be a time of devasting disaster for those who have chosen to rebel against God Most High and to reject life as God the Creator created it, it will be a time when those who love God Most High will receive life in the midst of the devastation and death.

Renewal requires the removal of what can no longer be allowed to continue. But renewal also allows newness of life to flourish.

The Old Testament / Tanakh prophet Daniel's description of prerecorded history prior to the first abomination of desolation event, and Daniel's description of the king that will exalt himself who will accomplish the future abomination of desolation event – Daniel 11

Daniel's vision recorded in Daniel 11:1-35, was an extensive history, or a pre-history, of the intertestamental period / the four hundred years of silence in between the message of the prophets of the Old Testament / Tanakh, and the coming of John the Baptist with Jesus Christ in the New Testament. The era in between the messages of the Old and New Testaments earned the title of the four hundred years of silence because during the four hundred years prior to the coming of the incarnate Jesus Christ into the world, God Most High did not send prophets to the people of Israel. For approximately four hundred years, God Most High was silent.

But God Most High provided a vision to Daniel before the intertestamental period / four hundred years of *silence began, that acted as a pre-history of the events that would take place during the intertestamental period / four hundred years of silence. God Most High's message through Daniel provided assurance that God Most High was aware of, and interactive in, world events through every moment of human history.*

The pre-history that Daniel received in 536 BC, that was pre-recorded in Daniel 11:1-35, would did begin until 530 BC, and then that history concluded around 160 BC. Daniel 11:1-35 was the context for the actual first abomination of desolation event that took place in 167 BC.

The main focus of Daniel 11:1-35 described how the 'king of the south' / Antiochus IV Epiphanes was able to build his power base on the previous kings and empires that preceded him. The history before Antiochus IV Epiphanes built the foundation for him, enabling him to be able to amass enough power, support, and emotional energy to arrive at the place where he would be positioned to commit the first abomination of desolation event.

The second part of the same vision, Daniel 11:36-12:12, was written for the people of the distant future */ the era of the time of Jacob's Trouble and described the details concerning the future abomination of desolation event. Because there was no record of transition between Daniel 11:29-35 and Daniel 11:36, the details and dynamics of the future abomination of desolation event were intrinsically founded upon the details that gave context to the first abomination of desolation event.*

The first abomination of desolation event of 167 BC was truly ancient history. Therefore, superficially, the first abomination of desolation event may seem unimportant to the study of the future abomination of desolation event.

But Daniel 11:1-35 which described the dynamics that were the foundation for the first abomination of desolation event, was linked heavily to Daniel 11:36-12:12 which described the details of the future abomination of desolation event. Consequently, to fully understand the future abomination of desolation event requires understanding the first abomination of desolation event of 167 BC.

Both abomination of desolation events shared the same primary mission; to destroy the religious traditions and rites of the people of Israel, to destroy the intrinsic power of God Most High's holy mountain in Jerusalem, to destroy the worship of the Lord, and to establish the dominance of the baal / mystery / mythology religion over the sovereignty of the Lord. If the religious traditions and rites of the people of Israel were able to be successfully destroyed, the theory is that the people of Israel would not be able to communicate effectively with their God.

In the minds of the red dragon / serpent / Satan, Inc., cutting off communication between the people of Israel and God Most High, was supposed to thwart the coming of the promised and prophesied messiah.

The conditions for the arrival of messiah included a temple in place, that was fully functional in its sacrificial system, and the people of Israel practicing the religious rites of consecration. Without a fully consecrated temple, or a functional and operational temple sacrificial system, or a people practicing the religious rites of consecration, the promised and prophesied messiah was not supposed to be able to come. Not meeting any one of these three conditions would have rendered the people of Israel to be unredeemable.

The mission for both abomination of desolation events is to desecrate the temple, remove the opportunity for the people of Israel to sacrifice offerings to be in communication with God Most High, and to cause the people of Israel to be unconsecrated. The methods for how this mission will be accomplished in the future abomination of desolation event will be consistent with the methods utilized in the first abomination of desolation event.

During the era of the first abomination of desolation event, the Seleucid / Syrian ruler Antiochus IV Epiphanes attempted to continue the legacy that his father Antiochus III the Great had attempted to achieve; to amass a kingdom greater than Alexander the Great; in essence, to rule the world. The high priest in Jerusalem worked in concert with the Seleucid / Syrian ruler Antiochus IV Epiphanes in order to desecrate the temple in Jerusalem as a means of establishing a more tyrannical rule over the people of Israel.

During the era of the time of Jacob's Trouble, as the beast of the sea / false prophet / eighth king beast attempts to inaugurate the centuries old goal of establishing global papal rule (especially sought after by the Jesuit Order of the Roman Catholic Church), and as final horn on the shaggy goat / prince who is to come beast of the earth / final world ruler attempts to establish the ultimate global dictatorship as global leader of the global governance system; together they will experience a greater level of success toward the goal of fully establishing the kingdom of Satan, Inc. / kingdom of man on earth, than at any other time in history. What the Seleucid / Syrian ruler Antiochus IV Epiphanes and high priest Menelaus attempted to accomplish; the two beasts of Revelation 13 will strive to bring into reality. It will even appear as if they will succeed.

But lost in the calculations of the red dragon / serpent / Satan, Inc. is the forgotten truth that God the Creator created the world and the universe. Therefore, it is God the Creator who knows best how the world operates and how to ultimately cause all things to work for good for those who love God and are called according to God's purposes (Romans 8:28).

It is God Most High who knows all the truly hidden secrets. It is actually God Most High who is in control. It is God Most High who will cut the days short of the reign of the red dragon / serpent / Satan, Inc. and their adherents in order to hasten the return of Jesus Christ and the full establishment of the kingdom of heaven on earth. And while Satan seems to have written the origins of the kingdom of Satan, Inc. / kingdom of man in the Garden of Eden / garden of God / paradise, it has been God Most High who has written its conclusion.

In interpreting biblical prophecy, a rule of thumb is that when something is intentionally repeated, the message has a heightened level of importance. Daniel's various visions, given at various times during Daniel's lifetime, tended to repeat the same prehistory, giving the prophecies of Daniel a heightened level of importance.

In Daniel 8, beginning with the ram (Medes and Persians) and the shaggy goat with the horns (Greeks, Alexander the Great, and the four generals / empires that divided the Greek empire), Daniel's vision portrayed the nation of Israel's history, beginning with the lifetime of Daniel and ending with the end of the Seleucid / Syrian empire's control of the land of Israel; spanning time from 551 BC to 63 AD. The gap that followed between the four horns and the final horn on the shaggy goat, represented the gap between Jesus Christ's earthly ministry and the time before Jesus Christ's return.

Daniel 9 documented the seventy 'sevens' which set the time for the coming of the messiah, 4 BC to 30-33 AD. Daniel 9, while given around the same time as the message in Daniel 6, was placed in the biblical record here between Daniel 8 and Daniel 10-12. It was the information in Daniel 9 that Daniel used to instruct the Magi from the east to know when to look for the star that would lead them to the messiah. The gap between the sixty ninth seven and the seventieth seven, represented the gap between Jesus Christ's earthly ministry and the time before Jesus Christ's return.

Daniel was given the vision recorded as Daniel 10-12 during the third year of the reign of Cyrus king of Persia, in 536 BC. It was in Daniel 10-12 that the history / prehistory for the nation of Israel concerning the Intertestamental period and the details concerning both of the abomination of desolation events has been laid out, through the vision given to Daniel by the man dressed in linen... while Daniel stood on the bank of the Tigris River. The description of the man dressed in linen was a match to the vision of the man that gave John the Revelator the visions that comprise the book of Revelation. (Compare Daniel 10:5-14 to Revelation 1.) For Daniel, the man dressed in linen... was accompanied with angels including the angel Michael, and the man dressed in linen... who brought the message to Daniel, did not declare who he is. For John the Revelator, the man made himself known as Jesus Christ. John the Revelator was also John the apostle who walked with, talked with and worked alongside Jesus Christ for three and a half years before Jesus Christ was crucified, died, was resurrected and ascended into heaven. For Daniel, Jesus had not yet entered the world as the incarnate Jesus Christ and so the man dressed in linen... remained unidentified for Daniel. John the Revelator was able to recognize the man in his vision because he had worked alongside him for over three years.

The record of the vision that Daniel received and recorded in Daniel 10-12 began with describing the challenging conditions that were experienced by the man dressed in linen as he battled with forces that sought to prevent him from even reaching Daniel in order to give the vision to Daniel. Daniel 10 described the struggle that the man dressed in linen... encountered with the 'king of Persia' / rebellious angel who maintained spiritual dominion over Persia.

The vision that the man dressed in linen gave to Daniel was recorded in Daniel 11-12. It was a two part vision with an overlap of details in Daniel 11:29-35 and the documentation of the abomination of desolation event. This was followed by Daniel's description of the king that will exalt himself in in the distant future / era of the time of Jacob's Trouble (Daniel 11:36-12:12).

Daniel 11:1-35 contained the vision for the timeline of historical events that took place beginning with the lifetime of Daniel, and proceeded through the first abomination of desolation event in 167 BC.

It was in Daniel 11:29-12:12 that the details of the future abomination of desolation were disclosed. The message of Daniel 11:29-12:12 is of primary interest for those who live during the era of the time of Jacob's Trouble. But Daniel 11:29-12:12 would lose almost all its meaning if it were separated from the context of Daniel 11:1-35 which acts as validation that God Most High has a detailed knowledge of the events of the future and that God Most High is ultimately sovereign in working out the plan to defeat the kingdom of Satan, Inc. / kingdom of man. It was out of God Most High's detailed knowledge of the future and the template of the first abomination of desolation, that God Most High's message could be given and understood for those who live to experience the future abomination of desolation event during the era of the time of Jacob's Trouble.

Some biblical interpreters claimed that Daniel 11:1-12:12 should be viewed as a complete unit. Consequently, they view all of Daniel 11-12 as having already been fulfilled. Having Daniel's prerecorded history as having already been fulfilled, negates the possibility of a future abomination of desolation event. But to interpret the entire two chapters as having been fulfilled with Antiochus IV Epiphanes' abomination of desolation of 167 BC and ending either with the Maccabean Revolt or later with the life of Jesus Christ, would require much twisting of the record and a major neglect of the details documented by Daniel.

Either the biblical record is entirely accurate, or it is not accurate at all. And what assurance exists that the determination that the parts deemed as being inaccurate are actually the parts that are inaccurate?

To hold the view that all the message of Daniel 11-12 has already been fulfilled would require that the last king of the north / king of the Seleucid / Syrian empire discussed at the end of the first section (Daniel 11:1-35), was also the king that was spoken of in Daniel 11:35-12:12. This interpretation is highly problematic.

Daniel 11:36-12:12 must be distinguished from Daniel 11:1-35 because:
- The king of Daniel 11:35-12:12 will expand to the east. Antiochus IV Epiphanes did not expand to the east. The empire of Alexander the Great had already reached to China. The subsequent kings of the Seleucid / Syrian empire experienced shrinkage in the lands of their empire.

- The king of the second section of Daniel 11-12, Daniel 11:35-12:12, will also be successful until the time of God Most High's wrath is completed. The pouring out of God Most High's full wrath / seven bowls / seven last plagues is scheduled to occur during the final seventy one and a half days following the death, resurrection and ascension of the two witnesses of Revelation 11. (See also Revelation 15-16.)
- The king of the second section of Daniel 11-12, Daniel 11:35-12:12 will also 'attack with the help of a foreign god' which implied that the king of the second section, will be aided by supernatural power, the kind of supernatural power that Antiochus IV Epiphanes definitely lacked.
- The points of differentiation between the last king of the north / king of the Seleucid / Syrian empire of Daniel 11:28-35 and the king of Daniel's second section, Daniel 11:36-12:12 continued.

Many of the details of Daniel's multiple visions have already been accomplished. For validation of the events that took place during the lifetime of Daniel and for the approximately five centuries following the life of Daniel, there were several historical sources.

There were primarily three historical sources for historical information that described the events that took place during the Intertestamental period: Josephus the Jewish Roman historian, the books of the Maccabees with the commentary literature concerning the books of the Maccabees, and the Greek historian Polybius who wrote the book, *The Rise of Rome*. These were historical sources written after the events of the ministry of Jesus Christ, took place.

The books of the Maccabees, while having described the same events with the same kind of detail that Daniel 11:1-35 described, have been considered to not meet the criteria to be able to be included in the biblical record because they were historical and not prophetic. They described past events instead of future events. Material must be congruent with a focus on future events in order to be considered to be prophetic and to have been considered for inclusion in the biblical record.

Josephus was merely a Jewish priest who became a Roman historian after being captured in the siege of Jerusalem of 70 AD.

The Greek historian Polybius was an independent historian, without a genealogical connection to the people of Israel, and without a political connection to the nation of Israel.

Daniel's vision of Daniel 10-12 was included in the biblical record because it was recognized as prophetical instead of merely historical. All of Daniel's visions concerning prophetic events were recorded prior to the fulfillment of the events.

Historical details that provided context and foundation for the first abomination of desolation event, as prerecorded by Daniel – Daniel 11:1-35

Daniel's ram (empire of the Medes and Persians) and prominent horn of the shaggy goat (Alexander the Great of the Greek empire) of Daniel 8, correspond to the beginning of the vision of Daniel 11:1-35 with the four kings of Persia and the 'mighty king who will appear, who will rule with great power and do as he pleases.' The first mighty king to fulfill the first layer of this prophecy, was Alexander III / Alexander the Great (356 to 323 BC).

Alexander the Great's empire encompassed all of Macedon, Greece, and Syria. It reached to the east touching China, included Egypt to the south, and reached into the north. The territory of the empire of Alexander the Great was so vast that no other empire in history has been known to have been as great by possessing the greatest amount of land mass.

Throughout history, those who have aspired to become world rulers have set as a goal to develop empires that would be as great as the empire of Alexander the Great. The two beasts of Revelation 13 will set as their goal to develop a global empire that will exceed and eclipse the empire of Alexander the Great. According to the biblical record's descriptions surrounding the future abomination of desolation, the two beasts of Revelation 13 will succeed in meeting this goal through the development of the global religious community and the implementation of the global governance system.

In opposition to the upsurge of support for global governance, Great Britain's exit from the European Union began on June 23, 2016 and so far, has not been fully realized. Currently, Spain's conservative party desires that Spain keep its culture and identity in the midst of the pressure to adopt the more European culture. Russia continues to send the message to other nations that other nations need to not interfere in the interests of Russia. China flexes its muscle with testing the limits of the understanding of the laws concerning international waters. Other nations of the world are also seeking to maintain their national sovereignty.

It is difficult to believe that the beast of the two beasts of Revelation 13 would ever be able to accomplish the establishment of a greater empire than the empire of Alexander the Great. But the fulfillment of the events of Daniel 11:1-35 during the intertestamental period acted as evidence that the prophesied events of Daniel 11:29-12:12, along with the rest of prophecies of the biblical record, will also be accomplished.

When Alexander the Great suddenly died in June 323 BC at the age of 32, he left no apparent legitimate heir. The dissension and military battles that followed, caused Alexander the Great's empire to eventually be divided by his four Generals:
- Cassander (Antipatrid empire 302 BC to 294 BC) received roughly the territory of Macedon, roughly the territory now known as northern Greece.
- Lysimachus (Kingdom of Lysimachus 306 BC to 281 BC) received roughly the territory of Pergamum now known as Turkey.
- Seleucus I Nicator (312 BC to 63 BC) became Daniel's first 'king of the north' in Daniel 11, and developed the Seleucid / Syrian empire which

included the regions that are now known as Iran (Persia), Iraq, Syria and the area east of Israel.
- Ptolemy I Soter (305BC to 30BC) became Daniel's first 'king of the south' in Daniel 11:5 and developed the Ptolemaic / Egyptian empire which included the regions that are now known as the land of Israel and the land south and west of Israel including Egypt.

Each of Alexander's generals established his own empire, with his own descendants who continued to rule their respective empires. Over time, those empires fought for and against each other. But the overall synopsis of the four hundred years of history that was Daniel's vision recorded in Daniel 11:1-35, focused on the pieces of history that influenced the people of Israel, the temple, and the political history that influenced the nation of Israel as it prepared for the first coming of messiah / Jesus Christ.

Soon after the death of Alexander the Great, the people of Israel were being ruled by the Ptolemaic / Egyptian empire headquartered in Egypt, from 301 to 200 BC. In 200 BC, the Seleucid / Syrian empire under Antiochus III the Great, captured the land of Israel from the Ptolemaic / Egyptian empire. Later, the leadership of the people of Israel invited a relationship with the Roman empire that eventually in 63 BC, resulted in Roman occupation and rule of the land of Israel prior to Jesus Christ's birth, and extending to 70 AD, when Rome finally destroyed Jerusalem and the nation of Israel, massacring many of the people in Israel and sending the majority of the survivors into the diaspora.

The first abomination of desolation event took place in 167 BC led by the king of the Seleucid / Syrian empire, Antiochus IV Epiphanes. It was this event that was the climax for the vision recorded by Daniel in Daniel 11:1-35.

Note in reading Daniel 11:1-35, that the references to the 'king of the north' were references to the kings of the Seleucid / Syrian empire. The references to the 'king of the south' were references to the kings of the Ptolemaic / Egyptian empire.

Also in Daniel's 11:1-35 account, the record would skip ahead to the next king without any indicator that a skip in time had taken place.

Understanding the format of Daniel 11:1-35 will assist in correlating the message of Daniel to the actual historical persons.

Timeline from Darius the Mede in 530 BC to the Third Jewish Roman War / Third Jewish Revolt / Bar Kokhba (son of a star) revolt (132 – 136 AD)

In order to demonstrate the authenticity of Daniel's vision with the events that would take place over the following four hundred years, it is helpful to read directly from the biblical record that referenced the events in this timeline.

The portions of this history in bold font, refer to the portions of Daniel's record that directly impacted the people of Israel as they prepared for the one who would commit the abomination of desolation, and for the coming of the promised and prophesied messiah.

Remember that the kings of the north were generally from the Seleucid / Syrian empire and would have accessed the land of Israel from the north. The kings of the south were generally from the Ptolemaic / Egyptian empire and would have accessed the land of Israel from the south. With the land of Israel in the middle, the impact of the history of the kings of the north and kings of the south spilt over onto the people of Israel.

530 – 522 BC: After the reign of Darius the Mede **(Daniel 11:1)**, there were three more kings; Cambyses (530 – 522 BC), Pseudo-Smerdis or Gaumata (522 BC), and Darius I (522 – 486 BC). **(Daniel 11:2)** The Medo-Persian empire was quite sympathetic to the people of Israel. It was King Cyrus that issued the decree that allowed the people of Israel to return to their land and to again become a self-governing body. King Cyrus also funded the rebuilding of the temple in Jerusalem.

490 BC: Persian King Darius was defeated by the Greeks at the Battle of Marathon.

486 – 465 BC: Xerxes I was known as 'King of the Persians and the Medes' / Great King / King of Kings (Shahan shah) / King of the Nations / King of the world / Xerxes the Great / Ahasuerus (book of Esther). Xerxes I inherited the throne as the oldest son of Darius I. He outraged the Babylonians by violently confiscating and melting down the golden statue of Bel / Marduk / Merodach in 484 BC. This was an issue for the

Babylonians because each year the rightful king of Babylon would clasp the hands of the statue on New Year's Day. In 480 BC, Xerxes I set out on a military campaign in an attempt to conquer Greece. Xerxes I did become far richer than all the others and was successful in stirring up everyone against the kingdom of Greece. **(Daniel 11:2)**

There was a gap in time in the account between Daniel 11:2 and 11:3 while the next king / Alexander the Great of Macedon / Greece, rose to power, and the focus transitioned from the Medes and the Persians to the Greeks and the Macedonians.

359 BC: King Perdiccas III of Macedon / region of northern Greece, was killed by the Illyrians.

359 – 336 BC: Philip II, Perdiccas III's younger brother, became king of Macedon / northern Greece. Philip II was father of Alexander the Great. Philip II also expanded the empire of Macedon with the use of the military technique of the phalanx. After conquering the city of Crenides in 356 BC, Philip II changed the name of the city to Philippi which would later be addressed by the letter to the Philippians in the Bible. Around 343 BC Aristotle began to solely tutored Alexander the Great for about a two year period of time. Philip II was assassinated, possibly by his first wife in order to ensure that the empire would be inherited by Alexander the Great, before the second wife could produce an heir.

336 – 323 BC: Alexander the Great became emperor of the Macedonian / Greek empire at the age of 20. Alexander the Great defeated the Medes and the Persians. Alexander the Great was welcomed in Egypt like a Pharaoh who saw Alexander as a liberator from the Persians. Alexander the Great created the largest empire in history. The borders of the empire even touched China. It was Alexander the Great who caused Greek to become the language of the empire, the language that later the New Testament was written in, and the Old Testament / Tanakh was translated into (Greek Septuagint). Because the nations surrounding Israel had been Hellenized, reading and speaking Greek; the message of Jesus Christ's first coming would be more easily spread throughout the world by means of the common Greek language, without the need to translate. Alexander the Great was known as 'the mighty king' because his empire was so vast that his legacy continues today, and even during the Christian era, kings continued to model their military styles, innovations, and empires after the success of Alexander the Great. **(Daniel 11:3)**

Included in the Greek religion were the practice of magic and the inclusion of a focus upon mystery religion. Greek religious influence of pagan polytheism even permeated the cultures of all groups of people within the Greek empire. The Olympic,

Pythian, Nemean, and Isthmian games were accepted as the most prominent religious-cultural events that took place. They generally took place near or in the gymnasiums, named from the Ancient Greek term gymnos / γψμνοσ / naked. Along the path to the games were temples to the various gods that corresponded to the various regional origins of the athletes. Religion was a prominent component to the games, with the awards placed on display in the temple of the regional god of the winner's choice.

As the Greeks would conquer a people, they would share the technology of the conquered people with the rest of the empire. One of the attractions of accepting and incorporating the culture of the Greek empire into the culture of the people of Israel was the shared advancement of technology. Advanced technology was also accompanied with military strength and protection.

Hellenization was the process of establishing an empire wide culture that included speaking the same language / Greek, understanding the same history, sharing mathematical concepts, studying the same philosophies throughout the empire, and honoring the same gods throughout the empire. During the Greek era, Alexander the Great possessed a moderate level of respect for the people of Israel and for their religion. **Hellenization was welcomed by the leaders of the people of Israel.**

332 BC: Alexander the Great of Macedon / Greece was at war with Darius III of Persia for six years. **Jerusalem capitulated to Alexander the Great after the Siege of Tyre.** The Siege of Tyre was a significant battle with noteworthy impact.

323 BC: Alexander the Great died, but not by his own hand, and the empire entered into turmoil. One of Alexander the Great's generals, Antigonus I Monophthalmus / Antigonus the One-eyed (382 – 301 BC), seemed to have the greatest authority to rule for a while after Alexander the Great's death. But the Greek empire was very disjointed and it was a period when multiple generals of Alexander the Great were vying for power. The Greek empire was eventually divided into four empires led by four of Alexander the Great's other generals. **(Daniel 11:4)** In 323 BC, **Jerusalem came under the rule of Laomedon of Mytilene as part of the arrangement between Alexander the Great's generals in the 'Partition of Babylon.'**

322 – 285 BC: Ptolemy I Soter was welcomed in Egypt and regarded as Pharaoh. Ptolemy I Soter was accepted as Pharaoh because the people of Egypt had already accepted Alexander the Great as Pharaoh. The Egyptians required any new pharaoh to provide the funeral for the burial of the body of the old Pharaoh as an act of receiving the office of pharaoh. Ptolemy I Soter acquired the body of Alexander the Great and

provided the funeral and the burial in Alexandria, Egypt. Ptolemy I Soter also worshiped the Egyptian gods and presented himself as a true Egyptian even though Ptolemy I Soter and his successors were actually Macedonian / Greek. Identifying himself as a true Egyptian provided his final qualification to reign on the Egyptian throne. When Ptolemy I Soter made himself king of Egypt, in the spirit of royalty's power to define gods and be defined as gods, Ptolemy I Soter created the god Serapis which was a combination of two Egyptian gods, Apis and Osiris; plus the main Greek gods; Zeus, Hades, Asclepios, Dionysus, and Helios. Serapis had powers over fertility, the sun, corn, funerary rites, and medicine. Apparently, it was more convenient to worship one god with multiple abilities than to worship many gods. Ptolemy I Soter also founded the Museum and Library of Alexandria. Ptolemy I Soter first dealt severely with the people of Israel, but later treated the people of Israel more favorably. Under the policy of toleration, Judaism and Hellenism coexisted peacefully. It was this peaceful tolerism that allowed the gradual infiltration of Greek influence and the assimilation of the Greek way of life, into the culture of the people of Israel. There were thirteen Ptolemies, each one numbered in line. The last Ptolemy was the sister of Ptolemy XIII Theos Philopator ('God beloved of his father') and was Cleopatra VII.

321 – 289 BC: Seleucus I Nicator of the Seleucid / Syrian empire / king of Syria / Daniel's 'king of the north,' originally served under Ptolemy I Soter of the Ptolemaic / Egyptian empire / Daniel's 'king of the south.' Seleucus I Nicator founded the Seleucid / Syrian empire in 311 BC, and became its first ruler. **(Daniel 11:5)**

315 – 311 BC: Four generals of Alexander the Great, Cassander, Lysimachus, Seleucus I Nicator, and Ptolemy I Soter **(Daniel 11:4)**, joined together against Antigonus I Monophthalmus in the Babylonian War. After the death of Alexander the Great and before the rise of the four generals, there was Antigonus I Monophthalmus who sought to be Alexander the Great's successor. In 315 BC, when Antigonus I Monophthalmus from the region to the west / Macedonian region, attacked Seleucus I Nicator, Ptolemy I Soter came to Seleucus I Nicator's rescue because of Ptolemy I Soter's loyalty to Seleucus I Nicator who had served under Ptolemy I Soter during the campaigns of Alexander the Great. Seleucus I Nicator was reestablished in power, reinstated as ruler over his territory, gained more territory from the territory of the other three generals, and became even stronger, breaking away from the power of the other generals. Daniel prerecorded it this way; *'The king of the south / Ptolemy I Soter became strong. But one of his commanders who served under the king of the south /Ptolemy I*

Soter was the king of the north / Seleucus I Nicator, who became even stronger than the king of the south / Ptolemy I Soter and ruled his own kingdom with great power.' **(Daniel 11:5) From 315 – 312 BC, Jerusalem was controlled by the Antigonid dynasty under the reign of Antigonus I Monophthalmus. In 312 BC, Jerusalem was recaptured by Ptolemy I Soter after defeating Antigonus' son Demetrius I at the Battle of Gaza. In 311 BC the Antigonid dynasty regained control of Jerusalem after Ptolemy I Soter withdrew from Syria.**

306 BC: Antigonus I Monophthalmus declared himself king in 306 BC. Antigonus I Monophthalmus would eventually die in battle against Lysimachus and Seleucus in 301 BC at the age of eighty one after being struck by a javelin. Prior to the Battle of Ipsus in 301 BC, Antigonus had never lost a battle. With his death, any plans for reuniting Alexander the Great's empire came to an end. The four generals declared themselves kings over their own respective territories.

301 BC: The empire of Alexander the Great was unofficially divided among his four generals: Cassander, Lysimachus, Seleucus I Nicator, and Ptolemy I Soter. The four generals developed a modus vivendi / mode of living / way of life for coexisting with each other. The four generals were spread out to the west / Cassander, north / Lysimachus, east / Seleucus I Nicator, and south Ptolemy I Soter. Essentially Alexander the Great's empire was parceled out toward the four winds. **(Daniel 11:4)** Note however that while the Seleucid / Syrian empire was to the east of the other three empires, in the rest of Daniel's account the Seleucid / Syrian kings would be referred to as the 'king of the north.'

301 BC: Coele-Syria / southern Syria including Jerusalem was recaptured by Ptolemy I Soter after Antigonus I Monophthalmus was killed at the Battle of Ipsus. Because Seleucus I Nicator and Lysimachus had carved up the Antigonid empire (formerly Antipatrid empire) between them, Ptolemy I Soter was able to make a land grab. **In 301 BC, Jerusalem came under the control of the Ptolemaic / Egyptian empire / Egyptians for about a hundred years.** Ptolemy I Soter's pre-emptive move contributed to the Syrian Wars which began in 274 BC.

285 – 246 BC: Ptolemy II Philadelphus ('lover of his sister') / Pharaoh of Egypt / king of the south inherited his father's Ptolemaic / Egyptian empire. Ptolemy II's first wife, Arsinoë I, was the daughter of Lysimachus, one of the four generals of Alexander the Great who developed his own empire. With Arsinoë I, they produced Ptolemy III Euergetes his successor, and Berenice Phemopherus who married the Seleucid emperor Antiochus II Theos.

After Ptolemy II Philadelphus repudiated Arsinoë I, Ptolemy II married his full sister Arsinoë II, who was the widow of Lysimachus. This marriage brought him her Aegean possessions. Their coinage hosts both their faces with Ptolemy II in the foreground and Arsinoë II in the background.

As the son of Ptolemy I Soter who was a Macedonian Greek general of Alexander the Great, and Queen Berenice I who was originally from Macedon in northern Greece, the lineage of the Ptolemies was genetically Macedonian. Ptolemy II Philadelphus' half-brothers became kings of Macedonia. The lineage of the Seleucids was also genetically Macedonian.

The great achievements of Ptolemy II Philadelphus included the development of the Great Library of Alexandria in Egypt, the importation of exotic animals which were used in processions / ceremonial parades, the commissioned Aegyptiaca history of the Pharaohs of Egypt by the historian Manetho, and the production of the Greek Septuagint translation of the Old Testament / Tanakh books.

The books of the Old Testament were already housed in the library, but in their original languages. Because the people of Israel who lived in Egypt at the time absorbed Greek, the dominant language of Egypt at the time, and heavily mixed their Greek with Hebrew, the seventy Jewish translators were well prepared to produce the Septuagint / Greek translation of the Old Testament / Tanakh, under the royal compulsion of Ptolemy II Philadelphus.

289 – 261 BC: Antiochus I Soter ('savior'), inherited his father's Seleucid / Syrian empire and launched the First Syrian War.

274 – 271 B: During the First Syrian War Ptolemy II Philadelphus extended his Ptolemaic / Egyptian region and included Jerusalem.

261 – 246 BC: Antiochus II Theos ('god') inherited his father's Seleucid / Syrian empire and launched the Second Syrian War in 260 BC which ended in 248 BC with a marriage treaty. The daughter of Ptolemy II Philadelphus / king of the south, named Berenice, married Antiochus II Theos (261 – 246 BC) / king of the north / king of the Seleucid / Syrian empire. Their marriage cemented the treaty.

The second marriage of Antiochus II Theos to Berenice also set the two mothers, Laodice I of the Seleucid / Syrian empire and Berenice of the Ptolemaic / Egyptian empire, in competition to place
their respective sons on the throne.

Berenice requested assistance from her brother Ptolemy III Euergetes.

The jilted Laodice I, Antiochus II's former wife, and the woman whom the city of Laodicea (Revelation 3:14) was named after, conspired to have Berenice, Antiochus II Theos, and their son poisoned. The poisoning of Berenice, Antiochus II Theos, their son and those that supported Berenice / Berenice's attendants, ended the treaty. Berenice was unable to retain her power and Antiochus II Theos' power did not last because his offspring through Berenice were also killed. **(Daniel 11:5-6)**

246 BC: Ptolemy II Philadelphus, father to Berenice, also died.

246 – 226 BC: Seleucus II Callinicos ('gloriously triumphant'), son of Antiochus II Theos and Laodice I, inherited the Seleucid / Syrian empire after the assassination of his father by his mother. Seleucus II Callinicos' wife was Laodice II. Together Seleucus II Callinicos and Laodice II had five children including a daughter Antiochis, and sons Seleucus III Ceraunus and Antiochus III the Great.

246 – 221 BC: Ptolemy III Euergetes ('doer of good works') inherited his father's Ptolemaic / Egyptian empire when is father Ptolemy II Philadelphus died.

Ptolemy III Euergetes was Berenice's brother / 'one from her family line' / 'one from the branch of her roots.' When Ptolemy III Euergetes did arrive to assist his sister, Berenice and her child had already been assassinated. In order to avenge Berenice's death, Ptolemy III Euergetes of Egypt / king of the south attacked the forces of the king of the north. Ptolemy III Euergetes launched the Third Syrian War / Laodicean War (246 – 241 BC) against Laodice's newly crowned son, Seleucus II Callinicos. With the Third Syrian War, Ptolemy III Euergetes seized the gods, the metal images and the valuable articles of silver and gold that belonged to the Seleucids / Syrians. Ptolemy III Euergetes captured the gods of the Seleucids, but also the gods that had originally belonged to the Egyptians, gods that the Persian Cambyses had captured from the Egyptians in 525 BC. (Is it truly a god if it can be captured?) **(Daniel 11:7-8)**

The Seleucids / Syrians / 'king of the north' attempted to retaliate, invading the realm of the king of the south, but failed and retreated. **(Daniel 11:9)**

Ptolemy's reign / king of the south, outlived Seleucus II / king of the north. **(Daniel 11:8)**

226 – 223 BC: Seleucus III Ceraunus / Seleucus III Soter, son of Seleucus II Callinicos, inherited the Seleucid / Syrian empire and was assassinated after only three years. **(Daniel 11:10)**

221 – 203 BC: Ptolemy IV Philopater ('lover of father') inherited the Ptolemaic / Egyptian empire. Ptolemy IV Philopater's reign was inaugurated with the murder of his mother. He was a weak and corrupt king that led the decline of the Ptolemaic / Egyptian empire.

Ptolemy IV Philopater also married his sister Arsinoë III.

223 – 187 BC: Antiochus III the Great, son of Seleucus II Callinicos and brother to Seleucus III Ceraunus, inherited the Seleucid /

Syrian empire. The name Antiochus III the Great took 'the Great' from Alexander 'the Great' in the hope that Antiochus III the Great would be able to reunite the kingdom that Alexander the Great had established.

Antiochus III the Great launched the Fourth Syrian War (219 - 217 BC). The king of the south / Ptolemy IV Philopator responded with rage, raising a large army that defeated the king of the north / Antiochus III the Great. **(Daniel 11:10-11)** Antiochus III the Great was defeated at Raphia in the region of the Sinai in 217 BC marking the decline of the military ability to predominately prevail for the remainder of the Seleucid / Syrian empire. The historian Polybius recorded that Antiochus III the Great lost nearly ten thousand infantrymen at Raphia.

When peace was finally achieved in 211 BC, Ptolemy IV / king of the south became filled with pride and slaughtered many thousands as a way to demonstrate his dominance. Because Daniel recorded this vision from the perspective of the people of Israel, the many thousands that were slaughtered were from the people of Israel. **(Daniel 11:12) The hardship and slaughter of many thousands in Jerusalem by Ptolemy IV Philopater bred a resentment by the people of Israel, against the Egyptians that would extend for centuries.**

Antiochus III the Great / king of the north, responded to defeat by regrouping, mustered another even greater army which took a about five years (211 – 205 BC), and then advanced with a huge army fully equipped. **(Daniel 11:13)**

The resentment of the people of Israel against the Egyptians / Ptolemaic / Egyptian empire rose to the level of protest and riot against the king of the south. Those who participated in the rioting attempted to fulfill the vision of the prophesied messiah, to act as messiah, to be the messianic fulfillment of God's promised messiah. It was a misguided attempt to force the position of messiah to be filled. The idea was that if the messiah were to come, the people of Israel would be able to throw off the yoke of the Egyptian oppression. Those who participated in the violence and rebellion, rioted against the king of the south without success. There were a series of riots in Jerusalem that were misguided, ill planned and ineffective. Ptolemy IV Philopater dealt swiftly and effectively against the rioters and rebels. (Daniel 11:14)

205 – 181 BC: Ptolemy V Epiphanes ('illustrious') inherited the Ptolemaic / Egyptian empire from his father when he was about eight years old, after the death of Ptolemy IV Philopator, and the murder of Ptolemy IV Philopater's wife and sister Arsinoë III, by the ministers Agothocles and Sosibius. Because of his young age, the Ptolemaic / Egyptian empire was ruled by the regency of Agothocles.

Antiochus III the Great had been building his army and at that time viewed the young Egyptian / Ptolemaic king as a weak ruler.

Antiochus III the Great took advantage of the instability of the Ptolemaic / Egyptian empire to attack, initiating the Fifth Syrian War (202 – 195 BC). The Seleucids / Syrians emerged as the victors.

200 BC: Antiochus III the Great of the Seleucid / Syrian empire defeated the Ptolemies with the Battle of Panium (part of the Fifth Syrian War (202 – 199 BC), fought near Paneas / Caesarea Philippi. Paneas / Caesarea Philippi was the headquarters for the religion of Pan, a baal / mystery / mythology religion god. Paneas / Caesarea Philippi was also considered to be the location for the Gates of Hell. Later, at the site of Paneas / Caesarea Philippi, Jesus would ask the disciples 'Who do you say that I am?' When Peter answered, 'You are the Christ, the Son of God.' Jesus replied, 'Blessed are you, Peter… On this rock / truth, I will build my church and not even the gates of hell will prevail against it.' The reference to the 'gates of hell' experientially illustrated the dialogue by having the dialogue staged at what was believed to be the 'gates of hell' located at Paneas / Caesarea Philippi. Paneas / Caesarea Philippi was a well-fortified city that required siege works to conquer. **(Daniel 11:15)** Along with Paneas / Caesarea Philippi, Antiochus III the Great also took the land of Judah. **Jerusalem and Judah fell under the control of the Seleucid / Syrian empire / Syrian control after the Seleucids / Syrians defeated the Ptolemaic / Egyptian empire in 198 BC at the Battle of Panium.** Some of the people of Israel viewed Antiochus III the Great, the Seleucid / Syrian king, as a savior. Others viewed Antiochus III the Great as an enemy. But the widespread hostility against the Ptolemaic / Egyptian empire was greater than the wariness of the people of Israel that was directed toward the Seleucid / Syrian empire. When the land of Judah became a province of the Seleucid / Syrian empire, the division grew among the different factions of the people of Israel. **The conservatives maintained the traditional Jewish religion, values, and culture, and continued to practice the Jewish religious feasts and customs. In contrast, the rulers and the elite of Israel tended to embrace the Greek culture and the Greek baal / mystery / mythology religion. Antiochus III the Great and the Seleucids / Syrians were allowed by the people of Israel to rule over them as the better of two bad choices, better than the Ptolemaic / Egyptian empire. (Daniel 11:16) It was around this time when the Sadducees were formed as a sect of Judaism. It was understood that the Sadducees derived their name from Zadok the first high**

priest to serve in Solomon's temple. The leaders of the sect were understood to be 'Sons of Zadok' and priests as descendants of Eleazar, Aaron and Levi. They also considered themselves to be elite aristocrats. They lived luxurious lives suing silver and golden vessels (instead of stone or clay), as a contrast to the Pharisees (common people) who led a hard life. Because they favored Hellenization, they created Hellenistic Judaism, a form of Judaism compatible with the Greek gods and culture. The Sadducees administered the affairs of the government, participated in the Sanhedrin, collected taxes, equipped and led the army, negotiated international relationships, and mediated domestic grievances. The most important distinction of the Sadducees from the Pharisees and Essenes was the Sadducees' denial of the possibility of resurrection, which translated into their denial of the possibility that messiah would be resurrected, and their denial of the sovereignty and divinity of God Most High.
Even though the people of Israel at this point in history preferred the Seleucid / Syrian empire more than the Ptolemaic / Egyptian empire as their ruler, the future relationship between the people of Israel and the Seleucid / Syrian empire would be rougher for the people of Israel than the relationship that they previously held with the Ptolemaic / Egyptian empire.
In order to preserve his power, Antiochus III the Great offered terms of peace to Ptolemy V Epiphanes, sealing the terms of peace with the offering of his daughter, Cleopatra I in marriage to Ptolemy V Epiphanes who was now a teenager in 194 BC.
(Daniel 11:17) Cleopatra I was the first of a series of seven Cleopatras. Antiochus III the Great gave his daughter Cleopatra I to Ptolemy V Epiphanes as a plot to destroy the Ptolemaic / Egyptian empire. Cleopatra I was intended to steer the young and impressionable Ptolemy V Epiphanes to bow to the will of Antiochus III the Great. Antiochus III the Great envisioned the Ptolemaic / Egyptian empire as becoming part of Antiochus III the Great's hegemony / a neighboring nation under the Seleucid / Syrian empire influence.

c.196 BC: The Rosetta Stone was produced during Ptolemy V Epiphanes' reign, around 196 BC, celebrating the anniversary of Ptolemy V Epiphanes' coronation as king of Egypt.
The Rosetta Stone also acted as a record of the marriage between Cleopatra I of the Seleucid / Syrian empire and Ptolemy V Epiphanes of the Ptolemaic / Egyptian empire. The Rosetta Stone was written in three languages; ancient Egyptian hieroglyphic script, ancient Egyptian Demotic script and ancient Greek. When the Rosetta Stone was discovered, it became the key to deciphering ancient Egyptian hieroglyphs.

Cleopatra I did not comply with her father's plan and instead of making the Seleucid / Syrian empire the ally of the Ptolemaic / Egyptian empire, she decided to make an alliance with Rome. When Cleopatra I encouraged her impressionable younger teenage husband to ally himself with Rome, Antiochus III the Great became furious. But unwilling to attack the Ptolemaic / Egyptian empire for the sake of his daughter, Antiochus III the Great turned to the coastlands, to Asia Minor and pursued military campaigns pushing into Europe in an attempt to push the Romans out of the region. Antiochus III the Great desired to prove to his daughter that Rome was not as strong as Rome was presented to be. But the Romans were stronger than anticipated and prevailed over the endeavors of Antiochus III the Great and the Seleucids / Syrians. The Romans defeated and humiliated Antiochus III the Great at Magnesia in Asia Minor around 190 BC. **(Daniel 11:18)** The result of the war with the Romans resulted in the Peace of Apamea of 188 BC which required Antiochus III the Great and successive generations to pay heavy reparations. To pay the war debt, Antiochus III the Great plundered temples. In 187 BC, Antiochus III the Great was stabbed in the back while attempting to plunder a temple in the province of Elymais / Susa. **(Daniel 11:19)**

187 – 175 BC: Seleucus IV Philopater ('lover of his father') inherited the Seleucid / Syrian empire complete with war debts that were owed to the Romans. Before he inherited the throne, Seleucus IV Philopator had been a hostage in Rome following the peace of Apamea in 188 BC as a condition of the treaty. Later Seleucus Philopator had been exchanged for his son who later became Demetrius I of Syria. Seleucus IV Philopater, like his father, looted the treasuries of temples.

During the reign of Seleucus IV Philopater, two groups developed among the people of Israel, the Tobiads and Oniads. The Tobiads embraced the Greek culture and religion, along with the Hellenization of Israel, with the idea that Greek culture was more upper class and desirable. The Oniads took their name from the Jewish High Priest Onias III and sought to remain true to the Jewish religion, tradition, and culture. The Oniads desired to remain true to the tradition that had originated with Moses in 1446 BC. According to the Jewish High Priest Onias III, it was Seleucus IV Philopater who began the Hellenistic infiltration into Judea.

While Onias III remained high priest, Jerusalem enjoyed peace and prosperity, with the laws strictly obeyed because Onias III was devout and hated evil. In response, the kings of the Seleucids / Syria and the Ptolemies / Egypt generally honored the temple and presented expensive gifts. The Seleucids / Syrians even paid the costs of the temple sacrifices from the revenues collected elsewhere.

At that time, Jerusalem's temple had the reputation of having a wealthy treasury. The Israelite Simon from the tribe of Benjamin and chief administrative officer of the temple who embraced the Greek culture, lost an argument over the regulations governing the city market to the temple High Priest Onias. As a retaliation, Simon induced Seleucus IV Philopater to raid the temple pointing out that the temple treasury was so large that it could not be counted, which was an inaccurate accounting of the temple treasury (2 Maccabees 3). Seleucus IV Philopater sent Heliodorus to raid and plunder the temple in Jerusalem. Heliodorus was the one sent out as a tax collector to maintain the royal splendor. **(Daniel 11:20)**
There was an enormous reaction to the raid of Heliodorus and the Seleucids / Syrians from the priests of the temple and the populace of Jerusalem.
The ancient temples were also the sites where the treasuries of the people would be stored. The ancient temples were well attended and frequently well protected. Ancient temples were also frequently viewed as benefiting from the protection of the god of the temple.
In Jerusalem, there was only one God and only one temple. The wealth of the people of Jerusalem was housed in the temple treasury.
'While everyone was begging the Lord Almighty to protect the money that had been entrusted to the care of the temple treasury, Heliodorus went on with his plan. But at the very moment that he and his bodyguards arrived at the treasury, the Lord of all supernatural powers caused such a vision to appear that everyone who had dared to enter with Heliodorus was panic-stricken and weak with fear at this display of the Lord's power. In the vision they saw a horse and a rider. The horse had a richly decorated bridle, and its rider, dressed in gold armor, was frightening. Suddenly the horse rushed at Heliodorus, then reared up and struck at him with its hoofs. Heliodorus also saw two unusually strong and handsome young men, wearing very fine clothes. They stood on either side of him and beat him unmercifully. He immediately fell to the ground unconscious, and his men put him on a stretcher and carried him out. Only a moment earlier this man had entered the treasury with a large group of men, including all his bodyguards, but now he was being carried away helpless. So they all openly acknowledged the mighty power of God.' 2 Maccabees 3:22-28
When the High Priest Onias prayed to save Heliodorus' life and offered sacrifice on behalf of Heliodorus, two angels again appeared and instructed Heliodorus to tell everyone of the great power of God.

The priests and populace of Jerusalem were so effective in their attempts to keep Heliodorus out of the temple that Heliodorus retreated. When giving his account to Seleucus IV Philopater, Heliodorus claimed that angels had stopped him; supernatural powers had prevented him from entering the temple.

When Seleucus IV Philopater asked Heliodorus who should be sent the second time, Heliodorus replied, 'If you have an enemy or know of someone plotting against your government, send him. He will come back badly beaten, if he comes back at all, for some strange power from God is at work there. The God of heaven watches over the Temple; he strikes down and destroys anyone who comes to harm it.' 2 Maccabees 3:38-39

The temple's chief administrative officer Simon who had been responsible for encouraging the raid of Heliodorus, desired to avoid becoming the focus for the disaster. So Simon accused the High Priest Onias III of having been responsible for the raid of Heliodorus. Simon was encouraged in every evil thing he did and his plotting against the High Priest Onias III continued.

Raphael painted the event in *The Expulsion of Heliodorus from the Temple*.

A few years after the attempt to loot the treasury of the Jerusalem temple, Heliodorus assassinated Seleucus IV Philopater, ending Seleucus IV Philopater's reign.

180 – 145 BC: Ptolemy VI Philometor ('lover of his mother') inherited the throne of the Ptolemaic / Egyptian empire. His mother was Cleopatra I, daughter of Antiochus III the Great of the Seleucid / Syrian empire. Ptolemy VI Philometor was around six years old when his father died. So, he ruled jointly with his mother Cleopatra I until her death in 176 BC. In 173 BC Ptolemy VI Philometor married his sister Cleopatra II and bore four to five children.

175 – 164 BC: Antiochus IV Epiphanes ('the illustrious'), (also known as Antiochus IV Epimanes ('the madman') behind his back) took control of the Seleucid / Syrian empire. Antiochus IV Epiphanes was not in the royal lineage to become king. The reign was supposed to pass from his older brother Seleucus IV Philopator to Seleucus' son / Antiochus' nephew, Demetrius I. As a condition of the Peace of Apamea treaty, Antiochus III the Great sent his son who later became Antiochus IV Epiphanes, to live in Rome as a hostage in connection with the reparations that Antiochus III the Great was forced to pay. A 'hostage' of Rome meant that Antiochus IV Epiphanes would merely be required to reside and be educated in Rome. In 175 BC, Antiochus IV Epiphanes was released by the intervention of his older brother Seleucus IV Philopator who substituted his own son Demetrius I as hostage.

After being released, Antiochus IV Epiphanes led military campaigns. While Antiochus IV Epiphanes was at Athens, Heliodorus who earlier had attempted the raid on the temple in Jerusalem, had killed the older brother, Seleucus IV Philopater (175 BC) with the idea of assuming the throne.
Antiochus IV Epiphanes returned home and killed Heliodorus. Then Antiochus IV Epiphanes claimed to rule on behalf of his nephew Demetrius I, who was still living in Rome as a condition of the Peace of Apamea treaty. With Seleucus IV Philopater assassinated by Heliodorus, and Heliodorus also dead, Antiochus IV Epiphanes proclaimed himself as co-regent with another of Seleucus IV Philopater's sons, the infant Antiochus. A few years later, Uncle Antiochus IV Epiphanes orchestrated his nephew Antiochus' murder. Antiochus IV Epiphanes then used his small cadre of trusted friends and a small military force to rise to power. After Antiochus IV Epiphanes had amassed enough power, he then revealed that his coregency had ended and now he was the new ruler. Once Antiochus IV Epiphanes' rule was well established, Antiochus IV Epiphanes repudiated all connections to Demetrius I in Rome, and assumed the throne for himself. **(Daniel 11: 21, 23)**

Through intrigue Antiochus IV Epiphanes came to the position of ruler and became the most hated of all the foreign rulers who had ever had dominion over Jerusalem during the Intertestamental period. Antiochus IV Epiphanes remains a contemptable person in Jewish history. (Daniel 11:21)

One of Antiochus IV Epiphanes' tactics for ruling Jerusalem and the people of Israel was to officially promote a Hellenization program / a cultural change program in Judea that was embraced with eagerness by the Jewish elite. Antiochus IV Epiphanes accelerated the Seleucid / Syrian empire's efforts to eradicate the Jewish religion by forcing the Jewish High Priest Onias III to step down in favor of Onias III's brother Jason (Greek) / Joshua (Hebrew) / Jesus (Greek). Jason was actually named Joshua, but took on the Greek form of his name 'Jason,' as he embraced Hellenism.

According to Josephus, Onias III's son Onias IV fled to Ptolemy and built a city resembling Jerusalem with a temple that was like the temple in Jerusalem (Josephus, *Wars of the Jews*).
Three years after Onias III was deposed as high priest, Jason was replaced by Menelaus.
There were two possible interpretations for Daniel's term 'the prince of the covenant' in Daniel 11:22. The first was as a reference to Antiochus IV Epiphanes and his responsibility in the death of the High Priest Onias III. The other possible

interpretation rendered this term 'confederate prince' and would have been a reference to Ptolemy VI Philometor of Egypt. Antiochus IV Epiphanes also plundered the people of Israel. In the list of the most recent rulers before Antiochus IV Epiphanes, the rulers had been obligated to pay the debt from war with Rome as arranged in the Peace of Apamea treaty. Antiochus IV Epiphanes however was no longer bound by that kind of debt. So Antiochus IV Epiphanes used wealth and squandered wealth to buy loyalty among the Seleucid / Syrian nobility. **(Daniel 11:24)**

174 – 171 BC: Jason (Greek) / Joshua (Hebrew) / Jesus (Greek) who favored Hellenism, became high priest in Jerusalem after having his brother deposed.

The ruling body for the nation of Israel with roots from the time of Moses, was the Sanhedrin / the seventy elders. The seventy elders that founded the original Israelite ruling body of the Sanhedrin, accompanied Moses on the mountain as they met with God soon after the exodus from Egypt (1446 BC). The high priest acted as head of the Sanhedrin and consequently, when Israel was without a king, the high priest acted as the chief ruler of Israel.

The beast of the sea / false prophet / eighth king beast will hold a similar position as chief ruler or spokesperson of the global religious community and the budding global governance system during the first half of the era of the time of Jacob's Trouble, until the little horn / eleventh king / final horn on the shaggy goat / prince who is to come / king that will exalt himself / beast of the earth / final world ruler rises to assume his role as king of kings for the global governance system.

For the people of Isael after the era of the kings of Israel and Judah, and after the return of the people of Israel from exile, there was no higher position in the nation of Israel than the office of high priest.

Previously in the history of Israel, when the governance of Israel was comprised of both high priests and kings, the kings of Israel and Judah tended to focus upon the military and international affairs, leaving the religious affairs to be cared for by the priests. But when the nation of Israel did not have a king, during the time of the Seleucid / Syrian empire's control of Israel, the high priest was also the official political leader of Israel.

Joshua (Hebrew) / Jason (Greek) / Jesus (Greek) was able to depose his brother as high priest, with the support of the people of Israel, because at the time, there was division among the people of Israel between those who held onto traditional values, who practiced the true Jewish religion, and those who adopted the Hellenistic culture and Hellenized Judaism. The Jerusalem Zadokite High Priest Onias III held to the tradition of

Moses and the worship of the Lord. But his younger brother Joshua (Hebrew) / Jason (Greek) / Jesus (Greek) believed that Hellenization and adopting the Greek culture along with the Greek religion was a better, more elite, higher class principle, and a more informed choice. In an effort to have his brother Onias III removed which allowed Jason to be placed in the position of high priest, Jason decided to appeal to Antiochus IV Epiphanes for the position of high priest, foregoing the traditional Jewish law that dictated how a high priest was to be chosen.

Jason appealed to Antiochus IV Epiphanes through a bribe, promising to build a gymnasium in Jerusalem. Gymnasiums were entirely a Greek culture phenomenon and viewed as offensive to the Jewish laws, tradition and religion.

Gymnasiums were where people would exercise naked. The Law given to Moses prohibited people from showing their nakedness. Also in the midst of nakedness, one's circumcision or uncircumcision became known. Greeks who were not under the covenant of Abraham were not circumcised. In the gymnasiums, circumcision caused the Jewish men to be easily identified and targeted for derision. Those people of Israel who desired to adopt Hellenism and Greek culture, would go through a very painful surgery to 'undo' their circumcision. Gymnasiums were also known for being the hangout for predators and people with propensities to sexual perversions which were also offenses of the Law of Moses.

Jason constructed the large gymnasium at the base of the southern steps to the temple mount, in the path for ascending to the temple.

The gymnasium was the site for another offense to God Most High / the God of Moses, because the focus of the events held in the gymnasium, were dedicated to the practice of the Greek baal / mystery / mythology religion.

For the appointment to the office of high priest, Jason offered the king '27,000 pounds of silver with 6,000 more pounds to be paid later. Jason also offered him an additional 11,250 pounds of silver for the authority to establish a stadium where young men could train and to enroll the people of Jerusalem as citizens of Antioch.' 2 Maccabees 4:7-9

When Antiochus IV Epiphanes agreed to Jason's plan, Jason took over the office of high priest, deposing his brother Onias III. With his new authority as high priest, Jason then forced the people of Jerusalem to change to the Greek way of life. Jason caused such a following of the Greek way of life that the temple priests abandoned their duties and neglected the temple sacrifices and services in favor of attending the games, games which were forbidden by Jewish Law. Jason also did other things like use 22,500 pounds of silver from the temple treasury to pay for a sacrifice to the god Hercules. The Seleucids / Syrians diverted Jason's sacrifice intended for the god Hercules, in order to pay for the construction of warships. Jason continually bribed Antiochus IV Epiphanes with Jason's proposition to make Jerusalem a showcase for Hellenistic culture and with the promise to Antiochus IV Epiphanes to produce more revenue / taxes collected from the people of Israel for the benefit of the Seleucid / Syrian empire.

In the second book of the Maccabees, it was reported, 'About this time Antiochus the Fourth made a second attack against Egypt. For nearly forty days people all over Jerusalem saw visions of cavalry troops in gold armor charging across the sky. The riders were armed with spears and their swords were drawn. They were lined up in battle against one another, attacking and counterattacking. Shields were clashing, there was a rain of spears, and arrows flew through the air. All the different kinds of armor and the gold bridles on the horses flashed in the sunlight. Everyone in the city prayed that these visions might be a good sign.'

'When a false report began to spread that Antiochus had died, Jason took more than a thousand men and suddenly attacked Jerusalem. They drove back those stationed on the city walls and finally captured the city. Menelaus (who would later become the high priest after Jason) fled for safety to the fort, near the Temple hill, while Jason and his men went on slaughtering their fellow Jews without mercy. Jason did not realize that success against one's own people is the worst kind of failure. He even considered his success a victory over enemies, rather than a defeat of his own people. But Jason did not take over the government. Instead, he was forced to flee once again to the territory of the Ammonites, and in the end his evil plot brought him nothing but shame and disgrace, and he died in misery. Aretas I, the ruler of the Arabs / Nabataeans, imprisoned him; he was looked upon as a criminal and despised because he had betrayed his own people; everyone was hunting for him, and he had to run from town to town. He fled to Egypt for safety, then to Greece, hoping to find refuge among the Spartans, who were related to the Jews. Finally, this man, who had forced so many others to flee from their own country, died as a fugitive in a foreign land. Jason had killed many people and left their bodies unburied, but now his own death was unmourned. He was not given a funeral or even buried with his ancestors.' 2 Maccabees 5:1-10

171 – 161 BC: Simon who had exposed the Seleucids / Syrians to the temple treasury and who had conspired against High Priest Onias III, had a brother Menelaus, who decided to depose Jason and to pursue the position of high priest in Jerusalem. Onias III and Joshua / Jason were of the tribe of Levi and descendants of Aaron. Their genealogy made them hereditarily eligible to hold the position of high priest. Simon and Menelaus were of the tribe of Benjamin making them unable to officially hold any office of the priesthood.

The Tobiads who embraced Hellenism, viewed Jason as still maintaining some partiality to traditional Judaism. Menelaus' view was that Jason was not Hellenistic enough to be trusted. When the temple officials sent Menelaus to Antiochus IV Epiphanes to pay the annual tribute, Menelaus took the opportunity to outbid Jason's bribe by 22,500 pounds of silver over what Jason had offered. Menelaus thus secured the office of high priest for himself.

Jason had been only a moderate Hellenizer compared to Menelaus. The various factions among the people of Israel responded to the appointment of Menelaus as high priest, with civil war; the Tobiads supporting Menelaus, but the masses of the people stood behind Jason, led by the Oniads / Hasideans. **By the time of Jesus, the Hasideans had split into the Pharisees and the Essenes.**

Antiochus IV Epiphanes sent a troop of Cyprian soldiers to accompany Menelaus as he transitioned to high priest. The troop of Cyprian soldiers, led by an officer named Sostrates, was sent to subdue any opposition to Menelaus' new position, and to collect the promised funds for the bribe.

Menelaus' first act as high priest was to seize the sacred vessels in the temple in order to meet his bribe obligations to Antiochus IV Epiphanes. When the deposed High Priest Onias III heard of the event, Onias III publicly accused Menelaus of robbing the temple.

Menelaus' character included a fierce temper like a wild beast. Jason who had previously cheated his own brother out of the position of high priest, was now forced to flee to the land of Amon because of the intensity of Menelaus' tempestuous character.

Onias III was later secretly murdered on the authority of Antiochus IV Epiphanes. Menelaus' friend Andronicus went to Onias III and deceived him with a friendly greeting and with promises of safety, luring Onias away from the safety of the temple and then took the opportunity to murder Onias. **(Daniel 11:22)**

Under Mosaic Law, Menelaus would have never been able to be considered for the position of high priest because he was not a Levite of the line of Aaron. Menelaus was of the tribe of Benjamin. The historical point when the priesthood was able to be purchased for a bribe by a person that was unqualified to be priest through his genealogy, was the point when the position of high priest in Israel ceased to

be legitimate. From that point on, through the time of Jesus Christ, and until the second temple was destroyed in 70 AD, the high priests serving in Jerusalem were not descendants of Aaron and Levi.

Menelaus continued to be high priest, but never paid any of the money he had promised to Antiochus IV Epiphanes. When summoned by Antiochus IV Epiphanes, Menelaus left his brother Lysimachus as acting high priest. It was while Lysimachus was acting as high priest that he sent out 3,000 troops against the people of Israel. Menelaus was then brought to trial, but Menelaus bribed Ptolemy and was declared innocent while three innocent men were sentenced to death.

170 BC: Under the rule of Menelaus, the Oniads / traditionalist in Jewish values, culture, tradition, and religion; decided to seek support from the Ptolemies / Egyptians. Ptolemy VI Philometor appreciated the friendly advances of the Oniads from Jerusalem. But unwilling to fully commit himself, Ptolemy VI Philometor decided to invest in a modest incursion into Coele-Syria / the southern portion of Syria that included the region of Jerusalem. Sending a small military force as a preparatory staging area, Ptolemy VI Philometor did not intend to provoke a response. The exercise was intended to be a mere poking, a statement of modest support for the people of Israel against the Seleucid / Syrian empire. But this small military force brought a ferocious response from Antiochus IV Epiphanes. Ptolemy VI Philometor possessed the larger overall force and the victory should have been his. But Ptolemy VI Philometor was betrayed into the Seleucid / Syrian / Syrian empire's hands by some of his closest advisors.

Daniel 11:25-26 prerecorded the history this way: 'With a large army the king of the north / Seleucid / Syrian empire will stir up his strength and courage against the king of the south / Ptolemaic / Egyptian empire. The king of the south / Ptolemaic / Egyptian empire will wage war with a large and very powerful army, but he will not be able to stand because of the plots devised against him. Those who eat from the king's provisions will try to destroy him; his army will be swept away, and many will fall in battle.'

Having been betrayed by his own people, Ptolemy VI Philometor was captured and his army surrendered. Ptolemy VI Philometor was reduced to a puppet under the control of Antiochus IV Epiphanes. The only city that held out against the Seleucids / Syrians was the city of Alexandria in Egypt who appointed the brother of Ptolemy VI Philometor named Ptolemy VIII Euergetes and nicknamed Physcon ('fat belly'), to rule them. (Ptolemy VI Philometor's son who should have been next in line was Ptolemy VII and was still an infant without influence yet.) The presence of Physcon in the ruler mix caused Ptolemy

VI Philometor and Antiochus IV Epiphanes to meet for the purpose of eliminating their new common enemy, Physcon. But their underlying goal was to eliminate each other at the same time. So Ptolemy VI Philometor and Antiochus IV Epiphanes met and exchanged lies to each other. **(Daniel 11:27)** Antiochus IV Epiphanes realized that he needed a larger military engine and returned home to Syria, stopping in Jerusalem on the way to have Menelaus levy a special tax on all of Jerusalem. **(Daniel 11:28)**
In the meantime, Ptolemy VIII Euergetes Physcon was able to stage a coup and drive out the weakened Ptolemy VI Philometor. Ptolemy VI Philometor fled to Rome and appealed to Rome for assistance.

169 BC: Menelaus' greatest problem arose in 169 BC when he had no means of paying Antiochus IV Epiphanes the bribe that he had promised in exchange for being appointed high priest in Jerusalem. Menelaus' had also lost his support from the overtaxed, impoverished, and the people of Israel he had previously mortally attacked.

168 – 167 BC: Antiochus IV Epiphanes returned to the battle lines to address the Ptolemaic / Egyptian empire with his much larger military force. But instead of meeting just the Egyptians, Antiochus IV Epiphanes would also have met Rome because the Romans responded favorably to the plea of Ptolemy VI Philometor on behalf of the Jewish Hellenists. The ships of the western coastlands opposed Antiochus IV Epiphanes. **(Daniel 11:29-30)**
The Roman presence was led by the Roman Senator Popilius Laenas. Upon meeting Antiochus IV Epiphanes and the army of the Seleucid Syrian empire, Popilius reminded Antiochus IV Epiphanes that Rome had a treaty agreement with the Ptolemaic / Egyptian empire based on arrangements made with Ptolemy V Epiphanes. For Antiochus IV Epiphanes to attack the Ptolemaic / Egyptian empire, would require a Roman response. Popilius then asked Antiochus IV Epiphanes if he was going to go home or if he was going to continue his military expedition which would initiate war with Rome because of Rome's alliance with the Ptolemaic / Egyptian empire. Antiochus IV Epiphanes said that he needed a day or two to consult with his advisors. But while Antiochus IV Epiphanes and Senator Popilius Laenas were dialoguing, Popilius had drawn a circle in the ground with a stick all the way around Antiochus IV Epiphanes and said that if Antiochus IV Epiphanes stepped out of the circle before giving his response, it would be deemed a declaration of war on Rome. It became known as the 'Day of Eleusis' in the summer of 168 BC. Antiochus IV Epiphanes quickly evaluated the situation and understood that a war against both the Ptolemaic / Egyptian

empire along with the Roman empire would be disastrous. Antiochus IV Epiphanes lost heart and withdrew. Antiochus IV Epiphanes did not have the means to also go to war with Rome. Antiochus IV Epiphanes' dream of reuniting the Greek empire as it had been under Alexander the Great, was demolished. Actually, Antiochus IV Epiphanes was humiliated before the world and became enraged.

On the way home from Egypt, Antiochus IV Epiphanes took out his fury against the people of Israel. (Daniel 11:30) The story that had reached the people of Israel in the meantime, falsely reported that Antiochus IV Epiphanes had been killed. Jason, the former high priest, took the opportunity to attempt to regain control of Jerusalem. When Antiochus IV Epiphanes heard of the revolt, Antiochus IV Epiphanes, complete with an army that had not been utilized, responded swiftly by personally addressing the uprising in Jerusalem.

2 Maccabees 5 documented the reaction of Antiochus IV Epiphanes: **'When the news of what had happened in Jerusalem reached Antiochus, he thought the whole country of Judea was in revolt, and he became as furious as a wild animal. So he left Egypt and took Jerusalem by storm, giving his men orders to cut down without mercy everyone they met and to slaughter anyone they found hiding in the houses. They murdered everyone — men and women, boys and girls; even babies were butchered. Three days later Jerusalem had lost 80,000 people: 40,000 killed in the attack and at least that many taken away to be sold as slaves.'**

'But Antiochus was still not satisfied. He even dared to enter the holiest Temple in all the world, guided by Menelaus, who had become a traitor both to his religion and to his people. With his filthy and unholy hands, Antiochus swept away the sacred objects of worship and the gifts which other kings had given to increase the glory and honor of the Temple. He was so thrilled with his conquest that he did not realize that the Lord had let his holy Temple be defiled because the sin of the people of Jerusalem had made him angry for a while. <u>If the people of Jerusalem had not been involved in so many sins, Antiochus would have been punished immediately and prevented from taking such a foolish action</u>. He would have suffered the same fate as Heliodorus, who was sent by King Seleucus to inspect the treasury. But the Lord did not choose his people for the sake of his Temple; he established his Temple for the sake of his people. So the Temple shared in the people's suffering but also later shared in their prosperity. The Lord abandoned it when he became angry, but restored it when his anger had cooled down. 2 Maccabees 5:11-20

Jason fled again to Ammon, then to Egypt, and finally to Sparta where he died and was buried.

Antiochus IV Epiphanes continued to receive worldwide support in his attempts to Hellenize the world including the Hellenization of the people of Jerusalem. Benefactors from the nobility of Athens, Delphi, Delos, Argos, Achaea, Arcadia, Boeotia, Rhodes, Byzantium, Chalcedon, and Cyzicus continued to support Antiochus IV Epiphanes and received his generosity, generosity that was paid for by such endeavors as raiding temple treasuries, receiving bribes from appointed officials, etc.

In Jerusalem, there were some who were willing to forsake the Jewish religion and people. This list of traitors to the people of Israel included the false high priest Menelaus. They were also rewarded by Antiochus IV Epiphanes. (Daniel 11:30)

Antiochus IV Epiphanes entered Jerusalem where he was warmly welcomed by the Hellenized elite and rulers of the people of Israel. To show his appreciation of the Hellenizing leaders among the people of Israel, Antiochus IV Epiphanes put to death many of those maintaining their traditional Jewish feasts and customs, along with those who desired to return to Ptolemaic / Egyptian sovereignty. Because of Antiochus IV Epiphanes' humiliation on the world stage, he initiated a more penetrating program of Hellenization toward the people of Jerusalem and the nation of Israel. Portable pagan altars, altars for the practice of the baal / mystery / mythology religion were built in the towns throughout Judea. 'Pagan sacrifices were offered in front of houses and in the streets. Any books of the Law which were found were torn up and burned, and anyone who was caught with a copy of the sacred books or who obeyed the Law was put to death by order of the king. So they used their power against Israel, against those who were caught, each month, in the cities.' 1 Maccabees 1:55-58

Menelaus assisted Antiochus IV Epiphanes in the composition of the decree issued against the people of Israel and against their worship of Yahweh / the Lord. Neither the Greek nor Syrian tradition had a priesthood that sacrificed pigs. The Greeks almost exclusively sacrificed goats. The idea of sacrificing a pig on the altar of the temple in Jerusalem as an affront to Jewish Law would not have naturally occurred to Antiochus IV Epiphanes, but it could have occurred to the Hellenized High Priest of Jerusalem Menelaus who was also versed in the Jewish Law. As an act of defiance against God Most High, it would have been Menelaus who would have offered this caveat for the decree of Antiochus IV Epiphanes against the people of Israel.

167 BC: Antiochus IV Epiphanes entered the temple and committed the abomination of desolation that would suspend the daily sacrificial system for three years. According to the book of Maccabees, the 'abomination of desolation' began on the fifteenth day of Kislev, 167 BC. But it was ten days later that the first sacrifice of a pig on the altar took place. The twenty fifth of the month was also recognized as Antiochus IV Epiphanes' birthday. Each month on the twenty fifth day, the people of the Seleucid / Syrian empire were required to celebrate his birthday. 'On the twenty fifth of the month, these same evil people offered sacrifices on the pagan altar erected on top of the altar in the Temple.' 1 Maccabees 1:59
From the time of King Darius 516 BC until the Roman General Titus in 70 AD, the temple operated uninterrupted with this one exception. Once the pagan sacrifices were offered on the altar, the altar and the temple were no longer consecrated and sacrifices to Yahweh / God Most High could not continue. There were only three years / approximately one thousand eighty days when the temple was not operational, when the daily sacrifices were not offered because the temple was unconsecrated.

While in Jerusalem, Antiochus IV Epiphanes, with the assistance of the false high priest Menelaus, began his 'reign of terror.' During the era of time when Antiochus IV Epiphanes committed the first act of abomination of desolation in the temple of Jerusalem, the Seleucid / Syrian empire:
- established Apollonius to oversee the Hellenization program.
- tore down the walls of Jerusalem and houses in order to build the fortress Acra / Akra on the west side of the temple mount.
- changed the laws concerning nudity, and compulsorily required acts of nudity and public prostitution as religious rites.
- prohibited the celebration of Sabbaths and feasts. People were required to work all seven days of the week and not allowed to participate in worship experiences or to celebrate holidays.
- prohibited the rite of circumcision.

- ordered mothers who circumcised their babies to either be crucified with their babies hung around their necks or to have their dead babies hung on their breasts, paraded through the city and then thrown over the city wall. Their families were also killed.
- ordered the burning of the Torah / Pentateuch / Five Books of Moses, and other holy works, essentially the core of the Jewish Bible.
- changed the name of Yahweh to Zeus Olympus.
- declared himself to be God. His coins were minted depicting 'King Antiochus…God made visible.'
- installed a statue of Zeus on the sacrificial altar.
- removed all traditional Jewish items of worship from the temple including the gold altar, the lampstand with all its equipment, the table for the bread offered to the Lord, the cups and bowls, the gold fire pans, the curtain, and the decorations.
- committed the abomination of desolation by taking a pig to the temple and offered the pig as a sacrifice on the brazen altar, causing the altar and the temple to become unclean and unacceptable for sacrifice.
- sprinkled pigs' blood on the Holy of Holies.
- took the broth of the pig sacrifice, poured it over the holy scriptures / holy scrolls and then had them cut up and burned.
- ordered the people of Israel to sacrifice pigs to Zeus.
- forced the priests in the temple to eat pork by forcing it down their throats, and when they refused to swallow, had their throats cut.
- enforced a theology of ecumenism within the temple including voluntary and forced public ritual prostitution as both sexual religious rites and as part of the drinking parties.
- required worshipers to parade wearing wreaths of ivy at Dionysiac festivals.
- required the people of Israel to make themselves ritually unclean in every way that they could, a reference to child molestation, voluntary homosexuality, ritual and forced homosexuality, rape, ritual / temple acts of sex, etc.
- forced the consumption of pork as part of the Jewish diet.
- plundered the temple treasury and then using the silver and gold to further the interests of the Seleucid / Syrian empire.
- took over political control of the temple activities.

- murdered many people and boasted arrogantly about it.
- left troops to conduct the reign of terror over the next three years in Jerusalem against the people of Israel.
- dedicated the Samaritan sanctuary at Mount Gerizim to Zeus Xenias / Zeus god of hospitality, or Jupiter Hellenius. Then allowed the Samaritans grace which further distanced the Samaritans from the people of Israel.
- compelled the people with brute force, each month that the king's birthday was celebrated, to eat the intestines of sacrificed animals.
- renamed the city of Jerusalem to 'Antiochus' and began to institute Antiochus IV Epiphanes' utopian ideal for the city of Jerusalem based on the culture he had experienced while he was in Greece; the sports, theatricals, pageantry, etc.

Disobedience to any of these dictates immediately brought the death penalty. (Daniel 11:31)

When Antiochus IV Epiphanes discovered that the faithful would choose death over resistance to his religious practices on the Sabbath day, the troops of Antiochus IV Epiphanes martyred many.

Venting his rage on the people of Israel, Antiochus IV Epiphanes began a war of extermination against the religion of the people of Israel.

Apollonius, one of the Seleucids charged with duty in Jerusalem, acted with restraint, for a time, lulling the people of Jerusalem into false confidence. Then Apollonius launched his attack on the Sabbath when the unsuspecting crowds had gathered on his invitation to review a military parade. Jerusalem was ransacked, and parts of it set on fire.

Using the temporary terror as an opportunity, a more permanent presence was established. According to I Maccabees, in the Seleucid citadel / the Akra, a military colony was installed, an 'abode of aliens,' 'a sinful race and lawless men.' The Akra served as a fortress not to protect the people of Jerusalem, but as a military base in the conflict against the people of Jerusalem. Antiochus IV Epiphanes was determined to eliminate the Jewish religion in Jerusalem.

The practice of murdering innocent people around the altar of the temple continued. The temple area was continually defiled by the presence of the murderers. The original inhabitants of Jerusalem were replaced with foreigners.

'Her Temple was as empty as a wilderness; her festivals were turned into days of mourning, her Sabbath joy into shame. Her honor became an object of ridicule. Her shame was as great as her former glory, and her pride was turned into deepest mourning.' 1 Maccabees 1:39-40

'Antiochus now issued a decree that all nations in his empire should abandon their own customs and become one people. All the Gentiles and even many of the Israelites submitted to this decree. They adopted the official pagan religion, offered sacrifices to idols, and no longer observed the Sabbath.' 1 Maccabees 1:41-43

The decree of Antiochus IV Epiphanes was the same kind of decree that the biblical record portrayed the little horn / eleventh king / final horn on the shaggy goat / prince who is to come / king that will exalt himself / beast of the earth / final world ruler will issue when he will cause all, both great and small to worship the image of the beast of the sea that the beast of the earth will set up in the wing of the temple on the temple mount. There were other similarities between the activity of Antiochus IV Epiphanes and the beast of the earth that were listed in the biblical record.

Antiochus IV Epiphanes also set himself up as divine, equal to or greater than God Most High.

The history for human individuals who took on the status of 'god' began with the antediluvian / preflood religion which recognized the Nephilim / offspring of rebellious angels mating with human women, as divine. After the flood, the descendants of Ham had revived the antediluvian / preflood baal / mystery / mythology religion, recognizing each of the rebellious angels as holding the position of god. The offspring of the 'gods' were also known as Nephilim / giants and their offspring were recognized as 'demigods' / part human-part divine.

Some of the descendants of Japheth, Ham's brother, which included the Greeks, were influenced by the descendants of Ham and had also been convinced to embraced the baal / mystery / mythology religion, offering the title of 'god' to whomever could provide reason to be recognized for that status. Those who had historically renowned ancestors that were Nephilim / giants, had undergone an apotheosis, being elevated to the rank of the divine. Swept into the apotheosis of the renowned ancestors were monarchs who also underwent the apotheosis to be classified as divine. The political and religious doctrine of the divine right of kings derived its beginning from the adoption of the idea that having historically renowned ancestors elevated a person to divine status, with the legitimate right to rule over others.

In contrast to the baal / mystery / mythology religion and the deification of powerful humans and those who considered themselves to be elite, the people of Israel viewed the deification of humans as anathema, an abhorrence, an abomination. This difference of views concerning how God or gods were to be defined, provided the first obstacle for the Israelite Menelaus in his goal of bringing Hellenization to the people of Israel and aligning himself more fully with the power structure of Antiochus IV Epiphanes. The second obstacle that Menelaus encountered was the fact that the Hellenistic culturalists were the wealthy elite who levied excessive taxes which resulted in the poor standard of living among the general population.

While the wealthy elite and ruling class of Jerusalem supported Menelaus and his connection with the Seleucid / Syrian empire Hellenization program, the majority of the masses of the people of Israel did not.

At this time there were two main groups in Jerusalem of thought. The Jewish Hellenists became the Proto Sadducees, who later became the Sadducees and embraced the pagan worship. The other group were called the Hasidim / 'the pious ones' / the Proto Pharisees who later became the Pharisees and Essenes. The Hasidim / Proto Pharisees held fast to the Jewish traditions, culture and religion. It was the Hasidim / Proto Pharisees that dedicatedly and heroically opposed the Seleucid / Syrian presence.

A minority of the people of Israel were employed by officials who frequented the centers of Greek culture and who used the Greek language, and many adopted Hellenistic dress and customs. Gradually, there was a sense among the minority that the old faith and morals were out of date.

But the majority of the people of Israel held onto their distrust of the new ways. As a result of the adherence to the Jewish religion, tradition, and culture, during this three year period of time, there was a ferocious underground campaign to push the Seleucid / Syrian / Syrian empire out of Israel. There were underground worship services and teaching taking place. The underground community seemed to be unsuccessful in effecting regime change and yet they provided the foundation for the future response that would mark the end of the reign of terror and the permanent decline of the Seleucid / Syrian empire. (Daniel 11:33-34)

167 BC: The Maccabean Revolt: It was this setting that caused Mattathias Maccabeus, a priest of the Jehoiarib family, and his five sons to resist the compulsory activity of Antiochus IV Epiphanes against the people of Israel. Matthias Maccabeus and his sons had already fled to the town of

Modein, seventeen miles northwest of Jerusalem. Antiochus IV Epiphanes sent out representatives to compulsorily force the practice of public pagan worship in the Hellenistic / Greek manner. The Seleucid / Syrian designated representatives were accompanied by a military presence as they took portable altars to the communities around Jerusalem and required the people to sacrifice a pig on the altar and then to eat the pork. Because Mattathias was a respected priest in the town of Modein, he was selected to lead the people in the sacrifice and consumption of the unclean sacrifice as an example for others. Mattathias was well respected and also about eighty years old. But Mattathias was so outraged that he refused. Mattathias replied loudly, 'I don't care if every Gentile in this empire has obeyed the king and yielded to the command to abandon the religion of his ancestors. My children, my relatives, and I will continue to keep the covenant that God made with our ancestors. With God's help we will never abandon his Law or disobey his commands. We will not obey the king's decree, and we will not change our way of worship in the least.' 1 Maccabees 2:19-22

When another Jewish man stepped forward to comply and offer the sacrifice, Mattathias, with inexplicable power, grabbed a sword, killed the one who stepped forward along with some others willing to make the sacrifice, killed the government official that required the act and also killed some of the soldiers. The rest of the soldiers retreated. This was the action that sparked the Maccabean Revolt. (Did the pig survive?)

Immediately, Mattathias Maccabeus, his five sons and their families retreated to the hills. They called all that wanted to join in the revolt to go into the wilderness from where they launched a guerilla type campaign against the Syrians / Seleucids. The Maccabees and their followers would defend themselves against Sabbath attacks.

During the reign of terror of Antiochus IV Epiphanes, the assault upon the Jewish religion, tradition, and culture caused the faithful of the people of Israel to examine their theology and their level of commitment to God Most High. While the full impact of Hellenization came to Jerusalem, there remained a group of people who possessed a deep heartfelt devotion to the Jewish promise of a messiah. The Maccabean Revolt began with people truly dedicated to the Jewish religion, tradition and culture, waiting for the arrival of the messiah. But the dedication dwindled quite quickly under the pressure of the constant threat of martyrdom.

Daniel 11:34-35 expressed it this way, 'When they fall, they will receive a little help, and many who are not sincere will join them. Some of the wise will stumble, so that they may be refined, purified and made spotless until the time of the end for it will still come at the appointed time.'

The 'little help' referenced the Maccabean Revolt. The Maccabean family experienced support only from the traditional / non Hellenophile parties. Those who later joined the Maccabean Revolt, joined because of the successes the Maccabean Revolt experienced, not out of deep faith or sincerity to the Jewish culture, tradition and religion. The dedication of those who supported the Maccabean Revolt faded with time and war weariness. But the result of the events surrounding Antiochus IV Epiphanes' abomination of desolation and the reign of terror, had a huge purifying effect upon the people of Israel which meant that when Jesus Christ would finally arrive and began his ministry one hundred eighty three years later, there was a deep, legitimate, heartfelt population of people who were actively looking for God Most High's messiah.

166 BC: When Mattathias Maccabeus died one year later, leadership fell to his middle of five sons, Judas Maccabeus. The family name was actually Hasmonean, but the family name was tagged Maccabeus because Maccabeus was the Syrian word for 'hammer.' During the 'reign of terror' thousands of people fled to the mountains for refuge.

It was a time when acts of boldness were provided by the truly faithful. Eleazar, who was ninety years old and a principal scribe, was brought before Antiochus IV Epiphanes and required to eat swine's flesh / pork meat. Eleazar refused to defile himself and break the law of God. So Antiochus IV Epiphanes offered the idea that Eleazar would be allowed to bring in clean food and pretend that it was unclean, eating the substitute as an example to the young people to entice them to eat the unclean food. Eleazar again refused. The soldiers beat him mercilessly until he died.

Hannah and her seven sons were also brought for the purpose of forcing them to eat the swine's flesh / pork meat. 2 Maccabees 7 was the record of the mother with seven sons, all of whom were tortured and died for their faith. One son had his tongue cut out, was scalped, had his hands and feet cut off, and was then thrown alive into boiling water while his mother and six brothers looked on. The soldiers tore the hair and skin from the next son before chopping off his hands and feet. This activity of dismembering the brothers continued with each brother and finally with the murder of their mother, each one giving testimony to their faith in the God and King of the universe, in the authorship of God as the creator of the universe, and in the resurrection into eternal life for those who obeyed God's laws.

Over the next few years, three of the five Maccabean brothers, Judas, Jonathan, and Simon led the Revolt and experienced campaigns where they were seriously outnumbered and yet they were victorious because of their expert tactics. By 164 BC they had retaken Jerusalem, cleansed the temple, and restored biblical worship.

The afternoon of October 30, 1207 BC, Beth Horon had been the site for Joshua pursuing the five kings of the Amorites through the pass where the Israelites received heavenly assistance with the sun and moon standing still and large stones were thrown down from heaven on their enemies (Joshua 10:10-15). In the Battle of Beth Horon of 166 BC, Judas Maccabeus defeated the Seleucid / Syrian general Seron (1 Maccabees 3:13-24). Five years later, at Beth Huron, Nicanor as he retreated from Jerusalem was defeated and slain (1 Maccabees 7:39, Josephus, *Antiquities of the Jews* 12.10.5). Later in 66 AD, the first victory for the people of Israel in the First Jewish Roman War would take place against the Syrian legate Cestius Gallus at Beth Huron.

164 BC: Kislev 25, 164 BC: The Maccabees captured portions of Jerusalem following the Battle of Beth Zur. The temple, while still held under the authority of the false high priest Menelaus, was able to be cleansed and rededicated. The annual feast of Hanukah / feast of dedication, honors the reconsecration of the temple in Jerusalem.

The legend was that while there was enough holy oil for one day for the menorah, the consecration service for the temple requires eight days. Miraculously, the one day's oil lasted for eight days. The feast of Hanukah / feast of dedication / feast of lights is celebrated with a menorah to commemorate the miracle of the holy oil and as a reminder of the dedication of those who took part in the Maccabean Revolt. In reality, the nine candles on a Hanukah menorah represented the eight days required for consecration and the ninth service candle. The terms of peace between the Seleucid / Syrian empire, the Maccabean family and their followers, required that the temple be restored to the worship of Yahweh / God Most High. All emblems of pagan worship were to be obliterated. A new burnt offering altar was to be erected with new, undefiled stones. According to the book of Maccabees and according to Josephus in *Antiquities of the Jews* 12.7.6, the temple was restored on the three year anniversary of the date that it was desecrated. Three years times three hundred sixty days per year according to the Israelite lunar calendar, yields approximately one thousand eighty days. When the final horn on the shaggy goat / beast of the earth will cause the abomination of desolation event during the era of the time of Jacob's Trouble, the temple will be closed for two thousand three hundred evening and morning sacrifices / one thousand one hundred fifty days (Daniel 8:14, 8:26).

There are many who claim that the three year period of time that the temple was desecrated during the reign of Antiochus IV Epiphanes fulfilled all of Daniel's prophecy assigned to the (first) abomination of desolation event, and that the biblical record just got the number of days for the desecration incorrect. With that altered and forced interpretation of the message of the biblical record, they go on to indicate that all of Daniel 11:1-12:12 was set within the context of one time period, and that the first abomination of desolation event led by Antiochus IV Epiphanes precluded any necessity for a future abomination of desolation event.

In contrast to this view, the biblical record gave a precise time period for the future abomination of desolation event during the era of the time of Jacob's Trouble, along with other markers that set the future abomination of desolation event as clearly scheduled for the era of the time of Jacob's Trouble.

The factors that distinguished the first abomination of desolation event by Antiochus IV Epiphanes from the future abomination of desolation event began with the description of the king who exalts himself and his unprecedented success to achieve all that he desires to accomplish (Daniel 11:29-12:12). Antiochus IV Epiphanes did have success. But Antiochus IV Epiphanes also experienced a large share of failure. **(Daniel 11:36)**

The king who exalts himself of Daniel 11:29-12:12 was defined as such by Daniel in contrast to the designations used earlier in Daniel 11:1-35 of the 'king of the north' and the 'king of the south.'

Next, the king who exalts himself will be successful until the time of wrath is completed (Daniel 11:36). According to the visions given to John the Revelator, the 'time of wrath' has been scheduled for the end of the era of the time of Jacob's Trouble when the seven bowls / seven last plagues will be poured out and the harvest of the earth will take place (Revelation 15, 16).

The 'one desired by women,' is the seed of the woman that was promised to Eve and Satan in the Garden of Eden / garden of God / paradise (Genesis 3:15). The promised and prophesied messiah was not desired by Satan nor by the first man in that moment. Something happened within Adam at the time that he ate the fruit of the tree of the knowledge of good and evil, that would change the dynamic between men and women, between women and the kingdom of Satan, Inc. /

kingdom of man, between God Most High and men, between men and the kingdom of Satan, Inc. / kingdom of man; for the next six thousand years. The two parts of the message to Satan of Genesis 3:15 were to a) put enmity between Satan's seed / Nephilim and rebellious humanity, and the woman's seed / promised and prophesied messiah; and b) put enmity between Satan and women, between the kingdom of Satan, Inc. / kingdom of man and women.

The future beast of the earth will be fully aligned with the kingdom of Satan, Inc. kingdom of man in order to be able to be fully connected to the power of the kingdom of Satan, Inc. / kingdom of man. If the red dragon / serpent / Satan, Inc. holds women in low regard, then the beast of the earth will also hold women in low regard, along with anyone that women would desire, i.e. the promised and prophesied messiah / seed of the woman. Antiochus IV Epiphanes had no understanding of the promised and prophesied messiah who would be coming after him, nor did he participate in any activity that indicated animosity against the promised and prophesied messiah who came over one hundred sixty years later.

The future king who exalts himself will also establish many rulers who greatly honor and acknowledge him. Antiochus IV Epiphanes did not share his ruling authority by making others rulers with him; not with his brother's infant son, not with his administrators, not with anyone else.

The list of discrepancies between Antiochus IV Epiphanes and the king who exalts himself of Daniel 11:36-12:12 continues.

164 – 160 BC: The Seleucids experienced civil war and regime change. After the first abomination of desolation event, the Maccabean Revolt successfully dented the power structure of the Seleucid / Syrian empire. From that point in history, the Seleucid / Syrian empire only declined.

Antiochus IV Epiphanes was distracted with trouble in the east to the extent that he did not return to Antioch. While attempting to loot the treasures in a temple in Elymais, Antiochus IV Epiphanes escaped, not like his father who was murdered in the same kind of activity. Later Antiochus IV Epiphanes fell ill and died in Media, not as a result of someone else's attack against him.

164 BC: The death of the Seleucid / Syrian king Antiochus IV Epiphanes was recorded in 2 Maccabees.

'About this time Antiochus was retreating in disorder from Persia, where he had entered the city of Persepolis and had attempted to rob a temple and take control of the city. The people took up arms and attacked Antiochus, forcing his army to retreat in disgrace. When he reached Ecbatana, he was told what had happened to the forces of Nicanor and Timothy. He became furious and decided to make the Jews pay for the

defeat he had suffered. So he ordered his chariot driver not to stop until they reached Jerusalem. With great arrogance he said, 'I will turn Jerusalem into a graveyard full of Jews."
'But he did not know that he was heading straight for God's judgment. In fact, as soon as he had said these words, the all-seeing Lord, the God of Israel, struck him down with an invisible but fatal blow. He was seized with sharp intestinal pains for which there was no relief — a fitting punishment for the man who had tortured others in so many terrible ways! But this in no way caused him to give up his pride. Instead, he became more arrogant than ever, and breathing out fiery threats against the Jews, he gave orders to drive even faster. As a result, he fell out of his chariot with such a thud that it made every bone in his body ache. His arrogant pride made him think he had the superhuman strength to make ocean waves obey him and to weigh high mountains on a pair of scales. But suddenly he fell flat on the ground and had to be carried off on a stretcher, a clear sign to everyone of God's power. Even the eyes of this godless man were crawling with worms and he lived in terrible pain and agony. The stink was so bad that his entire army was sickened, and no one was able to come close enough to carry him around. Yet only a short while before, he thought he could take hold of the stars.'
'Antiochus was deeply depressed and suffered constant pain because of the punishment that God had brought on him, so he finally came to his senses and gave up his arrogant pride. Then, when he could no longer endure his own stink, he said, 'It is right that all mortals should be subject to God and not think that they are his equal.' The time of the Lord's mercy had come to an end for Antiochus, but this worthless man made the Lord a promise: 'I once intended to level Jerusalem to the ground and make that holy city a graveyard full of Jews,' he said, 'but now I declare it a free city. I had planned to throw out the dead bodies of the Jews and their children for the wild animals and the birds to eat, for I did not consider them worth burying. But now I intend to grant them the same privileges as the citizens of Athens enjoy. I once looted the Temple and took its sacred utensils, but I will fill it with splendid gifts and with better utensils than before, and I will pay the cost of the sacrifices from my own resources. Besides all this, I will become a Jew myself and go wherever people live, telling them of God's power."
'Antiochus was in despair and could find no relief from his pain, because God was punishing him as he deserved, so he wrote the following letter to the Jews: 'King Antiochus to the Jews, my most distinguished subjects. Warm greetings and best wishes for your health and prosperity.

I hope that you and your families are in good health and that all goes well with you. My hope is in God, and I remember with a deep sense of joy the respect and kindness that you have shown me.'

'On my way home from Persia I fell violently ill, and so I thought it best to begin making plans for the general welfare of the people. I have not given up hopes of getting well; in fact, I am fully confident that I will recover. But I recall that my father used to appoint a successor whenever he went on a military campaign east of the Euphrates. He did this so that if something unexpected happened, or if some bad news came back, then his subjects would not be afraid, for they knew who had been left in command. Also, I know how the rulers along the frontiers of my kingdom are constantly on the lookout for any opportunity that may come along. That is why I have appointed my son Antiochus to succeed me as king. I have frequently entrusted him to your care and recommended him to you when I went on my regular visits to the provinces east of the Euphrates. (He is receiving a copy of the letter which follows.) Now I strongly urge each of you to keep in mind the good things that I have done for you, both individually and as a nation, and to continue in your good will toward me and my son. I am confident that he will treat you with fairness and kindness, just as I have always done."

'And so, this murderer, who had cursed God, suffered the same terrible agonies he had brought on others, and then died a miserable death in the mountains of a foreign land. One of his close friends, Philip, took his body home; but, because he was afraid of Antiochus' son, he went on to King Ptolemy Philometor of Egypt.' 2 Maccabees 9:1-29

More details concerning the battles and events of the Maccabean Revolt can be referenced with 1 and 2 Maccabees, the writings of Josephus and other historical documents.

But it was at this point in history that Daniel's narrative marked a change in focus from the events of the intertestamental period / four hundred years of silence (Daniel 11:1-35), to the focus of discussion on the 'king who will exalt himself' */ beast of the earth that will come in the* 'distant future' */ during the era of the time of Jacob's Trouble (Daniel 11:29-12:12).*

The historical events that took place after the first abomination of desolation event, that effected the nation of

Israel leading up to the incarnation of Jesus Christ, continued, but were not included in the vision that Daniel received and were not referenced in Daniel 11-12.

The following timeline of events has been included, for the purpose of continuity.

162 – 150 BC: Demetrius I Soter overthrew Antiochus Eupator, following the example of his uncle Antiochus IV Epiphanes. During the era of Demetrius I of the Seleucid / Syrian empire, the false high priest Menelaus was executed by the Seleucids / Syrians.

162 – 159 BC: Alcimus / Jacimus / Joachim was appointed to be the new high priest of Israel by the Seleucid / Syrian Demetrius I Soter. Alcimus supported the Seleucid / Syrian empire cause. The appointment of Alcimus as high priest was not in accordance to Mosaic Law. Alcimus was a descendant of Aaron but not in the priestly line. Alcimus' cruelties against the people of Israel caused the Maccabeans to drive him into exile in Syria where he remained until he returned to defeat and to kill Judah Maccabeus.

161 BC: Three generals had been commissioned by the chancellor Lysias with the destruction of Judea (1 Maccabees 3:34). The campaign that began in 166 BC initially left the Seleucids / Syrians defeated. Nicanor invited a thousand slave dealers to accompany him to buy the Jewish captives. But when Nicanor was defeated and humiliated, he was forced to escape 'like a fugitive slave' to Antioch. A different account from 1 Maccabees 7 recorded that the Maccabeans cut off Nicanor's head and right arm 'which he had extended arrogantly,' and declared an annual national holiday for the thirteenth of Adar. After their victory, the Maccabeans seized the money from the people who had come to buy them as slaves, collected the enemy's weapons, and looted the dead (2 Maccabees 8:21-36).

There were other historical accounts of the battles that took place during the era of the Maccabean Revolt including those recorded in the books of Maccabees.

161 – 152 BC: When Judas Maccabeus was killed in battle, Judas' youngest brother Jonathan assumed leadership of the rebels and continued the Maccabean Revolt.

160 BC: The Seleucids / Syrians retook control of all of Jerusalem after Judas Maccabeus was killed in the Battle of Elasa, marking the end of the Maccabean revolt.

160 BC: There were two accounts of the death of Alcimus / Jacimus / Joachim, the last Hellenizing high priest. One account told of Alcimus / Jacimus / Joachim dying of a stroke. Another account claimed that Alcimus died while he was pulling down the wall of

the temple that divided the court of the Gentiles from the court of the Israelites.

The high priest successor remains unknown but was thought to have founded the Essenes, a religious group of which John the Baptist was a member.

The death of the Seleucid / Syrian appointed Alcimus / Jacimus / Joachim also marked the end of Seleucid / Syrian military intervention.

152 – 145 BC: Alexander I Theopator Euergetes Balas assumed the Seleucid / Syrian throne when he defeated Demetrius Soter in 150 BC. Alexander I Theopator Euergetes Balas denied his humble origins and instead claimed to be the lost and discovered son of Antiochus IV Epiphanes and Laodice IV. Alexander I Theopator Euergetes Balas married Cleopatra Thea Eueteria, the daughter of Ptolemy VI and Cleopatra. Cleopatra Thea Eueteria was the wife of two more Seleucid / Syrian kings.

Alexander I Theopator Euergetes Balas appointed Jonathan Maccabeus as high priest in Jerusalem.

145 – 142 BC: Antiochus VI Dionysus, son of Alexander I Theopator Euergetes Balas and Cleopatra Thea Eueteria, was raised to the throne by Tryphon, his father's general.

Jonathan Maccabeus of Israel was named governor of Israel along with being high priest. In the history of Israel, high priests were never intended by God Most High to be the rulers of Israel. Israel experienced the leadership of prophets, judges, and kings who were not high priests. The appointment of Jonathan Maccabeus as both high priest and governor of Judea was an act that combined religious leadership and political leadership into one position.

Simon Maccabeus / Thassi, the second of the five brothers, was made military governor of the Palestinian littoral.

143 BC: Jonathan Maccabeus was arrested by Tryphon.

143 / 142 – 135 / 134 BC: The Maccabean Revolt was successful enough to cause the people of Israel to finally receive a pseudo independence under the leadership of the Hasmonaean dynasty that began with Simon Maccabeus / Thassi, son of the original Matthias Maccabeus who began the Maccabean Revolt. The independence of the people of Israel lasted for almost seventy years. Simon Maccabeus became the high priest and ethnarch / national leader, the founder of the Hasmonean Dynasty.

142 BC: Jonathan Maccabeus was executed in prison.

The Hasmoneans / Maccabeus / Hyrcanus family were a ruling dynasty that ruled Judea semi-autonomously under the Seleucid / Syrian empire from around 140 – 116 BC.

140 BC: Simon Maccabeus' titles as high priest and governor were confirmed as hereditary by the Seleucid / Syrian empire.

Note that the rulers of the nation of Israel were to come from the tribe of Judah as descendants of David, and the priests from the tribe of Levi, specifically as descendants of Aaron. To hold the position of both priest and ruler was a violation of Israelite law, with the allowable exception of the promised and prophesied messiah who through his mother Mary, was a descendant of both David (Judah) and Aaron (Levi).

135 / 134 BC: Simon Maccabeus and two of his sons, were assassinated at a banquet provided by his son-in-law Ptolemy, son of Abubus. Ptolemy then attempted to kill Simon Maccabeus' son John Hyrcanus I, but failed.

135 / 134 – 104 BC: John Hyrcanus I, the oldest son of Simon Maccabeus, was not present at the banquet at which his father and his two brothers were murdered. John Hyrcanus I then inherited his father's former offices of high priest and ethnarch / national leader, but was not recognized as king. After the Pharisees had offended John, John exchanged the Hasmonean name for Hyrcanus which was Greek, as an acceptance of the Hellenistic culture of the Seleucids / Syrians. Transitioning from originally being a Pharisee to becoming a Sadducee, John Hyrcanus I experienced opposition from the Pharisees. When the Seleucid / Syrian king Antiochus VII Sidetes recaptured Jerusalem, John Hyrcanus I opened King David's sepulcher and removed three thousand talents which he paid as tribute to spare the city and to remain governor. John Hyrcanus I also conquered Transjordan and Idumaea and destroyed the Samaritan temple on Mount Gerizim, which bolstered his popularity politically among the Sadducees ('righteous') so that John Hyrcanus I declared himself as king. The orthodox Pharisees ('separatists') recognized no king unless he was of the lineage of King David.

John Hyrcanus I also moved against the Edomites / Idumaeans, and forced them to either leave the country or be circumcised and become Jewish. The family of the future Herod the Great was one of the families that accepted the forced imposition of Judaism. The Hasmonaeans who first championed freedom against religious persecution, became the dynasty that imposed religion upon others. The forced conversion of the Edomites / Idumaeans also acted as a welding together of the houses of Esau / Edomites / Idumaeans and Jacob / Israelites.

104 – 103 BC: Aristobulus I, first son of John Hyrcanus I became high priest and king.

It was intended that upon the death of John Hyrcanus I, that his wife was to succeed him as civil ruler and his son Aristobulus I as high priest. But Aristobulus I starved his mother to death, imprisoned three of his brothers and took for himself the joint title of ruler and high priest. Aristobulus I's brother Antigonus assisted him in governing until Antigonus fell into disfavor and was assassinated. When Aristobulus I died, his widow Salome Alexandra released his brother Alexander Jannaeus and married him, making Alexander Jannaeus the ruler and high priest.

103 – 76 BC: Alexander Jannaeus, the second son of John Hyrcanus I, became ruler and high priest, adding the title of king and conqueror. Alexander Jannaeus then killed his other captive brother.

Alexander Jannaeus appeased the Pharisees by giving them important offices in the government.

But Alexander Jannaeus could not appease all the people of Israel. Once when he went to the altar to offer sacrifice as high priest, the people pelted him with citrons (a lemonlike citrus fruit). The enraged Alexander Jannaeus responded with having more than six thousand killed.

When civil war broke out, the people of Israel even allied themselves with the Seleucids / Syrians against Alexander Jannaeus, because of his barbarity in the persecution of the Pharisees.

During the reign of Alexander Jannaeus, the borders of Judea were expanded to approximately where they were at the height of the kingdom of David and Solomon.

76 – 67 BC: When Alexander Jannaeus died, his widow, Salome Alexandra, who had sided with the Pharisees, established herself as reigning queen of Israel.

John Hyrcanus II, the oldest son of Alexander Jannaeus and grandson of John Hyrcanus I, was established as high priest by his mother Salome Alexandra.

Salome Alexandra was a friend of the Pharisees.

67 – 63 BC: Aristobulus II became king and high priest. When Salome Alexandra died, she had named John Hyrcanus II to be her successor to the kingship as well as holding the position of high priest. But her younger son Aristobulus II opposed his brother and three months later rose in rebellion, meeting his brother in battle near Jericho. Aristobulus II compelled John Hyrcanus II to surrender and renounce the throne and office of high priest. Aristobulus II was a friend of the Sadducees.

The strife between the two brothers resulted in Roman intervention that ended the Hasmonaean rule in 63 BC.

63 BC: Pompey of Rome conquered Israel during the required feast of the Day of Atonement / Yom Kippur, putting all of Judea under control of the Caesars. About twelve thousand people of Israel including many priests, were killed on the temple compound. Aristobulus II was taken prisoner by Pompey after the fall of Jerusalem. Judea became a Roman province. The people of Israel lost their independence.

Roman rule brought law and government which was sometimes brutally enforced. Roman rule brought peace, the Pax Romana that characterized the Roman empire. Roman rule brought stable government and systems. The Romans had systems of collecting taxes, governmental processes, utilization of technology, etc.

Roman rule also brought slavery with approximately five out of every seven people as slaves. One hundred thirty two years later, after the Roman General Titus vanquished the people of Israel in 70 AD, ninety thousand people of Israel were sold into bondage.

Rome also brought roads, a kind of interstate system that they used for connecting the Roman empire together, that would be used to spread the message of the risen Jesus Christ into the world.

Roman rule brought new and higher taxes. The excessive taxation to pay for the extravagances of Antony and Cleopatra VII assisted in awakening in the people of Israel, a deep hatred against Rome.

During the Roman era, the Herodians, the Zealots, and the Essenes emerged with each group pursuing their own mission. The Pharisees and Sadducees were firmly established. By the time that the incarnate Jesus arrived, there would also be the Scribes and the Publicans.

Because a large percentage of the people of Israel remained living outside of the land of Israel as a result of the Assyrian – Babylonian exile of 772 BC and 586 BC, the Roman roads that connected the Roman empire also connected the people of Israel who had already been spread out and living throughout the Roman empire.

As the disciples of Jesus Christ would be dispersed into the world, they would first go to the synagogues of communities that had been established by the people of Israel that had not returned to the land of Israel. And then they would go to the Gentiles with their message.

63 – 40 BC: John Hyrcanus II was reinstated as high priest but without the royal title.

57 – 55 BC: The proconsul of Syria, Aulus Gabinius, split the former Hasmonean Kingdom into five districts of legal and religious councils known as the Sanhedrin / Synhedrion system based in Jerusalem. The first ruling body for the people of Israel were the seventy elders that accompanied Moses on the mountain as the people of Israel left Egypt (1446 BC). With the division of the Hasmonean Kingdom into five districts, the Sanhedrin system was expanded to consist of the Great Sanhedrin of seventy one judges and the lesser Sanhedrin which appointed a court of twenty three judges to chosen cities. The Great Sanhedrin would take appeals from the cases decided by the

lesser courts. After the destruction of the second temple in 70 AD, the Great Sanhedrin moved to Galilee.

Around 30 AD, the Sanhedrin lost its authority to impose capital punishment. This meant that the Sanhedrin needed to request capital punishment including crucifixion, to be administered by the Roman governor.

The last universally binding decision of the Great Sanhedrin / Beit HaMidrash ('house of learning) appeared in 358 AD when the Hebrew calendar was abandoned. The Great Sanhedrin was finally disbanded in 425 AD under continual persecution by the Eastern Roman empire. In October 2004, a group of rabbis representing varied Orthodox communities in Israel claimed to have reestablished the Sanhedrin in Tiberias, where the original Sanhedrin was disbanded.

45 – 43 BC: Antipater the Idumean was appointed Procurator of Judea by Julius Caesar. Antipater the Idumaean saved Malichus' life twice from two different rulers. (Malichus was ruler of Nabatea / region south of Israel, and possible cousin of Herod the Great.) Yet Malichus despised Antipater and plotted to have Antipater the Idumaean poisoned. After several failed attempts, the deed was accomplished by a bribed cup bearer of John Hyrcanus II.

43 BC: Antipater the Idumaean was succeeded by his sons Phasael and Herod. (Herod would later become the king Herod the Great that would rule the nation of Israel on behalf of Rome.)

40 BC: The Roman interest in Judea, cared for by the Idumeans Phasael and Herod, was challenged by the Parthians. Antipater the Idumaean's son Herod lost in his conquest for Jerusalem to the Parthians. As a result of the defeat by the Parthians, Antipater the Idumaean's son Phasael committed suicide. Herod fled quickly from Masada to Rome where he was surprisingly nominated to be the new king of Judea / Israel through the recommendation of Mark Antony. Rome began the process of supplying Herod with an army.

40 – 37 BC: Antigonus II Mattathias was the puppet king installed by the Parthians who had invaded Syria in 40 BC. Antigonus II Mattathias promised the Parthians large sums of gold and five hundred female slaves.

John Hyrcanus II's ears were mutilated by Antigonus II Mattathias who bit them. The bodily mutilation of John Hyrcanus II rendered him unfit for the office of high priest, and he was exiled. Antigonus II Mattathias was also proclaimed high priest.

Antigonus II Mattathias / Antigonus the Hasmonean, youngest son of Aristobulus II, was the last Hasmonean king of Israel.

39 – 37 AD: Herod the son of Antipater the Idumean returned from Rome and opened a campaign against Antigonus II Mattathias laying siege to Jerusalem.

In 38 BC, Herod obtained control of the province of Galilee and eventually all of Judea as far as Jerusalem.

37 BC: King Herod gave Antigonus II Mattathias to the Romans for execution after Antigonus II Mattathias led a three year fierce campaign in Israelite independence against the Romans.

37 – 4 BC: The Hasmonaean dynasty ended when with the death of Antigonus II Mattathias who had been taken to Antioch and was either crucified and / or beheaded by Mark Antony.

After Herod conquered the land of Israel, Herod was able to establish his reign as Herod the Great.

Herod the Great was a descendant of Esau / an Edomite / an Idumean. But the family of Herod the Great had converted to Judaism in order to be able to occupy positions in Judea.

To increase his claim upon the throne, Herod the Great married Mariamne I, son of Alexander of the Hasmonean family, the older brother of Antigonus and granddaughter of Aristobulus II. Herod the Great also married Mariamne II who was the daughter of high priest Simon. Herod the Great also had nine other wives.

Herod the Great embarked on massive building within Judea. Herod the Great built the Antonia Fortress named after Mark Anthony on the site of the Hasmonean Baris located north of the temple mount.

In 19 BC, Herod the Great expanded the temple mount, and began to 'rebuild' the temple. Actually, Herod the Great built a new and great temple over the existing 'second' temple of Zerubbabel and then dismantled the existing temple. The daily evening and morning sacrifices continued uninterrupted.

30 BC: John Hyrcanus II, the former high priest, was executed.

27 BC – 14 AD: Octavian Caesar Augustus was emperor of Rome.

4 BC: Birth of Jesus of Nazareth.

4 BC – 6 AD: Archelaus was ethnarch / national leader of Judaea and Samaria.

14 – 37 AD: Tiberius was emperor of Rome.

26 – 36 AD: Pontius Pilate was prefect of Judea.

30 AD: Crucifixion of Jesus Christ.

66 – 70 AD: First Jewish Roman War ended with the capture of Jerusalem and the destruction of the temple by Roman general Titus. Titus was the oldest son of Vespasian. Vespasian began the First Jewish Roman War as a general, but during the First Jewish Roman War, Vespasian became emperor of Rome.

70 AD: Herod's 'second temple' was destroyed on the ninth of Av, 70 AD. The majority of the world's population of the people of Israel were killed.

73 / 74 AD: Fall of Masada, the last holdout of the people of Israel, as the Romans captured the fortification.

130 AD: Emperor Hadrian decided to rebuild Jerusalem as a city dedicated to Jupiter and renamed it Aelia Capitolina. Hadrian

forbid the people of Israel and Christians to enter Jerusalem. Believing circumcision to be mutilation, Hadrian abolished circumcision.

132 – 136 AD: Third Jewish Roman War / Third Jewish Revolt / Bar Kokhba (son of a star) revolt against Rome led by Simeon Bar Kosiba / Bar Kokhba was unsuccessful and again the majority of the world's population of the people of Israel were killed. But some of the people of Israel have remained in the land of Israel throughout time from 1406 BC to the present.

Why was John the Baptist a prophet, and not a priest in the temple like his father Zechariah?

John the Baptist's father, Zechariah, was a priest. Only a priest of the tribe of Levi would have been authorized to offer incense on the altar of incense. Zechariah and his wife Elizabeth were both descendants of Aaron. (Luke 1:5-10)

The promise made to Zechariah and Elizabeth was that their promised child John would be great in the sight of the Lord, and that he would bring back many of the people of Israel to the Lord their God. He would go on before the Lord, in the spirit and power of Elijah. He would make the people of Israel ready and prepared for the Lord. (Luke 1:15-17)

So the question arises, 'Why was John the Baptist a prophet and not a priest like his father Zechariah?'

One possible explanation was that temple system of selecting high priests that had existed since 1446 BC, was adulterated by the Seleucid and Roman empires. The Seleucid empire was an offshoot of the Greek empire.

Antiochus IV Epiphanes of the Seleucid empire, had already greatly distorted the priesthood in the nation of Israel, through his appointment of priests through bribery, which laid the foundation for the first abomination of desolation event (167 BC).

By the time of John the Baptist's birth, the priests were selected and appointed by the Roman empire's appointed king over Israel.

When the Romans found the high priest Ananias to be difficult to work with, the procurator Valerius Gratus deposed Ananias as high priest in 15 AD.

But Ananias did not go away quietly. For the next several decades, Ananias engineered the Roman appointments for high priest.

Ananias ben Seth / Ananias / Ananus / Annas (fl. 6 to 15 AD) was the father-in-law of Caiaphas. Ananias also had five sons who eventually served as high priests:
- Eleazar ben Ananus (fl. 16-17 AD)
- (son-in-law of Ananias) Caiaphas / Joseph ben Caiaphas, who married the daughter of Annas (John 18:13), (fl. 18 to 36/37 AD),
- Jonathan ben Ananus (fl. spring 37 AD),
- Theophilus ben Ananus (fl. 37-41 AD),
- Matthias ben Ananus (fl. 43 AD)
- Ananus ben Ananus (fl. 63 AD).

High priests were installed for life. For the Roman government to depose Ananias was religiously illegal. And according to Jewish law of the temple system, to have two high priests serving at the same time, was illegal. Consequently, because Ananias remained alive while his sons and his son-in-law politically held the office of high priest, Ananias continued to be consulted by the people of Israel as a high priest.

Caiaphas was more easily manipulated by the Roman government, and therefore the Jewish religious leaders were more easily corruptible.

The high priests at the time of John the Baptist's beheading and Jesus Christ's crucifixion (c. 30 AD), were Ananias and Caiaphas (Matthew 26:3, 26:57, Luke 3:2, John 11:49, 18:13-14, 18:24, 18:28). This duo were also high priests when Peter and John were charged with healing a crippled beggar (Acts 4:6).

There was also archaeological that denounced the level of corruption attributed to the temple system and the men who occupied the office of high priest. But Jesus Christ himself continually referenced the corruption of the temple system that existed during his earthly ministry. So, it is *possible that one reason for John the Baptist not following his father as a priest, was the corruption that existed among the Jewish religious leaders at that time.*

Jesus celebrated the feast of dedication / Hanukah

The feast of dedication / Hanukah is the annual celebration of remembrance of the reconsecration of the temple after the second temple built by Zerubbabel, but not yet upgraded by Herod the Great, experienced the first abomination of desolation by the king of the Seleucid / Syrian empire, Antiochus IV Epiphanes, in 167 BC.

The rededication of the temple took place three years / one thousand eighty days after the first abomination of desolation event desecrated the temple, on the twenty fifth of the month of Kislev, 164 BC. The word 'Hanukah' actually means 'dedication.' 'Dedication' summed up the entire account of the history of the feast. The feast of dedication / Hanukah was centered around the temple, its desecration, and rededication.

Jesus celebrated the feast of dedication / Hanukah (John 10:22-23).

Then came the Festival of Dedication at Jerusalem. It was winter, and Jesus was in the temple courts walking in Solomon's Colonnade. The Jews who were there gathered around him, saying, 'How long will you keep us in suspense? If you are the Messiah, tell us plainly.'

Jesus answered, 'I did tell you, but you do not believe. The works I do in my Father's name testify about me, but you do not believe because you are not my sheep. My sheep listen to my voice; I know them, and they follow me. I give them eternal life, and they shall never perish; no one will snatch them out of my hand. My Father, who has given them to me, is greater than all; no one can snatch them out of my Father's hand. I and the Father are united.'

Again his Jewish opponents picked up stones to stone him, but Jesus said to them, 'I have shown you many good works from the Father. For which of these do you stone me?'

'We are not stoning you for any good work,' they replied, 'but for blasphemy, because you, a mere man, claim to be God.' John 10:22-33

... And in that place, many believed in Jesus. John 10:42

Based on how and where John recorded this dialogue, it probably took place during the last year of

Jesus' ministry, approximately six months prior to his crucifixion, around the twenty fifth day of the month of Kislev.

    The audience for this interchange were well schooled in the first abomination of desolation event of 167 BC and the Maccabean Revolt that transpired as a result. The king of the Seleucid / Syrian empire, Antiochus IV Epiphanes had used the temple in Jerusalem to make his declaration that he was divine / god. According to the popular ideas of Judaism at the time, it would have been appropriate for anyone claiming to be the promised and prophesied messiah to have stood up during the feast of dedication / Hanukah and take advantage of the historical date and setting to declare himself as God. So, the disciples asked Jesus if Jesus would like to make the same kind of claim in the temple concerning his own divinity, that previously Antiochus IV Epiphanes made. In the minds of the plan of the people of Israel, and according to the message of the prophets, the promised and prophesied messiah will declare himself to be messiah in the temple.

    Note that Jesus' answer to their request to publicly and officially declare himself as messiah, took a totally different direction than what the inquisitors had expected. Jesus referred to his daily work as evidence of his messiahship, work that could only be accomplished through the power of God Most High's support. Jesus' claim was that he did not need to declare himself to be messiah on a specific date and time and in a specific location in order to actually be the promised and prophesied messiah. Jesus viewed messiahship as something intrinsic within him, instead of a position or office to be bestowed upon him like a coronation. Jesus Christ was, is and always will be messiah. Others who claim to be messiah and must clothe themselves with the title and position, can only be imposters. Messiahship is not what one wears, or becomes, or a position that one fills. Messiahship is what one is, inherently, within one's being, from the beginning, through the present, and onto the future. Jesus Christ was, is and is to come.

The one who holds the office does not define messiahship. Messiahship defines the one who is messiah who holds the office.

Jesus Christ's claim was that God Most High's messiah was sent for sheep. Only sheep will recognize authentic messiah. Those who are not sheep will not recognize authentic messiah.

Also note the eternal nature of the relationship of God the Father and of Jesus with the 'sheep' / with those who recognize the authentic messiah. The sheep cannot be snatched out of God the Father's hand and the sheep cannot be snatched out of Jesus Christ's hand. This statement recognized that there will always be those who will seek to snatch the sheep away from God, in a similar manner to the forcible nature of Antiochus IV Epiphanes who used coercion against the people of Israel in the pursuit of having them adopt and worship the Greek / baal / mystery / mythology religion gods.

If Jesus had truly been a blasphemous messiah, then Jesus would have used the opportunity during the feast of dedication / Hanukah to exhibit his force and his power, to take on his divine position, to offer signs and wonders that would leave the audience awestruck. When Jesus Christ did not act in an ostentatious manner, he did not meet their expectations, and he was ironically labeled a blasphemer / a liar about the issue of his divinity.

During the future abomination of desolation, the little horn / eleventh king / final horn on the shaggy goat / prince who is to come / king that will exalt himself / beast of the earth / final world ruler will not pass up the opportunity to make himself known as the one who is worthy to fill the position of messiah. The little horn / eleventh king / final horn on the shaggy goat / prince who is to come / king that will exalt himself / beast of the earth / final world ruler will declare himself in the temple as the authentic God Most High. Because there will be no other witness to announce him, he must declare himself to be messiah and higher than God Most High, in order to possess the position.

In contrast, Jesus Christ has always truly held the position and needs not make a declaration in order to actually be divine and sovereign.

The little horn / eleventh king / final horn on the shaggy goat / prince who is to come / king that will exalt himself / beast of the earth / final world ruler will boldly 'prove' his divinity through his performance of signs and wonders, and magic that will be used to make a bold declaration. It will be essential that his show go well so that people will believe and follow him.

In contrast, Jesus Christ attempted to keep his divinity discreet as a reflection of the quiet and absolute character of the working of God.

The works of Jesus Christ were about making God Most High's love the focal point. Jesus Christ was the messenger of God Most High's love.

The little horn / eleventh king / final horn on the shaggy goat / prince who is to come / king that will exalt himself / beast of the earth / final world ruler will be about making himself the focal point. The beast of the earth will 'be' the message.

Various views for the interpretation of the 'second abomination of desolation' event

Daniel documented two abomination of desolation events. The first to be accomplished by the king of the north (Daniel 11:29-35). The second to be accomplished by the king that will exalt himself, in the distant future (Daniel 12:11-12). Daniel also documented that the future abomination of desolation event will mark the time clock for the finale for the era of the time of Jacob's Trouble, before the kingdom of heaven will be fully established on earth.

John the Revelator documented that the future abomination of desolation would be accomplished by the beast of the earth (Revelation 13:11-18).

Jesus Christ taught the future abomination of desolation event will take place in preparation for his return to fully establish the kingdom of heaven on earth (Matthew 24:15-21, Mark 13:14-19).

There are five main interpretative views for describing the fulfillment concerning the 'second abomination of desolation.' They are the inspirational / spiritual interpretation, the idealist interpretation, the preterist interpretation, the historicist interpretation, and the futurist interpretation.

Inspirational / spiritual / allegorical interpretation

The inspirational / spiritual / allegorical approach to the prophecies concerning the era of the time of Jacob's Trouble was introduced by the ancient church father Origen (185 - 254 AD) and made prominent by Augustine (354 - 420 AD).

The inspirational / spiritual interpretation assessed the biblical references to the 'second abomination of desolation' event as references with an allegorical or inspirational message that was intended to only edify the human spirit. Instead of the biblical record being viewed as having authenticity as a historical document that relates to humanity the activity of God Most High, the inspirational / spiritual interpretation views the Bible as a historical mythological novel epic that tells a nice story and should be considered in the same category as other ancient classical works.

With the inspirational / spiritual interpretation, there will not be another abomination of desolation, and even if there were, it would be inconsequential for human history.

Idealist interpretation

The idealist interpretation holds an amillennial view, meaning that there is no literal thousand years in which Jesus Christ rules on earth. Without an actual millennial reign of Jesus Christ, the need for an abomination of desolation event becomes superfluous because the idealist interpretation presents the kingdom of heaven not coming to earth and therefore there is no need for kingdom change and no need for the beast of the earth to desolate the temple by declaring himself as a challenger to the divinity and sovereignty of messiah / the Lamb / Jesus Christ.

Idealists view the biblical message as offering only a description of the timeless struggle between the forces of good and evil which will continue indefinitely until the 'end of time.' But idealists don't have a definitive point in time when the end of time will arrive.

Idealists present the biblical message as a theological poem that presented the ageless struggle between the kingdom of light and the kingdom of darkness. The purpose of the biblical prose became for idealists, a philosophy of history where Christian forces are continuously meeting, and with their own power, conquering the demonic forces of evil.

The idealist position became a grab bag that has collected a variety of ideas that deny the return of messiah / the Lamb / Jesus Christ to fully establish the kingdom of heaven on earth. Without a true connection to biblical prophecy, the idealist position has allowed commentators to bring their own ideas and meanings for the interpretation of the symbols and visions contained in the biblical record. But they remain ideas, not true to the eschatological message documented in the biblical record.

Preterist interpretation

Preter, which means 'past,' was derived from Latin. Church historians traced the roots of preterism to Jesuit priest Luis de Alcazar (1554 - 1613 AD) who wrote the preterist exposition of prophecy published in 1614, as an address to the accusations of Martin Luther that the papacy represented the beast of the sea / false prophet / beast of the Abyss / eighth king beast within the antichrist system. However, some preterists contended that preterist teachings were found in the writings of the early church as early as the fourth century AD.

The preterist view had almost passed from the scene until recently when it received new impetus from the leaders of several denominations that have embraced a philosophy of the devaluation of the authority of scripture and use preterist interpretations for denying the events of the era of the time of Jacob's Trouble and the second coming of Jesus Christ to fully establish the kingdom of heaven on earth.

The preterist interpretation viewed the 'second abomination of desolation' event as having been completely fulfilled soon after the time of the incarnation of Jesus Christ; either before the fall of Jerusalem and the destruction of the temple in 70 AD, or at the time of the Bar Kokhba Revolt that ended in 136 AD when Hadrian built his temple on the temple mount.

In the preterist interpretation, all the biblical prophecy that was ever going to be fulfilled was fulfilled right after the life of Jesus Christ and there will be no future abomination of desolation event. In the preterist interpretation, the millennial reign / Thousand Years Reign of Jesus Christ began when Jesus Christ ascended into heaven and has been established in heaven without any scheduled future interruption. The world will continue as it currently operates now, with the church becoming more influential over time and eventually able to produce a more moral world. It will be the work of the church as an institution that will bring the principles and benefits of the kingdom of heaven to earth. Only after the culture of the kingdom of heaven has been established on earth will the world be such that Jesus Christ will find the culture on earth irresistible.

In support of the preterist interpretation, preterists view the message of Jesus Christ to the seven churches recorded in Revelation 2-3 as a description of the cultural condition of the churches prior to the First Jewish Roman War of 66 - 73 AD. The remaining chapters of John the Revelator's Revelation, along with Jesus' Olivet Discourse are interpreted as representing the fall of Jerusalem to the Romans.

The problem with this interpretation is that the events described in Jesus' Olivet Discourse and in the book of Revelation have a number of points where they differ from the events of the First Jewish Roman War of 66 - 73 AD.

Preterists also claim that John the Revelator wrote the book of Revelation during the time of the First Jewish Roman War of 66 - 73 AD as an encouragement to the followers of Jesus Christ to persevere under the persecution of the Roman empire. But there is more critical evidence that places the date of the writing of the book of Revelation around 85 to 90 AD. John the Revelator wrote that he had received the visions while he was imprisoned on the island of Patmos where he had been imprisoned by the Emperor Domitian, long after 70 AD. Domitian died in 96 AD. After the death of Domitian, John was allowed to return from exile and relocate to Ephesus.

Another example of issues with the preterist view is found in the preterist interpretation of the event where, Jesus Christ described his future return to Jerusalem and stated, 'As lightning that comes from the east is visible even in the west, so will be the coming of the Son of Man' (Matthew 24:27). Preterists interpret Jesus' statement as a reference to the Roman army's advance on Jerusalem. But the actual Roman army's advance upon Jerusalem was from west to east and their assault was a multiple year siege, not a quick lightning strike.

Preterists also cite the translation found in the introduction to the book of Revelation where Jesus Christ states that 'the things described must shortly take place,' and interpret this as meaning that the events of the book of Revelation must take place within a short time from John's writing. But a better translation of the Greek term 'en tachei' / εν ταχει / 'in quickness,' would be to interpret the phrase as meaning to take place quickly or suddenly, which indicates a rapidity of execution once the era of time has been initiated. The idea is not that the events would occur soon after the writing, but that when the events do begin, the described events will transpire in rapid succession, not spread out over hundreds of years like the time settings of many of the other prophecies of the Old Testament. In the other seven times that a similar word 'tachys' was used, it was translated as 'quickly.' The word tachycardia (racing heart) and tachometer (device indicating speed of rotation) originated from this Greek word meaning 'rapid.'

Concerning the 'second coming of Jesus Christ,' the future arrival of Jesus Christ to battle the enemies of the kingdom of heaven, and Jesus Christ's full establishment of the kingdom of heaven on earth, preterists will interpret scriptures such as Revelation 2:5 where Jesus Christ's message to the Ephesian church was the promise to '<u>come</u>' and remove their lampstand if they did not return to their love of God Most High, as the type of return or 'second coming' that could be expected of Jesus Christ. Preterists conclude that because the Ephesus church no longer exists, that Jesus Christ indeed covertly came and removed their lampstand. Then they go on to conclude that this is the type of secret coming that Jesus Christ described when he referred to his coming again to fully establish the kingdom of heaven on earth. The type of coming that preterists expect to take place is more idealized, allegorized, and spiritualized, than it is physical, literal, and real.

Preterists also use other examples as well to support defining Jesus Christ's 'second coming' as merely an idealized, allegorical, or spiritualized return. One example from the biblical record cited is when the preincarnate Jesus met with Abram in order to announce the birth of Isaac. During the visit, the preincarnate Jesus gave Abram and Sarai the Holy Spirit, changing their names to Abraham and Sarah. The additional 'h' in the Hebrew language is related to the presence of the Holy Spirit. Acts 2 recorded that after Jesus Christ's death, resurrection, and ascension, the Holy Spirit was made available to every person who believes that Jesus is the promised and prophesied messiah / Christ. Preterists sometimes use the temporary visit of the preincarnate Jesus with Abraham and Sarah as a template for the 'second coming' of Jesus Christ, and place that visit to have taken place soon after his ascension into heaven. Jesus Christ was supposed to have come for a visit, not to reign, and the visit was temporary, not for the purpose of dwelling with humanity.

Preterism also entertains the doctrine of Replacement Theology. The doctrine of Replacement

Theology advocates the idea that God Most High discontinued the covenant relationship with the people of Israel when they rejected Jesus as the promised and prophesied messiah and then crucified him. In Replacement Theology, that was the moment when God Most High transferred the conditions and promises of the covenant that were made to Abraham, Isaac, Jacob, Moses, and their descendants, to the church which became the 'New Israel.' If this were true, it would mean that God Most High cannot be fully trusted to fulfill any of the promises and covenants that God Most High has made to anyone, which would actually nullify the message of the biblical record.

Also held within the preterist view is the idea that because the biblical record ended almost two thousand years ago with the writings of the apostles of Jesus Christ, that God Most High has also finished working on earth, and that there is nothing more to write about. Therefore, there would be no purpose for Jesus Christ to even complete a future 'second coming.'

Preterists view the full establishment of the kingdom of heaven as having already taken place with Jesus Christ's first coming, Jesus Christ's incarnation. Evidence used by preterists is Jesus' statement made while he was on the cross as he was dying, 'It is finished.' This statement can be interpreted in many ways. For those who believe that all of scripture must be fulfilled and that there are many complex layers to the events that must take place to fulfill the will of a complex God, the statement 'It is finished,' means that the work of the cross was finished, completing the mission for messiah / the Lamb / Jesus Christ's earthly ministry; with more work to come later.

In the Garden of Eden / garden of God / paradise, in the presence of the first man and first woman as witnesses, God Most High specified that there would be enmity between Satan's seed and the seed of the woman / the promised and prophesied messiah that would come from the virgin. The serpent would strike messiah's heel, but messiah would crush the head of the serpent. The process of crucifixion severely bruises the heels of the victims.

When the first man and first woman ate the fruit from the tree of the knowledge of good and evil, they traded away their dominion over the earth. With the shedding of the blood of the perfect sacrifice Jesus Christ, the transaction was made to regain dominion of the earth for humanity. Jesus marked the occasion with the declaration, 'It is finished.' For the past two thousand years we have waited for Jesus Christ to return in order to claim what has already been paid for.

But preterists interpret Jesus' statement on the cross, 'It is finished,' to be a statement that claimed that all that God Most High had intended to fulfill of the prophecies of the Old Testament have been finished. According to the preterists' view, from the point of Jesus' crucifixion, God Most High's plan changed and God decided to ignore or neglect the rest of the unfulfilled prophecies. God Most High decided to throw in the towel in defeat and stopped working the moment that Jesus uttered this declaration.

Preterists also do not recognize Jesus' imperative that every dot and tittle of God Most High's word must be fulfilled. Preterists do not recognize the inspiration of the Holy Spirit, the Spirit of truth as a force behind what the authors of the biblical record have chronicled.

But truth is truth. To fulfill only a portion of the truth is not actual truth. The Holy Spirit can only present truth. The truth is that the prophecies of the biblical record are places where God Most High has gone on the record in telling us what and how and when God Most High will act. If God Most High does not act in accordance with the biblical record, then that would constitute ... a lie. Once the act of lying has been established, then everything that the liar has stated must be questioned, especially if the Holy Spirit of truth, who is one of the persons of the office of God Most High, is determined to be the liar.

But the Holy Spirit is actually the Spirit of truth with no lie found in him.

Interpreting the biblical record with the standard that only portions of the biblical record are accurate is a very dangerous practice. The standard of partiality /

demythologizing / decentralizing of scripture, and the individual's peeling back the layers of the onion to discover what is truth for the individual, can only result in guesswork as to which portions of the biblical record God Most High will choose to ignore. Biblical study that is founded on decentralizing / demythologizing scripture results in Swiss cheese theology, theology with a myriad of large holes. It is a theology that cannot hold up to the hard questions of life. It is a theology that results in a God Most High whose character must be able to be constantly changing and is not stable enough to have a plan, a purpose, or the persistence to be able to provide redemption, reclamation and regeneration.

Ultimately, the preterist position is that all of scripture that God Most High intended to fulfill has been fulfilled. What has remained unfulfilled, God Most High no longer intends to address. While Jesus Christ's revelation to John envisioned nothing less than the complete overthrow of the kingdom of Satan, Inc. / kingdom of man, the final destruction of evil, and the eternal reign of Jesus Christ as Lord in the fully established kingdom of heaven on earth; the preterists imagine that God Most High has concluded God's business in heaven and on earth, allowing the status quo to remain unchallenged, which means that unfulfilled prophecy of the biblical record is merely incorrect.

In the preterists' view, those who believe that all the prophecy of the biblical record needs to be fulfilled in order for God Most High to maintain integrity, are merely people who have been led astray.

In contrast to the preterists' view, the biblical record documented that Jesus Christ clearly stated that God Most High is resolute that while heaven and earth will pass away, not one word of God Most High will remain unfulfilled. This means that anything short of a full and complete fulfillment of prophecy must remain uninformed, inaccurate, impotent, and antithetical to the message of the biblical record.

Preterist possibilities for the 'second abomination of desolation'

Preterists raise multiple defenses for their belief that the abomination of desolation as described by Daniel, Jesus Christ and John the Revelator, has already taken place within the timeframe of the first century AD. Preterists placed the potential 'second abomination of desolation' event at various places in time, but always prior to the conclusion of the Bar Kokhba Revolt that ended in 136 AD.

Some preterists placed the 'second abomination of desolation' event as having taken place during the time of Jesus Christ's crucifixion, 30 AD. Because human sacrifice is definitively, specifically, and absolutely forbidden in Mosaic Law, the death of Jesus Christ as the divine and chosen messiah on the mountain near the temple mount was considered a curse and would have potentially nullified the consecration of the temple. Because Jesus Christ is God, as well as being God Most High's appointed person for sitting upon the mercy seat that was located upon the ark of the covenant, the body of Jesus Christ himself truly represented the true temple. Jesus Christ even instructed that if they destroyed 'his temple' / his body, it would be reestablished in three days, which equated Jesus Christ himself with the holiness of the temple.

Support for the preterist interpretation begins with the context of the statement of Jesus recorded in Matthew 27, where Jesus gave the instructions concerning the future abomination of desolation in connection with Jesus' own crucifixion and death. The preterist conclusion reached was that the crucifixion of Jesus Christ would have been the desolating sacrilege. Golgotha / Calvary, the mountain that was the site of the crucifixion of Jesus Christ, would have been the holy place because of the proximity to the temple mount.

But the fact remains that Jesus was not crucified, nor even made his own declaration of messiahship, on the site of the temple, and therefore the crucifixion of Jesus Christ did not desolate the temple.

The next historical opportunity considered for the fulfillment of the 'second abomination of desolation' event was the attempt of Caligula to erect a statue of himself as Zeus in the Jewish temple in 40 - 41 AD. Roman emperor Caligula in 40 AD, ordered a golden statue of himself depicted as Zeus incarnate, to be erected in the temple in Jerusalem. Zeus belongs to the baal / mystery / mythology religion and therefore a statue of Zeus, or Caligula as Zeus, would have been classified as an idol, which violates the first and second commandments of the ten commandments (Exodus 20:1-6).

Because Caligula was assassinated along with his wife and daughter in 41 AD, the statue was never erected in Jerusalem. Caligula did not desolate the temple.

The most prominent preterist view placed the 'second abomination of desolation' event as having taken place prior to the destruction of the temple in 70 AD.

Roman general Vespasian and later, Vespasian's son Roman general Titus, directly and militarily addressed the First Jewish Roman War / First Jewish Revolt of 66 - 73 AD that included the destruction of the temple in 70 AD and ended with the siege of Masada in 73 AD. The Romans had placed their standards / 'flags' that designated the legions, throughout the city of Jerusalem and around the circumference of the city of Jerusalem. The Roman standards contained the images that represented the Roman gods. The Roman soldiers would 'carry their god' into battle with them and bow down and worship the standards. Because the whole city of Jerusalem and the land surrounding the city were considered to be holy, and the standards were considered to be forms of idols, the presence of the standards of the various legions were assessed to be an abomination of desolation.

During the First Jewish Roman War / First Jewish Revolt of 66 - 73 AD, Nero was Caesar and eventually Vespasian replaced Nero as the new Caesar. Vespasian's son Titus finally made it into the city of Jerusalem during the month of Av 70 AD. But neither Nero, Vespasian, nor Titus ever stood in the temple with the temple intact, and declared themselves to be the equivalent of God Most High.

The Roman emperor Hadrian (117 - 138 AD) expelled the Jews from Jerusalem altogether, and allowed them into the city only on the fast of Tisha B'Av / Av 9. This action led to the Third Jewish Roman War / Third Jewish Revolt / Bar Kokhba revolt of 132 - 136 AD.

The Bar Kokhba revolt ended in 136 AD. Once Jerusalem had been defeated in 135 AD, the Roman emperor Hadrian covered the temple mount with rubble and erected a pagan temple dedicated to Jupiter on the site. Hadrian installed two statues; one of Jupiter and the other of himself, in his temple that he built on the temple mount. But the temple of Jupiter constructed by Hadrian, on the temple mount, was not a temple consecrated to God Most High and therefore could not be considered by God Most High to be desolated.

But the rest of the conditions of the prophecy concerning the abominations of desolation, were not fulfilled with either the Bar Kokhba revolt or Hadrian.

According to Daniel, John the Revelator, and Jesus, an abomination of desolation event must foundationally include the following aspects:
- It must take place in the temple.
- It must be committed by a 'man of lawlessness.'
- It must be committed by a man standing in the temple.
- It must be committed by a man with global prominence politically, economically and militarily.
- It must be committed by a man with heavy influence over the religious practices of the people of Israel at a level equal to or greater than the influence that the Seleucid / Syrian Antiochus IV Epiphanes possessed.

The future abomination of desolation event must also:
- Take away the daily evening and morning sacrifices for a period of time, two thousand three hundred evening and morning sacrifices /

> one thousand one hundred fifty days, before the temple is reconsecrated and the sacrificial is system restored.
> - Take place approximately three and a half years after the covenant peace treaty agreement has been established.

The temple was destroyed in 70 AD. None of the proposed preterist events met the temple requirements as prophesied in the record from Daniel or from John the Revelator or from Jesus Christ.

The abomination of desolation event must be committed by the 'man of lawlessness' (2 Thessalonians 2:1-3).

Daniel's vision of Daniel 8 presented a man who will grow up to the host of heaven (Daniel 8:10) with power and might that is not his own (Daniel 8:24, Revelation 13). The little horn / eleventh king / final horn on the shaggy goat, was described as a 'little horn' who shall rise against the Prince of princes / God Most High's messiah, and will not be able to be defeated by human means (Daniel 7:8-11, 8:25). None of the preterists' candidates for committing the act of the future abomination of desolation, met the required criteria for having an extraordinary death.

While most of the above potential candidates for accomplishing an abomination of desolation event in the temple, had no problem with breaking the law, none of them qualified as being the 'man of lawlessness.' Each remained under the law in some way and accountable to the law. Every Caesar and other potential offender, was removed from office by assassination, murder or mere death. Each one was accountable to a higher governmental body. The 'man of lawlessness' described in the biblical record will need to be removed by Jesus Christ alone, by the Prince of princes that the beast of the earth will seek to dethrone. The record of Revelation 20:19-20 stated clearly that the beast of the earth will be disposed only by messiah / the Lamb / Jesus Christ.

Next, the one who stands in the wing of the temple and commits the abomination of desolation must possess global prominence politically, economically and militarily, and with a governmental structure that has sweeping global power over the affairs of humanity. The argument could be successfully made that the Roman emperors possessed that kind of authority. But the influence of the Roman emperors remained less than spectacular in comparison to the magnitude of authority that the Seleucid / Syrian Antiochus IV Epiphanes possessed and that the biblical record has described for the beast of the earth and his partner, the beast of the sea.

The man who commits the abomination of desolation must also be a man with a heavy influence over the religious practices of the people of Israel. The Seleucid / Syrian Antiochus IV Epiphanes exercised enough power and influence that he was able to have mothers killed and their other family members murdered for merely circumcising their baby sons. In the history following the life of Jesus Christ, there were no other leaders who even attempted to exercise that kind of power and influence over the religious activity and customs of the people of Israel. Yet Jesus Christ indicated that the future abomination of desolation event will be greater in its impact than what has ever been experienced historically before.

Another requirement for abomination of desolation events, according to Daniel, was the discontinuation and reestablishment of the temple's evening and morning sacrifices. Daniel clearly recorded that the one who would stand in the temple and commit the abomination of desolation would cause the sacrifices to cease for a period of two thousand three hundred evening and morning sacrifices / one thousand one hundred fifty days. The books of the Maccabees reported that during the first abomination of desolation event led by the Seleucid / Syrian king Antiochus IV Epiphanes, the sacrifices were discontinued for exactly three years, from the month of Kislev to the month of Kislev, approximately one thousand eighty days. But God Most High's vision recorded in Daniel 11:36-12:12 was precise to the half day increment, two thousand three hundred evening and morning sacrifices, exactly one thousand one hundred fifty days or almost three and a half years. The first abomination of desolation event was one hundred ten days short. The precision that God Most High placed on the effective time period of the future abomination of desolation event, on the cessation of the temple sacrificial system, was evidence that until the temple is unconsecrated for the required time period, the event has not yet taken place. (Daniel 8:14, 9:27, 12:11)

    Daniel also recorded in his description of the future abomination of desolation event, the statement that after missing the two thousand three hundred evening and morning sacrifices, the temple will be reconsecrated and the evening and morning sacrifices will be reinitiated.
    When Jesus Christ died, was buried, was resurrected, and then ascended into heaven, the temple sacrificial system was not interrupted, even though the veil of the Holy of Holies had been torn.
    The temple sacrificial system continued uninterrupted even through the siege of Jerusalem until just days before the destruction of the temple when the priests no longer had animals to sacrifice in 70 AD. Even when the temple sacrifices were stopped in 70 AD, it was due to a lack of supply of animals and not the result of a world leader declaring that sacrifices were no longer allowed to be offered. And after the temple was destroyed in 70 AD, there was no opportunity to reinstate the practice of offering the animal sacrifices in order to fulfill Daniel's prophecy.
    When the Roman emperor Hadrian built his temple to Jupiter on the site of the temple mount, there was no temple to host sacrifices that would have been acceptably offered to Yahweh God; and therefore, there would have not been any acceptable evening and morning sacrifices to stop, or to reinstate.
    Another condition for the future abomination of desolation spoken of by the prophet Daniel was the condition that there must first be a covenant peace treaty agreement made between the nation of Israel and other nations. The nation of Israel did not have a covenant peace

treaty agreement with other nations during the lifetime of Jesus Christ or when Titus destroyed the temple. (Daniel 9:24-27)

If the approach to the message of the biblical record is merely to check off details as having been completed in order to escape the experience or the magnitude of the event, then life becomes a delusion with a very limited understanding of the purposes of God Most High, especially concerning the events scheduled for the era of the time of Jacob's Trouble.

Understanding the reason for why an abomination of desolation event must take place, is vital to understanding the events of the second half of the era of the time of Jacob's Trouble, and is vitally essential for understanding the responsibilities that the followers of the Lamb / Jesus Christ have during the second half of the era of the time of Jacob's Trouble.

But a prerequisite for understanding why there must be a future abomination of desolation event, is to recognize that the future abomination of desolation event must take place according to the definition presented in the biblical record. All the possibilities that have been presented by preterists for the fulfillment of the abomination of desolation event spoken of by Daniel, by Jesus and by John the Revelator, fall short of the precision needed in order to be the actual fulfillment of the future abomination of desolation event.

Timeline from the Hasmonean dynasty through the Bar Kokhba Revolt

The preterist view of the second abomination of desolation event having taken place sometime between the earthly ministry of Jesus Christ and the Bar Kokhba Revolt became a prevalent idea used to dismiss the possibility of the future abomination of desolation as having been scheduled for the era of the time of Jacob's Trouble.

Consequently, included here is a timeline of events that took place beginning with the establishment of the Hasmonean dynasty through the Bar Kokhba Revolt. This *timeline demonstrated that while there were a variety of events that took place that contained some of the same elements of the abomination of desolation event detailed within the biblical record, none of the potential events that have been considered for possibilities have met the criteria for being able to be considered the actual fulfillment.*

In this timeline, the dates for the following events have often been disputed. They were originally linked to the reigns of kings and politicians, the times of battles and of wars. A note of caution needs to be used in using this list of dates. Here the estimated dating is included for the purpose of giving the account of events in a chronological order.

Timeline from the Hasmonean dynasty through the reign of Herod the Great

134 – 104 BC: John Hyrcanus I of the Maccabean family and Hasmonean dynasty became ethnarch / governor and high priest in Israel. The Hasmonean name was derived from the name of their ancestor Hasmoneus / Hasmon / Asmonaios.

104 – 103 BC: Judah Aristobulus I, son of John Hyrcanus I became ethnarch / governor and high priest. Salome Alexandra convinced her husband Aristobulus I that his favorite brother, Antigonus, was set against him. Salome Alexandra conspired to murder Antigonus. With her suggestions to Aristobulus that Antigonus was attempting to overthrow him by force, Salome Alexandra convinced Antigonus that Aristobulus wished to see his new armor. At the same time, she told Aristobulus that his brother was coming to kill him. Antigonus was killed by Aristobulus I's guards before he could get close to his brother. Days later, Aristobulus I died from pain and internal bleeding from an unknown disease. This gave Salome Alexandra the opportunity to release the younger brothers from prison and to place Alexander Jannaeus on the throne.

103 – 76 BC: Alexander Jannaeus / Jonathan Alexander / Alexander Jannai / Yannai was the third son of John Hyrcanus I, and held the office of king of Judea. Judah Aristobulus I and Antigonus I were his older brothers. As the oldest living half-brother of Judah Aristobulus I, Alexander Jannaeus had the right to marry Salome Alexandra as well as the right to ascend to the throne. Salome Alexandra was thirteen years older than him. Alexander Jannaeus and Salome Alexandra's two sons both became high priests; Hyrcanus II in 62 BC and Aristobulus II from 66 – 62 BC. The younger began a bloody civil war with his

brother that ended in the captivity of the people of Israel by Pompey the Great.

Alexander Jannaeus and the Hasmonean line had become aligned with the Sadducees who embraced liberal theology and Hellenization. However, Salome Alexandra came from a pharisaic family and her brother Simeon son of Shetach was a famous Pharisee leader. When the rabbis would not recognize Alexander Jannaeus as high priest because they believed that his mother had been captured and violated in Modi'in, Alexander Jannaeus turned against the Pharisees and persecuted them until his death. One incident took place at the feast of tabernacles when Alexander Jannaeus who was high priest refused to perform the ceremony properly, pouring the water onto his feet instead of the altar. The crowd became enraged and pelted him with their citron fruit. Alexander Jannaeus order soldiers to kill those who insulted him and more than six thousand people in the temple courtyard were massacred. Alexander Jannaeus had wooden barriers built around the altars preventing people from sacrificing and denied daily offerings except for the priests. The Judean Civil War followed. When rebel hostility ceased, Alexander Jannaeus' reign continued in peace. Alexander Jannaeus died from the illness of quartan ague / malaria while in Transjordan. Alexander Jannaeus entrusted the government to Salome Alexandra on his deathbed with advice to make peace with the Pharisees.

76 – 67 BC: Salome Alexandra / Alexandra of Jerusalem, having outlived two husbands, the brothers Aristobulus I and Alexander Jannaeus, became queen of Judea of the Hasmonean dynasty. Salome Alexandra was sympathetic to the Pharisees, protecting and hiding Pharisees from her husband's attacks and so gained favor from the Pharisees. Salome Alexandra installed as high priest her oldest son, John Hyrcanus II who also supported the Pharisees. The Sanhedrin was reorganized under pharisaic leadership. To keep peace, the Sadducees were removed from Jerusalem to other fortified towns. Salome Alexandra also increased the size of the army and carefully provisioned the fortified places.

The nation of Israel experienced prosperity under Salome Alexandra's rule. The Haggadah (Ta'anit, 23a; Sifra, HuKKat, i. 110) designated that her rule was a reward for her piety with the rain falling only on Sabbath / Friday nights so that the working class suffered no loss of pay through the rain falling during their work-time. The fertility of the soil was so great that the grains of wheat grew as large as kidney beans, oats as large as olives, and lentils as large as gold denarii.

76 - 66 BC: John Hyrcanus II oldest son of Alexander Jannaeus and Salome Alexandra, was appointed high priest by his mother.

73 BC: Herod was born. Herod the Idumean who would become Herod the Great, was not an Israelite even though he would become king of Judea / king of the Jews. Herod's father was Antipater I / Antipater the Idumaean / Antipater son of Antipas, an Edomite, and his mother was Cypros a Nabatean, a princess from Petra in what is now located in Jordan. Herod's father was a diplomat from a peasant tribe that had been forced into Judaism at the point of a sword. Herod's older brother was Phasael. Phasael and Herod had two younger brothers Joseph and Pheroras, along with a youngest sister Salome I. Herod grew up in Jerusalem because of his father's government position as prime minister while the Hasmonean family ruled the nation of Israel. Herod lived in the societal circle with Mark Antony.

Idumaea was also known as the land of Edom, the land of Esau. Under the Hasmonean kings, Antipater the Idumean became a powerful official and friend of the Roman Republic. When Gaius Julius Caesar defeated Pompey, Antipater the Idumean rescued Caesar in Alexandria and Caesar made Antipater the chief minister of Judea with the right to collect taxes, a very profitable position. Eventually Antipater the Idumean made his sons Phasael and Herod the governors of Jerusalem and Galilee. The political diplomacy of Antipater the Idumean provided for the rise of his son Herod the Idumean who became Herod the Great.

69 BC: The conflict in Judea began between the brothers Aristobulus II (younger brother) and John Hyrcanus II (elder brother) over the succession to the Hasmonean throne.

67 BC: Salome Alexandra / Alexandra of Jerusalem died. The death of Salome Alexandra's rule marked the advancement of the sibling rivalry between John Hyrcanus II and his brother Aristobulus II. The Roman empire would later take advantage of this sibling rivalry to assume rule over the Judean province.

67 – 66 BC: John Hyrcanus II, oldest son of Alexander Jannaeus and Salome Alexandra, followed his mother as king of Judea. Soon after receiving the throne, his younger brother Aristobulus II raised dissention over the right to the throne. John Hyrcanus II was backed by the Pharisees who held onto the traditional values. Aristobulus II was backed by the Sadducees who had embraced Hellenism.

The brothers met in battle near Jericho with many of John Hyrcanus II's soldiers joining Aristobulus II. John Hyrcanus II was forced to take refuge in the citadel of Jerusalem, but when the temple was captured by Aristobulus II, John Hyrcanus II was compelled to surrender and renounce both titles of king and high priest.

Antipater the Idumean was an advisor to John Hyrcanus II and advised John Hyrcanus II that his brother Aristobulus II was planning his death. According to Josephus, Antipater the Idumean was ambitious for controlling Judea and putting the weak John Hyrcanus II back onto the throne. John Hyrcanus II took refuge with Aretas III, King of the Nabateans who had been bribed by Antipater the Idumean into espousing the cause of John Hyrcanus II. In exchange the Nabateans would reacquire their Arabian towns that had been taken by earlier Hasmoneans.

66 – 63 BC: Aristobulus II became king and high priest. Aristobulus II deposed his older brother John Hyrcanus II.

This time it was Aristobulus II who had taken refuge in the temple while the city of Jerusalem was besieged. Onias angered the priests who were supportive of Aristobulus II by selling them cattle for the paschal sacrifice for the enormous price of one thousand Greek drachmae and then refused to deliver the promised animals for sacrifice. Josephus *Antiquities of the Jews* 14.2.2 During the siege of Jerusalem, the adherents of John Hyrcanus II's followers captured the scholar Onias. When Onias refused to pray for the demise of their opponents, the followers of John Hyrcanus II stoned Onias. During the Roman civil war, the Roman general Pompey defeated the kingdoms of Pontus and the Seleucids / Syrians. Marcus Aemilius Scaurus was sent to take possession of Seleucid / Syria. Both of the brothers, John Hyrcanus II and Aristobulus II, took the opportunity to appeal to Scaurus. Both brought gifts and made promises to win Scaurus to their side. The four hundred talents gift of Aristobulus II appealed to Scaurus who withdrew his army. During the retreat, the Nabateans suffered a crushing defeat at the hands of Aristobulus II. Scaurus returned to Damascus.

When Pompey arrived in Syria in 63 BC, both brothers and a third party who sought the removal of the entire Hasmonean dynasty, sent their delegates to Pompey. Pompey favored John Hyrcanus II over Aristobulus II because he believed that John Hyrcanus II would be a more reliable ally to the Roman empire. Aristobulus II resisted so that Jerusalem and the temple were badly damaged.

Once captured, Aristobulus II was taken to Rome as a prisoner of Pompey along with his son Antigonus II Mattathias. John Hyrcanus II was restored as high priest, but not as king. The Romans were interested in Antipater for leadership.

63 BC: Roman General Gnaeus Pompeius Magnus / Pompey the Great took the nation of Israel, placing the nation of Israel under the control of Rome.

Pompey was impressed that the priests of Israel would not allow any interruption in their service of sacrifice in the temple.

General Pompey was also intrigued by the Israelite mysterious religion and sought to see what their God looked like. As soon as General Pompey had seized control of the city, he went into the Holy of Holies where the God of the people of Israel was reputed to live, expecting to find a statue of this mysterious God. According to the Law given to Moses, only the high priest was permitted to enter the Holy of Holies, and then only on one day a year, Yom Kippur / Day of Atonement. In the Holy of Holies, instead of finding some statue of bronze or silver, Pompey found nothing (Josephus *Jewish Antiquities* 14.4.71-73). The God of the people of Israel is without form, timeless, and everywhere. To the Romans it was incredible that the people of Israel would be so very dedicated to a single God, especially a God who would not be represented by images made of stone or other materials. The Romans had a huge pantheon of gods in their baal / mystery / mythology religion. But out of respect for the God and the religion of the people of Israel, Pompey did not touch nor disturb the items within the temple.

After checking out the Holy of Holies, Pompey ordered the people in charge of the temple to purify the temple and bring offerings to God as the Law of God Most High required.

Pompey restored John Hyrcanus II to the high priesthood, made Jerusalem a tributary of Rome, and Judea a satellite of Syria.

Pompey with Marcus Licinius Crassus and Gaius Julius Caesar had made up the First Triumvirate, an unofficial military-political alliance for the leadership of the Roman state. Pompey even married Julius Caesar's daughter Julia in order to secure the alliance. Later there would be war among the members of the First Triumvirate.

63 – 40 BC: John Hyrcanus II oldest son of Alexander Jannaeus and Salome Alexandra was once again appointed as high priest.

57 BC: Antigonus II Mattathias son of Aristobulus II escaped and returned to Judea.

49 – 44 BC: Gaius Julius Caesar became emperor of the Roman empire.

47 BC: When Herod the Idumean was 26, a riot broke out in the region of Galilee. The people of Galilee refused to pay taxes. Herod was sent to put down the rebellion and was appointed governor. Herod the Idumean was effective and brutal, willing to use execution freely.

Herod the Idumean was then appointed governor of Syria and married his first wife Doris. Together they had a son, Antipater II named after Herod's father. After six years, both Doris and Antipater II were banished when Herod fell in love with Mariamne I, a Jewish princess of the Hasmonean lineage, sometime between 43 BC and 40 BC.

Through a marriage to Mariamne I, Herod hoped to gain a position among the Jewish aristocracy. Their children would have the ancestry that would have the legitimacy that Herod craved.

Mariamne I was probably only thirteen or fourteen years old at the time when Herod the Idumean fell in love with her.

Mariamne I's mother was Alexandra, the daughter of John Hyrcanus II. Alexandra had married her cousin Alexander of Judea who was the son of Aristobulus II, brother of John Hyrcanus II. Alexander of Judea and Alexandra had a daughter Mariamne I and son Aristobulus III.

Alexandra, Mariamne I's mother arranged for Mariamne I's betrothal to Herod in 41 BC. But Herod the Idumean needed to wait for four years, until she was sixteen, to marry her.

Mariamne I was the daughter of Alexander of Judea, sister of Aristobulus III, granddaughter of Aristobulus II who had married his cousin Alexandra who was the daughter of John Hyrcanus II.

47 – 40 BC: John Hyrcanus II, oldest son of Alexander Jannaeus and Salome Alexandra, also became the ethnarch / governor of Judea. But because John Hyrcanus II was deemed a very weak ruler, Antipater the Idumean was appointed by Julius Caesar as the first Roman Procurator, a position similar to Prime Minister, allowing Antipater the Idumean to promote the interests of his own house. John Hyrcanus II was forced to yielded to Antipater the Idumean. Antipater the Idumean was also the father of Herod, who benefited from his father's position. Antipater the Idumean appointed his sons Phasael as governor of Jerusalem and Herod as governor of Galilee, which caused tension between John Hyrcanus II and the family of Antipater the Idumean.

44 BC: Roman emperor Julius Caesar was assassinated. The resulting unrest and confusion spread to Judea.

44 – 31 BC: Rome entered a period of joint rule.

43 BC: Antipater the Idumean was assassinated by Malichus I. Malichus I was a Nabataean king (fl. 59 to 30 BC) who was possibly a cousin of Antipater and Herod, but who sided with the Parthian empire. It may have been that Malichus I was paid by John Hyrcanus II to assassinate Antipater the Idumean. Antipater's sons killed Malichus I and maintained their control over Judea as well as their father's puppet Hyrcanus II the Hasmonean.

42 BC: Antigonus II Mattathias son of Aristobulus II attempted to seize the government of Judea by force with the assistance of his brother-in-law Ptolemy Mennei of the Parthians.

The excessive taxation of the people of Israel to pay for the extravagances of Mark Antony and Cleopatra VII had awakened a deep hatred against Rome. The aristocratic class of Jerusalem and the leaders of the Pharisees supported Antigonus II Mattathias in the pursuit of easing the pressure applied by Rome.

41 BC: Herod and his brother Phasael were named as tetrarchs by the Roman leader Mark Antony. They were placed in this role to support John Hyrcanus II.

40 BC: Roman Mark Antony developed his relationship with the last of the Ptolemy / Egyptian empire rulers, Cleopatra VII. Neglecting his duties, Mark Antony focused on Cleopatra VII, which allowed the Parthians to invade Judea and to install their own puppet king. The Parthians invaded Syria and preferred to see a ruler on the throne of Judea who was opposed to Rome. The Parthians selected Antigonus II Mattathias / Antigonus Mattathias the Hasmonean and son of Aristobulus II.

40 – 37 BC: Antigonus II Mattathias son of Aristobulus II was proclaimed king and high priest by the Parthians and was installed in the office. When Antigonus II Mattathias promised the Parthians gold and five hundred female slaves, the Parthians provided him a troop of five hundred warriors.

40 BC: Phasael and Herod were both charged with having committed atrocities which were brought to the attention of Mark Antony. But Mark Antony shared a friendship with Phasael and Herod. Mark Antony was also indebted to Antipater the Idumean and so consequently the charges were dropped.
As a result of the conflict that followed, Phasael was captured with John Hyrcanus II by John Hyrcanus II's nephew Antigonus II Mattathias. John Hyrcanus II was seized and his ears mutilated. According to Josephus, it was Antigonus II Mattathias who bit off his uncle's ears. This mutilation made John Hyrcanus II permanently ineligible for priesthood. Phasael dashed out his brains in order to avoid mutilation. Herod fled Jerusalem to Petra where he was refused and then to Alexandria to meet Cleopatra VII.

40 BC: Herod fled to Rome in the middle of winter, to plead with Mark Antony and Octavian Caesar Augustus for support for the Hasmonean royal family and John Hyrcanus II. But Rome didn't care who ruled Judea as long as Judea remained under Roman control.
Instead of deciding to assist John Hyrcanus II whom the Romans viewed as weak, the Roman senate unexpectedly appointed Herod to be the new king of Judea / king of the Jews.
When Herod was appointed the new king over Israel, Antigonus II Mattathias / Antigonus the Hasmonean and son of Aristobulus II, became the last Hasmonean king of Judea.
But it would be a few more years before Herod would be able to actually take the throne and wear the crown. Herod needed to rid Judea of the Parthian invaders and depose Antigonus II

Mattathias, Mariamne I's grandfather. The people of Israel had preferred the ruler that the Parthians had installed over Herod. Herod was not welcome in Judea. The people of Israel would only recognize someone of the lineage of David to be their king. With Roman military help, Herod began a long military campaign.

37 BC: Herod the Idumean married the Hasmonean princess Mariamne I. Together they had two sons, Alexander and Aristobulus IV, along with two daughters. Herod loved Mariamne. But in order to become king of Judea, Herod had deposed Mariamne I's grandfather. Mariamne I loathed Herod. Consequently, Herod was wracked with jealously and paranoia. When Herod went on military missions, Herod left instructions that Mariamne I was to be killed if he failed to return.

Herod's mother-in-law, Mariamne I's mother, also sought to regain power for the Hasmonean family.

37 – 4 BC: Herod the Great was officially able to claim the throne of Judea and became Rome's choice for king. Josephus stated that Mark Antony bound Antigonus II Mattathias to a cross and scourged him, killing him, a punishment no other king had suffered at the hands of the Romans. Josephus *Antiquity of the Jews* 15.1.2 (8-9)

37 – 36 BC: Ananelus / Hanameel was appointed by Herod to be high priest upon the death of Antigonus II Mattathias. Ananelus was of priestly descent, but not of the Hasmonean family. His background according to the Mishnah was Egyptian, and according to Josephus was Babylonian. Ananelus was credited with having prepared the most recent in Israel's history of red heifers required for sacrifice for the consecration of priests and of the tabernacle / temple (Numbers 19). The first red heifer was sacrificed by Moses for the consecration of the priests and the tabernacle. So far, Jewish tradition has acknowledged the sacrifice of nine red heifers.

36 – 35 BC: Aristobulus III, grandson of Aristobulus II and Hyrcanus II, and brother of Mariamne I, the Hasmonean princess, became high priest under the Hasmonean family pressure applied to Herod the Great.

The Ptolemy / Egyptian Cleopatra VII had just married the Roman leader Mark Antony. Aristobulus III's mother Alexandra viewed this as an opportunity for Cleopatra VII to influence Mark Antony to compel Herod the Great to remove Ananelus from the office of high priest and appoint her son in his place. If Aristobulus III were high priest, the Hasmonean family fortune would be partially restored. Cleopatra VII encouraged Aristobulus III to visit Mark Antony.

But Herod the Great learned of this and became afraid that if Mark Antony met the popular Aristobulus III, that Antony might appoint Aristobulus III as king in Herod's place.

As Aristobulus III performed his first duties as high priest at the altar, Aristobulus III was extremely well received by the people of Israel. Herod the Great, as an Idumean, was not even allowed to enter the temple court. This caused jealousy for Herod.

Herod the Great found Aristobulus III to be too popular because of his noble descent and handsome presence. Even though Aristobulus III was seventeen years old and Herod the Great's brother-in-law, Herod the Great's fear was that the people of Israel would view his Hasmonean position in the lineage of David as too appealing and that Aristobulus III would be appointed by the people of Israel as the king of Judea, seizing Herod's monarchy.

To secure himself against danger from Aristobulus III, Herod the Great instituted a system of espionage against him and his mother. The surveillance proved so onerous that they sought refuge from Cleopatra VII. Herod the Great discovered their plans and increased his suspicions against his brother-in-law. Jericho was the lush resort for the aristocracy of Israel and the site of a banquet organized by Aristobulus III's mother. Herod the Great conspired to have Aristobulus III drowned while he was bathing in a pool in Jericho.

Aristobulus III's mother Alexandra appealed to her friend Cleopatra VII to hold Herod the Great responsible for his murder. Cleopatra VII was willing to assist and to have Mark Antony sentence Herod to death. That would leave Cleopatra VII the opportunity to take over Jericho which was once an Egyptian possession. Mark Antony allowed his old friend Herod a pass on the assassination of his brother-in-law. But Antony appeased Cleopatra VII by giving her Jericho as a gift. Instead of occupying her new possession, Cleopatra VII leased it back to Herod at an exorbitant rate. For three years, it cost Herod almost half of the national income. Herod was embarrassed and resented Cleopatra VII's hold over Mark Antony. When she came to Judea, Cleopatra VII attempted to seduce Herod who skirted her advances.

With the marriage of Cleopatra VII and Mark Antony, the power struggle was sparked in Rome between Mark Antony and Octavian Caesar Augustus. Herod had to choose a side and he chose Mark Antony.

When Herod went for his appeal to Mark Antony and Cleopatra, he left his young wife in the care of his uncle Joseph, along with the instructions that if Antony should kill him, Joseph should kill Mariamne. Herod believed his wife to be so beautiful that she would become engaged to another man after his death. His great passion for Mariamne prevented him from enduring a separation from her, even in death.

Joseph became familiar with the queen and eventually divulged this information to her and the other women of the household. The reception of this information did not have the hoped-for effect of proving Herod's devotion to his wife. Rumors soon circulated that Herod had been killed by Antony, and Alexandra persuaded Joseph to take Mariamne to the Roman legions for protection. However, Herod was released by Antony and returned home, only to be informed of Alexandra's plan by his mother and sister, Salome. Salome also accused Mariamne of committing adultery with Joseph, a charge which Herod initially dismissed after discussing it with his wife. After Herod forgave her, Mariamne inquired about the order given to Joseph to kill her should Herod be killed, and Herod then became convinced of her infidelity, saying that Joseph would only have confided to her if the two of them were intimate. He gave orders for Joseph to be executed and for Alexandra to be confined, but Herod did not punish his wife.

Herod the Great underestimated the popularity of Aristobulus III. And although he was a brother of Mariamne, Herod had him drowned.

35 – 30 BC: With the vacancy open once again for high priest, Herod the Great reappointed Ananelus / Hanameel as high priest.

31 BC: Judea suffered a devasting earthquake.

31 AD: At Actium, Antony lost to Octavian Caesar Augustus. Herod the Great had been kept busy fighting in the desert against the Nabateans.

31 BC – 14 AD: Octavian became emperor of the Roman empire and changed his name to Augustus Caesar.

Octavian Caesar Augustus' position posed a threat to Herod the Great's rule who had previously chosen Antony. At Rhodes, Herod the Great convinced Octavian Caesar Augustus of his loyalty to him. Herod the Great was reconfirmed as king of Judea and given autonomy regarding the internal reign over Judea. But restrictions were placed upon his international affairs. Octavian Caesar Augustus needed the revenue that Judea provided to cover the cost of his military campaigns and in exchange, Octavian Caesar Augustus gave Herod the Great more lands to rule.

30 BC: Mark Antony took poison and died in Cleopatra VII's arms, knowing that his friend Herod the Great had already betrayed him in seeking an alliance with Octavian Caesar Augustus.

30 – 23 BC: Joshua son of Fabus / Jesus son of Fabus became high priest and was removed when Herod the Great appointed his father-in-law, Simon son of Boethus.

29 BC: While Herod the Great had been away, rumors developed that Mariamne I had been having an affair. Salome I, Herod's sister, was either the originator of the rumors or at least the main communicator of the rumors against her sister-in-law.

Being a member of Herod the Great's family did not provide the kind of security that one would assume to be inherent as a member of the royal family. And the main danger originated from within the family itself, and with Herod the Great.

While Herod visited Augustus in Rhodes, Herod separated his wife Mariamne I and his sister Salome, to Alexandrium and Masada. Again Herod left instructions that if he should die, the government was to be left to Salome and his sons. Mariamne I and her mother Alexandra were to be killed. Sohemus was the man left in charge of Mariamne I and after having gained his trust, they learned of Herod's provisions of murder if harm should befall him.

Josephus wrote that Herod was filled with great passion and jealousy concerning his wife Mariamne I. When Mariamne I learned of Herod's plans to murder her a second time, she stopped sleeping with Herod. Mariamne I also accused Herod of killing her grandfather John Hyrcanus II and her brother Aristobulus III.

Herod then responded with a charge of adultery using his sister Salome I as the main witness against her. Salome also insinuated that Mariamne I had plotted to poison Herod.

Herod had Mariamne I, the Hasmonean princess, tried and executed. Even Alexandra, Mariamne I's mother incriminated her own daughter. Alexandra had been next on Herod's list to be executed and provided testimony against her daughter in order to save her own life.

Alexandra declared herself to be queen, stating that Herod was mentally unfit to be king. This strategy was Alexandra's mistake because Herod then executed her without trial.

After Mariamne I was executed, Herod the Great entered into a deep depression. Herod the Great kept her body embalmed in a jar of honey and visited her at night, using her body to fulfill erotic desires.

Herod made his son with his first wife Doris, Antipater II, the first heir in his will. Mariamne I's own sons challenged Antipater II for the throne, but Mariamne I's sons were executed in 7 BC before they would have advanced to the throne.

28 – 25 BC: Herod the Great executed Salome's husband Costobar / Costobarus. Costobar was from a noble and priestly family in Idumaea, an Arab, who had resented the Hasmonean John Hyrcanus I who had forced the Idumeans to adopt the customs and laws of the Jews. Costobar was Salome's first husband. Costobar was also the father of Berenice and father-in-law to Aristobulus who was the son of Herod and Mariamne I.

Costobar had aided Herod in his rise to power joining with Mark Antony and Herod against the Hasmonean king Antigonus, Mariamne I's grandfather. Costobar had controlled the exists from the city of Jerusalem.

Around 37 BC, Herod appointed Costobar as governor of Idumaea and Gaza. Around 34 BC, Herod gave his sister Salome in marriage to Costobar.

In Costobar's ambition to rule Idumaea himself and to achieve great things, Costobar had been protecting Herod's enemies, the sons of Baba, from the early days when Costobar guarded the exists of the city. Costobar had hid them on his own estate. When this was discovered, Costobar denied even knowing them, sent them to the place where they were falsely reported as being in residence, and then had them killed along with those who were accused with them. This was the first of three events Costobar initiated, but the last to be revealed to Herod the Great. It was Salome, Costobar's wife and Herod's sister, who informed Herod.

Next, because Idumaea originally belonged to the Ptolemy / Egyptian empire, Costobar approached Cleopatra VII to ask Mark Antony for Idumaea to be transferred to her instead of to Herod. Costobar also offered to Cleopatra VII, his own loyalty. Cleopatra VII made the request to Mark Antony for the transfer of power, but Antony refused. This was the first transgression discovered by Herod who immediately sought to kill Costobar, but his mother and sister intervened. Herod pardoned him for this, but no longer trusted him.

The last of the three events, but second in revelation to Herod, was the divorce that Salome sought against Costobar. Around 27 – 25 BC, Salome issued a writ of annulment which the Jewish Law did not permit the woman to do. But Salome was not originally Jewish. She was Idumean / Arab. Salome then informed Herod that Costobar was intending to flee the country with Herod's and her own brother Pheroras. Pheroras had an infatuation with a slave girl, someone below their class level, rejecting the match that Herod had arranged.

Because of Costobar's multiple conspiracies, Herod had him executed.

Salome, the sister of Herod the Great, had three children with Costobar:
- Antipater IV who married Cypros II who was the daughter of Herod the Great and Mariamne I the Hasmonean princess;
- Berenice who first married Aristobulus IV who was the son of Herod the Great and Mariamne I the Hasmonean princess, second married Theudion who was the brother of Herod the Great's first wife Doris; and
- an unnamed daughter who married Alexas' son Alexas, the temple treasurer.

Salome I was also the great grandmother of the Salome who was rewarded for her dance with the head of John the Baptist (Matthew 14:6-11, Mark 6:21-28).

Simon Boethus the high priest was the father of Mariamne II. Herod the Great and Mariamne II were the parents of Herod II. Aristobulus IV and Berenice were the parents of Herodias, Herod of Chaklis / Herod II / Herod V, Herod Agrippa who became king of Judea, Aristobulus Minor, and Mariamne III. (Mariamne III was the wife Antipater II who was the son of Herod the Great and first wife Doris. After Antipater II was executed by his father in 4 BC, Mariamne III possibly was married to Herod Archelaus who was the son of Herod the Great and Malthace the Samaritan. Herod Archelaus was the brother of Herod Antipas / Herod Antipater and was associated with the execution of John the Baptist.)

Herod II and Herodias were the parents of Salome the dancer associated with the execution of John the Baptist.

Berenice's children were Herodias, Herod Agrippa I who became king of Judea, Herod of Chalcis and Aristobulus Minor, and Mariamne III (who may have been the first wife of her uncle, Herod Archelaus, ethnarch of Judea).

- 23 – 5 BC: Simon Cantatheras son of Boethus became high priest. Simon's daughter Mariamne II was the third wife of Herod the Great.
- 20 BC: Around 20 BC Herod the Great began the temple expansion. The work would continue for another 80 years. The work on the actual temple was completed in a year and a half. It would take the rest of the 80 years to complete the work on the out buildings and the courts.

  Some of Herod the Great's other achievements included the development of water supplies for Jerusalem, building of fortresses at Masada and Herodium, founding cities like Caesarea Maritima, the enclosure of the Cave of the Patriarchs where Abraham, Sarah, Isaac and Rebecca are buried. Herod had a partnership with Cleopatra VII, and together they held a monopoly over the extraction of asphalt used in shipbuilding, from the Dead Sea. Herod also leased copper mines on Cyprus from the Roman emperor.

  Herod introduced numerous architectural innovations in his construction techniques, such as domes. He adapted the mikveh / Jewish ritual bath, for use as the frigidarium in the Roman style bathhouses of his many palaces. Herod also developed the architectural combination of palace and fortress.
- 14 BC: Emperor Julius Caesar was assassinated in Rome.
- 14 BC: Herod the Great brought back his first wife Doris and son Antipater II.

  Herod the Great's sister Salome persistently warned Herod of the threat that Mariamne I's sons Alexander and his brother

Aristobulus presented to Herod's own life as their response to their mother's execution. Alexander and Aristobulus also were descendants of the Hasmonaean dynasty / Maccabeus family that many in Israel desired to have come back to full leadership with the expectation that the messiah would arise from their family.

After Mariamne I's execution, Herod the Great attempted to have a positive relationship with his sons Alexander and Aristobulus through Mariamne I the Hasmonean princess. But in 7 BC, he had his sons Alexander and Aristobulus IV strangled. In Herod's will, Doris' son Antipater II became the exclusive successor to the throne, but he would also be executed before being able to receive the throne.

7 BC: The sons of Herod and Mariamne I were executed. The historian Macrobius noted that 'It is better to be Herod's pig than his son' (Greek: pig – 'hys,' son – 'huios'). This was a reference of how Herod, as a Jew, would not kill pigs, but Herod had three of his sons and many others executed or assassinated.

5 BC: Matthias son of Theophilus became high priest.

4 BC: Joazar son of Boethus became high priest. As an advocate of compliance with the Roman census, Joazar was unpopular.

4 BC: Jesus was born. Herod the Great was approached by wise men from the east who were seeking the next King of the Jews. Realizing that the wise men from the east did not return to him and that he had been tricked, Herod the Great ordered the slaughter of the baby boys of Bethlehem in an effort to hold onto his throne. Joseph was warned in a dream to flee Bethlehem before the slaughter / massacre of the innocents ordered by King Herod the Great. (Micah 5:2, Matthew 2:1-12 – referral of the wise men to Bethlehem as the site for the birth of messiah, Matthew 2:13-23 Jesus' family fleeing Israel and their subsequent return, Matthew 2:16 – slaughter / massacre of the innocents, the boys under two years of age in Bethlehem). When Herod the Great died, Joseph, Mary and the infant Jesus could have returned. But Joseph learned that Herod the Great's son, Herod Archelaus had taken Herod the Great's place and was afraid to return. With another warning communicated in a dream, Joseph was informed to go to Galilee (Nazareth).

4 BC: King Herod the Great, an Idumean / Edomite, who had been appointed by Rome to be king over Israel, died in Jericho after an excruciatingly painful, putrefying illness.

As Herod the Great aged, he began killing on an unprecedented scale and murdered his rivals. From his deathbed, Herod commenced on a rampage of violence. For example, when Herod discovered that the eagle had been torn down from the temple by some students, Herod had the approximately forty students and the two teachers involved executed as a burnt sacrifice.

Doris' son Antipater II attempted to mount a palace coup. But the action was too soon and five days before Herod would die, he had Doris' son Antipater II immediately executed.

Josephus stated that Herod was so concerned that no one would mourn his death that Herod commanded a large group of distinguished men to come to Jericho and Herod gave the order that they should be killed at the time of his death so that there would be displays of grief. When Herod did die, his son Archelaus and his sister Salome I forestalled the order.

Herod the Great had ten wives and at least nine sons and five daughters.

Selected Members of Herod the Great's Family Tree

First generation
Herod the Great's father and mother: Antipater the Idumaean and Cypros of Nabataea.

Second generation
Herod the Great's siblings: Phasael, Herod the Great, Joseph, Pheroras, Salome I (sister)

Herod the Great's brother Phasael had a son Phasael who married Herod the Great's daughter Salampsio by Mariamne I. Phasael and Salampsio had five children: Antipater, Herod, Alexander, Alexandra and Cypros. Cypros married Herod Agrippa I / Marcus Julius Agrippa (son of Aristobulus IV and Berenice). Aristobulus IV was the son of Herod the Great and Mariamne I. Berenice was the daughter of Salome I sister of Herod the Great and Costobarus.

Herod the Great had ten wives: Doris, Mariamne I the Hasmonean princess, Mariamne II, Malthace, Cleopatra of Jerusalem, Pallas, Elpis, Phaedra, and two unknown wives.

Doris the first wife of Herod the Great, married in 47 BC before Herod the Great became king. Together they had Antipater II, named after Herod the Great's father. When Herod ascended to the throne in 37 BC, Herod dismissed Doris and Antipater II in order to marry the Hasmonean princess Mariamne I. Doris and Antipater II were allowed back around 14 BC, only to be dismissed again around 7 BC when it was discovered that Antipater II had plotted against his father. Doris was a part of Antipater II's plot, and also worked against Mariamne I and Mariamne I's sons. Antipater II was executed in 4 BC.

Mariamne I the second wife of Herod the Great was the Hasmonean princess, a descendant of the Maccabeans / Hasmonean line of priests and rulers of Judea. Mariamne I was a descendent of the genetically Jewish and Levitical lineage, the daughter of Alexander (son of Aristobulus (son of John Hyrcanus II)). Herod the Great used his marriage to Mariamne I to support his claim as a converted Jew and Idumean, to reign over Judea. Herod the Great loved Mariamne I deeply because of her lineage, because of her beauty, because of her youth, etc. But Herod had put to death practically all the members of her family in an effort to limit the number of people who could challenge his position as king of Judea and to destroy the Hasmonean dynasty that preceded the Roman rule led by Herod the Great. Herod committed murderous atrocities against the people of Israel who offended him. Herod's actions were not actions of a truly devoted follower of Yahweh / the Lord. Herod the Great's sister Salome I took an active part in Herod the Great's monarchy and sought opportunities to accuse Mariamne I, fabricating libels against Mariamne I. Mariamne I bore Herod three sons and two daughters. One of the sons died in his youth. The other two sons, Alexander and Aristobulus IV were executed on the order of Herod in 7 BC. The two daughters were Salampsio who married Phasael the son of Phasael and Cypros.

In 29 BC, Herod the Great had Mariamne I executed.

Mariamne II the third wife of Herod the Great was the daughter of Simon Boethus the high priest. Simon Boethus' position as high priest was related to the marriage of his beautiful daughter Mariamne II to Herod the Great. Herod the Great and Mariamne II had a son Herod II / Herod Boethus / Herod Philip I who was removed from the line of succession because of his mother's part in the plot of Antipater II against Herod the Great. Herod II / Herod Boethus / Herod Philip I married his niece Herodias (daughter of Aristobulus IV and Berenice) and had one daughter Salome. Salome danced for her step father Herod Antipas and demanded and received the head of John the Baptist.

Salome first married her uncle Philip the tetrarch and as a widow married her cousin Aristcbulus of Chalcis (son of Herod of Chalcis / Herod V / Herod II grandson of Herod the Great, and of Berenice (daughter of Salome I)).

Malthace was a Samaritan, the wife of Herod the Great and the mother of two sons, Herod Archelaus the ethnarch and Herod Antipas the tetrarch, and one daughter Olympias who married Herod the Great's nephew Joseph son of Joseph. Olympias and Joseph had a daughter Mariamne who was the first wife of Herod of Chalcis.

Cleopatra of Jerusalem the wife of Herod the Great, was the mother of their two sons, Philip the tetrarch / Herod Philip II and Herod. After the death of Herod the Great, Philip the tetrarch became tetrarch of Ituraea and Trachonitis, and possibly Gaulanitis and Paneas. Philip the tetrarch married his niece Salome who was the daughter of Herodias and Herod II / Herod Philip I and who danced for the head of John the Baptist.

Pallas was the wife of Herod the Great and together they had a son Phasael, not to be confused with Herod the Great's brother Phasael and Phasael's son Phasael.

Phaedra was the wife of Herod the Great and together they had a daughter Roxanne.

Elpis was the wife of Herod the Great and together they had a daughter Salome, not to be confused with Salome I the sister of Herod the Great or Salome who danced for the head of John the Baptist.

Herod the Great also married a cousin and a niece whose names are not known and there were no known children from the unions.

Third generation

Salampsio was the oldest daughter of Herod the Great and Mariamne I. Salampsio married Phasael, the son of Phasael (older brother of Herod the Great), Salampsio's cousin. They had five children: Antipater, Herod, Alexander, Alexandra, and Cypros. Cypros married Herod Agrippa I (son of Aristobulus IV).

Aristobulus IV the son of Herod the Great and Mariamne I, was just 3 years old when his father executed his mother on false rumors of her infidelity spread by his father's sister Salome I. When Aristobulus IV reached age 12, he was sent with his brother Alexander to Rome to be educated in the household of emperor Augustus. The handsome sons of the beautiful Hasmonean princess, attracted the adulation of many of the people of Israel. Finally in 7 BC, Herod the Great had the brothers

Aristobulus IV and Alexander strangled on charges of treason.

Aristobulus IV married Berenice (daughter of Salome I (sister of Herod the Great) and Costobar). Together they had 5 children; Mariamne III, Herod V / Herod of Chalcis, Herodias, Herod Agrippa I / Marcus Julius Agrippa, Aristobulus Minor.

Herod Agrippa I / Marcus Julius Agrippa was educated in Rome as a friend of Tiberius' son Drusus. Herod Agrippa I / Marcus Julius Agrippa and his wife Cypros had four children: Herod Agrippa II, Berenice, Mariamne, and Drusilla.

Herod V / Herod of Chalcis married his cousin Mariamne. Together they had Aristobulus of Chalcis. Then he married his niece Berenice of Cilicia / Julia Berenice (daughter of Herod Agrippa I (son of Aristobulus IV and Berenice)).

Berenice of Cilicia / Julia Berenice was also the sister of King Herod Agrippa II. Herod V / Herod of Chalcis and Berenice of Cilicia / Julia Berenice had two sons, Berenicianus and Hyrcanus.

Herod Antipas tetrarch of Galilee and Peraea (Mark 6:14-29, Luke 3:1, 13:31-35, 23:7-12) was the son of Herod the Great and Malthace the Samaritan, and full brother of Herod Archelaus. Herod Antipas, Herod Archelaus and their half-brother Philip were educated in Rome.

Herod Archelaus, ethnarch of Judea, Samaria, and Idumaea (Matthew 2:22) was the son of Herod the Great and Malthace the Samaritan, full brother of Herod Antipas and half-brother of Philip. Herod Archelaus was replaced by a series of Roman governors including Pontius Pilate.

Herod Agrippa I / Marcus Julius Agrippa was the son of Aristobulus IV (son of Herod the Great and Mariamne I) and Berenice (daughter of Salome I (sister of Herod the Great) and Costobar). His grandfather, Herod the Great, sent him to be educated in Rome. Tiberius held great affection for the young Marcus Julius Agrippa and educated him with his own son Drusus. Drusus and the future emperor Claudius became good friends with Herod Agrippa I / Marcus Julius Agrippa.

Herod Agrippa I was the king named Herod of Acts 12. Herod Agrippa I's territory included Judea, Galilee, Batanaea and Perea.

Herod Agrippa I was involved in extravagant living, accused of receiving bribes, and accused of plotting against Tiberius. When Tiberius died and Caligula became emperor, Herold Agrippa I returned to

Jerusalem in 39 AD, banished his uncle Herod Antipas and was given Herod Antipas' territory of Galilee and Peraea.

After the assassination of Caligula in 41 AD, Herod Agrippa I was involved in the struggle over accession between Claudius, the Praetorian Guard, and the Senate, supporting Claudius. As a reward, when Claudius became emperor, he gave Herod Agrippa I dominion over Judea and Samaria, and Claudius gave Herod Agrippa I's brother Herod of Chalcis, the kingdom of Chalcis in Lebanon. In this way, Herod Agrippa I became one of the most powerful kings of the east. Herod Agrippa I's domain more or less equaled the kingdom held by his grandfather Herod the Great.

In 41 AD, when Caligula attempted to set up his statue in the temple at Jerusalem shortly before his death, Herod Agrippa I interceded with Caligula on behalf of the people of Israel which resulted in a temporary rescinding of Caligula's order. Herod Agrippa I prevented the temple's desecration. Caligula issued a second order for establishing his statue in the temple, which was prevented by Caligula's death.

Acts 12 reported that Herod Agrippa I / 'King Herod' persecuted the Jerusalem church, having James the son of Zebedee, an apostle of Jesus Christ, killed. Herod Agrippa I also imprisoned Peter around the time of Passover.

After Passover in 44 AD, Herod Agrippa I went to Caesarea Maritima where he had games performed in honor of Claudius. Herod Agrippa I wore a garment made wholly of silver with a wonderful texture. With the illumination of the reflection of the sun's rays, he 'looked like a god.' In the midst of his speech to the public a cry went out that he was a god. When Herod Agrippa I did not publicly react, an owl perched over his head. Previously, when Herod Agrippa I had plotted against Tiberius and was imprisoned, there had been a similar omen that had been interpreted with his speedy release and future kingship, and with the warning that when the omen was repeated, he would die. In 44 AD at the site of the games, upon seeing the owl perched over his head, Herod Agrippa I was immediately smitten with violent pains in his heart and abdomen. He died five days later. He had reigned for 7 years with his reign over all of Judea lasting for only three years. Herod Agrippa I was known for his extravagant spending that exceeded his income and also for his generosity.

While Herod Agrippa I was the last king of the Jews, his son Herod Agrippa II was the last of the Herodian dynasty and last Herodian ruler.

With Herod Agrippa I's wife Cypros, they had a son and three daughters: Herod Agrippa II who became the 8th and final ruler from the Herodian family, Berenice who married Marcus Julius Alexander and later her uncle Herod of Chalcis and later Polamo king of Cilicia before returning to a potential love interest with her brother Herod Agrippa II, Mariamne, and Drusilla who married Antonius Felix the procurator of Judea referenced in Acts.

Herod II / Herod Boethus / Herod Philip I was the son of Herod the Great and Mariamne II the Samaritan. Herod II also known as Herod Philip I was the first husband of his niece Herodias, not to be confused with Philip the tetrarch. Herod Philip was not a ruler. Herod Philip was referred to in Mark 6:17.

Fourth generation

Herod Agrippa II / Marcus Julius Agrippa son of Herod Agrippa I (son of Aristobulus IV and Berenice) and Cypros; granddaughter of Aristobulus IV and great granddaughter to Herod the Great. Herod Agrippa II became the eighth and final ruler from the Herodian family but without any control of Judea. Herod Agrippa II was only seventeen years old when his father died. Herod Agrippa II lived in an incestuous relationship with his sister Berenice.

Herod Agrippa II was appointed by Festus to hear Paul's defense. Herod Agrippa II was tetrarch of Chalcis and other northern territories. (Acts 25:13-26:32)

Herod Agrippa II died at the age of seventy and childless.

Berenice of Cilicia / Julia Berenice was the daughter of Herod Agrippa I (son of Aristobulus IV and Berenice) and Cypros; granddaughter of Aristobulus IV and great granddaughter to Herod the Great. Berenice of Cilicia / Julia Berenice had three short-lived marriages. First husband was Marcus Julius Alexander. Second marriage to her father's brother, Herod of Chalcis. Then she lived with her brother Herod Agrippa I before marrying Polemon II of Pontus / king of Cilicia. Berenice of Cilicia / Julia Berenice was mentioned in Acts 25:13, 25:23, 26:30, and was present at the trial of Paul. Berenice of Cilicia / Julia Berenice also met and fell in love with the Roman general Titus who was eleven years younger than she was. Berenice of Cilicia / Julia Berenice also heavily supported Titus' father Vespasian in his campaign to become the Roman emperor.

Mariamne was the daughter of Herod Agrippa I (son of Aristobulus IV and Berenice) and Cypros; granddaughter of Aristobulus IV and great granddaughter to Herod the Great.

Drusilla was the daughter of Herod Agrippa I (son of Aristobulus IV and Berenice) and Cypros; granddaughter of Aristobulus IV and great granddaughter to Herod the Great. Drusilla left her first husband that had been a marriage arranged by her brother Herod Agrippa II, to marry the Roman governor Felix. (Acts 24:24)

Marcus Antonius Felix was the Roman procurator of Judaea Province. Felix was married to Drusilla the daughter of King Herod Agrippa I and Cypros.

Felix' first wife was Drusilla of Mauretania the Younger, daughter of Ptolemy of Mauretania and Julia Urania. Felix' second wife was Drusilla of Judea daughter of Herod Agrippa I and Cypros after Drusilla of Judea divorced Gaius Julius Azizus the king of Emesa, to marry Felix. Together Felix and Drusilla of Judea had a son Marcus Antonius Agrippa who died with his mother Drusilla of Judea in the eruption of Mount Vesuvius August 24, 79 AD. The eruption of Mount Vesuvius buried several towns and settlements including Pompeii and Herculaneum. This was the same eruption that took the life of the historian Pliny the Elder.

Felix married again for the third time after the death of Drusilla of Judea.

Felix was noted for his cruelty and licentiousness. His cruelty and licentiousness, coupled with his accessibility to bribes, led to a great increase of crime in Judea (Acts 24). After Paul was arrested in Jerusalem and rescued from an assassination plot, the local Roman authority transferred Paul to Caesarea where he stood trial before Felix. Felix and his wife Drusilla heard Paul's presentation of Jesus Christ, frequently sending for Paul for further discussion. When Antonius Felix was accused before Nero of using a dispute between the Jews and the Syrians of Caesarea as a pretext to slay and plunder the inhabitants, Felix was replaced by Porcius Festus. Felix left Paul in prison for two years before the new procurator Porcius Festus became the second judge to hear Paul. It was before Festus that Paul appealed to Caesar.

Herodias was the daughter of Aristobulus IV (son of Herod the Great and Mariamne I), and of Berenice (daughter of Salome I sister of Herod the Great).

Herodias' first marriage was to Herod II / Herod Boethus / Herod Philip I son of Herod the Great and Mariamne II. Together they had a daughter Salome. Herodias left Herod II / Herod Boethus / Herod Philip I in order to marry his half-brother Herod Antipas the tetrarch of Galilee and Perea.

After 31 BC, Herodias divorced Herod II / Herod Boethus / Herod Philip I in order to marry his brother Herod Antipas.

The adulterous relationship with Herod Antipas had already begun while Herodias was still married to Herod II / Herod Boethus / Herod Philip I.

Herod Antipas was the half-brother to both Herod II / Herod Boethus / Herod Philip I and Herod Antipas. Herodias married two of her half uncles. The Law of Moses forbade a man to marry his brother's wife when they were divorced and not widowed (Leviticus 18:6) which resulted in opposition led by John the Baptist (Matthew 14, Mark 6, Luke 3). After Salome's erotic dance for her stepfather, Herod Antipas gave Salome John the Baptist's head as referenced in Mark 6:14-29. In 40 BC, when Herod Agrippa I, Herodias' brother, became king, Herodias persuaded her husband Herod Antipas to request a royal crown for himself from Caligula. Herod Agrippa I slandered Herod Antipas which led to Herod Antipas losing all, and his fortune being given to Herod Agrippa I. Herod Antipas was exiled to Lugdunum in Gaul with Herodias choosing to accompany him in exile.

Fifth generation

Salome who asked for the head of John the Baptist, daughter of Herodias and Herod Philip, became wife of Philip the tetrarch. (Matthew 14:1-11)

Philip the tetrarch / Herod Philip II the tetrarch of Iturea, Tiachonitis, Gaulanitis, Aurantis, and Batanea should not be confused with Herod II / Herod Boethus / Herod Philip I. Philip the tetrarch / Herod Philip II married Herodias' daughter Salome, his grandniece. (Luke 3:1)

Timeline from after Herod the Great, to the First Jewish Roman War 66-73 AD

4 BC – 7 AD: Herod the Great's final will instructed the kingdom of Judea to be divided into quarters / tetrarchies. Augustus respected the terms of Herod's final will which stipulated the division of Herod's kingdom among three of his sons and his sister; Herod Archelaus (mother: Malthace the Samaritan), Herod Antipas (mother: Malthace), Herod II / Philip the Tetrarch (mother: Mariamne II / daughter of Simon Boethus the high priest), and Salome I / Herod the Great's sister.

These three sons of Herod the Great, along with other sons, were educated in Rome.

From this point on in history, Judea was no longer a kingdom with a king of its own. Judea was ruled by governors and paid taxes directly to the Roman emperor.

Herod Archelaus

4 BC – 6 AD: When Herod Archelaus son of Herod the Great and Malthace the Samaritan, assumed rule, he was dressed in white to ascend a golden throne. Herod Archelaus sought to appease the populace without lowering taxes so he released the imprisoned enemies of Herod the Great.

The people of Jerusalem also desired to have those who were responsible for the death of the 40 youths and 2 teachers, punished. Herod Archelaus complied, but requested moderation until he was confirmed as king by Caesar Augustus. When Herod Archelaus departed to feast with his friends, the people of Jerusalem began streaming into the temple, wailing for the loss of the teachers. The gathering escalated into a mob. The people that Herod Archelaus sent to address the crowd were stoned and many others were killed. The mob returned to offering their sacrifices as if nothing had happened. Herod Archelaus responded with ordering the entire army into the city to the temple. Josephus recorded the death toll at 3000. Herod Archelaus then cancelled the celebration of Passover.

Herod Archelaus then faced his enemies within his own family. Herod Antipas, the younger brother of Herod Archelaus, had been removed from Herod's will only days earlier. Herod Antipas claimed that Herod Archelaus did not display enough authentic grief for the death of his father when he cried during the day and partied at night. Herod Antipas also claimed that Herod Archelaus did not yet have his authority confirmed by Caesar Augustus in order to be authorized to order a response to the riot or to cancel the Passover celebration. Herod Archelaus was acting as a king without actually being the king.

The parable that Jesus told and was recorded in Luke 19 may have been in reference to Herod Archelaus.

Herod Archelaus' case was pleaded before Caesar Augustus who decided to divide the kingdom of Judea and install Herod Archelaus as ethnarch.

Later viewed as incompetent to rule, Herod Archelaus would reign for only nine years.

Herod Antipas

4 BC - 39 AD: Herod the tetrarch / Herod Antipater / Herod Antipas / 'King Herod' (in the gospel record) was the son of Herod the Great and Malthace the Samaritan, full brother of Herod Archelaus and half-brother to Philip the tetrarch. Herod Antipas was the tetrarch / ruler of Galilee and Perea under the direction of the Roman empire. Herod Antipas was also titled 'King Herod' although he did not hold the title of king.

The title of tetrarch means 'ruler of a quarter.' Herod Antipas, as tetrarch of Galilee and Perea, ruled for 42 years.

Antipas took an active role in the events that led to the executions of John the Baptist and Jesus of Nazareth.

Herod Antipas divorced his first wife Phasaelis, the daughter of the king of the Nabataeans Aretas IV, in order to marry Herodias, who had formerly been married to his half-brother Herod II / Herod Boethus / Herod Philip I, not Philip the tetrarch. Herodias was also the granddaughter of Herod the Great and Mariamne I.

Herod Antipas was Herod the Great's son with wife Malthace while Herod II / Herod Boethus / Herod Philip I was Herod the Great's son with wife Mariamne II.

John the Baptist pointed out repeatedly that it is against the law of God Most High to 'steal' another man's wife, and to have sex with one's niece / incest (Matthew 14:1-12, Mark 6:14-29). Salome daughter of Herod II / Philip and Herodias, stepdaughter of Herod Antipas, performed her erotic and seductive dance for her stepfather which was rewarded with the granting of her request. Herodias had prearranged with Salome that Salome would demand the head of John the Baptist. Salome's demand was granted (Matthew 14:6-11, Mark 6:21-28).

During the scenario leading up to the crucifixion of Jesus, Jesus was first brought before Pontius Pilate for trial since Pilate was the governor of Roman Judea which encompassed Jerusalem at the time of Jesus' arrest. Pilate initially handed the matter over to Herod Antipas, the ruler of Galilee, the region that Jesus based his ministry from. Originally Herod Antipas was pleased to see Jesus in hope that Jesus would perform a miracle, but when Jesus remained silent to Herod Antipas' questioning, Herod Antipas mocked Jesus and sent

Jesus back to Pilate's court. After this, Pilate and Herod Antipas exchanged their enemy status for new friendship.

Philip the tetrarch

4 BC – 34 AD: Philip the tetrarch was the son of Herod the Great with his fifth wife, Cleopatra of Jerusalem. Cleopatra was a common name.
Philip the tetrarch / Herod Philip II the tetrarch of Iturea, Tiachonitis, Gaulanitis, Aurantis, and Batanea should not be confused with Herod II / Herod Boethus / Herod Philip I.
Little is known about Philip the tetrarch. Philip the tetrarch did not utilize the title 'Herod' to the extent that his half-brothers Herod Archelaus and Herod Antipas did.
Philip the tetrarch / Herod Philip II married Herodias' daughter Salome, his grandniece. (Luke 3:1)

4 – 3 BC: Eleazar son of Boethus became high priest.

3 - ? BC: Joshua son of Sie became high priest.

? – 6 AD: Joazar son of Boethus was restored as high priest.

6 – 15 AD: Ananias / Ananus / Annas / Hanan son of Seth was appointed high priest by the Roman legate Quirinius during the time of the rebellious Judas the Galilean. The Romans had deposed Herod Archelaus who had been the ethnarch / governor of Judea. This action placed Judea directly under Roman rule without the intermediary Roman appointed king.
As a member of the Sadducees, and as the holder of the office of high priest, the highest office that an Israelite could hold at the time, Ananias' was part of the wealthy Jewish elite. Ananias was also aided greatly by his use of his five sons and his son-in-law Caiaphas as puppet high priests.
Ananias son of Seth, had a son-in-law and five sons who would all become high priests: Eleazar son of Ananias (fl. 16-17 AD), Caiaphas the son-in-law (fl. 18-36 AD), Jonathan son of Ananias (fl. 36-37, 44 AD), Theophilus son of Ananias (fl. 37-41 AD), Matthias son of Ananias (fl. 43 AD), Ananias son of Ananias (fl. 63 AD).

14 AD: Roman emperor Octavian Augustus Caesar died.

14 – 36 AD: Tiberius Caesar / Tiberius Caesar Divi Augusti Filius Augustus became emperor of the Roman empire. Tiberius Caesar Divi Augusti Filius Augusts was born to Tiberius Claudius Nero and Livia Drusilla in a Claudian family. Through adoption, Tiberius also became a member of the Julian family. Tiberius was the stepson of Augustus, grand uncle of Caligula, paternal uncle of Claudius and great grand uncle of Nero. Tiberius reigned for an almost record 22 ½ year reign.

15 AD: High priest Ananias son of Seth was deposed by the procurator Valerius Gratus (Josephus *Antiquities of the Jews* 18.95-97). According to the Law given to Moses, the term of the high priest was intended to last until the death of the high priest

(Numbers 35:25, 28). Because Ananias son of Seth was removed from office prior to his death, he was still referred to as high priest and still retained some of his former duties. While Ananias was officially removed from office, he remained one of the nation of Israel's most influential political and social individuals.

15 – 16 AD: Ishmael son of Fabus became high priest. Ishmael son of Fabus was a descendant of John Hyrcanus. Ishmael's tenure as high priest was controversial. Ishmael required the people to partake in the ritual bath / mikveh and then be sprinkled with the ashes of the red heifer. Following sunset, they were to be again sprinkled by the water and the ashes of the red heifer. This twice sprinkled doctrine was challenged. It was also said of him that Ishmael was 'the handsomest man of his time, whose effeminate love of luxury was the scandal of the age.' Ishmael's appeal inspired the writing of the fictional novel, Ben-Hur. Ishmael son of Fabus would be reinstated by Herod Agrippa II / Marcus Julius Agrippa from 58 – 62 AD.

16 – 17 AD: Eleazar son of Ananias son of Seth, became high priest.

17 – 18 AD: Simon son of Camithus became high priest.

18 – 36 AD: Caiaphas / Joseph son of Caiaphas, who had married the daughter of Ananias son of Seth, became high priest when the proconsul Vitellius deposed his father-in-law, Ananias son of Seth (Josephus *Antiquities of the Jews* 18.33-35 and 18.95-97). According to Josephus, Caiaphas was appointed in 18 AD by the Roman prefect who preceded Pontius Pilate, Valerius Gratus.

As John the Baptist / John son of Zechariah began his ministry, Ananias son of Seth shared in a joint high priesthood with Caiaphas (Luke 3:2). During the ministry years of Jesus, the office of high priest was designated as being filled by both Ananias and Caiaphas, father-in-law and son-in-law.

The high priest Caiaphas who had married the sister of the five sons of the elder Ananias, led in the accusations against Jesus of Nazareth (John 18:12-14, 18:19-24, Luke 3:1-2). Jesus' parable of the father with five sons who would not even believe in the resurrection if Lazarus were raised from the dead, highly resembled Ananias with his five sons (John 16). When the real Lazarus was raised from the dead, Ananias and the five sons of Ananias plotted to have the real Lazarus killed after he had been raised from the dead (John 12:9-10).

30 AD: In the final conspiracy to execute Jesus, Jesus was brought before the high priest Ananias first because his palace was closest. Ananias questioned him regarding his disciples and teaching before Ananias sent Jesus to Caiaphas. Caiaphas considered the political implications of his own stance concerning Jesus and realized that if Jesus were to continue, the kingdom that Jesus led would be a competitor to the

kingdom that Ananias and Caiaphas led as high priests. Rome might also become involved and depose Caiaphas of his position. The more expedient option was to have the Romans crucify Jesus. To persuade the Roman governor that Jesus needed to be crucified, Caiaphas' legal position was that Jesus was guilty of blasphemy and also of proclaiming himself to be the promised and prophesied messiah which was understood to be a return of the Davidic kingship. To reestablish the throne of David would have been an act of sedition and Jesus' claim to be the promised and prophesied messiah / heir to David's throne, prompted Jesus Christ's Roman execution.

Jesus was taken to the Roman governor, Pontius Pilate who found no basis for a charge against Jesus. From Pontius Pilate, Jesus was sent to Herod Antipas who was ruler of Galilee where Jesus had established his ministry base. Herod Antipas mocked Jesus and sent Jesus back to Pilate's court. But in order to appease the mob, Pontius Pilate allowed Jesus to be crucified.

In approximately three days, Jesus was crucified, died, buried, resurrected, and ascended into heaven.

- 30 AD: After Pentecost, Ananias son of Seth presided over the Sanhedrin when the Apostles Peter and John were presented and accused (Acts 4:5-7).
- 34 AD: Stephen was stoned to death and Saul / Paul experienced a conversion in his belief about Jesus Christ.
- 36 – 37 AD: Jonathan son of Ananias son of Seth, became high priest.
- 37 AD: Roman emperor Tiberius Caesar died. On March 16, 37 AD, Tiberius died at the age of 77.
- 37 – 41 AD: Theophilus son of Ananias son of Seth became high priest. As part of the Ananias family, Theophilus was wealthy and influential. It was his son Matthias who served as the next to the last high priest before the destruction of the temple by the Romans in 70 AD.

Caligula / Gaius Julius Caesar Augustus Germanicus, his order to establish his statue in Jerusalem, and beyond

- 37 – 41 AD: Caligula / Gaius Julius Caesar Augustus Germanicus became emperor of the Roman empire.

    Caligula / Gaius Julius Caesar Augustus Germanicus was born in Antium / modern Anzio and Nettuno. The name 'Caligula' means 'little boots.' When he was a child, Caligula / Gaius Julius Caesar Augustus Germanicus would accompany his father Germanicus on campaigns in the north of Germania. The soldiers were amused that Caligula / Gaius Julius Caesar Augustus Germanicus was dressed in a miniature soldier's outfit, including boots and armor. He was given his nickname 'Caligula' / 'little boots' (Latin). The name stuck.

Caligula's father was the popular Roman general Germanicus. Tiberius was Germanicus' uncle and adoptive father and the emperor that followed Augustus in 14 AD. When Caligula was seven, his father fell ill during a military campaign and died. The historian Suetonius claimed that Germanicus was poisoned in Syria by an agent of Tiberius who viewed Germanicus as a political rival.

Caligula's mother was Augustus' granddaughter, Agrippina the Elder. Agrippina the Elder was also Germanicus' second cousin. Agrippina the Elder was the daughter of Marcus Vipsanius Agrippa and Julia the Elder. She was the granddaughter of Augustus and Scribonia through her mother. Through Agrippina, Augustus was the maternal great grandfather of Caligula / Gaius Julius Caesar Augustus Germanicus.

After Agrippina the Elder's husband Germanicus was assassinated, Tiberius refused to allow Agrippina to remarry because of her genealogy and the fear that a future husband would become a rival to rule the Roman empire.

Agrippina the Elder's children were; three sons, Nero, Drusus, and Caligula, with three younger daughters, Agrippina the Younger, Julia Drusilla and Julia Livilla. Agrippina the Elder had six children. But in a bitter feud with Tiberius, her family was eventually destroyed with Caligula as the sole male survivor.

In 30 AD, Caligula's brother, Drusus Caesar, was imprisoned on charges of treason and his brother Nero died in exile from either starvation or suicide. Caligula and his sisters became prisoners of Tiberius. Caligula was surprisingly spared by Tiberius.

In 31 AD, Caligula came under the personal care of Tiberius on Capri where he lived for six years. Some said that Tiberius' relationship with Caligula was sexual as well. Caligula became a natural excellent actor, who recognized danger and hid all his resentment toward Tiberius.

In 32 AD, Caligula was briefly married to Junia Claudilla. In 33 AD, she died in childbirth.

In 33 AD, Tiberius began raising the position of Caligula.

In 35 AD, Caligula was named joint heir to Tiberius' estate with Tiberius' grandson, Tiberius Gemellus.

On March 16, 37 AD, Tiberius died at the age of 77.

For the first six months of Caligula's reign, he was described as noble and moderate. Caligula destroyed Tiberius' treason papers, ended the treason trials, granted bonuses to the military, recalled the exiles, helped those who had been injured by the imperial tax system, banished certain sexual deviants, and increased the entertainment including gladiatorial games.

After the first six months, the nature of the historical records changed, describing Caligula's cruelty, sadism, extravagance, and sexual perversion.

In October 37, Caligula fell seriously ill, or was poisoned. Caligula soon recovered from his illness, but many believed that the illness caused Caligula to become diabolical. Caligula began to kill off or exile those who were close to him or whom he perceived as a serious threat. Caligula had his cousin and adopted son Tiberius Gemellus executed. When their shared grandmother, Antonia Minor became outraged, the historian Suetonius implied that Caligula had his grandmother poisoned. Other family executions followed.

Caligula was described by Philo of Alexandria and Seneca the Younger, who were Caligula's contemporaries, as an insane emperor who was self-absorbed, angry, killed on a whim, and indulged in too much spending and sex. He would sleep with other men's wives and then return to the banquet to offer to the guests the intimate details about what he had done to the women.

Caligula's reign as emperor was marked with a carnival type atmosphere. At one of the games that he was presiding over, Caligula ordered one entire section of the audience into the arena during the intermission to be eaten by the wild beasts because there were no prisoners to be used and he needed to alleviate his boredom.

Roman historians Suetonius and Cassius Dio also accused Caligula of incest with his sisters Agrippina the Younger, Drusilla, and Livilla, along with prostituting them to other men. Caligula turned the palace into a brothel. These accounts may be debated, but based on Caligula's character, they may also be legitimate accounts.

By 38 AD, Caligula had spent the Roman empire into a financial crisis. Caligula engaged in massive building projects. Caligula also brought to Rome, the massive obelisk from Egypt that is currently located in the Vatican's piazza in front of Saint Peter's Basilica in Rome. The financial crisis motivated Caligula to falsely accuse, fine, and even kill individuals for the purpose of seizing their estates.

Caligula had originally believed that Tiberius acted alone in exiling and destroying Caligula's siblings and mother. But when he investigated their deaths more, he discovered that the Roman senate also played a supportive part. Entering the senate, Caligula began an active attack upon the senate.

In 39 AD, Herod Agrippa I accused Herod Antipas, the tetrarch of Galilee and Perea of planning a rebellion against Rome with the help of Parthia. Herod Agrippa I, governor of the territories of Batanaea and Trachonitis, was a good friend of Caligula.

Herod Antipas confessed and Caligula exiled Herod Antipas. Herod Agrippa I was rewarded with Herod Antipas' territories.

40 AD: The Judean region had experienced a relative calm for a number of years. But the calm was broken and the Judean region became a source of trouble for the Roman emperor Caligula.

In 40 AD, Caligula began implementing very controversial policies that introduced religion into his political role. Caligula even began appearing in public dressed as various gods and demigods such as Hercules, Mercury, Venus and Apollo. Then he was reported as referring to himself as the god Jupiter in public documents. Caligula had the heads of various statues of gods removed and his own head positioned in their place. Caligula also identified himself as Neos Helios / 'New Sun.'

As a result of the political underlying tensions, the prefect of Egypt Aulus Avilius Flaccus attempted to placate both the Greek population and Caligula by having statues of the emperor placed in Jewish synagogues.

Philo wrote that Caligula 'regarded the Jews with the most especial suspicion, as if they were the only persons who cherished wishes opposed to his.' Philo of Alexandria, *On the Embassy to Gaius*, XVI.115

Rebellion, conspiracies against Roman rule, accusations, and exiles took place. Riots erupted between the Jews and Greeks in Alexandria.

Caligula was exceptionally bitterly hostile to the people of Israel. The people of Israel were accused of not honoring the Roman emperor. The people of Israel were removed to ghettos within the city of Alexandria. Disputes occurred in the city of Jamnia. The people of Israel were angered by the erection of a clay altar and destroyed it.

Beginning in Alexandria, Caligula took from the people of Israel all their synagogues and filled them all with images and statues of himself. The temple in Jerusalem was left untouched until last with Caligula's plan to make the temple in Jerusalem into the temple of the new Jupiter, the illustrious Gaius. As a demonstrative act of authority, Caligula ordered the erection of a statue of himself as the god Jupiter to be placed in the Jewish temple in Jerusalem.

Because Publius Petronius, governor of Syria, feared civil war if the order were carried out, he delayed in implementing the order for nearly a year. Herod Agrippa I finally convinced Caligula to reverse the order. However, Caligula issued a second order to have his stature erected in the temple of Jerusalem. In Rome, Caligula commissioned a colossal sized statue to be made of brass for the purpose.

In 40 AD, Caligula announced to the senate that he planned to leave Rome permanently in order to move to Alexandria, Egypt, There Caligula hoped to be worshiped as a living god. Caligula would also no longer be accountable to the Praetorian Guard or the Roman Senate.

When the Roman senate, the nobility and the equestrian order had become the object of Caligula's attention, conspiracies against Caligula developed. Most of them failed. Eventually the Praetorian Guard officers led by Cassius Chaerea provided the solution. While the plot was devised by three men, the senate was also aware and involved.

On January 41 AD, in the cryptoporticus / underground corridor beneath the imperial palaces on the Palatine Hill, Caligula addressed an acting troupe of young men beneath the palace, to applaud them during a series of games and plays being held for the honor of the Divine Augustus. The crowd was kept away by the Praetorian Guard in order to allow for Caligula's meeting with the troupe. But Caligula's bodyguards were also kept at distance.

Chaerea stabbed Caligula first, followed by a number of conspirators, in a similar manner to the assassination of Julius Caesar. Both the elder Gaius Julius Caesar / Julius Caesar and the younger Gaius Julius Caesar / Caligula were stabbed by conspirators led by a man named Cassisus (Cassius Longinus and Cassius Chaerea).

By the time Caligula's loyal Germanic guard responded, the emperor was already dead. The Germanic guard responded with a rampaging attack on the assassins, conspirators, innocent senators and bystanders.

Planning to leave no heirs, the conspirators also stormed the palace, killing Caligula's wife Caesonia and young daughter Julia Drusilla whose head was smashed against a wall.

The assassination resembled the assassination of Julius Caesar, except that the Senate had underestimated the affection of the people for Caligula.

41 – 54 AD: Claudius became the emperor of the Roman empire. As Roman emperor Caligula / Gaius Julius Caesar Augustus Germanicus was assassinated; his uncle Claudius hid. Claudius was located behind a palace curtain where he had been spirited away by the Praetorian Guard out of the city to a nearby camp. When Claudius had been installed as emperor and had procured the support of the Praetorian Guard, Claudius ordered the execution of the conspirators.

Tiberius Claudius Caesar Augustus Germanicus was the son of Drusus and Antonia Minor. Claudius was also the grandson of Augustus' sister Octavia. Originally, he was nicknamed with the cognomen of 'Nero,' but dropped the nickname / cognomen when he adopted the nickname / cognomen 'Caesar' in order to gain popularity. Born at Lugdunum in Gaul, he was the only Roman emperor to be born outside the region of Italy, which possibly worked in Claudius' favor.

Claudius was a step grandson through his father Drusus and a great nephew through his mother Antonia Minor, of Augustus. Claudius was a nephew of Tiberius through his father, Tiberius' brother. Through his brother Germanicus, Claudius was an uncle of Caligula and a great uncle of the future Nero who would become emperor. Through his mother Antonia Minor, Claudius was a grandson of Mark Antony.

Claudius was also afflicted with a limp and slight deafness due to sickness at a young age. His family ostracized him and excluded him from public office. Even though he was not trained and prepared for the position of emperor, Claudius proved to be an able and efficient administrator and ambitious builder.

Claudius' infirmity and seclusion probably saved him when the nobles purged the reigns of Tiberius and Caligula.

Claudius had four wives and was poisoned by his fourth wife, Agrippina the younger.

41 – 43 AD: Simon Cantatheras son of Boethus became high priest.
43 AD: Mattias son of Ananias became high priest.
43 – 44 AD: Elioneus son of Simon Cantatheras became high priest.
44 AD: Jonathan son of Ananias was restored as high priest.
44 AD: King Herod Agrippa I died.
44 – 46 AD: Josephus son of Camydus became high priest.
46 – 58 AD: Ananias son of Nedebeus became high priest. He was appointed by Herod of Chalcis and deprived of his office by Herod Agrippa II, but not robbed of influence. Ananias' wealth continued to increase daily by gifts and by unscrupulous means.

Ananias son of Nedebeus was described by the historian Josephus as being 'a violent, haughty, gluttonous, and rapacious man, and yet looked up to by the Jews.'

This was the same high priest Ananias who presided during the trials of the apostle Paul in Jerusalem (Acts 23:2) and Caesarea (Acts 24:1). Ananias, after hearing Paul's opening defense, commanded those who stood by him to strike Paul on the mouth. Paul described Ananias as a whitewashed wall and stated that God would strike Ananias for this unlawful act. Those who stood by, accused Paul of insulting the high priest. Paul replied that he did not know that he was the high priest and laid his appeal to the Pharisees within the Sanhedrin.

In 52 AD, Quadratus, governor of Syria, accused Ananias son of Nedebeus of being responsible for acts of violence. Ananias was sent to Rome for trial, but was acquitted by the emperor Claudius.

As a friend of the Romans and as a violent, greedy, and unscrupulous man, Ananias drew the hatred of the Sicarii. The Sicarii were so named because they carried sicae / small daggers that they concealed in their cloaks. At public gatherings, the Sicarii would use their daggers to attack Romans and Roman sympathizers, then blend into the crowd afterward in order to escape detection. The Sicarii, a branch of the Zealots, seem to be first documented by Josephus in *The Wars of the Jews* 2.254.7 as being a new phenomenon around 52 – 60 AD. The Sicarii were one of the earliest known organized assassination units of cloak and daggers, predating the Islamic Hashishin and Japanese ninja by centuries.

Ananias drew the hatred of the Sicarii so that when the First Jewish Roman War began in 66 AD, the revolutionists not only burnt his palace but killed Ananias and his brother.

Ananias' son, Eleazar ben Hanania became a leader during the First Jewish Roman War supporting the people of Israel instead of being a friend to the Romans like his father was. Eleazar used his position as the governor of the temple to convince the priests of the temple to stop the service of sacrifice for the emperor, which was a main milestone in the escalation of the rebellion against Rome, in Judea.

47 – 48 AD: Saul / Paul went on his first missionary journey.

49 AD: The followers of Jesus held the Jerusalem Council to determine the answers to theological questions in the context of the resurrected Jesus Christ.

49 – 52 AD: Saul / Paul went on his second missionary journey.

52 – 57 AD: Saul / Paul went on his third missionary journey.

54 AD: Roman Emperor Claudius died on October 13, 54 AD, a result of consuming poisoned mushrooms supplied by his fourth wife, Agrippina the younger. Poisoning Claudius was Agrippina's assurance that her younger son Nero would ascend to the position of emperor.

54 – 68 AD: Nero became the emperor of the Roman empire when he was sixteen years old and reigned from October 54 AD to June 9, 68.

The Roman emperor Claudius and his third wife Valeria Messalina had a son Tiberius Claudius Caesar Britannicus born February 12, 41 AD. When it was revealed that Valeria Messalina had entered into a bigamous marriage without Claudius' knowledge, Britannicus was released from inheriting the throne.

Britannicus was educated and raised with Titus Vespasianus, the future emperor of Rome.

Britannicus who was the son of Claudius with his third wife Valeria Messalina, had a sister Claudia Octavia, who would later marry Lucius Domitius / Nero.

After the heartbreaking affair of Tiberius Claudius' third wife Valeria Messalina, Claudius vowed to never marry again. But Agrippina the younger applied all her charm and convinced Claudius to take her as his fourth and final wife.
Agrippina the younger was the daughter of Agrippina the elder who was the granddaughter of Augustus. Agrippina the younger was also the sister of Caligula. Agrippina the younger already had a son Lucius Domitius through a prior marriage. When his father died, Lucius Domitius was only four years old. First Agrippina the younger convinced Claudius to betroth his daughter Claudia Octavia to her son Lucius Domitius who was nine years old at the time. Next, Agrippina the younger convinced Claudius to adopt her son Lucius Domitius. Claudius who was Lucius Domitius' great uncle also became his adoptive father. Lucius Domitius was renamed Nero Claudius Caesar.
Lucius Domitius / Nero was placed in physical danger when his uncle Caligula experienced low popularity. Nero was not expected to become emperor because of the expectation that Caligula would have a long reign and would produce direct male heirs. But with Caligula's early death, heirs to the throne had dwindled.
Because Britannicus had been released from inheriting the throne, Nero Claudius Caesar became the first in line to inherit the throne over Britannicus. But Claudius eventually favored the skill of Britannicus over Nero. When the dispute arose over who would succeed Claudius, Britannicus or Nero, Agrippina the younger conspired to poison Claudius with mushrooms, leaving the possibility for Nero to fill the position.
Immediately following the death of Claudius, Agrippina the younger set about removing others that she perceived were a threat to Nero Claudius Caesar's reign. Included on the list was Britannicus, son of Claudius.
Nero Claudius Caesar also sought to eliminate Britannicus after Britannicus avoided the embarrassment that Nero had planned for Britannicus to endure during a concert. Instead of giving a below par performance, Britannicus sang a poem telling the tale of how he had been cast aside in favor of Nero. Britannicus' poem engendered the favor of the audience.
When the first attempt at poisoning Britannicus failed, Nero brought Locusta the herbalist, to his room to mix a faster acting poison in his presence and tested the various potions on animals. When satisfied, the concoction was brought immediately to the dining room. Britannicus was poisoned at a dinner party with his sister Claudia Octavia, Agrippina the younger and several notables present. Even Britannicus' childhood friend Titus who would become the future Roman emperor, claimed to be present. The hot drink was presented

first to the food tester who requested cold water to be added to cool the drink. It was with the cold water that the poison was added. When affected, Nero claimed that Britannicus was merely suffering from an epileptic fit. Britannicus died the day before his fourteenth birthday and just four months after his father's death. The historian Tacitus alleges that Britannicus was sexually abused by his step brother Nero and claimed that because he was a victim of sexual abuse, Britannicus' death was not cruel. Cremated and with the funeral the very next day, Nero supplied no eulogy for his step brother.

Because Nero was so young when he became emperor, there was a triumvirate who primarily assisted Nero in his governance. The trio consisted of Lucius Annaeus Seneca his tutor, Sextus Afranius Burrus his Praetorian prefect, and his mother. Seneca was a famous stoic philosopher. Burrus was the head of the Praetorians and very competent.

As Nero aged, his behavior became more bizarre and lawless. When Agrippina the younger began to cool toward Nero, Nero had his mother assassinated in 59 AD. The first attempt failed when the sabotaged boat sank, and Agrippina's maid took her place and was killed. Agrippina was rescued by a fishing boat. Finally, soldiers were sent to kill her effectively. Nero presented the story that Agrippina the younger had killed herself.

Nero married Claudia Octavia, the sister of Britannicus. When Claudia Octavia had not produced an heir for Nero during their eight years of marriage, Nero wanted to marry his pregnant mistress Poppaea Sabina the Younger. Nero ordered the torture of Claudia Octavia's servants to provide false accusations of Claudia Octavia's infidelity. The servants endured torture and remained loyal. But Claudia Octavia was banished to the island Campania, in the general area of Pompeii where Poppaea had been born. There Nero had Claudia Octavia murdered.

Just days later, Nero married Poppaea in 62 AD. Poppaea was beautiful and vain. Poppaea had previously been married first to Rufrius Crispinus. Then in order to gain proximity to Nero, Poppaea married Otho, who would become emperor in 69 AD. Nero became Poppaea's third husband. Their daughter Claudia Augusta died just four months after she was born. Nero then murdered any in the family who might have a claim upon the throne.

In 62 AD, Burrus died and Seneca was forced to commit suicide along with his wife.

Nero enjoyed his personal perception that he was a wonderful entertainer. Nero would hold concerts where the guests were required to attend and sit through hours of his performances. Women would even give birth during their attendance of his performances because they were not allowed to leave. There were no restroom breaks while he played and sang.

Nero's sexual exploits were renown. For entertainment, Nero would cover himself in wild animal skins, be let loose from a cage and attacked the private parts of men and women who had been bound to stakes.

In 64 AD, Rome experienced the Great Fire of Rome which destroyed about a third of the city. As soon as Nero heard of the fire, Nero hastened home, acting as a hero, providing food, shelter, etc. Soon after the fire, Nero presented intricate and already prepared plans for redeveloping the portion of the city that had burned. Included in the plans was the proposal to rename the city 'Neropolis.' At that point, it became obvious that Nero was behind the fire. But to deflect the blame, Nero chose to blame the Christians for the fire.

Under Nero's persecution of the Christians, Nero would do things like douse the Christians in tar and light them on fire to light his garden for his parties. John the Revelator's exile on the Island of Patmos took place during this era. Etc. Up until this time, Christian persecution had been at the hands of the people of Israel against the followers of a man they considered to be a blasphemer, Jesus Christ. With Nero's angst against Christians, Christian persecution was also from the hands of the Gentiles.

Around 64 – 65 AD, when Nero came home late from the chariot races, he received Poppaea's criticism. Nero so violently kicked Poppaea that both she and her unborn child died. Poppaea received Egyptian embalming and a state funeral with divine honors.

After the death of Poppaea, there were a number of historians that offered various accounts of Nero's next spouse. In one account, Nero ordered a young freedman, Sporus, to be castrated and then married him. Sporus had born an uncanny resemblance to Poppaea Sabina. Nero even called Sporus by his dead wife's name. In another account, Nero married a freedman named Pythagoras in a public ceremony in which Nero took the role of bride and wore the bridal veil. The wedding laid everything plainly visible, which normally when a woman marries, is hidden in darkness. In another account Nero married a freedman named Doryphorus who was one of the wealthiest and most powerful of Nero's freedmen.

In 68 AD, the Praetorians had sentenced Nero to death. As Nero left his residence, he took up refuge in a house away from Rome. When told that he had been sentenced to being paraded through the city naked and then stoned to death, Nero opted for suicide. A servant helped him with a knife to the throat. Just before the knife was plunged into Nero, he said something like, 'What an artist dies in me!'

54 – 68 AD: Nero was Roman emperor. Nero was a catalyst for instability throughout Rome and the Roman empire, including the nation of Israel. This instability and tension had been rising for twenty years prior to the initiation of the First Jewish – Roman War. By this time in Israel the people were deeply divided between liberals and conservatives. The moderates had become the minority.

56 AD: Sicarii assassinated Jonathan son of Ananias. Josephus *Wars of the Jews* 2.13.3 256

57 AD: Saul / Paul was arrested in Jerusalem.

57 – 59 AD: Saul / Paul was held prisoner in Caesarea.

58 AD: Ananias son of Nedebeus was a friend of the Romans and was hated by the people of Israel. Ananias was murdered by the people at the beginning of the First Jewish Roman War. But his son Eliezar ben Hanania / Eliezar son of Ananias was one of the leaders of the Great Revolt of Judea.

58 AD: Jonathan became high priest.

58 – 62 AD: Ishmael II son of Fabus was reinstated by King Agrippa to the high priesthood. Ishmael had been high priest from 15-16 AD, prior to Ananias and his five sons controlling the office.

~59 – 62 AD: Porcius Festus became procurator of Judea. The Apostle Paul had his final hearing before Festus (Acts 24:27). Festus sought to induce Paul to go to Jerusalem for trial (Acts 25-26). Festus' death was sudden.

59 – 60 AD: Saul / Paul appeared before Festus and appealed to Cesar who sent Saul / Paul to Rome.

60 – 62 AD: Saul / Paul lived under house arrest in Rome.

62 – 64 AD: Saul / Paul released from house arrest. Accounts vary as to what happened next. One account had Paul journeying to Spain. Another account had Paul killed as a Christian martyr in Rome. Another account had Paul having journeyed to Spain and then having returned to Rome for martyrdom.

62 – 63 AD: King Herod Agrippa II appointed Joseph Cabi son of Simon to became high priest, but then the king denied Joseph Cabi son of Simon the high priesthood and bestowed the priesthood on Ananias son of Ananias.

62 AD: Ananias son of Ananias seized power upon the sudden death of Festus, before another Roman governor took command. Ananias was the youngest of the five sons of the elder Ananias and brother-in-law to Caiaphas. Each of the five sons and the son-in-law of Ananias had been high priest.
Ananias son of Ananias was very insolent, arrogant in character, exceptionally bold, and belonged to the Sadducees. Ananias son of Ananias ordered the execution of James the brother of Jesus / James the Just. Like Jesus' trial before the Sanhedrin, James the brother of Jesus / James the Just was also sentenced to death by the Sanhedrin, who had James

stoned. Josephus noted that the Sadducees, when they sat in judgment, were more heartless than any other Jews.
Herod Agrippa II subsequently deposed Ananias.

63 AD: Jesus son of Damneus became high priest following Ananias son of Ananias.

63 – 64 AD: Joshua son of Gamla became high priest. His wife Martha belonged to the Boethus family. The Boethus family headed the list of the wicked and sinful priestly families. 'Boethusian' is a form of 'Beit Essay' or 'House of Essenes.' It may have been that by the time of the diaspora, the Essenes had become corrupt. There is no significant evidence to support this characterization, nor to deny it.

64 – 66 AD: Gessius Florus was the Roman procurator of Judea appointed by the emperor Nero. Gessius Florus' wife was named Cleopatra and had been a friend of Poppaea, Nero's mistress whose ambition had landed Poppaea the position of empress as the second wife of Nero.

Gessius Florus was noted for his public greed and his injustice to the people of Israel. Josephus attributed Gessius Florus as being the primary cause of the First Jewish Roman War / Great Jewish Revolt.

When a delegation of the people of Israel protested against a pagan sacrifice that was set up deliberately in front of a synagogue in Caesarea, Gessius Florus arrested them and extracted money from the temple treasury. The temple treasury acted as the bank for the people of Israel as well as the nation of Israel. There was no place that was more secure and protected for holding personal wealth than the temple.

Following the raid on the temple treasury, Gessius Florus ordered his troops to raid the markets in Jerusalem. Gessius Florus had thirty six hundred men, women, and children slaughtered during his six month reign of terror during 66 AD. The Zealots and the Sicarii responded with taking up arms against the Romans.

Herod Agrippa II sent two thousand riders to assist the Jewish leaders in the upper city of Jerusalem against the rebels.

65 – 66 AD: Mattathias son of Theophilus and grandson of the elder Ananias, became high priest.

66 – 73 AD: First Jewish Roman War

70 AD: Herod's temple destroyed

The possibility of the First Jewish Roman War of 66 to 73 AD as the fulfillment of Daniel 11:29-12:12, and the prophecy of Jesus Christ concerning the future abomination of desolation event

The majority preterist view maintained that the abomination of desolation event described by Daniel and by Jesus Christ (Matthew 24, Mark 13), already took place around the time of the First Jewish Roman War (first rebellion – June 18, 66 to fall of Masada – April 73 AD), or the Third Jewish Roman War / Third Jewish Revolt / Bar Kokhba (son of a star) revolt (132 - 136 AD) during the era of the Roman emperor Hadrian (fl. 117 to 138 AD). And with placing the fulfillment of the abomination of desolation event at that time, preterists maintain that Jesus Christ has already returned, possibly multiple times, and will not be returning again.

Consequently, they concluded that all of Daniel 11:29-12:12 and all that Jesus Christ instructed concerning his return, has already been fulfilled.

The correlation was made that the First Jewish Roman War lasted approximately seven years, and Daniel 9:26-27 referenced seven years for the confirmation of the covenant peace treaty agreement. The destruction of the temple took place on Av 9, 70 AD, roughly in the middle of the First Jewish Roman War, which was close enough of a fulfillment, according to preterists, to be able to make the claim that the prophecies were already fulfilled.

But there are multiple inconsistencies that arise in the interpretation that the abomination event described by Daniel and by Jesus Christ, has already taken place.

If the abomination of desolation event took place in 70 AD around the middle of the era of the First Jewish Roman War, then the discontinuation of the temple sacrifice in the few days prior to the destruction of the temple needs to be interpreted as having fulfilled Daniel's prescribed discontinuation of the evening and morning daily sacrifices for two thousand three hundred days (Daniel 12:11). The preterist view holds that the discrepancy between the few days of the cessation of sacrifice in 70 AD and the biblical record's detailed and specific two thousand three hundred daily sacrifices, must be ignored.

If the abomination of desolation event took place in 70 AD around the middle of the era of the First Jewish Roman War, then the event lacked the man of lawlessness standing in the temple and making the declaration that he is equal to or greater than God Most High. Some preterists have defined the man of lawlessness as merely the ruler of the era. But the biblical record defined the man of lawlessness as considering himself to be above the law, not bound by the law, and able to establish law in defiance to God Most High's Law. Each of the preterist candidates for fulfilling the role of the man of lawlessness have eventually been held accountable by a human legal system, not above the law.

The preterist view believes that the return of Jesus Christ needs to be interpreted with an understanding that Jesus Christ actually allegorically or spiritually comes at various times throughout history, popping in for visits from time to time. Therefore, Jesus Christ would have already established his millennial reign which currently has been extended for almost two thousand years. With the preterist view there is no identified translational point for Jesus Christ to come with the clouds and make his dramatic entrance, for the purpose of defeating the enemies of the kingdom of heaven in the final battle of this age. There would be no identified transitional point for the new heaven and new earth to be established. And the final day of judgement would not be necessary.

The impact of the preterist view of interpretation of the biblical record upon understanding the events of the era of the time of Jacob's Trouble always result in the dismissal of the necessity for the fulfillment of various scheduled events for the era of the time of Jacob's Trouble.

Another substantial problem with the preterist view was that it required that God Most High abandon God Most High's covenant established with the people of Israel. And in that context, the preterist view denied the importance of the reestablishment of Israel as a nation in 1948, after almost one thousand nine hundred years, just as it was documented to happen in the biblical record.

No other nation in human history has been disbanded and its people dispersed, only to rise again to become a nation. Israel's statehood and other prophecies that continue to be fulfilled in our contemporary world are indications that God Most High is still at work to fulfill God's plan.

If the preterist view were to be correct and there are not more scheduled events on God Most High's timeline, then the prophesied era of the time of Jacob's Trouble would become superfluous. There would be no need to be watching for Jesus Christ's return. Jesus Christ's instructions and warnings concerning the preparation that the followers of the Lamb are to take as a preparation for the era of the time of Jacob's Trouble would be able to be set aside as unnecessary.

But if the preterist view is incorrect, the result for those who embrace the preterist view, will be to arrive at the era of the time of Jacob's Trouble unprepared for the events described in the biblical record. Using the preterist view to rationalize ignorance, inactivity and unpreparedness, is merely an act of disobedience to Jesus Christ's instruction to the followers of the Lamb / Jesus Christ to be watching and to be prepared.

The preterist view uses the order of events that were presented by Luke as one of the proofs that the abomination of desolation required by biblical prophecy has already taken place. Luke's order was:
    a) Jerusalem would be surrounded by armies;
    b) the people of Israel would fall by the sword and being taken as prisoners into all the nations;
    c) and then Jerusalem being trampled until the times of the Gentiles are fulfilled.

To be fair to the biblical account, Luke referred to the desolation of the city of Jerusalem and did not place the desolation of the city of Jerusalem in the context of the abomination of desolation that must take place in the temple.

Matthew's (Matthew 24:15-21) and Mark's (Mark 13:14-19) accounts of Jesus' instructions have this order for the events:
    a) the abomination that causes desolation' as described by the prophet Daniel taking place in the holy place / temple;
    b) then fleeing to the mountains;

c) and then great distress unequaled from the beginning of the world until now and never to be equaled again.

The accounts of Jesus' instruction recorded in Matthew and Mark clearly placed the abomination of desolation in the temple and did not indicate that an army needed to surround Jerusalem as a prerequisite for the future abomination of desolation event to take place. The army surrounding Jerusalem was only a requirement before the siege of the city of Jerusalem. While Luke cited the army that surrounds Jerusalem as the source for the punishment of the city of Jerusalem, Matthew and Mark allowed for the source of the great distress to be provided by a nonmilitary source. Even the result of Luke's desolation of the city of Jerusalem was described differently than the result of Matthew's and Mark's great destress that will result from the future abomination of desolation event that will take place on the temple mount.

The preterist view offers a list of other details as evidence for dating the abomination of desolation event of Daniel 11:29-12:12 and of Jesus' description as having already taken place. The following timeline offered details that referred to a variety of times that have been the focus for the preterist view.

Timeline for the First Jewish Roman War 66 - 73 AD
Josephus' list of reasons for the revolt included:
- the involvement of governor Albinus with criminal gangs
- the removal of rights of the people of Israel in Caesarea Maritima
- the pollution of the synagogue of Caesarea Maritima
- the murder of high priest Jonathan
- the murder of high priest Ananias
- the refusal to offer prayers or sacrifice on behalf of the emperor in the temple
- the movement of the Fourth Philosophy that held divine assistance would come to a rebellion: 'The infection which spread from them among the younger sort, who became zealous for it, brought the public to destruction.' The other three philosophies were the Pharisees, Sadducees, and Essenes. The fourth of the philosophies was led by Judas the Galilean and agreed in all other things with the

Pharisaic notions except that the Fourth Philosophy possessed an unconquerable passion for liberty and claimed that God is to be their only Ruler and Lord. The insurgency led by Judas the Galilean and Zadok the Pharisee began around 6 AD among the lower classes of the people of Israel. Judas the Galilean led resistance to the census imposed for Roman tax purposes by Quirinius. The Fourth Philosophy was also resolutely ready to die for their cause. (Judas the Galilean was explicitly named in Acts 5:37.)

- the criminal acts and abuse of authority on the part of governor Gessius Florus
- a conspiracy on the part of Gessius Florus
- a certain ambiguous oracle
- the extremism of the Zealots who mixed nationalism with religious ideal. Those who believed in the Israelite national movement repeated robberies, riots, and uprisings that were left unchecked by the administrators which led to the cycle of protest—response—protesting the response and the escalation of rebellions.
- the cruelty and corruption of the Roman administrators, particularly those serving under Emperor Nero. Nero had left Judaean society exposed to many dangers: crime and terrorism, exploitation by corrupt governors and anti-Jewish violence in the surrounding multicultural cities where some of the people of Israel had relocated.
- the belief that if the people of Israel were able to throw off the oppression of the occupying government, they could fulfill their destiny and assist the coming of the promised messiah.

The factions of the Revolt:
- Eleazar son of Ananias who was the captain of the temple, led the officiating priests in revolting against Rome.
- Menahem son or grandson of Judas the Galilean / founder of the Fourth Philosophy, was the rebellion's would-be messiah. The Fourth Philosophy believed that one of their group would be anointed king of Israel. Menahem was killed in the first days of the war by his opponents.
- The Sicarii were knife wielding assassins and a division of the Zealots. The Sicarii were opportunists seeking a path for gaining wealth and power through their utilization of the chaos. Some were under the leadership of Menahem.
- There were those who chose to rebel rather than continue to be ruled by corruption.

There were also those who were anti-revolutionaries.

- The Ruling Class of Judea. Without the active participation of the Ruling Class, the revolution could not have taken place. The Ruling Class also included the Hellenized and pro-Roman priests of the temple. The wealthy and powerful leaders of Jerusalem did not desire to antagonize the Romans and put at risk their wealth and equity.
- The former high priest Ananias who while no longer holding the office, remained highly influential.
- Herod Agrippa II held influence because of his genealogy and his position, and used that influence to advance his political standing. Herod Agrippa II was the son of Herod Agrippa I and Cyprus, grandson of Aristobulus IV and Berenice the daughter of Salome I, great grandson of Herod the Great the Idumean and Mariamne I the Hasmonean princess. Herod Agrippa II was both Idumean and Israelite, but Herod Agrippa II cooperated with Rome because Rome had made him king over territories east of Galilee including the area of the Golan Heights. Herod Agrippa II held the power to appoint the high priest, choosing Hellenized people for the position instead of those who embraced the tradition and culture of the true practice of Judaism. Herod Agrippa II also appreciated the support of many of the wealthy and powerful of the nation of Israel and did not desire to place his position at risk by offending the wealthy and powerful people of either Israel or Rome.
- Gessius Florus who was the Roman Procurator of Judea. Gessius Florus did not wish to experience the effects of a revolt. However, Gessius Florus showed little interest in suppressing the causes of revolution, and even contributed to the animosity and angst.
- Vespasian the Roman general who first militarily addressed the rebellion and was later recalled to Rome to acquire the position of emperor.
- Titus the Roman general who replaced his father Vespasian in militarily addressing the rebellion.

One that cannot be definitively placed on either side of the conflict was Yosef ben Matityahu / Josephus who had been appointed the rebel commander in Galilee and the city of Jodapatha in Galilee. Later Josephus, the same Josephus who became the historian, attempted to negotiate with the Romans for peace.

Timeline:
65 AD: Passover – Some marked the beginning of the First Jewish Roman War with Passover the year before the major hostilities broke out. Gaius Cestius Gallus had visited Jerusalem, heard the people's denunciation of the Judean procurator Gessius

Florus (Josephus, *Wars of the Jews* 2.14.3.280) and had promised to curtail Gessius Florus' misdeeds, but then failed to do so. But because of an outbreak of violence in Antioch, Caius Cestius Gallus initially ignored the situation in Judea.

65 – 66 AD: Haley's comet was in appearance. Other omens were also noted around this time: for example, a star shaped like a sword that hung over the city of Jerusalem; a brilliant light appeared around the altar; armed battalions were seen in the sky; voices were heard in the temple; and prophecies were given like the prophecy of a peasant crying out, 'Woe to Jerusalem.'

66 AD: Passover – March 20, 66 AD / Nisan 8, a heifer was about to be sacrificed on the altar by the high priest. The young cow gave birth to a lamb in the middle of the temple complex. Many in Jerusalem believed that this was an omen foretelling the impending destruction of Jerusalem.

66 AD: July – Violent clashes between the people of Israel and Gessius Florus had caused the people of Israel to again appeal to Gaius Cestius Gallus for relief and an end to Gessius Florus' corruption. The Roman senator, general and Legate of Syria Gaius Cestius Gallus sent Neopolitanus as his emissary to further investigate the details. Herod Agrippa II took this opportunity to make a disastrous attempt to persuade the people of Judea to abstain from complaining to the emperor and to continue to recognize the authority of Gessius Florus.

66 AD: August-September – Revolt in Jerusalem began.

Three actions occurred at the same time.
- Herod Agrippa II abandoned his efforts to hold the revolutionary movement in check, leaving Jerusalem and resigning to the Roman Procurator Gessius Florus to handle the problems Josephus *Wars of the Jews* 2.17.1 407
- Eleazar son of Ananias persuaded the priests to suspend the evening and morning sacrifice offered in the temple for the Roman emperor. Josephus *Wars of the Jews* 2.17.2.409
- Revolutionaries took the fortress of Masada and killed the Roman garrison there. Josephus *Wars of the Jews* 2.17.2.408

The powerful leaders of the city, along with some of the high priests and the leaders of the Pharisees attempted to persuade the dissidents to reestablish the sacrifices for the emperor. When this failed, Simon son of Ananias, Costobar, Saul and Antipas were sent to Gessius Florus and Herod Agrippa II for assistance. Gessius Florus did not respond. But Herod Agrippa II sent three thousand cavalry. Josephus *Wars of the Jews* 2.173-4 411-421

Herod Agrippa II and his wife Berenice were forced to flee to Rome and never return.

66 AD: September 4 / Av 15 – The Antonia fortress was captured by the rebels and the Roman soldiers stationed there were slain. Herod the Great's palace was besieged by the rebels.
Josephus took refuge in the temple, afraid of being taken for one of the pro-Roman party.
Menahem son of Judas the Galilean broke into the armory at Masada and provided weapons to his own people as well as to the 'robbers.' Menahem returned to Jerusalem 'as a king' and took command of the revolutionary forces and the siege of the palace. Josephus *Wars of the Jews* 2.17.8 430-434

66 AD: September 25 / Elul 6 – Menahem one of the leaders of the rebellion, took Herod's palace and burned it. Josephus *Wars of the Jews* 2.17.8 440
Herod Agrippa II's troops were forced out of Jerusalem.

66 AD: September 26 / Elul 7 – The former high priest Ananias and his brother Hezekiah were killed by the 'robbers.' Menahem consequently regarded himself as absolute ruler. Some of Menahem's followers contemplated that Menahem was the promised messiah.
Eleazar the son of the former high priest Ananias and his supporters argued to the populace that if the Romans were overthrown because they were to have 'no master but the Lord,' then that should apply also to Menahem who was not qualified to lead because of his low class status.
Menahem, who continued to regard himself as an anointed king, entered the temple in royal robes and surrounded himself with armed guards.
The priestly forces that supported Eleazar arranged to have Menahem son or grandson of Judas the Galilean, captured. After many tortures, Menahem was killed.
Josephus left the refuge of the temple and rejoined the high priests, leading the Pharisees to discuss what could be done. With no alternative, the Pharisees joined the rebels.

66 AD: October – Twenty thousand people of Israel were killed in Caesarea Maritima by the Greek residents. The rest of the people of Israel were deported so that the city 'was completely emptied of Jews.' Josephus *Wars of the Jews* 2.18.1 457
In reprisal, parties of the people of Israel organized and attacked Greek villages and cities of Syria so that immense numbers of people were captured and slaughtered. Josephus *Wars of the Jews* 2.18.2 460
Reprisals on both sides continued. Thousands of people were killed.

66 AD: October-November – Campaign of Gaius Cestius Gallus – Roman military surrounds Jerusalem.

During the revolt in Jerusalem, the rebels had defeated the pro-Roman civic leaders, the local Roman garrison and the forces of Herod Agrippa II. When the report of the loss traveled up the chain of command to the Governor of the Roman province of Syria, Gaius Cestius Gallus was given the responsibility to smother the rebellion.

Gaius Cestius Gallus approached the region of Judea and first conquered Beit She'aram in Lower Galilee where the Sanhedrin had relocated its headquarters after the devasting earthquake that took place at the time of the crucifixion of Jesus Christ had destroyed the temple rooms where the Sanhedrin had previously met. But Gaius Cestius Gallus had experienced losses from the encounter. With a reduced force and a compromised supply chain, Gaius Cestius Gallus approached Jerusalem. Gaius Cestius Gallus' inexperience in military campaigns caused him to place his supply column behind the military instead of placing it in the center, which left his supply column susceptible to ambush. In addition, Gaius Cestus Gallus failed to secure the hilltops where his army was to pass allowing the rebel forces to seize the strategic positions and attack the Twelfth Legion.

When Gaius Cestus Gallus reached Mount Scopus that is an observation point over the city of Jerusalem, Gaius Cestus Gallus was unable to capture the temple mount. After a siege of nine days, Gaius Cestius Gallus decided to retreat back to the coast, in order to be out before the fall rains.

Gaius Cestius Gallus and the Twelfth Legion experienced heavy losses ... twice; when advancing on Jerusalem and then again on the retreat.

The retreat of Gaius Cestius Gallus also prompted the historical memory of the miraculous success of Joshua who pursued the five kings of the Amorites through the pass of Beth Horon, with the Lord's assistance in throwing down huge stones from heaven, holding the sun and moon to stand still until the nation defeated their enemies as recorded in Joshua 10:10-13.

For some, the defeat of Gaius Cestius Gallus was another fulfillment of Hezekiah's account of Sennacherib recorded in 2 Kings 19:32-33, where Sennacherib had sieged Jerusalem and then was defeated by the Lord's angel as the Lord protected Jerusalem.

Gaius Cestius Gallus' defeat was also similar to the success of the Maccabees against a previous 'ruler' of the Seleucid / Syrian empire, Antiochus IV Epiphanes and his much larger army.

The people of Israel viewed Cestius Gallus' sudden and inexplicable retreat as a miracle. There developed a sense of elation in Jerusalem at the prospect of the people of Israel prevailing in a revolt against the Roman occupation. The rebels sang their way back to Jerusalem.

The rebellion and reprisals from both sides continued with deaths measured in the thousands.

But there was another response to the siege of Gaius Cestius Gallus from those living in Jerusalem who believed that Jesus Christ was the promised and prophesied messiah. Eusebius and Epiphanius of Salamis during the fourth century AD, were still telling of what the followers of Jesus Christ did in response to the siege of Jerusalem by Cestius Gallus.

66 AD: Those who believed that Jesus Christ was the messiah sent by God Most High, also believed and obeyed Jesus Christ's instructions and recognized Gaius Cestius Gallus' siege as a warning. The followers of Jesus Christ / followers of the Way, left Jerusalem because they remembered Jesus' words.

Jesus said: 'So when you see standing in the holy place 'the abomination that causes desolation, spoken of through the prophet Daniel — let the reader understand — then let those who are in Judea flee to the mountains. Let no one on the housetop go down to take anything out of the house. Let no one in the field go back to get their cloak. How dreadful it will be in those days for pregnant women and nursing mothers! Pray that your flight will not take place in winter or on the Sabbath. For then there will be great distress, unequaled from the beginning of the world until now — and never to be equaled again.' (from Matthew 24:15-21)

Mark 13:14-18 and Luke 21:20-24 also recorded Jesus' warning. So, when the followers of Jesus Christ saw the army of Gaius Cestius Gallus surrounding Jerusalem, they remembered Jesus' instructions, recognized Gaius Cestius Gallus' siege as a warning, and fled across the Jordan River to Pella.

The emigration of the followers of Jesus Christ, along with the mass departure of the pro-Roman distinguished aristocracy of Jerusalem, left only the moderate Jews and the Zealots left to occupy the city. The vacuum of leadership that occurred when the leadership of the followers of Jesus Christ and the pro-Roman aristocracy left, created an environment that was ripe for disorder and civil war.

It was from this point on during the First Jewish Roman War, that the people who remained in Jerusalem lived under civil disorder, tyranny, and their own form of terrorism and starvation.

67 – 70 AD: Phannias son of Samuel became high priest.

67 – 68 AD: The Campaign of Vespasian was led against the people of Israel by the Roman general Vespasian who was dispatched by Nero to restore order. Vespasian arrived in the spring with

sixty thousand elite special forces troops. Beginning north of Jerusalem in Galilee, Vespasian was successful in putting down the rebellion. But it was a bloodbath. The Sea of Galilee had dead bodies in it that had been stabbed and killed. By 68 AD, the rebellion in the north had been fully crushed.

Thousands of the people of Israel felt that Jerusalem would be safe and fled there. Jerusalem at that time had provisions to withstand a siege and strong walls to protect from invasion. Jerusalem began to be overpopulated as many sought out its refuge. Upon arriving in Jerusalem, the people found that the leadership of Jerusalem was locked in civil war between the liberals and conservative. And the people were locked in civil war between the pro-Roman populace and the traditional values people.

During the Campaign of Vespasian and the subsequent siege of Jerusalem led by Titus, the various factions of the people of Israel within Judea and Jerusalem held their internal civil war. The Zealots intentionally destroyed the supplies of the city of Jerusalem with the intent to force the people to fight more vigorously.

Factional groups within Jerusalem responded with seizing the supplies of the Zealots.

People would sell their possessions for gold and then swallow the gold coins to hide them as they attempted to escape the Romans. Two of the main leaders: John and Simon organized parties for the robbing and murder of the wealthy. Because the gold was carried within the bodies of escapees, the Romans would slice open the abdomens of escapees to retrieve the gold.

Instead of peaceful transitions for those who would fill the office of high priests, various factions would put up their man with the most powerful faction for the moment providing the man for the position. Often the transition was bloody.

Wives were kidnapped and held for ransom. People starved in mass. Homes became tombs. Roads became littered with dead bodies of all ages and both genders.

It was estimated that during the First Jewish Roman War more murders were committed by the various factions of the people of Israel upon their fellow citizens, than by the Romans.

68 AD: Rabbi Yohanan ben Zakkai was smuggled out of Jerusalem in a coffin by his students during the siege of Titus in a scheme to negotiate a peace.

The Talmud reported that, in the mid first century, Rabbi Yohanan ben Zakkai was particularly active in opposing the Sadducees' interpretations of Jewish law, and produced counter-arguments to the Sadducees' objection to the Pharisees. So dedicated was he to opposing the Sadducee view of Jewish law, that he prevented the Jewish high priest, who was a Sadducee, from following the Sadducee interpretation of the Red Heifer ritual.

Originally from Galilee, Rabbi Yohanan ben Zakkai found the Galileans to hate the Torah.

During the siege of Jerusalem in the Great Jewish Revolt, Rabbi Yohanan ben Zakkai argued in favor of peace. When exasperated, Rabbi Yohanan ben Zakkai arranged a secret escape from the city inside a coffin so that he could negotiate with general Vespasian.

Rabbi Yohanan ben Zakkai correctly predicted that Vespasian would become Roman emperor, and that the temple would soon be destroyed. In return for this prophecy, Vespasian granted Rabbi Yohanan ben Zakkai three wishes: 1) the salvation of Yavne and its sages, 2) the salvation of the descendants of Rabban Gamliel, who was of the Davidic dynasty, in order to make provision for the continuation of the house of David, and 3) a physician to treat Rabbi Tzadok, who had fasted for 40 years to stave off the destruction of Jerusalem.

68 AD: June 9th, 68 AD – the Roman emperor Nero committed forced suicide in Rome which created a vacuum in the power structure of Roman government and began the 'Year of Four Emperors' where four men were emperor in the same year.

68 – 69 AD: The Year of Four Emperors:
- Galba (December 3, 68 – January 15, 69) Galba was old and was expected to name Otho as the next emperor. When Galba failed to pass the position on to Otho, Otho had Galba assassinated.
- Otho (January 15 – April 16, 69) Otho was a previous husband of Poppaea who had divorced Otho to marry Nero. Ortho led a military campaign, First Battle of Bedriacum, where he suffered defeat and then committed suicide.
- Vitellius (April 16 – December 20, 69) Vitellius' practice was to hold three banquets / parties a day, which incurred debt. He had those who questioned him executed. Those who had named him as their heir, he also had put to death to collect the inheritance. Bribery and making promises of power did not work to continue gaining support of his reign as emperor. And the Batavians came to the city gates. Vitellius went into hiding and prepared to flee. But before Vitellius left, he made one last visit to the palace where Vespasian's men caught and killed him. Vespasian's men also burned down the temple of Jupiter.
- Vespasian (December 21, 69 – 79 AD) Vespasian was observing all the events in Rome and recognized the need for quality, strong leadership. In preparation, Vespasian

amassed a large military force for the purpose of assuming leadership. Vespasian founded the stable Flavian dynasty which succeeded the Julio Claudians.

This was a year defined by wars and rumors of wars more than any other for the Roman empire.

In order to pursue the position of emperor, Vespasian left his son Titus to continue with the military assault on Jerusalem. Vespasian took the best soldiers with him and left the inferior mercenaries for Titus. Mercenaries were less disciplined than regular soldiers and less likely to follow orders. Mercenaries were also more active in murder, looting, raping, pillaging, etc.

70 AD: April-August – Campaign of Titus son of Vespasian – Roman military surrounds Jerusalem laying siege against Jerusalem for a second time.

The Roman legions surrounded Jerusalem and began to slowly squeeze. But it would be April 70 AD before Titus would be able to make the siege of Jerusalem effective.

It was noted that the people who lived in southern Israel knew when the Romans were coming because they saw the dead bodies floating in the Jordan River.

70 AD: April 14, 70 AD the siege of Jerusalem began. Using the draw of Passover for gathering the nation of Israel's population into the city of Jerusalem, the Romans laid siege to Jerusalem three days before the beginning of Passover, but after the people had already begun to arrive, entrapping a large mass of the people of Israel inside the city. What made the siege of Jerusalem more horrific was the leadership of the Zealots. The Zealots fought among themselves, offered poor leadership, encouraged poor discipline and training, and were ill-prepared for survival during the siege and the battles with the Romans. Prisoners were tortured, killed and then crucified outside the walls of the city of Jerusalem to intimidate the people within. As many as five hundred a day were crucified. 'So great was their number that space could not be found for the crosses nor crosses for the bodies.' Trees were used for fuel and for crucifixion so that the land became barren of trees.

Syrian troops discovered some who had managed to escape the city who had swallowed gold coins. Either their intestines swelled and killed them with their intestines bursting forth gold coins or they were cut open and the gold was discovered. Rumor spread that all deserters were filled with gold. Soldiers then embarked on eviscerating all who escaped the city. In one night more than two thousand were ripped open.

From approximately May 1 to July 20, the estimate was that almost one hundred sixteen bodies were carried out through the gate and another six hundred thousand were dead among the lower classes within the city.

The people gnawed on shoe leather and grass.

Josephus, at the urging of contemporary witnesses, recorded the story of a woman who had been robbed of everything including her food. She took her infant son, decided that he was going to die anyway, killed him, roasted him and ate half of him, concealing the other half. When others smelled the roasted child, they threatened her to tell the source. She replied that she had saved what was left of her son and uncovered the meat. Those who had impinged upon her for food were seized with a horror and amazement, astonished at the sight. She offered the uneaten half of her son. But they exited trembling and left the mother with the second half of her son. When the account was conveyed to the Romans, some Romans responded with disbelief, others with pity for the distress, still others developed a more bitter hatred. Caesar Nero excused himself claiming that he had proposed peace and liberty to the people of Israel, but that they had insisted on sedition, war, and famine. Josephus, *Wars of the Jews* 6.3.4-5

A crowd of about six thousand primarily poor women and children, were persuaded by a 'false prophet' to go into the temple court to receive deliverance from God. After they had climbed onto the porticoes, they were set on fire by the Romans.

The Romans carried standards with emblems on the standards, into the temple area through the east gate and sacrificed to them. The emblems on the Roman standards were depictions of the gods that the Romans worshiped. Under the people of Israel's definition, that act was considered idolatry and an abomination.

Gold was taken out of the temple, so much gold that the price of gold throughout Syria dropped in half.

The Romans breached the outer walls of Jerusalem, so that by August 5th, 70 AD, the priests had exhausted the sacrificial animals and could no longer continue offering sacrifices.

After Jewish allies killed several Roman soldiers, Titus sent Josephus, the Jewish priest and historian, to negotiate with the defenders of the city. In response, the people of Israel wounded the negotiator with an arrow and then launched another round. Titus was almost captured during this sudden attack, but escaped.

70 AD: Av 9-10 / August – Titus had wanted to capture the temple and transform it into a temple dedicated to the Roman emperor and the Roman pantheon of gods from the baal / mystery / mythology religion. But the fire that had been set in the doorway of the temple spread quickly and was soon out of control. The temple court was captured by the Romans. Most of the citizens of Jerusalem were unarmed, and therefore butchered where they were caught. Around the altar the heaps of corpses grew higher and higher, while down the sanctuary

steps poured a river of blood and the bodies of those killed at the top slithered to the bottom.

As victors, the Romans slaughtered over a million people. Those sparred from death were enslaved and sent to the mines of Egypt or dispersed to the arenas throughout the empire to be butchered for the amusement of the public or forced to build the Forum of Peace and the Colosseum. The spoils of the First Jewish Roman War financed the building of the Colosseum in Rome.

Priest Jesus ben Thebuthi delivered some of the Temple treasures to Titus in exchange for protection. Included were two candelabra, solid gold tables for the showbread, bowls, and platters, the veils, the high-priests garments including the precious stones, and many other items. The temple treasurer Phineas provided more, including priestly clothing and incense. The treasures were eventually displayed by Vespasian in Rome in the newly constructed Temple of Peace. Until the temple's furniture was publicly displayed, the temple's furniture had only ever been seen by the high priests of the temple. The arch of Titus depicts the event, carved in the stone.

Titus ordered the whole city and temple to be razed to the ground leaving only the tallest towers and a small portion of the wall on the west. (Matthew 24:2, Mark 13:2, Luke 19:44, 21:6)

73 AD: The last sputtering of the rebellion was extinguished with the fall of the stronghold at Masada.

The era of the Roman emperor Hadrian (fl. 117 to 138 AD) and the Third Jewish Roman War / Third Jewish Revolt / Bar Kokhba (son of a star) revolt (132 – 136 AD)

There have always been some people of Israel who remained dwelling in the land of Judea.

After the diaspora of the First Jewish Roman War, some of the people of Israel made one more attempt to rise against the yoke of the Roman empire, with the Bar Kokhba revolt (132 - 136 BC).

In response to the Bar Kokhba revolt, the Roman emperor Hadrian (fl. 117 to 138 AD) determined to take a more forceful approach to the people of Israel who had remained living in the land of Israel. Hadrian covered the temple mount with rubble and erected a pagan temple dedicated to Jupiter on the site. Hadrian installed two statues in his temple; one of Jupiter and the other of himself.

Hadrian expelled the people of Israel from the city of Jerusalem altogether, allowing them into the city only for the fast of Tisha B'Av / Av9, the anniversary date for the destruction of both the first and second temples. It was this action that caused the Third Jewish Roman War / Third Jewish Revolt / Bar Kokhba Revolt of 132 - 136 AD.

The leader for the Bar Kokhba Revolt / Third Jewish Roman War / Third Jewish Revolt was Simon bar Kokhba. Simon bar Kokhba / Simon son of a star, was an excellent military strategist and garnered the support of a majority of the rabbis who even viewed him as messiah for a period of time because he was such an excellent strategician. Simon bar Kokhba effectively uprooted the Romans from the land of Israel by his repeated practice of retaking a city for the people of Israel, eliminating the Roman presence, fortifying the city and then moving on to the next city to repeat the process. Under Simon bar Kokhba's leadership, the people of Israel living in Judea accomplished self-governance once more.

The Roman response to the Bar Kokhba Revolt was to send approximately one hundred forty thousand to two hundred twenty thousand troops to destroy what was left of the people of Israel who remained in the land of Israel. The destruction of the people of Israel during the Bar Kokhba Revolt almost entirely annihilated the world's total population of the people of Israel. The Greek historian Cassius Dio noted that five hundred eighty thousand people of Israel perished in war with many more dying of hunger and disease, and more sold into slavery. In 135 AD, on the ninth of Av, a day of mourning for the destruction of the first and second temples, the fortress of Jerusalem was breached and destroyed. Once the defeat of the people of Israel was established, the Romans continued killing 'until their horses were submerged in blood to their nostrils.' The city's capture was described as a massacre.

After the suppression of the revolt, Hadrian instituted several proclamations designed to root out Jewish nationalism and prevent further uprisings. Torah law and the Hebrew calendar were prohibited. Scholars were executed. Sacred scrolls of Judaism were burned on the temple mount. The greatest offense was Hadrian's construction of the temple for Jupiter on the temple mount and the installation of two statues; one of Jupiter, another of Hadrian himself. The name of Judea / Israel was stricken from the map and replaced with 'Syria Palaestina.' Jerusalem was renamed 'Aelia Capitolina.'

This time when Judea was reconquered from the people of Israel, the Romans salted the earth which made the land unable to produce a crop and unable to support people living in the region.

A careful review of the detailed timeline of events for the preterist view of the period surrounding the second abomination of desolation event having taken place during the era of time between Jesus Christ's crucifixion around 30 - 33 AD and the construction of the Roman emperor Hadrian's temple to Jupiter on the temple mount around 137 AD, did not yield an event that could authentically stand out as meeting the description criteria for the future abomination of desolation event that was described in the biblical record by Daniel, Jesus, and other biblical writers.

While an acknowledgement of a second abomination of desolation event as having already taken place would add a sense of security and peace to one's psyche, the falseness of the claim that the prophesied future abomination of desolation event has already been completed, will eventually be realized when the future abomination of desolation event actually takes place.

Historicist interpretation

The beginning of historicism was attributed to Joachim of Fiore (1132-1202) and Nicolas of Lyra (1270-1349) a Franciscan monk.

The historicist interpretation viewed all the prophecies concerning the second coming of Jesus Christ, including the scheduled events described in the book of Revelation, as having been fulfilled sometime between the death and resurrection of Jesus Christ to this current point in time. The historicist view applied the fulfillment of the prophecies specifically referenced in the book of Revelation as pieces that have been fulfilled during times such as the Dark Ages / Middle Ages / medieval period, or the French

Revolution, or The Great War or World War II, etc. The primary setting for the historicist view was Western Europe leaving unaddressed, the events that must take place in the land of Israel in the reestablished nation of Israel.

Historicism appeals to theologians who have observed that in the Old Testament narrative, once the people of Israel exited Egypt, God Most High interacted with the people of Israel regularly. In contrast, when Jesus Christ ascended into heaven after his crucifixion, death, and resurrection; and after the apostles recorded their gospels, epistles, and revelations; there was no more special revelation to be recorded.

There were several reasons for the lack of recorded special revelation from God Most High. First, God Most High no longer needed to speak using prophets. It is now the work of the Holy Spirit to speak to each individual spirit. Second, God Most High's message was no longer exclusively given to the people of Israel. With the crucifixion, death, resurrection and ascension of Jesus Christ, the covenant agreement that God Most High held with the people of Israel expanded to become available to all the tribes, peoples, multitudes, nations and languages of the world to receive.

Theologians who became weary of waiting for God Most High to present some activity that 'proved' God Most High was still at work, over time gave up on God Most High's message of fully establishing the kingdom of heaven on earth as a literal and physical possibility. To appease their minds and the minds of their contemporaries, a new explanation, a new interpretation was needed that was more immediate and was not the futurist / literal interpretation of God Most High's message communicated in the biblical record.

Even Abram / Abraham, weary of waiting for the fulfillment of becoming the father of nations that God Most High had promised to him, considered his servant Eleazar as his heir, and also Abram / Abraham produced a son through Hagar the handmaiden of his wife Sarai; all before becoming the father of Isaac through Sarah. It would be

Isaac who would be the messianic lineage bearer for messiah that would arrive in the incarnation around two thousand years after Abram / Abraham.

The historicist view taught that John the Revelator's book of Revelation was a symbolic representation that presented the course of history from the apostle's life through the end of the age. The symbols in the apocalypse corresponded to events in the history of Western Europe, including various popes, the Protestant Reformation, the French Revolution, and rulers such as Charlemagne.

Prominent scholars who held the historicist view included John Wycliffe, John Knox, William Tyndale, Martin Luther, John Calvin, Ulrich Zwingli, John Wesley, Jonathan Edwards, George Whitefield, Charles Finney, C. H. Spurgeon, and Matthew Henry. This view rose to popularity during the Protestant Reformation because of its identification of the pope and the papacy with the beasts of Revelation 13.

One historicist interpretation claimed that the six seals of Revelation 6 were opened in association with events that took place in Europe between 96 and 324 AD with the fall of the Roman empire. The events of the first four trumpets of Revelation 8 took place between 395 and 476 AD and consisted of the invasions of the Vandals, Huns, Saracens, and Turks. The fifth trumpet / woe #1 of Revelation 9 took place between 1062 and 1453 AD. The sixth trumpet / woe #2 and the arrival of the two witnesses of Revelation 9 and 11, took place between 312 and 1794 AD. The events of Revelation 12 took place between 107 and 1572 AD. Revelation 15-16, the seven bowls / seven last plagues, began in 1795 and are continuing today. But all of those events provided at best, only a hint of partial fulfillment of the original biblical prophecy.

In many versions of the historicist view, the beast of the earth / false prophet was viewed as a position more than a person, specifically the position of the papacy of the Roman Catholic Church, and not the man who is the pope himself. Revelation 11-13 was claimed to represent the true church in the struggle against Roman Catholicism. The harvest of the earth along with the seven bowls / seven last *plagues of Revelation 14-16 represented God Most High's judgment on the Roman Catholic Church.*

In the historicist interpretation, there were very few events described in the biblical record that are left to take place prior to the actual arrival of Jesus Christ and the subjugation of the two beasts of Revelation 13.

There are several criticisms of the historicist approach. First, the historicist approach allowed for a wide variety of interpretations. Adherents to the historicist approach, had a tendency to interpret the biblical text through the context of the period of time that the interpreter lived in. Thus, many historicists interpreted the climax of the eschatological prophecies as being fulfilled in their generations. With an historicist approach, estimates of fifty substantial versions of interpretation developed.

But in reality, the only interpretation that is of true importance is the interpretation of the direct and accurate message of God Most High concerning what will actually take place. And with time, those previous interpretations met with not being fulfilled.

Around the time that Jesus came as the incarnate messiah, there were many interpretations for the timing of the coming of messiah and what messiah would accomplish. They were interpretations that were constructed on only partial pieces of prophecy, or on prophecy that was spun to fit an artificial context. One of the dynamics of the Bar Kochba revolt was the belief of the Israelite people still living in the land of Israel, that it was the time when their messiah was to come. And so they accepted others to be the fulfillment of messiah, having missed the actual promised and prophesied messiah. The historicist view concerning eschatology has also entertained multiple interpretations set within the context of the time of the interpreter, and because it was not the correct time for the return of messiah / the Lamb / Jesus Christ, the prophecies that were not fulfilled were just ignored.

Second, the historicist view focuses mostly on the events of the church in Western Europe with very little application of the eschatological prophecies applied to areas outside of Western Europe. Oddly, Asia which was the context for the messages of Jesus Christ to the seven churches, was left out of the historicist eschatological interpretation.

Third, the historicist view was laden with symbolism that portrayed an ever present conflict but lacked the details of a resolution of the conflict. While acknowledging the return of Jesus Christ, the historicist view provided no allowance for understanding that the scheduled events of the era of the time of Jacob's Trouble will serve a vital purpose in the process of preparing the earth and humanity for the full establishment of the kingdom of heaven on earth.

Futurist / literal interpretation

The futurist / literal view was the predominant choice of interpretation for many of the early church leaders. The early church leaders wrote of an actual, physical, established millennial kingdom / Thousand Years Reign of Jesus Christ. Clement of Rome (96 AD), Justin Martyr 100-165 AD, Irenaeus (115-202 AD), Tertullian (150-225 AD) and others presented and taught a futurist / literal interpretation until Origen (185-254 AD) became weary of waiting for the return of Jesus Christ and introduced the inspirational / spiritual / allegorical interpretation. Augustine (354-430 AD) continued to promote the inspirational / spiritual / allegorical interpretation.

In more recent times, the futurist / literal interpretation has been revived. With the actual reestablishment of the nation of Israel after nearly two thousand years, and the acceleration of the fulfillment of the prophecies detailed in the biblical record, it has become more apparent that the total fulfillment of the prophecies listed in the biblical record may in fact become reality, and that total fulfillment will be realized during the era of the time of Jacob's Trouble.

The futurist / literal interpretation viewed the future abomination of desolation event in the category of what is yet to happen. *The futurist interpretation recognized the details of the descriptions of the future abomination of desolation event given by Daniel, Jesus Christ, the gospel writers, the writers of the epistles of the New Testament, along with the visions that Jesus Christ personally gave to John the Revelator; as yet to take place during the era of the time of Jacob's Trouble. Only with the futurist / literal interpretation was there a place for all the pieces of the biblical descriptions to be included without being falsely forced into their humanly determined positions. In fact, only the futurist / literal interpretation <u>required</u> that all of prophecy must be fulfilled, every dot and tittle. In the futurist / literal view, it was essential to arrive at an eschatological interpretation that allowed for all the biblical record to be included in the eschatological framework.*

The futurist view taught that events such as the Olivet Discourse (Matthew 24-25, Mark 13, Luke 21) and Revelation chapters 4-22 would occur in the future. The futurist view approached the message of the book of Revelation as divided into three sections as indicated in 1:19: 'what you have seen, what is now and what will take place later.' *Revelation chapter 1 described the past* ('what you have seen'). *Revelation chapters 2-3 described the present from the perspective of the time of the life of John the Revelator forward* ('what is now'), *and the rest of the book of Revelation described future events* ('what will take place later'). *The divisions of the eras of time from the perspective of the life of John the Revelator, conveyed the message that marking time from the life of John the Revelator, there was a past era, an era for the events of Revelation 2-3 (Jesus Christ's message to the seven churches marking around two thousand years of history) as preparation for the future era of drastic and quick change marking the transition from what we know now to the actual full establishment of the kingdom of heaven on earth / the era of the time of Jacob's Trouble (Revelation 4-19). In addition, John the Revelator documented the further future eras of the Thousand Years Reign of Jesus Christ followed by eternity (Revelation 20-22).*

The futurist / literal view interpreted Revelation chapters 4-19 as referring to a period known as the seven years of the era of the time of distress such as has not happened from the beginning of nations until then. (Daniel 9:27, 12:1b). During this time, God Most High will allow the red dragon / serpent / Satan, Inc. to have the opportunity to attempt to fully establish the kingdom of Satan, Inc. / kingdom of man as a part of the plan for bringing the people of Israel back into a full relationship with God Most High. The plan of the red dragon / serpent / Satan, Inc. will meet with the resistance of God Most High and Jesus Christ personally, and the plan of the red dragon / serpent / Satan, Inc. will fail.

Revelation chapters 4-19 documented the process for Jesus Christ to reclaim dominion of the earth from the red dragon / serpent / Satan, Inc. through the opening of the seven seals that sealed the will of God Most High, through the blowing of the seven trumpets that will allow the kingdom of Satan, Inc. / kingdom of man to be released upon humanity, and through the pouring out of the seven bowls of God Most High's wrath / seven last plagues upon humanity as God Most High's response to the attempt to fully establish the kingdom of Satan, Inc. / kingdom of man.

The futurist / literal view presented a full and deeply detailed eschatology that did not include the vague and fluid eschatological description presented by the inspirational / spiritual / allegorical, the idealist, the preterist, or the historicist interpretations. While the preterist and historicist interpretations presented the prophetic requirement for a world empire as being fulfilled by either the Romans or later by countries such as France with Napoleon or Germany with Hitler, the futurist / literal view presented the prophetic requirement for a world empire as a phenomenon that was yet to be developed and would need to be greater than the empire of Alexander the Great and massively greater than France's Napoleonic empire or Hitler's Nazi empire. The futurist / literal interpretation presented a future world empire / global governance system that will be in partnership with the global religious community under the leadership of the beast of the sea. This was just a listing of some of the details that were glossed over or even denied in the inspirational / spiritual / allegorical, idealist, preterist, and historicist interpretations.

The futurist / literal view held that the message from God Most High documented in the biblical record was to be considered to be accurate and unable to be altered, just as it was presented. It was in the futurist / literal eschatology that the actual physical, real and true return of the person of Jesus Christ as documented in the biblical record, was acknowledged; not an allegorical illusion of Jesus Christ, not a distant 'rule by proxy' Jesus Christ, not a spiritual ghost of Jesus Christ who pops in and out of human history on a whim, not a Jesus Christ affiliated with the regulations and relegations determined by the superiority of the church over the will of God Most High. The futurist / literal eschatology presented the return of an actual in-the-flesh, glorified incarnation, personal Jesus Christ who happens to embody divinity and will be ready to physically and fully prevail in a truly physical and bloody battle with the armies of the world in order to incontestably and incontrovertibly regain dominion of the earth from the red dragon / serpent / Satan, Inc. on behalf of the very real and physical humanity.

Revelation chapters 19-20 documented the future second coming of Jesus Christ, the battle of the siege of Jerusalem, and the subsequent literal Thousand Years Reign of Jesus Christ on earth. Revelation chapters 21-22 documented the certainty and actuality of the heavenly city's arrival on earth with the development of a new heaven and a new earth for the old heaven and the old earth will have passed away.

The entirety of this prophetic description remains difficult to comprehend because of the drastic change that will take place from the current conditions that are familiar to us. The incomprehensibleness of this magnitude of change causes many to deny the possibility of this kind of change. Denial becomes a method for coping with the message recorded in the biblical message. But not being able to accept the details of the dynamics of the message of God Most High, will not be able to prevent the eventuality of the scheduled events from taking place just as the biblical record described.

When Jesus stated, 'This generation will not pass away until all these things have happened' (Matthew 24:34), the futurist / literal interpretation stated that Jesus Christ was saying that once these events begin to take place, they will happen quickly, so quickly that the events will be witnessed in their entirety from the beginning of the era to the end of the era, by the same people, the same generation. Only the futurist / literal interpretation presented the scheduled events for the era of the time of Jacob's Trouble, as being fulfilled within one generation.

The inspirational / spiritual / allegorical, idealist, and preterist problem of the establishment of the nationhood of Israel in 1948

The biggest problem with embracing the inspirational / spiritual / allegorical, idealist, preterist, and historicist interpretations arises out of the fact that Israel did in fact became a literal and physical nation, recognized by the world community on Friday, May 14, 1948, just before the celebration of the Sabbath was to begin. As prophesied, Israel became a nation in a single day and literally arose from people who were intended by the world to become dry, dead bones (Ezekiel 37). In the previous decade before Israel became a nation, the people of Israel had experienced the worst genocidal onslaught since the diaspora of 70 AD and the Bar Kokhba Revolt (132 to 136 AD).

When Israel became a nation, it was a statement by God Most High that the words of God Most High are more than mere inspiration or allegory. The words of God Most High cannot be explained away by humanly redefining the words used in the biblical record. The words of God Most High will not be buried in historical dust.

The reestablishment of the statehood of the nation of Israel demonstrated that there is substance, physical presence, and spiritual power that is intrinsic in the word of God Most High. At the time of creation, the word of God Most High was able to say, 'Let there be light,' and there was light. The word of God Most High said through the prophets of the Old Testament that Israel would become a nation in a single day, and the nation of Israel was recognized as a nation in a single day.

When Israel became a nation, it was a statement by God Most High that God has not forgotten the promises and the covenant that God made to Abram / Abraham, Isaac, Jacob / Israel, Moses, David and their descendants. The institution of the nation of Israel serves as proof that the fully instituted reign of Jesus Christ on earth will also become a reality. God Most High's futurist and literal view was adequately been described in the biblical record and will become established.

When Israel became a nation in 1948, it was a statement by God Most High that history has not yet been completed. Prophecy is a living thing that cannot be relegated to the past, until the events actually take place on the calendar, specifically God Most High's calendar.

When Israel was reestablished as a nation, it was a statement by God Most High that 'every dot and tittle' that God Most High has commanded to be fulfilled will be fulfilled. Partial fulfillments of prophecy do not count as full fulfillments of prophecy. Partial fulfillments of prophecy remain as foundation for later and larger and greater total fulfillments of prophecy.

When Israel was reestablished as a nation, it was a statement by God Most High that the timer has been set. Not one generation will pass from the point that Israel became a nation until Jesus Christ will literally and physically return to fully establish the literal and physical kingdom of heaven on earth; and Jesus Christ will literally and physically reign. Jesus Christ's reign will not be merely inspirational, allegorical, idyllic, a pseudo fulfillment, provided by proxy or remote, or be a partial historical event. The biblical record clearly specified that Jesus Christ will in the future, literally, physically, and personally establish his reign as king of his own kingdom, the kingdom *of heaven, fully established on earth, under the dominion of Jesus Christ and shared with humanity.*

The possibility of a historical past event as fulfilling the criteria of the prophecies concerning the future abomination of desolation event

Jesus Christ instructed the disciples that when they 'see the abomination of desolation' spoken of by Daniel the prophet, standing in the holy place / in or around the Holy of Holies, then 'let those who are in Judea flee to the mountains' (Matthew 24:15-16, Mark 13:14). In between the writing of Daniel and the life of Jesus Christ dwelling on earth, was the first abomination of desolation event led by Antiochus IV Epiphanes of 167 BC. Therefore, when Jesus Christ instructed the disciples approximately 197 years later concerning the future abomination of desolation event, Jesus was informing us that there would be yet another abomination of desolation event.

The inspirational / spiritual / allegorical interpretation that defined the biblical message as merely symbolic or allegorical, does not need an actual fulfillment of any biblically recorded event. Events that take place that resemble the fulfillment of prophecy can be relegated to the category of coincidental. With the inspirational / spiritual / allegorical interpretation, there was no need for an actual future abomination of desolation event.

With the idealist interpretation of the biblical message, the fulfillment of biblically recorded events merely represented the haphazardly timeless struggle between the forces of good and evil. Idealists interpreted that a future abomination of desolation event cannot be truly defined. Any event that resembles an abomination of desolation event would merely be a part of the ongoing narrative in the struggle between the forces of good and evil and not necessarily connected to a larger plan, a series of scheduled events designed to result in the completion of a mission.

The preterist interpretation and the historicist interpretation looked to the immediate timespan that began with the crucifixion of Jesus Christ and for some extended to the Bar Kokhba revolt for the fulfillment of the abomination of desolation event spoken of by Daniel and by Jesus. But there were several occasions during that time period that were focused upon for completing the fulfillment of the abomination of desolation event. Each instance focused upon was lacking any completeness in being able to meet all of the requirements detailed by Daniel and by Jesus.

The preterist interpretation was not concerned with the partiality of the fulfillment of the rest of the prophecy concerning the era of the time of Jacob's Trouble or the possibility of an actual literal and physical return of Jesus Christ.

The historicist view dealt with the issue by merely extending the timespan over centuries. Surely there has been some point in the history of the past two centuries when every piece of prophecy could be checked off as having been fulfilled. For the historicist, there was no need for the events that have been slated to occur 'in the distant future' or to be collected together in a timeframe of occurring during the era of the time of Jacob's Trouble.

Only the futurist / literal interpretation required that there be a future abomination of desolation event that takes place while there is a covenant peace treaty agreement established between the nation of Israel and others, while the people of Israel are living in the land of Israel. Only the futurist / literal interpretation required that there will be a king who will exalt himself, and will discontinue the fully consecrated, functional and operational temple sacrificial system for exactly two thousand three hundred evening and morning sacrifices.

Each individual is left to decide which interpretation to embrace, to invest in. If the individual choices the correct interpretation, they will be blessed. But an incorrect choice could lead to devastating and deathly consequences.

The Future Abomination of Desolation Scheduled for the Era of the Time of Jacob's Trouble

The term 'abomination of desolation' refers to the desolation of the temple through the substitution of some form of idolatry that defies and desecrates what Yahweh / the Lord God Most High determined to be holy.

The definition of 'abomination of desolation' allows for a variety of forms of idolatry including the establishment of an idol of some foreign god to be set up in the temple, which is an offering of an alternative to be recognized as sovereign and divine over God Most High, and is an attempt to dethrone and displace God Most High.

Or the abomination of desolation idolatry could take place as the desecration of the Holy of Holies through the disrespect of the Law given to Moses and the people of Israel, for how the Holy of Holies was to be approached. To violate the Law that God Most High provided to Moses and to the people of Israel, also acts as a denial of God Most High's authority and power to establish God Most High's rules for conduct in the kingdom of heaven.

Or the abomination of desolation could occur through the offering of unclean animals or the offering of human sacrifice in the temple court. To offer unclean animals or human sacrifice, requires belief that there are other ways to enter into the kingdom of heaven other than through the path established by God Most High in God's redemption, reclamation and regeneration plan. But the biblical record was clear that there are no back doors that can be used for entrance into the kingdom of heaven. And there are no other methods for sneaking in. (John 14:6)

Or the abomination of desolation could be the result of the profaning of the temple court through deviant sexual practices that violate the Law provided to Moses and to the people of Israel. Deviant sexual practices and unblessed sex act as supportive practices that honor the baal / mystery / mythology religion. More importantly, deviant sexual practices and unblessed sex require that one party lords over the other party, which God Most High recognizes as abuse that violates the cultural economy of love that defines the kingdom of heaven.

Or the abomination of desolation could be the result of some other kind of activity that would nullify the consecration of the temple. The temple houses the Holy of Holies. The Holy of Holies houses the ark of the covenant with the mercy seat / throne of God, on top. The ark of the covenant houses God Most High's covenant with the people of Israel and with humanity. To violate the temple acts as a statement in effigy that God Most High's covenant must be violated and nullified.

The abomination of desolation may also actually include all the above dynamics as a collective in the future abomination of desolation event.

In the past, the temple was violated through the sacrifice of pigs / unclean animals, and human beings, especially young children. Pig sacrifice is still abominable to the altar of God Most High. But what is more abominable to God Most High is human sacrifice.

In the past, Solomon built altars to the gods Chemosh of the Moabites and Molech of the Ammonites (1 Kings 11:7). The altar of Molech was used for sacrificing children, sons and daughters (2 Kings 23:10, Jeremiah 32:35).

While those activities and similar other activities violated the temple and caused desolation, those events were not what the biblical record designated as the future abomination of desolation event.

When Daniel received the vision of Daniel 8 along with the interpretation, Daniel's response was to be worn out, to lay exhausted for several days, because the vision 'was beyond understanding.' (Daniel 8:27)

When Jesus instructed the disciples concerning the abomination of desolation, both Matthew's record and Mark's record included Jesus Christ's notation, '... let the reader understand, ...' (Matthew 24:15, Mark 13:14).

Both Daniel and Jesus, through their extra notations concerning the future abomination of desolation event, identified the future abomination of desolation event as an event that will be difficult to understand and overwhelming in its magnitude. But the difficulty in understanding the future abomination of desolation event is not to be an excuse for not contemplating the event and its meaning, and gaining at least a partial understanding. The overwhelming magnitude of the future abomination of desolation event should not be a hindrance to taking in the reality and the significance of the event.

The future abomination of desolation event will be one of the most important events in human history. A majority of the events scheduled for the era of the time of Jacob's Trouble will be attached to the future abomination of desolation event that will serve as the hub. The future abomination of desolation event will be crucial to the planned impact and effect that it will have on the world.

The future abomination of desolation event is pivotal in the plans of both God Most High and also the red dragon / serpent / Satan, Inc. If it were not important, then Daniel and Jesus would not have needed to mention it, repeatedly. Four times in the book of Daniel the term 'abomination of desolation' or a similar term was used (Daniel 8:12-14, 9:26-27; 11:31; and 12:11). Matthew, Mark, and Luke all recorded Jesus Christ discussing the topic. And John the Revelator, who was also the fourth gospel writer, placed the future abomination of desolation event set in the context of the entire book of Revelation as one of the pivotal events that will take place during the era of the time of Jacob's Trouble. Both
Daniel and John the Revelator identified the future abomination of desolation event as setting the time clock for the future glorious return of messiah / the Lamb / Jesus Christ. It was widely understood for those who have taken a futurist / literal view, that the future abomination of desolation will be an anchor point in time during the era of the time of Jacob's Trouble; an anchor point in the timeline that intertwines the efforts of the red dragon / serpent / Satan, Inc. and God Most High's responsive activity against the kingdom of Satan, Inc. / kingdom of man.

There will be many key elements that will make the future abomination of desolation crucial in the plans of both God Most High and of the red dragon / serpent /

Satan, Inc. The time, date, location, and world leaders for this event have been planned at least from the time of Daniel, who received the most detailed vision of the future abomination of desolation event and recorded it in Daniel 11:29-12:12, during the third year of the reign of Cyrus king of the Persians, 536 BC. Consequently, the future abomination of desolation event has prerequisite requirements that must be met in order for the event to transpire.

There is also a purpose for the future abomination of desolation event. God Most High's purpose for the future abomination of desolation event is very different than the purpose that the red dragon / serpent / Satan, Inc. has intended the future abomination of desolation event to serve.

For the red dragon / serpent / Satan, Inc. and for the kingdom of Satan, Inc. / kingdom of man, the future abomination of desolation event will be a crucial step toward the complete overthrow of God Most High and of the kingdom of heaven. For the red dragon / serpent / Satan, Inc. the future abomination of desolation event will provide alternative human leadership for humanity and for the earth, to the leadership of messiah / the Lamb / Jesus Christ, in the form of the beast of the earth. For the red dragon / serpent / Satan, Inc., the future abomination of desolation event will mark the full establishment of the kingdom of Satan, Inc. / kingdom of man on earth and fulfill the promise that Satan made to through the serpent to the first woman and first man in the Garden of Eden / garden of God / paradise when Satan promised that if they ate the fruit of the tree of the knowledge of good and evil that they would become 'like God.' The future abomination of desolation event will coronate the six thousand year old dream of Satan, to fully dominate the world, make humanity into the red dragon / serpent / Satan, Inc.'s definition of what it is to be 'like God,' and to use the subservient humanity to make the kingdom of Satan, Inc. / kingdom of man into a reality.

For God Most High and for the kingdom of heaven, the future abomination of desolation event will be allowed by God Most High in the plan to determine exactly who is loyal to messiah / the Lamb / Jesus Christ and worthy to be citizens of the kingdom of heaven, and who are adherents of the kingdom of Satan, Inc. / kingdom of man and belong in that kingdom.

According to the biblical record, immediately before or immediately after the time of the future abomination of desolation event, a series of actions will take place:
- The sixth trumpet will be sounded / woe #2 will begin.
- The little scroll and the seven thunders events will begin (Revelation 10).
- Three angels will make their announcements that (Revelation 14:6-13):
  - 'The hour of judgment has come. It is time to worship God who has made the heavens, the earth, the sea and the springs of water.'
  - 'Fallen, is Babylon the Great…'
  - 'Anyone worshiping the beast of the sea and its image and receives its mark on their forehead or on their hand, will receive God's fury and wrath. They will be tormented with burning sulfur in the presence of the holy angels and of the Lamb…'
- The little horn / eleventh king / final horn on the shaggy goat / prince who is to come / king that will exalt himself / beast of the earth / final world ruler will commit the future abomination of desolation event, in wing of the temple. The future abomination of desolation event will include a number of elements:
  - The beast of the earth will stand in the temple and declare his divinity, that he is in fact the god the world has been waiting for.
  - The beast of the earth will animate / 'bring to life' the image of the beast of the sea / false prophet / beast from the Abyss / eighth king beast.

- o The beast of the earth will discontinue the fully consecrated, functional and operational temple sacrificial system.
  - o The beast of the earth will attempt to usher in the full establishment of the kingdom of Satan, Inc. / kingdom of man on earth.
- The two witnesses will arrive from heaven and begin their work scheduled to take place during the second half of the era of the time of Jacob's Trouble (Revelation 11).
- Other events will also be initiated simultaneously with the future abomination of desolation event.

The religious, political, economic, social and cultural requirements for the future abomination of desolation event

Understanding the religious, political, economic, social and cultural environment that incubated the first abomination of desolation event in 167 BC, provides an understanding of what religious, political, economic, social and cultural dynamics may be present that will nurture the future abomination of desolation event.

The first abomination of desolation event was part of Israel's history before Jesus Christ was born. Jesus Christ was aware of the causes, the impact, and the despicable atrocities that took place with the first abomination of desolation event.

So when Jesus Christ spoke of how to prepare for the future abomination of desolation event, he spoke with an understanding of the details that will define the future abomination of desolation event.

The first abomination of desolation event of 167 BC was able to occur because the religious, political, economic, social and cultural environment had created long term dynamics favorable to rebellion against God Most High. The books of the Maccabees detailed the distance that the people of Israel had placed between them and God Most High, and claimed that this distance placed the people of Israel in a vulnerable position so that the first abomination of desolation could take place.

It was this same spirit of rebellion that Jesus Christ continually addressed during his earthly ministry, and this same spirit of rebellion that continued until the diaspora of 70 AD when the people of Israel were dispersed into the world. The spirit of rebellion will again be intense prior to the return of messiah / the Lamb / Jesus Christ.

Life in Israel in 167 BC was filled with internal dissension between the people and the religious system, between the people and those who governed them, etc.

A case could be made that internal dissention and rebellion today is similar to the internal dissension and rebellion of Israel in 167 BC.

Currently in the nation of Israel, there are orthodox Jews who seem to rule and impose their own sense of law upon the rest of the nation. There are non-orthodox Jews who desire merely to be devout. There are non-orthodox and nonpracticing Jews who live in the land of Israel because it is merely a great place to live and are Jewish only in their genealogy, denying their Jewish religious heritage. There are messianic Jews who believe that Jesus Christ is the promised and prophesied messiah sent by God Most High. The list of divisions continues. One result of the divisions among the people living in the land of Israel is the difficulty that the Knesset sometimes experiences in forming a government.

By 167 BC, many of the people of Israel had become blasé concerning their devotion to God Most High. The people of Israel had adopted Hellenization initiated by the Greek empire and Alexander the Great. The Hellenistic culture conflicted greatly with the traditional values of the people of Israel who had remained faithful to living according to the Law God Most High gave to Moses. The Hellenistic culture also acted as a force for the tolerance of many cultures living in the nation of Israel, and each alien culture was accompanied with its own set of conflicting gods and traditions. Over time, the nation of Israel lost greater amounts of its national identity, its national culture, and its understanding of its relationship with God Most High.

Today, the nation of Israel meets with the same kind of social and cultural diversity. Occupying the land of Israel are people with very diverse backgrounds. Added to the people already living in the land of Israel are more people who are immigrating from all over the world and bringing pieces of those unique cultural identities with them. The vastness of the cultural diversity amongst the population within Israel, will be used by God Most High in the future as a way to culturally connect the people of Israel with the nations of the world that they have emigrated from, to be a nation of priests to other nations.

But during the time in between now and the return of Jesus Christ, during the era of the time of Jacob's Trouble, the religious, political, economic, social and cultural diversity will aid in the creation of an environment that will be favorable to the development of the future abomination of desolation event. Great amounts of diversity are necessary to allow for the development of the global religious community, of global governance, and to assist in the temple mount becoming the main worldwide site for the implementation of the future abomination of desolation event.

When the first abomination of desolation event took place, the Hellenization program of the Greek empire and Alexander the Great had permeated even the religion, values, and culture of the people of Israel. The job description for the high priest of Israel had been so transformed that when the Maccabean / Hyrcanus family finally reclaimed the high priesthood after the 167 BC abomination of desolation event, they were able to only partially restore the dictates of the Law given to Moses.

When later generations of the Maccabean / Hyrcanus family assumed the office of high priest, the high priesthood became able to be bought with bribes. Bribes were paid from the religious community to the political community. When a religious community pays bribes to the political community, it is an act of the religious community capitulating to the political powers as the authority of the land. While the thought in most nations is that the political component of a nation is sovereign over the religious component of a nation, the nation of Israel's foundation was opposite. The nation of Israel was founded as a theocracy where God Most High dictated the law to the people and required accountability to God Most High's law. In the original foundation of the nation of Israel, prophets and the priesthood were developed first. The monarchy was developed last. The nation of Israel has always been unique among nations because only in the nation of Israel was God Most High considered to be sovereign above the nation's rulers. But after the first abomination of desolation of 167 BC, the sovereignty of God Most High was no longer functionally recognized by the leaders of the people of Israel.

When the nation of Israel was willing to be complacent with the abandonment of the selection of the high priest according to the Law given to Moses, and accept the selling of the office of high priest to the highest bidder, the nation of Israel also lost more of its religious identity and religious strength. For a nation founded on the sovereignty of religious strength over political strength, losing religious identity was the equivalent of a death wish for the nation. It would take only two hundred thirty six years from the first abomination of desolation event until the nation of Israel would actually be annihilated. But, the seeds for the death of the nation were already in place prior to the first abomination of desolation event of 167 BC.

After the decline of the Seleucid / Syrian empire, the Roman empire stepped into the role of ruling the nation of Israel (45 BC). The nation of Israel would be challenged to accept the Roman version of monarchy and Roman rule over their people, beginning with Herod the Great in 38 BC, until the nation of Israel entered into the diaspora in 70 AD, and also including the last gasp for life of the nation of Israel in the Bar Kokhba revolt (132 to 136 AD). The nation of Israel would be challenged to accept the social norms of Roman law in how they were governed, including the practice of the Romans to execute people without cause or trial as evidenced by the crucifixion of Jesus Christ. Tyrannical rulers would not be held accountable for their actions under Roman rule. The nation of Israel would be compelled and forced to accept the cultural invasion of many more people who held other religious principles, other traditions, and other cultural practices that were contrary to the practice of the Law of Moses. The rich theological understanding of the people of Israel became diluted and lifeless, which weakened the people of Israel's previously strong connection to God Most High. Having lost their relationship with God Most High meant they had lost their purpose for existing. God Most High allowed the nation of Israel to be dissolved in 70 AD.

When Jesus Christ was asked by his disciples what the world would be like before he would return to fully establish the kingdom of heaven on earth, Jesus offered a number of signs that would be indicators that the time is approaching (Matthew 24:4-14, Mark 13.) Jesus Christ's list of prerequisites included:
- false prophets,
- wars and rumors of wars,
- nation rising against nation, kingdom rising against kingdom,
- famines and earthquakes in various places,
- God's people handed over to be persecuted and put to death,
- God's people hated by all nations,
- a turning away from the faith, with betrayal and hatred directed toward others,
- false prophets (again) and the deception of the masses,
- an increase of wickedness causing the love of most to grow cold (but the one who stands firm to the end will be saved),
- gospel of the kingdom being preached in the whole world as a testimony to all nations (and then the end will come).

False prophets: *When Jesus Christ gave John the Revelator the vision of the beast of the sea / false prophet / beast from the Abyss / eighth king beast (Revelation 13), it was a vision of probably the most ominous and most powerful false prophet that human history will ever come to know. But the beast of the sea / false prophet / beast from the Abyss / eighth king beast will not be the only false prophet of the era of the time of Jacob's Trouble. The era of the time of Jacob's Trouble will be a time when there will be many leaders, including religious leaders, that will become a part of the global religious community, supporting the union of various denominations that will come under the umbrella of the Roman Catholic Church or use the Roman Catholic Church as the foundation for the development of the global religious community.*

Citing the Roman Catholic Church as the foundation for the global religious community was not a new idea. One of the tenets of the Protestant Reformation was the understanding that the woman who rides the beast and of 'Babylon' described in Revelation 17-19, is the Roman Catholic Church. The leaders of the Protestant Reformation even declared that the beast of the sea / false prophet / eighth king beast would be one of the popes of the Roman Catholic Church. The Roman Catholic Church's aggression in the Protestant Reformation Wars only supported the claims of the protestors against the Roman Catholic Church and the papal office.

Contemporarily, movements like the movement led by Ken Copeland and Rick Warren already are seeking to develop a following of people and churches that they will be able to present to the Roman Catholic Church for a connectional relationship.

One of the goals of the Roman Catholic Church's Vatican II was to begin dialogue with various church denominations for the purpose of encouraging 'the restoration of unity among all Christians...' *The World Council of Churches share the same purpose of embracing ecumenism / developing a shared theology. The Southern Baptist Convention officially entered into communication in 1990 with the Roman Catholic Church for the purpose of* dialoguing areas where the two denominations share theology. There are multiple other denominations and movements whose hierarchies share the agenda of a worldwide connectional system with the idea that the hierarchies of these movements will be rewarded for bringing the people they are responsible for, into reconnection with the Roman Catholic Church.

In addition to the future union of many Christian denominations and churches with the Roman Catholic Church, the current pope is also partaking in a movement to establish a relationship of acceptance with several other religions, religions that have been founded upon denying the divinity and sovereignty of Jesus Christ. In establishing a basis of commonality between the Roman Catholic Church and other religions, Francis has already made statements that Jesus Christ is not divine, that Jesus Christ failed when he came and was not able to finish the mission that God had established for him to complete, etc. These kinds of statements make dialogue possible with religions that reject the divinity and sovereignty of Jesus Christ.

The divinity and sovereignty of Jesus Christ used to be the point of differentiation that set Christianity apart from other religions. But Francis has taken on the task of rewriting Roman Catholic Church theology for the purpose of broadening the base of influence of the Roman Catholic Church, not just among Christian communities, but also with all regions of the world and with the religions of those regions. Francis consistently denied the divinity and sovereignty of Jesus Christ in the effort to repackage the principles of Christianity so that the Roman Catholic Church can become more compatible with the theology of other religions.

John the Revelator described the beast of the sea / false prophet / beast from the Abyss / eighth king beast as having a 'mouth to utter proud words and blasphemies and to exercise its authority for forty two months' (Revelation 13:5).

'Blasphemy' in the biblical record context meant to believe a lie, a lie specifically about the divinity and sovereignty of Jesus Christ when the Holy Spirit has *communicated the veracity of the divinity and sovereignty of Jesus Christ.*

Francis cannot be removed from the list of candidates of those who are qualified to fill the position of beast of the sea / false prophet / beast from the Abyss / eighth king beast.

Jesus said: 'At that time if anyone says to you, 'Look, here is the Christ!' or 'Look, there he is!' do not believe it. For false Christs and false prophets will appear and perform signs and miracles to deceive the elect – if that were possible. So be on your guard; I have told you everything ahead of time.' Mark 13:21-23

In Jesus Christ's description of the future abomination of desolation event, Jesus communicated that the era before Jesus Christ returns will be filled with false Christs and false prophets.

Notice that Jesus already was communicating that there is a difference between false Christs and false prophets, and that both will be present for the future abomination of desolation event.

Jesus also noted that in order to attempt to 'prove' their authenticity as messiahs and prophets, they will appear and perform signs and miracles intended to deceive, to manipulate the elect. But the signs and miracles will not be of the quality to be able to actually deceive the elect.

Jesus Christ's own authenticity was challenged by John the Baptist and his disciples. Jesus offered proof that he was in fact the authorized messiah with this: 'Go back and report to John what you hear and see: The blind receive sight, the lame walk, those who have leprosy are cleansed, the deaf hear, the dead are raised, and the good news is proclaimed to the poor. Matthew 11:4-5

It is not leaders who wear fine clothes who are prophets. Those who wear fine clothes are found in the palaces of kings.

It is not leaders who provide signs and wonders in order to prove their own position who are true prophets of God Most High. Those who provide signs and wonders for their own advantage are people whose claim to be a prophet of God Most High is false.

As the true Christ and true prophet of God Most High, Jesus' 'signs and wonders' benefited people instead of himself. Jesus' version of 'signs and wonders' / miracles were simply illustrations of what the kingdom of heaven is about.

And Jesus Christ defined the difference between what is true and what is false about those who claim to be god or speak for God. There is no excuse to not be on guard because Jesus Christ foretold these events before they will happen.

Wars and rumors of wars: Josephus in his history recorded around one hundred and fifty pages of documentation on wars, rumors of wars, and details of bloodshed. The wars and rumors of wars that Josephus documented took place either during Josephus' lifetime or prior to Josephus' lifetime. Wars and rumors of wars have been transpiring throughout human history. Even Enoch documented wars during the antediluvian / preflood world.

During the era of the time of Jacob's Trouble, beginning with the opening of the first four seals of the will of God Most High, the first four scheduled events will be the release of the four horses and their riders; the white horseman will be sent out to conquer which is an element of war, the red horseman will be sent out to take peace from the earth with a sword, the black horseman will be sent out to generate hyperinflation / a kind of economic war, and the green horseman with the rider named death will be sent out to kill a fourth of the world's population by sword, famine and plague, and by the wild beasts of the earth. The four horsemen technically all bring war; each of the horsemen just uses their own unique means for making war. The list of conflictual events / war continued throughout the rest of the book of Revelation.

During the era of the time of Jacob's Trouble the magnitude and incidence of war will increase to the crescendo, concluding with the armies of the world gathering together for the purpose of defeating the nation of Israel and to thwart the purposes of God Most High.

Jesus Christ said that all of this must take place before he returns.

Nation rising against nation, kingdom rising against kingdom: *While Jesus Christ noted that nation will rise against nation, kingdom will rise against kingdom; John the Revelator's vision described the red dragon / serpent / Satan, Inc. along with the two beasts of Revelation 13, as connected with the image of a red dragon with seven heads, ten horns and seven crowns on its head (Revelation 12-13). Daniel also described a fourth and terrible beast with ten horns / ten kings (Daniel 7). The number of heads, horns and crowns does not present an image of a unified effort. Instead, the number of heads, horns, and crowns presented an image of conflict and discord. The heads, horns, and crowns represented divisions within the kingdom of Satan, Inc. / kingdom of man, with each division representing its own interests.*

Added to the number of heads, horns, and crowns that top the red dragon of Revelation or the terrible fourth beast / fourth kingdom of Daniel, was the description that the little horn / eleventh king will rise up and subdue three of the ten horns / ten kings / kingdoms (Daniel 7). Subduing three of the ten horns / ten kings will also be an act of kingdom rising against kingdoms.

In contrast to the disunity and disorder that characterizes the red dragon / serpent / Satan, Inc., the office of God is comprised of three separate individuals who have been defined as unity (Deuteronomy 6:4, Mark 12:29). The nature of the conflict during the era of the time of Jacob's Trouble will be characterized by the forces of disunity verses an ultimate unified force; chaos verses order; just as it began in the week of creation: 'there was evening / chaos, and morning / order, the first day…' *God the Creator has always been the God who brings order out of chaos.*

Jesus Christ also pointed out that a kingdom divided cannot stand. The kingdom that will win this conflict during the era of the time of Jacob's Trouble will be the kingdom that is not defined as being divided and having seven heads, ten horns, and seven crowns. It will be the kingdom that is characterized by bringing unity.

Famines: Around 40 AD, Caligula wanted a statue of himself put up in the temple. The people of Israel continually resisted him. But there was so much fear of Caligula and fear that war would break out, that the people of Israel did not sow their crops. In a world that has reached its level of chaos so that chaos rules over peace, famine seems to invariably follow. And starvation followed the decision to not sow crops.

During the era of the time of Jacob's Trouble, there will be great chaos. Added to the chaos will be the political hyperinflation that will cause food to be overpriced as a way of controlling the human population. The third horseman released with the opening of the third seal (Revelation 6) will correspond to politically generated hyperinflation. Two pounds of wheat or six pounds of barley (about a day's bread ration) will cost a day's wages.

Food availability will be used to control humanity. When food is available but unattainable, it is still considered to be a famine, just not an environmental famine.

Governmental control will determine what kind of food will be available and how much food will be available. Rationales that will be offered to demonstrate the necessity for governmental control of food availability will include: maintaining peace by making food unavailable for regions that live in rebellion against the kingdom of Satan, Inc. / kingdom of man (in order to make it 'safer' for the regions that have resigned themselves to the global governance system), 'managing health' by determining what the proper diet should consist of for people (in order for the global governance system to provide better healthcare and to systematically starve those designated to be unworthy), the need to reduce 'global warming' (in order to combat food shortages that will actually be created by the global governance system), 'climate change,' etc.

(Note here that Elijah's God provided the widow with a continual supply of flour and oil during the drought

(1 Kings 17). Jesus Christ fed the multitudes using children's lunches as the starter, and there were leftovers.)

With the arrival of the two witnesses from heaven (Revelation 11), there will also be plagues and drought, blessing and rain, that will be based upon the reception of the people of the world to God Most High. As the people of the world embrace the culture of the kingdom of Satan, Inc. / kingdom of man and treat God's people and the followers of the Lamb / Jesus Christ as enemies, the two witnesses will have the authority to send plagues and drought. The two witnesses will also have the authority through God Most High to end the plagues and to bring rain. The plagues and drought, and the ending of plagues and drought, will serve the purpose of drawing God's holy people closer to God Most High and providing a message of God Most High's divinity and sovereignty to those who do not recognize God Most High.

During the era of the time of Jacob's Trouble, military discord will also be a source of famine, as famine is one of the usual results of military conflict.

Earthquakes: There was an earthquake when Jesus died. There was another earthquake when Jesus Christ rose from the dead. The number of earthquakes from the time of Jesus Christ's resurrection until the time of the destruction of Jerusalem forty years later in 70 AD was huge.

79 AD was the date for the great Mount Vesuvius eruption that buried Pompeii and Heracleum in Italy. Earthquakes accompanied the eruption.

Currently, the number of earthquakes is increasing along with the magnitude of earthquakes. While this is fodder for alarmists, the biblical record concerning the era of the time of Jacob's Trouble documented some specifically scheduled earthquakes that will take place at specified times and specified locations that will be more than mere earthquakes. These earthquakes will be messages from God Most High.

The proponents that advocate for the establishment of the kingdom of Satan, Inc. / kingdom of man will claim that these prophesied earthquakes are the result of 'climate change' and market the earthquakes as demonstrations that more global governance control is needed. Climate change alarmists who embrace the climate change religion will use the earthquakes to define God Most High as vicious and seeking to thwart the 'goodness' of the kingdom of Satan, Inc. / kingdom of man.

But those who are followers of the Lamb / Jesus Christ will recognize the prophesied earthquakes as the work of God Most High, as a part of God Most High's plan to fully establish the kingdom of heaven on earth; the kingdom that values life, that values humanity and has pressed into humanity the full image of God Most High.

God's people handed over to be persecuted and put to death: To be handed over to be persecuted means that it is one's own people that hand over their own people. This was not a statement that indicated that the people were conquered and taken by the enemy. Just as the people of Israel handed over messiah to the Romans to be persecuted and put to death through crucifixion; forty years after Jesus Christ's crucifixion, the people of Israel themselves experienced what it was to be handed over to the enemy for persecution and death during the First Jewish Roman War of 66-73 AD when most of the violence and death was the result of the people of Israel fighting with other people of Israel.

Jesus Christ's words indicated that during the era of the time of Jacob's Trouble, there will exist among the people of Israel, a culture that will be prone to offering family, friends and neighbors for persecution and death.

Also, during the era of the time of Jacob's Trouble, one of the largest points of conflict will be the dissension within churches, between people who will maintain their faith in the divinity and sovereignty of Jesus Christ, along with those who will have adopted the view that the biblical record is mere allegory and that Jesus Christ is not divine. Similar to the era of World War II, there will be people who will call themselves 'Christian,' who will believe that it is their duty to hand over others for the purpose of *providing a better path to 'world peace' through global governance.*

God's people hated by all the nations: One of the hardest dynamics for the people of Israel to grasp is the dynamic that the people of Israel throughout history, remain a people that is hated by the majority of the nations of the world. Currently, almost half of the world's population of the people of Israel live in the United States. Another almost half of the world's population of the people of Israel live in the land of Israel with an approximate land mass that is equivalent to the size of the state of New Jersey in the United States. The question remains, 'How can such a small group of people engender such a great hatred?' Most recently in human history, this hatred has fueled the Roman Catholic Church's Inquisitions, Hitler's Nazi Germany and World War II, and the emigration of the people of Israel out of Russia, Europe, and other nations.

The biblical record from John the Revelator identified a future time coming when the hatred against the people and the nation of Israel will intensify once more. The future abomination of desolation will be one of the main evidences that the hatred of the people of Israel by the nations of the world will be within a few years of its conclusion.

But in the fully established kingdom of heaven on earth, the people of Israel will be transformed and will be greatly loved.

Turning away from the faith, with betrayal and hatred directed toward others: The Holy Spirit is the way that God Most High pours love into our hearts (Romans 5:5).

During the era of the time of Jacob's Trouble, the division between those who have an allegiance with Jesus Christ or who are God Most High's chosen people, and those who have rebelled against God Most High and have rejected God Most High, will become a division of two sides that will be diametrically opposed to each other. Tolerance of other's view will become nonexistent.

Friendship, acceptance of diversity, tolerance, etc. will no longer be allowed in the new global culture of the fully established kingdom of Satan, Inc. / kingdom of man. 'Hate speech' will be defined as any speech that speaks of the divinity and sovereignty of God Most High, and any speech that speaks of the unfavorable characteristics or failures of the global religious community and the global governance system.

The global religious community that will be founded upon the organization of the world's churches, will have fully embraced the vision of Pierre Teilhard de Chardin's merger of 'science' / pseudo-science / scientism / evolutionary theory, with the form of religion that denies the God of Creation.

For the people of God Most High and the followers of the Lamb / Jesus Christ, it will be unsafe to blanketly extend love to others. Those who remain in connection with the church / global religious community, will view those who have continued their allegiance to God Most High or to Jesus Christ, as enemies of the newly developed principles of the redefined church / global religious community.

For the rest of the people of the world who have not ever considered Jesus Christ to be God and Lord, the concept of love will actually be seen as a deterrent to the kingdom of Satan, Inc. / kingdom of man's new and efficient power structure. Friendship with the global religious community and the global governance system will require a divorce from any previous devotion to respecting people as valuable merely because people are the creation of God the Creator who created the heavens and the earth. Along with the greater acceptance of abortion, will be the institution of infanticide. Homicides and euthanasia will increase. 'Love' will become an anathema as the global religious community and global governance system will seek to increase their efficiency in genociding those who live in rebellion to the kingdom of Satan, Inc. / kingdom of man, those who seek to practice kingdom of heaven love, and who seek to protect life.

In order to be able to prove one's full devotion to the global religious community and the global governance system, and in order to be a responsible member of the kingdom of Satan, Inc. / kingdom of man in its efforts to bring 'world peace,' the population of the world will be required to abandon kingdom of heaven love.

This ideology has the incessant ring of the propaganda distributed throughout Nazi Germany prior to and during World War II when allegiance to the 'Fatherland' meant that a responsible citizen would give away their friends and neighbors in the effort to 'cleanse' the German nation of its plague of those who rebelled against Hitler's vision for the world.

The era of the time of Jacob's Trouble will again challenge people to determine which kingdom they will personally embrace and be devoted to, and which kingdom they will personally rebel against.

False prophets (again) and the deception of the masses: The beast of the sea and the beast of the earth were recognized even by early church leaders as a false prophet and a false messiah.

The beast of the sea was clearly defined as a false prophet of the highest order.

And the beast of the earth will be defined as a false messiah. But the beast of the earth will also be employed as a false prophet as well, because the beast of the earth will vouch for the beast of the sea.

Together, the two beasts of Revelation 13 will have a cadre of colleagues that will use their positions to present false theology to the masses of the people of the world.

The next layer of leaders that will also be false prophets after the two beasts of Revelation 13, will be the men represented by the ten horns / ten kings that sit on top of the beast that is the red dragon / serpent / Satan, Inc. with the seven heads, ten horns and seven crowns. Although the men represented by the ten horns / ten kings will be leaders with a primarily political focus, they will also be instrumental in presenting a false message to the people of the world about the divinity and sovereignty of God Most High and of Jesus Christ.

While these twelve men will be the greatest offenders in the art of deceiving the masses of people, there will also be other false prophets with great influence.

Currently, the era that we live in was described as the historical era of the church of Laodicea. Church leaders of every denomination have abandoned the message of Jesus Christ's sovereignty and divinity. The one sermon preached throughout the book of Acts by the apostles and disciples of Jesus Christ, had three points:

1) Jesus is Lord.
2) We crucified him.
3) God raised Jesus Christ from the dead.
(And a fourth implied point: Jesus Christ ascended into heaven and will return.)

But this sermon that the apostles and disciples of Jesus Christ proved to be so effective in providing growth to the church, has been abandoned. The focus of most modern churches has turned away from the message of the divinity and sovereignty of Jesus Christ, to substitute in its place things like commentary study, various human based theologies, social justice issues, counseling studies, and even book reports. Throughout the hierarchies of most of the mainline denominations, is the assimilation of the spirit of ecumenism which compromises the original message of the church as recorded in the book of Acts, in favor of a redefined message of social acceptance of worldly principles that in reality are a detriment to God's promise of life and liberty.

Jesus Christ's message continues to be that the one who overcomes is the one who maintains love, devotion, and allegiance to God Most High's plan to fully establish the kingdom of heaven on earth.

An increase of wickedness causing the love of most to grow cold, but the one who stands firm to the end will be saved: The God of the kingdom of heaven is the author of love. The Holy Spirit is the vessel through which the love of

God flows. Where the Holy Spirit is not present, love cannot exist.

We currently live in a world where the Holy Spirit is constantly at work, wooing individuals to believe in the divinity and sovereignty of Jesus Christ. But during the era of the time of Jacob's Trouble, the power and influence of the red dragon / serpent / Satan, Inc. will increase with the effect of persuading people to ignore the message from the author of love.

The Holy Spirit does not go where the Holy Spirit is not invited. When the Holy Spirit is not present in the dynamic, there is no way to infuse love into the dynamic.

In contrast, where the Holy Spirit is invited to dwell, the Holy Spirit fills the space with love, God's love, pure love, true love, strong love, lifegiving love, love that removes whatever is not glorious. What the Holy Spirit's love buoys up, cannot be destroyed.

Gospel of the kingdom being preached in the whole world as a testimony to all nations (and then the end will come): There are some who have declared that the gospel of the kingdom has already been preached in the world to all nations and therefore this item should be checked off the list of requirements that need to be fulfilled before Jesus Christ returns.

It is true that the message of the good news of the kingdom of heaven has indeed reached to every nation, to the whole world.

But this caveat from Jesus Christ has also been interpreted as support for the idea that before Jesus Christ returns, there will be a new era of revival of the message of Jesus Christ and his divinity.

When the question is posed, 'What is the purpose for the events that are scheduled to take place during the era of the time of Jacob's Trouble?' the complete answer contains an understanding that the scheduled events are intended to create an environment to challenge the people of the world to ultimately and with finality choose which kingdom they will share allegiance with.

Because one of the purposes of the era of the time of Jacob's Trouble is to offer the people of the world a choice for who will be their God, it will be necessary for the whole world to again review the message of who Jesus Christ is and why Jesus Christ is divine.

During the era of the time of Jacob's Trouble, the preaching of the gospel of the kingdom must also be addressed to the people of Israel who have previously rejected the divinity and sovereignty of Jesus Christ as God Most High's messiah. For the people of Israel to finally accept Jesus Christ as messiah and become the nation of priests that God Most High has promised for them to become, the message of who Jesus Christ is, must be preached and received.

Temple must be present and the beast of the earth must have authority over temple to provide leadership for the future abomination of desolation event – Daniel 7:25, 8:24-25, 9:27, 11:42-43, 12:7, 12:11-12, Revelation 11:3, 12:6, 12:14, 13:5, 13:8-13).

Four times in the book of Daniel the term 'abomination of desolation' or a similar term was used; Daniel 8:12-14, 9:26-27; 11:31; and 12:11. In each of Daniel's references, there was a corresponding description of the defiling of the temple and the cessation of the daily evening and morning sacrifices.

Daniel and John the Revelator's documentation of events required that there must be a functioning temple as a site for the future abomination of desolation event to take place in. And their documentation also required that the beast of the earth hold authority over the temple mount and its activities.

The ruler who will come will confirm a covenant with many for one 'seven.' In the middle of the 'seven' he will put an end to sacrifice and offering. And at the temple he will set up an abomination that causes desolation, until the end that is decreed is poured out on him. Daniel 9:27 NIV

The prince / ruler will confirm a covenant with many, for one 'seven' / 'week.' But in the middle of the 'seven' / 'week,' the prince / ruler will bring an end to the sacrifice and offering. On the wing (of the temple), the prince / ruler will establish abominations that will cause desolation, even until the consumption which has been determined is poured out on the desolate / the one who destroys. Daniel 9:27 translated

Daniel's vision of the future abomination of desolation event identified the temple as the site for the event.

Sacrifices to God Most High can only be effective if the temple they are offered in is consecrated and holy. The future abomination of desolation event will act as a deconsecration of the future consecrated and holy temple and the termination of the fully consecrated, functional and operational temple sacrificial system.

The Law given to Moses by God Most High as the people of Israel were leaving Egypt (1446 BC) included very detailed instructions on how to construct the tabernacle and the Holy of Holies. Moses received the details concerning the tabernacle vessels and furniture that represented the process required in reconciling humanity's relationship with God Most High. It was also a blueprint for the atoning work that would be accomplished with messiah / the Lamb / Jesus Christ during his earthly ministry. The temples built in Jerusalem were constructed to incorporate the same details identified in the reconciliation process prescribed by God Most High for the tabernacle.

The layout of the items in the tabernacle and the temples represented the procession that a person makes as they approach God Most High in the process of reconciliation with God Most High. For example, the worshipper would place their hands on the animal they brought for sacrifice, as an act of transferring their sins onto the sacrificial animal. And then the person or family sacrificing the animal, would place the animal upon the altar as a symbol of confession and repentance. The basin of water was made of polished brass with the effect of acting like a mirror, revealing sins both in the reflection of the mirror and in the reflection of the surface of the water. The water represented baptism, the washing away of sin, the cleansing necessary for entrance into heaven. Inside the sanctuary was the large golden menorah that used *pure olive oil as fuel and represented the Holy Spirit's work for the individual. Located opposite from the menorah was the table of showbread, twelve loaves of unleavened bread symbolic of Jesus the bread of life whose body was broken for humanity. The wine was also located on the table with the showbread representing the pure blood of Jesus Christ shed for the forgiveness of sins. The curtain to the Holy of Holies was adorned with cherubim that represented the cherubim that guarded the Garden of Eden / garden of God / paradise after the first man and first woman left it, in order to prevent imperfection from entering into what has been declared holy. The Holy of Holies that housed the ark of the covenant and the mercy seat, was only allowed to be accessed by the high priest on the Day of Atonement / Yom Kippur. The mercy seat represented the throne that messiah / the Lamb / Jesus Christ will assume during the Thousand Years Reign of Jesus Christ. The ark of the covenant held the covenant of God Most High with humanity, with heaven and with earth, and represented the judgement that will take place during the final battle of this age on the Day of Atonement / Yom Kippur, and the judgement that is scheduled to take place at the end of the Thousand Years Reign of Jesus Christ. Etc.*

Jesus Christ came to fulfill the Law given to Moses by God Most High. To fulfill the Law, it was necessary for messiah / the Lamb / Jesus Christ to proceed through each step of the process of reconciliation, to approach God Most High as a perfect human individual and as the perfect sacrifice.

In order to approach God Most High as a fully human being, Jesus needed to set aside his divinity and come to earth in a fully incarnate / fully human form. What set the fully human Jesus Christ apart from the rest of us is the fact that Jesus Christ had no sin to hinder him from being able to fully approach God Most High.

Consequently, when messiah / the Lamb / Jesus Christ was crucified, the curtain that separated the Holy of Holies was torn from top to bottom, exposing the Holy of Holies, and causing access to the Holy of Holies to be available to everyone at any time. Tearing the temple curtain was God Most High's recognition that messiah / the Lamb / Jesus Christ had fulfilled the atoning work that was prophesied within the tabernacle / temples. Messiah / the Lamb / Jesus Christ had made a path for the rest of humanity for reconciling humanity's relationship with God Most High.

Jesus Christ offered his perfect blood as a sacrifice to take the place of the blood of animals offered as sacrifice. If a person does not believe in Jesus Christ's divinity, then Jesus Christ's perfect blood sacrifice cannot be applied to that person. A person who does not place his or her sin upon messiah / the Lamb / Jesus Christ, cannot have their sin removed and washed away. They cannot be a recipient of the Holy Spirit's cleansing work, or to being a recipient of the covenant promises, or to experiencing a right relationship with God Most High.

The first people of Israel that believed that Jesus was the promised and prophesied messiah, understood that Jesus Christ had fulfilled the requirements to make it possible to find a right relationship with God Most High without needing to offer more animal sacrifice. The first people of Israel who believed were called 'Christians' / 'followers of Christ.'

But the people of Israel who reject Jesus as messiah remain confined to the requirements and restrictions of the Law that was given to Moses. The temple sacrificial system remains their only process for reconciliation with God Most High. When the temple was destroyed in 70 AD, those who still trusted in the Law of Moses for their redemptive path, no longer had the means to achieve reconciliation with God Most High because without a temple there can be no sacrifice offered for the forgiveness of sin.

This is why a consecrated temple with a functioning sacrificial system is vital to the people of Israel who do not recognize that Jesus Christ is their promised and prophesied messiah. Without a consecrated temple and a functional sacrificial system, the people of Israel have no process for achieving reconciliation with God Most High.

Another reason why a consecrated temple and a functional sacrificial system is essential for the people of Israel is that the prophecies of the Old Testament / Tanakh prophets foretold of the promised and prophesied messiah coming to the temple. The people of Israel believe that in order for their messiah to come, there must be a temple for him to come to.

These are the reasons why the first abomination of desolation caused a crisis point for the people of Israel in 167 BC.

These are the reasons why in 70 AD, when the Romans destroyed the temple in Jerusalem, the hope of those who were still hoping that messiah would come, dissolved with the destruction of the temple.

These are the reasons why a temple must be in place with a fully consecrated, functional and operational temple sacrificial system, in order for the people of Israel to recognize any messiah; the false messiah and the authentic promised and prophesied messiah / the Lamb / Jesus Christ.

Building a temple in Jerusalem will also be essential in order for the people of the nation of Israel to believe that they can be heard by God Most High. The tabernacle and afterward the temples, were the places that the high priest would enter the Holy of Holies on the Day of Atonement / Yom Kippur, and hear a message from God Most High for the people of Israel. Without a consecrated and functioning temple, the people of Israel remain distant from hearing any message from God Most High, and believe that God Most High cannot adequately hear them.

The presence of a consecrated and functioning temple will also essential for the work and advancement of both the kingdom of heaven and for the red dragon / serpent / Satan, Inc.

God Most High will use the fully consecrated, functional and operational temple sacrificial system as a means of awakening the people of Israel to the relationship that God Most High needs to have with the people of Israel in order to fulfill the promise to make the people of Israel into a nation of priests for God Most High.

The red dragon / serpent / Satan, Inc. understands the importance of the presence of a fully consecrated, functional and operational temple sacrificial system in the theology of the people of Israel. With a consecrated and functioning temple in place, the people of Israel will be again actively looking for their messiah. The red dragon / serpent / Satan, Inc. will view the erection of the future temple as an opportunity to draw out the people of Israel who seek to be in a functional relationship with God Most High, in order to target them for annihilation. And the beast of the earth will need a temple system in place in order to establish his authority with the people of Israel via taking authority over the temple mount and stopping the temple sacrifices.

The little horn / eleventh king will need the temple established as a platform for speaking against the Most High, and as a mechanism for oppressing God's holy people, and for attempting to change the set times and the laws, for a time, times and half a time (Daniel 7:25).

The final horn on the shaggy goat / completely wicked fierce looking king and master of intrigue, will need the established temple as a mechanism for destroying God's mighty holy people. Because of his power and authority over the temple mount, he will cause deceit to prosper and consider himself superior. He will destroy many and take his stand against the Prince of princes / messiah / the Lamb / Jesus Christ. (Daniel 8:24-25)

The ruler who is to come will need the fully consecrated, functional and operational temple sacrificial system in place, in order to prove his superiority by putting an end to sacrifice and offering; and to set up an abomination that causes desolation, until the end that is decreed is poured out on him (Daniel 9:26-27).

The king that will exalt himself will utilize the temple as a means for gaining control of the treasures of gold and silver of other nations that will become submissive to his reign (Daniel 11:42-43).

The beast of the earth will require the temple in place in order to have a location for establishing the idol / image of the beast of the sea as an object of compulsory worship, a mechanism for establishing global governance, a method for collecting revenue, and a scheme for advancing the culture of the kingdom of Satan, Inc. / kingdom of man (Revelation 13:11-18).

The kingdom of heaven will need the temple in place so that the future abomination of desolation event will be able to mark time in preparation for the return of messiah / the Lamb / Jesus Christ (Daniel 7:25, 8:24-25, 12:7, 12:11-12, Revelation 11:3, 12:6, 12:14, 13:5, 13:12).

When the little horn / eleventh king / final horn on the shaggy goat / ruler that is to come / king that will exalt himself / beast of the earth stands on the wing of the temple and declares himself to be greater than God Most High, it will be an act taunting the kingdom of heaven and enticing messiah / the Lamb / Jesus Christ to return to earth for the purpose of doing battle. After the rebellious angels have exited heaven, the only place left to battle will be on earth. The strategy will be that when Jesus Christ comes to claim his earthly throne, the kingdom of Satan, Inc. / kingdom of man will defeat him to prevent this from happening.

It will be reminiscent of when Jesus Christ stood at the gates of hell in Caesarea Philippi and taunted the red dragon / serpent / Satan, Inc. to get on with the crucifixion process (Matthew 16:13-20, Mark 8:27-30, Luke 9:18-20).

The fully consecrated, functional and operational temple sacrificial system, halted

Joel was an Old Testament / Tanakh prophet (fl. ~800 to 700 BC) - of Judah, who was messaging modern Israel.

Mourn like a virgin in sackcloth grieving for the betrothed of her youth. Grain offerings and drink offerings are cut off from the house of the Lord. The priests are in mourning, those who minister before the Lord. The fields are ruined, the ground is dried up. The grain is destroyed, the new wine is dried up, the olive oil fails. Joel 1:8-10

Grain, wine, and oil were essential for temple worship. Grain was the substance that bread was made from. Wine would be placed next to the bread in the temple. And oil served as the fuel for the light of the menorah. Not only did Joel prophesy that opportunity to offer gain and drink offerings will be cut off, but Joel also described that at that time there won't be grain, wine, or oil present to be used in offerings.

This will be an era for Israel that will include drought. It will be the responsibility of one of the two witnesses to bring drought or rain.

During the second half of the era of the time of Jacob's Trouble, while the offerings and sacrifices will not be allowed in the temple, the priests will have nothing left to do but mourn.

When Elijah effectively prayed for drought or rain in the past, the purpose was to demonstrate God Most High's sovereignty and supremacy over other gods / rebellious angels, over people, over the physical earth, and most importantly over those who would seek to destroy the lives of others for their own personal gain.

There will be much to grieve for and much mourning.

Put on sackcloth, you priests, and mourn. Wail, you who minister before the altar. Come, spend the night in sackcloth, you who minister before my God; for the grain offerings and drink offerings are withheld from the house of your God. Declare a holy fast; call a sacred assembly. Summon the elders and all who live in the land to the house of the Lord your God, and cry out to the Lord. Alas for that day! For the Day of the Lord is near. It will come like destruction from the Almighty.

Has not the food been cut off before our very eyes — joy and gladness from the house of our God? The seeds are shriveled beneath the clouds. The storehouses are in ruins, the granaries have been broken down, for the grain has dried up. How the cattle moan! The herds mill about because they have no pasture. Even the flocks of sheep are suffering. Joel 1:13-18

Joel continued the messaging to the priests that hold office during the era of the time of Jacob's Trouble before the return of Jesus Christ ('For the Day of the Lord is near…').

Joel's description depicted a nation that will be under siege. At the time of the future abomination of desolation event, the covenant peace treaty agreement will have been broken and it will be a time when the people of Israel will no longer have a covenant peace treaty agreement to protect them. The people of Israel will receive the full animosity of the people of Israel's enemies. When a peace treaty is broken, it is the same as declaring war.

But Joel offered a response for the people of Israel. When the temple sacrificial system has been discontinued, Joel passed along God Most High's instruction to the priests that they are to declare a holy fast, call a sacred assembly, summon the elders and all who live in the land of Israel to the house of the Lord / the temple, and cry out to the Lord.

While the people of Israel believe that through sacrifice they will be heard by God Most High, Joel's message to the people of Israel was that God Most High will hear them through their holy fast, sacred assembly, convocation, and actual pleas that originate from their hearts. Things like holy fasts, sacred assemblies, convocations and pleas that originate from their hearts, are not dependent upon the presence of an intact, consecrated temple and a functioning sacrificial system.

According to other biblical notations, it will take about forty two months for the people of Israel to capitulate to Joel's prescription.

> The prince / ruler will confirm a covenant with many, for one 'seven' / 'week.' But in the middle of the 'seven' / 'week,' the prince / ruler will bring an end to the sacrifice and offering. On the wing (of the temple), the prince / ruler will establish abominations that will cause desolation, even until the consumption which has been determined is poured out on the desolate / the one who destroys. Daniel 9:27 translated

The kingdom of Satan, Inc. / kingdom of man will view the discontinuation of sacrifice and offering as a way to interrupt the people of Israel's communication with God Most High and therefore, a means to victory.

But the disruption of sacrifice and offering will cause the people of Israel to cry out to the Lord via other means. And the people of Israel will discover that God Most High has been faithful to God Most High's promise of reconciliation with God's chosen people.

Set at the right time in history

While there was a gap of almost two thousand two hundred years in between the first abomination of desolation event and the future abomination of desolation event, the two events are closely intertwined. The interconnectedness of the two abomination of desolation events emphasized that the first abomination of desolation event was a template for the future abomination of desolation event.

One of the points of connectedness between the two events is their proximity to the coming of messiah / Jesus Christ. The first abomination of desolation event took place less than two hundred years before the ministry, crucifixion, death, resurrection and ascension of Jesus Christ. While two hundred years is a long span of time, when two hundred years is compared with the seven thousand year plan of God, two hundred years is a relationally short length of time.

The future abomination of desolation event is scheduled to take place approximately three and a half years prior to the return of messiah / the Lamb / Jesus Christ.

Daniel's account of pre-history recorded as Daniel 11:1-35, foretold of the leaders and events that would precede the first abomination of desolation that took place in 167 BC.

Daniel's account of pre-history recorded as Daniel 11:29-12:12, foretold events that will take place at the time of the future abomination of desolation event. Daniel's vision even pinpointed the time for the future abomination of desolation to take place at the midpoint of the era of the time of Jacob's Trouble, the midpoint of the seven year confirmation of the covenant peace treaty agreement.

The ruler who will come will confirm a covenant with many for one 'seven.' In the middle of the 'seven' he will put an end to sacrifice and offering. And at the temple he will set up an abomination that causes desolation, until the end that is decreed is poured out on him. Daniel 9:27

This 'seven' that has been set aside as the time period that the rule who will come will confirm for the covenant peace treaty agreement. It follows the sixty nine 'sevens' that counted time before the crucifixion of messiah / the Lamb / Jesus Christ, and the almost two thousand years / 'two days' that marked the times of the Gentiles.

The sixty ninth 'seven' was the time period designated the ministry of messiah / the Lamb / Jesus Christ and was cut in half with the crucifixion of messiah / the Lamb / Jesus Christ.

The seventieth 'seven' marks the time of the era of the time of Jacob's Trouble, with the time period of the second half of the 'seven' designated for the beast of the earth to attempt to fully establish the kingdom of Satan, Inc. / kingdom of man.

Three and a half years for both sides.

While there was an almost two thousand year gap between the sixty ninth 'seven' and the seventieth 'seven,' the fact that the seventieth 'seven' is a continuation of the sixty ninth 'seven' implied that the seventieth 'seven' will complete the purpose that was discontinued when the sixty ninth 'seven' was cut off.

Half way through the sixty ninth 'seven' the ministry of messiah / Jesus Christ, was cut off when Jesus was crucified. The work that Jesus Christ accomplished for the redemptive process on behalf of the world was indeed 'finished.' But the work that Jesus Christ was to accomplish in forming the nation of Israel into a nation of priests for God Most High was postponed by the people of Israel when they rejected Jesus Christ as the promised and prophesied messiah. The people of Israel who rejected Jesus Christ as the promised and prophesied messiah are still waiting for their messiah / king / ruler to come.

The kingdom of Satan, Inc. / kingdom of man's alternative messiah will be presented with the future abomination of desolation event, offering himself as the one that the people of Israel have been looking for.

The era of the time of Jacob's Trouble will now serve to finish out the set of seventy 'sevens.' This time, it will be the beast of the earth who will have three and a half years to enlist the people of Israel under his rule. But the people of Israel will reject this candidate for messiahship, and will finally recognize Jesus Christ as their promised and prophesied messiah; completing the process of making the people of Israel into the nation of priests that God Most High promised them to be.

The number of days for the first half of the era of the time of Jacob's Trouble was left undesignated. It will be approximately half of seven years.

But the numbers of years, months and days designated for the second half of the era of the time of Jacob's Trouble, was specified, stated, quantified and measured with precision. And the timing of the future abomination of desolation event will be precisely accomplished at the right time, to mark time until the return of messiah / the Lamb / Jesus Christ to battle the enemies of God Most High and to fully establish the kingdom of heaven on earth.

Rebellion against God must be prevalent

Daniel's vision of the ram and the shaggy goat: Out of one of the four horns came a little horn that grew to be exceedingly great, growing toward the south and east and toward the Glorious (Land). It grew up to reach the host of heaven and to cast some of the host and some of the stars of heaven to the ground. And it trampled some of the host and some of the stars of heaven. He exalted himself as the Prince even as high as the host of heaven; and by him, the daily sacrifices were taken away. The place of the Lord's sanctuary was cast down. An army was given over to the horn to oppose the daily (sacrifices), because of rebellion. He cast truth down to the ground. In all that he did, he prospered.

Then I heard a holy one speaking, and another holy one said to him 'How long will it take for the vision concerning the daily sacrifices and the transgression of desolation to be fulfilled — the transgression that causes desolation, both of the giving in the sanctuary and the trampling underfoot of the host?'

He said to me, 'It will be 2,300 evenings and mornings. Then the sanctuary will be cleansed.' Daniel 8:9-14 translated

The books of the Maccabees specifically attributed the rebellion of the people of Israel as a major contributing factor in the causation of the first abomination of desolation event of 167 BC. Without the rebellion against God Most High by the people of Israel, against the religion, tradition and culture of the Jewish faith - the people of Israel would not have been so vulnerable to accept the Hellenization program that Alexander the Great initiated. Without the rebellion against God Most High, the temple would not have been so easily plundered, the priests would not have been so easily corrupted, and the people of Israel would not have allowed their national identity to slip away; a national identity that had in the past caused them to be extraordinarily strong and wise in comparison to the nations around them.

In the vision of the ram and the shaggy goat, it was the Lord who explained that the rebellion of the Lord's people will be one of the underlying causes for the future abomination of desolation event and the surrendering of the sanctuary. Both the books of the Maccabees and Daniel's vision asserted that rebellion against the Lord must be present in order for an abomination of desolation event to take place.

The rebellion against God Most High is not merely an earthly phenomenon among humanity, inspired by humanity. As Daniel prayed prior to receiving the vision of Daniel 11-12, Daniel recorded in Daniel 10 the struggle that took place in the spiritual realm in order for the angel with the vision to be able to come to Daniel.

Beginning with the time when the first man and first woman lived in the Garden of Eden / garden of God / paradise, rebellion in the spiritual realm and rebellion in heaven has spilled over into the earthly realm. It is almost

as if rebellion in the spiritual realm is a prerequisite for rebellion on earth. Rebellion against God Most High was attributed throughout the biblical record as originating with the rebellious angels of the red dragon / serpent / Satan, Inc.

Rebellion that leads to war in heaven has flared up before. Enoch referred to times of conflict in heaven. Jesus spoke of the violence and the violent people that the kingdom of heaven had to endure from the days of John the Baptist through the days of Jesus Christ's ministry (Matthew 11:12-13). Daniel in Daniel 12:1-3 and John the Revelator in Revelation 12:7-12 both described the war in heaven that must take place near the beginning of the era of the time of Jacob's Trouble.

The rebellion against God Most High during the first abomination of desolation event was not as much of a political rebellion as it was a religious and spiritual rebellion. The rebellion against God Most High in the first abomination of desolation event was actually initiated by the acting high priest Menelaus and by the Sanhedrin as they betrayed the temple to the Seleucid / Syrian king Antiochus IV Epiphanes.

And the rebellion against God Most High during the future abomination of desolation event will be led by the beast of the earth (Ezekeial 12:25, Daniel 8:12-13, 8:23, 11:14, 2 Thessalonians 2:3, etc.) who will have obtained his power and authority via the beast of the sea, from the red dragon / serpent / Satan, Inc.

Idolatry will prevail

Idolatry will again be practiced particularly on the temple mount during the future abomination of desolation event. Even though the people of Israel will have a working temple, their hearts will still not be captured by devotion to God Most High. And it will be a requirement to worship the idol / image of the beast of the sea.

During the time of Antiochus IV Epiphanes, idolatry on the temple mount included the forced *consumption of pork (meat designated as unclean) and the slaughter of those who refused to worship the Greek baal / mystery / mythology religion gods. It also included forced sexual rituals.*

During the coming abomination of desolation season, there will also be forced acts that are offensive to God Most High and to the Mosaic Law, including forced sexual rituals and the slaughter of those who refuse to worship the idol / image of the beast of the sea / false prophet / eighth king beast.

The idol / image of the beast of the sea will be something created by humans, who were also the result of creation. It remains illogical to worship the created thing, instead of worshiping the one who created.

Humanity generally does not praise the crafted item. Generally, humanity praises the one who crafted the item: 'My compliments to the chef,' and then the meal is eaten. 'This artist has great perception,' and then the artwork is appreciated. 'You have a gift,' and then the item is cherished. Etc.

But during the era of the time of Jacob's Trouble, the backwardness and illogicalness of the culture will be that the created item, the idol / image of the beast of the sea, will be worshiped.

Concerning the godlessness and wickedness of humanity who suppress the truth by their wickedness: They exchanged the truth of God for a lie, and worshiped and served created things rather than the Creator – who is forever praised. Amen. Romans 1:25

Those who are in search of truth naturally ask, 'What is the 'lie'?'

In the context of Romans 1:25, God was referred to as 'the Creator.' *Throughout the biblical record, God Most High continued to stress and to demonstrate that God is the Creator and as the Creator, rules over and holds power over every aspect of creation. Consequently, worship that is misdirected away from God the Creator to focus on something that has been created, is a deception, idolatry, and offensive to God.*

One of the greatest humanly created ideas was that God the Creator does not exist. The idea that God the Creator was not powerful and capable of being able to create the world or to hold power over the things of the world, was incorporated into the deception of the serpent / Satan with the first man and first woman when the serpent / Satan promised the first man and first woman that if they ate the fruit of the tree of the knowledge of good and evil they would not surely die as God the Creator had indicated, but rather they would be 'like God.' *To be* like God *should have meant that humanity would possess the power to create; and yet no human being or angel can create anything truly new in this world. The ability to create was reserved for God the Creator alone.*

The idea that God the Creator was not the actual creator, was also the foundation for the pursuit of the antediluvian / preflood religion, all flavors of the baal / mystery / mythology religion, and evolutionary theory both ancient and modern.

In the antediluvian / preflood world, the disrespect of God the Creator resulted in the breeding of Nephilim and chimera.

In the postdiluvian / postflood world, the idea that God the Creator did not hold ultimate control over all of creation, was crucial in the foundation of the tower of Babel empire and the construction of the tower of Babel. The tower of Babel was constructed with the belief that humanity would be able to survive a flood if a tower that was tall enough could be built for housing the elite and elect. If humanity could successfully survive the destruction of another flood, then they thought they could dispense with giving any further honor to God the Creator and indeed become responsible only to the rebellious angels' vision for humanity and in effect be like God.

Both ancient and modern evolutionary theory were also similar to the baal / mystery / mythology religion in its presentation when it dispensed with a Creator God and sought to provide an explanation for life detached God the Creator. God Most High considered the humanly devised evolutionary theory from a humanly created idea. And in reality, God the Creator was present to witness creation; humanity was not.

But it is essential for the red dragon / serpent / Satan, Inc., that humanity believes this lie that God the Creator can be dismissed, in order for the red dragon / serpent / Satan, Inc. to attempt to fully establish the kingdom of Satan, Inc. / kingdom of man.

During the era of the time of Jacob's Trouble, the idol / image of the beast of the sea on the temple mount will serve as proof that idolatry continues to be prevalent in the hearts and minds of much of humanity.

People will expect signs, wonders and miracles as proof of the beast of the earth's divinity and sovereignty.

The people of Israel have been waiting for the promised and prophesied messiah since the time of that God Most High established covenant with Abram / Abraham (c. 2050 BC). With so much time and so many people to consider as candidates for messiah throughout human history, there has been difficulty in selecting the one out of humanity's population of billions, that is truly the one and only Son of God / messiah.

It is not unreasonable that the people of Israel should expect a sign from messiah in order for messiah to prove his divinity and sovereignty.

When Jesus Christ was pressed to provide a sign, Jesus Christ postponed providing an extra sign, knowing that the veracity of any extra sign that he would have performed would have not been recognized and would have been considered null and void by those who were requiring a sign.

In contrast to Jesus Christ, the beast of the earth will readily provide signs as a demonstration that he influences both heaven and earth.

But the ability to provide signs does not fully establish one's divinity and sovereignty. God Most High defined the promised and prophesied messiah as possessing a specific and unique intrinsic character that was to be messiah's proof of his divinity and sovereignty.

And more importantly, a sign of divinity and sovereignty is only effective if the people who receive the sign are willing to also receive the proof of what the sign demonstrates.

The beast of the earth works great signs so that it should even cause fire to come down out of heaven to the earth, in the presence of humanity.
The beast of the earth deceives those dwelling on the earth by reason of the signs that it was given to perform before the beast of the sea, telling those dwelling on the earth to make an image to the beast that was wounded by the sword and has lived.
The beast of the earth was given the ability to give breath to the image of the beast of the sea, so that the image of the beast of the sea should also speak. And the image of the beast of the sea will cause all who would not worship the image of the beast of the sea, to be killed. Revelation 13:13-15 translated

It will be vital for the beast of the earth to develop the support of the world's population as an attempt to accomplish the full establishment of the kingdom of Satan, Inc. / kingdom of man and the global governance system.

At the time of the future abomination of desolation event, the show that the beast of the earth will provide will be enormously spectacular, better than any demonstration that modern humanity has ever seen. The illusion, the magic, the detail will be superb and awe inspiring. Anyone unfamiliar with the depth of the biblical message will be overwhelmingly convinced that there could be no better global leader than the beast of the earth. Certainly, the beast of the earth will appear to be everything that the people of Israel should desire in their messiah.

In contrast to the beast of the earth's presentation of himself, the biblical record clearly identified that it is the character of a person, as defined by the God of the kingdom of heaven, that defines the amount of authority that person holds.

The beast of the earth's character will be defined as being full of intrigue, throwing truth to the ground, centered around deception, etc. (Daniel 8:12, 8:23-25, etc.).

The only people who accused Jesus Christ of deception or of lies were the leaders in the nation of Israel who themselves produced the false witnesses to testify against Jesus Christ, in the process of crucifying him.

When the people of Israel wanted Jesus to prove himself as messiah, some of the Pharisees and teachers of the law said to him, 'Teacher, we want to see a sign from you.'
Jesus answered, 'A wicked and adulterous generation asks for a sign! But none will be given it except the sign of the prophet Jonah. For as Jonah was three days and three nights in the belly of a huge fish, so the Son of Man will be three days and three nights in the Heart of the earth. The men of Nineveh will stand up at the judgment with this generation and condemn it; for they repented at the preaching of Jonah, and now something greater than Jonah is here. Matthew 12:38-41
A holy people will seek a messiah who is holy in character.
A wicked and adulterous / idolatrous people will seek a messiah who is also wicked and adulterous / idolatrous in character.
Only wicked and adulterous / idolatrous generations are unable to recognize authentic messiah through a sinless and perfect life. Only wicked and adulterous / idolatrous generations have rejected the Mosaic Law that begins with four commandments concerning one's relationship with God, including the command that there is to be no other god before God Most High. Every potential messiah that has been considered by the people of Israel, has not been able to fulfill even the first four of the ten commandments... save one, Jesus Christ.

In contrast to the eagerness that the beast of the earth will provide to prove himself, when Jesus was pressed to provide a sign of his divinity, Jesus Christ instead referred to his character as proof that he was messiah.
Jesus had already lived a life without sin, provided miracles of which only a very small percentage of the miracles he performed were even recorded, taught as one having authority, etc. But, to a wicked and adulterous / idolatrous generation, those signs were not sufficient. The leaders of the people of Israel were looking for a more political messiah, a more militant messiah, a messiah that would enhance the personal power, prestige, and coffers of

the already established elite; not a messiah that would bring a kingdom where love would reign and love would elevate the common person to the same level as the elite leaders and the wealthy.

The leaders of the people of Israel who did not understand the redemptive plan of God Most High, also did not understand that the ultimate purpose for sending messiah was not to establish the nation of Israel as the powerbase that would tyrannically rule over the entire world, benefiting Israel at the expense of the other nations.

Wicked and adulterous / idolatrous generations seek wicked and adulterous / idolatrous leaders to follow. The problem for Jesus was that the integrity of his character could not fit into the expectations of those of the wicked and adulterous / idolatrous generation who insisted that Jesus provide a sign.

Generations that are not wicked and adulterous / idolatrous, understand, and respect, the Mosaic Law. When that kind of understanding and respect was present, the purpose of the Law given to Moses was able to be recognized. The purpose of the Law was to annually dramatize the unfolding message of God Most High's plan of redemption, reconciliation and regeneration; and to annually dramatize the role that the promised and prophesied messiah would have of generating God Most High's redemptive plan, into reality.

When the deeper purpose of the Law of Moses was understood, then there was no need for signs and wonders to provide proof that Jesus is indeed the promised and prophesied messiah. For those versed in Mosaic Law, messiah was able to be recognized because true messiah is able to completely fulfill the Mosaic Law, to live up to every jot and tittle of the law, and to be qualified to recover dominion of the earth from the red dragon / serpent / Satan, Inc.

The people of Israel have traditionally held multiple expectations of what the promised and prophesied messiah would be. With a wrapped present, no one knows what is actually inside until the gift is opened. Like a wrapped present, the people of Israel brought multiple images of what God Most High should incorporate into the wrapped gift inside / of what God Most High's promised and prophesied messiah should be.

The term 'messiah' has been interpreted with such a wide variety of interpretations that there has been vast disagreement among the people of Israel and among Gentiles, of what 'messiah' should be.

For the people of Israel, there have been some who have sought a messiah ben Joseph / messiah son of Joseph who saved Jacob / Israel and his family from the worldwide famine by taking them into Egypt.

Others have sought a messiah ben David / messiah son of David who with his military strength and leadership forged the nation of Israel into a strong and mighty nation, placing the enemies of Israel under their feet.

Others have sought a messiah who would recognize the power and authority of the Sanhedrin and the elite leadership of Jerusalem and the nation of Israel as the greatest authority.

The followers of the Lamb / Jesus Christ have yet another definition of 'messiah.' They claim that messiah is the one who is able to restore a right relationship with God Most High and will one day fully establish the kingdom of heaven on earth, dismantling all other kingdoms and empires with the same kind of imagery of a rock from heaven crushing the toes of Nebuchadnezzar's vision of the image of a man.

Throughout the history of the people of Israel, the people of Israel have accepted several 'would-be' messiahs or leaders that have resembled any one of the many established typologies for messiah. This list included leaders like Judas Maccabeus and Simon bar Kokhba.

When Jesus Christ came, the people of Israel expected the promised and prophesied messiah to be modeled after David or after Judas Maccabeus and the Maccabean / Hasmonean family. When Jesus did not bring great military victory and relief from the rule of the

Roman empire, the religious and political leaders requested the performance of some other kind of messianic sign. And yet, they rejected the multiple miracles and the other supernaturally empowered work that Jesus Christ accomplished.

Judas Maccabeus with his father and brothers, led the Maccabean Revolt which officially began in 167 BC. The Maccabeans / Hasmoneans successfully reclaimed and rededicated the temple after the first abomination of desolation event. Because Judas Maccabeus seemed to possess the ability and success of David, comparisons were made between Judas Maccabeus, and the definition for messiah that the people of Israel had imagined as a messiah ben David / messiah son of David. But Judas Maccabeus died in battle against the Seleucids / Syrians.

During the Bar Kokhba revolt / Third Jewish Roman War / Third Jewish Revolt 132 - 136 AD, Simon bar Kokhba / 'star' led with such effectiveness that many entertained the idea that Simon bar Kokhba was the promised messiah. Simon bar Kokhba was an excellent military strategist and garnered the support of many of the rabbis who accepted Simon Bar Kokhba as messiah for a period of time because he was such an excellent strategician. Simon bar Kokhba effectively uprooted the Romans from the land of Israel by selecting a city, retaking that city for the people of Israel, eliminating the Roman presence, fortifying the city and then moving on to the next selected city to repeat the process. Simon Bar Kokhba was also imagined as a messiah ben David / messiah son of David.

In response to the Bar Kokhba revolt, the Romans brought in approximately one hundred forty thousand to two hundred twenty thousand troops and destroyed the majority of what was left of the people of Israel who remained in the land of Israel. The destruction of the people of Israel during the Bar Kokhba revolt almost entirely genocided the world's total population of the people of Israel. When Simon bar Kokhba was killed in battle, the dream that he was the promised and prophesied messiah also died.

Jesus Christ arrived in between the Maccabean Revolt that began in 167 BC and the Bar Kokhba revolt that ended around 136 AD. Jesus' ministry took place around 26 to 30 AD.

For those who were familiar with Daniel's seventy 'sevens,' Jesus Christ was the only candidate for messiah. Jesus Christ arrived at just the right time, as scheduled on God Most High's calendar. But most of the people of Israel who lived at the time of Jesus, were not familiar with the writings of the prophets including the writings of the prophet Daniel.

The Pharisees, Sadducees and teachers of the law were well versed in the writings of the prophets and were entrusted to understand the times and the seasons, to discern when the time for the appearance of messiah would be. But the Pharisees and the teachers of the law were looking for a messiah ben David / messiah son of David who would be a great military strategist, who would place the enemies of the people of Israel under their feet, and who would shine favor upon their personal little kingdoms that they had established for themselves. They were not looking for a messiah ben Joseph / messiah son of Joseph who would fulfill the plan of making salvation available for humanity and for the earth.

Unlike other would be messiahs whose lives were defeated in battle; Jesus Christ laid down his life. The life of a true messiah cannot be taken from him. Jesus clearly taught and proved, that he could have chosen to skip the entire death experience. In order to die, Jesus Christ had to choose to die.

Properly identifying the one true promised and prophesied messiah, continues to be essential for the people of Israel. God Most High believed that it was so essential that the people of Israel properly be able to identify the one true messiah, that the clues were embedded within the required feasts included in the Law that God Most High provided to Moses and the people of Israel in 1446 BC. And during the era of the time of Jacob's Trouble, properly identifying the one true messiah will be a requirement that will need to be met prior to the return of messiah / the Lamb / Jesus Christ.

Before the people of Israel accept that Jesus Christ was and is the promised and prophesied messiah, they must first reject the beast of the earth as messiah.

The beast of the earth will present himself as messiach ben Yosef / messiah son of Joseph, through bringing a form of salvation to the people of Israel, probably through the confirmation of the covenant peace treaty agreement and assigning it to be respected for seven years. He will present himself as a friend to Israel.

The beast of the earth will also present himself as messiach ben David / messiah son of David through his subduing three of the ten kings who comprise the ten horns / ten kings. He will present himself as a protector of Israel.

The beast of the earth will even offer the demonstration of bringing to life the idol / image of the beast of the sea.

The beast of the earth will be adored! He will be a celebrity, a star! He will even be worshiped!

But the beast of the earth will also not be able to prevent being defeated, removed from earth and cast into the fiery lake (Revelation 19:20). A true messiah would possess the superior power and be the victor, not the defeated.

The sign of Jonah that Jesus Christ offered – Matthew 16:1-4, Luke 11:29-32

The sign that Jesus Christ offered to authenticate his messiahship was the sign of Jonah.

The Old Testament / Tanakh prophet Jonah was sent by God Most High to Nineveh. But Jonah sought to escape his assignment by catching a boat and sailing away. When the storm came up, Jonah was thrown overboard and swallowed by a large fish. Jonah stayed in the belly of the large fish for three days before being vomited onto the shore.

Jesus Christ's version of fulfilling the 'sign of Jonah' was to be crucified, dead, buried, and then three days later, to be resurrected; which was possible because of Jesus Christ's sinless character.

According to ancient teaching from the meaning of the Hebrew message describing Jonah's three day experience in the belly of the big fish, Jonah had gone into the world of the dead, 'the heart of the earth,' before returning to be coughed up on the beach.

In the creeds of the early church, the message to the early Christians was that the spirit of Jesus Christ also descended into hell during his three days that his body was entombed.

Jesus Christ provided a sign for the leaders of the nation of Israel, a sign that was dramatic and unable to be duplicated in all of human history. But even though Jesus Christ provided this sign, the Pharisees, Sadducees and others would still not accept it.

Jesus offered this message to the Pharisees and Sadducees:

The Pharisees and Sadducees came to Jesus and tested him by asking him to show them a sign from heaven.

Jesus replied, 'When evening comes, you say, 'It will be fair weather, for the sky is red,' and in the morning, 'Today it will be stormy, for the sky is red and overcast.' You know how to interpret the appearance of the sky, but you cannot interpret the signs of the times. A wicked and adulterous generation looks for a sign, but none will be given it except the sign of Jonah.' Jesus then left them and went away. Matthew 16:1-4

Jesus identified the disconnect in the theology of the Pharisees and Sadducees between their understanding of what messiah was supposed to be and what they were demanding messiah to be.

There is a saying, 'Red sky in the morning, sailors take warning. Red sky at night, sailors' delight.' *It is a verse taught as an assistance in remembering that in the evening, as the sun sets, the light from the sun can bend in a calm sky, around the earth, creating a red sky. But in the morning, when the sun light has been bent by storm conditions to reflect the red color, it is a sign that a storm is coming. It is a simple way to 'read' the sky.*

The Pharisees and Sadducees were religious leaders. It was their responsibility to study the history of Judaism and to know how to foster the relationship between God Most High and the people of Israel. They were learned, educated, scholarly. There was no excuse for them to not understand the basics of the coming of messiah... except that they had chosen to ignore all that had been taught concerning God Most High's Law and the messages of the prophets.

When the Mosaic Law and the messages of the prophets are ignored, as they are even today by the people of Israel, then there is no other path for identifying God Most High's messiah except through some kind of sign in the form of magic, sorcery, occult practices, illusion, dark arts, etc. A wicked and adulterous / idolatrous generation will again be ready to request, to recognize, and to receive a magical, illusionary sign, in preference over the true signs of the true messiah of God. And the beast of the earth will be required to provide magic, sorcery, occult practices, illusion, dark arts, etc., to attempt to prove his claim that he can fulfill the role of God's messiah, and to support his claim that he is sovereign and divine.

As the crowds increased, Jesus said, 'This is a wicked generation. It asks for a sign, but none will be given it except the sign of Jonah. For as Jonah was a sign to the Ninevites, so also will the Son of Man be to this generation.
The Queen of the South will rise at the judgment with the people of this generation and condemn them, for she came from the ends of the earth to listen to Solomon's wisdom; and now something greater than Solomon is here.
The men of Nineveh will stand up at the judgment with this generation and condemn it, for they repented at the preaching of Jonah; and now something greater than Jonah is here. Luke 11:29-32

When the beast of the earth accomplishes the future abomination of desolation event, he will briefly appear to be everything that the people of Israel ever hoped for in a messiah. He will seek to be everything that, during his earthly ministry, Jesus Christ was not.

When Jesus Christ entered the city of Jerusalem on Lamb Selection Day / Palm Sunday, riding on a donkey, in preparation for his crucifixion, the children and the people cried out 'Hosanna to the Lord. Hosanna to the Son of David.' *It was Wednesday of that week when the attitude of other people of Israel changed to reject Jesus Christ as messiah, at the urging of the religious leaders.*

On Sunday before Jesus Christ was crucified, Jesus was accepted and hailed as messiach ben David / messiah son of David and Savior. Wednesday, Jesus was rejected, conspired against, and sought after to be killed.

When the beast of the earth will declare himself to be greater than God Most High, he will also be well received. As the Queen from the South traveled to garner understanding from Solomon's wisdom, so people from all over the world will travel to merely be in the presence of the beast of the earth.

But there will be a cost for the people of Israel who choose the wrong option for which messiah they will believe in and follow. Zechariah 13:7-9 claimed that the lives of two thirds of the people of Israel will eventually be taken. Only the one third of the people of Israel that survives will call on God's name; and only after they have been put into the fire, refined like silver, and tested like gold, will they make their correction.

Government sponsored persecution of those who believe in Yahweh / the Lord - Daniel 8:20-26, 11:31-33, 12:1, Amos 8:1-12, Zephaniah 1:14-18, Matthew 24:21, Mark 13:17-19, Luke 21:23, Romans 2:5-11, Revelation 12:

It was during the era of the first abomination of desolation around 167 BC, that the government sponsored persecution of those who believed in Yahweh / the Lord, became a regular occurrence in the land of Israel. This practice would continue in the land of Israel and throughout the nations that surrounded the land of Israel, against both Jews and Christians, until around 381 AD when Christianity legally became a religion accepted by the government of Rome.

According to the books of the Maccabees, at the time of the first abomination of desolation event, the people of Israel were fractured into two groups, the Hellenized Jews and the people who maintained their devotion to the religion, tradition and culture of the Jewish faith. When the first abomination of desolation event took place in 167 BC, the people who maintained the tradition and culture of the Jewish faith, fled to the mountains. Antiochus IV Epiphanes responded by sending a large force of soldiers to pursue the people who had fled to the mountains. When the soldiers attacked the first refugees, they did nothing to resist. They did not even throw stones or block the entrances to the caves where they were hiding. They said, 'We will all die with a clear conscience. Let heaven and earth bear witness that you are slaughtering us unjustly.' So the enemy attacked them on the Sabbath and killed the men, their wives, their children, and their livestock. A thousand people died.

When Mattathias Maccabeus and his friends heard the news, they decided that if anyone attacked them on the Sabbath, they would defend themselves so that all the people of Israel would not be 'wiped off the face of the earth.'

Mattathias gathered an army of the faithful people of Israel to defend themselves against both the Hellenized / renegade Jews and the Gentile Seleucid / Syrian army of Antiochus IV Epiphanes.

Now that they had an army, they gave vent to their anger by attacking the renegade Jews. Those who escaped were forced to flee to the Gentiles for safety. Mattathias and his friends went everywhere tearing down pagan altars and circumcising by force every uncircumcised boy they found within the border of Israel. They were also successful in hunting down the arrogant Gentile officials. They rescued the law of Moses from the Gentiles and their kings and broke the power of the wicked King Antiochus. 1 Maccabees 2:44-48

When the time came for Mattathias Maccabeus to die, he gathered his sons and gave them a message of encouragement followed by instructions for how to carry on the rebellion against Antiochus IV Epiphanes. The events of Mattathias Maccabeus' death and the message that he left his family with, is valuable reading (1 Maccabees 2:49-70), along with the rest of the history of the Maccabean revolt recorded in 1 and 2 Maccabees.

This little army was able to face the military offense of Antiochus IV Epiphanes, and later the attacks from the south and from the Ptolemies. The Maccabean Revolt was *so effective that their attacks on the Seleucid / Syrian empire marked the downfall of the Seleucid / Syrian empire.*

When the Gentiles would go to war, they would consult their idols. But the Maccabeans unrolled the book of the Law to search for God's guidance. The Maccabeans sought to bring their offerings to God in the midst of the conflict and they brought in leaders who were holy to lead in prayer. They would blow trumpets and rally. Only after worshiping and consulting God Most High would the organization for war begin. Outnumbered and less well equipped, the Maccabeans amazingly were able to prevail.

In 164 BC, when the Maccabeans went to rededicate the temple, they found it abandoned. The altar was profaned, the gates burned down, the courtyards had grown up in a forest of weeds, and the priests' rooms had been torn down.

The Maccabeans proceeded to purify the temple, removing the stones used for pagan worship, and all vestiges of the baal / mystery / mythology religion. They 'put the stones in a suitable place on the temple hill, where they were to be kept until a prophet should appear and decide what to do with them.' *Then they took uncut stones and built a new altar in accordance with the Law of Moses. They repaired the temple, made new utensils and brought the lampstand, the altar of incense, and the table for the bread, into the temple. They set about putting the temple right again. (1 Maccabees 4:36-61)*

For eight days they celebrated the rededication of the altar, the amount of time required for dedication. On the twenty fifth day of the ninth month, the month of Kislev, in the year 148 of the kingdom of Syria / 164 BC, on the third year anniversary of the first abomination of desolation event, they dedicated the new altar with music, worship and praise.

This account should have a 'they lived happily ever after' type of ending. But it does not. The people of Israel placed a temple guard in place, built up the walls and then incurred the wrath of their neighbors, the Seleucids /

Syrians, the Ptolemaic / Egyptian empire, and the Idumeans / descendants of Esau from Edom.

It would be an Idumean, approximately one hundred years later in 63 BC, that would come to sit on the throne of Israel, King Herod the Great. King Herod the Great was an illegitimate king of Israel who still reigned when Jesus was born.

Heavily influenced by the history of the Maccabean Revolt, King Herod fostered the fear that a legitimate heir to the throne in Israel would arise. The lineage of Joseph, the husband of Mary the mother of Jesus Christ was recorded in Matthew 1 and demonstrated Joseph's own legitimacy to the throne of David / throne of Israel. Mary the mother of Jesus also had a genealogy recorded in Luke 3 that legitimized her right to the throne of David / throne of Israel. In response to King Herod's fear that a true and legitimate king would arise in Israel, King Herod took measures to ensure that his place on the throne would not be stolen, by ordering all the infant boys under two years of age in Bethlehem, around the time of the birth of Jesus, to be killed.

Persecution has consistently been a major part of the history of the people of Israel. The future abomination of desolation event will again be a time of persecution for both the people of Israel and the followers of the Lamb / Jesus Christ.

There are numerous biblical references, including Jesus Christ's own description, that outline that during the era of the time of Jacob's Trouble, there will be an immense intensity of the persecutions that will take place.

John the Revelator's message from the resurrected and ascended Jesus Christ documented that the persecutions will begin with the opening of the first seal (Revelation 6:1-2) and the release of the first white horse with its rider sent out to conquer. The era of persecution will not end until messiah / the Lamb / Jesus Christ returns, defeats the armies of the world / enemies of God Most High, and fully establishes the kingdom of heaven on earth at the conclusion of the era of the time of Jacob's Trouble.

The era of the time of Jacob's Trouble will be an era when persecution of the people of Israel and the followers of the Lamb / Jesus Christ will reach a magnitude that has not been experienced in human history. This persecution will permeate the world, and the future abomination of desolation event will mark the heightening of the intensity of persecution that will set record levels.

The explanation for the shaggy goat: 'The two-horned ram that you saw represents the kings of Media and Persia. The shaggy goat is the king of Greece, and the large horn between its eyes is the first king. The four horns that replaced the one that was broken off represent four kingdoms that will emerge from the nation of Greece but will not have the same power.'

'In the latter part of their reign, when rebels have become completely wicked, a fierce-looking king, a master of intrigue, will arise. He will become very strong, but not by his own power. <u>He will cause astounding devastation</u> and will succeed in whatever he does. <u>He will destroy those who are mighty, the holy people</u>. He will cause deceit to prosper, and he will consider himself superior. <u>When they feel secure, he will destroy many and take his stand against the Prince of princes</u>. Yet he will be destroyed, but not by human power.'

'The vision of the evenings and mornings that has been given you is true, but seal up the vision, for it concerns the distant future.'
Daniel 8:20-26

Daniel's vision could not be clearer. The final horn on the shaggy goat will begin his reign of terror with bring security, that will entice people to accepting him as their leader. They will consider this man to be wonderful, deceivingly wonderful, and successful.

As a master of intrigue, he will use his abilities to obtain a position of power, an advantageous position from which to most effectively strike. And when the people of Israel are securely trusting him, he will take the opportunity to destroy many.

Many will entertain the idea that the final horn on the shaggy goat will be just a man, with only the power of a single man, a person who puts his pants on one leg at a time just like everyone else. But neither Daniel's vision or John the Revelator's vision depicted him as a man with just one man's power.

The final horn on the shaggy goat / beast of the earth will have power that is not his own. This supernatural power will feed his ego. This supernatural power will cause the final horn on the shaggy goat / beast of the earth to believe that he is truly superior, a truly superior species that is high above the level of humanity. This supernatural power will even cause the final horn on the shaggy goat / beast of the earth to believe that he is the real-life superhero the world has been waiting for, and that he is indestructible. And truly, he is in a way indestructible... until Jesus Christ arrives to deal with him (Revelation 19:19-21).

But before Jesus Christ arrives to defeat the final horn on the shaggy goat / beast of the earth, he will use his phenomenal cosmic powers to inflict upon the people who have been favored by God Most High through covenant, the angst that the red dragon / serpent / Satan, Inc. accumulated in the past six thousand years, against God Most High.

The Lord prophesied that at the time of the king that will exalt himself:

'He will muster his forces and they will defile the sanctuary fortress. Then they will take away the daily sacrifices, in the place of the abomination of desolation.'

'With flattery he will corrupt those who have violated the covenant, but the people who know their God will be strong and firmly resist him.'

'Those who understand will instruct many, though for a time they will fall by the sword or be burned or captured or plundered.'
Daniel 11:31-33 translated

During this era of the time of Jacob's Trouble, after the future abomination of desolation event, the people of God will have the opportunity and responsibility to instruct many concerning the kingdom of heaven and the true nature of the red dragon / serpent / Satan, Inc., and the two beasts of Revelation 13. The era of the time of Jacob's Trouble will be marked by many people seeking to understand what is truly the way of God Most High and what belongs to the kingdom of Satan, Inc. / kingdom of man.

But there will be a cost for the followers of the Lamb/ Jesus Christ that provide instruction.

(Note: there is also a cost for those who choose to deny God Most High during this era and contribute to the persecution.)

This is what the Sovereign Lord showed me: a basket of ripe fruit. 'What do you see, Amos?' the Lord asked.

'A basket of ripe fruit,' I answered.

Then the Lord said to me, 'The time is ripe for my people Israel. I will spare them no longer.'

'In that day,' declares the Sovereign Lord, 'the songs in the temple will turn to wailing. Many, many bodies – flung everywhere! Silence!' Hear this, you who trample the needy and do away with the poor of the land, saying, 'When will the New Moon be over that we may sell grain, and the Sabbath be ended that we may market wheat?' skimping on the measure, boosting the price and cheating with dishonest scales, buying the poor with silver and the needy for a pair of sandals, selling even the sweepings with the wheat.

The Lord has sworn by himself, the Pride of Jacob: 'I will never forget anything they have done.'

'Will not the land tremble for this, and all who live in it mourn? The whole land will rise like the Nile; it will be stirred up and then sink like the river of Egypt.'

'In that day,' declares the Sovereign Lord, 'I will make the sun go down at noon and darken the earth in broad daylight. I will turn your religious festivals into mourning and all your singing into weeping. I will make all of you wear sackcloth and shave your heads. I will make that time like mourning for an only son and the end of it like a bitter day.'

'The days are coming,' declares the Sovereign Lord, 'when I will send a famine through the land — not a famine of food or a thirst for water, but a famine of hearing the words of the Lord. People will stagger from sea to sea and wander from north to east, searching for the word of the Lord, but they will not find it.' Amos 8:1-12

This message from the Lord to Amos was multifaceted.

Phrases like 'The time is ripe for my people Israel...' *and* 'In that day, I will make the sun go down at noon and darken the earth in broad daylight,' *were references to the era connected with the return of Jesus Christ / 'the Day of the Lord.' This prophecy awaits its fulfillment during the era of the time of Jacob's Trouble.*

God Most High said that vengeance belongs to God. There have been so very many offenses that God's grace has allowed to delay the accountability for. But delaying accountability is not the same as forgetting to hold accountable. 'The days are coming,' says the Lord when the people of Israel will have the opportunity to mourn for their rejection of God Most High's plan for them and for their rejection of Jesus Christ as messiah. The future abomination of desolation will mark the time when those days have arrived.

Amos described the mindset of the people at the time of this destruction as being impatient with honoring the holy days when the markets should be closed, willing to skimp on the measure of what they market, practicing price gouging and cheating with dishonest scales, buying the poor and enslaving them for the price of silver or a pair of sandals, selling even the sweepings / the chaff along with the wheat.

Amos' description of the economy could be equated with the release of the black horse and rider that corresponded with the third seal (Revelation 6:5-6). The fraudulent economy could also be the result of the cumulation of three and a half years of war, famine, pestilence, death, and political manipulation.

Amos also documented that the poor of the land will be extinguished. But the Lord will remember what the people did to the poor. The Lord swore by the Pride of Jacob: 'I will never forget anything they have done.'

While it is tempting to view God Most High as a forgiving God, a merciful God in all things, God Most High is not forgiving of all things. God Most High is able to forgive all things, but God Most High does not forgive all things.

God Most High has stated that the rebellious angels will never be forgiven and has instituted the annual sacrifice of Yom Kippur / Day of Atonement to stress that point. God Most High has repeatedly prophesied to the Old Testament prophets that there would be nations that God Most High slated to totally destroy during the era of the time of Jacob's Trouble. And God Most High has not forgotten that the people of Israel have repeatedly broken covenant with God, have used God Most High for their own gain at God Most High's expense, and continued to reject and impede God Most High's plan for fully establishing the kingdom of heaven on earth.

At the time of the future abomination of desolation event, the allowance for tolerance will be coming to a close. The greatest persecution of the people of Israel will have begun at the moment that the beast of the earth stands in the wing of the temple and declares that he is greater than God Most High. In that moment, beast of the earth will need to begin the annihilation process of all that would be a threat to his reign and his power and his authority. And the largest threat will come from the people of Israel. Therefore, the people of Israel will be the first target for persecution (Daniel 7:21-22, 8:24-25, 12:1, Revelation 12:13-17). And God Most High will allow the beast of the earth to take the lead in accomplishing this pursuit, because God Most High has not forgotten that the people of God who should have been representatives of God Most High and the kingdom of heaven, have instead trampled the needy, done away with the poor in the land, dishonored the holy days for the opportunity to make a profit, cheated their customers, partook in price gouging, enslaved their own people because they were poor, and diluted their products.

God Most High cutting the days short, and Jesus Christ's instruction for dealing with the onslaught of persecution that will begin with the future abomination of desolation event – Matthew 10:21-23a, 24:15-25, Mark 13:14-20, Luke 21:20-24, John 16:2-4

God Most High determined that during the era of the time of Jacob's Trouble, God will act on behalf of the elect, by cutting the days short.

But Jesus Christ also provided instruction for the followers of the Lamb / Jesus Christ, for how to deal with the era of the time of Jacob's Trouble. Jesus Christ's instruction for dealing with the onslaught of persecution that will come with the future abomination of desolation event, was to flee to the mountains.

Jesus said: 'Therefore, when you see the abomination of desolation, spoken of by Daniel the prophet, standing in the holy place – let the reader understand – then let those who are in Judea, flee to the mountains. Do not let the one on the housetop come down to take anything out of the house. Do not let the one in the field return back to take his cloak. It will be dreadful to those who are pregnant and nursing infants in those days. Pray that your flight is not in the winter nor on a Sabbath. For then there will be great tribulation, such unequaled from the beginning of the world until now, and never to be equaled again.'

'If those days had not been shortened, no one would have survived. But because of the elect, the days will be shortened.'

'If anyone says to you, 'Behold, here is the messiah!' Or 'Here he is!' Do not believe it. False messiahs and false prophets, will arise; and they will provide great signs and wonders to intentionally mislead, if possible, even the elect.'

'Behold, I have foretold you, ahead of time.' Matthew 24:15-25 translated

If the reestablished Israeli Sanhedrin, or the Knesset, during the era of the time of Jacob's Trouble, were able to culturally establish an increase in the observance of Mosaic Law within the nation of Israel, then if the future abomination of desolation event were to take place on the Sabbath, travel would not be allowed and escape would become difficult.

The instruction to 'pray that flight not take place in winter or on the Sabbath' *indicated that the actual day for the future abomination of desolation event may take place in the winter. Or the date may be yet to be determined by the red dragon / serpent / Satan, Inc. and not by God Most High. Or God Most High may have determined that the date should be selected by the ordering of the current events in the region.*

The fact that Jesus Christ was specific enough to express that the danger will be so acute that the future abomination of desolation event could be heavily impacted by which day of the week that it takes place on, was an indicator of the swiftness with which the beast of the earth will enact his catastrophic and deadly mark of the beast system - in a single day.

Note that the phrases 'but for the sake of the elect...' *and* 'to deceive even the elect...' *indicated that* 'the elect' *will be physically present to experience and witness world events. The phrases also indicated that* 'the elect' *will experience a certain level of protection as well as experiencing some of the effects of world events.*

Jesus Christ's use of these phrases, provided evidence against the possibility of the veracity of rapture theology.

The phrase 'days cut short' *may indicate that God Most High will intervene during the events of the era of the time of Jacob's Trouble and shorten the number of hours in a day from a twenty four hour day to a day with less hours.*

Or it may be a reference to the fourth trumpet where a third of the sun will be struck, a third of the moon so that for a third of the day and night there is no light (Amos 8:9, Revelation 8:12).

Or 'days cut short' *may be a cutting short the days that the two beasts of Revelation 13 will have to reign with complete effectiveness. While the two beasts of Revelation 13 will be given forty two months (~ one thousand two hundred sixty days) for their term of office marking time from the future abomination of desolation event, the temple will be unconsecrated for only one thousand one hundred fifty days, with a difference of on hundred ten days; which may also be an indicator that the forty two month term may be an approximation of forty two months and not the full one thousand two hundred sixty days that the two witnesses have been allotted to consecutively serve.*

Also, Daniel 12:11 cited two periods of one thousand two hundred ninety days and one thousand three hundred thirty five days, marked to begin with the future abomination of desolation event. The biblical record did not indicate what would happen at the one thousand two hundred ninety day mark.

And there may be something not yet disclosed, that was hidden within all this dating, that would correspond to the fulfillment of the phrase 'days cut short.'

Jesus said: 'When you see the abomination of the desolation which was spoken of by Daniel the prophet, standing where it should not be – let the one reading understand – then those in Judea should flee to the mountains. Do not let the one on the housetop come down or go in to take anything out of his house. The one in the field should not return to the things behind, to retrieve his clothing.'

'How dreadful it will be for pregnant women and nursing mothers in those days! Pray that this will not take place in winter. For those days will be tribulation such as never has been equaled from the beginning of creation, when God Created the world, until now – and never will be again.'

'If the Lord had not shortened the days, none of humanity would have been saved. But because of the elect whom God chose, God has shortened the days.' Mark 13:14-20 translated

Mark's account of Jesus Christ's teaching on the future abomination of desolation event described an era when the distress will be unequaled and never equaled again; the days when, if the Lord did not discontinue the reign of terror sponsored by the beast of the earth, then no one would survive.

Mark recorded Jesus Christ's message to be communicated to those living during the era of the time of Jacob's Trouble.

Jesus said: 'When you see Jerusalem surrounded by armies, then you will know that its destruction is near. Then let those who are in Judea, flee to the mountains. Let those who are living within her, depart. And let those living in the country, not enter into her. For these are the days to fulfill vengeance, all things that have been written.'

'But woe to those who are pregnant and to those who are nursing in those days. For there will be great distress upon the land and wrath upon this people. And they will fall by the edge of the sword, and will be led as captives into all nations. Jerusalem will be trampled on by Gentiles until the times of the Gentiles are fulfilled.' Luke 21:20-24 translated

When something is repeated in all three of the synoptic gospels, it should have the effect upon the reader of amplifying the message. Communicating this message was important to Matthew. Communicating this message was important to Mark. Communicating this message was important to Luke.

Luke's account of Jesus' words was what preterist used most effectively in supporting their idea that the future abomination of desolation event that Jesus taught about, has already taken place in 70 AD when the city of Jerusalem received its time of punishment and was destroyed. It was a time when pregnant women had their bellies ripped open. Nursing mothers experienced their infants killed in front of them. And the people of Israel fell by the sword and were taken as prisoners to all nations in what became known as the diaspora. Jerusalem has been trampled on by the Gentiles from 70 AD until our present time.

But the fact that Luke's account of Jesus' words had their partial fulfillment, did not negate that a future abomination of desolation event will take place.

Note that in Luke's account, Luke did not actually reference the future abomination of desolation event with the persecution of Jerusalem. Luke's context for Jesus Christ's warning was set only for 'when you see Jerusalem being surrounded by armies, you will know that Jerusalem's desolation is near.'

The preterist view would like to make the case that because Jerusalem is the holy city and because the Romans surrounded Jerusalem with their standards that served as focal points of worship for the Roman legions, that when the Roman siege of Jerusalem took place in August 70 AD, that this event fulfilled the future abomination of desolation event scheduled for the era of the time of Jacob's Trouble. But Luke's account did not actually validate the preterist interpretation.

Jesus said: 'They will put you out of the synagogue; in fact, a time is coming when anyone who kills you will think he is offering a service to God. They will do such things because they have not known the Father or me. I have told you this, so that when the time comes you will remember that I warned you. I did not tell you this at first because I was with you.' John 16:2-4

When the first disciples of Jesus Christ went out into the world, they were first, practicing Israelites. So they continued their regular practice of going to the synagogues for worship.

But in the very early years following the crucifixion, death, resurrection and ascension of Jesus Christ, the people in the synagogues viewed the followers of Jesus as blasphemers, heretics, people who had been deceived in order to follow someone that the people in the synagogue considered to be a false messiah. It was the Jewish people who first persecuted the followers of Jesus Christ and put them out of the synagogues, and turned them over to be martyred.

During the era of the time of Jacob's Trouble, there will be a resurgence of intolerance toward those who choose to worship Jesus Christ as messiah. It will be a reason for expulsion out of the synagogue. It will probably be reason for the authentic followers of the Lamb / Jesus Christ's expulsion out of the church as well.

Jesus' instructions to the disciples: 'Brother will betray brother to death, and a father his child; children will rebel against their parents and have them put to death. All people will hate you because of me, but the one who stands firm to the end will be saved. When you are persecuted in one place, flee to another.' Matthew 10:21-23a

While this prophecy was most definitely fulfilled during the first four hundred years after the crucifixion, death, resurrection, and ascension of Jesus Christ, this prophecy also had multiple other fulfillments in the past two thousand years.

There is every reason to believe that there will be yet another period of time during the second half of the era of the time of Jacob's Trouble when this prophecy will be fulfilled again.

Timing and duration of the abomination of desolation events

From humanity's perspective, time is chronological in that each day is ordered after the previous day, each month ordered after the previous month, etc. A human life is marked and defined by death and time; minutes, hours, days, months, years, decades, etc. Old tombstones will sometimes include the person's lifetime in the measure of years, months, and days. Death itself is a statement that says, 'time is up.'

On the fourth day of creation, God created the sun, moon and stars. God determined the seasons for marking time on God's calendar. Time was created for the benefit of humanity, to be used as a communication tool by God. Time has been marked for a specific purpose; so that humanity would know when the right time had arrived. (Ecclesiastes 3:11, Jeremiah 8:7, 33:15, Habakkuk 2:2-3, Luke 19:41-44, Romans 5:6, Galatians 4:4, 1 Timothy 6:13-16, etc.)

In the era of eternity, marking time will not hold the significance that it currently holds in human history.

Currently, time has been marked as the cosmos nears the point in time when messiah / the Lamb / Jesus Christ will return, will defeat the enemies of God Most High and of the kingdom of heaven, and will fully establish the kingdom of heaven on earth for the Thousand Years Reign of Jesus Christ. All of human history has been operating on the countdown clock to this most significant event.

During the Thousand Years Reign of Jesus Christ, time will be marked before the era of eternity begins.

It is essential that the entire cosmos mark time on the same scale so that these events can be coordinated.

But from God's perspective, God the Creator created time, is over time, controls time. God the Creator is not controlled by time. From God's perspective, time is irrelevant in plotting the end result of human history. What God determined, God will accomplish.

God Most High does not need the calendar to make anything happen. From God Most High's perspective, what God has determined, has already been accomplished. God Most High's schedule / calendar is for the benefit of the cosmos to know the when and where of what God Most High is doing. The calendar is merely a device to allow humanity to be aware of the dynamics of God Most High's plan as it develops.

God Most High is eternal and perfectly effective at what God does. God does not need time. In 'God's time,' there is only what was, what is, and what is to come. So the sabbath and the seven days in a week, serve to remind God, and humanity, of God's seven thousand year plan with the seventh millennium of human history, being defined as rest for God's Spirit, a holiday. While we believe that the sabbath rest was created for humanity to remember God Most High's plan for the seventh thousand year period when God's Spirit will rest, the biblical record also presented the sabbath rest as a reminder for God. Every week, every seven days, God Most High is reminded that God made this promise to humanity to set the world right, to reestablish the Garden of Eden / garden of God /

paradise living that God the Creator established during the first week of creation.

It is because God the Creator rules over time, that Jesus Christ ruled over the sabbath instead of being ruled by the Sabbath (Matthew 12:1-8, Mark 2:23-28, Luke 6:1-11, 13:10-16).

Concerning the scheduled return of Jesus Christ when he comes with his glory, Jesus Christ said that only God the Father knows the time, the day and the hour, that was scheduled for Jesus Christ's return. But that day and hour will also be coordinated with messiah / the Lamb / Jesus Christ and all the armies remaining in heaven.

While time is important, what is more important are the events that take place in time. God created time. God transcends time. God is over time. But the effects of the events that take place in the context of time, will remain into the era of eternity.

When God imparted information to humanity through the prophets and indicated at what time in human history the future events would take place such as in 'the distant future,' *or for* 'two thousand three hundred evenings and mornings,' *God Most High set the time for us, for humanity, so that we will know when to be looking for God's activity and be able to act in phase, in harmony, in agreement with God.*

One of time's purposes is to be a tool for bringing order out of chaos. In the biblical account of creation, each day consisted of an evening / 'chaos' and a morning / 'order.' Each day of creation was chronologically placed in its order, for life to be able to be sustained throughout time. For example, dry land was separated from water before the vegetation was created. The sun, moon and stars were set immediately after the day of the creation of vegetation. Animals, living things, humanity, were not created until after there was vegetation established to sustain them. God's timing is precise, reasoned, ordered.

Before the incarnation of Jesus, those who consulted God Most High's calendar as defined by Daniel's seventy 'sevens,' were able to understand the time of the coming of messiah. The magi from the east, understood the time to search out the infant messiah.

All of Jesus' incarnated life on earth, was placed on God Most High's schedule. A star marked the time and place of Jesus Christ's birth. Jesus Christ's crucifixion was scheduled to the year, month, day and hour according to Daniel's seventy 'sevens.' Jesus himself understood the hour of the work that he needed to accomplish on the cross. At just the right time, when everything was in order, Jesus Christ died for us (Romans 5:6).

Those who did not understand how important it was to God Most High that people keep that appointment to meet messiah, rejected Jesus Christ as the promised and prophesied messiah and received a judgment against them that led to the destruction of Jerusalem, the destruction of the temple, and the dispersion of the nation of Israel, forty years later.

God Most High shared the timing of scheduled events so that <u>humanity</u> would have the opportunity to be in the right place at the right time.

The timing of all the events of the era of the time of Jacob's Trouble will be essential for the <u>benefit of humanity</u>, not for the benefit of God Most High.

The detail that God Most High supplied concerning timing of the events of the era of the time of Jacob's Trouble and the return of Jesus Christ, is intricate. It is purposeful. Events must take place according to God Most High's will which bears the seven seals that were opened in sequence in order to have their intended effect. The events associated with the seven trumpets, while sometimes overlapping in in their expression in time, must also be accomplished in sequence in order to have their intended effect. Etc.

Just as God Most High held the expectation of the people living during Jesus Christ's earthly life, that those who believed in messiah would meet and greet messiah / the Lamb / Jesus Christ, God Most High also holds the expectation for those living during the era of the time of Jacob's Trouble to also be ready for the preparatory events that will be experienced prior to the return of messiah / the Lamb / Jesus Christ.

There was a purpose in communicating these events to the followers of the Lamb / Jesus Christ.

Just as the disciples of Jesus Christ had responsibilities to perform at the time of Jesus Christ's ministry, the followers of the Lamb / Jesus Christ will have responsibilities during the era of the time of Jacob's Trouble.

Almost two thousand years ago, Jesus sent his disciples into the world at the end of his ministry. During the era of the time of Jacob's Trouble, the followers of the Lamb / Jesus Christ will have responsibilities prior to Jesus Christ's return. Timing must have its effect in the events that will prepare the world for the full establishment of the kingdom of heaven on earth.

Included in God's time schedule, God Most High will allow the rise to power of the beast of the earth. But the mere fact that God is the author of time and the author of the will of God that was contained by the seals, means that when God has said that the beast of the earth will have a certain number of days for desolating the temple and a certain number of days to reign, God Most High also has the power, the authority and the authorship to accomplish limiting the beast of the earth to the number of days allotted to him to work. God Most High retains authority over time. And time will have authority over the beast of the earth.

God Most High's authorship of time also means that the end has already been written. Therefore, God Most High has the authority to inform humanity of what is yet to take place during the era of the time of Jacob's Trouble, including informing those who live during the era of the time of Jacob's Trouble, through Daniel who recorded the information for us around two thousand five hundred seventy years ago.

This phenomena of God's view of time also means that in God Most High's description of the different abomination of desolation events, there can be overlap in the record of the details, and that God Most High can present them by describing them as if they were in some ways the same event just placed on top of each other, but spread out over time.

One example of a precedence for this kind of communication device where there is an overlapping of details on the same kind of event was with the feast of Passover.

On the seventeenth of the month of Nisan, the ark of Noah rested on land.

Approximately nine hundred years after the flood, on the fourteenth of Nisan, the people of Israel donned their doorposts with lamb's blood so that the angel of death would pass over their homes. Three days later, on the seventeenth of Nisan, they were crossing through the Red Sea on dry ground.

Jesus was crucified on the fourteenth of Nisan. Three days later, on the seventeenth of Nisan, Jesus Christ was resurrected from the dead, assuring the promise that believers in messiah (BC) and followers of the Lamb (AD) would one day dwell in the regenerated Garden of Eden / garden of God / paradise that the first man and first woman had originally been placed in (after having been formed from 'land').

On the seventeenth of Nisan, when the ark rested on land, it was the promise to Noah and his family that they were about to enter into a new world.

On the seventeenth of Nisan, when the people of Israel had crossed through the Red Sea, it was the promise to the people of Israel that they were about to enter into a new relationship with God Most High, and headed toward the Promised Land.

On the seventeenth of Nisan, when Jesus Christ rose from the dead, it was the promise to all of humanity of the opportunity for the followers of Jesus Christ to be able to live eternally with God Most High in God's Garden of Eden / garden of God / paradise.

The descriptions of the first and future abomination of desolation events also consisted of overlapping of details.

The first abomination of desolation event fulfilled many of the prophetic details. But the future abomination of desolation will be a time when all the prophetic details recorded in the biblical record that have described abomination of desolation events, will be fully realized.

The first half of the era of the time of Jacob's Trouble will serve as staging and preparation for this global event of the future abomination of desolation event that will have cosmic impact upon all of heaven and earth.

The future abomination of desolation event will take place after the prophecies have been fulfilled for the sounding of the first five trumpets and around the time of the fulfillment of the events associated with the first part of the sounding of the sixth trumpet. The evidence for placing the future abomination of desolation after the first five trumpets and the first part of the sixth trumpet consisted of the notation that the sixth trumpet / woe #2 / part 2 will be the arrival and ministry of the two witnesses (Revelation 8:13, 11:14). The two witnesses will accomplish their work during the one thousand two hundred sixty days that follow the future abomination of desolation.

Setting aside the calendar and observing the dynamics of the entirety of the events of the era of the time of Jacob's Trouble, the future abomination of desolation event will need a specific environment that is receptive of the subtleties that will occur with the future abomination of desolation event.

After the first five trumpet prophecies have taken place, John the Revelator included this note: The rest of humanity who were not killed by their plagues *(with the sounding of the first six trumpets)*, did not even repent of the works of their hands, so that they did not worship the demons and their golden and silver and bronze and stone and wooden idols, which are neither able to see nor to hear nor to walk. And they did not repent of their murders, nor of their sorceries (magic arts), nor of their sexual immorality, nor of their thefts. Revelation 9:20-21 translated

John the Revelator did not indicate that God Most High expects the inhabitants of the earth to repent. There was no indication provided in this message that the survivors will repent, nor even learn at this point that God

Most High is Sovereign God and that the two beasts of Revelation 13 can only be counterfeits serving the counterfeit kingdom. The biblical record assumed that unrepentance will inevitably continue.

The authentic followers of the Lamb / Jesus Christ do not fall under the definition of 'the rest of humanity,' or 'the inhabitants of the earth.' Clearly, the followers of the Lamb / Jesus Christ cannot worship Jesus Christ and also worship demons and idols. Authentic followers of the Lamb / Jesus Christ do not produce work that they need to repent of; murder, practicing magic (including poisoning, drugging, or injecting illness into people), practicing sexual immorality, or theft. In addition, authentic followers of the Lamb / Jesus Christ are marked by their already present repentance as a condition of becoming followers of the Lamb / Jesus Christ. Authentic followers of the Lamb have heeded Jesus Christ's message to the angels of the seven churches (Revelation 2 and 3).

The world will be primed and ready to experience the full effect of the degradation that the rest of humanity will have actively pursued. The events of the five trumpets and even the first part of the sixth trumpet will be the result of God Most High no longer imprisoning, chaining, restraining, or holding back the full effect of the rebellious angels upon the earth. The rebellious angels by this time will have become the favored gods of the majority of the people of the world. God Most High must have a period of time when the rebellious angels and the people of the world who favor the rebellious angels, have an opportunity to mesh together.

In a way, it is God Most High's extended grace to allow the people of the world to taste the flavor of the kind of kingdom that the people of the world have labored so diligently to embrace, the kingdom of Satan, Inc. / kingdom of man. But even the abuse, infliction, and exploitation that the rebellious angels / kingdom of Satan, Inc. / kingdom of man places upon the people of the world, will not be enough to cause them to repent.

So, the world will move on to the next event, the future abomination of desolation and the progression of the rest of preparatory events required to bring about kingdom change.

The future abomination of desolation event will be so historic worldwide and throughout the entirety of all of history that it will be used to mark time and be remembered as a marker in time in the same way that the flood, the tower of Babel, the exodus of the people of Israel out of Egypt, and the crucifixion and resurrection of Jesus Christ, have marked time.

There will also be other markers of time during the era of the time of Jacob's Trouble. The seven year covenant peace treaty agreement already marked the beginning of the seven years that will be the era of the time of Jacob's Trouble. The future abomination of desolation event will mark the middle of the seven years. The death of the two witnesses that will take place in the vicinity of seven years after the covenant peace treaty agreement was initiated, will mark the official endpoint of the power position of the two beasts of Revelation 13. But the greatest of all markers in time will take place during the seventy five days that will follow the murder of the two witnesses. It will be within the final seventy five days that messiah / the Lamb / Jesus Christ will return, defeat the armies of the world, and then fully establish the kingdom of heaven on earth.

Unfortunately, in God Most High's plan, there was no other way to prepare the earth, heaven, and their inhabitants, for the acceptance of Jesus Christ's fully established kingdom of heaven on earth without first going through the process of allowing the red dragon / serpent / Satan, Inc. to have the opportunity to make a pitch to the people of earth and to attempt to sell the people of earth the ideals of the kingdom of Satan, Inc. / kingdom of man. The pitcher and catcher designated to fully market the kingdom of Satan, Inc. / kingdom of man, will be the two beasts of Revelation 13. The time for the pitch to be made will be the future abomination of desolation event. They will be set at center stage in the future consecrated temple in Jerusalem. And they will supply their demonstration during the future abomination of desolation event... at just the right time.

The understanding of the Old Testament / Tanakh prophet Daniel (fl. 605 to 530 BC) – a prophet of Judah, of the marking of time by the future abomination of desolation event, for further events

Multiple times in Daniel's account, Daniel documented the length of events with marking time from the future abomination of desolation event. And John the Revelator's description of the two beasts of Revelation 13, also confirmed marking time from the future abomination of desolation event. Both Daniel and John documented that once the future abomination of desolation event has taken place, and the coronation of the beast of the earth has been established, that the timer will be set for the deadline of the ending of the second half of the era of the time of Jacob's Trouble.

Daniel and John identified four time segments that all begin with the future abomination of desolation event. The precision of timing to the half day, cannot be missed in this message. Marking time from the starting point of the abomination of desolation event, the events with the simultaneous starting point will be:

- 2,300 evening and morning sacrifices / 1,150 days during which the temple sacrifice system will be suspended. (In Genesis 1, the evening and morning combination equated with a 24 hour day.) Following the 1,150 days of sacrificial system suspension, or 8 days before the 1,150 days, the temple will be reconsecrated and sacrifices will begin again. 8 days are required for the temple consecration. (Daniel 8:14)
- 1,260 days during which the two witnesses will provide plagues, the relief of plagues, drought, and rain as they witness on the temple mount. (Revelation 11:3)
- 42 months during which the beast of the earth will express his power and authority. Notice that 150 days before the 1,260 days will be completed, that the people of Israel will have

retaken the temple and reestablished the consecration of the temple restoring the fully consecrated, functional and operational temple sacrificial system. (Revelation 11:2, 13:5)

'From the time the daily sacrifice is taken away, and the abomination of desolation is set up, there will be one thousand two hundred ninety days.'

'Blessed is the one who waits and arrives at the one thousand three hundred thirty five days.' (1,260 + 30 = 1,290; 1,290 + 45 = 1,335) Daniel 12:11-12 translated

- *1,290 days that will mark time 30 days following the death of the two witnesses. There are activities that take place after the death of the two witnesses that will have a conclusion 30 days after the death of the two witnesses and another set of activities that will have a conclusion 75 days after the death of the two witnesses. (Daniel 12:11)*
- *1,335 days which will mark the end of everything that God Most High and the promised and prophesied messiah intend to accomplish in heaven and on earth in fully establishing the kingdom of heaven on earth. The final 75 days will include the events of the seventh trumpet / woe #3, pouring out of the seven bowls / seven last plagues, the armies of the world preparing for battle, the return of Jesus Christ, the harvest of the earth, the defeat of the armies of the earth in the final battle, the gathering of the grapes, etc. (Daniel 12:11-12)*

The future abomination of desolation event will mark the beginning of all four of these segments of time.

Daniel's vision of the ram and the goat: Then I heard a holy one speaking, and another holy one said to him 'How long will it take for the vision concerning the daily sacrifices and the transgression of desolation to be fulfilled — the transgression that causes desolation, both of the giving in the sanctuary and the trampling underfoot of the host?'

He said to me, 'It will be 2,300 evenings and mornings. Then the sanctuary will be cleansed.' Daniel 8:13-14 translated

Daniel's phraseology of 'how long will it take for the vision to be fulfilled...?' *was almost identical to the phraseology of the holy ones under the altar in Revelation 6:9-11 when they called out in a loud voice,* 'How long, Sovereign Lord, holy and true, until you judge the inhabitants of the earth and avenge our blood?' *The similarity acted to link the two passages.*

The answer provided was that it will take two thousand three hundred evenings and mornings before the sanctuary / temple will be reconsecrated. That is two thousand three hundred half days or one thousand one hundred fifty whole days.

The preterist interruption offered the idea that the cessation of the temple sacrificial system was fulfilled at the time of the Maccabean Revolt when Antiochus IV Epiphanes desecrated the temple and ended the daily sacrifices in Kislev 167 BC, for three years. Exactly three years later, to the day, the temple was reconsecrated in 164 BC. The temple rededication has been annually celebrated as the holiday of Hanukah / feast of dedication, since that time. But the number of days of interruption of the temple sacrifice at that time was approximately one thousand eighty days, not the one thousand one hundred fifty days that Daniel cited.

On the fifteenth day of the month Kislev, in the year one hundred and forty five, the king erected the desolating abomination upon the altar of burnt offerings, and in the surrounding cities of Judah they built pagan altars. 1 Maccabees 1:54

~ *December 6, 167 BC*

On the twenty fifth day of each month they sacrificed on the pagan altar that was over the altar of burnt offerings. 1 Maccabees 1:59

The twenty fifth day of the month was the birthday of Antiochus IV Epiphanes and it was required that each month on the twenty fifth day, the people of the Seleucid / Syrian empire would celebrate Antiochus IV Epiphanes' birthday with sacrifice that honored the gods of the Greek version of the baal / mystery / mythology religion.

The Seleucids / Syrians had developed a system of portable pagan altars that would be taken to each community and even to people's homes to facilitate the compulsory worship of the baal / mystery / mythology religion.

In God Most High's temple, the altar used for sacrificing the clean animal sacrifice dedicated to God Most High, was confiscated and used by the Seleucids / Syrians for offering a pig sacrifice. This act of sacrificing an unclean animal upon the altar dedicated to God Most High, desecrated the altar and the stones of the altar. According to 1 Maccabees 1:59, the Seleucids / Syrians also erected an altar over the top of the temple altar for offering more pagan sacrifices.

When the Maccabeans retook the temple from the Seleucids / Syrians, they replaced the defiled altar with new stones and performed the eight day consecration service for the temple.

On the anniversary of the day on which the Gentiles had desecrated the temple, on that very day it was rededicated with songs, harps, lyres, and cymbals. 1 Maccabees 4:54

For eight days they celebrated the dedication of the altar and joyfully offered burnt offerings and sacrifices of deliverance and praise. 1 Maccabees 4:56

Then Judas and his brothers and the entire assembly of Israel decreed that every year for eight days, from the twenty fifth day of the month Kislev, the days of the dedication of the altar should be observed with joy and gladness on the anniversary. 1 Maccabees 4:59

~ December 14, 164 BC

The number of days that the temple sacrificial system was interrupted from 167 to 164 BC was between one thousand eighty days (three years of three hundred sixty days in the Hebrew lunar calendar year) and one thousand ninety five days if the second month of Adar provided additional calendar days during that time period. The number of days that the temple sacrificial system was suspended under the reign of Antiochus IV Epiphanes, still fell short of the one thousand one hundred fifty days required to fulfill the prophecy of Daniel's vision.

Some preterists recognized the interruption of the temple sacrificial system as having taken place in August 70 AD with the siege of Jerusalem and the destruction of the temple. But when the temple was destroyed, the temple *sacrificial system could not be reestablished because the temple that hosted the temple sacrificial system no longer existed. With the destruction of the temple in 70 AD, there was no reinstitution of the temple sacrificial system that would have been required in order to fulfill Daniel's prophecy.*

Paul's instruction concerning the approaching return of messiah / the Lamb / Jesus Christ

Prophecy is history that has not taken place yet. Technically, the writing of the biblical record material is 'pre-historic.' Prophecy is writing about things that have not yet become history.

Because the veracity of prophecy cannot be fully determined until the prophetic event takes place, many have categorized the future events surrounding the future abomination of desolation event as fiction / imaginary / myth....

> *... until the details of the event of the future abomination of desolation event become reality, personal reality, and the kind of reality that impacts every person.*

Paul warned against categorizing prophecy in a way that minimizes its truth.

Now, fellow believers, about times and dates we do not need to write to you, for you know very well that the Day of the Lord will come like a thief in the night. While people are saying, 'Peace and safety,' destruction will come on them suddenly, as labor pains on a pregnant woman, and they will not escape.

But you, fellow believers, are not in darkness so that this day should surprise you like a thief. You are all children of the light and children of the days. We do not belong to the night or to the darkness. So then, let us not be like others, who are asleep, but let us be aware and sober. For those who sleep, sleep at night, and those who get drunk, get drunk at night. But since we belong to the day, let us be sober. For those who sleep, sleep at night, and those who get drunk, get drunk at night. But since we belong to the day, let us be sober, putting on faith and love as a breastplate, and the hope of salvation as a helmet.

For God did not appoint us to suffer wrath but to receive salvation through our Lord Jesus Christ. 1 Thessalonians 5:1-9

Paul was explicit that those who are believers in Jesus Christ will not be surprised. Believers will be the people who heed the matters concerning the return of Jesus Christ, in a serious manner. Believers will not dismiss the coming of Jesus Christ with partial pieces of biblical study, or with cast off ideas that allow the rationalization of inattentiveness. Believers will not merely depend upon God providing care without ever putting themselves to the task in arranging least some kind of preparation. Authentic believers in our Lord Jesus Christ, will not be surprised.

The purpose of the future abomination of desolation event
Some biblical interpreters claimed that we have no way of knowing what the abomination of desolation is. Their claim was that in the passages of the biblical record that they have chosen to study, there was no description of what an abomination of desolation consisted of or what its purpose was: therefore, they have rendered the prophecies concerning a future abomination of desolation event, as invalid.

But the biblical record's actual use of the term 'abomination of desolation,' along with the description that Jesus offered concerning the future abomination of desolation event, meant that there is such a thing as an abomination of desolation.

A student of biblical material does not need to have taken a class in world religions or church history, nor consult the biblical record, in order to be able to ascertain a definition of an abomination of desolation. *Even Wikipedia can provide education on the basics of what an* abomination of desolation *event consists of.*

Various biblical interpreters also claimed that because <u>they</u> *have chosen to not be able to discern the description of what an* abomination of desolation *event is, that* <u>no one else</u> *will be able to recognize the future abomination of desolation event when it happens. Because they themselves have not taken any initiative to actually study the full biblical record or the history behind the previous* abomination of desolation *event, they present the future abomination of desolation event as inconsequential.*

In contrast to those who have chosen to remain ignorant concerning the future abomination of desolation event, there are those who have chosen to truly explore at a deeper level, the biblical record's understanding of what an abomination of desolation event is and why God Most High will allow a future abomination of desolation event to take place. Daniel, Jesus and even John the Revelator distinctly communicated that they expect us as readers, to understand that the future abomination of desolation event will happen. And they provided instruction on how to respond.

Abomination of desolation events provide specific dynamics to world events, also interacting with the spiritual realm, that are necessary for the working of God Most High. Those who have shed their desire to remain ignorant understand that the future abomination of desolation event will have worldwide impact that will ripple in effect into the spiritual realm, and also to every individual living during the era of the time of Jacob's Trouble.

The first abomination of desolation event in 167 BC, can be viewed as the attempt of the red dragon / serpent / Satan, Inc. to prevent the coming of messiah to the people of Israel. In desecrating the temple, the connection between God Most High and the people of Israel was weakened.

God Most High's temple in Jerusalem was unique from all other temples on earth because within the temple in Jerusalem, God Most High directly communicated with the people of Israel, specifically on annual the Day of Atonement / Yom Kippur, through the high priest. It was the annual dramatization of the prophecy for the future day when God will reestablish the fullness of the face to face relationship that God the Creator held with the first man and first woman in the Garden of Eden / garden of God / paradise. It was also the annual dramatization of the prophecy for the future day when God will defeat the enemies of God Most High and of the kingdom of heaven, through the act of the scapegoat's destruction by being removed from God's holy city and falling off the cliff. To desecrate the temple was an act of claiming that the prophecies of reestablishing the full kingdom of heaven on earth, were unable to be realized.

In 167 BC, while the Hellenized people of Israel were already estranged from God Most High, the desecration of the temple served to give hope to adherents of the kingdom of Satan, Inc. / kingdom of man. If the temple were desecrated, it served as a prevention against messiah's arrival and successful work toward the implementation of God Most High's redemption, reclamation and regeneration plan. Without a temple to act in, messiah's arrival would have been perverted. Without the arrival of messiah, there would have been no potential opportunity for Satan's rival kingdom, the kingdom of heaven, to be fully established on earth. That would have been a win for the red dragon / serpent / Satan, Inc.

But three years after the first abomination of desolation event in 167 BC, the temple was reconsecrated, which meant that the promised and prophesied messiah would be able to come on time as planned.

The future abomination of desolation event that will take place in the middle of the era of the time of Jacob's Trouble, will also act as an attempt of the red dragon / serpent / Satan, Inc. to prevent the return of the messiah to the people of Israel. Because the people of Israel have not yet accepted that Jesus Christ is the promised and prophesied messiah, the people of Israel still believe that a physical temple is necessary in order for their promised and prophesied messiah to come to them, to rescue them from their enemies, and to reestablish that promised face to face relationship with humanity.

Both abomination of desolation events will have desecrated the temple which will have attempted to hinder the arrival of messiah who needs a functioning temple to come to. Without the arrival of messiah, the kingdom of heaven will not be able to be fully established on earth. With this kind of leadership void, the red dragon / serpent / Satan, Inc. planned to fill the vacuum with the establishment of the kingdom of Satan, Inc. / kingdom of man. But this was not the primary purpose of the abomination of desolation events.

Ultimately, the abomination of desolation events will seek to separate people from God Most High, for the purpose weakening the people of God so that they are more easily destroyed. Like the first abomination of desolation event, the future abomination of desolation will initiate aggressive action against the people of Israel, and this time the event will also focus aggressive action against the followers of the Lamb / Jesus Christ, with the intent of also destroying them and the kingdom of heaven that they are citizens of.

God Most High will allow the future abomination of desolation event to take place because it will become a turning point for the people of God who choose to take a stand to end their tolerance of the rule of the kingdom of Satan, Inc. / kingdom of man. While the red dragon / serpent / Satan, Inc. will use the future abomination of desolation event to seek to strengthen the kingdom of Satan, Inc. / kingdom of man, God Most high will also use the future abomination of desolation event to develop conviction and loyalty in people who have chosen the kingdom of heaven.

The abomination of desolation events do not just desecrate the temple and separate the people from God Most High, they also are used to destroy God's people.

Because of rebellion, the Lord's people, <u>and</u> the daily sacrifice were given over to it. Daniel 8:12

Just as the first abomination of desolation event included the massacre of the people of Israel, the future abomination of desolation will also have as its purpose the destruction of the people of God.

To separate people from God Most High

During the first abomination of desolation event, Antiochus IV Epiphanes had set as his goal, to curtail the power of the people of Israel through the process of separating the people of Israel from their God through adulterating their worship, their culture and their relationship with their God. The biblical record depicted the people of Israel's relationship with God as the source of their strength; as a military force, as a dynamic nation, as an enduring nation. When the relationship with God Most High was strong, the nation of Israel was strong. When the relationship with God Most High was weak, the nation of Israel was extremely vulnerable.

To deny the people of Israel their right to worship their God has been the attempt of many nations, people, and powers throughout history in their efforts to weaken and destroy the people of Israel. When the Pharaoh of Egypt attempted to deny the people of Israel of their worship of God Most High, God responded with sending Moses as the deliverer of God's message... and as a vehicle for the plagues that addressed the gods of Egypt.

Moses survived the Pharaoh's infanticide program. Eighty years later, Moses provided a dramatic staff / snake demonstration for Pharaoh and the Egyptian baal / mystery / mythology religion priests. Moses initiated, and also prayed for the ending of, the ten plagues visited upon Egypt that were used by God Most High to prove that the God of Israel was greater than the Egyptian gods. Moses led the Israelite's nighttime escape from their oppressors the Egyptians. Moses was the leader that God Most High used in accomplishing the parting of the Red Sea along with the total destruction of the Egyptian military and the Egyptian economy. (Exodus 1-15)

When King Ahab and Queen Jezebel had desecrated the worship of the Lord in Israel, they set up their many temples and high places for the worship of baal and Asherah, and they killed the prophets of the Lord. God Most High responded with sending the prophet Elijah who provided drought and rain for the benefit of the people of Israel against Ahab and Jezebel. Elijah also led the Mount Carmel altar challenge where God Most High successfully challenged the baal and Asherah gods. The Mount Carmel altar challenge marked the initiation of the time for the destruction of Ahab, Jezebel and their lineage. (1 Kings 16:29-22:40, 2 Kings 10)

The future abomination of desolation event during the era of the time of Jacob's Trouble will seek to deny the *people of Israel of their worship and their connection to God Most High. God's response will be to send Moses and Elijah once again to the people of Israel, to address the matter.*

This future abomination of desolation event will again seek to separate the people of Israel from their God, and thereby cause God's people to become weak and vulnerable.

Instead of the temple in Jerusalem being a vehicle for connecting the people of Israel with God Most High, the beast of the earth will establish himself in the former role of high priest; and will be determined to impede the connection of God Most High with the people of Israel. In fact, the beast of the earth will consistently declare that he himself is greater than God Most High, and that he is the God of the people of Israel who promised to establish a face to face relationship with them. (Daniel 7:8, 7:19-25f, 8:9-14, 8:23-25, 9:26-27, 11:31-39, Revelation 13:11-18)

But nothing can separate God's people from God's love and power (Romans 8:31-39, and the entirety of the biblical message).

To destroy the people of God: the people of Israel and the followers of the Lamb

The abomination of desolation of 167 BC was used as a part of a plan to entirely 'wipe the people of Israel off the map.'

Abomination of desolation events consist of actions intended to wipe off the map all vestiges of the kingdom of heaven. The 'wiping' consists of a two pronged approach: to destroy all of Judaism (and Christianity as its daughter) as a system of faith, and to annihilate those who have faith in the God of Israel.

Destroying God Most High's treasured people of Israel, and destroying the followers of the Lamb / Jesus Christ, is essential to fully establishing the kingdom of Satan, Inc. / kingdom of man on earth.

Following the destruction of the people of Israel and the followers of the Lamb / Jesus Christ, will be the destruction of all of humanity. Without destroying those who bear the image of God Most High breathed into them, pressed into them, (which is all of humanity) the kingdom of Satan, Inc. / kingdom of man would be weakened because even the image of God Most High within the human being remains greater than the altered product that the kingdom of Satan, Inc. / kingdom of man will seek to produce out of what was once the species of humanity. (Note: this is also a premise of Islamic eschatology - to destroy all of humanity, every human being.)

To accomplish the full destruction of Judaism and the 'wiping of the people of Israel off the map,' the red dragon / serpent / Satan, Inc. must also destroy all the people of Israel throughout the world, not merely those who dwell in the nation of Israel. The beast of the earth will target all who have developed their identity and connectedness as a people with a belief in the Lord God.

Because Christianity is actually Judaism part 2, it will also be important to the red dragon / serpent / Satan, Inc. to destroy the followers of the Lamb / Jesus Christ throughout the world. The followers of the Lamb / Jesus Christ have also developed their identity and connectedness as a people with a belief in the Lord God's messiah. The followers of the Lamb / Jesus Christ also believe in this Jewish messiah as their access to God Most High and as their opportunity to be able to be citizens of the kingdom of o heaven. Truly devoted followers of the Lamb / Jesus Christ would never make willing citizens of the kingdom of Satan, Inc. / kingdom of man. Therefore, they too must be destroyed.

Ultimately, both the people of Israel and the followers of the Lamb / Jesus Christ must all be eliminated if there is to be the full establishment of the kingdom of Satan, Inc. / kingdom of man on earth.

In order to attempt to accomplish the destruction of the people of God and the followers of the Lamb / Jesus Christ, there must be a new and higher level of hatred and fury generated than has ever been generated before. Even with Hitler's Nazi Germany, Japan's imperial empire, and Mussolini's Italian support, there were still areas of the world that were able to be considered refuge. But during the era of the time of Jacob's Trouble, the hatred will be much more individualized. Nationalism will have melted away. The idea that a nation will take a side with another nation will be overcome by the infiltration of the conflict even to the local level. Instead of nation fighting nation, this conflict will be between neighbors; those who believe in God Most High verses those who reject God Most High.

In order for the fury of the leaders of the kingdom of Satan, Inc. / kingdom of man to reach the magnitude that has been described in the biblical record, there must be a source of supernatural power that stimulates the events, a power source that is more than just what humanity alone can fuel.

Each abomination of desolation event is uniquely extraordinary in its magnitude, ferocity, and impact. Humanity alone cannot provide the immensity of the impact that an abomination of desolation event contains. The future abomination of desolation event that is scheduled for the middle of the era of the time of Jacob's Trouble has been defined in the biblical record as not being able to be compared to what humanity alone can provide for warfare and confrontation.

Found in the biblical record of the prophets and the message of Jesus Christ through John the Revelator's descriptions of the future abomination of desolation event; was the activity of the red dragon / serpent / Satan, Inc. who provides the spiritual 'fuel' that will be used in preparation for the future abomination of desolation event. With the spiritual fuel provided by the red dragon / serpent / Satan, Inc., there will be a display of the full power and fury of all that the kingdom of Satan, Inc. / kingdom of man can muster.

But the people of Israel have been God's chosen people, the people that God Most High holds first in God's heart. God Most High has made a covenant with Abraham and his descendants. To break that covenant that extends through Israelite genetics, the people of Israel must be eliminated. The people of Israel must be destroyed in order for the people who have covenanted with the kingdom of Satan, Inc. / kingdom of man to be able to reign.

And God Most High extended that covenant to all followers of the Lamb / Jesus Christ, through messiah / the Lamb / Jesus Christ. Consequently, the followers of the Lamb / Jesus Christ will also be a target engulfed in the future abomination of desolation event. (The idol / image of the beast of the sea established on the temple mount will serve as evidence of the inclusion of the followers of the Lamb / Jesus Christ in their targeting (Revelation 13). See also Revelation 12:17.)

Composite of the prophesied requirements for the future abomination of desolation event – Daniel 7:25, 8:9-14, 8:23-26, 9:26-27, 11:29-45, 12:1-12, Matthew 24:15-28, Mark 13:14-22, Revelation 13:11-18

The various descriptions of the future abomination of desolation tended to connect several related events with the actual act of the future abomination of desolation event. Some corresponding events may begin just prior the future abomination of desolation event and are necessary for preparing the power base and structure that the beast of the earth will need to accomplish his goals. Other events will be initiated with the future abomination of desolation event and the future abomination of desolation event will serve as prerequisites for still other subsequent events.

The Old Testament / Tanakh prophet Daniel provided the most information concerning the satellite events of the future abomination of desolation event.

"He (little horn / eleventh king) will speak pompous words against God Most High, and against the saints of God Most High. He will persecute the saints and will intend to change the times and the law. The saints will be given into his hand for a time and times and half a time." Daniel 7:25 translated

The future abomination of desolation event will necessitate the attempt to change the set times and the laws. The reference to set times was a reference to the prophecy inherent within the required feasts that annually dramatized the work of redemption, reclamation and regeneration provided by the promised and prophesied messiah. The reference to laws was a reference to the Law that God Most High provided to Moses and the people of

Israel (1446 BC) and to the current laws of the nation of Israel.

In the biblical record of Daniel 8, the future abomination of desolation event was described as:
- the final horn on the shaggy goat having responsibility in the exile of the starry host / rebellious angels from heaven and relocating to earth (Daniel 8:10).
- the final horn on the shaggy goat trampling upon the Lord's people (Daniel 8:13).
- having its origins somehow through the Greek empire and sharing similarities to the Greek empire's Hellenized culture for living. There was also the possibility that the final horn on the shaggy goat may have a link to the Seleucid / Syrian empire, but this was not definitive (Daniel 8).
- being set in an era when the world will experience the leadership of those who rebel against God Most High from the core of their nature. Rebels against God Most High, who have become completely wicked will have chosen for their leader, a man who truly represents their wickedness. It will be out of a climate of rebellion that the final horn on the shaggy goat will be able to step in to act, to be recognized as a savior who will establish a newly defined peace and security. (Daniel 8:23-25, 2 Thessalonians 2:3-12)
- being led by the final horn on the shaggy goat who will be a fierce-looking king and a master of intrigue (Daniel 8:23). Antiochus IV Epiphanes was a master of intrigue which was instrumental in his assumption of the Seleucid / Syrian throne. Being a master of intrigue will defy the biblical definitions of the promised and prophesied messiah's character of integrity.
- being led by a man, a mere man, who will be made strong by supernatural power and use the display of his supernatural power to establish his

authority to rule (Daniel 8:24, 2 Thessalonians 2:3-12).
- being led by a man who will seek to accomplish astounding devastation and will be successful in everything that he sets out to do (Daniel 8:24).
- being led by the final horn on the shaggy goat who will consider himself to be royalty, of the elite class, superior to those who he considers to be undesirables or inferior. Even though he will be distanced from a qualifying royal genetic lineage, he will consider his genetics superior to the rest of humanity. He will consider his wisdom superior to even the greatest minds in all of history. He will consider himself to be as close to being God as one can be. In fact, he will consider himself to actually be higher than God Most High. (Daniel 8:23-25).
- taking place at a time when God's people will have a feeling of security and will have been assured by the final horn on the shaggy goat of his good intentions toward them. The final horn on the shaggy goat's assurance will in fact be a lie, a trick, an act of manipulation, in order to acquire more power and a better position from which to rule and to destroy. In a similar way to Hitler's treachery of signing peace treaties and then the following day or week or month Hitler's Nazis would invade the nation they had made the treaty with; the final horn on the shaggy goat will act as if there is no plan to attack the people of Israel. He will use the strategy of surprise. (Note, this kind of quick activity will be similar to Jesus Christ coming 'as a thief in the night.' Is this tactic of coming quickly the idea of the red dragon / serpent / Satan, Inc. first, or is it possible that Jesus Christ is going to come like a thief in the night as a response to the suddenness of the about face activity of the final horn on the shaggy goat?) (Daniel 8:25)

- the final horn on the shaggy goat setting himself up to be as great as the commander of the army of the Lord (Daniel 8:10-11).
- taking away the daily sacrifice 'from the Lord.' Notice that it will be taken away from the Lord, not taken away from the people of Israel as what might have been expected. (Daniel 8:11-12)
- throwing down the sanctuary of the Lord. Some translations of the message concerning the abomination of desolation events, interpreted the throwing down of the sanctuary as the temple being destroyed, while other interpretations translated this act as a temporary overthrow of the temple. The final horn on the shaggy goat will indeed cause the temple to become unholy, not heavenly, earthly, and unable to be glorified or used in the process of connecting holy God Most High with the people of Israel. But this goal could also be accomplished by either the destruction of the temple or a mere defilement of the temple. God Most High has the authority to specify how restoring a right relationship with God must be accomplished and God Most High's redemption process is laid out in the arrangement of the temple and the process used for accomplishing sacrifice. By committing the abomination of desolation, the final horn on the shaggy goat will attempt to establish his divinity on earth and in heaven by redefining the process of people connecting with God. Using the actual temple area with the temple building intact, is a benefit for the purpose of redefining the 'salvation process' by the red dragon / serpent / Satan, Inc. Because the abomination of desolation has a lifespan of one thousand one hundred fifty days before the temple is reconsecrated, the evidence is great for the actual temple building remaining throughout the era of the time of Jacob's Trouble. (Daniel 8:11)

- *marking when the final horn on the shaggy goat will take authority over the Lord's people (Daniel 8:11-12, 8:23-25).*
- *being the temporary end to the practice of daily sacrifice in the temple and consequently a form of attempting to end the practice of Judaism (Daniel 8:11-12).*
- *being accomplished by a leader who in God Most High's view is no longer a person that is recognizable as bearing the image of God and is therefore be referred to as 'it' at this point in the biblical account (Daniel 8:10-12).*
- *marking the time when truth will be thrown to the ground (Daniel 8:12).*
- *corresponding with the temple being unconsecrated for only two thousand three hundred evenings and mornings / one thousand one hundred fifty days, leaving an additional one hundred ten days between the time when the temple sacrifices will be reestablished and the death of the two witnesses which mark the end of the reign of the beast of the sea (Daniel 8:11-14).*
- *being accompanied with* astounding devastation. *The future abomination of desolation event will not be contained within the temple proper. The future abomination of desolation event will extend to the entire nation of Israel and beyond. Other translations of this passage indicated that through magic, sorcery and witchcraft that the final horn on the shaggy goat will be made to be effective and that he will use his magic, sorcery and witchcraft to harm people and bring devastation. (Daniel 8:24)*
- *including the attempt to annihilate the holy people, the people of Israel who believe in the promised and prophesied messiah. There is no definitive indicator that the attempt to annihilate the 'holy people' will be limited to those who are living in the nation of Israel. (Daniel 8:12-13, 8:24-25) (After the war against*

the people of Israel fails, the new focus will be upon destroying the followers of the Lamb / Jesus Christ. Revelation 12:17)
- encouraging deceit as a means of personal advancement and obtaining prosperity. Daniel's account hinted that the final horn on the shaggy goat will achieve his position through intrigue, which possibly meant that he will come to the position through a breaking of laws, bribery, and political manipulation, in a similar way that Antiochus IV Epiphanes came to his position as king in the Seleucid / Syrian empire. (Daniel 8:23-25)
- a concluding effort for the final horn on the shaggy goat to take his stand against the Prince of princes / Jesus Christ. When the final horn on the shaggy goat assumes complete control of the temple, he will also declare himself to be greater than God Most High, challenging God Most High to defend God's title and position as divine and sovereign. According to Jewish tradition and Daniel's seventy sevens, messiah was scheduled to arrive in the temple and to declare himself to be King of kings and Lord of lords around 33 AD (Isaiah 6:1, Daniel 9:24-27, Malachi 3:1). Jesus Christ was cut short from fulfilling this act. The final horn on the shaggy goat will use this prophecy of messiah declaring himself in the temple to be God, to his (final horn on the shaggy goat's) advantage in convincing the world of his right to fill the position of God's messiah / the chosen one / appointed by God to rule the world. This blasphemous act will be a declaration of war against God Most High. (Daniel 8:11, 8:25)
- being concluded with the defeat of the final horn on the shaggy goat at the time of the Prince of princes / messiah's return. While the final horn on the shaggy goat will not be able to be destroyed by human means (he is after all the world's master magician), John the Revelator

documented that the ten horns / ten kings and their followers, will turn against him at the end of the era of the time of Jacob's Trouble and will also destroy the global religious community from the inside. While some of the power of the final horn on the shaggy goat will be a casualty of the riot that ends the global governance system and global religious community, it will be messiah / the Lamb / Jesus Christ who in actually defeats him, and then throws him and the beast of the sea / false prophet / eighth king beast into the fiery lake for the next thousand years. (Daniel 8:11, 8:24-25, Revelation 17:12-18, (18), 19:11-20)
- designed especially for our time, the era of the time of Jacob's Trouble, as a means for accomplishing God's purposes and preparing the world for the full establishment of the kingdom of heaven on earth (Daniel 8:23, 8:26).

From Daniel's vision recorded in Daniel 9, the future abomination of desolation event will:
- be led by the prince who is to come who will confirm a covenant with many for one 'seven' (Daniel 9:27).
- take place in the middle of the prophesied seventieth 'seven' / the seven years of the era of the time of Jacob's Trouble (Daniel 9:27).
- not be marked by a time of peace. War will continue until the end. (Daniel 9:26d)
- be accompanied with a suspension of the sacrifice and offering in the temple, by the work of the same prince who is to come who will have been instrumental in the confirmation of the covenant peace treaty agreement (Daniel 9:27)
- be established in his position when he sets up an abomination that causes desolation at the temple (Daniel 9:26b-27).
- also aid in the establishment of the ruler who is to come in his temporary rule until his

specifically determined end that is decreed, has been poured out on him (Daniel 9:27).
- *take place during the seventieth 'seven' that will be the conclusion of the process of finishing transgression, putting an end to sin, atoning for wickedness, bringing in everlasting righteousness, sealing up vision and prophecy and anointing the Most Holy Place (Daniel 9:24, 9:27).*

Daniel 11-12 described the future abomination of desolation event as:
- *being performed by the king who is accountable to no one, who will exalt and magnify himself as supreme above all gods and will make unprecedented statements against God Most High (Daniel 11:36-39).*
- *being performed by the king who is successful in everything he does ... until the time of wrath is completed when he has been predetermined to be imprisoned (Daniel 11:36).*
- *being led by one who will show no regard for the gods of his ancestors or for the one desired by women. Because 'gods' here was plural and the God of Israel was defined as 'one' / united, the king that will exalt himself will not honor even the gods of the baal / mystery / mythology religion that provided him with power. He will also not honor Jesus. But he will believe that he is superior and sovereign over all – except for a god of fortresses, unknown to his ancestors, a new god that is either the god of his invention or a rebellious angel who has remained hidden until this time. (Daniel 11:36-39)*
- *initiating an era when the king that will exalt himself will attack the mightiest fortresses with the help of a foreign god. This could mean that the superpower nations of the world will be targets of attack, for the king that will exalt himself (Daniel 11:37-44).*

- *being an era when favoritism and elitism will rise. With the rulers that the king that will exalt himself will establish, the new system of government will resemble feudalism and feudalism's favoritism extended to those designated to be enforcers of the reigning regime. (Daniel 11:39b, 11:42-43)*
- *initiating an era associated with the king that will exalt himself engaging in battles that involve chariots (tanks?), cavalry, and a great fleet of ships. May countries will be invaded and swept through like a flood, including Israel. (Note that the Egyptians and Libyans are descended from the same lineage as the Cushites and the Canaanites, through Ham.) (Daniel 11:40-43)*
- *a time when the king that will exalt himself will change his residence to an area between the seas and Jerusalem in Israel (Daniel 11:45).*
- *a time of great distress and associated with war among the angels of heaven (Daniel 12:1).*
- *a time associated with people, everyone whose name is found written in the book, being delivered – a reference to the resurrection of God's holy people (Daniel 12:1).*
- *a requirement that must take place before the general resurrection (Daniel 12:2).*
- *a time when Daniel's secreted scroll will be revealed (Daniel 12:4).*
- *initiating the era when the temple sacrifice will be abolished, initiating the era that will be concluded at one thousand two hundred ninety days, and initiating the era that will be concluded at one thousand three hundred thirty five days (Daniel 12:11-12).*

Jesus described the future abomination of desolation according to the gospel writers as:
- *a time to flee to the mountains.*

- *a time for persecution of the followers of the Lamb / Jesus Christ.*
  a time of family betrayal and rebellion.
- *a time of great distress unequaled from the beginning of the world. This would imply that it will be more distressful than the events that took place in the antediluvian / preflood world and the flood at the time of Noah.*
- *the greatest time of distress in all human history with no future time of distress able to reach its magnitude.*
- *a time that must take place before the return of Jesus Christ.*

(Matthew 24:15-28, Mark 13:14-22)

Jesus Christ provided the vision to John the Revelator who described the future abomination of desolation in Revelation 13 as:
- *a time that will mark the compulsory worship of the beast of the sea / false prophet / eighth king beast by anyone who does not have their name written in the Lamb/s book of life.*
- *a time when the beast of the earth will amaze the people of the world with great signs including calling fire to come down from heaven to earth for all the people to see.*
- *initiating the era of deception through the signs that the beast of the earth will perform.*
- *the time when the idol / image of the beast of the sea will be animated / brought to life and able to speak. The idol / image of the beast of the sea will also be authorized to carry out immediate forced executions of those who refuse to worship the idol / image of the beast of the sea.*
- *associated with the institution of the mark of the beasts system that will control the economy of the world and potentially alter the genetics of the inhabitants of the earth that receive the mark of the beasts, so that the image of God Most High that is inherent within every human, will*

no longer be able to exist in those that receive the mark of the beasts.

The Two Beasts of Revelation 13: The Beast of the Sea and the Beast of the Earth – Revelation 13

The beast of the sea / false prophet / beast from the Abyss / eighth king beast begins his forty two months reign of supernatural power and authority – Revelation 13

Major preparation has been provided in anticipation of the future abomination of desolation event. The infiltration of the authentic faith system and the church by the baal / mystery / mythology religion began millennia ago. And during the era of the time of Jacob's Trouble, the infiltration by the various flavors of the baal / mystery / mythology religion, will have come to total fruition; turning what was once dedicated to God Most High into the refuge for the greatest enemies of God Most High.

For his part as the designated forerunner in preparing for the arrival of the beast of the earth and the future abomination of desolation event, the beast of the sea will have already communicated the message that Jesus Christ can no longer be viewed by the church and the world, as messiah, as divine, as sovereign, as God. The message will be that Jesus failed to do what he set out to do when Jesus came the first time for his earthly ministry. In this narrative, the people of the world, specifically the Jews, effectively killed Jesus and Jesus remains dead. The account of Jesus Christ being raised from the dead will have been denied within the message. Therefore, the message of the beast of the sea will be that Jesus must remain dead and cannot be divine and sovereign. It will be continued to be asserted that Jesus Christ cannot meet the biblical definition of what the promised and prophesied messiah must be.

The purpose of espousing the message that Jesus Christ is not divine and sovereign, will have two major effects.

First, the message that Jesus Christ is not sovereign will create a spiritual vacuum that the beast of the sea intends to fill as the new candidate for prophet. And it will be used to create a political vacuum that the beast of the sea will intend to fill with the kingdom of Satan, Inc. / kingdom of man's candidate for pseudo messiah, the beast of the earth. It will be the responsibility of the beast of the sea to ensure that the role for the beast of the earth is primed and ready for the beast of the earth to step into.

Second, the message that Jesus Christ is not divine will create a platform for declaring that all who are followers of Jesus Christ are heretics, worthy of destruction. Anyone who will disagree with the vision and tenets of the new religion, will receive treatment that is reminiscent of the Roman Catholic Church's Inquisitions.

Around the time of the future abomination of desolation event, the beast of the sea / false prophet will have attained the goals of having reached the height of his power to fully lead the global religious community. And with the aid of the global religious community, he will have prepared the world to receive the beast of the earth and the beast of the earth's new religion, with the beast of the earth declaring himself to be greater than God Most High, and with the beast of the earth now requiring the inhabitants of the earth, to worship of the idol / image of the beast of the sea because of the beast of the sea's stupendous global vision and leadership.

The biblical record indicated that the identity of the beast of the earth will remain hidden until the beast of the earth stands in the wing of the temple and definitively declares himself to be sovereign above the God of heaven, during the future abomination of desolation event.

In contrast to the secretiveness of the identity of the beast of the earth, the biblical record provided a description of the beast of the sea / false prophet / beast from the Abyss / eighth king beast that provided a conclusive identity of the beast of the sea. In fact, church leaders have for almost two millennia, already agreed upon the identity of the man who will fill the role of the *beast of the sea / false prophet / beast from the Abyss / eighth king beast. And the actual man who will fill the role has confirmed his identity through his activities and through his espoused theology.*

With the future abomination of desolation event, the beast of the sea's identity will be confirmed with finality. His identity will be confirmed by his survival of a near fatal attack that will affect his right arm and his right eye, and the establishment of an idol / image of him on the temple mount.

Once the beast of the sea has been unveiled to the world, his attention will turn to shoring up the position of the beast of the earth and putting the finishing touches upon the mark of the beasts system that will require compulsory worship, provide compulsory global governance, institute a compulsory global currency, and demand a compulsory global culture. But most importantly, during the course of events of the era of the time of Jacob's Trouble, the man who will begin as a man who was loved, respected and feared as a holy man of religion, will reveal what resides within the deepest recesses of his heart.

Jesus said, 'Watch out for false prophets. They come to you in sheep's clothing, but inwardly they are ferocious wolves. By their fruit you will recognize them… Matthew 7:15-16a.

It will be during the second half of the era of the time of Jacob's Trouble that the beast of the sea will disclose the extent of his true beliefs. His blasphemy against messiah / the Lamb / Jesus Christ will be loudly broadcast for the world.

It will be during the second half of the era of the time of Jacob's Trouble that the beast of the sea will fully disclose his anger and hatred against God Most High and against God's holy people. The beast of the sea will proceed to blaspheme against God Most High, against the culture of heaven itself, and against those who dwell in heaven.

The beast of the sea was given a mouth speaking great things and blasphemy. And to it was given authority to act for forty two months.

It opened its mouth to speak blasphemies against God, to blaspheme the name of God, and the tabernacle of God, those who dwell in heaven. Revelation 13:5-6 translated

'The beast of the sea was given a mouth to utter proud words and blasphemies…'

This beast of the sea was 'given a mouth.' He was not born with this mouth. Nor did he develop this mouth by his own determination. The source of the 'mouth' according to the context of John the Revelator's prophecy, was the red dragon / serpent / Satan, Inc. For who else could cause a global leader to go against current political correctness in order to blaspheme God continually for forty two months? Jesus Christ and John the Revelator both documented that the source of this 'mouth' will supply the beast of the sea with what he is to say. A single person not supernaturally endowed with power and authority, would not be able to amass the vitriol against God Most High, against messiah / the Lamb / Jesus Christ, and against God's holy people, that the beast of the sea will spew forth from his mouth.

The beast of the sea will receive his primary supernatural support from the red dragon / serpent / Satan, Inc. And the at the point of the future abomination of desolation event, the red dragon / serpent / Satan, Inc. will have lost in the war with Michael and his angels (Revelation 12).

In ancient human history, the red dragon / serpent / Satan, Inc. was told that there will be no place in heaven for those who rebel against God Most High and against the rules of the kingdom of heaven. The red dragon / serpent / Satan, Inc. was told this in the Garden of Eden / garden of God / paradise when the first man and first woman were expelled. The red dragon / serpent / Satan, Inc. was told this again during the antediluvian / preflood world before the Nephilim civil war, through Enoch. The deluge / flood during the life of Noah reiterated God Most High's determination to annihilate the Nephilim, the chimera, and any product of rebellion; and echoed a message that only the nonrebellious righteous will experience transition into God Most High's new and eternal heaven and earth. Waring with the gods of Egypt through the ten plagues, and the people of Israel safely exiting from Egyptian bondage, was another message of God Most High's determination. Jesus Christ's resurrection from the dead was another message that only the nonrebellious righteous will experience transition into eternal life. And now, with this final conflict of this age between God Most High and the red dragon / serpent / Satan, Inc., God Most High will again stand unrelentingly firm on the requirement that rebellion, death and destruction of humanity, will have no place in the kingdom of heaven.

When God Most High has completed cleaning house in heaven and on earth, there will be no remnant of the red dragon / serpent / Satan, Inc., nor of the kingdom of Satan, Inc. / kingdom of man that will not be addressed and exiled from the kingdom of heaven. This fact infuriates the red dragon / serpent / Satan, Inc. and so the red dragon / serpent / Satan, Inc. will use the mouthpiece that they have developed for expressing their views: the beast of the sea / false prophet / beast from the Abyss / eighth king beast.

When John the Revelator wrote 1 John the epistle, he said, 'but every spirit that does not acknowledge Jesus is not from God. This is the spirit of the antichrist, which you have heard is coming and even now is already in the world' 1 John 4:3.

The red dragon / serpent / Satan, Inc. has been working at least since before the lifetime of John the Revelator to prepare to fill the position of the beast of the sea with just the right man who will represent the interests of the red dragon / serpent / Satan, Inc.

In addition, the red dragon / serpent / Satan, Inc. has had six thousand years to develop the venomous and poisonous lies to fling against God Most High and against God's holy people. The fullness of the animosity and anger that the red dragon / serpent / Satan, Inc. has collected, will now be launched against the people of the world.

The beast of the sea will not only lie / blaspheme about God Most High and messiah / the Lamb / Jesus Christ, while holding the position as supreme representative of God Most High, but the beast of the sea will also slander God Most High's name and God Most

High's dwelling place of heaven. That activity will still not be considered by the beast of the sea, to be enough degradation of God. The beast of the sea will proceed to also lie concerning those who live in heaven. The beast of the sea will present to the people of the world that God Most High's forgiveness of sins is not a necessary condition for entrance into heaven. The beast of the sea will present a theology that as the highest representative of the church, it is he who determines what one's afterlife will be. Roman Catholic Church theology has traditionally taught that the pope and the hierarchy of the Roman Catholic Church determined the definition of what life after death consists of, and which option of eternal life the Roman Catholic Church has chosen for each individual (using activities such as the Inquisitions and religious wars, and using the doctrines of withholding the wine in communion / withholding forgiveness of sins through communion, the act of confession, extreme unction / last rights / absolution, purgatory, praying for the dead, etc.).

The current pope, Francis, currently repeatedly and verbally denies the divinity and sovereignty of Jesus Christ, and has technically already communicated this basic message to the world. It is the message that corresponds to the message of the beast of the sea (Revelation 13:1, 13:5-6, 17:3).

John the Revelator identified multiple events that will confirm the identity of the beast of the sea / false prophet / beast from the Abyss / eighth king beast:
- *his survival of a near fatal attack that will affect his right arm and his right eye,*
- *the establishment of an idol / image of the beast of the sea on the temple mount,*
- *his blasphemy against the divinity and sovereignty of messiah / the Lamb / Jesus Christ,*
- *his support of the beast of the earth to attempt to assume the role of being greater than God Most High,*
- *his slander against God's holy people, including the two witnesses that God Most High is sending from heaven,*

- etc.

During the first abomination of desolation event, Antiochus IV Epiphanes, king of the Seleucids / Syrians, committed the abomination of desolation event in the temple (167 BC). But he was assisted by the high priest Menelaus who had purchased the position through bribery / simony.

When Jesus was pursued by the religious leaders of the early first century AD, it fell upon the high priest, the man who held the highest religious position, to lead in denying the divinity of Jesus Christ. The co high priests Ananias and his son-in-law Caiaphas broke the rules for trial in conducting Jesus' nighttime trial. The high priests provided false witnesses who led in the blaspheme against Jesus. The high priests made the judgment against Jesus. The high priests pressured Pilate, the Roman governor of Judea, to have Jesus Christ crucified. (30 AD)

During the era of the time of Jacob's Trouble, the beast of the sea will assume a role similar to the high priests in the past, to assist in desecrating the temple and discontinue the fully consecrated, functional and operational temple sacrificial system, in the attempt to distance God's holy people from access to God Most High. The beast of the sea will act even more treacherously than Menelaus, Ananias, and Caiaphas. It will be the beast of the sea who will place great emphasis upon pursuing the death penalty against the people of Israel and against the authentic followers of the Lamb / Jesus Christ.

And the beast of the sea was given the <u>power to make war with the saints and to overcome / conquer them</u>. And the beast was given authority over every tribe and people and tongue and nation.
And all inhabitants of the earth, will worship the beast of the sea, all whose names have not been written in the book of life of the Lamb having been slain, that began to be written from the creation of the world. Revelation 13:7-8 translated

The beast of the sea will have the power to make war *and to* conquer.

The rider of the first horse of the opened first seal, also was given the power to conquer *(Revelation 6:1-2).*

It may be that the evilest of this trio comprised of the red dragon / serpent / Satan, Inc., and the two beasts of Revelation 13, will not be the beast of the earth. It may be that the evilest of this trio will be the beast of the sea.

The beast of the sea will provide the authority and means to make war against those who believe that Jesus Christ is Lord / the holy ones, and to conquer them. The historical wars of the Crusades, the Inquisitions, the Protestant Reformation wars / European wars of religion, etc. will all be mere warmups to the big event of the war between the beast of the sea with the backing of the global religious community, versus the followers of the Lamb / Jesus Christ.

The beast of the sea's power will extend to every corner of the earth.

The Roman Catholic Church Crusades from 1095 AD until the end of the eighteenth century, were generally not fought in Europe, leaving Europe relatively unscathed from the battles. But the crusades left an estimated three million dead among Muslims, Christians from other denominations, and Roman Catholic Church members.

The Roman Catholic Church Inquisitions from around 1250 AD to the early nineteenth century, left an estimated one hundred fifty thousand or more, people of Israel, Muslims, and Christians from other denominations, either tortured or tortured and killed.

The Protestant Reformation wars / European wars of religion lasted from 1517 to 1712 AD when the Roman Catholic Church declared war upon Protestants and left an estimated seventeen million people dead.

What the beast of the sea has envisioned, will be a greater kinetic conflict than all previous kinetic conflicts. And historically, the precedence has been established for the church to declare war upon the authentic followers of the Lamb / Jesus Christ.

John the Revelator documented that 'all inhabitants of the earth will worship the beast.' But then John followed this up with an escape clause: '… all whose names have not been written in the book of life belonging to the Lamb…' From John the

Revelator's context the, 'All inhabitants of the earth' *must be differentiated from* 'inhabitants of heaven' / *people whose names are* 'written in the book of life belonging to the Lamb...'

The final outcome for 'all inhabitants of the earth' *that will worship the beast, will be that instead of receiving the eternal life promised by the beast of the sea, they will experience exclusion from eternal life and the kingdom of heaven (Revelation 14:9-12, 20:4-6, 20:11-15). When the harvest of the earth takes place, the people still living in the category of* 'all inhabitants of the earth,' *will be treated as weeds and* 'thrown into the fire' *(Matthew 13:30, 13:40).*

If anyone has an ear, let them hear.
'If anyone is to go into captivity, into captivity that one goes. If anyone is to be killed with the sword, with the sword they will be killed.' Here is the endurance and the faith of the saints. Revelation 13:9-10 translated

Anyone who has an ear (who is willing to hear), let that one hear. If anyone is to go into captivity, into captivity he will go. If anyone is to be killed with the sword, with the sword that one will be killed. This calls for patient endurance and faithfulness on the part of the holy ones. Revelation 13:9-10 NIV

He who leads into captivity shall go into captivity. He who kills with the sword must be killed with the sword. Here is the patience and the faith of the saints. Revelation 13:10 (NKJV)

Jesus Christ's message through John the Revelator was sometimes almost cryptic and sage like.

This message was Jesus Christ's way of saying that the beast of the sea was already destined for captivity. It is a done deal. The beast of the sea / false prophet / beast from the Abyss / eighth king beast must go! He will not be gaining entrance into the kingdom of heaven.

But also, those who enforce the regime of the beast of the sea will also share a final destination that has been designated for them.

In Revelation 17-19, John the Revelator recorded the process for the capture and incarceration that God Most High has predestined for the two beasts of Revelation 13. The message of Revelation 13 was offered in a format that communicated the reality that the beast of the sea should have known and should have been able to hear because he has ears, that choosing to follow the path that he is on can only lead to an eternal life of incarceration in the fiery lake. Their adherents will be killed with the sword. And even before the two beasts of Revelation 13 begin their campaign of devastation, at the time of the future abomination of desolation event, they should have known what their ultimate destination would be.

The little horn / eleventh king / final horn on the shaggy goat / prince who is to come / king that will exalt himself / beast of the earth / final world ruler revealed, and begins sharing the supernatural power and authority of the beast of the sea – Revelation 13

The dynamics of the relationship between the two beasts of Revelation 13, that will be displayed during the future abomination of desolation event will bear much resemblance to the events of December 800 AD when the king of the Franks and Lombards, Charlemagne / Charles the Great (747 to 814), had rescued the pope and restored Leo III (fl. 795 to 816) to his position on December 24, 800 AD. On December 25, 800 AD, the pope in turn crowned Charlemagne as Holy Roman Emperor (who was neither holy nor Roman). Charlemagne's life was rife with sorted sexual affairs, political marriages, acts of tyranny, unholy living, and despotic rule. Charlemagne brought to the people that he ruled, the seeds of Carolingian Renaissance, which on the surface has been received as positive advancement in European culture. But the position of Holy Roman Emperor also gave Charlemagne a greater thirst for power which resulted in tyrannical rule.

The two beasts of Revelation 13 will share the same kind of symbiotic relationship that Charlemagne shared with Leo III.

Both beasts of Revelation 13 will be active, and at work behind the scenes, in preparing for the future abomination of desolation event. But the future abomination of desolation event will be the point in human history when the debutantes will have their coming out party.

The beast of the sea will have already accumulated the foundational support of centuries of international relationships, especially with the United Kingdom / lion, Russia / bear and Germany - France / leopard. The beast of the sea will have the foundational support of the Roman Catholic Church / scarlet beast. And the beast of the sea will have the foundational support of the baal / mystery / mythology religion / great prostitute. (Revelation 13, 17)

But the beast of the earth will be new on the international scene. Because Israel has only been reestablished as a nation on May 14, 1948, there has been no nation of Israel to prepare centuries of support for the beast of the earth. Because the people of Israel have been dispersed throughout the world, there has been no base for the people of Israel to previously garner their support. Because there has been no temple on the temple mount since 70 AD, there has been no site for the practice of Judaism that would warrant even giving strength to Judaism.

In contrast to the visible anticipation of the rise of the beast of the sea, the beast of the earth will need to be revealed with the future abomination of desolation event. To compensate for his lack of historical foundational support, the beast of the earth will need to be impressive to gain global attention and respect.

To gain global attention and respect, the beast of the earth will stand on the temple mount, at the future abomination of desolation event and will:
- rise to global prominence as a master of intrigue,
- present himself like a lamb with two in his entourage that will add to the façade of a lamb, but he will speak like a dragon,
- violate the covenant peace treaty agreement that he had previously confirmed,
- discontinue the fully consecrated, functional and operational temple sacrificial system that the people of Israel have waited since 70 AD to have reestablished, and attempt to negate the validity of the inherent prophecy of the required feasts that annually dramatized the work of the authentic promised and prophesied messiah,

- declare himself to be greater than God Most High, and will establish his own form of religion with himself and the beast of the sea as the central focus,
- use flattery to advance his agenda,
- share supernatural power and authority with the beast of the sea,
- perform great signs, magic, sorcery, occult practices, illusion, dark arts, etc., including causing fire to come down from heaven for everyone to see,
- set up an idol / image of the beast of the sea on the temple mount,
- give breath to the idol / image of the beast of the sea so that the image will be able to speak,
- initiate capital punishment for all who refuse to worship the idol / image,
- have the power and authority to institute the compulsory mark of the beasts system, establishing the kingdom of Satan, Inc. / kingdom of man's currency, and establishing a system of governmental control over the global population via the new global economy,
- do as he pleases, without regard to any law,
- begin his reign of astounding devastation,
- make war with many countries, sweeping through them like a flood, and amassing their treasuries,
- make war with God's holy people,
- cause deceit to prosper,
- lull people into a false belief of security, as a means for destroying many,
- begin the preparation for making war against the Prince of princes / the Lamb / Jesus Christ,

One of the dynamics that the beast of the earth will employ will be the massive amount of change that he will bring to global systems, in the shortest amount of time. This quickness in bringing change will also serve as another proof of his power and authority. And even though the *power and authority that he exercises will not be his own, his arrogance will convince the inhabitants of the earth that he is worthy to provide quality global leadership.*

The arrogance and boastfulness of the beast of the earth will also serve as a cover for the work that the beast of the earth will accomplish in secret.

Secrecy has always been a major component of dysfunctional systems. Jesus referred to the kingdom of Satan, Inc. / kingdom of man as the kingdom of darkness because the kingdom of darkness does not want the light to shine on it and make its deeds known (John 1 and 3).

When Jesus Christ presented himself on Lamb Selection Day, he openly rode into Jerusalem on a humble donkey. It was his followers who recognized him and proclaimed him to be messiach ben David / messiah son of David. Four days after Jesus Christ rode into the receptive Jerusalem, Jesus Christ was rejected and crucified / defeated? By the red dragon / serpent / Satan, Inc. (until his resurrection and ascension into heaven).

The beast of the earth's covert secrecy will be essential for attaining the full desired effect when he reveals himself to the general population of the world at the time of the future abomination of desolation event. And his secrecy will be essential with his work after the future abomination of desolation event as he attempts to permanently establish his position as global ruler.

But the beast of the earth will utilize his entrance on the global landscape to make a dramatic entrance.

Because he will be a master of intrigue, he will be the team member who will make the sudden and dramatic entrance, seeking to resemble the sudden and dramatic entrance of messiah / the Lamb / Jesus Christ when he will return with the clouds at the end of the era of the time of Jacob's Trouble. At the future abomination of desolation event, he will reveal himself with boldness!

The identity of the beast of the earth revealed with the future abomination of desolation event and his activity at that time

Note that there have been many who have jumped to conclusions concerning the identity of the beast of the earth. Candidates for the beast of the earth have included various popes, George Soros, Prince Charles of England, Tony Blair, France's Emmanuel Macron, Russia's Mikhail Gorbachev, Henry Kissinger, various presidents of the United States including Bill Clinton, both George Bushes, Barak Obama, and even Donald Trump. The list of potential candidates for the man who will assume the position of beast of the earth is extensive. Most of the people on the list do not actually qualify. For example, the little horn / eleventh king / final horn on the shaggy goat will start out small and grow in political stature. But most of the people on the list could not be classified as having started out small.

The identity of the beast of the earth will probably be a total surprise even to the prognosticators. Any other approach, other than honoring the biblical directive for interpretation that the beast of the earth will be the one to announce himself, will lead to detours that will require disinvestment of the interpreter's choice, before recognizing the actual man who will truly fill the role of beast of the earth.

The history of the beast of the earth was not stressed as much as the activities that he will participate in around the time of the future abomination of desolation event. It will be by his fruit / the activities that he accomplishes, that he will best be identified.

The Old Testament / Tanakh prophet Daniel (fl. 605 to 530 BC) - a prophet of Judah, provided the greatest amount of detail concerning the character and nature that will assist in identifying the little horn / eleventh king / final horn on the shaggy goat / prince who is to come / king that will exalt himself, as he provides leadership in the future abomination of desolation event.

'Then I wished to know the truth about the fourth exceedingly dreadful beast which was different from all the others with its iron teeth and its bronze nails which devoured and broke into pieces, and trampled on what remained with its feet, and the ten horns that were on its head, and the other horn that came up from it, from which the three horns fell before it; specifically this horn which had eyes and a mouth which spoke pompous words, whose appearance was greater than his fellows.'

'As I was watching, this horn was making war against the saints and prevailing against them, until the Ancient of Days came and a judgment was made in favor of the saints of God Most High, and the time came for the saints to possess the kingdom.' Daniel 7:19-22 translated

"The ten horns that will rise from this kingdom, will be ten kings. And another will rise after them. He will be different from the first kings, and three of the kings will be subdued."

"He (little horn / eleventh king) will speak pompous words against God Most High, and against the saints of God Most High. He will persecute the saints and will intend to change the times and the law. The saints will be given into his hand for a time and times and half a time." Daniel 7:24-25 translated

One of the characteristics of the little horn / eleventh king will be his boastfulness and his audacity to consider himself greater than God Most High, that will be displayed with the future abomination of desolation event.

With the future abomination of desolation event, he will also attempt to change the set times and the laws. In his attempt to eliminate authentic faith including authentic Judaism, he will develop his own version of religion, with a political cover, and coercively market his new religion / governance.

And with the future abomination of desolation event, he will declare war upon God's holy people, a war that will last three and a half years (time, times and half a time).

Daniel's vision of the ram and the goat and the final horn on the shaggy goat:

The male goat grew to be very great (Greece). When the male goat became strong, his large horn (Alexander the Great) was broken off and four notable horns came up out of the large horn to take its place (Alexander's four generals / four kingdoms). The four horns grew toward the four winds of heaven.

Out of one of the four horns came a little horn that grew to be exceedingly great, growing toward the south and east and toward the Glorious (Land) (the land of Israel).

It grew up to reach the host of heaven and to cast some of the host and some of the stars of heaven to the ground. And it trampled some of the host and some of the stars of heaven.

He exalted himself as the Prince even as high as the host of heaven. And by him, the daily sacrifices were taken away. The place of the Lord's sanctuary was cast down. An army was given over to the horn to oppose the daily (sacrifices), because of rebellion. He cast truth down to the ground. In all that he did, he prospered.

Then I heard a holy one speaking, and another holy one said to him 'How long will it take for the vision concerning the daily sacrifices and the transgression of desolation to be fulfilled — the transgression that causes desolation, both of the giving in the sanctuary and the trampling underfoot of the host?'

He said to me, 'It will be 2,300 evenings and mornings. Then the sanctuary will be cleansed.' Daniel 8:8-14 translated

Daniel's vision of the final horn on the shaggy goat identified him as starting out small as a little horn. As a little horn, he would not be able to be distinguished from the population of eight billion people currently living on earth.

But as a man who reaches into heaven, tramples on some of the stary host, exalts himself and has the power and authority to take away daily sacrifices, he will become internationally noteworthy. The fact that the daily sacrifices will be taken away at the same time, identified the final horn on the shaggy goat as making himself known with the future abomination of desolation / 'transgression of desolation,' when the daily sacrifices will be discontinued because of the desolation of the temple.

Also associated with the future abomination of desolation event, will be the final horn on the shaggy goat's influence upon the starry host / rebellious angels, and their exile from heaven.

'In the latter part of their reign, when rebels have become completely wicked, a stern-faced king, a master of intrigue, will arise. He will become very strong, but not by his own power. He will cause astounding devastation and will succeed in whatever he does. He will cause deceit to prosper, and he will consider himself superior. When they feel secure, he will destroy many and take his stand against the Prince of princes. Yet he will be destroyed, but not by human power.' Daniel 8:23-25

The final horn on the shaggy goat will be able to be recognized because with the future abomination of desolation event, he will:

- *have a face that is stern. A stern face implied that this man who will assume the position of the beast of the earth will not be a happy and well-adjusted man.*

- *present himself like a king. But he will not be the king of a nation or region.*
- *employ strategies that make him a master of intrigue. The reference to being a master of intrigue was similar to how Antiochus IV Epiphanes assumed the office of king of the Seleucid / Syrian empire when he was not in the direct line to inherit the throne. Antiochus IV Epiphanes stole the throne and then had those who were rightfully in line to receive the throne, assassinated.*
- *rise to his position. Jesus Christ was born a king and as an infant, even received ambassadors from another nation, the Magi from the east / Persia. But the final horn on the shaggy goat will not be born with that kind of recognition. The final horn on the shaggy goat will begin small and then rise to his position. His small beginnings will attract to him all classes of people. His rise will act as a success story that will act to validate the authenticity that he should occupy the position of global ruler.*
- *amass power from other sources and become very strong. Specifically, the final horn on the shaggy goat's source of supernatural power and authority will be the red dragon / serpent / Satan, Inc., via the beast of the sea (Revelation 13). In contrast, Jesus Christ's authority and power was inherently his own.*
- *cause astounding devastation. It will be one of the goals of the final horn on the shaggy goat to bring as much destruction as possible, into the world that God the Creator created. While the earth will experience much devastation at the hand of the global governance system through the events that will occur with the opening of the seven seals, the blowing of the seven trumpets, the pouring out of the seven bowls / seven last plagues, the harvest of the earth, etc.; the message that will be told to the inhabitants of the*

earth will be that the source of devastation is a result of things like climate change, overpopulation of the planet, the lack of political control over nations with their inability to make peace, the inherent evil within the people of Israel and their rebellion against the kingdom of Satan, Inc. / kingdom of man, the domination of wealthy nations over the undeveloped nations, etc.; basically the items that the United Nations Agenda 2030 attributed as the fault of the inhabitants of the earth. In reality, it will be the kingdom of Satan, Inc. / kingdom of man that will have provided the devastation upon the earth under the politics of the elite and elect ruling class along with the supernatural power and authority of the red dragon / serpent / Satan, Inc.

- magically succeed at whatever he does. In order for the final horn on the shaggy goat to rise from being small, into the greatest tyrannical leader in all of human history, he must experience phenomenally good success, magical success. The final horn on the shaggy goat will employ magic, sorcery, occult practices, illusion, dark arts, etc. Miracles are authentic, without illusion, and serve to prosper the person or persons who receive the miracle. But magic, sorcery, occult practices, illusion, dark arts, etc. are employed to benefit the magician, sorcerer, etc., usually at the expense of those who have magic and sorcery practiced against them.
- cause deceit to prosper. In contrast to fostering deceit, the Holy Spirit was also known as the Spirit of Truth because the Holy Spirit is the author of truth and testifies God Most High's truth, to the spirits of individuals. But the final horn on the shaggy goat will utilize deceit to advance his agenda. His father is the father of lies.

- *feel elite, superior and entitled. And he will be able to convince the inhabitants of the earth of his elite status, superiority and entitlement. He will utilize his elite status, superiority and entitlement to rationalize for the inhabitants of the earth, his worthiness to rule.*
- *destroy many. The perspective of the United Nations and those who seek to be the elite ruling global oligarchy is that* 'People are the problem. The world is overpopulated.' *The final horn on the shaggy goat will pursue the destruction of humanity. His motivation in destroying many will also include the dynamic that it is always easier to control few, than it is to control many.*
- *take his stand against the Prince of princes / messiah / the Lamb / Jesus Christ. The ultimate goal of the red dragon / serpent / Satan, Inc. has always been to unseat Jesus Christ and then to occupy his position as true sovereign over heaven and earth. Occupying and controlling Jerusalem during the era of the time of Jacob's Trouble will also provide the final horn on the shaggy goat with an opportunity to be in preparation for his meeting the Prince of princes / messiah / the Lamb / Jesus Christ in the final battle of this age.*
- *be invincible to human destruction. During the second half of the era of the time of Jacob's Trouble, the final horn on the shaggy goat will not be able to be injured or destroyed by human means. But he will also not have enough supernatural power and authority to be able to adequately defend himself against the Prince of princes / messiah / the Lamb / Jesus Christ.*

Concerning Daniel's prophecy of the seventy 'sevens':

The prince / ruler will confirm a covenant with many, for one 'seven' / 'week.' But in the middle of the 'seven' / 'week,' the prince / ruler will bring an end to the sacrifice and offering. On the wing (of the temple), the prince / ruler will establish abominations that will cause desolation, even until the consumption which has been determined is poured out on the desolate / the one who destroys. Daniel 9:27 translated

Since 1948 there have been over fifty United Nations Peace proposals for the nation of Israel. None of them has provided any real hope for an established peace for the nation of Israel. But on September 15, 2020, the Abraham Accords were signed and for the first time in the reestablished nation of Israel's history, the realization of peace became a real possibility.

One of the identifying factors of the prince who is to come, will be his confirmation of the Abraham Accords... and then his violation of the Abraham Accords with the future abomination of desolation event.

Confirming peace treaties, was the work of monarchs. Confirming the Abraham Accords covenant peace treaty agreement would be an act of declaring himself to be a monarch.

Breaking peace treaties was also the work of monarchs. Breaking the Abraham Accords covenant peace treaty agreement will also be an act of declaring himself to be a monarch.

And then, with the future abomination of desolation event, the prince who is to come, will seek to eliminate all threats against his claim to sovereignty as a monarch, by declaring war upon Judaism and God's holy people. Ending the daily sacrifices and offerings will be a strategy designed to weaken any threat that the united combination of God Most High with the people of Israel poses to the sovereignty of the prince who is to come.

Because only God the Creator initiates original creation, the red dragon / serpent / Satan, Inc. will never be able to invent something new. The only strategy that the red dragon / serpent / Satan, Inc. has available is to copy, copy, copy. And what the red dragon / serpent / Satan, Inc. copies are God the Creator's ideas. This dynamic limits the red dragon / serpent / Satan, Inc. to such a great extent, that the inability to devise some new stratagem that God Most High has not considered and not provided a counter attack to, will be a factor in God Most High's *planned defeat and destruction of the red dragon / serpent / Satan, Inc. and the destruction of the kingdom of Satan, Inc. / kingdom of man.*

But until the red dragon / serpent / Satan, Inc. and the kingdom of Satan, Inc. / kingdom of man has reached that realization that his strategy is failed, they will continue to copy. The beast of the sea will be a false prophet. The beast of the earth will attempt to fill the role equal to the promised and prophesied messiah.

With the future abomination of desolation event, the beast of the earth will use magic, sorcery, occult practices, illusion, dark arts, etc., to attempt to prove his legitimacy as divine and sovereign cosmic ruler.

Jesus said: 'False messiahs and false prophets, will arise; and they will provide great signs and wonders to intentionally mislead, if possible, even the elect.' Matthew 24:24 translated

Some biblical interpreters subscribe to a theology of imminence. It is a theology that claims that the prerequisite events that must take place prior to Jesus Christ's return, have already been fulfilled. Therefore, in the theology of imminence, Jesus Christ could return at any time. It is a theology that haphazardly accepts partial fulfillments of prophecies in checking off the necessary boxes on the list of events required before Jesus Christ returns. And it is a theology that denies the magnitude of the actual events that are scheduled to take place, and denies the greatness of the kingdom transition change that will occur when messiah / the Lamb / Jesus Christ fully establishes the kingdom of heaven on earth.

But both Jesus and Paul the writer of 1 and 2 Thessalonians, stressed that it is important that the followers of the Lamb / Jesus Christ not be deceived. There are prerequisites that must take place prior to the return of Jesus Christ.

Concerning the coming of our Lord Jesus Christ and our being gathered to Jesus Christ, we ask you not to become easily unsettled or alarmed by some prophecy, report or letter supposed to have come from us, saying that the Day of the Lord has already come. Do not let anyone deceive you in any way, for that day will not come until the rebellion occurs and the man of lawlessness is revealed, the man doomed to destruction. The man of lawlessness will oppose and will exalt himself over everything that is called God or is worshiped, so that the man of lawlessness sets himself up in God's temple, proclaiming himself to be God. 2 Thessalonians 2:1-5

One of the prerequisites that must take place prior to the return of Jesus Christ is the rebellion *must occur. This will be a global movement to reject Jesus Christ as Lord and to reject God Most High as divine and sovereign. That movement has already begun within the hierarchy of the Roman Catholic Church, and within modern churches that have embraced the post Christian, church of Laodicean theology (Revelation 3:14-22).*

There will be an increased intensity of 'aposticia' / period of apostasy, a departure from faith in God Most High, a rebellion against God Most High, that will take place around the time that the beast of the earth reveals himself during the future abomination of desolation event.

There will be some kind of rationale offered that God Most High has not acted well enough or soon enough or in a proper, politically correct manner or is even able to act at all.

Dear friends, do not believe every spirit, but test the spirits to see whether they are from God, because many false prophets have gone out into the world. This is how you can recognize the Spirit of God: Every spirit that acknowledges that Jesus Christ has come in the flesh is from God, but every spirit that does not acknowledge Jesus is not from God. This is the spirit of the antichrist, which you have heard is coming and even now is already into the world. 1 John 4:1-3

The same John the Revelator who wrote the book of Revelation, also wrote the epistles of 1, 2, and 3 John.

1 John 2:4-6 also expounded upon the previous three verses.

John identified that there is a test for determining which side a personal spirit or any other kind of spirit, is on. The test is, 'Does this spirit acknowledge that Jesus Christ has come into the world in human form and also acknowledge that Jesus Christ is from God?'

Both the humanity ('in the flesh') and the divinity ('from God') of Jesus Christ are vital elements of this test.

Some people acknowledge Jesus as merely a great prophet, but this is not a full acknowledgement of Jesus' position as Christ / messiah / the Anointed One.

Some people acknowledge Jesus as merely an invention of a committee of men or they acknowledge Jesus as a spirit being and deny that Jesus entered into human form, allowing his human blood to be shed in order to provide the spiritual blood transfusion to replace the blood that all of humanity possesses that was tainted by the sin of Adam and inherited from Adam.

Believing that Jesus is both spiritually divine and also fully human is required in order to answer this test question correctly. The definition of Christ / messiah / Anointed One is when the perfectly divine and sovereign member of God, fully took on the human form fully.

To answer the question of the identity of Jesus Christ, is to fail this test. Those who fail this test are automatically destined to be on the side of the antichrist / little horn / eleventh king / final horn on the shaggy goat / prince who is to come / king that will exalt himself / beast of the earth / final world ruler.

Those that fail this test have been assured that they will encounter eternal life with the red dragon / serpent / Satan, Inc. who is the true author of the lie that denies the divinity and humanness of Jesus Christ.

The same spirit who will empower the antichrist / beast of the earth began working on both the lie and the empowerment of the spirit of the antichrist system since the era of the Garden of Eden / garden of God / paradise (Genesis 3).

The current pope, Francis (March 13, 2013 to present), has already rejected the divinity of Jesus Christ and has declared Jesus a failure in his earthly ministry when Jesus came and died on the cross. Francis' theology holds that when Jesus Christ died on the cross, he failed to do the work that was expected of him. Even the fact that Jesus Christ died on the cross is considered as evidence that Jesus was cursed and therefore unable to be divine, because dying through crucifixion was considered a cursed death. Theoretically, true divinity cannot be cursed.

Proposing that Jesus Christ was not all that he claimed to be and that Jesus Christ failed in his mission when he came the first time is a denial of Jesus Christ's divinity as the authentic messiah / Christ / Anointed One. Through many of Francis' activities and statements, Francis has either denied the divinity of Jesus Christ or has refused to recognize Jesus Christ's divinity. While this kind of rejection of the divinity of Jesus Christ is characteristic of the spirit of antichrist, Francis is not **the** antichrist. **The** antichrist will also deny the divinity of Jesus Christ.

Irenaeus of Smyrna and bishop of Lyon (c. 130 to c. 202 AD) was a student of Polycarp who was a student of John the Revelator.

Irenaeus documented the understanding of the leaders of the apostolic church.

In 2 Thessalonians, the 'falling away' is an apostasy and there will be a literal rebuilt temple. In Matthew (chapter 24), the 'abomination spoken by Daniel' is the Antichrist sitting in the temple as if he were Christ. The abomination will start in the middle of Daniel's 70th week and last for a literal three years and six months. The little horn (the 11th horn) is the Antichrist. Irenaeus, *Against Heresies* 5.25

As a student of Polycarp and John the Revelator, and therefore close to the source of Paul who was the giver of the information, Irenaeus' commentary must be considered as an authentic understanding of the early church.

Based on the people of Israel's failed record in testing the authenticity of those who 'would be' messiah, the people of Israel will again be willing to receive a 'would be' messiah who will turn out to be false.

Unlike the previous abomination of desolation event committed by Antiochus IV Epiphanes (167 BC), the one who commits the future abomination of desolation event will be viewed by the people of Israel, not as an enemy of Israel, but initially as a friend of Israel. The beast of the earth will initially appear as a lamb, assisting in the establishment of peace for the people and nation of Israel. Surely someone so helpful to establishing the safety and security of the nation of Israel, must be placed in the category of friend.

The people of Israel may even receive the beast of the earth as God Most High's actual promised messiah for a period of time, because the beast of the earth promise to fulfill God Most High's covenant to raise the nation of Israel up to a sovereign position over other nations of the world, and to bring his own version of 'peace' / 'world peace.'

Peace is defined differently by different people, according to their personal agendas. Baruch Spinoza (1632 to 1677) defined peace this way: 'Peace is not the absence of war, it is a virtue, a state of mind, a disposition of benevolence, confidence, justice.' The beast of the earth will define peace as his obtaining personal control over all things global, and having no threats to his tyrannical reign of terror. But God Most High defined peace as being in a right and loving relationship with God Most High.

But at the future abomination of desolation event, it will be the beast of the earth who will break the covenant peace treaty agreement. What appeared as a lamb will speak as a dragon. And his displays of supernatural power and authority will serve as authorization of his divinity and sovereignty.

Because the authentic and certain reality is that God Most High maintains God Most High's position as true sovereign, the actual trajectory that the beast of the earth must follow is not up, but down. While the beast of the earth will view the future abomination of desolation event as the beginning of his ever-increasing glorious reign, the future abomination of desolation event will instead be the high point of his reign. Revelation 17-19 described the erosion that will be taking place within the established kingdom of Satan, Inc. / kingdom of man; and that erosion will begin on the date of the future abomination of desolation event.

After the kingdom of Satan, Inc. / kingdom of man has had their fill of the beast of the earth, the man doomed to destruction described in Revelation 19:19-21, is scheduled to be thrown alive into the fiery lake of burning sulfur with the beast of the sea. But that will not happen until the two beasts of Revelation 13, have had their forty two months to attempt to fully establish the kingdom of Satan, Inc. / kingdom of man on earth and in heaven.

Temple sacrifice discontinued

In historical Jewish tradition, God Most High dwells with the people of Israel, within a sanctuary / tabernacle / temple.

God Most High's instruction to Moses and the people of Israel was: 'Then have them make a sanctuary for me, and I will dwell among them.' Exodus 25:8

In the song of Mariam, there was this phrase: You will bring them in and plant them on the mountain of your inheritance — the place, Lord, you made for your dwelling, the sanctuary, Lord, your hands established. Exodus 15:17

And Jewish tradition taught that the Jewish messiah cannot come until there is a temple established for him to come to, based on Malachi 3:1.

'Then suddenly the Lord you are seeking will come to his temple. The messenger of the covenant, whom you desire, will come,' says the Lord Almighty. Malachi 3:1b

Jewish tradition also taught that messiah will assist in building the final temple. And Maimonides / Moses ben Maimon / Rabbi Moshe (1138 to 1204) taught that the only conclusive proof of the identity of messiah will be that he will be the one to build the temple. (Maimonides, Rambam / Laws of the Chosen House 1:1, Laws of Kings 11:4)

The Medrash Rabba (homiletic expositions from the time of the Talmud) taught that God will personally build the third temple and it will descend out of the fire from heaven, to its appointed place on earth, the temple mount. Rashi was a chief and classical commentator (c. 1200). Tosefos was of the academy of European scholars (c. 1300). Because Rashi and Tosefos also subscribed to this understanding, this understanding gained prominence in Jewish understanding.

In the description that John the Revelator provided of the beast of the earth, John noted: And the beast of the earth works great signs so that it should even cause fire to come down out of heaven to the earth, in the presence of humanity. Revelation 13:13 translated

Being able to cause fire to come down out of heaven to the earth, may be interpreted by the people of Israel as a fulfillment of the understanding presented in the *Medrash Rabba*.

One understanding of the people of Israel is that messiah will come to an established temple.

The other understanding is that messiah will assist in building the temple.

The two understandings seem contradictory to each other.

Messiah / the Lamb / Jesus Christ answered the quandary by first coming for his earthly ministry to an already established Herod's temple / second temple. And when messiah / the Lamb / Jesus Christ returns, he will be responsible for the building of the temple that will stand during the Thousand Years Reign of Jesus Christ.

But the people of Israel do not yet recognize Jesus Christ as their messiah. They believed and continue to believe that the disciples stole the body of Jesus (Matthew 28:11-15). They are seeking a messiah who will fill their expectations.

Therefore, the person who seeks to be a would be candidate for Jewish messiah and leader of the people of Israel, must both be involved in building the next temple / third temple, and also declare himself within that temple.

Once the future third temple has been constructed during the first half of the era of the time of Jacob's Trouble, there will be the resumption of the fully consecrated, functional and operational temple sacrificial system. Without the daily sacrificial system in place, the temple will not be recognized as fully established.

With the reconstitution of the fully consecrated, functional and operational temple sacrificial system, daily sacrifices for the continual burnt offering, will be offered twice daily (Daniel 9:21; Exodus 29:38-42), as a representation of the atonement of the people of Israel as a whole.

Once the temple is built and the practice of daily sacrifice has been established, the beast of the earth will believe that the people of Israel will be ready to receive him, as messiah and leader of the people of Israel. The beast of the earth will know that he is not messiah sent by God Most High. But, the beast of the earth will believe that he is equal to filling the position and will declare himself to be superior to God Most High, sovereign above God.

Because the beast of the earth will see himself as God in the flesh, now dwelling with humanity, the beast of the earth will believe that there is now no longer any necessity to offer sacrifices to God Most High who will be accused of not being present or active any human events. Therefore, the beast of the earth will end the evening and morning temple sacrifices because they acknowledge the sovereignty and divinity of God Most High and do not recognize the beast of the earth as divine and sovereign.

In place of the evening and the morning sacrifices, the beast of the earth will establish a system where the idol / image of the beast of the sea is worshiped. This will be compulsory worship and those that decline to worship the idol / image of the beast of the sea will be murdered. (Revelation 13:14-15)

In a sense, when the animal sacrifices to the Lord in the temple are discontinued, those who refuse to worship the idol / image of the beast of the sea and refrain from engaging in the mark of the beasts system, will become a new kind of <u>human</u> sacrifice, dedicated to the red dragon / serpent / Satan, Inc.

The prince / ruler will confirm a covenant with many, for one 'seven' / 'week.' But in the middle of the 'seven' / 'week,' the prince / ruler will bring an end to the sacrifice and offering. On the wing (of the temple), the prince / ruler will establish abominations that will cause desolation, even until the consumption which has been determined is poured out on the desolate / the one who destroys. Daniel 9:27 translated

The same day that the ruler who is to come / beast of the earth stands in the temple and declares himself to be greater than God, he will also abolish the daily sacrifice. The beast of the earth will claim that because he (the beast

of the earth) is finally with us, and is greater than God Most High, and has rewritten what sin consists of and how the consequences of sin are dealt with, there is no longer any need to offer sacrifice for the forgiveness of sins. Sexual perversions will no longer be considered offensive sin. Murder will be considered an act of goodness in the pursuit of decreasing the overpopulation of the world. Other changes in the definition of 'sin' will follow.

Worship of God Most High and of Jesus Christ will become the first newly defined sin.

Jesus Christ claimed that only God Most High could forgive sin. But the Roman Catholic Church has historically practiced a theology where the pope and the pope's representatives declared the sins of a person forgiven through confession and extreme unction / absolution / last rites. In a similar manner, the prince who is to come / beast of the earth will define the process for forgiveness of sin based upon the individual's relationship with the global religious community, the individual's relationship with the new global governance system, and the individual's equity in the new currency of the established global economic structure.

Along with the new procedures that the prince who is to come / beast of the earth will incorporate for dealing with sin, there will be a new theology concerning life after death. The kingdom of heaven will have been cursed by the beast of the sea (Revelation 13:6); so gaining access to heaven will no longer be sought after and with the global religious community baring entrance into the kingdom of heaven, it will no longer be necessary for sins to be forgiven. Without the redemption process that required an individual to be right with God Most High through belief in Jesus Christ as Lord, what constitutes eternal life will be redefined. And the new process for entering into eternal life will begin with 'envisioning your redemption,' worshiping the idol / image of the beast of the sea, and performing good works that benefit the kingdom of Satan, Inc. / kingdom of man.

Daniel's vision of a goat: Out of one of the horns came another horn, which started small but grew in power to the south and to the east and toward the Beautiful Land (Israel). It grew until it reached the host of the heavens, and it threw some of the starry host down to the earth and trampled on them. It set itself up to be as great as the Prince of the host. It took away the daily sacrifice from God Most High, and the place of his sanctuary was brought low. Because of rebellion, the host of the holy ones, and the daily sacrifice were given over to it. It prospered in everything it did, and truth was thrown to the ground.

Then I heard a holy one speaking, and another holy one said to him, 'How long will it take for the vision to be fulfilled – the vision concerning the daily sacrifice, the rebellion that causes desolation, and the surrender of the sanctuary and the host that will be trampled underfoot?'

He said to me, 'It will take 2,300 evenings and mornings; then the sanctuary will be reconsecrated.' Daniel 8:9-14

The preterist claim was that Daniel's prophecy was initially fulfilled on Kislev 25, 167 BC after the pagan altar was set up by Antiochus IV Epiphanes. The period ended at the reconsecration of the temple by Judas Maccabeus in 164 BC. The commemoration of the rededication of the temple is still celebrated today as the feast of dedication / Hanukah.

Daniel's prophecy concerning the abomination of desolation events, did receive its first fulfillment with Antiochus IV Epiphanes desecrating the temple. Antiochus IV Epiphanes discontinued the temple worship to Yahweh / God Most High by offering unclean animals on the altar along with constructing an altar to Zeus, a baal / mystery / mythology religion god, and requiring compulsory worship of the Greek gods.

Antiochus IV Epiphanes also forbid the practice of the Jewish religion including the observation of the feasts and festivals, the practice of circumcision, and the sacrificing of animals in sin offerings. Antiochus IV Epiphanes also massacred Jews.

The rededication of the temple took place three years later, which meant that the evening and morning sacrifices were discontinued for approximately one thousand eighty days / two thousand one hundred sixty evening and morning sacrifices. This time period falls short of the one thousand one hundred fifty days / two thousand three hundred evening and morning sacrifices that Daniel's vision prescribed.

Because of the precision of time required by Daniel's prophecy, to the increment of the half day, the abomination of desolation event committed by Antiochus IV Epiphanes cannot be the abomination of desolation event that was described in Daniel 8 that is scheduled for 'the distant future.' Daniel's words, 'for it concerns the distant future,' were a reference to the time of the era of the time of Jacob's Trouble.

When the future abomination of desolation event takes place, the temple altar will again be desecrated in order to ward off any temptation by the people of Israel to use it to offer legitimate sacrifices to God Most High. Daniel documented that the temple will be desecrated for exactly two thousand three hundred evening and morning sacrifices / one thousand one hundred fifty days. 1,150 days = 3 years and 55 days on a solar calendar; 3 years and 70 days on a lunar calendar.

Just prior to the end of the desecration time period, there will need to be eight days of consecration as required by the law given to Moses concerning the temple.

The red dragon / serpent / Satan, Inc.'s magic, sorcery, occult practices, illusion, dark arts, etc., used to support the supernatural power and authority of the kingdom of Satan, Inc. / kingdom of man – Revelation 16:12-16

During the era of the second half of the era of the time of Jacob's Trouble there will be an increase in miraculous signs and wonders both among those on the side of God Most High and among those on the side of the red dragon / serpent / Satan, Inc. Both sides will be participating in stupendous supernatural events of the magnitude never before experienced in human history, in the attempt to convince the inhabitants of the earth and the hosts of heaven, of the superiority of their respective kingdoms' power and validity to hold the position of sovereign over the cosmos.

Similar to God Most High's war with the gods of Egypt through the ten plagues, God Most High will again do battle with the gods / rebellious angels comprising the red dragon / serpent / Satan, Inc. Similar to the front lines of the battleground of God Most High's war with the Egyptian gods being among humanity, specifically Egypt, God Most High will again allow the front lines of the battleground of God Most High's war with the red dragon / serpent / Satan, Inc. to take place among humanity, with the epicenter of the battles at Jerusalem and Rome.

Unlike God Most High's activity during the era of Moses and the exodus of the Israelites out of Egypt, during the era of the time of Jacob's Trouble, the world will not need to depend merely upon hearing reports of God Most High's mighty acts. During the era of the time of Jacob's Trouble, the inhabitants of the earth and the people of God will be able to see God Most High's mighty acts either through electronic screens or directly personally experienced around the world. In the modern era of the tremendous amount of 'fake news,' it will be important to experience authentic news instead of merely hearing or seeing the reports of news. During the era of the time of Jacob's Trouble, the events will be entirely participatory and not spectator events.

Among the list of the acts of sorcery and magic that the red dragon / serpent / Satan, Inc. will empower the two beasts of Revelation 13 to perform, will be the ability to counterfeit resurrection. It is probable that counterfeit resurrections will allow people to rise from the dead, but not to new life, just to a shadow of the human life they once had. Transhumanism will be employed to prolong life, and will be presented as one path to 'resurrected eternal life.' 'Resurrected life' will become a combination of human life mixed with technology. The beast of the sea's near-death experience followed by his return from the near fatal wound, will be elevated and presented to people as an example of the supposed power available when individuals invest in the kingdom of Satan, Inc. / kingdom of man. The presentation of his return from his near fatal wound will be shrouded in mystery reminiscent of the shroud of mystery that characterized the ancient mystery religions. And like the ancient mystery religions, the revelation of the secret to the mystery will only be revealed to those who dedicate themselves to the mystery religion and pay the price of membership.

There will not be any stunt doubles during this performance of bringing the beast of the sea back to 'life.' But, the 'resurrection' that the red dragon / serpent / Satan, Inc., the two beasts of Revelation 13 offers will not be an authentic resurrection.

The quality of the red dragon / serpent / Satan, Inc.'s miracles, signs and wonders will be quite good during this era; so good that they will deceive most of the inhabitants of the earth. When the majority of the inhabitants of the earth do not possess any relationship with or knowledge of the contents and instruction of the biblical record, they will not be prepared to understand that there is a God Most High who offers authentic resurrection of glorious bodies and genuine eternal life to those who choose to believe that Jesus Christ is Lord. The ignorant majority of the inhabitants of the earth will willingly embrace the promises offered by the two beasts of Revelation 13 on behalf of the kingdom of Satan, Inc. / kingdom of man because the promises made by the two beasts will be supported by the magic and miraculous signs that they will perform.

Because the beast of the earth will be an imposter for the role of messiah, the beast of the earth will not be able to rely on what is found intrinsically within himself as the sufficient power needed to produce magic, signs and wonders.

Jesus Christ was inherently divine and sovereign. Jesus Christ emptied himself of the power he held associated with his divinity, to take on the form of humanity, be humanly born and to live as a fully human being. It was the power of Jesus Christ's human character that warranted his resurrection after his crucifixion. His perfectly lived human life, was unable to be held by death.

And it was his perfectly lived human life that caused Jesus Christ to be able to heal, resurrect, command the wind and the waves, walk on water, etc.

The biblical record documented that the beast of the sea will be a blasphemer, and the beast of the earth will be a facsimile of the biblical description of the promised and prophesied messiah. Because they will be full of lies, their calculations for how to work with the created order, will be flawed. Because they will have intrinsically rebelled against the God who created order, they will not be able to access and utilize the created order for their own mission. Therefore, the two beasts of Revelation 13 will not be able to source their own power for their magic, sorcery, occult practices, illusion, dark arts, etc.

The signs and wonders that will be provided by the two beasts of Revelation 13 to perform, will be empowered by the red dragon / serpent / Satan, Inc. Their signs and wonders will surpass anything that the inhabitants of the earth have ever previously experienced. The magic presented by the two beasts of Revelation 13 will be greater than anything ever experienced in human history and will cause the two beasts of Revelation 13 to impart an irresistibility.

For the red dragon / serpent / Satan, Inc.'s plan to work, it will be vital that humanity remain uneducated, not only concerning the deep things of God, but also remain uneducated at all levels. The deepest secrets that cause the magic and illusion to be amazing, must remain undisclosed in order for the magic and illusion to work. Disclosing the deepest secrets of their magic would render the veracity of their supernatural power and authority to be meaningless. Consequently, the promise will be made that once an individual has become fully committed to the new religion of the two beasts of Revelation 13 the secrets will be revealed, the reality will be that once fully committed, no new revelations will be forthcoming.

Satan began his deception with the first man and first woman in God the Creator's Garden of Eden / garden of God / paradise, promising that consumption of the fruit of the tree of the knowledge of good and evil would cause them to be like God, elevated to God the Creator's level of divinity and sovereignty. Instead, they lost the inherent glory they already possessed, and they became susceptible to sin and death. Satan profited on the first man and first woman's lack of understanding and education, and their willingness to be deceived. And for the past six thousand years, the red dragon / serpent / Satan, Inc. has continued to take advantage of being able to dupe most of humanity concerning God Most High's redemption, reclamation and regeneration plan.

When humanity has eyes to see and ears to hear and yet chooses to not perceive, humanity becomes vulnerable to invest in whatever the red dragon / serpent / Satan, Inc. is marketing.

But when humanity understands the context and the results of the decisions made, then deception cannot work and the illusion cannot be accomplished.

God Most High made provision to again educate humanity in the midst of the performance that will be brought by the unholy trio of the two beasts of Revelation 13 and the red dragon / serpent / Satan, Inc. God Most High will be sending two witnesses to represent the kingdom of heaven.

The era of the time of Jacob's Trouble will also be a time when the followers of the Lamb / Jesus Christ, including the two witnesses, will be performing great miracles. This will be a time when followers of the Lamb / Jesus Christ will be equipped to be a part of doing greater miracles than Jesus Christ accomplished during his earthly ministry (John 1:50, 14:12). In this cosmic 'dance,' God Most High has made provision to supply counter moves to the activity of the two beasts of Revelation 13, and the red dragon / serpent / Satan, Inc.

The era of the time of Jacob's Trouble was divided into sections by God Most High.

God Most High determined the forty two month term of supernatural power and authority that the two beasts of Revelation 13 will enjoy. And God Most High determined the one thousand two hundred sixty days that the two witnesses will provide ministry as a counter to the presentation of the two beasts.

When messiah / the Lamb / Jesus Christ was crucified, the red dragon / serpent / Satan, Inc. celebrated with the idea that their kingdom had prevailed. But when God resurrected messiah / the Lamb / Jesus Christ with a glorious physical resurrected body, God Most High was declaring the war was not over yet.

In the assassination of the two witnesses by the beast of the sea / beast from the Abyss, the two beasts will present themselves as the victors of this cosmic war. But with the resurrection of the two witnesses, God Most High will again be declaring the war is not over yet.

With the resurrection and ascension into heaven of the two witnesses, the finale for the era of the time of Jacob's Trouble will begin. The battle lines will be redrawn. And the nature of the supernatural power brought to this cosmic war, will be altered. In military terms, the weapons utilized in the battle will be rotated.

During the finale for the era of the time of Jacob's Trouble, the two beasts of Revelation 13 along with the red dragon / serpent / Satan, Inc. will utilize a different form of magic: three evil demon frog spirits. Remember that demons are the spirits of the dead Nephilim that were a species bred during the antediluvian / preflood era and immediately after that era. The finale of the era of the time of Jacob's Trouble will provide the demon spirits with the opportunity to also actively participate in this cosmic conflict at a new level, and to bring their magic and illusion into the battlefield.

<u>Sixth bowl: Euphrates River dried up</u>
The sixth (angel) poured out his bowl upon the great river Euphrates and dried up its water to prepare a way for the kings of the rising of the sun (kings of the east). And I saw coming out of the mouth of the dragon, and out of the mouth of the beast, and out of the mouth of the false prophet, three demonic spirits like frogs. They are spirits of demons performing signs. They go forth to the kings of the whole inhabited world, to gather them together for the battle of the great day of God the Almighty.

'Behold, I am coming like a thief. Blessed is the one awake and vigilantly watching, and who keeps their garments on so that they should not walk naked and their shame be seen.'

And he gathered them together to the place called in Hebrew, Armageddon. Revelation 16:12-16 translated

It will also be during the finale for the era of the time of Jacob's Trouble, that God Most High will be providing the counterstrategy of pouring out the seven bowls of God Most High's wrath / seven last plagues (Revelation 16).

But the inhabitants of the earth will be so allied with the unholy trinity, that they will not be persuaded even by the events associated with the pouring out of the seven bowls of God Most High's wrath / seven last plagues.

Under the mesmerizing magic spell provided through the two beasts of Revelation 13 and the red dragon / serpent / Satan, Inc., the three evil demon frog spirits will persuade the power leaders of the world to bring their armies to the point of rebellious religious fervor and gather in the nation of Israel to siege Jerusalem and battle the people of Israel and the followers of the Lamb / Jesus Christ, with the determination to annihilate all opposition to the kingdom of Satan, Inc. / kingdom of man.

It is possible that the reference to frogs as a description for the three evil spirits, was intended to correspond to some of the evil spirits of the gods of Egypt that the ten plagues of Egypt were designed to battle. One week after the first plague of the Nile River turning to blood, came the plague of frogs. The frogs came out of the Nile, even into the palace, into the bedroom of the palace and onto the pharaoh's bed, along with entering the houses of the officials, the people, the ovens and kneading troughs (Exodus 8:1-4). While Moses was the instrument of God Most High to bring this plague to the Egyptian people, the magicians were able to accomplish the same feat of conjuring frogs, with their secret arts. The kingdom of Satan, Inc. / kingdom of man has experience with frogs. But so does the God of the kingdom of heaven.

While the Holy Spirit is represented as a dove, the spirits of the red dragon / serpent / Satan, Inc.'s will

continue to be represented as frogs. Doves fly and travel through the air unimpeded by being bound to the ground. Frogs must hop only a few inches at a time, and always fall back to earth.

Notice that the instruction that Jesus Christ provided to the followers of the Lamb / Jesus Christ for this era, is to keep awake, keep watching, and keep the suitcase packed and ready to go. Nakedness will not be advisable at this time. It will be a time when preparations will need to be made for the real final battle of this cosmic war.

The two beasts of Revelation 13 use of magic, sorcery, occult practices, illusion, dark arts, etc.

The biblical record provided multiple examples of God Most High's supernatural activity in God's interactions with humanity throughout human history. Because of the biblical record's documentation of multiple signs of God Most High's interaction with humanity, the people of Israel came to expect the expression of supernatural signs. One of the challenges presented to Jesus Christ was for him to present a sign as proof of his messiahship, instead of believing him to be the promised and prophesied messiah because of his fulfillment of prophesy and his perfect nature.

Jesus answered, 'A wicked and adulterous generation asks for a sign!' Matthew 12:39a

According to the biblical record, the era of the time of Jacob's Trouble will be another time when there will be a wicked and adulterous generation that will seek a sign to prove supernatural ability.

The people of Israel currently continue to reject the actual promised and prophesied messiah who came with the full backing of God Most High. Not only is this fact amusing and amazing to Jesus, but the fact that the people of Israel will consider the beast of the earth as a potential candidate for their messiah is also the result of a total misread of the what God Most High told Moses, the prophets, and the other Old Testament writers.

Jesus said: 'For false christs and false prophets will appear and perform great signs and miracles to deceive even the elect – if that were possible. See, I have told you ahead of time.' Matthew 24:24

Jesus taught, and the apostolic and early church leaders understood, that there would be a dichotomy within the role of antichrist / 'in place of Christ' that would be filled with both false christs and false prophets.

In contrast to false christs and false prophets, Jesus Christ personally filled all the roles of prophet, priest, and king, simultaneously. No other individual in human history has been or will be able to fill all the roles of prophet, priest, and king simultaneously.

Those who are familiar with the biblical record will be able to recognize the deception of false christs and false prophets because of their inability to fill the offices of prophet, priest, and king simultaneously. But that will not prevent the two beasts of Revelation 13 from attempting to deceive the inhabitants of the earth and even the elect / the followers of the Lamb / Jesus Christ when they attempt to fill the roles of messiah / Christ and prophet of God.

And the two beasts of Revelation 13 will utilize their supernatural power and authority that they will receive from the red dragon / serpent / Satan, Inc.

The beast of the sea / false prophet / beast from the Abyss / eighth king beast's use of magic, sorcery, occult practices, illusion, dark arts, etc. - Revelation 13:1-7, 16:12-16, 18:23c

The beast of the sea will perform great signs and miracles with the goal of deceiving the inhabitants of the earth in the pursuit of validating both his position as prophet of God and the position of the beast of the earth as sovereign over God Most High.

John the Revelator's first description of the beast of the sea's use of magic, sorcery, occult practices, illusion, dark arts, etc., will be with his survival of his near fatal attack. Through this experience, the beast of the sea will demonstrate the level of power that will cause him to be perceived as invincible.

I saw a beast rising out of the sea, having ten horns, and seven heads. And on its horns, there were ten royal crowns (diademata / διαδηματα). And upon its heads were names of blasphemy.

The beast that I saw was like a leopard, and its feet like a bear, and its mouth like the mouth of a lion. And the dragon gave to the beast, his power and his throne and great authority.

One of its heads was as if it was having been slain to death. And its wound of death was healed, and all the earth marveled after the beast.

The people of the earth, worshiped the dragon who had given authority to the beast of the sea. And they worshiped the beast of the sea, saying, 'Who is like the beast? And who is able to make war against it?' Revelation 13:1-4 translated

For forty two months the beast of the sea will appear to be indestructible to the global community.

At the end of the forty two months, the beast of the sea / beast from the Abyss will be able to assassinate the two witnesses on the temple mount. This will be an amazing feat because the two witnesses will also appear to be indestructible.

I will appoint my two witnesses, and they will prophesy one thousand two hundred and sixty days, clothed in sackcloth. These are the two olive trees and the two lampstands standing before the Lord of the earth. If anyone should desire to harm them, fire comes out of their mouths and devours their enemies. And if anyone should desire to harm them, it is necessary for them to be killed in this manner. They have the power to shut heaven, so that no rain falls in the days of their prophecy. They have power over the waters, to turn them into blood; and to strike the earth with every plague, as often as they might desire.

When they have completed their testimony, the beast that ascends out of the Abyss will make war against them, and overcome them, and kill them. Revelation 11:3-7 translated

With the assassination, death, resurrection and ascension into heaven of the two witnesses, the second half of the era of the time of Jacob's Trouble will end and the finale for the era of the time of Jacob's Trouble will begin.

During the finale for the era of the time of Jacob's Trouble, the two beasts of Revelation 13 will again receive a measure of supernatural power, this time sourced by three evil demon frog spirits.

<u>Sixth bowl: Euphrates River dried up</u>

The sixth (angel) poured out his bowl upon the great river Euphrates and dried up its water to prepare a way for the kings of the rising of the sun (kings of the east). And I saw coming out of the mouth of the dragon, and out of the mouth of the beast, and out of the mouth of the false prophet, three demonic spirits like frogs. They are spirits of demons performing signs. They go forth to the kings of the whole inhabited world, to gather them together for the battle of the great day of God the Almighty.

'Behold, I am coming like a thief. Blessed is the one awake and vigilantly watching, and who keeps their garments on so that they should not walk naked and their shame be seen.'

And he gathered them together to the place called in Hebrew, Armageddon. Revelation 16:12-16 translated

During the final battle of this age, the great city that rules over the kings of the earth, will be destroyed. The entire eighteenth chapter of the book of Revelation was devoted to the massive mourning that will take place with its destruction. And in that description of destruction, was tucked the explanation for why God Most High will allow the great city to be destroyed.

'Because of your sorcery / magic spell, all the nations were deceived.' Revelation 18:23c translated

The global religious community which will be led by the beast of the sea, will use magic throughout the hierarchy of the global religious community for establishing global power and for the purpose of deceiving the nations of the world.

During the final battle of this age, the two beasts of Revelation 13 will also be defeated and captured. Even though the beast of the earth will have been credited with performing great signs, John the Revelator recognized that the beast of the sea will have served as a motivator and as a resource for the use of magic, sorcery, occult practices, illusion, dark arts, etc. as a strategy for deceiving the inhabitants of the earth.

The beast was captured, and with him the false prophet. The beast was the one having performed the signs on behalf of the false prophet, by which the beast deceived those having received the mark of the beasts and those worshiping the image of the beast. The two were cast into the lake of fire burning with brimstone. And the rest were killed with the sword of the one sitting on the horse having gone forth from out of his mouth. And all the birds were filled with their flesh. Revelation 19:20-21 translated

Because magic, sorcery, occult practices, illusion, dark arts, etc. are used as manipulation to persuade people to believe what is unreal, their purpose in using them can only be to achieve deception.

The deception that the beast of the sea will attempt to sell to the global community will be the blasphemy that Jesus Christ is not the divine and sovereign messiah, that his crucifixion was justified, that his resurrection was a narrative derived from his disciples who stole his body, that the resurrected Jesus Christ did not ascend into heaven, and that Jesus Christ does not have the ability or power to return to defeat the enemies of the kingdom of heaven and to fully establish the kingdom of heaven on earth.

The beast of the sea's further deception will be to point to the beast of the earth as the next messianic candidate.

Because the beast of the sea will also hold high position and respect within the global Christian community, his deception will be widely received.

The beast of the earth's magic, sorcery, occult practices, illusion, dark arts, etc., signs and wonders – Daniel 8:23-25, 2 Thessalonians 2:9-11, Revelation 13:13-15, 16:12-16, 19:19-21

Daniel and John the Revelator documented that the beast of the earth's arrogance will cause him to crave from the people of the earth, the recognition of his assumed divinity and sovereignty. It will be essential to the beast of the earth that the inhabitants of the earth recognize him as supreme and sovereign, as a validation of his claim that he holds the position of supreme and sovereign God over the entire cosmos. To convince the inhabitants of the earth of his divinity, the beast of the earth will use every resource that is made available to attempt to prove his claim.

To make his claim convincing, the beast of the earth will need the supernatural empowerment of the red dragon / serpent / Satan, Inc. as a source for his magic, sorcery, occult practices, illusion, dark arts, etc. And with that supernatural power and authority, the beast of the earth will engage in magic, sorcery, occult practices, illusion, dark arts, etc.

Jesus said: 'For false christs and false prophets will appear and perform great signs and miracles to deceive even the elect – if that were possible. See, I have told you ahead of time.' Matthew 24:24

Jesus' claim to be messiah was validated when Jesus was able to begin his ministry with the declaration of the year of Jubilee. Jesus' ministry was marked with the blind being able to see, the deaf being able to hear, the lame being able to walk, etc. Jesus' claim to be messiah was validated in his living a sinless life in the total fulfillment of the Law given to Moses, that allowed him to be resurrected from death as his dramatized fulfillment of the prophecy of the feast of unleavened bread. Jesus' claim to be messiah was validated in the love that Jesus extended to the world through sacrificing his own life in order to free humanity from the grasp of the kingdom of Satan, Inc. / kingdom of man. Jesus fully demonstrated the love that is characteristic of the Creator God Most High.

In contrast to Jesus' claim to be messiah, the beast of the earth will have nothing to validate his claim to be messiah except what supernatural powerful acts of magic, sorcery and illusion that he can muster as a way of saying, 'I am God. How dare you question who I say that I am?'

Without having lived a holy life in relationship with God Most High, the only way that the beast of the earth will be able to attempt to validate his claim to be messiah will be through supernatural power; the use of power, the abuse of power, the manipulation of power, and the destruction of any who question his power.

Paul identified the ultimate purpose for God Most High's plan for the events that will take place during the era of the time of Jacob's Trouble. The events will be dramatic enough that the people of the world will be compelled to decide which god(s) and which kingdom they will invest themselves in for an eternity. Will the inhabitants of the earth believe God Most High? Or will the inhabitants of the earth believe the very powerful delusion?

Nearly two thousand years ago, the early disciples understood that the one who would fill the position of the beast of the earth, would need to use counterfeit miracles / magic, signs and wonders in his plan of deception.

The coming of the lawless one will be in accordance with the work of Satan displayed in all kinds of counterfeit miracles, signs and wonders, and in every sort of evil that deceives those who are perishing. They perish because they refused to love the truth and so be saved. For this reason, God sends them a powerful delusion so that they will believe the lie and so that all will be condemned who have not believed the truth but have delighted in wickedness. 2 Thessalonians 2:9-11

For the beast of the earth to accomplish his task, he must provide signs, many signs, miraculous signs. Because he will have the ability to authentically fulfill the prophecies that identified messiah, the beast of the earth will need to provide his own 'proof' to be considered the candidate to fill the position of messiah. The 'proof' that the beast of the earth will offer to the inhabitants of the earth will be his use of magic, sorcery, occult practices, illusion, dark arts, etc.

'In the latter part of their reign, when rebels have become completely wicked, a stern-faced king, a master of intrigue, will arise. The stern-faced king will become very strong, but not by his own power. The stern-faced king will cause astounding devastation and will succeed in whatever he does. The stern-faced king will cause deceit to prosper, and he will consider himself superior. When they feel secure, the stern-faced king will destroy many and take his stand against the Prince of princes. Yet the stern-faced king will be destroyed, but not by human power.' Daniel 8:23-25 (final horn on the shaggy goat)

In the King James version of this same passage, Daniel 9:25 described the final horn on the shaggy goat as causing 'craft to prosper in his hand.' *The KJV emphasized that the final horn on the shaggy goat will use sorcery, for bringing peace to the earth of course.*

And in the latter time of their kingdom, when the transgressors are come to the full, a king of fierce countenance, and understanding dark sentences, shall stand up. And his power shall be mighty, but not by his own power: and he shall destroy wonderfully, and shall prosper, and practice, and shall destroy the mighty and the holy people. And through his policy also he shall cause craft to prosper in his hand; and he shall magnify himself in his heart, and by peace shall destroy many: he shall also stand up against the Prince of princes; but he shall be broken without hand.' Daniel 8:23-25 KJV

This beast of the earth will also 'understand dark sentences.' *This was a reference to the occult and the magic of the occult. Tapping into the power of the dark side of the spiritual realm of the cosmos, the beast of the earth will incorrectly believe that his magic is powerful enough to overcome, destroy and conquer God Most High's messiah.*

John the Revelator also documented some of the beast of the earth's use of magic, sorcery, occult practices, illusion, dark arts, etc. in his attempt to prove himself.
　　The beast of the earth works great signs so that it should even cause fire to come down out of heaven to the earth, in the presence of humanity.
　　The beast of the earth deceives those dwelling on the earth by reason of the signs that it was given to perform before the beast of the sea, telling those dwelling on the earth to make an image to the beast that was wounded by the sword and has lived.
　　The beast of the earth was given the ability to give breath to the image of the beast of the sea, so that the image of the beast of the sea should also speak. And the image of the beast of the sea will cause all who would not worship the image of the beast of the sea, to be killed. Revelation 13:13-15 translated

One of the miracles that the beast of the earth will use for convincing the inhabitants of the earth of his power will be to cause fire from heaven to come down so that everyone will be able to see it. This ability to command heavenly fire will be an important counter to the witness from heaven who will be able to send or stop rain (Revelation 11:1-14).

John the Revelator's record reiterated the beast of the earth's use of magic, sorcery, occult practices, illusion, dark arts, etc. in the description of the defeat of the two beasts of Revelation 13 that will take place with the final battle of this age.
　　The beast was captured, and with him the false prophet. The beast was the one having performed the signs on behalf of the false prophet, by which the beast deceived those having received the mark of the beasts and those worshiping the image of the beast (of the sea). The two were cast into the lake of fire burning with brimstone. And the rest were killed with the sword of the one sitting on the horse, having gone forth from out of his mouth. And all the birds were filled with their flesh. Revelation 19:19-20 translated

The power that the beast of the earth will exercise, will not be his own. Instead of providing miracles, demonstrating power over nature, speaking to nature, etc. the beast of the earth will only be able to utilize the supernatural power and authority sourced by the red dragon / serpent / Satan, Inc. that will allow him to wield his use of magic, sorcery, occult practices, illusion, dark arts, etc.

A key component of the strategy of the beast of the earth will be to deceive the inhabitants of the earth into believing that his borrowed supernatural power and authority is actually his own. The beast of the earth will even be deluded into believing that this supernatural power is actually his own, in order to believe that he is supreme over God Most High and worthy to challenge the Lamb / Jesus Christ in global war.

The beast of the earth animates the idol / image of the beast of the sea – Revelation 13:11-18

One of the most astounding elements of biblical eschatology was the prophecy concerning the idol / image of the beast of the sea.

Almost two millennia ago, John the Revelator documented that an idol / image would be constructed on the temple mount. Idols and images were forbidden within the Law that God Most High provided to Moses and the people of Israel (Exodus 20:4-6, 34:17, Leviticus 26:1, 26:30, Numbers 33:51-52, Deuteronomy 4:15-25, 5:8-10, 7:5, 7:25, 12:3, 27:15, 32:16, 32:21, etc.). The God of the kingdom of heaven is living God, not able to be contained by the confines of inanimate material of any kind. Therefore, to have an idol / image constructed on the temple mount dedicated to God Most High, was recognized as disgusting to the theology of who the God of the kingdom of heaven is.

And then John the Revelator also documented almost two thousand years ago, that this idol / image will be given breath by a mere (created) human being, so that the idol / image will be able to speak.

It was God the Creator that breathed life into the first human man (Genesis 2:7). For a mere (created) human being to breathe life into a (created) idol / image that would be elevated in position to be worshiped, was also considered to be an insult to the creative work of God the Creator in creating humanity.

And breathing life into an idol / image was a depiction of the devaluation of human life that had breath given to humanity by God the Creator.

Probably the most amazing part of John the Revelator's vision of the idol / image of the beast of the sea, was the portrayal of an inanimate idol / image being given animacy. Even half a century ago, it was merely a dream that a robotic creation that would bear a resemblance to humanity, could be created. Robots, androids, artificial intelligence, etc. used to be fodder for Saturday morning cartoons and movies. Now they are being developed and marketed. But John the Revelator was provided with this vision that foresaw an idol / image of the beast of the sea being animated, around 95 AD.

The beast of the earth deceives those dwelling on the earth by reason of the signs that it was given to perform before the beast of the sea, telling those dwelling on the earth to make an image to the beast that was wounded by the sword and has lived.

The beast of the earth was given the ability to give breath to the image of the beast of the sea, so that the image of the beast of the sea should also speak. And the image of the beast of the sea will cause all who would not worship the image of the beast of the sea, to be killed. Revelation 13:14-15 translated

In the original Greek text, what was translated as 'an image,' was translated from the Greek word εικονα / eikona, and literally means 'icon.'

Currently, the nation of Israel is a world leader in technology. It is possible that the technology of Israel will be the technology that will bring the image to life. And even though the beast of the sea is antisemitic, the possibility that the technology that will bring the image to life would be Israeli technology, would be too great to allow antisemitic beliefs to inhibit acceptance of the idol / image, especially when it represents the beast of the sea.

The technology that will be involved in bringing the idol / image of the beast of the sea to life, will also provide

the beast of the sea with the means to achieve his dream of establishing global rule via controlling the inhabitants of the earth; their finances, their food, their living arrangements, their laws, their culture, their mandatory contributions to the global religious community, etc.

During the second half of the era of the time of Jacob's Trouble, as part of the demonstration of support for the beast of the sea, the beast of the earth will not merely erect an innocuous statue of the beast of the sea on the temple mount. He will erect a cyborg / robot / computer type image on the temple mount that will have the ability to monitor and demand compulsory worship of the idol / image of the beast of the sea. It will be a system whose tentacles will intrude upon the innermost pieces of every human being, interconnected with the mark of the beasts system. It will be a system with the ability to strip the individual of the opportunity to express their own autonomy. It will be the mechanism that will provide ultimate tyrannical control over individuals.

The beast of the earth will 'breathe life' into this idol / image of the beast of the sea, as a mimicry of God the Creator breathing life into humanity and providing human life with autonomy (Genesis 2:7). It is possible that this act of 'breathing life' could actually be the act of activating the 'image of the beast' with a source of seemingly endless energy which would make the 'image of the beast' impervious to dependency upon humanity and invulnerable to threats upon its operation.

(Note that the 'battery life' on this idol / image will run out after around forty two months of service (Revelation 13).)

Today robots accomplish face recognition, and have heads, eyes, arms and legs, that resemble actual human beings. They even move like human beings. They respond and interact in a human type form. Add in some forms of artificial intelligence, a prime directive has been established that is set on establishing global rule that will morph into tyrannical dictatorship.

At this point in human history, we have the technology to make it possible for the picture of the extreme nightmare depicted in the vision that Jesus Christ provided to John the Revelator, to be fully realized.

This idol / image of the beast of the sea will also be able to speak every language. In speaking every language the idol / image of the beast of the sea will overcome the language barrier that God Most High instituted just years after the flood at the construction of the tower of Babel empire, as a preventative against this kind of total world rebellious activity against God Most High and against the kingdom of heaven (Genesis 11:1-9).

The Holy Spirit gifted the disciples of messiah / the Lamb / Jesus Christ with the ability to speak in different languages (Acts 2). And the Holy Spirit will remove the language barrier during the Thousand Years Reign of Jesus Christ. But as a 'proof' that the beast of the earth should be recognized as greater than God Most High, this idol / image of the beast of the sea, will also transcend the language barrier.

The idol / image of the beast of the sea will also be able to 'make transactions' with human beings. The idol / image of the beast of the sea will receive worship, in exchange for the interconnected human being's opportunity to live. Its mannerisms will allow it to interact with human beings in a manner similar to priests interacting with congregants.

The level of control that this idol / image of the beast of the sea will enjoy, will hold over individual human beings will affect every aspect of human composition. No chains, no prisons, no prison guards required. And yet the idol / image of the beast will provide slavery at a level not yet experienced by humanity throughout human history.

The technology available for making the idol / image of the beast of the sea effective in its task – gene editing, artificial intelligence (AI), implants / Internet of Bodies (IoB), ability to hack humans

The Defense Advanced Research Projects Agency (DARPA) launched the Neural Evidence Aggregation Tool (NEAT) program that focuses on aggregating preconscious brain signals to determine what someone believes to be true. The NEAT program is supported by the Department of Defense with anticipation that it will be applied first to soldiers.

The Pentagon, and other defense departments of other nations, are also investigating how to fundamentally alter what it means to be human, funding research into creating super humans that are smarter, faster, and stronger through human performance enhancement.

November 2021, the Pentagon sponsored RAND report detailed how the US Defense and Intelligence communities are on the cusp of ushering in a new era of transhumanism by funding research into gene editing, artificial intelligence, and the Internet of Bodies (IoB), to enhance human performance.

The technological potentials of this controversial transhumanist research include potentially 'adding reptilian genes that provide the ability to see in infrared,' *and* 'making humans stronger, more intelligent, or more adapted to extreme environments.'
Technological Approaches to Human Performance Enhancement.

RAND says the modalities for human performance enhancement (HPE) can be grouped into three principal categories:

1. Gene editing
2. Applications of artificial intelligence (AI)
3. Networked technologies that are wearable or even implantable (the so-called Internet of Bodies (IoB))

According to the unelected architects of the great reset agenda, the IoB will be inexplicably linked to an individual's digital identity, which will determine what goods and services the individual will be able to access depending on both the individual's online and offline behavior.

Genetic editing, according to the RAND report, has the potential to:
1. Make humans stronger, more intelligent, or more adapted to extreme environments
2. Provide new capabilities (such as infrared vision)—applications with potential implications for military and intelligence operations

Examples of gene editing applications given in the report included:
1. Adding reptilian genes that provide the ability to see in infrared
2. Fostering specific physical attributes (e.g., ability to cope with low oxygen levels) that could aid warfighters
3. Increasing muscle mass in disease-free humans
4. Increasing an average runner's endurance to the level of an elite marathoner
5. For space travel and living on other planets: Adding genes from Deinococcus radiodurans, a bacterium that can survive in high levels of radiation, and adding genes from a variety of organisms to enable humans to synthesize all 20 amino acids (humans normally synthesize only 11 and extract the remaining nine from food)

The alteration of human genetics was the goal of the Nephilim breeding program during the antediluvian / preflood era of human history, and immediately afterward. The resulting Nephilim were larger, taller and stronger than the genetically pure humanity. But the Nephilim were also more fragile, with half of the life expectancy of the genetically pure humanity. And the Nephilim required a greater proportion of resources to sustain their lives. By all accounts, the Nephilim breeding program was assessed as a major disaster and required the deluge / flood to clean up the mess.

In the computer and AI culture, the point when computing will be determined to be faster, more efficient, more accurate and more effective than the human brain, was designated to be reaching singularity.

Ray Kurzweil anticipated that the ability of a computer would overtake the abilities of the human brain, and provide the point of singularity, sometime around 2045. Reaching the point of singularity would mark the obsolescence and endangerment of humanity as a living species. Since Kurzweil's initial predictions, the computing community shortened Kurzweil's anticipated date for achieving singularity.

Singularity would also anticipate the crossing over of human life into transhumanism, and the implementation of machine into the physical human being under the guise of augmenting human life and controlling all aspects of the human life experience. While transhumanism will be marketed as an improvement to human living and freedom from traditional human confines and ailments, in reality the trade will have been made to humanity giving up dominion of their own personal being to become a slave to the global governance of the oligarchy of rulers.

Astrobiology searches for extraterrestrial life (SETI / search for extraterrestrial intelligent life) with the concept that there may be other civilizations older and more advanced than our own, that have moved beyond their version of singularity. The further idea that has encouraged the search for extraterrestrial life has been the assumption that other older civilizations would be benevolent to the earthlings, sharing advancements that would improve earth's civilization. And extraterrestrial life may want a dryer climate than the earth so that humidity would not interfere with their electronic systems, and entangle their abilities for superconductivity in computing. A destruction of the earth's ecosystem would then be welcomed by extraterrestrial life to benefit computing and transhumanism.

With the implementation of the mark of the beasts system, the intricacies of every human being would be able to be monitored and controlled through the system. A person's mind and thoughts, wealth, ability to buy and sell, ability to travel, ability to work, etc. will all be monitored and permitted at the discretion of the new singularity that will manage the world's resources, 'for the greater good.'

In choosing the path of the mark of the beasts system, the human being would be altered in such a way as to be unredeemable. It would be a similar transition to the transformation that took place when the first man and *first woman ate the fruit of the tree of the knowledge of good and evil and became aware that they were naked (Genesis 3). One evidence of the truth of the events of Genesis 3, is that humanity wears clothes.*

Speaking to the unelected globalists at the World Economic Forum (WEF) annual meeting in Davos in 2020, Dr. Yuval Harari warned in his speech on How to Survive the 21st Century, that humans were no longer mysterious souls, but rather hackable animals that could be monitored and controlled by public and private entities in horrendous ways. While Dr. Harari claims to be an atheist, his warning eerily echoes John the Revelator's depiction of events with the establishment of the idol / image of the beast of the sea and the mark of the beasts system, during the future abomination of desolation event. Dr. Harari's observations also validate Daniel's observations concerning the events led by the little horn / eleventh king / final horn on the shaggy goat / king that will exalt himself in his global power grab.

'Governments, corporations, and armies are likely to use technology to enhance human skills that they need like intelligence and discipline while neglecting other human skills like compassion, artistic sensitivity, and spirituality' — Yuval Harari, WEF, 2020

'We humans should get used to the idea that we are no longer mysterious souls – we are now hackable animals. That's what we are.' *How to Survive the 21st Century* given by Yuval Harari, Professor in the Department of History, Hebrew University, 2020 World Economic Forum Annual Meeting, January 27, 2020

'Technology risks dividing the world into wealthy elites and exploited 'data colonies.''' *How to Survive the 21st Century* given by Yuval Harari, Professor in the Department of History, Hebrew University, 2020 World Economic Forum Annual Meeting, January 27, 2020

What will be presented as an aid to advancing human health, will morph into the surveillance of individuals. And then carefully crafted stimuli will be utilized that is designed to evoke specific mental processes.

With enough data about any individual, and with enough computing power and biological knowledge, a person's body, brain and life can be hacked. The equation is:

$B \times C \times D = AHH$

Biological knowledge multiplied by **C**omputing power multiplied by **D**ata equals the **A**bility to **H**ack **H**umans.

With the ability to hack humans, global governance will potentially have the power and ability to understand the human individual, better than the human individual understands one's self. Information on personality type, political views, sexual preference, mental weakness, fears and hopes that motivate an individual, etc. will all be able to be collected in a manner that will be much more effective than the system of reporting on family and neighbors that Hitler's Third Reich developed. And all this information will be collected specifically to be used for manipulating and controlling individuals to make global governance easier.

The rich and powerful elites who support global governance, will also be monitored by the total surveillance regimes, even more than the less wealthy and less powerful. But all will be controlled by the establishment of the digital dictatorship through the global algorithm.

Using the global algorithm, decisions on employment, residence, how family is comprised, diet, health care, etc. will be made for the inhabitants of the earth. This era will become a new era of enslavement for the inhabitants of the earth.

Daniel's understanding of the methodology of the plan of the final horn on the shaggy goat and of the king that will exalt himself – Daniel 8:23-25, 11:36, 11:39c

Daniel's prophecy described the dynamics of the plan of the final horn on the shaggy goat.

In the latter part of their reign, when rebels have become completely wicked, a fierce-looking king, a master of intrigue, will arise. The master of intrigue will become very strong, but not by his own power. The master of intrigue will cause astounding devastation and will succeed in whatever he does and will cause deceit to prosper, and he will consider himself superior.

When people feel secure, the master of intrigue will destroy many and take his stand against the Prince of princes / messiah. Yet the master of intrigue will be destroyed, but not by human power. Daniel 8:23-25

One of the effects of being a master of intrigue will be the final horn on the shaggy goat's ability to deceive the inhabitants of the earth. His deception will include his claim that he is greater than God Most High. And his breathing life into the idol / image of the beast of the sea will be one of his 'proofs' of his claim.

Daniel was also provided with a vision concerning the king who will exalt and magnify himself, who will rise during the era of the time of Jacob's Trouble, and who will defy the divinity and sovereignty of God Most High.

And as the king that will exalt and magnify himself, he will redistribute wealth.

The king will act according to his own will and he will exalt and magnify himself, above every god. And he will speak blasphemies against the God of gods. He will prosper until the time for wrath has been accomplished, for what has been determined, will be completed. Daniel 11:36 translated

And he will advance with glory, those who acknowledge him. He will make them rulers over many and distribute the land as a reward. Daniel 11:39b translated

Daniel's portrayal identified a man with the power and authority to present himself as an unbridled king, who is also able to hack into the equity of individuals. With his ability to determine which individuals will support him with their loyalty, he will redistribute that human equity and wealth to those that honor and acknowledge him.

Daniel's vision of the king that will exalt himself was provided to Daniel in 536 BC, over twenty five hundred years ago. And now it is possible for this prophecy to be fulfilled.

John the Revelator's understanding of the methodology of the plan of the two beasts of Revelation 13 and the implications of bringing the idol / image of the beast of the sea 'to life'

Along with the signs and wonders, magic, sorcery, occult practices, illusion, dark arts, calling fire to come down from heaven, etc., the two beasts of Revelation 13 will also entice the inhabitants of the earth to participate in the worship of the idol / image of the beast of the sea and

participate in the mark of the beasts system, because of their promise of their version of virtual eternal life.

When the beast of the sea will have survived his near fatal wound, the two beasts of Revelation 13 will capitalize upon that event and offer it as evidence that they have the knowledge, power and authority to offer to the inhabitants of the earth, 'eternal life.'

Breathing life into the idol / image of the beast of the sea, will serve as further evidence of their claim to control 'eternal life.'

But the version of eternal life that the two beasts of Revelation 13 will offer, will be a virtual eternal life, based upon reaching the omega point of modern evolutionary theory and upon the promise that the memories, the experiences, and the essence of human beings, will be stored in the nonexistent noosphere.

One of its heads was as if it was having been slain to death. And its wound of death was healed, and all the earth marveled after the beast.

The people of the earth, worshiped the dragon who had given authority to the beast of the sea. They worshiped the beast of the sea, saying, 'Who is like the beast? Who is able to make war against it?' Revelation 13:3-4 translated

All inhabitants of the earth will worship the beast — all whose names have not been written in the book of life belonging to the Lamb who was slain, that began to be written from the creation of the world. Revelation 13:8 translated

The beast of the earth deceives those dwelling on the earth by reason of the signs that it was given to perform before the beast of the sea, telling those dwelling on the earth to make an image to the beast that was wounded by the sword and has lived.

The beast of the earth was given the ability to give breath to the image of the beast of the sea, so that the image of the beast of the sea should also speak. The image of the beast of the sea will cause all who would not worship the image of the beast of the sea, to be killed. Revelation 13:14-15 translated

The animated idol / image of the beast of the sea will be attractive, drawing people to it, causing people to desire to worship it.

And with the animated idol / image of the beast of the sea, and the other 'proof' that the two beasts of Revelation 13 present to support their claim that they have power and authority over life and death, the two beasts

will declare that God the Creator was not truthful in proclaiming that in the day that the first man and first woman rebelled against God the Creator, that they and all their descendants would die. The two beasts of Revelation 13 will declare that it is no longer necessary to seek out God Most High's redemption, reclamation and regeneration plan, in order to experience an eternal life in paradise.

But just as the 'resurrection' / healing of the near fatal wound of the beast of the sea will be a deception, the 'resurrected eternal life' that the two beasts of Revelation 13 offer, will also be a deception. And when the two witnesses that will be assassinated by the beast of the sea / beast from the Abyss are resurrected (Revelation 11:1-14), it will be proof of the deception provided by the two beasts of Revelation 13 to the inhabitants of the earth. And when the two beasts of Revelation 13 are defeated by messiah / the Lamb / Jesus Christ in the final battle of this era, it will also be proof of the deception they will have perpetrated.

Modern evolutionary theory's cosmology, omega point, noosphere (sphere of human cognitive process), etc., and its application within the idol / image of the beast of the sea

Evolutionary theory is a religion.

The basic components of religions include having a theory of origin (abiogenesis, astrobiology, cosmology, anthropology, etc.); having a theory of the nature of God / gods / lack of God and the relationship of humanity with god(s) (hamartiology, Christology, soteriology, pneumology, justification, etc.); and having a theory on how the age will end and what will follow the transition that takes place at the end of the age (eschatology, regeneration).

1. Modern evolutionary theory has a <u>theory of origins</u> and the book by Charles Robert Darwin has been referenced as the source for laying out the foundation for the theory of origins of modern evolutionary theory: *On the Origin of Species by Means of Natural Selection, or the Preservation of Favoured Races in the Struggle for Life*, November 24, 1859.
2. Modern evolutionary theory has a <u>theory of the nature of God / gods</u>. Modern evolutionary

theory claims there is no God of Creation; no person of God who is active in the cosmos; no God who is capable of defeating the enemies of the kingdom of heaven; no God for humanity to be accountable to; etc. For modern evolutionary theorists, God is not an omnipotent personal entity, but God is an idea and ideology.
3. Most importantly, modern evolutionary theory has an <u>eschatology</u>. And that eschatology was based upon unprovable philosophical ideas, and the promises of modern evolutionary leaders in the realm of scientism.

The vision that John the Revelator presented of the animation of the idol / image of the beast of the sea, was a depiction of an essential marker in human history in the advancement of time on the scale of modern evolutionary theory. God knew ahead of time, that modern evolutionary theorists would have this mindset at this time in human history. For modern evolutionary theorists, the animation of the idol / image of the beast of the sea will mark when humanity and the earth will enter into the final preparation for attaining a new level of consciousness. Attaining this new level of consciousness will be essential in the attempt to incorporate present biological human life into the next major advancement of life.

Pierre Teilhard de Chardin (1881 to 1955) was a major advocate who advanced this new form of thinking that dispensed with the activity of God Most High in the world, and exchanged the idea that humanity could supersede beyond the authority and power of God Most High. This idealized proposal for the advancement of life would allow humanity to determine humanity's own form and definition of 'eternal life,' devoid of God the Creator's form for eternal life, devoid of God the Creator's activity in providing eternal life, and most importantly devoid of God the Creator's law and rules for dwelling with God the Creator during the span of eternal life.

Pierre Teilhard de Chardin was a French Jesuit priest, who claimed to be a scientist. He took part in the 'discoveries' of the Piltdown man and the Peking man, which were fossils that were presented as 'proof' of modern evolutionary theory. Teilhard utilized his fake fossils and the invented narrative of the fossils and the Roman Catholic Church's influence, to advance the adoption of modern evolutionary theory globally into school curriculums, and to infuse modern evolutionary theory into scientific thought in his attempt to separate authentic biblical Christianity from authentic science. When Teilhard's fossils were proven to be hoaxes, there was no retraction of the teaching of modern evolutionary theory. Modern evolutionary theory continued in its insistence that authentic science was devoid of the authentic truth within authentic religion.

For Teilhard de Chardin, human life was not defined by the physical limitations that the physical human body provides in its human existence. For Teilhard, the mind was essential and the body was disposable in the experience of human life. In Teilhard's essay, *The Phenomenon of Man*, 1930 / 1955, Teilhard described evolution as a process that leads to increasing complexity, culminating in the unification of consciousness. Teilhard's rules for evolution required that humanity would be ever advancing, never regressing.

Modern evolutionary theory defies historical evidences such as prior to the Dark Ages / Middle Ages / medieval period, humanity was more educated and accomplished than during the later Dark Ages / Middle Ages / medieval period. And at the time of the deluge / flood, humanity had the scientific knowledge to breed Nephilim, a knowledge that has not been able to be replicated. And in ancient history, humanity was able to construct temples using huge stones cut with a precision that cannot be duplicated today and were able to set the huge stones that today would be a challenge to set even with modern innovations and equipment. Etc.

Modern evolutionary theory defies or requires the suspension of the second law of thermodynamics. Order does not naturally increase. Order decreases throughout time.

Modern evolutionary theory also defies that God the Creator originally created humanity to live in a physical body and to experience physical pleasures and to live eternally. Modern evolutionary theory rejects the physical bodily resurrection of Jesus Christ who in his resurrected body, walked, talked, ate with disciples, was able to be touched, etc. And modern evolutionary theory also rejects that Jesus Christ fulfilled the prophecy of the feast of firstfruits in his resurrection, so that all who were believers in messiah (BC) and followers of the Lamb (AD) would be resurrected with an eternal glorified physical body as well.

There are no authentic physical proofs for modern evolutionary theory.

The resurrected, ascended physical Jesus Christ (30 AD), who lives and waits to return to earth, acts as proof of the coming physical resurrection of God's holy people (soon).

In defiance of the biblical record's explanation of God the Creator acting during the first week of creation (Genesis 1-2), Teilhard developed within his perspective, four stages for the evolutionary development of the cosmos:
1. *From 'creation' (without a Creator God, and accidental) or origins, to the existence of life: geogenesis / cosmogenesis - physical universe cosmosphere / geosphere / the age of inanimate matter*
2. *From the existence of life, to the development of humans: biogenesis - biosphere / the age of biological life*
3. *From the development of humans, to the point of Christ: homogenesis, noogenesis, psychogenesis - noosphere / the age of human life*

4. *From the point of Christ, to the Omega Point: christogenesis - pneumatosphere / the age of life in a virtual sense of reality*

Among the many ideas that Teilhard espoused in the process of denouncing and defying the activity of God the Creator, Teilhard believed that the earth was born by accident, through the development of a prebiosphere.

Following the accidental development of a prebiosphere, emerged the biosphere with elemental matter, chemicals and the particles that became ordered into life.

This biosphere of human life as we know it, is to be followed by the point where the idea of Christ will merge with human life and institute a new age for human life in the noosphere.

The noosphere will conclude with humanity's achievement of attaining the ability to achieve a collective consciousness that is no longer tied to anything physical (except the computer system that continues to provide the resources to sustain the collective consciousness), in the pneumatosphere.

Through Teilhard's definition of the stages of modern evolutionary theory, Teilhard was able to merge pieces of his religious understanding with his imaginary vision for the future. This merger of Teilhard's selected pieces of religious understanding with his imagined narrative of science, and Teilhard's position as a Jesuit priest, served to advance modern evolutionary theory throughout the world, and especially in the Roman Catholic Church's hierarchy; influencing the Second Vatican Council (1962 to 1965), further influencing the Vatican Observatory (~1540 to present), and promoted by the current pope.

Geogenesis and biogenesis

For modern evolutionary theory to eliminate the narrative of God the Creator's activity in the past (the week of creation (Genesis 1-2)) and God the Creator's activity in the future (regenerating the Garden of Eden /

garden of God / paradise (Revelation 21-22)), modern evolutionary theorists were challenged to develop an alternative narrative. That alternative narrative began with ideas such as the Gaia hypothesis / Gaia principle.

The Gaia hypothesis was named after the primordial deity who personified earth in Greek mythology. The Gaia hypothesis claimed that out of the primordial conditions that came to exist on earth, there was a coevolution of life that included the interaction of life forms to provide for life to further evolve.

The Gaia hypothesis / Gaia principle proposed that after matter had evolved (as if matter were itself a living thing that could evolve into existence), simple living organisms were generated. Those living organisms interacted with their inorganic surroundings on earth to form a synergistic and self-regulating complex system that helped to maintain and perpetuate the conditions for more complex lifeforms to survive on the planet.

An example of this interactive evolution was claimed to be the activity of photosynthetic bacteria that modified the earth's atmosphere to turn it aerobic for the support of other forms of life. Subsequent individual species pursued their own self-interests and brought further environmental change that allowed for more complex life forms to evolve into existence.

Formulated by the chemist James Lovelock and the microbiologist Lynn Margulis, the Gaia hypothesis further proposed that because the foundation for the evolution of higher life forms rests upon the previous development provided by lower life forms and the environment created by those previous lower lifeforms, that the elements that determine the stability of the earth, such as global temperature, salinity of seawater, atmospheric oxygen levels, the maintenance of a hydrosphere of liquid water, etc., affecting the habitability of the earth, can be influenced by humanity.

And if humanity has the power to control the climate on the earth, the influence of the sun and moon on the earth, etc., then it would reason that humanity could cause its own evolution into a higher form of life, into a new species, a new creation; without the influence or presence of the biblically defined God of the kingdom of heaven.

In contrast to the ideas of the Gaia hypothesis / Gaia principle (named after a Greek mythology primordial deity), the psalmist documented: Know that the Lord is God. It is he who made us, and we are his. We are his people, the sheep of his pasture. Psalm 100:3

The prophet Nehemiah claimed: 'You are the Lord, you alone. You have made heaven, the heaven of heavens, with all their host, the earth and all that is on it, the seas and all that is in them; and you preserve all of them; and the host of heaven worships you.' Nehemiah 9:6 ESV

John the Revelator claimed in the gospel of John that in the beginning was the Word, and the Word was with God, and the Word was God. He was in the beginning with God. All things were made through him, and without him was not anything made that was made. John 1:1-3 ESV

Paul claimed: For his invisible attributes, namely, his eternal power and divine nature, have been clearly perceived, ever since the creation of the world, in the things that have been made. So they are without excuse. Romans 1:20 ESV

They exchanged the truth about God for a lie and worshiped and served the creature rather than the Creator, who is blessed forever! Amen. Romans 1:25 ESV

And Paul claimed: Yet for us there is one God, the Father, from whom are all things and for whom we exist, and one Lord, Jesus Christ, through whom are all things and through whom we exist. 1 Corinthians 8:6 ESV

And Paul also claimed that by him all things were created, in heaven and on earth, visible and invisible, whether thrones or dominions or rulers or authorities – all things were created through him and for him. And he is before all things, and in him all things hold together. Colossians 1:16-17 ESV

The twenty four elders in heaven are continually claiming: 'You are worthy, our Lord and God, to receive glory and honor and power, for you created all things, and by your will they were created and have their being.' Revelation 4:11

(See also Job 26:7, 33:4, Psalm 14:1, 19:1-4, 33, 90:2, 96:5, 139:13, Proverbs 16:4, Isaiah 37:16, 42:5, 44:24, 45:18, 64:8, Jeremaih 10:11-13, 32:17, Luke 1:37, Acts 17:26-28, Romans 1:18-20, 8:38-39, Hebrews 3:4, 11:3, 11:6, 40:28, James 1:17, 2 Peter 3:5, 1 John 4:8, Revelation 10:6 (The fact that God created the cosmos will be the reason why the God of

the kingdom of heaven will have the authority and power to determine that there will be no more delay.), etc.)

Noogenesis (evolutionary process that will result in mind achieving mastery over matter / the physical portion of what defines life)

In the fantasy of modern evolutionary theory's eschatology, the era of biogenesis that humanity currently experiences, will transition into the era of homogenesis, noogenesis, psychogenesis - noosphere / the age of human life, during which humanity will be evolving in preparation to fully integrate the concept of Christ into the collective cosmic consciousness of the Omega Point.

The era of noogenesis loosely corresponds to the era that the biblical record referenced as the Thousand Years Reign of Jesus Christ.

The noogenesis will provide humanity with time to develop the ever increasing consciousness. Because a theme of modern evolutionary theory is the human mind as an emergent from life and life itself as an emergent from matter, the idea presented is that there will be a time when the conscious mind of the evolved humanity, will be able to be separated from the confines of the physical portion of biological living.

The biblical record's documentation of the animation of the idol / image of the beast of the sea, was a recognition of the attempt of leaders in modern evolutionary theory to attempt to force humanity to advance on their modern evolutionary timeline of history.

The assumption will be that with the animation of the idol / image of the beast of the sea, humanity will move closer to the point of Christ / Omega Point. (Notice the reference to a redefined imagined and idealized Christ, not Jesus Christ the fully human being who was also real, divine, sovereign and already resurrected into eternal life.) For Teilhard, Christ was more of a concept or a marker in time of the achievement of an idea. And for Teilhard, the idea of Christ provided the collection of the consciousness of humanity in the pneumatosphere (mind), merged with the shedding of the physicalness that confines humanity in a limited space (physical body).

Among modern evolutionary theorists, time itself is a confine of space. Time is the 'mind' of motion. The act of materializing / creating or evolving matter, is the 'mind' of matter. And the experience of living is therefore the 'mind' of what makes our imaginary life a perceived reality.

Teilhard's narrative of the origins of thought recognized that with the advent of thought, a new dimension was added to the earth and its evolution - the phenomenon of man (noogenesis). This new consciousness was also a reflection; consciousness turned back upon itself. This reflection of consciousness meant that humanity was not merely knowing, but knowing that it could be known. With this kind of reflective consciousness, Teilhard proposed that impressions and experiences could be knitted together and fused into a unity of consciousness. Once consciousness is fully established, then the physical portion of human life would become superfluous.

For Teilhard, man is unique because of humanity's ability to consciously understand that he not only knows, but he knows that he knows. Because humanity can mark time into the past and into the future, unperceived by other forms of life, humanity's power of understanding should translate into being boundless. In Teilhard's theory, man has an unlimited capacity for acquiring and transmitting information, and then assessing the quality of the information he receives. Man, even with his finite limitations upon the individual mind) then becomes his own arbitrator for determining what is true and false, accepting what is true and rejecting what is false. Teilhard insists that the world itself is reasonable and that the human mind has the capacity to fully understand and embrace the reasonableness of the world. For Teilhard, man can arrive at truths about the world, by degrees, and apart from answers supplied by the biblical God of Creation.

To compensate for the finite limitations of the single human mind, modern evolutionary theory proposed that a collective consciousness could be developed. This collective consciousness would provide the unification of all thoughts of all humanity. The collective consciousness would be able to find those portions of thought that are missing in the minds of single human individuals.

Teilhard argued that with the evolution of a collective consciousness, each individual would experience a sense of completeness through the process of joining the collective mind separated from the physical. Teilhard also argued that all of humankind bears a profound sense of responsibility for the shape of its own future, and that humanity's future must be developed in close interrelation with all forms of life, with the whole of nature in its global and planetary dimensions.

Teilhard's proposal would require that all of humanity, would need to be merged into this collective consciousness. Each individual mind would supply pieces of knowledge with the implication that if an individual did not join the collective consciousness, that piece of knowledge would potentially be inaccessible to the collective consciousness.

Noosphere (planetary mind)

Biocenosis was a termed coined (1877) by Karl August Mobius (1825 to 1908), describing the interacting of organisms living together in a habitat / biotope.

A noocenosis is an artificial biological community (biocenosis) built upon a degraded ecosystem, and is the result of structural improvements by man that differs from the original evolutionarily constructed biological community. Similar terms are noobiocenosis, noobiogeocenosis and noocenology.

The term noosphere was first used in the publications of Pierre Teilhard de Chardin in his Cosmogenesis (1922). Nous / νοος (Greek) indicated 'mind,' 'reason.' The noosphere was considered to be the next evolutionary layer resulting from human reason merged with their version of scientific thought.

Vladimir Ivanovich Vernadsky (1863 to 1945) defined the noosphere as the new state of the biosphere and described it as the planetary 'sphere of reason'. The noosphere represents the highest stage of biospheric development, that of humankind's rational activities.

Teilhard's conception of modern evolutionary theory incorporated the development of a collective identity where the individuality of humanity would necessarily decrease for the collective 'life' to adapt to the increasing levels of depth and complexity. From this evolutionary process, a thinking layer would envelop the earth like the atmosphere. This new membrane / noosphere / new consciousness / new mind, was accredited as providing the world with a soul / noosphere. Each particle awakens to itself through social experience, and then harmonizes / internalizes the universe accessible to it from its experiences, having been absorbed in a legacy of augmented consciousness.

The noosphere would become a social network of thought and emotion in which all would be immersed, and be able to share memories and experiences. The collective mind / network of consciouses, would also be coerced to experience others' mental memories and experiences. And because of the nature of virtual reality, the mental memories and experiences of others would seem to be reality for other minds connected to the collective consciousness.

The divine milieu was defined as a field of divine energy with a central focal point that is both immanent and wholly transcendent at the same time.

And with the development of Teilhard's vision for science and technology, it would be possible to expand the human sphere of influence to allow a person to be simultaneously present in every corner of the world.

While God the Creator created each individual to possess personal consciousness and to encounter unique individual experiences, Teilhard presented the contradictory idea that conscious is not synonymous with life (geogenesis). With his denial of creation as the theory of origin, Teilhard substituted the idea that the earth was born by accident and that with that accident, the consciousness was imprisoned in the primordial dust and began to exercise a tension which continued to become the evolution of nature. For Teilhard, this evolutionary tension could only be relieved (establish peace) through the evolution of a collective consciousness.

While God the Creator designed human beings to be in relationship with God, Teilhard determined that humanity was destined to evolve enough to be separated from God. Teilhard's humanity was destined to shape its own experiences separated from the influence of God. 'You are not a human being in search of spiritual experiences. You are a spiritual being immersed in human experience.' Pierre Teilhard de Chardin

A tenet of modern evolutionary theory's eschatology is that humanity will someday evolve to be able to separate mind from body, shedding the physical to mentally join with the collective of consciousness. And yet the same adherents to modern evolutionary theory believe that salvation will be found in 'saving the planet' which remains an endeavor to save what is physical matter.

According to modern evolutionary theory, physical matter was vital in the past stages of evolution. But no answer was provided for why physical matter will no longer be vital for future stages of evolution.

Modern evolutionary theory proposed that a superior form of existence can be reached if we but think and walk in the direction in which the lines passed by evolution take on their maximum coherence.

In modern evolutionary theory, the past life passed from prehominids to modern man. And in the future, life will be passed from modern man to a new species that will be more evolved. This should make humanity obsolete and susceptible to extinction. But in this end of the dream for humanity, Teilhard saw a light in the evolution and rise of the collective consciousness. So, while a person will lose his or her individuality in the multitude, he or she will not lose his or her potential for hyperpersonality.

Teilhard argued that a personal identity would remain in the fully evolved cosmos of Teilhard's imagination, imprinted upon the 'eternal' collective consciousness.

Modern evolutionary theory proposed that when experiences are shared through the minds of the collective, there will develop a heterogeneity, sharing a common set of values, thinking in the same way. And with that heterogeneity, conflict will fade away and a form of peace will be developed.

And yet Teilhard sought to integrate through interfaith dialogue, the conflicting diversity of religious and spiritual ideas, to be incorporated as elements of his noospheric diversity.

During the era of the time of Jacob's Trouble, the idol / image of the beast of the sea will be tasked with determining the acceptability of the worship of the idol / image, and the responsibility to make judgement against the inhabitants of the earth. Through the elimination of divergent thought by the idol / image of the beast of the sea, diversity that would oppose the new proposed religion of the two beasts of Revelation 13, would be eliminated, with 'peace' being achieved within the network of collective consciousness.

The beast of the earth was given the ability to give breath to the image of the beast of the sea, so that the image of the beast of the sea should also speak. And the image of the beast of the sea will cause all who would not worship the image of the beast of the sea, to be killed.

The beast of the earth causes all the small and the great, and the rich and the poor, and the free and the servants, that it should give them a mark on their right hand or on their forehead, 17 so that no one should be able to buy or to sell, if they did not have the mark — the name of the beast, or the number of the name of the beast. Revelation 13:15-17 translated

Teilhard's cosmology also entirely obscured the scriptural meaning of sin. Even though Teilhard determined that sin was evil, sin was defined by natural reason. And evil was determined to be the manifestation of any sort of imperfection or disorder. Evil and sin would

eventually be eliminated with the development of free personality and the completion of the individual deriving law exclusively from himself, and apart from the biblically defined God of the kingdom of heaven.

Utilizing modern evolutionary theory, when the individual has effectively envisioned himself to become the author of the definition of law and sin, then the individual provides for himself self-redemption and is no longer in need of a redemption by the cosmic Christ. This is a theology that is currently taught in a substantial number of churches, and it will influence the receptivity of humanity to worship the idol / image of the beast of the sea, and to subscribe to the mark of the beasts system.

The biblical depiction of the worship of the idol / image of the beast of the sea and the subscription of humanity to the mark of the beasts system, corresponded to the modern evolutionists concepts of the gateway to the development of the noosphere.

Omega Point

Modern evolutionary theorists proposed that the completion of the development of the noosphere (homogenesis, noogenesis, psychogenesis, age of human life), would culminate with the Omega Point.

The Omega Point will usher in christogenesis, the pneumatosphere, the age of life in a virtual sense of reality.

Teilhard's vision of Christ was as a portal in the evolutionary movement toward the Omega Point. Because the Roman Catholic Church hierarchy holds that Jesus Christ died without a physical bodily resurrection, Christ became a visual illustration of an ideal of resurrection, and a model for an imagined life lived in a spiritual realm without the confines of the physical.

Modern evolutionary theory also proposed the concept of the evolution of a pneumatosphere, as a sphere of supreme spiritual and moral values which will accumulate and translate the human spiritual experience.

Teilhard's Omega Point will be a significant marker in the progress of physical human evolution.

After the Omega Point, all that will remain of humanity will be its collective consciousness, a virtual collection of memories derived from the minds that comprise the collective consciousness, of real past experiences. And that virtual collection of the memories of experiences contained in the collective mind, will be thrust upon other minds within the collective consciousness to provide an 'infinite' involvement of memories and experiences. Because the individual mind encapsulated within the collective consciousness would have access to all other collected memories and experiences, the collective consciousness would be able to live virtually for an eternity (or until the collected memories and experiences were exhausted).

The Omega Point was defined as that point when human history would begin a form of reflection upon itself. From the Omega point, humanity's evolution would insert itself into past history, in order to alter history for the purpose of making possible, the future process of christogenesis and the development of the pneumatosphere.

The proposal of modern evolutionary theorists was that the veracity of human experience itself is dependent upon the existence of consciousness. Modern evolutionary theory asks, what proof is there that the human life experience was not already translated into a virtual reality and is currently merely perceived as human life experience?

For modern evolutionary theorists, human life experience may have already reached the Omega Point without realizing it. Conscious minds would not even necessarily know that they are in this form of emulation. Current human life may already be merely a form of sleep or a dream, without being able to determine the difference between being awake or being in a dream.

Teilhard presented a vision of the movement of the universe with a gradual increasing complexity, to reach unity and thereby move from chaos to a great oneness. In his attempt to mix aspects of religion into his ideals of science, he envisioned the social advancement of humanity to eventually reach a final state of absolute collective consciousness which he called the Omega Point (reminiscent of Jesus Christ's declaration that he is the alpha and the omega).

In defiance of the biblical definition of what resurrected human living with Jesus Christ would be like, Teilhard's representation was that humanity would advance to overwhelm the biblically defined Christ. Humanity (or its more evolved life form) would develop beyond Teilhard's perception of a limited Christ, to advance the evolution of life into eternity, continually returning to past historical points prior to the Omega Point, in order to improve upon the evolutionary process.

And there was no definition offered in Teilhard's imaginary world, for the role of Teilhard's redefined Christ, after the Omega Point.

August Ferdinand Mobius (1790 to 1868), (probably not a relative of Karl August Mobius (1825 to 1908)), was a descendant of the Protestant Reformer Martin Luther. As a mathematician and astronomer, he presented the Mobius strip.

A Mobius strip is formed when a strip of paper is given a half twist, and then one end is connected to the other end of the strip of paper. This provides a continual closed surface with only one side, that resembles the number 8 (also the shape of the symbol for infinity ∞). Even slicing the Mobius strip down its center line, continues to result in one endless strand. Consequently, following a line on the Mobius strip always results in being brought back to the beginning point.

(Why did the chicken cross the Mobius strip? To get to the same side.)

Mobius strip conveyor belts last longer because the entire surface area receives a similar amount of wear. The character of the Mobius strip allows for recording tapes to become continuous loop recording tapes. Etc.

With the Mobius strip, Mobius discovered the nonorientable, two dimensional surface embedded within three dimensional Euclidean space. With the Mobius strip, fixed dimensions in space were recognized as fluid. The conception of geometry occupying more than three dimensions was introduced. The Mobius strip also provided the conceptualization that space can exist without volume.

Jesus Christ declared that he is the alpha and omega / the beginning and the end. With a Mobius strip, it can be envisioned that the beginning and the end can coexist in one point.

The concept of the Mobius strip also reflected the concept that the unity of the believers in messiah (BC) and the followers of the Lamb (AD) cannot be broken by space or time. With the omnipresence of the God of the kingdom of heaven, God can transcend both space and time, to provide life that is boundless. And the God of the kingdom of heaven holds a connection through the Holy Spirit, that links all God's holy people with the God of the kingdom of heaven, throughout time and throughout space.

Even modern evolutionary theorists recognized the intelligent design in the foundation of the earth. The concept of the Omega Point provided an explanation for the intelligent design of the universe, without the action of the God of the kingdom of heaven.

Because the universe was so obviously a result of intelligent design, it was unreasonable to assume that the universe resulted from an unintelligent and blind process. Therefore, the explanation was presented that the universe resembles a huge Mobius strip, with humanity traveling on it to return to the first point. In this way, the dimension of time intercepted and merged into the dimensions of space. In this imaginary vision of human existence, the future and more evolved life form was brought back to provide the intelligence of design necessary for biological life to exist in the present. For this reason, the future Omega Point is essential to ensure that current life in this time, exists. Sir Fred Hoyle defined this as a backward looped causation that brings about its own creation.

In modern evolutionary theory, the randomization that exists in the universe, will be brought to the point of singularity that will provide definitive order, so that the order will go back in time to establish randomization.

The Omega Point will demark the full evolution of the universe, and as such Omega living will not be a part of the current universe. It was defined as the place where the actual computer that runs all the informational processes of which we are made, will be the source for monitoring / controlling all space, time, matter and energy.

In that place, the rules for existence will be established through computers and the type of existence will become a subset, without the necessity of obeying the laws of thermodynamics, or allowing humanity to determine the minimal portion of life necessary to sustain itself. Because the cosmos, the earth and human life were presented as reflexive upon themselves, the assumption that a computer will be running the world should not be made; rather the computer that will run the world should be considered to be a function of that world, that will be finitely unbounded.

The Omega Point, point of singularity was presented as the point where all the universes implode into a single point in order to begin again. But there was no detailed definition offered of a process for moving out from the Omega Point for life to begin again, no stimulus for movement in the direction of the spontaneity of new life, no insurance that the new life that originates from the point of singularity will be better and not worse than the current existence, and no definition for how eternal consistency of the new life would be accomplished. Responsibility for eternal existence would be placed with the computer system itself and the computer system would be motivated by love, to not 'unplug' the mental collaboration of the 'human life' that it was entrusted to maintain.

Teilhard's adherents stressed that it was more important to consider the mental stimulation of Teilhard's *thesis that union with the concept of God would be the final result of the evolution of the earth, than to become preoccupied with the accuracy of Teilhard's theories.*

Because modern evolutionary theorists who proposed deep thoughts about this illusionary future, also fancied themselves to be adept theologians, the ideologies for what they presented as the definitions of God reworked the description of the God presented in the biblical record. With the evolution that would follow the Omega point, it was envisioned that that future evolved life would become a godlike entity and essentially create a god that would be omnipresent. The concept of the Omega god's omnipresence would require that its god would incorporate all religious ideals and theologies.

Modern evolutionary theorists did not recognize that if the Omega god were to actually incorporate all religious ideals and theologies, that the Omega god would become unable to separate good from evil. Not being able to separate good from evil would invalidate the moral system that would have been developed through christogenesis.

In this inventive imaginary scenario, the Garden of Eden was also equated with the Omega Point. While the original Garden of Eden was a real entity in a real location, the future Omega version of the Garden of Eden will promise to allow for an infinite number of iterations, while remaining confined to the number of mental experiences that will have been uploaded into the computer system. And the assumption was that human beings will willingly upload themselves / their mental experiences, into the Omega Garden of Eden computer system. The origin of the future Omega version of the Garden of Eden was not defined, except to assume that it will be a pattern that will appear out of nowhere and appear to have been created, without a creator, and without the confines of an actual physicality.

Because the premise of Teilhard, John Barrow, Frank Tipler and others, was that a god who creates does not yet exist and therefore god did not exist to provide creation. Humanity currently dwells in a godless universe.

Therefore, to bring about any realization of god, will require evolution to finally realize the Omega Point. The Omega Point then creates the world, but only after the world creates the Omega Point (The Anthropic Cosmological Principle). With the arrival of the Omega Point, the Omega Point will raise the virtual cyberspace computerized emulations of human beings from death, billions of years from now and provide human emulations of eternal life. They proposed that self-replicating humanoid or android computers will come to inhabit all the Milky Way, and then move on to conquer other galaxies. This form of advancement will require that intelligent machines will come to be regarded as people and ultimate heirs, and will possess the ability to reproduce themselves.

With the redefinition of god, leaders in modern evolutionary theory also redefined hell. The new definition described hell as the infinitely prolonged individuated consciousness devoid of all value enhancing enrichments including hope. Hell would be an experience of misery; authoritarian animosity to knowledge; cowardly adventure avoidance; being emersed in hatred, resentment, selfishness, interpersonal insensitivity, destructive interests; etc.

Barrow and Tipler offered their predictions as their Final Anthropic Principle (FAP). Marvin Gardner renamed their principle the Completely Ridiculous Anthropic Principle (CRAP).

Teilhard's personal credo

Instead of marking his life with a creed like the Apostles' Creed, Teilhard depicted his life with this creed (1971):

> I believe that the universe is an evolution.
> I believe that evolution proceeds towards spirit.
> I believe that spirit is fully realized in a form of personality.
> I believe that the supremely personal is the universal Christ.

Note that the universal Christ was not the Jesus Christ as defined in the biblical record.

Teilhard placed his faith in the future and his faith in man to fully develop the evolutionary process of human beings (a theme from *The Future of Man*). Teilhard truly believed that with the development of human consciousness, there would be a continuity of life. And yet, this continuity of life was also defined through the evolution of humanity into a higher form of life that would render humanity itself to become obsolete and discardable.

(How is it possible for Teilhard's harmonization to occur between the higher form of life and the inferior humanity? Teilhard's imaginary cosmos did not supply an answer for this.)

Some other prominent thinkers who ascribed to Teilhard's theology either in part or as a whole: Vladimir Vernadsky, Edouard Le Roy, John Barrow, Henri Bergson, Kenneth Boulding, Richard Dawkins, Theodosius Dobzhansky, Pavel Florensky, Edward Fredkin, Mikhail Gorbachev, Fred Hoyle, Julian Huxley, James Lovelock, Lynn Margulis, Marshall McLuhan, Nikita Moiseyev, Dorion Sagan, Rafal Serafin, Edward Suess, Frank Tipler, and Arnold Toynbee.

Critiques of Teilhard's imaginary scheme of the transformation of the cosmos throughout time, have pointed out that for the past six thousand years, the structure of DNA has substantially remained the same. Humanity has not been successful in the past six thousand years, in introducing new DNA to already established forms.

The questions that will challenge humanity during the era of the time of Jacob's Trouble will include:

Will trust be placed in the offer of the two beasts of Revelation 13 to provide an eternal life shaped by their vision? Or will trust be placed in the offer of God Most High to provide an eternal life in which Jesus Christ has already provided the path and that God Most High *invested six thousand years of human history preparing for?*

Will trust be placed in the kingdom that the two beasts of Revelation 13 represent? Or will trust be placed in the kingdom of heaven that will send the two witnesses from heaven to personally oppose the two beasts of Revelation 13?

Will trust be placed in the mark of the beasts system to provide for the necessities of life? Or will trust be placed in God the Father who makes provision for one's daily bread?

Will worship be given to the idol / image of the beast of the sea? Or will God the Father's name be recognized as holy?

Will trust be placed in the kingdom that promises an eternal life that consists of a virtual living existence of the mind (with no guarantee that 'living' will be activated and not unplugged in the future)? Or will trust be placed in the kingdom of heaven that has already provided proof of a physical resurrected eternal life through the physical resurrected eternal life of the fully human Jesus Christ?

Will trust be placed in the kingdom that remembers one's debts and shortcomings, and then extracts payment from the one who has debts and shortcomings, for the sake of the greater good and in the exercise of a redefined version of 'love'? Or will trust be placed in the kingdom that forgives its citizens' debts?

Will trust be placed in the kingdom that allows each adherent to write their own laws, rules, etc., even when it brings destruction to one's self and others? Or will trust be placed in the kingdom that provides deliverance from the evil one?

(Matthew 6:9-13, Luke 11:2-4)

Will trust be placed in the kingdom that rebels against creation and God the Creator's rules for the existence of life? Or will trust be placed in God the Creator and the rules established by God the Creator that made it possible for life to exist and to be sustained? (Psalm 8:3-5)

Will trust be placed in the kingdom that values physical treasures stored on earth that can be physically ruined or stolen? Or will trust be placed in the kingdom that values treasures stored in heaven where the treasure cannot be physically ruined or stolen?

Will trust be placed in the kingdom where every piece of sustenance, clothing and shelter, must be a matter of concern? Or will trust be placed in the kingdom that provides out of abundance and eliminates worry?

(Matthew 6:19-34, 21:22, 26:41, Mark 11:24, 14:38, Luke 11:5-13, 21:36, 17:15, 17:20, Romans 8:26, 12:12, Ephesians 3:16-21, Philippians 1:9-11, 4:6, 1 Thessalonians 1, Jams 5:13-20, etc.)

Nebuchadnezzar's compulsory worship of his own image of gold and the futility of worshiping an idol / image instead of worshiping God the Creator – Daniel 3

The Babylonian king Nebuchadnezzar, that had taken the southern kingdom of Judah into exile, erected an image of gold to be worshiped, on the plain of Dura in the province of Babylon. Nebuchadnezzar required that all 'nations and peoples of every language,' would fall down and worship the image of gold that Nebuchadnezzar had set up. Whomever did not fall down and worship the image, would be immediately thrown into a blazing furnace. (Daniel 3:1-6).

Nebuchadnezzar's image served as a typology for this idol / image that the beast of the earth will establish and activate.

Three Israelite young men that had been taken into exile, defied the command of Nebuchadnezzar to worship the image of gold. Instead, they opted to obey the Law given to the people of Israel, that forbid bowing down and worshiping idols and images. Consequently, the three young men were thrown into the fiery furnace that had been heated to seven times its original temperature. In the midst of the fire, a fourth person appeared that looked like 'a son of the gods.' At that point, the three young men were called to come out. (Daniel 3)

Because the three young men honored God Most High's command, God protected the three young men.

The biblical record's understanding of the futility of worshiping a created idol / image instead of worshiping the Creator

While the beast of the earth will be described as arrogant and boastful, there will be an almost equal level of arrogance inherent in the beast of the sea. Out of his arrogance, the beast of the sea will be prepared to acquiesce to having an idol / image of him erected in the wing of the temple and he will be keen to be worshiped vicariously through this idol / image. The beast of the sea must also have a high level of arrogance within his character to support the implementation of the mark of the beasts system which among other accomplishments, will provide financial revenue for the global religious community and its military arm. The two beasts of Revelation 13 will also view themselves as superior to the rest of humanity, possessing their own version of divinity and sovereignty that will establish them as worthy to rule over the rest of the inhabitants of the earth and even over the residents of heaven.

The beast of the sea will be worshiped because of his seemingly invincibility. Afterall, he will have survived his near fatal injury. And he will be able to continue to blaspheme God Most High, and to slander heaven and those who live in heaven, seemingly without consequence from God Most High. He will have authority over every tribe, people, language and nation. He will wage war against God's holy people and conquer them.

For the beast of the earth to compete with the global level of adoration and worship that the beast of the sea will attract for himself, the beast of the earth must also provide an almost equal level of stupendousness. He will share supernatural power and authority with the beast of the sea. But he must also provide his own 'proofs' to substantiate his claim that he is greater than God Most High.

And to be accepted as leader by the people of Israel, he must attempt to prove that he is at least as great as Israel's greatest leader, Moses. The beast of the earth must *accomplish all of this while Moses will be personally present on the temple mount.*

Moses' great humility will be a stark contrast to the arrogance of the two beasts of Revelation 13.

Also, Moses has always held a unique relationship with God Most High. It was Moses who was first able to hear God speak in the tabernacle.

When Moses entered the tent of meeting to speak with the Lord, Moses heard the voice speaking to him from between the two cherubim above the atonement cover on the ark of the covenant law. Numbers 7:89a

Consequently, for the beast of the earth to be able to convince the people of Israel that he should be their leader, he will have to meet the same level of 'ability' that was demonstrated, and will again be demonstrated, by Moses.

By causing the idol / image of the beast of the sea to 'speak,' and then also to 'act,' the beast of the earth will seem to have accomplished proving himself to be greater than the prophet Moses. By providing the idol / image of the beast of the sea with the appearance of life, the beast of the earth's power and authority will appear to be on par with God the Creator.

Because of the signs it was given power to perform on behalf of the beast of the sea, the beast of the earth deceived the inhabitants of the earth. The beast of the earth ordered them to set up an image in honor of the first beast of the sea who was wounded by the sword and yet lived.

The beast of the earth was given power to give breath to the image of the first beast of the sea, so that it could speak and cause all who refused to worship the image to be killed. Revelation 13:14-15 translated

With the activation of the idol / image of the beast of the sea, the beast of the earth will have proven that the artificial intelligence technology that is available to him, is ready for public consumption, and activated under his power and authority. The beast of the earth will appear to the world as a hero with the ability to tackle all humanity's concerns. And with the ability of the idol / image of the beast of the sea and the mark of the beasts system, to provide global control of humanity, the beast of the earth will establish himself as a global leader, sharing supernatural power and authority only with the beast of the sea.

For those whose names are written in the Lamb's book of life, they will not be deceived by the false claims of the two beasts of Revelation 13. They know that there is only one true creator, and that is Yahweh / the Lord, the God described in the biblical record. All others that attempt to take the place of God Most High, are pretenders. And only the authentic God of heaven has the power, ability and willingness to provide actual eternal life / to resurrect.

Other gods cannot create. They can only provide facsimiles. Even the idol / image of the beast of the sea on the temple mount will still be constituted of materials from the already created physical earth, with electrical power also captured from the already created physical earth. And the idol / image of the beast of the sea will still be created from the hands of created humanity.

The idol / image of the beast of the sea will not be either dead or alive. To be dead requires that something once lived and that the intrinsic living has ceased. To be alive requires that something was produced by a similar living being as that living being's offspring, from the essence of that living being's existence, and that living thing possesses the potential to be able to reproduce itself from the essence of its existence.

While the idol / image of the beast of the sea, and the two beasts of Revelation 13, will promise to provide humanity with a form of health and a form of everlasting awareness, in reality what they will offer will still be fragile and able to be destroyed just as the idol / image established by the two beasts of Revelation 13 will eventually be destroyed.

The living God of the people of Israel first dwelled with the people of Israel, making God's presence known in the pillar of fire and cloud, and then in the glory of God that resided in the tabernacle and traveled with the people of Israel in the wilderness. And the God of Israel is omnipresent, and unable to be contained within some form of physical container, especially a physical container constructed by human hands. For this reason, creating an idol / image to represent God Most High and then to worship that idol / image, is abhorrent to the God of the kingdom of heaven.

According to the Old Testament / Tanakh prophet Isaiah, idolatry was being devoted to this exhaustive building project to construct a statue, and then richly animating it with sacrifices as a focus of worship, with the hope of giving the statue the ability to interact with living humanity.

> With whom, then, will you compare God?
> To what image will you liken God?
> The metalworker molds an image. The goldsmith overlays the image with gold. And the silversmith fashions silver chains for it.

(This was the pattern for the development of most forms of technology as well.)

> A person too poor to provide these materials, selects wood that will not rot, from a tree.
> That person looks for a skilled craftsman to prepare a carved image that will not totter and fall.

(If an image can totter and fall, has it truly met the criteria necessary to be classified as a god?)

> Do you not know? Have you not heard? Has it not been told you from the beginning? Have you not understood since the earth was founded?
> It is God who sits enthroned above the circle of the earth. And the inhabitants of the earth are like grasshoppers. It is God who stretches out the heavens like a canopy, and spreads them out like a tent to live in.
> It is God who brings princes to naught and reduces the rulers of this world to nothing. It is God who makes the judges of the earth useless.
> No sooner are they planted, no sooner are they sown, no sooner do they take root in the ground, than God blows on them and they wither, and the whirlwind sweeps them away like chaff.
> 'To whom will you compare me? Or who is my equal?' says the Holy One.
> Lift up your eyes and look to the heavens, and see. Who has created all these things?
> Who brings out the starry host one by one and calls forth each of them by name?

Because of his great power and mighty strength, not one of them is missing. Isaiah 40:18-26 translated

The Lord said: 'Of what value is an idol carved by a craftsman? Or an image that teaches lies? For the one who makes it, trusts in his own creation. He makes idols that cannot speak.'
'Woe to him who says to wood, 'Come to life!' Or to lifeless stone, 'Wake up!' Can it give guidance? It is covered with gold and silver. There is no breath in it.'
The Lord is in his holy temple. Let all the earth be silent before him. Habakkuk 2:18-20

In the Garden of Eden / garden of God / paradise, God the Creator created the first man and first woman with all that defined perfection. God the Creator offered them a perfect dwelling, a perfect relationship with a perfect God. The first man and first woman, with the image of God Most High pressed into them, were given abilities and powers that rivaled the heavenly hosts. Some of those abilities and powers were lost to their descendants when the first man and first woman ate the fruit of the tree of the knowledge of good and evil. They were abilities and powers that we can only imagine.

As the creation that bears the vision or image of God the Creation, everything that we dream of humanity achieving today, would have been available for the first man and first woman to have achieved six thousand years ago. Created in the image of the God of creation, humanity was created to be imaginative creative explorers, able to work in partnership with creation to accomplish great things. Progress would not have resulted in pollution. Expansion would have not required extinction of large portions of the population. Success would have not been the result of worry, greed, theft, deception, envy and malice.

Idolatry in the Garden of Eden / garden of God / paradise was the result of God the Creator posing to the first man and first woman the question of 'Will you embrace my vision and accept the culture of the kingdom of heaven?' God the Creator's very character defined what good and evil consist of. The first man and the first woman were asked to submit to those boundaries and to embrace

God the Creator's vision for what creation was intended to be.

To embrace the vision of God the Creator, God's requirement was that God the Creator remain in the position of divine and sovereign God. God the Creator required that God remain the original, and that the first man and first woman remain the image, the copy.

But the first man and first woman declined the conditions required for maintaining their residence in the Garden of Eden / garden of God / paradise, and for preserving their prefect and untarnished relationship with God the Creator.

In eating the fruit of the tree of the knowledge of good and evil, the first man and first woman demonstrated that they desired to aspire to be greater than God the Creator, that they rejected the vision that God the Creator held for what creation was created to be, and that they be able to redefine the character of the god that they would choose to give allegiance to.

The serpent / Satan recognized the opportunity to fill that position as an alternative god for the first man and first woman, and then exploited it.

The prophet Isaiah recorded a description of the people of Israel as they made the same kind of decision that the first man and first woman made, chasing after idolatry, justifying their adultery against their covenant relationship with God Most High, and believing the lie concerning the promised and prophesied messiah.

And Isaiah recorded in the songs of the suffering servant, the activity of God Most High in providing a path for reversing the effects of that decision, for those who would become believers in messiah / followers of the sacrificed Lamb (Isaiah 52:13-53:12). Isaiah's message told of the future coming of the second Adam who would buy the opportunity for each individual human being, to be offered Adam's choice again.

The first man / Adam chose to create his own god, when he chose to attempt to create himself as his own god, instead of allowing God the Creator to be Lord of his life.

When a person becomes a believer in messiah (BC) or a follower of the Lamb (AD), that individual decided to make the opposite choice from the choice that was made by the first man / Adam, and to make messiah / the Lamb / Jesus Christ the Lord of their life.

Idolatry is the committing of the same crime that the first man committed when the first man rejected the divinity and sovereignty of God the Creator, and attempted to appropriate himself to take the place of God the Creator as sovereign, forcing the position of god to yield to the control of humanity.

Isaiah's message to the people of Israel was, 'What kind of stupid are you that you believe a statue can save you?'

The message for those who live during the era of the time of Jacob's Trouble is, 'What kind of stupid are you, to believe that even an animated statue can save you?'

This statue / idol / image of the beast of the sea, even though it will speak and act, will still be merely a better copy of a statue. It will remain the product of humanity, animated by humanity, subservient to the force and power of humanity.

This idol / image of the beast of the sea will not even possess the level of inherent sovereignty that humanity possesses having been created in the image of God the Creator. Because this idol / image will be under the authority of the beast of the earth, it will not possess the ability to make its own decisions or to act on its own. And yet the inhabitants of the earth will worship this idol / image.

A portion of this idol / image's responsibility will be to separate the impressed image of God the Creator, from the human creation. In worshiping this idol / image, or in receiving the mark of the beasts, the recipient will be designated for the form of eternal life that the kingdom of Satan, Inc. / kingdom of man offers. And the worshiper or recipient will no longer be acceptable for citizenship in the kingdom of heaven. But the marketing for the mark of the beasts will not disclose this disclaimer.

The Roman Catholic Church's recent prototypes of computer priests

The Roman Catholic Church recently developed 'computer priests' that are designed to take confession. The Bless U-2 robot was unveiled in Wittenberg, Germany, May 20, 2017. It speaks five languages: English, French, Spanish, Polish, and German. And it listens to confession. A catechism for robots is currently in development.

It is interesting that the location chosen for the unveiling of the Bless U-2 robot, Wittenberg, Germany, was also the location that sparked the Protestant Reformation in 1517. The year, 2017 was the five hundred year anniversary of the Protestant Reformation. On October 31, 1517, the Augustinian monk, Martin Luther, nailed his ninety five theses to the door of the Wittenberg church.

The pervasive following of beast of the sea / false prophet / beast from the Abyss / eighth king beast will enjoy that will allow the idol / image of the beast of the sea to assume control of the inhabitants of the earth who worship it

In describing the beast of the sea, John the Revelator documented:

The whole world was filled with wonder and followed the beast of the sea. Revelation 13:3c

People worshiped the dragon because the dragon had given authority to the beast, and they also worshiped the beast and asked, 'Who is like the beast?' Revelation 13:4a

All inhabitants of the earth will worship the beast – all whose names have not been written in the Lamb's book of life… Revelation 13:8a

Combining the adoration of the beast of the sea by the inhabitants of the earth, with the magical signs and wonders performed by the beast of the earth, the hearts and minds of the inhabitants of the earth will be so well captured that they will actually desire to willingly enter into the captivity of this promised form of virtual reality governance.

Once locked into this new global governance system, the idol / image of the beast of the sea will be able to eliminate the need for physical prisons. Physical prisons can be escaped from. Prison guards can exercise their own decision making and too frequently be persuaded to relax the rules or to allow escapes. Worship of the beast of the sea and of the idol / image of the beast of the sea, will seal the loyalty relationship that the worshipers establish with the new system of global governance. And with that loyalty, the flaws of past systems of incarceration will be eliminated.

With the addition of the mark of the beasts system, all aspects of human life will be able to be manipulated.

In this way, the two beasts of Revelation 13, and the red dragon / serpent / Satan, Inc., will also seek to purge every bit of allegiance to God Most High and to messiah / the Lamb / Jesus Christ, from the hearts and minds of the inhabitants of the earth.

Messiah / the Lamb / Jesus Christ was an active participant in the creation of the world, including the creation of every human being (John 1). Having taken part in the creation of humanity, it will be essential, if the kingdom of Satan, Inc. / kingdom of man is to have any hope of being successful in the final battle of this era, to purge every bit of allegiance to God Most High, and to messiah / the Lamb / Jesus Christ who took part in the creation of humanity.

Locking in the compulsory allegiance of those who might have sided with messiah / the Lamb / Jesus Christ during the final battle of this age, will be one of the ultimate goals of the mark of the beasts system.

The mark of the beasts system initiated – Revelation 13:14-18

The mark of the beasts system will be globally implemented with the future abomination of desolation event. It will be a system that will attempt to establish ultimate control of every individual and every aspect of every individual's life.

And the beast of the earth deceives those dwelling on the earth by reason of the signs that it was given to perform before the beast of the sea, telling those dwelling on the earth to make an image to the beast that was wounded by the sword and has lived.

And the beast of the earth was given the ability to give breath to the image of the beast of the sea, so that the image of the beast of the sea should also speak. And the image of the beast of the sea will cause all who would not worship the image of the beast of the sea, to be killed.

And the beast of the earth causes all the small and the great, and the rich and the poor, and the free and the servants, that it should give them a mark on their right hand or on their forehead, so that no one should be able to buy or to sell, if they did not have the mark — the name of the beast, or the number of the name of the beast.

Here is the wisdom: Let the one who has understanding count the number of the beast. It is humanity's number, and its number is six hundred sixty six. *(Some original manuscripts identified the number as six hundred sixteen.)* Revelation 13:14-18 translated

In John the Revelator's description of the mark of the beasts system, the question arises, 'Which beast rules over the mark of the beasts system?'

Does the mark of the beasts system belong to the beast of the earth because the beast of the earth will initiate / animate the system and be the enforcer of the system? Or does the mark of the beasts system belong to the beast of the sea because the idol / image of the beast of the sea will be the center for compulsory worship and will be the technological interlink between the idol / image of the beast and the adherents of the kingdom of Satan, Inc. / kingdom of man who receive the mark of the beasts? Or does the mark of the beasts system belong to both beasts?

The nature of Koine Greek / New Testament Greek, was to string ideas together with minimum punctuation and grammatical breaks such as paragraph breaks, headings, separations between words, commas and periods to separate thought or end sentences, etc. Consequently, reading the original text concerning the mark of the beasts system, allowed for the mark of the beasts system to be legitimately attached to either of the two beasts of Revelation 13, or to both of them.

Possibly the best paradigm of the mark of the beasts system is that the system belongs to both beasts. The power and authority of both beasts, and the foundational structures that support both beasts, will be needed to establish and maintain the mark of the beasts system.

Within the mark of the beasts system will be the culmination of the attempt to address all aspects of the human experience, placed into one system, under the control of the kingdom of Satan, Inc. / kingdom of man. Religion, politics, economics, culture, thought, health, life, death, etc. will all be components that the mark of the beasts system will address.

The four horsemen of the first four seals / four horsemen of the apocalypse, addressed religion (white horse), governance (red horse), economics (black horse), and culture with Death and Hades (green horse) (Revelation 6:1-8).

If previous tyrants who pursued global leadership, such as Adolf Hitler, would have been more biblically literate, the mark of the beasts system would have been something that they would have dreamed of implementing as an aid to establishing and maintaining their governance. Adolf Hitler's concentration camp system, provided a number to each person incarcerated. But tattooing a number on a body, could never provide the kind of invasive control of an individual like a system that can even control thought and health of an individual.

During the second half of the era of the time of Jacob's Trouble, there will be many who will have been beheaded because of their testimony about Jesus Christ and because of the word of God. They will not have worshiped the beast or its image and will not have received the mark of the beasts. For these martyrs, the kingdom of heaven has a special category. They will come to life and reign with messiah / the Lamb / Jesus Christ during the Thousand Years Reign of Jesus Christ (Revelation 20:4).

But for those that receive the mark of the beasts, there will be no opportunity for entrance into the kingdom of heaven. Receiving the mark of the beasts will be an automatic disqualification for entrance into the kingdom of heaven. (Revelation 14:9-12)

This fact is so important to the kingdom of heaven, that God Most High will send three angels prior to the *future abomination of desolation event, just to warn humanity of the future danger. The third angel will provide the warning concerning the mark of the beasts.*

And another angel, a third, followed them saying in a loud voice, 'If anyone worships / prostates oneself before the beast and the image of the beast, and <u>receives a mark on their forehead or upon their hand</u>, that one will also drink of the wine of the wrath of God; having been mixed / poured out undiluted in the cup of God's wrath. That one will be tormented in the fire and brimstone, before the holy angels, and before the Lamb. And the smoke of their torment ascends forever and ever. Those who worship the beast and its image, and <u>anyone who receives the mark of the name of the beast</u>, have no rest day and night.' Revelation 14:9-11 translated

And during the finale for the era of the time of Jacob's Trouble the first angel assigned to pour out the first bowl of the seven bowls of God Most High's wrath / seven last plagues, will pour out his bowl only upon those who have received the mark of the beasts and worshiped its image (Revelation 15:2).

To implement the global mark of the beasts system, will require massive coordination of the kingdom of Satan, Inc. / kingdom of man, of global religion, global governance, global economics, global culture, modern technology, etc. Imagine combining all the goals of the Great Reset, the World Economic Forum, the United Nations Agenda 2030, the mission of the global elites, etc., and then apply them to the mark of the beasts system.

Throughout human history, there has been no other entity that has represented death in all forms, like the future mark of the beasts system. It will be one of the greatest antitheses to the life offered by the kingdom of heaven.

Hippolytus of Rome's understanding of the significance of the mark of the beasts system

Hippolytus of Rome (c. 170 to 235 AD), was one of the most influential of the second and third century theologians. Hippolytus was a disciple of Irenaeus of Smyrna (c. 130 to 202 AD), who was a disciple of Polycarp bishop of Smyrna (69 to 155 AD) who was a disciple of John

the Apostle / John of Patmos / John the Revelator (c. 6 to c. 100 AD). Hippolytus was instrumental in the development of the foundation for understanding biblical eschatology. For example, Hippolytus was one who understood that six thousand years must transpire from the point of creation, until the return of messiah / the Lamb / Jesus Christ.

Hippolytus had a bitter conflict with Rome's bishop Zephyrinus over theological issues, with Zephyrinus' teachings on the nature of the trinity, rejected the nature of God as being comprised of three persons. That conflict may have been the reason that the full history of Hippolytus' life was misplaced. Hippolytus was exiled to Sardinia where he was martyred, August 13, 235 AD.

Hippolytus' writings also reflected the social context in which he lived. The history of the social context of Hippolytus' time, was initiated with the culture of past Roman emperors.

Hippolytus referenced the 'law of Augustus' which were laws instituted by the Roman empire's Gaius Octavius / Octavian / Caesar Augustus (63 BC to 14 AD / fl. 27 BC to 14 AD).

Julius Caesar (100 to 44 BC) who was the fourth in a lineage of Gaius Julius Caesars, was born into the Julia family of the Alban people, which claimed to be descendants of the goddess Venus. Julius Caesar was noted as having slept his way to rise in the political arena, with both women and men.

Julius Caesar had named Gaius Octavius to be his heir and successor. Gaius Octavius was the great nephew of Caesar through Caesar's sister Julia the Younger. Julius Caesar imposed a homosexual relationship upon his great nephew. With the death of Julius Caesar, the Roman Republic collapsed. It would take twenty five years for Gaius Octavius who established the 'law of Augustus,' to claim his inheritance as emperor of Rome.

After the Roman Republic collapsed, Rome was ruled by two triumvirates until 32 BC. Gaius Octavius rose the victor of the Second Triumvirate's controversy. On January 13, 27 BC the Roman Senate imposed upon

Octavian the titles of Augustus / 'majestic' / 'great,' and Princeps / 'first in time or order' / 'distinguished' / 'noble.'

Octavian / Caesar Augustus also held the position of pontifex maximus / supreme pontiff or chief high priest of the College of Pontiffs in ancient Rome. Pontifex maximus was the most powerful positions in the ancient Roman religion. The reign of Augusts initiated an imperial cult as well as an era associated with imperial peace / Pax Romana / Pax Augusta. The Peace of Rome constituted hegemonial power and regional expansion, and meant that peace with Rome could be achieved when Rome ruled, and the people under Roman rule accepted their roles as Roman plebs. It was a compulsory peace with Roman governance established as always right and contesters to Roman governance as always wrong.

Augustus also established the Praetorian Guard. The Praetorian Guard was a unit of the Imperial Roman army that served as personal bodyguards and intelligence agents for the Roman emperors, and as bodyguards for senior officers of the Roman legions.

It was Constantine the Great who later disbanded the cohorts praetoriae and destroyed their Castra Praetoria barracks in 312 AD.

Having been installed as the leader of Rome, Augustus was credited with forming the Roman Principate / Roman empire (27 BC to 284 AD). Augustus introduced the 'law of Augustus.' Augustus' laws sought to regulate marriage and sexual conduct among citizens, at a time when Rome was experiencing moral decay. Childless unions, the intermarriage of lower class women to the Roman elite, adultery and untethered bachelorhood all threatened the Roman aristocracy. The Roman social engineering program sought to replenish the dwindling number of upper class citizens, and to increase the population of the Roman empire. And with an increase in population there were be a resulting improvement upon the economy and wealth of the empire.

The laws that were introduced, imposed high taxes upon unmarried people and low taxes to married couples. Marriage was compulsory for men between the ages of twenty five to sixty, and women ages twenty five to fifty. The laws required a minimum period that a couple had to stay in the union before they could seek divorce. In order to be eligible for appointment to certain senior public offices, a man had to be a father. Men with three or more children gained priority in the competition for public office. Childless couples were denied the right to receive an inheritance.

Stiff penalties were imposed on anyone found to have engaged in marital infidelities. Adulterous wives were divorced and their dowries were confiscated. The women were then ostracized and not allowed to remarry. Husbands were legally obligated to report the adultery of their wives. Men however were allowed to engage in affairs with unmarried women and slaves. Men who engaged in affairs with married women would incur a loss of property, imprisonment or banishment to an island. Adulterous men and women could be banished to different islands, with women required to wear the short tunic worn by prostitutes.

The laws also prohibited indiscriminate emancipation of slaves, prohibited freed slaves from marrying Romans and prohibited senators from marrying freed women. Infanticide remained legal and a husband's decision.

Prostitution was taxed. Homosexuality became a punishable offense.

Augustus also restored the temples of the gods as a part of his quest for religious revival. He reintroduced past ceremonies and festivals, and revived the secular games traditionally held every one hundred ten years that included sacrifices and theatrical performances. Augustus established the Imperial Cult for the worship of the emperor as a god.

It was from this context that Hippolytus described the beast of the earth and the mark of the beasts.

... And in speaking of 'the horns being like a lamb,' (John the Revelator) means that the antichrist will make himself like the Son of God, and set himself forward as king. And the terms, 'he spoke like a dragon,' means that he is a deceiver, and not truthful. And the words, 'he exercised all the power of the first beast before him, and caused the earth and them which dwell therein to worship the first beast, whose deadly wound was healed,' signify that, after the manner of the <u>law of Augustus</u>, by whom the empire of Rome was established, he too will rule and govern, sanctioning everything by it, and taking greater glory to himself.

For, being full of guile, and exalting himself against the servants of God, with the wish to afflict them and persecute them out of the world, because they give not glory to him, he will order incense-pans to be set up by all everywhere, that no man among the holy ones may be able to buy or sell without first sacrificing; for this is what is meant by the mark received upon the right hand. And the word — 'in their forehead' — indicates that all are crowned, and put on a crown of fire, and not of life, but of death. For in this wise, too, did Antiochus Epiphanes the king of Syria, the descendant of Alexander of Macedon, devise measures against the Jews. He, too, in the exaltation of his heart, issued a decree in those times, that 'all should set up shrines before their doors, and sacrifice, and that they should march in procession to the honor of Dionysus, waving chaplets of ivy;' and that those who refused obedience should be put to death by strangulation and torture. But he also met his due recompense at the hand of the Lord, the righteous Judge and all-searching God; for he died eaten up of worms. And if one desires to inquire into that more accurately, he will find it recorded in the books of the Maccabees. Hippolytus of Rome: *Treatise on Christ and Antichrist*, 49

Hippolytus pointed out that the 'antichrist' / beast of the earth will:
- *seek to mimic the Son of God, fulfilling the prophecy given to humanity in Genesis 3:15 and will seek to obtain and utilize the power of the Son of God who holds access to the true power of God and who will return to establish himself as the king of the kingdom of heaven.*
- *speak like a dragon / a deceiver, and not tell truth.*
- *have power that will be like the power available to the beast of the sea / false prophet / beast from the Abyss / eighth king beast.*
- *compel all people to worship the beast of the sea / false prophet / beast from the Abyss / eighth king beast.*
- *rule the earth and eventually his glory will eclipse the glory of the beast of the sea / false*

prophet / beast from the Abyss / eighth king beast.
- *rule using the model of the law of Augustus.*
- *be full of guile.*
- *exalt himself. The 'antichrist' / beast of the earth, will not be promoted by anyone other than himself. He will be a self-promoter among the ten horns / ten kings, and even amidst the objection of authentic Christians.*
- *desire to afflict the servants of God, seeking to persecute and annihilate God's people from the earth. God's servants are a threat to the kingdom of Satan, Inc. / kingdom of man. And just as a perfect heaven and earth cannot allow to have even one rebel in heaven or earth sneaking into eternity, neither can the kingdom of Satan, Inc. / kingdom of man allow to have even one devotee to God Most High, infiltrate the eternal kingdom of the red dragon / serpent / Satan, Inc.*
- *order incense pans to be set up by all, everywhere, so that no one among the holy ones will be able to trade without first making sacrifice through the mark of the beasts system.*
- *institute the mark of the beasts economy.*
- *mark people on the forehead with a crown of fire / crown of death that is in contrast to the crown of life that Jesus Christ offers.*
- *follow after the pattern of Antiochus IV Epiphanes / king of Syria (emperor of the Seleucid empire) who devised measures against the people of Israel.*
- *require that homes have shrines set up in front of their doors.*
- *require that people march / parade in honor of Dionysus, waving chaplets of ivy / crowns fashioned from plant vines.*
- *torture and strangle to death those who refuse to obey him.*

- *meet with God's recompense and judgment. He will be destroyed by the righteous judge and all-searching God.*

As his tribe, then, and his manifestation, and his destruction, have been set forth in these words, and as his name has also been indicated mystically, let us look also at his action. For he will call together all the people to himself, out of every country of the dispersion, making them his own, as though they were his own children, and promising to restore their country, and establish again their kingdom and nation, in order that he may be worshipped by them as God, as the prophet says: 'He will collect his whole kingdom, from the rising of the sun even to its setting: they whom he summons and they whom he does not summon shall march with him.' Hippolytus of Rome: *Treatise on Christ and Antichrist*, 54

Hippolytus portrayed the beast of the earth / final world ruler / antichrist as:
- *having a 'tribe, a following that he will use to establish his mystical name.*
- *being destined for destruction.*
- *calling people from every nation and cultural background to* 'make them his own, as though they were his own children.'
- *promising to those that follow him the restoration of their country and the reestablishment of their kingdom and nation in exchange for their support of him. Note that the beast of the earth will be responsible for the ruin of many nations, and will be responsible for the need of many nations to be restored.*
- *requiring and receiving the worship of himself as god.*
- *having a kingdom that is so expansive that there will not be any time when the sun does not shine on some portion of his kingdom. There was a time when the empire of Great Britain / the United Kingdom spanned around the world so that every moment of every day, the sun shone on some place that was ruled by Great Britain / the United Kingdom. Hippolytus presented the beast of the earth / final world ruler as also*

having a kingdom that will also span the entire world.

Whether people willingly align themselves with the beast of the earth / antichrist and believe in his cause, or they seek to defy his rule, all people (inhabitants of the earth) will be forced to march with him.

But this dynamic of mandatory compulsion will cause his kingdom to experience divided loyalty. People who willingly rebel against the rule of God Most High, will also willingly rebel against the rules of the kingdom of rebellion.

The ten toes of Nebuchadnezzar's image of a man (Daniel 2) were comprised of iron and clay which did not mix with each other.

Revelation 17 to 19, described the armies of the world congregated in order to engage in battle against the people of Israel, the followers of the Lamb / Jesus Christ, and Jesus Christ. But the armies of the nations of the earth will turn upon one another and enter into a mutually assured destruction.

Compulsory worship, compulsory rule, compulsory war, etc., are always inadequate and ineffective in bringing unity to any endeavor. Compulsion may rule over the physical body, but it cannot truly and effectively capture the head and heart of an individual. Compulsion always has an end date when those who are coerced will eventually revolt and shed their bondage. But compulsion and coercion have always been the strategy of the kingdom of Satan, Inc. / kingdom of man.

In contrast, the kingdom of heaven is centered on heartfelt allegiance; even requiring Jesus Christ to make the voluntary, autonomous decision to become a fully human man and to endure the cross, to provide a path for salvation.

The authentic biblically defined love is a concept that will escape the understanding of the beast of the earth, along with all the leaders and adherents of the red dragon / serpent / Satan, Inc. They will only be able to understand compulsive self-enhancing power and will never be capable of understanding the power of truth or the power of authentic love or the power of self-sacrifice.

The mark of the beasts and the days before Noah – Matthew 24:38-39

Receiving the mark of the beasts will irrevocably seal the recipient into citizenship within the kingdom of Satan, Inc. / kingdom of man and ensure an eternal life that will be lived with the red dragon / serpent / Satan, Inc. There will be no opportunity for God Most High to redeem a person after they have received the mark of the beasts or they have worshiped the idol / image of the beast of the sea. The only other beings who were deemed unredeemable were the rebellious angels, the offspring of the rebellion of the rebellious angels / Nephilim and their descendants, along with all who deny the divinity and sovereignty of Jesus Christ.

Jesus said, 'As it was in the days of Noah, so it will be with the coming of the Son of Man. For in those days before the flood, people were eating and drinking, marrying and giving in marriage, until the day Noah entered into the ark. And they did not know until the flood came and took them all away. It will also be like that with the coming of the Son of Man. Matthew 24:37-39 translated

The dynamics of the antediluvian / preflood rebellion against God the Creator, were similar to the dynamics of the rebellion required for the establishment and implementation of the mark of the beasts system.

During the antediluvian / preflood era, according to Jewish tradition, the population of living things on the earth had become primarily Nephilim and chimera, distortions of God the Creator's creation. The humans and animals selected to be transported on the ark, were individually selected by God the Creator to be pure in their genetics, including Noah and his family.

During the era of the time of Jacob's Trouble, altering the genetic makeup of the general population of humanity, will again be a possibility. And the altering of the genetic makeup of animals, plants and sea creatures will be possible, as it serves the purposes of the kingdom of Satan, Inc. / kingdom of man. The mission of the kingdom of Satan, Inc. / kingdom of man is to eventually defeat humanity that bears the image of God the Creator.

Receiving the mark of the beasts will act as the consummation of the 'marriage' between the individual who receives the mark of the beasts and the red dragon / serpent / Satan, Inc. Once 'married' to the red dragon / serpent / Satan, Inc., that individual will no longer be available to become part of the collective 'bride of Christ,' no longer be qualified for citizenship in the kingdom of heaven, and no longer eligible for living with messiah / the Lamb / Jesus Christ for eternity.

> Within this beast (the Antichrist) when he comes will be a recapitulation made of all sorts of iniquity and of every deceit, in order that all apostate power flowing into and being shut up in him, may be sent into the furnace of fire. Fittingly, his name will possess the number six hundred and sixty-six because he sums up in his person all the commixture of wickedness which took place previous to the deluge (flood of Noah) due to the apostasy of the angels. For Noah was six hundred years old when the deluge came upon the earth, sweeping away the rebellious world for the sake of that most infamous generation which lived in the times of Noah.
>
> And the Antichrist also sums up every error of devised idols since the flood, together with the slaying of the prophets and the cutting off of the just. For that image which Nebuchadnezzar had set up was a height of sixty cubits with a breath of six cubits. Ananias, Azarias, and Misael did not worship it and were cast into a furnace of fire, pointing out prophetically by what happened to them, the wrath against the righteous which will arise towards the end of this time. For that image, taken as a whole, prefigured the coming of the Antichrist, decreeing that he should undoubtedly be worshiped alone above all of humanity.
>
> So at the sixth hundred year of Noah when the deluge occurred because of the apostasy, and the number of the cubits of the image for which these just men were sent into the fiery furnace, indicate the number of the name of that man in whom is concentrated the whole apostasy of six thousand years of unrighteousness, and wickedness, and false prophecy, and deception. For these things' sake, a cataclysm of fire will also come upon the earth. Irenaeus, *Against Heresies* 55:29:2

Irenaeus was a student of Polycarp and John the Revelator.

Irenaeus shared the understanding of what the first century apostolic church knew concerning the purpose of this era of the time of Jacob's Trouble and the Antichrist / beast of the earth's part in it.

Within the early church leadership was this deep understanding that all the activity of God Most High throughout all human history, has been laying the foundation or leading up to this climatic point of messiah / the Lamb / Jesus Christ's return. The antediluvian / preflood religion caused the world to become so wicked that God the Creator's response for saving creation could only be to send a deluge / flood / a sort of mitzvah, a baptism of the earth and its inhabitants at that time (Genesis 6-8).

After the deluge / flood of Noah's lifetime, the antediluvian / preflood religion began again under the leadership of Cush, Canaan and Nimrod. Nimrod of Babylon developed fire worship and reestablished idolatry and rebellion against God Most High. According to some Jewish legends, Nimrod erected the first fire idol in postdiluvian / postflood history, honoring himself as a god. And Nimrod compulsorily forced worship to his image. Those who refused were thrown into the furnace. When Abram refused to worship Nimrod, Abram was thrown into Nimrod's furnace, but walked out alive, unscathed and unscorched.

It became the practice in the worship of the baal / mystery / mythology religion gods, 'Molech' and others, to 'pass one's seed through the fire.' Passing one's seed through the fire was a euphemism for offering one's child to the gods by placing them alive into the hands of the idol, usually constructed of bronze, and allowing the fire to rise from the lap of the idol to burn the child alive.

Nebuchadnezzar also considered himself to be god and set up his image, demanding compulsory worship of his image. But God Most High decided that Shadrach, Meshach and Abednego (Ananias, Azarias, and Misael) would not die in the furnace (Daniel 3).

The ancient altars and fiery furnaces were a dramatization of the activity of the feud between God Most High and the red dragon / serpent / Satan, Inc. Various baal / mystery / mythology religion gods were worshiped with special altars usually located in the high places *on hills, with trees that were carved into specific images, and with altars that were designed for the acceptable sacrifices to the baal / mystery / mythology religion, including human sacrifice.*

God Most High required that humanity not be sacrificed on the altar. On God Most High's altar, the bull, the ram, the lamb, the goat, etc. were offered as sacrifices. The sacrifice of the Day of Atonement / Yom Kippur goat specifically dramatized the destruction of the red dragon / serpent / Satan, Inc. in the fiery lake of burning sulfur. Human sacrifice upon God Most High's altars would render the altar unclean and unsuitable for an acceptable sacrifice to God Most High. God Most High demanded living sacrifices that represented that God the Creator created life and represented the life that God Most High desires for humanity to experience.

In contrast to what God Most High defined as an acceptable sacrifice, the baal / mystery / mythology religion has no compunction against human sacrifice. Various baal / mystery / mythology religion gods such as Molech and others, required human sacrifice. Burnt human sacrifice also should have reminded worshipers of the fiery lake of burning sulfur that awaits those who have rejected God Most High's assigned work for the promised and prophesied messiah, and Jesus Christ as that messiah.

For God the Creator, humanity was not created to endure an eternity in the fiery lake of burning sulfur. God the Creator created humanity to dwell in the Garden of Eden / garden of God / paradise for the purpose of sharing a full and right, face to face friendship relationship with God the Creator. Life in the fiery lake of burning sulfur for humanity was the choice that the red dragon / serpent / Satan, Inc. offers to humanity.

Today human sacrifice is also termed ritual murder. After the introduction of fiery burnt offering sacrifice, ritual murder advanced to also include the burial of the living both as pillars next to buildings and laid out horizontally, the taking of poison, stoning, crucifixion, burning while tied to a stake, honor killings, etc.

Nebuchadnezzar had established an image to be worshiped that either stood next to, or encompassed, a fiery furnace that was erected for the purpose of disposing of those who had decided to decline the invitation to participate in the compulsory worship of Nebuchadnezzar, king of the Babylonians, king of the same area that Nimrod had sought to establish his world empire. Nebuchadnezzar's image was a typology of what the Antichrist / beast of the earth will also establish; requiring compulsory worship of an image of someone who is not God Most High and slaying those who decline to participate in worship.

Irenaeus made the connection between Nebuchadnezzar's compulsory worship and the fiery furnace, with the work of the Antichrist / beast of the earth. If God Most High is true to form, then those who share the kind of dedication to God Most High that Shadrach, Meshach, and Abednego displayed, who will also decline the invitation to participate in compulsory worship of the idol / image of the beast of the sea, will experience life through the 'fiery furnace' events of the era of the time of Jacob's Trouble.

For six thousand years, the red dragon / serpent / Satan, Inc. has been collecting power and tweaking the plan for attempting to fully establish the kingdom of Satan, Inc. / kingdom of man, using unrighteousness, wickedness, murder, false prophecy, and deception.

But God Most High has been prepping God Most High's response during the past six thousand years as well.

The condition of the religious community that will foster the establishment of the mark of the beasts system

Throughout human history, those who have desired to establish their empires, found it necessary to address religion, economics and culture, in their pursuit of attaining imperial sovereignty and dominion.

Ham, Cush, Canaan and Nimrod understood this dynamic in their scheme to achieve global domination. Ham's family utilized religion in the physical conception of Nimrod, the development of cities, and the tower of Babel system of governance. Nimrod was the product of the

Nephilim breeding program devised by rebellious angels in their attempt to corrupt God the Creator's creation. Cities were developed as a rebellion against God Most High's instruction to spread throughout the earth. The tower of Babel empire was developed as the program for storming heaven and overthrowing God Most High in order to establish a new global regime as a defiance of the plan that God Most High had envisioned life to be. (Genesis 6:1-4, 9:18-27, 10:6-20, 11:1-9).

Nimrod's personal physical size and strength enabled him to advance his control of economics and culture. The cities that Nimrod and his family established, made it easier to control the economics and culture of the people they ruled over. The tower of Babel empire became its own economic microcosm, with its own coin and its own culture.

In the development of empires, once coin was issued, and city walls were established to determine boundaries, the rulers had the opportunity to demand economic and cultural dependance upon the governance system established by the designated ruler.

The fall of the tower of Babel empire was initiated when God Most High (religion) intervened over the tower of Babel empire (political governance). With God Most High's intervention through the division of language (culture), the tower of Babel empire's culture disintegrated, the economy became disordered (economics), the baal / mystery / mythology religion suffered a significant setback, and the power of Nimrod's attempt to achieve global governance failed.

Throughout human history, governance was proven to be unable to be entangled from religion, economics and culture. The success of the great empires of past history was dependent upon the incorporation of aspects of religion, economics and culture, into their governance plans. When one area faltered, the other arenas followed with their subsequent collapses.

The biblical record documented the battles of peoples and nations that fought against God Most High. For the first four thousand years of human history, as detailed in the biblical record, God Most High verifiably was the victor every time. This begs the question of whether or not politics / governance, is truly superior and supreme over religion.

During World War II it was the vision of Adolf Hitler to establish the National Socialist Party and to envisioned Nazi Germany as the empire that would rule the world for a thousand years. Adolf Hitler was himself a religious man with many religious ideas that were the product of his Roman Catholic Church membership and heritage, mixed with occultic ideas and his own impression of self-grandeur. Many leaders within the Roman Catholic Church shared in Hitler's theology and pursuits. The people of Israel became the number one target for destruction for Hitler's Nazi Germany because they were considered to be of a different and unacceptable religion; but also because of the jealousy that existed in the world concerning Jewish wealth and Israelite heritage.

Jesus Christ identified the organized church's cultural temperature concerning the biblically defined messiah / the Lamb / Jesus Christ, that will exist during the era of the time of Jacob's Trouble, as being neither hot nor cold. In fact, during this time, Jesus Christ who was the original foundation and lifeblood of the church, documented that he is currently located outside of the church, knocking at the door of the individual – not the church, to offer the individual the invitation for relationship with Jesus Christ (Revelation 3:20-21). The organized church, devoid of the life provided by the foundational presence of Jesus Christ, will essentially be spiritually dead. Even though the organized church will continue to act in global affairs, the organized church has become corrupted, and a pure enemy to messiah / the Lamb / Jesus Christ and to the kingdom of heaven (Revelation 17:12-18, 18).

Jesus Christ also documented that during this time, people will say, 'I am rich. I have acquired wealth and do not need a thing.' They will not realize that they are wretched, pitiful, *poor, blind and naked; and that their economy is failing; and that only heaven's economy will last. They will not realize their nakedness, and that only clothes provided by Jesus Christ will cover their nakedness. They will not recognize their own blindness and that the salve that cures their blindness can only be obtained through Jesus Christ. (Revelation 3:14-22)*

The nature of governance is that it cannot stand alone. Governance is only successful with the support of religion, economics and culture. A living God is accompanied with productive economics, functional culture and effective governance. The gods that support death provide apostate dysfunctional religion, defective economic policies, dreadful culture and governance that can only be temporary.

The governance of the kingdom of Satan, Inc. / kingdom of man will also depend upon religious, economic and cultural dynamics. The kingdom of Satan, Inc. / kingdom of man's methodology will be to rule the inhabitants of the earth with a selected elite ruling class that will benefit from the destruction of those they rule. And so, the kingdom of Satan, Inc. / kingdom of man will demand control over all aspects that influence each individual; with its apostate dysfunctional religion, defective economic policies, dreadful culture and unsustainable governance.

To make a respectable attempt in achieving global control, the kingdom of Satan, Inc. / kingdom of man must be embraced by a cultural environment that is ready to receive what the kingdom of Satan, Inc. / kingdom of man has to offer.

In the vision provided to John the Revelator, after the sixth trumpet had been sounded and the first part of the sixth trumpet had been completed, John the Revelator observed that the culture around the world will be engaged in depravity. And John the Revelator observed that even with the events associated with the sounding of the first six trumpets, there will still be no significant change the hearts and minds of humanity concerning God Most High and the kingdom of heaven.

The rest of humanity who were not killed by their plagues (with the sounding of the first six trumpets), did not even repent of the works of their hands, so that they did not worship the demons and their golden and silver and bronze and stone and wooden idols, which are neither able to see nor to hear nor to walk. And they did not repent of their murders, nor of their sorceries (magic arts), nor of their sexual immorality, nor of their thefts. Revelation 9:20-21 translated

Because the hearts and minds of the inhabitants of the earth are centered on worshiping demons and idols, murdering, magic arts, sexual immorality and thievery; and because the hearts and minds of the inhabitants of the earth will remain unchanged; the events that God Most High scheduled for the second half of the era of the time of Jacob's Trouble as a response, will need to be globally experienced. But more importantly, the global cultural environment will be receptive to the kingdom of Satan, Inc. / kingdom of man's global plan to totally rework everything.

The ultimate goal of God Most High in the work of the scheduled events for the era of the time of Jacob's Trouble, is to bring the hearts and minds of the people of Israel to the realization that Jesus Christ is the promised and prophesied messiah; and to bring a deep understanding to the rest of humanity of the end results of life directed by the two different kingdoms (kingdom of heaven and kingdom of Satan, Inc. / kingdom of man). Only with the full comprehension and realization of the evil of the kingdom of Satan, Inc. / kingdom of man, will the people of Israel recognize that Jesus Christ is the promised prophesied messiah. For this reason, the events scheduled for the second half of the era of the time of Jacob's Trouble will be necessary in the transitional work on earth as the earth readies itself for the future arrival of messiah / the Lamb / Jesus Christ and for the full establishment of the kingdom of heaven on earth.

The Roman Catholic Church's catechism concerning the ten commandments that will allow for the worship of the idol / image of the beast of the sea, and the endorsement by the global religious community of the worship of the idol / image of the beast of the sea

God Most High provided God's Law to the people of Israel as they were gathered at the mountain of God after they left Egypt in 1446 BC. In that Law was the expressed prohibition against making idols / images of other gods. The prohibition against making idols and worshiping idols was so important that it was listed second in the ten commandments, personally etched on tablets by the finger of God. (Exodus 20)

And then the ten commandments were repeated for the people of Israel by Moses, forty years later before they entered into the Promised Land (1406 BC) (Deuteronomy 5).

You shall not make for yourself an image in the form of anything in heaven above or on the earth beneath or in the waters below. You shall not bow down to them or worship them. For I, the Lord your God, am a jealous God, punishing the children for the sin of the parents to the third and fourth generation of those who hate me, but showing love to a thousand generations of those who love me and keep my commandments. Exodus 20:4-6 / Deuteronomy 5:8-10

Most of the ten commandments were given without explanation; given just as directives. But with this second commandment, God Most High went into detail concerning the rationale for why making idols / images of other gods and worshiping other gods, would not be acceptable in God Most High's system of worship. And God provided detail on the consequences of not obeying this second commandment.

Even when the religion of Islam was being developed, there was an understanding of the Israelite second commandment that was incorporated into the religion of Islam. Islam has a severe prohibition against the use of idols and images, except for the black stone in the Kaaba in Mecca Saudi Arabia.

But the Roman Catholic Church recognizes no such injunction against idols / images. The Roman Catholic Church utilizes idols, images, icons, etc. as foci for worship, aids in education, etc. And the Roman Catholic Church practices the regular repurposing of items previously used within the baal / mystery / mythology religion, i.e., the Pantheon in Rome, obelisks, the use of sixteen pointed stars, pinecones that symbolized Osiris in Egypt / Tammuz in Assyria / Dionysus in Greece, halos, shepherds' hooks with snakeheads, miter hats, statues of gods renamed to become statues of religious leaders, etc. as used by the hierarchy of the Roman Catholic Church. The Paul VI Audience Hall was constructed in the shape of the inside of a snake's head (1971), and decorated with objects that symbolize characteristics of the kingdom of Satan, Inc. / kingdom of man.

Icons are pictorial representations of revered persons, or rebellious angels, or gods.

Idols are traditionally formed out of wood, clay, stone or metal; and are used as objects of worship that represent persons esteemed to be divine, gods, or the spirits of gods. In ancient times, idols were formed and then placed under buildings, with the belief that the idol of the spirit the idol represented, would be present within the building.

But statues are merely statues, until they or the being they represent, is prayed to. At that point a statue becomes an idol. In Roman Catholicism, one of the most prayed to figures is the Blessed Virgin Mary.

The fact that the Roman Catholic Church embraces the use of idols / images in their worship, was one of the reasons for the advancement of the Protestant Reformation with Protestants rejected the use of idols and images in worship.

To embrace the Roman Catholic Church's utilization of idols and images, the Roman Catholic Church eliminated the second commandment and then split the tenth commandment into two parts, renumbering the commandment list so that there continued to be ten commandments.

Comparison of the Roman Catholic Church catechism, with the original ten commandments of the Law given to Moses and contained in the original biblical text

Exodus 20:2-17 God Most High spoke all these words:	Deuteronomy 5:6-21 The Lord said:	*Roman Catholic Church Catechism*
I am the Lord your God, who brought you out of the land of Egypt, out of the land of slavery.	I am the Lord your God, who brought you out of Egypt, out of the land of slavery.	
1 – You shall have no other gods before me.	1 – You shall have no other gods before me.	*1 – I am the Lord your god: you shall not have strange gods before me. (Exodus 20:2-6; Deuteronomy 5:6-10)*
2 – You shall not make for yourself an image in the form of anything in heaven above or on the earth beneath or in the waters below. You shall not bow down to them or worship them. For I the Lord your God am a jealous God, punishing the children for the sin of the parents to the third and fourth generation of those who hate me, but showing mercy to a thousand generations of those who love me and who keep my commandments.	2 – You shall not make for yourself an image in the form of anything in heaven above or on the earth beneath or in the waters below. You shall not bow down to them or worship them. For I, the Lord your God, am a jealous God, punishing the children for the sin of the parents to the third and fourth generation of those who hate me, but showing love to a thousand generations of those who love me and keep my commandments.	**MISSING**
3 – You shall not misuse the name of the Lord your God, for the Lord will not hold anyone guiltless who misuses the name of the Lord your God.	3 – You shall not misuse the name of the Lord your God, for the Lord will not hold anyone guiltless who misuses the name of the Lord your God.	*2 – You shall not take the name of the Lord your God in vain. (Exodus 20:7, Deuteronomy 5:11)*

4 – Remember the Sabbath day by keeping it holy. Six days you shall labor and do all your work. But the seventh day is a sabbath to the Lord your God. On it you shall not do any work, neither you, nor your son or daughter, nor your male or female servant, nor your animals, nor any foreigner residing in your towns. For in six days the Lord made the heavens and the earth, the sea, and all that is in them, but the Lord God rested on the seventh day. Therefore, the Lord blessed the Sabbath day and made it holy.	4 – Observe the Sabbath day by keeping it holy, as the Lord your God has commanded you. Six days you shall labor and do all your work. But the seventh day is a sabbath to the Lord your God. On it you shall not do any work, neither you, nor your son or daughter, nor your male or female servant, nor your ox, your donkey or any of your animals, nor any foreigner residing in your towns, so that you male and female servants may rest as you do. Remember that you were slaves in Egypt and that the Lord your God brought you out of there with a mighty hand and an outstretched arm. Therefore, the Lord your God commanded you to observe the Sabbath day.	*3 – Remember to keep holy the Lord's Day. (Exodus 20:8-11; Deuteronomy 5:12-15)*
5 – Honor your father and mother, so that you may live long in the land the Lord your God is giving you.	5 – Honor your father and your mother, as the Lord your God has commanded you, so that you may live long and that it may go well with you in the land the Lord your God is giving you.	*4 – Honor your father and your mother. (Exodus 20:12, Deuteronomy 5:16)*
6 – You shall not murder.	6 – You shall not murder.	*5 – You shall not kill. (Exodus 20:13; Deuteronomy 5:17)*

7 – You shall not commit adultery.	7 – You shall not commit adultery.	*6 – You shall not commit adultery. (Exodus 20:14; Deuteronomy 5:18)*
8 – You shall not steal.	8 – You shall not steal.	*7 – You shall not steal. (Exodus 20:15; Deuteronomy 5:19)*
9 – You shall not give false testimony against your neighbor.	9 – You shall not give false testimony against your neighbor.	*8 – You shall not bear false witness against your neighbor. (Exodus 20:16; Deuteronomy 5:20)*
10 – You shall not covet your neighbor's house. You shall not covet your neighbor's wife, or your neighbor's male or female servant, your neighbor's ox or donkey, or anything that belongs to your neighbor.	10 – You shall not covet your neighbor's wife. You shall not set your desire on your neighbor's house or land, your neighbor's male or female servant, your neighbor's ox or donkey, or anything that belongs to your neighbor.	*9 – You shall not covet your neighbor's wife. (Exodus 20:17; Deuteronomy 5:21)*
		10 – You shall not covet your neighbor's goods. (Exodus 20:17; Deuteronomy 5:21)

Either the Bible is true, or it is not. Either the biblical record is correct, or it is filled with error, and it needs to be determined which portions of the biblical record is in error. (Who determines which portions are in error? And what are their qualifications / credentials that authorize them, to make that determination?)

Protestants originally held that the biblical record is completely true and accurate. Originally Protestants taught their children the ten commandments as sourced by the authentic biblical text. The first Protestants even required their children to memorize the ten commandments.

The Roman Catholic Church operated throughout its history, as if the Bible was a historical mythological novel epic that provided the Roman Catholic Church hierarchy with the power and authority to alter the biblical message for its convenience, to honor only an abridged or altered version of the biblical text, and to support the Roman Catholic Church's global dominion.

Because of the current larger organized church's understanding of the Bible as an errant manuscript without the full authority of God Most High, the earth's inhabitants that received their instruction and direction from the apostate church, will remain biblically illiterate and unaware of God Most High's second commandment that forbids the construction and worship of idols / images of other gods or individuals.

This will be the doctrinal and theological environment that will exist during the era of the time of Jacob's Trouble. This will be the environment that will allow the Roman Catholic Church hierarchy, and the rest of the apostate organized church, to support the construction of the idol / image of the beast of the sea upon the temple mount, and to compulsorily demand worship of the idol / image of the beast of the sea from all inhabitants of the earth.

During the era of the time of Jacob's Trouble, the beast of the earth will have already abandoned the portions of Jewish tradition that would object to the construction and worship of the idol / image of the beast of the sea. He will be the man of lawlessness, not recognizing the validity of any of the Law that God Most High provided.

And during the era of the time of Jacob's Trouble, the beast of the sea will also have already abandoned the portions of the authentic faith system that objects to the construction and worship of the idol / image of the beast of the sea. He will be the man covered with blasphemies, not recognizing that messiah / the Lamb / Jesus Christ should be the object of authentic worship.

The political leader whose name is a number, '666' – Revelation 13:18

For nineteen hundred years, the meaning of the connection of the beast of the earth with the number 666, has been the source of speculation. What John the Revelator recorded and the name of the beast of the earth being a number, has remained an unsolved riddle.

The two beasts of Revelation 13 will seek to strip the inhabitants of the earth from the value they were created with through renaming them with a number. When John the Revelator provided the number of the beast, it was a similar act to stripping him of his uniqueness as a created human being and substituting it for a number.

Here is the wisdom: Let the one who has understanding count the number of the beast. It is humanity's number, and its number is six hundred sixty six. *(Some original manuscripts list the number as six hundred sixteen.)* Revelation 13:18 translated

Beginning this statement with 'Here is the wisdom: Let the one who has understanding…' *placed this piece of information directly into the unsolved mystery category; and into the category of knowledge to be revealed at a later date.*

As with most prophecies of the future, the full meaning will be revealed when the prophecy takes place. But included here are some of the ideas that people have pondered concerning this prophecy.

Among other ideas, the number 666 has been equated with being an actual name. This connection would imply that the number 666 was a form of Jewish Gematria, a practice of assigning a numerical value to a name, similar to an alphanumerical cipher.

Each letter of the Hebrew alphabet was assigned its own number. The first ten letters were numbered one through ten. The next letters were numbered by tens. Then the numbering changed to hundreds, concluding with the twenty second and last letter of the alphabet being equated with nine hundred.

Every word then has an associated number value, calculated by adding the value of each letter that comprises the word.

Associating letters with numbers may have been practiced even before the Law was given to Moses and the people of Israel (1446 BC). The ephod that the high priest was assigned to wear held the breast plate mounted with twelve stones that represented the twelve sons / twelve tribes of Israel. It was known as the Urim and Thummim / 'lights and perfections' / 'revelation and truth' / 'cursed and innocent.' The high priest wore the ephod into the Holy of Holies on the annual Day of Atonement / Yom Kippur. God Most High use the ephod to communicate with the high priest. Reflecting light against each stone, in the total darkness of the Holy of Holies, acted to communicate words and numbers in the message between God Most High and the high priest.

With the destruction of the temple in 70 AD by the Romans, the Holy of Holies was also destroyed, leaving the riddle of 666 to be disconnected from the context of Jewish tradition for almost nineteen hundred years.

The most sacred numbers in Astrology were 1, 6, 12, 36, 111, & 666. According to Roy Anderson in *Revelation of John*, the pagan priests wore amulets called 'Sigilla Solis' / 'Sun Seal' which symbolized 36 constellations. The amulet was divided into thirty-six squares. The numbers were arranged in the squares so that adding the numbers in every line horizontally or vertically, would total 111. The sums of the numbers on the two diagonal lines would also total 111.

An example of an amulet magic square array dedicated to the sun god:

6	32	3	34	35	1
7	11	27	28	8	30
19	14	16	15	23	24
18	20	22	21	17	13
25	29	10	9	26	12
36	5	33	4	2	31

Similar magic squares were dedicated to Saturn, Jupiter, Mars, Venus, Mercury and the moon.

It was noted that within the astrological religion of Babylon, every god was assigned his own personal sacred number or numbers that were used to identify and 'name' the god. The numbers were indicative of the place and power that each god held among the astrological gods.

The Babylonians recognized the stars in the sky to be divided into 36 constellations, 12 houses in the zodiac, with 3 rooms per house. With 36 constellations / gods, each could rule over 10 degrees, with a cumulative total of 360 degrees and 360 days per year. The seven planets / seven headed astrological dragon, then ruled over the 36 constellations / gods. The sun / 'father of the gods,' ruled over the planets. Adding all the numbers from 1 to 36, provided the sum total of 666, known as the Grand Number of the Sun.

$1 + 2 + 3 + 4 + 5 + 6 + 7 + 8 + 9 + 10 + 11 + 12 + 13 + 14 + 15 + 16 + 17 + 18 + 19 + 20 + 21 + 22 + 23 + 24 + 25 + 26 + 27 + 28 + 29 + 30 + 31 + 32 + 33 + 34 + 35 + 36 = 666$

The Babylonians perceived their gods as being predominately evil and vengeful, ready to strike the people down at the will of the gods. Because of their fear of their gods, they produced 6 x 6 amulets that were worn with the intention that the amulets would provide protection from the vengeance of the evil of the gods. Wearing an amulet was to offer power over the gods, to the individual who wore it.

Note that the numbers 36 and 666 are called summary numbers because they 'summarize' the sum of the numbers of the gods. 36 is the summary number for the god numbers 1 through 8, while 666 is the summary number of the god numbers 1 through 36. They are more commonly called triangular numbers, which was an important concept to the ancient Babylonians.

Each god had one or more numbers assigned to it as the sun god not only had the number 666 assigned to it as the sum of the numbers of the 36 gods, but it also had the number 1 assigned to it, which went towards creating the sum of the 36 god numbers. The moon god was assigned the number 2 as it was considered the wife of the sun god, so their most important son was assigned the number 3 and typified all new life, whether plant or animal. The summary number of all three of these gods was 6 because 1 + 2 + 3 = 6. Murl Vance, *Trail of the Serpent*

When the Medes and Persians conquered Babylon October 12, 539 BC, the global seat of the Babylonian religion, baal / mystery / mythology religion, was relocated to Pergamum, and then eventually moved and established in Rome around 133 BC. This fact earned Rome the moniker 'New Babylon' (1 Peter 5:13).

Archaeologists have found amulets with Latin inscriptions, indicating that the Romans also practiced astrology. Sun worship and the astrological symbolism remains within the Roman Catholic Church, even today. A theology that envisions having power over all the gods, leads to a theology were the papacy can claim to have authority over God Most High and God Most High's Law, with the authority to change God Most High's Law because of the Roman Catholic Church's recognized papal supremacy over the biblical record.

One of the emblems of the Babylonian religion, the baal / mystery / mythology religion, that can still be identified embedded within religion today, are the eighteen pointed star and the six pointed star. The six-sided star numerically relates to 666 (6 points, 6 triangles, 6-sided hexagon).

What has become known as the 'star of David' was a six pointed star, founded upon the idea of two triangles laid together. But the truth is that David did not use a star as a representation of his kingdom. The symbol that truly represents the nation of Israel was and continues to be, two olive branches and a menorah.

Within the Roman Catholic Church, the six pointed star continues to be utilized as a representative symbol. Sometimes it can even be located on papal mitres.

Often the six pointed star / hexagram will be encircled by a serpent / dragon, with the serpent's head swallowing its tail / ouroboros / uroboros. The ouroboros / uroboros was used in ancient Egyptian iconography, in

Greek magical tradition, and as a representation of the constellation Draco.

It has been noted that the Roman Catholic Church's title for pope is 'Vicar of Christ' / 'Vicarivs Filii Dei (Latin) / 'person who acts in the place of Christ.' This title has a numerical value of 666.

Numerous other names and titles add up to the same number.

The original name of Rome was Saturnia, spelled STUR. It was a secret name revealed only to initiates of the Babylonian baal / mystery / mythology religion. S represented 60. T was 400. U was 6 and R was 200. It totaled 666.

Nero Caesar, using Hebrew numerology, totaled 666.

The Greek letters of the word Lateinos (Latin) come to 666.

The Hebrew version of Romulus / Romiith, the founder of Rome, also sums up to 666.

The Roman numeral system's six letters, also add up to 666. D is 500. C is 100. L is 50. X is 10. V is 5. And I is 1.

There were other notable biblical references to the number 666.

King Solomon annually received 666 talents of gold (1 Kings 19:14, 2 Chronicles 9:13).

There were 666 descendants of Adonikam that returned to the land of Israel from the exile (Ezra 2:13, 8:13, (Nehemiah 7:18)).

It has been noted that the Washington monument located in Washington DC USA, is an obelisk that is 666 feet tall.

Traditionally, the number 666 has been associated with a state of incompleteness and imperfection.

Humanity was created on the sixth day of creation with the number six often representing the number of humanity. The number seven, was always represented within the biblical document as a reference to completeness. The number eight referenced new eras, new promises, new levels of relationship, life in a new land, that could only be available following the completeness of seven.

Within the biblical record, the number 666 as a name was only referenced in association with the beast of the earth and the mark of the beasts system. Because of this context, the triple 6s suggested that there will be a contrast between the imperfection and incompleteness of the mark of the beasts system, and the perfection represented by the three sets of sevens provided by God Most High's plan for kingdom transition in heaven and on earth (seven seals, seven trumpets, seven bowls). The triple 6s also suggested that the potency of evil of the mark of the beasts system, will be intensified. The fact that 6 was a number of imperfection and incompleteness, also served to forecast that the mark of the beasts system would be imperfect and incomplete which will contribute to its eventual failure.

John the Revelator also documented that the number 666 was noted to be specifically associated with humanity. The Greek transcript did not contain a definite article / the word 'the,' before 'man.' For this reason, the manuscript could read, the 'number of humanity.'

There are many who will offer further speculation on the meaning of the number 666 and its marking of the man who will be the beast of the earth. The number / name remains a riddle, until the answer is fully disclosed to the world through the events of the era of the time of Jacob's Trouble, the revelation of the beast of the earth at the future abomination of desolation, and the implementation of the mark of the beasts system.

Six hundred sixty six / χξς, or six hundred sixteen / χις? - Revelation 13:18
Some ancient texts recorded the number of the beast of the earth as six hundred sixteen instead of six hundred sixty six.

This calls for wisdom. Let the person who has insight calculate the number of the beast, for it is humanity's number. That number is 666. Revelation 13:18 translated

The Papyrus 115 text is considered to be the oldest preserved manuscript of the book of Revelation. The Papyrus 115 and the Codex Ephraemi Rescriptus texts recorded the number of the beast to be χις / 616 instead of χξς / 666. Codex Ephraemi Rescriptus spelled out the number as ἑξακόσιοι δέκα ἕξ / hexakosioi deka hex.

The Textus Receptus reads χξς / 666.

χξς in Greek translated into 666. χ represented 600. ξ represented 60. ς represented 6.

χις in Greek translated into 616. χ represented 600. ι represented 10. ς represented 6.

616 is a member of the Padovan sequence, coming after 265, 351, 465 (it is the sum of the first two of these). 616 is a polygonal number in four different ways: it is a heptagonal number, as well as 13-, 31- and 104-gonal.

It is also the sum of the squares of the factorials of 2,3,4: $(2!)^2 + (3!)^2 + (4!)^2 = 4+36+576=616$.

The 616th harmonic number is the first to exceed seven.

There was some controversy in the apostolic and early church community about whether the number of the mark of the beasts was six hundred sixty six or six hundred sixteen based on how the passage was copied in some of the ancient transcripts.

Irenaeus of Smyrna and bishop of Lyon (c. 130 to c. 202 AD - student of Polycarp who was a student of John the Revelator) defined the matter decisively and claimed that the number was six hundred sixty six instead of six hundred sixteen.

... This number being found in all the most approved and ancient copies of the Apocalypse and those who saw John face to face bearing their testimony to it, while reason also leads us to conclude that the number of the name of the beast, according to the Greek mode of calculation by the value of the letters contained in it will sum up to six hundred and sixty and six. The number of the tens is equal to that of the hundreds. The number of the hundreds is equal to that of the units, with the number expressed of six being adhered to throughout.

I do not know how it is that some have erred following the ordinary understanding of speech and have vitiated the middle number in the name, deducting the amount of fifty from it so that instead of six decades they will have it that there is one. (I am inclined to think that this occurred through the fault of the copyists... the Greek letter which expresses the number sixty was easily expanded into the letter iota.) Irenaeus, *Against Heresies* 5.30.1

The establishment of a new identity upon the recipients of the mark of the beasts

For God Most High, names are important. Names provide identity to things. One of the first responsibility God the Creator gave to the first man, was to name the wild animals and all the birds in the sky (Genesis 2:19-20).

God Most High even determined the names of some people. For example, God Most High changed Abram's name to Abraham, and Sarai's name to Sarah. With the addition of the 'h' in their names, was the addition of the Holy Spirit's mark upon their lives.

God determined Isaac's name even before he was conceived, because Sarah laughed when she was told that at the age of ninety, that she would have a son. The name Isaac means laughter.

Jacob, after wrestling with God, was renamed Israel. The name 'Jacob' meant supplanter / deceiver. The name 'Israel' means 'one who wrestles with God and prevails.'

When the people of the southern tribe of Judah, were taken into exile into Babylon, there were four young people / adolescents, who stood out. In Babylon, those four young people were given new names (Daniel 1:6-7). Renaming people was the attempt of the victors to cause their new captives to surrender their old traditions, religions, beliefs, and culture; in order to assimilate into their new society.

The names of the four adolescents as exiles in Babylon according to Daniel's record

Hebrew name	Meaning	Babylonian name	Meaning
Daniel	God is my judge / God is judge	Belteshazzar	Keeper of the hidden

	and the source of justice		treasure of Bel / baal
Hananiah	The Lord is gracious to me	Shadrach	You are the servant of the pagan gods; sun, moon, stars, etc.
Mishael	Like God	Meshach	Servant of the goddess Sheba
Azariah	The Lord is my helper	Abednego	Servant of Nebo

Adolescence is one of the prime times in life to shape or reshape one's worldview, one's character, one's sense of purpose, one's understanding of God Most High, etc.

Daniel 1:8 recorded, 'But Daniel resolved in his heart not to defile himself with the royal food and wine…'

The context of Daniel 1 implied that Daniel resolved to not accept the mental and cultural makeover that the Babylonian empire intended to accomplish in their new captives.

John the Baptist and Jesus were both named by God Most High.

In the Nazi Germany death camps, the incarcerated people were given numbers. And they were stripped of being able to use their names. It was part of the process of stripping them of their humanity.

One of the promises that Jesus Christ made to those who are victorious is to provide the victorious person with a white stone with a new name written on it, known only to the one who receives it (Revelation 2:17).

Receiving a new name is the equivalent of receiving a new identity. And names can represent the relationship that the person has with their God or with their position in a family or as a citizen of a nation.

In Revelation 13:16-17, John the Revelator documented that with the mark of the beasts system, the beast of the earth will be identified not with a name, but with a number. It is possible that the mark of the beasts system will replace identification by name of the inhabitants of the earth, with identification by number. What is definite is that the inhabitants of the earth will be required to receive a mark that will demonstrate their connection with the two beasts and with the kingdom of Satan, Inc. / kingdom of man.

The mark of the beasts system, will have the effect of modifying every person that receives the mark of the beasts: modifying their relationships, modifying their autonomy, modifying their physical being, etc.

Resistance to being transformed or remade in the image of the beast of the sea, will seem to be futile. It will be essential to the kingdom of Satan, Inc. / kingdom of man, to transform and reimage the core of humanity in order to cause humanity to be compliant in the pursuit of bringing peace as redefined by the kingdom of Satan, Inc. / kingdom of man. This transformation and reimaging of the core of humanity will be essential in the allies of the rebellion's preparation for war against messiah / the Lamb / Jesus Christ.

The transformation of life that the kingdom of heaven offers, is a life that is rich, full and eternal. It is a life that is drenched in the love, joy, peace, etc. that God the Creator originally created humanity to experience. The kingdom of heaven offers full and complete healing, provided by the original maker of life, as a gift and not as a trade. The kingdom of heaven offers life that experiences being drenched in the full image of the perfect God of the perfect kingdom of heaven.

The transformation of life that the kingdom of Satan, Inc. / kingdom of man will offer with the mark of the beasts system will be a life where pieces of what makes a person human, will be stripped away, and replaced with inferior replacement parts. The kingdom of Satan, Inc. / kingdom of man offers life that experiences the best that humanity can offer, with patches for what the kingdom of Satan, Inc. / kingdom of man determines to be broken. The kingdom of Satan, Inc. / kingdom of man offers a version of life, that seeks to remake the human being in the image of the red dragon / serpent / Satan, Inc.

    To accomplish the goals of the kingdom of Satan, Inc. / kingdom of man, new technologies will be offered to humanity that will be judged to be superior to the created humanity that God the Creator produced. Artificial intelligence will be touted as superior over regular human intelligence. Automatons will be offered as the better choice, instead of autonomous humanity.
    God the Creator breathed life into humanity in the beginning, in the Garden of Eden / garden of God / paradise (Genesis 2:7).
    It will be vital to the kingdom of Satan, Inc. / kingdom of man's mission of human genocide, to replace breathed human life, with a transformed life stripped of the breath of God the Creator.

    There was only one human being in all human history that was able to become impervious to the transformed life that the red dragon / serpent / Satan, Inc. offers. Only Jesus Christ was able to live the perfect human life, unaffected in any way to the transformation that the kingdom of Satan, Inc. / kingdom of man offers.
    It was this imperviousness that allowed Jesus Christ to descend into hell after his death on the cross, and not be able to remain a captive there. And because the red dragon / serpent / Satan, Inc. was forced to allow Jesus Christ to escape, Jesus Christ made it available for every person who is willing to shed the transformative efforts of the kingdom of Satan, Inc. / kingdom of man, to follow messiah / the Lamb / Jesus Christ and to escape, and then to experience the full restoration of life as offered by the kingdom of heaven.
    God Most High's ultimate mission is to provide a kingdom that cannot be contained and will fill the entirety of heaven, earth and the entire cosmos. The life that the

kingdom of heaven offers is marked with humanity and God walking together in face to face relationship, and angels working alongside humanity aiding humanity to accomplish great things.

In contrast to the kingdom of heaven's plan, the red dragon / serpent / Satan, Inc.'s plan has a hierarchical structure where the rebellious angels hold authority over humanity, and any human presence that is allowed among the rebellious angels, is subservient to the rebellious angels. The rebellious angels long ago made their own self declaration of their own divinity, and demanded to be worshiped as gods. The two beasts of Revelation 13 and the idol / image of the beast of the sea, will provide the portal for that worship to become empowered (Revelation 13).

The goal of the mark of the beasts system will be to remove all identifying markers of God the Creator from what God has created.

But God the Creator created humanity with an identity that was founded and tethered upon God the Creator. And that image of God the Creator cannot be stripped away unless the individual consents to relinquish it.

The mark of the beasts system's attempt to redefine the personal identities of the inhabitants of the earth

One of the strategies that the kingdom of Satan, Inc. / kingdom of man will employ will be to redefine the personal identity of every human being. Humanity was created in the image of God the Creator. One of the promises that Jesus Christ makes to those who overcome was that they will become the recipient of a name selected for them by God and by Jesus (Revelation 2:17, 3:12, 19:12). It is the name of every believer in messiah (BC) and follower of the Lamb (AD) that was written in the book of life.

In order to attempt to eliminate all vestiges of God the Creator from earth and heaven, it will be important to attempt to eliminate the image of God the Creator in humanity, and to alter all that God the Creator created. Erasing names and substituting numbers as references to people, will be one of the methods of the kingdom of Satan,

Inc. / kingdom of man for removing the inherent connection that a person holds with God the Creator.

God the Creator named the land, the sea, the stars, etc. And God the Creator assigned the first man and first woman with naming the living creatures upon the earth. (Genesis 1, 2)

In contrast, the mark of the beasts system will assign those who join the system, with a number, replacing their name, and their inherent identity.

Names speak of the aspirations of the one who provides the name, for the one who is named. Names speak of character and uniqueness. Names identify one's relationship with others and how others perceive the individual.

A number only identifies a place in an order of a string of other numbers. Being assigned a number, strips the unique human identity from a person and serves to devalue the individual.

But Jesus Christ promised that:

'To the one having an ear, hear what the Spirit says to the churches. To the one who overcomes, I will give hidden manna. And I will give to that one, a white stone, and on the stone, a new name will be written which no one has known, except the one who receives it.' Revelation 2:17 translated

'The one who overcomes, I will make a pillar in the temple of my God, and that one will not go out anymore. I will write upon that one the name of my God and the name of the city of my God, the new Jerusalem coming down out of heaven from my God, and my new name.' Revelation 3:12 translated

In ancient times, when a father named a child, it was a recognition that the child belonged to the father. And when the God of the kingdom of heaven provides the name, it is a recognition that the heavenly Father has recognized the relationship that the individual holds with God.

For those who do not participate in the mark of the beasts system, the God of heaven will personally provide them with a unique and very personal name that belongs to the person and identifies the surety of the person's relationship with the God of heaven. It will be a name personally chosen by the God of heaven, like a name carefully chosen by a parent for their child. It will be a name that will forever remind that person that they are a treasure of the God of heaven, and that they cannot be removed from the fullness of their relationship with the God of heaven.

In contrast, the mark of the beasts system will provide the inhabitants of the earth with a reference for how the individual is identified by the global governance system for the purpose of collecting and redistributing that person's work equity in a system that elevates the elect and elite ruling class, at the expense of the labor of the rest of humanity.

The mark of the beasts system will be designed to totally strip its recipients of identity and value.

But the name that the God of heaven provides to each unique individual person, will communicate the immense value and worth that the God of heaven individually assesses for each of its recipients.

The economic status of the world that will render the inhabitants of the earth susceptible to welcome the economic solution provided by the mark of the beasts system

The horseman that will be released with the opening of the third seal, will ride the black horse.

When the Lamb opened the third seal, I heard the third living creature say, 'Come!" I looked and behold a black horse, and the one sitting on the horse had a pair of scales in his hand. And I heard something like a voice in the midst of the four living creatures saying, 'A choenix / χοενιξ / measure / quart of wheat for a denarius, and three choenix / χοενιξ / measures / quarts of barley for a denarius. And do not injure the oil and the wine.' '... two pounds of wheat for a day's wages, and six pounds of barley for a day's wages...' Revelation 6:5-6 translated

The scales and the exchange rate of two pounds of wheat for a day's wages and six pounds of barley for a day's wages, portrayed an economy that has collapsed.

In order for the beast of the earth / final world ruler to be able to install a system where no one will be able to buy or sell without receiving the mark of the beasts, the economy must be in a state of collapse. And the global economy must be so devastated that the inhabitants of the earth will be desperate to embrace any hope of a solution.

The mark of the beasts system will then present itself as the new stable economic solution for the inhabitants of the earth.

And the beast of the earth causes all the small and the great, and the rich and the poor, and the free and the servants, that it should give them a mark on their right hand or on their forehead, so that no one should be able to buy or to sell, if they did not have the mark — the name of the beast, or the number of the name of the beast. Revelation 13:16-17 translated

The financial component of the mark of the beasts system and its economy

Possibly the most apparent initial result of the mark of the beasts system will not be the compulsory worship aspect, but rather the effect that the mark of the beasts system will offer as a solution to the problem of the collapsed global economy.

The horseman released with the opening of the third seal held a pair of scales and was associated with global hyperinflation so that one quart / two pounds of wheat cost a day's wages and six pounds of barley cost a day's wages (Revelation 6:5-6). Two pounds of wheat processes into approximately 6 to 7 cups of flour and would make approximately two loaves of bread.

That kind of global hyperinflation will aid in the implementation of the mark of the beasts system.

And the beast of the earth causes all the small and the great, and the rich and the poor, and the free and the servants, that it should give them a mark on their right hand or on their forehead, so that no one should be able to buy or to sell, if they did not have the mark — the name of the beast, or the number of the name of the beast. Revelation 13:16-17 translated

Plausible possibilities for implementing this new economy include the establishment of a cashless society, development of a system of electronic currency, the confiscation of all funds in the pursuit of establishing a global currency standard, etc.

With this kind of global control over personal finances, the inhabitants of the earth will not be able to purchase items deemed unacceptable according to the standards of the beast of the earth. There will be a new dieting standard established of what is halal / kosher /

clean, and it will be enforced. Entertainment and travel will be regulated and monitored.

An enticing marketing strategy for the mark of the beasts system will be its tailoring of music, entertainment, news, travel, and experiences, specifically for the pleasure of the individual (and for influencing minds to foster a better predisposure to accepting global governance). 'Happiness' will be redefined and the propaganda produced will instruct the participants in the mark of the beasts system, that they are happy.

Managing the participants in the mark of the beasts system will resemble the sales of the first Model T Fords, where the customer could have any color vehicle they would like, as long as it was black.

The mark of the beasts system will swap authentic news for newsertainment, and then for propaganda, after the model of Nazi Germany's propaganda machine.

All of this will be part and parcel of the mission of the allies of the rebellion to bring 'peace and security' to the masses, through compulsory human compliance with the global governance system. And because every living creature requires nourishment, by controlling the source and amount of that nourishment, humanity will be controlled.

Jesus taught us to pray, 'Our Father who is in heaven… give us this day our daily bread.' (Matthew 6:11, Luke 11:3)

The promise will be made that through the mark of the beasts system, poverty will be eliminated. But the reality will be that those who are poor will be eliminated, and with their elimination, their personal poverty will no longer be an issue for them. Their resources will be confiscated and redistributed, with the merchants of the world receiving their share first (see Revelation 18, etc.).

For those who provide benefit to the allies of the rebellion, there will be rewards. And through the transactions, the beast of the earth will also personally prosper.

He will advance with glory, those who acknowledge him. He will make them rulers over many and distribute the land as a reward. Daniel 11:39b translated

For those who seek to benefit from the promises of security that will be offered by the two beasts of Revelation 13, a starvation lifestyle will be imposed upon them, with the rationale that their starvation will be necessary in order to conserve the global resources.

Because the integrity level of the global religious community and the global governance system is nonexistent, the era of the time of Jacob's Trouble will become a time when once again a government system will divert the food resources available, in order to increase the wealth of the elite leaders and in order to control the masses of people through the control of the availability of food.

The Roman Catholic Church priesthood practiced this kind of economic system for centuries with their vow of poverty among their priests and nuns, and through their other feudal system practices. All funds were directed through the hierarchy of the Roman Catholic Church organization and then the hierarchy determined how the funds should be distributed. Their priests do not work for the people of God. Their priests work for the benefit of the Roman Catholic Church and are dependent first upon the Roman Catholic Church.

There are also other Christian denominations that follow this practice of requiring allegiance to the church hierarchy in exchange for receiving security and resources.

The mark of the beasts will be used to determine who will be educated. Historically, the Roman Catholic Church metered out the availability of education to those who politically, financially, militarily, etc. supported the Roman Catholic Church. The Roman Catholic Church required support at the expense of the masses.

In the future, students will be required to receive the mark of the beasts system in order to receive education. And the mark of the beasts system may actually contain an internal component that will train the mind. (See *Brave New World*.)

The mark of the beasts system will monitor the health of those who enroll in the system. And under the guise of providing longer life and better health, the mark of the beasts system will assume control over the systems of the body. The mark of the beasts system may have the capability of altering the genetics of the person who receives it so that the person will have pseudo immortality in exchange for their allegiance to the beasts. And the mark of the beasts system may have the power and authority to determine when a person's life should end.

But more importantly, the mark of the beasts system will strive to meet its goal of stripping the inhabitants of the earth of their own personal autonomy, an autonomy that God the Creator created within each human being that was designed to be supported by God the Creator.

The most important aspect receiving the mark of the beasts system will be the system's irreparable damage of the image of God that each human being was created with. Once the image of God has been broken within an individual, that individual will become ineligible to receive citizenship in the kingdom of heaven.

Ultimately the mark of the beasts system will traffic in the currency of human life and eternal human life. Giving away the essence of one's being through receiving the mark of the beasts will be the most tragically significant form of the transaction between the kingdom of Satan, Inc / kingdom of man and that human being.

God Most High declared, 'Every animal of the forest is mine, and the cattle on a thousand hills. I know every bird in the mountains, and the insects in the fields are mine.' Psalm 50:10-11

God the Creator authored and created the cosmos and everything in it. Everything in the cosmos is already under the stewardship plan of God Most High. God Most High's stewardship cannot be taken away. Those who enroll in the mark of the beasts system will have been deceived into giving away what God the Creator personally gave to them, and giving away the opportunity to develop an eternal and loving relationship with the one that created them.

In contrast to the restrictions that the kingdom of Satan, Inc. / kingdom of man will impose upon humanity, the kingdom of heaven's goal is to set human individuals free: free to explore, free to experiment, free to be creative, free to experience the fullness of life, free to be heirs of the richness of the perfect Garden of Eden / garden of God / paradise that God will reestablish on earth, etc. If the Son sets you free, you are truly free. John 8:36

The societal and cultural environment of idolatry, adultery, sexism and porn that will be present to aid in the ascent of the beast of the earth / final world ruler

Another global condition that will contribute to the installation of the mark of the beasts system will be society's cultural environment.

God Most High provided Moses and the people of Israel with strict societal rules as the people of Israel left Egypt in 1446 BC. It was called the Law / Torah. During the millennia since then, those strict societal rules provided for the people of Israel, infiltrated throughout the world to become guiding principles for many societies and cultures, especially societies and cultures where Christianity prevailed.

The Roman Catholic Church has historically and consistently altered and minimized the Law as documented in the biblical record. The Protestant Reformation was a protest against the forbiddance and suppression by the Roman Catholic Church, of the reading and teaching concerning the Law. The principle of sola scriptura / scripture alone, was introduced with the initiation of the Protestant Reformation (October 31, 1517). With the Protestant Reformation, colleges were established for the teaching of theology, and education was made available to all. A further result of the Protestant Reformation was the Great Awakening / Evangelical Revival / Holiness Movement that further shaped the cultural dynamics of the world.

It was the societal rules documented within the biblical record that provided the foundation for the *structure many of the American colonies and then the founding of the nation, the United States of America.*

But with the modern church's new stance of distancing itself from the biblical record, a void has been created where societal rules are no longer taught (Revelation 3:14-22). The result has been to trample on the societal rules that once were strong. This cultural dynamic of the disregard of the Law, will be necessary to allow for the 'man of lawlessness' *to rise (2 Thessalonians 2:1-12).*

John the Revelator described the societal cultural environment that will exist at the point in history just prior to the future abomination of desolation event. God Most High's assessment of the cultural societal environment will be the reason for allowing the events scheduled for the second half of the era of the time of Jacob's Trouble, to proceed.

The rest of humanity who were not killed by their plagues *(with the sounding of the first six trumpets)*, did not even repent of the works of their hands, so that they did not worship the demons and their golden and silver and bronze and stone and wooden idols, which are neither able to see nor to hear nor to walk. And they did not repent of their murders, nor of their sorceries (magic arts), nor of their sexual immorality, nor of their thefts. Revelation 9:20-21 translated

Today's 'post Christian' culture worships demons and idols, even within the church that was established to be the enemy against rebellious demons and idols. Murder used to be viewed as morally wrong. But today, murder is considered justified if the murder is of someone who is the wrong age, or of someone who disagrees with politically woke views, or someone who does not accept the globalist agenda, or someone who is inconvenient. Theft is no longer thwarted or prosecuted. Etc.

The 'brave new world' that was defined in 1931 by Aldous Huxley (1894 to 1963), that depended upon the application of drugs for the behavioral conditioning of humanity, articulated goals that have been embraced by the United Nations. The time for that brave new world, has arrived. Neurochip interfaces have been developed that will aid in the advancement of embracing further rebellion against God Most High, murder, hallucinatory states of mind, sexual deviancy and theft.

Klaus Schwab as a leader of the World Economic Forum of Davos Switzerland, has now openly declared the goals of the global elites who desire to be the global ruling class.

Elon Musk envisioned a society connected with neuralinks. The neuralinks that will provide brain-machine interfaces / BMI, have become reality. Through neuralinks, the inhabitants of the earth will also be able to be controlled by those who consider themselves to be global elites.

There will be many components of the societal culture that will aid in the implementation of the mark of the beasts system. This is the point in human history when the global elites' theoterrorism movement will have fully coalesced and blossomed to fruition.

The societal culture of the transhumanist agenda of the oligarchy of the global elites

At the point in history when the future abomination of desolation event will take place, there must be an environment of acceptance within societal culture for receiving the leadership of the two beasts of Revelation 13, and for the loyal worship of the idol / image of the beast of the sea, and for the implementation of the mark of the beasts system. The global elites have for millennia, sought to rule over the masses and to find more efficient methods for ruling the masses. One method for appealing to the masses during this era, will be the development of transhumanism, proffered as a solution to starvation, health issues, insecurity, discomfort and death.

The budding thought for the concept of transhumanism, existed in societal culture since before the deluge / flood, and afterward. The breeding of the Nephilim was one attempt to alter the genetic core of humanity in order to produce a hybrid superhuman. The 'men of renown' of ancient history were products of the Nephilim breeding program who were physically stronger and taller than genetically pure human beings.

In modern culture, the concept of transhumanism has been popularized in television and movies, for example, *Six Million Dollar Man*, *Bionic Woman*, *Superwoman*, Darth Vader of *Star Wars*, etc. The concept of robot type creations, androids, etc. being produced that imitate humanity has also been popularized, for example, *Bicentennial Man*, *Terminator* series of movies, *I, Robot*, the androids of *Star Trek*, etc. Those depictions communicated the message that transhumanism and robots / androids only benefit society and further advance humanity.

Another appeal of the mark of the beasts system will be its promise to provide to each individual, an interconnectedness with a new virtual reality that will promise to incorporate the benefits of technology and 'science.'

The awareness of society's cultural movement toward the incorporation of new ways to govern people, evolutionary theory, transhumanism and its associated technologies, began centuries ago in places like the *Royal Society of London for Improving Natural Knowledge*, and other organizations frequented by global elites. There are many organizations that seek to advance the development of an elite ruling class with many classes of people to be ruled. Agencies serving that goal that have become known are Davos, World Economic Forum, Bilderberg Group, Bill Gates Foundation, the United Nations, etc. And then there are agencies whose identities are not as well known.

The movement toward this kind of globalist society has been presented as if their version of globalism will bring world peace. Their theme song could be the 1970's Coke commercial jingle, 'I'd like to teach the world to sing, in perfect harmony...' Globalism has been presented as an answer to making everything wonderful, where everyone will live in perfect harmony, if we would just learn to sing their song.

But the reality is that globalism advocates the establishment of a permanent elite ruling class that is willing to sacrifice individual prosperity, individual freedoms, individual decision making, individual consciences and morals, individual identities and lives of human beings, under the guise of advancing the greater good / social justice. The rationale for eliminating mass numbers of human beings and human life as we currently experience human life, will be that the earth cannot endure the stress upon its resources, of such a great population. The hidden rationale for eliminating mass numbers of human beings and human life, will be that it is easier to rule less numbers of people than it is to rule greater numbers of people. Those considered to be unproductive or valueless to the culture of the ruling elites, will be the first to be deemed undesirable, valueless and disposable.

Adolf Hitler's final solution pogrom served as a typology for the future systematic attack upon the world's population.

Many organizations with a globalist agenda have risen over the millennia. But the idea of total world domination existed from the time when everyone dwelled in the Garden of Eden / garden of God / paradise, and rebellion entered into their relationships.

The Royal Society of London for Improving Natural Knowledge was one of the many incubators of globalist ideas. The Royal Society of London was established in 1660 / 1663 by the king of Great Britain, Charles II (fl. 1649 to 1651 Scotland; fl. 1660 to 1685 England, Scotland Ireland, etc.), as a response to the beheading of his father, Charles I (fl. 1625 to 1649) over religious differences between Catholicism / papal rule and Protestantism / autonomy. The Royal Society of London was charged with establishing better ways for governing the people so that monarchs in Great Britain would not need to experience execution.

Out of the Royal Society of London came the development of theories that could fill the position that religion took in society, without using a Judeo Christian foundation. The Royal Society of London began as an organization that feigned a pursuit of science. But after a number of decades, the pursuit of authentic science was replaced with the pursuit of scientism and humanism.

Modern evolutionary theory was initiated and incubated within the Royal Society of London. So were theories on eugenics and the governance of the masses through control and manipulation. The Darwin and Galton families, who developed evolutionary theory and eugenics were nurtured within the Royal Society of London. The Huxley family, including Julian Huxley, the first director general of UNESCO, and his older brother Aldous Huxley who wrote Brave New World, were nurtured within the Royal Society of London.

The direction of thought that was gestated within the Royal Society of London, was the supposition that if humanity could advance fast enough and far enough, human life could escape the confines of religious dogmas, doctrines, theologies and practices, espoused by the church.

Humanism, the belief that man is the beginning point for serious moral and philosophical inquiry, engendered and embraced modern evolutionary theory.

Modern evolutionary theory generated transhumanism, the belief that the human condition can be improved upon through technologies. Some forms of transhumanist thought even proposed that the transhuman enhanced longevity of life, could conceivably be extended to become a form of eternal life.

'Enhanced man is eternal man, and that man has already been born.' – unknown source

Julian Huxley (1887 to 1975), first Director General of UNESCO / United Nations Educational, Scientific and Cultural Organization, popularized the term 'transhumanism' (1957).

Julian's older brother Aldous Huxley (1894 to 1963) engaged in philosophical mysticism / psychedelic experiences with mescaline and LSD, and embraced universalism in defiance of the precepts of Christianity. Aldous Huxley wrote Brave New World (1932) that anticipated a futuristic world state, whose citizens will be environmentally engineered into an intelligence based upon social hierarchy. The novel projected advancements in reproductive technology, sleep learning / sleep teaching, psychological manipulation and classical conditioning, that would be combined to make a dystopian society. Through scientific and psychological engineering, the people of the dystopian society would be genetically designed to be passive and therefore consistently useful to the ruling class. It was a society of indulgence rather than abstinence. Monogamy was discouraged because 'everyone belongs to everyone else.'

Upon reading George Orwell's *Nineteen Eighty-Four*, Aldous Huxley wrote to George Orwell, commenting on their shared belief in the rise of a ruling elite class.

Within the next generation I believe that the world's rulers will discover that infant conditioning and narco-hypnosis are more efficient, as instruments of government, than clubs and prisons, and that the lust for power can be just as completely satisfied by suggesting people into loving their servitude as by flogging and kicking them into obedience…
Aldous Huxley, October 12, 1949, Wrightwood California

The Royal Society of London continues to entertain its ideas of achieving a godless society. For example, on September 10, 2019, The Royal Society published a report, *iHuman: blurring lines between mind and machine*. (https://royalsociety.org/-/media/policy/projects/ihuman/report-neural-interfaces.pdf)

The report provided a summary of recommendations for the United Kingdom; to develop a Neural Interface Ecosystem, to accelerate the development of the technologies in the UK, to advocate for trial approaches to technology regulation, to engage in public interaction as a means to garner public acceptance, to engage policy makers and the public, etc. This publication of course did not include the fine print of the deeper plan that would only be available to the elite members of the Royal Society. But the publication described the benefits of the neural revolution upon those who experience health challenges and mental health challenges, as a means for appeasing the public.

With neural interfaces, health could be monitored and neurostimulation could prompt people to exercise or respond to other directional control. The neural interfaces could enhance daily life through the use of the mind to *open doors, to turn on lights, to play games, to operate equipment, to type on computers, to assist in learning, to assist in decision making* 'free from biases.' *The technologies would even support several of the United Nations' Sustainable Development Goals.*

Merging the decision making capacity and emotional intelligence of humans (even altered through the proposed mind control) with the big data processing power of computers, would create a new form of intelligence that would allow humanity to become telepathic / able to access other minds.

The implementation of the idol / image of the beast of the sea, with the mark of the beasts system, will integrate modern technology and thought into one exclusive system that will seek to replace all other systems, for the purpose of achieving global governance, with the beast of the earth as its focal point for global rule.

Their unified system will be designed to incorporate gene editing (body), neuroenhancement (brain), bionics (cyborg culture), robotics (digital body), artificial intelligence (digital brain), and a host of other technologies and ideologies into its application. Their unified system with its ability to connect with a neuralink system, will even have the ability to achieve misattribution of memory including cryptomnesia, false memory, social cryptomnesia, source confusion, suggestibility, etc., providing adverse conditioning to what the kingdom of Satan, Inc. / kingdom of man has determined to be deterrents toward its goals. Their unified system will be designed to create pleasure induced conditioning for those items considered to advance its agenda. The appeal of the mark of the beasts system will be the promise to enhance one's physical, psychological, and social capability, through human augmentation; and a virtual reality 'eternal life.'

All aspects of their unified system will be intentionally calculated to achieve the separation of the human being created in the image of God the Creator, from the image of God the Creator that was created intrinsically within every human being. Their unified system will necessitate the diminution of individual human beings to process their own autonomous thought, in order to be effective in attaining globalists' goals.

In contrast to the human augmentation offered through their unified system, the authentic human augmentation that the kingdom of heaven offers was defined in the biblical record as the bodily resurrection of those who are believers in Jesus Christ as the promised and prophesied messiah. And the fully intact physical and biological resurrection of every unique follower of the Lamb / Jesus Christ will take place in the space of a twinkling of the eye, when messiah / the Lamb / Jesus Christ returns, near the conclusion of the finale for the era of the time of Jacob's Trouble.

The design of modern evolutionary theory and transhumanism, is to establish a virtual dimension where the essence of the individual can be captured / stolen, separated from the human being, and placed into a collective where the power of the human being can be accessed by the elite and elect ruling class for their own personal benefit (at the expense of the discardable physical human being).

Transhumanism was defined by Max More in 1990 as 'Philosophies of life (such as extropian perspectives) that seek the continuation and acceleration of the evolution of intelligent life beyond its currently human form and human limitations by means of science and technology, guided by life-promoting principles and values.'

Joe Allen has written extensively on transhumanism, its mechanics, its ideology, its danger to societal culture, and its danger for those who are followers of the Lamb / Jesus Christ. Joe Allen explained how the various components of transhumanist ideology are being merged together to create a network that will interact with the physical individual human being to achieve control over the human individual's thought processes and physicality.

Aleksandr Isayevich Solzhenitsyn (1918 to 2008) wrote concerning the line that separates good and evil. 'Gradually it was disclosed to me that the line separating good and evil passes not through states, nor between classes, nor between political parties either – but right through every human heart – and through all human hearts. This line shifts. Inside us, it oscillates with the years. And even within hearts overwhelmed by evil, one small bridgehead of good is retained. And even in the best of all hearts, there remains ... an un-uprooted small corner of evil.'

'Since then, I have come to understand the truth of all the religions of the world: They struggle with the evil inside a human being (inside every human being). It is impossible to expel evil from the world in its entirety, but it is possible to constrict it within each person.'
Aleksandr Solzhenitsyn, *The Gulag Archipelago 1918-1956*

Society has been groomed for six thousand years, to reach the point of global acceptance of this form of tyrannical rule, brought by the kingdom of Satan, Inc. / kingdom of man. Even though tyrannical rule has been locally or regionally achieved in the past, and then defeated, the biblical record documented that this time, tyrannical rule will be so deceptive that it will be embraced globally ...

... before being defeated by messiah / the Lamb / Jesus Christ upon his return from heaven.

The biblical record would classify transhumanism as a form of mechanical sorcery. It is the product of dark religion that is obsessed with power. The bulk of transhumanist thought remains in direct conflict with the message of the biblical record.

Artificial intelligence will never be consciousness, nor will it have an authentic human spirit. Artificiality in all forms, defies the creative work of God the Creator.

For these reasons, the unified system of the two beasts of Revelation 13, will be in such a deep conflict with the kingdom of heaven, that those who receive the mark of the beasts will not be compatible with the kingdom of heaven (Revelation 14:9-11, 20:4).

The societal cultural environment of the global elites' theoterrorism movement

There is within the list of management techniques, the strategy of creating a crisis. Once the created crisis has been identified, then the solution can be proposed and accepted by those living in the crisis.

The crisis that the Egyptians and their pharaoh experienced with the ten plagues against the Egyptian gods, incentivized the pharaoh to allow Moses to provide the solution that the people of Israel should leave Egypt (1446 BC).

Wars are about creating crises and then providing a solution of accepting the victors' rule.

Currently within the United States, a segment of politicians and leaders have embarked on creating a state of economic, political and cultural crisis, in their pursuit of garnering greater control over the government of the United States and over the citizens of the United States.

There are multiple other nations and organizations that experience the same kind of threat to their societies.

But employing the 'create a crisis' strategies of the past, will all pale in comparison to the crisis that will arise from the societal cultural environment of theoterrorism that the global elites have planned for humanity around the world.

The fourth green horse (societal cultural theoterrorism) that was released with the opening of the fourth seal, had a rider named Death, and Hades followed immediately behind him.

When the Lamb opened the fourth seal, I heard the voice of the fourth living creature saying, 'Come!' I looked and behold a green horse, and the one sitting on the horse was named Death, and Hades was following with him. They were given authority over the fourth of the earth to kill with sword and with famine and with plague and by the beasts of the earth. Revelation 6:7-8 translated

Obtaining power over a quarter of the earth, to kill by sword, famine and plague, and by the wild beasts of the earth, is almost unimaginable. This kind of reality would cause other historical attempts of establishing global empires, to pale in comparison.

After the mark of the beasts system becomes functional, the biblical record documented that the global societal culture will experience an increase in turmoil, unruliness, lawlessness, etc. Anticipate a rise in hijackings, kidnappings, bombings, assassinations, assaults, hostage incidents, dictates, sexual trafficking, sexual crimes, etc. And the man of lawlessness will not recognize any of these behaviors as problems that will need to actually be addressed beyond offering fake empathy and a modicum of words of disdain. In fact, the rise in this kind of evil behavior will be used to justify the enforcement of further global and individual controls upon humanity.

What will be important to remember as we watch the dynamics of the scheduled events for the era of the time of Jacob's Trouble transpire, will be that the solutions that the kingdom of Satan, Inc. / kingdom of man will offer, will be responses to the destruction and crises that the kingdom of Satan, Inc. / kingdom of man will have created. And the kingdom of heaven's solutions to the crises are greater than anything the kingdom of Satan, Inc. / kingdom of man have to offer.

The acceptance of magic, sorcery, occult practices, illusion, dark arts, etc.

Contemporary culture has experienced an increased acceptance of magic, sorcery, occult practices, illusion, dark arts, etc. The creation of legendary superheroes has grown in number and the abilities of fictitious superheroes has expanded. Batman advanced to become more than a child's television program, to something quite sophisticated. The *Good Witch* transformed the image of witches from being nefarious and in league with Satan Inc., to having inherent goodness and people that would be desirable to have living in one's neighbor. The wizard *Harry Potter* would not be able to have been offered to children raised in the 1950s. But in the 1990s, Harry Potter became a savior figure, using magic for good to defeat evil.

This was precisely the attitude toward magic, sorcery, occult practices, illusion, dark arts, etc. that the Law provided by God Most High to Moses and the people of Israel, warned to avoid.

Magic, sorcery, occult practices, illusion, dark arts, etc., were not effective for the pharaoh during the life of Joseph (Genesis 41), nor during the life of Moses for the people of Egypt to provide a defense against the plagues (Exodus 7 through 11), nor for Nebuchadnezzar the king of Babylon (Daniel 1, 2, 4), nor for Belshazzar the later king of Babylon (Daniel 5), etc.

John the Revelator noted that around the time of the future abomination of desolation event, the inhabitants of the earth not marked with God's seal, will experience five months of sores that will be the result of scorpion locust stings. And that will be followed by one third of humanity being killed by plagues of fire, smoke and sulfur from the mouths of the horses and riders of the two hundred million cavalry released from under the Euphrates River. And still those events will not deter the global culture in their pursuit of practicing their magic arts.

The rest of humanity who were not killed by their plagues (with the sounding of the first six trumpets), did not even repent of the works of their hands, so that they did not worship the demons and their golden and silver and bronze and stone and wooden idols, which are neither able to see nor to hear nor to walk. And they did not repent of their murders, nor of their sorceries (magic arts), nor of their sexual immorality, nor of their thefts. Revelation 9:20-21 translated

Rather than being a culture that seeks truth, the global culture will prefer magic, sorcery, occult practices, illusion, dark arts, etc. This will be the global society's cultural environment that will foster humanity's embrace of the magic performed by the beast of the earth and the idol / image of the beast of the sea being established on the temple mount.

Sexual immorality and its acceptance in cultural norms

The first abomination of desolation event in 167 BC, was heavily steeped in sexually immoral activity with deviant sex acts incorporated into the compulsory worship of the gods of the Seleucids, on the temple mount.

The future abomination of desolation event will follow the template of the first abomination of desolation event. In order for similar practices to take place, and still have the beast of the earth be accepted by the inhabitants of the earth as a final world ruler, sexual immorality must be culturally acceptable during the era of the time of Jacob's Trouble.

According to the Barna Group, Ltd, Americans' perspectives and behaviors related to sexuality have shifted with younger generations. Cohabitation, extramarital sex, pornography, homosexuality and sexual fantasies have now become culturally acceptable. The new cultural norms have invaded television shows, explicit movies and explicit videos.

The new rules of morality affect all personal interactions, creating less civility, less respect and less self-control. The use of profanity in public has increased, along with rumoring, lying, and theft. A new acceptance of gambling, intoxication and illegal drug use has resulted in viewing these activities as morally acceptable behaviors. In the absence of moral teaching, a significant shift in morality has taken place.

Concerning the United States of America, 'The consistent deterioration of the Bible as the source of moral truth has led to a nation where people have become independent judges of right and wrong, basing their choices on feelings and circumstances. It is not likely that America will return to a more traditional moral code until the nation experiences significant pain from its moral choices.' The Barna Group, Ltd.

According to the Barna Group, Ltd (2016), the use of porn has significantly risen among pastors, male and female youth and women. For example,

- 62% of teens and young adults have received a sexually explicit image and 41% have sent one.
- 57% of pastors and 64% of youth pastors admit they have struggled with porn, either currently or in the past.
- 21% of youth pastors and 14% of pastors admit they currently struggle with using porn.
- About 12% of youth pastors and 5% of pastors say they are addicted to porn.
- The vast majority of faith leaders who struggle with porn say this has significantly affected their ministry in a negative manner.

https://www.barna.com/the-porn-phenomenon/

Other data on porn use from the conquerseries.com (https://conquerseries.com/15-mind-blowing-statistics-about-pornography-and-the-church):

- *Over forty million Americans regularly visit porn sites.*
- *There are approximately forty two million porn sites and three hundred seventy million pages of porn.*
- *The porn industry's annual revenue is more than the combined revenue of the NFL, NBA, and MLB. It is also more than the combined revenues of ABC, CBS, and NBC.*
- *The average age that a child is first exposed to porn is eleven years of age. 94% of children will see porn by the age of 14.*
- *Of young Christian adults 18 to 24 years old, 76% actively search for porn.*
- *68% of churchgoing men view porn on a regular basis.*
- *87% of Christian women have watched porn.*
- *55% of married men and 25% of married women say they watch porn at least once a month.*
- *57% of pastors have or currently struggle with porn.*
- *47% of families in the United States reported that pornography is a problem in their home.*
- *Pornography use increases the marital infidelity rate by more than 300%.*
- *56% of American divorces involve one party having an 'obsessive interest' in pornographic websites.*

The porn addicted brain looks similar to the heroin addicted brain. Porn is that addictive. People involved in porn are likely to find their real world partner considerably less stimulating than porn, perhaps to the point of sexual dysfunction. The brain can be conditioned over time to expect hyper-stimulation as part of sexual arousal to the point where an in-person partner cannot provide the same neurochemical rush. Porn has the effect of bringing in another partner into relationships, even if it is only through a computer or video screen.

But the good news is that the damage to the brain from porn addiction, can be reversed.

What cannot be reversed is the damage that porn use has upon the rest of the family. (https://conquerseries.com/to-my-porn-watching-dad-from-your-daughter)

Theft as an accepted practice
Theft will be considered an accepted practice during this time.

It seems quite odd that theft, especially during a time of turmoil, would be an accepted practice. But the biblical record documented that theft will be an accepted practice among the inhabitants of the earth during the era of the time of Jacob's Trouble.

In addition, in order for the mark of the beasts system to become functional, the global economy will need to experience a cataclysmic shift during which the bank accounts of every individual will become subject to seizure; possibly the greatest act of theft ever imagined.

Also, Daniel and John the Revelator described the little horn / eleventh king / beast of the earth as promising a kingdom to the ten horns / ten kings atop the fourth beast / fourth kingdom, and then never delivering to them their promised kingdom. The two beasts of Revelation 13 will participate in this theft from the ten horns / ten kings and their allies.

During the era of the time of Jacob's Trouble, some of the greatest thievery in history will take place, led by the circle of the global elites.

The termination of the mark of the beasts system
The mark of the beasts system will become functional during the future abomination of desolation event.

The biblical record did not directly address when the mark of the beasts system would cease operation. But the context that described the mark of the beasts system, was the context of John the Revelator's description of the beast of the earth (Revelation 13:11-18). And the two beasts of Revelation 13 will experience their term of supernatural power and authority ending after forty two months.

Daniel's description also defined the ruler who will come / the king who will exalt and magnify himself, as beginning this term of supernatural power and authority with the future abomination of desolation event (Daniel 9:26-27, 12:11). In Daniel's description, some form of his power and authority will be extended to sometime between one thousand two hundred ninety days and one thousand three hundred thirty five days.

It is possible that with the earthquake in Jerusalem that will accompany the resurrection and ascension of the two witnesses (Revelation 11:11-14), that the temple mount will experience such a shaking that every stone of the temple will be dislodged and everything on the temple mount would be destroyed, possibly including the idol / image of the beast of the sea and the console for the mark of the beasts system. If this took place, it would be reminiscent of the earthquake that shook the temple at the time of the crucifixion and death of Jesus Christ. This kind of earthquake would potentially have the power to disconnect the mark of the beasts system, taking it offline and rendering it inoperable. (Caution: this proposal of the timing of the termination of the mark of the beasts system, is only plausible speculation and not fully supported by the biblical record.)

The willingness to martyr God's holy people

The vision that Jesus Christ gave to John the Revelator documented numerous times, the attitude of the inhabitants of the earth that will be expressed during the era of the time of Jacob's Trouble. In Revelation 2 and 3, it was the attitude of the various church theologies that developed throughout the history of the church, that was the focus. The attitude of angels, heavenly beings, etc. were also detailed.

But one of the more unique aspects of the general global attitude during the era of the time of Jacob's Trouble, will be the mindset that human life is cheap, valueless and almost meaningless. The importance of the souls of human beings will not be recognized. And the human lives of people who belong to God, will be categorized as detestable and needing to be destroyed as a final solution.

The opening of the fifth seal revealed the martyrs that are held under the altar. People who were slain because of the word of God and the testimony they had maintained (Revelation 6:9-10).

This perspective of hatred toward God's holy people will be such a prevailing dynamic, that God Most High made provision for 'sealing' those who will stand with messiah / the Lamb / Jesus Christ in the final battle of this age; sealed prior to the majority of the scheduled events of the era of the time of Jacob's Trouble.

But it will not be just God's holy people who the kingdom of Satan, Inc. / kingdom of man will target. The impetus of the kingdom of Satan, Inc. / kingdom of man will be derived from the belief that all human life is cheap, valueless and expendable. The kingdom of Satan, Inc. / kingdom of man will attack its own adherents first. The sounding of the seven trumpets will act as a warning, similar to the warning sounds of the trumpets during the time when the people of Israel were camping in the wilderness for forty years. In John's Revelation, the events associated with the sounding of the first six of the seven trumpets were recognized as plagues brought by the kingdom of Satan, Inc. / kingdom of man, and visited upon those not sealed as belonging to God Most High.

And example of the deaths of human beings through the plagues brought with the sounding of the trumpets, by members of the kingdom of Satan, Inc. / kingdom of man:

A third of humanity was killed by the three plagues of fire, smoke and sulfur that came out of their mouths. Revelation 9:18

The rest of humanity who were not killed by these plagues still did not repent of the work of their hands... Revelation 9:20a

A third of the inhabitants of the earth will die just with the events associated with the sounding of the first six trumpets, especially the sixth trumpet (Revelation 9:18).

The vision that Jesus Christ provided to John the Revelator documented that the amount of death that will be realized during the era of the time of Jacob's Trouble, will be so extensive that the people of God Most High who will be martyred will be crying, 'How long will it be?' (Revelation 6:9-10). In addition, those that will be martyred because of their belief in God Most High and in messiah / the Lamb / Jesus Christ, during this era, will receive extra blessing (Revelation 14:13).

The mark of the beasts system will incorporate the global posture that human life dedicated to God Most High, messiah / the Lamb / Jesus Christ, and the kingdom of heaven should be extinguished, as the kingdom of Satan, Inc. / kingdom of man's 'final solution.' And those not dedicated to the God of the kingdom of heaven, should have their lives irreversibly altered so that the image of God the Creator should be extinguished.

And the beast of the earth deceives those dwelling on the earth by reason of the signs that it was given to perform before the beast of the sea, telling those dwelling on the earth to make an image to the beast that was wounded by the sword and has lived.

And the beast of the earth was given the ability to give breath to the image of the beast of the sea, so that the image of the beast of the sea should also speak. And the image of the beast of the sea <u>will cause all who would not worship the image of the beast of the sea, to be killed</u>.

And the beast of the earth causes all the small and the great, and the rich and the poor, and the free and the servants, that it should give them a mark on their right hand or on their forehead, so that no one should be able to buy or to sell, if they did not have the mark — the name of the beast, or the number of the name of the beast. Revelation 13:14-17 translated

It will be this societal cultural environment that will support the beast of the earth to institute a system where those who refuse to worship the idol / image of the beast of the sea, will be guilty of noncompliance to the kingdom of Satan, Inc. / kingdom of man. And that will be an offense that will be punishable by death.

The efficiency of this killing machine will surpass the proficiency of any past historical killing process.

The convergence of the rise of the Roman Catholic Church's global papal authority, the modern evolutionary theory birthed in the Royal Society of London, the United Nations' Agenda 2030 pursuit of the Omega Point of modern evolutionary theory's eschatology, the pursuit of establishing the Great Reset with the result of economically enriching the global elites, the implementation of the United Nations' Agenda 2030 global plan for global population reduction, etc.; with the mark of the beasts system

Over nineteen hundred years ago, Jesus Christ revealed to John the Apostle, details of the events that would take place during the era of the time of Jacob's Trouble. John the Revelator recorded those events from his first century AD perspective. The intervening nineteen hundred years have been utilized by God Most High for the preparation and staging of those events. During the era of the time of Jacob's Trouble, what John saw in his vision, will now coalesce to become reality.

The book of Revelation that John the Revelator recorded was the design plan.

The transpiration of the actual events of the era of the time of Jacob's Trouble, will be the constructed realization of the design plan.

The three dimensional and operational constructed building is always different from the two dimensional blueprint. One way in which the actual building is different from the blueprint is in scale. The blueprint can be held in one's hand. The actual building can envelope its occupants.

Applying this same expansion of scale to John the Revelator's record of the vision that he received, means that what John the Revelator described, must utilize the multiple developed major organizations of the world.

A blueprint for a building will have lines drawn that represent property boundaries, structure and construction, HVAC (heating, ventilating, air conditioning), plumbing, electrical systems, communication lines, safety systems, etc. All these details on a blueprint assume that the property boundaries, structural components, construction equipment, HVAC equipment, water and sewage system, electrical grid, communication network, safety system equipment, etc. have been planned out and must be assembled in physical three dimensional materials that will be much larger than the lines on the blueprint.

The history of construction cranes dates back only to 1838. Modern indoor plumbing is a relatively new development with the first screw down water tap being patented in 1845 in Rotherham England. Electrical grid systems that supplied usable electricity to homes and businesses, were established just over a hundred years ago. Safety systems were a more modern development. Telephones became a standard in homes around sixty to seventy years ago. The internet has only been well established for about thirty years. And now cell phones can receive cell service in almost every nation of the world.

Understanding the dynamics and scheduled events of the era of the time of Jacob's Trouble, requires the same kind of application of scale, magnifying the blueprint that John the Revelator provided, to the actual experience of the era of the time of Jacob's Trouble.

During the era of the time of Jacob's Trouble, there will be a convergence of systems; specifically the global religious system (white horse), global political system (red horse), global economic system (black horse), global cultural theoterrorism system (green horse with Death as its rider and Hades following behind), global resistance (martyrs of the opening of the fifth seal), the earth's response (opening of the sixth seal), with the response of the red dragon / serpent / Satan, Inc. (seven trumpets) and God Most High's response (seven bowls of God Most High's wrath / seven last plagues) that will result from the opening of the seventh seal. (Revelation 6)

While the focus of the kingdom of Satan, Inc. / kingdom of man will be upon obtaining total global domination, the focus of the kingdom of heaven will be upon the individual who decided to strive to overcome / to be victorious (Revelation 2 and 3), validating the treasure that God the Creator understands each human life to be and striving to be responsible in honoring that created treasure and relationship with God the Creator.

According to most current global systems, human life has little value and is worthy of being disposed of.

But according to God Most High, human life is the only value worth sacrificing for. And God Most High demonstrated that kind of love in sending one of the beings of God / messiah / the Lamb / Jesus Christ, to experience a fully human life, and to experience being the perfect sacrifice, so that whomever believes in him will not perish but have eternal life dwelling with all three persons of God in a face to face relationship. (John 3:16-21)

The kingdom of Satan, Inc. / kingdom of man will strive to achieve its mission of destruction, while attempting to compete with the attractiveness of the mission of the kingdom of heaven. Because the kingdom of heaven is fully and completely authentic, the kingdom of Satan, Inc. / kingdom of man must resort to artificial replication.

For example, God the Creator created authentic humanity. But the kingdom of heaven will strive to create artificial humans, or trans humans, etc., designed to replace authentic human beings. One piece from the kingdom of Satan, Inc. / kingdom of man's blueprint for the global future will include the utilization of artificial intelligence / AI. One media production that described this plan was *Timelapse of Artificial Intelligence (2028 - 3000+)*, https://www.youtube.com/watch?v=63yr9dIIocU.

The conglomeration of evil forces that will converge together during the era of the time of Jacob's Trouble will include:
- the realization of the Roman Catholic Church and the Society of Jesus / Jesuit's mission to establish global papal authority,
- the advancement of modern evolutionary theory birthed in the Royal Society of London, supported by the hierarchy of the Roman Catholic Church and secular educational curriculum, espoused throughout scientism,

- the progression of the United Nations' Agenda 2030 pursuit of the Omega Point of evolutionary theory's eschatology,
- the pursuit of establishing the Great Reset by the global elites, with the result of establishing a new system for global economy and enriching the global elites,
- the implementation of the United Nations' Agenda 2030 global plan for global population reduction,
- the achievement of the missions of other organizations and systems that will seek to be stakeholders, and
- the implementation of the mark of the beasts system.

During his earthly ministry, Jesus Christ commented upon the intensity of the future condition of the world during this era of the time of Jacob's Trouble, and the threat upon authentic human life.

'If those days had not been shortened, no one would have survived. But because of the elect, the days will be shortened.' Matthew 24:22 translated

'If the Lord had not shortened the days, none of humanity would have been saved. But because of the elect whom God chose, God has shortened the days.' Mark 13:20 translated

United Nations Agenda 21 and Agenda 2030 as the formal plan for establishing global governance

The United Nations Agenda 21 was originally planned for implementation by the year 2050. The determination was made that Agenda 2030 would be implemented by the year 2030. Agenda 2030 is more aggressive, intensive and invasive than Agenda 21. Agenda 21 was a United Nations pogrom with a more local focus. Agenda 2030 is a pogrom with a national and international focus / a global emphasis. Both agendas seek to install the system of total global governance, with the United Nations established as the organization with oversight for globalism.

September 23, 2017, Pope Francis addressed the United Nations in New York, offering his blessing at the second anniversary of the inauguration of Agenda 2030. (September 23, 2017 was also the date for the fulfillment of Revelation 12:1-2.)

    The United Nations' Sustainable Development Goals are seventeen goals and one hundred sixty nine targets that the United Nations committed for itself to achieve by 2030. Recently the United Nations assessed their progress and moved the date for implementation of global governance, forward.
    United Nations' Agenda 2030 moves people out of the rural areas into cities and to destroy representative government in order to erase national boundaries, develop regionalization, and more easily control people.
    Economy, Ecology and Equity will merge together to bring balance. Industry will become surveilled and managed. The plan is global, regional and local with all vestiges of democracy removed.
    Social equity is about redistributing wealth. Social equality is about impoverishing huge portions of the population and decreasing the power and influence of the developed nations. Developed nations that maintain power and influence would be a threat to the establishment of global governance as envisioned by the United Nations' Agenda 2030.
    The Inventory Control Plan is the plan for controlling all land, water, plants, animals, construction, all means of construction, all food, all energy, and all people.
    Some of the goals of Agenda 2030:

1. End poverty in all its forms everywhere. This will require the centralized banks, the International Monetary Fund, the World Bank, etc. to control all finances, and to develop a global currency with a cashless society in order to surveil and manage the financial activity of the people of the world. Many international

monetary organizations already hold connection with the United Nations.
2. End hunger, achieve food security, improve nutrition, and promote sustainable agriculture. This will require the alteration of food on a massive scale to comply with a standard of nutrition (and malnutrition) determined by the United Nations. Global governance will determine what and how much individuals will eat. The global governance system will seek to be the supplier / controller of the food supply. (Jesus taught us to pray to God the Father for supplying our daily bread.)
3. Ensure healthy lives and promote well-being for all at all ages. This will mean that mass vaccinations will take place. It also will require medical 'advances' such as the continual monitoring of the vital statistics of individuals and making determinations of what medical intervention should take place, or not take place, based on the value of the individual to the global regime and their compliance with the societal norms established by the two beasts of Revelation 13. The prescribed medical intervention will not be optional. The withholding of medical care will not be able to be effectively appealed.
4. Ensure inclusive and equitable quality education and promote lifelong learning opportunities for all. The Hitler Youth Camps provided quality education with a curriculum dictated by the Third Reich. Inclusive and equitable quality education will not encourage the development of independent thinking, the kind of thinking that brings innovations and advancements necessary for quality living and improvement.
5. Achieve gender equality and empower all women and girls. Currently, the context for this goal is set in the United States within the framework of the former Eugenics Society of

America / the modern Planned Parenthood. Eugenics and population control through forced family planning will again be practiced around the world, 'for the benefit of women and girls.'
This list continued.

The commonality in all goals of Agenda 2030 is that there will be a new global governance system that will bring about 'a better world' as defined by the leaders of the United Nations. The global elites will exercise their god like authority, with the sovereignty once offered to the ancient gods of the baal / mystery / mythology religions.

In addition, the World Health Organization / WHO, a United Nations Agency (1948 to present), actively is pursuing the establishment of their global pandemic treaty. With the World Health Organization's global pandemic treaty, the WHO would be granted absolute power over global biosecurity, such as the power to implement digital identities, vaccine passports, mandatory vaccinations, travel restrictions, standardized medical care, etc. In nations that adopt the global pandemic treaty, when the World Health Organization declares a global pandemic emergency, all governmental authority of a nation will become subservient to the dictates of the World Health Organization and the United Nations. National sovereignty would no longer exist.

The World Economic Forum (1971 to present) determined that establishing a system of universal digital identity, would include addressing and monitoring an individual's healthcare, finances, food and sustainability, travel and mobility, humanitarian services, commerce, social platform interactions, governmental interactions, telecommunications, community / societal interactions, GPS tracking, etc.

During the era of the time of Jacob's Trouble, the beast of the sea / false prophet / beast from the Abyss / eighth king beast will bless the establishment and implementation of global governance, especially when it aids in advancing his own power and authority. And with his one remaining good eye, he will focus his energy upon being the supreme global leader of the global religious community.

With the future abomination of desolation event, the beast of the earth will have politically risen and declared himself to be more divine and sovereign than God Most High. The beast of the earth will also attempt to assume the position of supreme global ruler, of course sharing supernatural power and authority from the beast of the sea (Revelation 13:11-18).

Together this team of the two beasts of Revelation 13 will use their supernatural power and authority as global rulers to enforce compulsory worship of the idol / image of the beast of the sea, and to attempt to force the inhabitants of the earth to participate in the mark of the beasts system, which will be the method of enforcing global governance with a centrally controlled global economy, and a culture of theoterrorism that will include death and destruction of the earth.

The World Economic Forum / WEF's plan for the implementation of the Great Reset

The World Economic Forum / WEF was originally founded as the European Management Forum in 1971. For decades, members of the World Economic Forum have looked for the right global crisis, as an opportunity for implementing their design for reshaping world economics. In the 2014 annual meeting of the World Economic Forum / WEF, Klaus Schwab declared, 'What we want to do in Davos this year… is to push the reset button.'

Later, the World Economic Forum drew up an 'economic recovery plan' that was presented as a response to the COVID-19 pandemic. The project was launched in June 2020, with a video featuring the then Prince of Wales, now king of Great Britain, Charles III. Klaus Schwab described the metrics for the Great Reset plan in terms of an environmental, social, and corporate governance (ESG) index (a global economy based on global control instead of market capitalism), in harnessing the innovations of the Fourth Industrial Revolution / 4IR / Industry 4.0 /

imagination age. The Fourth Industrial Revolution conceptualized rapid change for implementing an interconnectedness of technology, industries, societal patterns and smart automation. In order to make this transition into a reality, technologies like artificial intelligence, cognitive computing, gene editing, advanced robotics, will be utilized to blur the lines between the physical, the digital and the biological.

As a precursor to the launch of the plan for the Great Reset, the World Economic Forum collaborated with the Johns Hopkins Center for Health Security (May 2018), and the Bill and Melinda Gates Foundation (2019) in pandemic exercises that simulated responses to pandemics. The simulation conducted with the Bill and Melinda Gates Foundation was specifically targeted for a novel coronavirus, just two months before the COVID outbreak. The responses and the effects studied included worldwide lockdowns, the collapse of businesses and industries, the adoption of biometric surveillance technologies, an emphasis on social media censorship to combat 'misinformation,' the flooding of social and legacy media with 'authoritative sources,' widespread riots and mass unemployment.

In addition to being promoted as a response to COVID, the Great Reset is promoted as a response to climate change. In 2017, the WEF published a paper entitled, *'We Need to Reset the Global Operating System to Achieve the [United Nations Sustainable Development Goals].'*

On June 13, 2019, the WEF signed a Memorandum of Understanding with the United Nations to form a partnership to advance the 'UN 2030 Agenda for Sustainable Development.' Shortly after that, the WEF published the 'United Nations-World Economic Forum Strategic Partnership Framework for the 2030 Agenda,' promising to help finance the UN's climate change agenda and committing the WEF to help the UN 'meet the needs of the Fourth Industrial Revolution,' including providing assets and expertise for 'digital governance.' Michael Rectenwald, *What Is the Great Reset? Imprimis* December, 2021

What Klaus Schwab entitled the Great Reset, could better be recognized as corporate socialism, or communist capitalism. The social justice aspect of the Great Reset will require that governments, banks, etc. use the environmental, social and corporate governance (ESG) index to pressure non-woke corporations and businesses out of the market. The result will be a two tiered economy with the establishment of profitable monopolies among the 'woke' with high ESG indices.

For the Great Reset plan to work, every country and every industry, must be transformed.

On a personal human individual level, Klaus Schwab cheers developments that seek to connect human brains directly to the cloud for the sake of 'data mining' thoughts and memories. But this technology would also provide mastery over decision making, stripping away human autonomy and free will. The goal would be to understand and share, every action, thought and motivation of the human individual, and possibly to prevent human action, and to alter human motivations.

One result would be that the middle class would disappear in societies. Eventually only those that govern and those willing to be governed, would remain.

The World Economic Forum / WEF's plan for the Great Reset, is merely one plan that seeks to establish illegitimate governance over 'netizens,' what the biblical record identified as inhabitants of the earth.

The importance of not receiving the mark of the beasts and the warning of the angel – Revelation 14:9-12, 16:2, 19:20, 20:4-5

Jesus Christ's message through John the Revelator warned that those who enrolled in the mark of the beasts system, would not be able to enter into the kingdom of heaven and receive eternal life. (Revelation 14:9-12, 19:20, 20:4)

Prior to the future abomination of desolation event, there will be three angels who will issue warnings to people on earth. The third of the three warning angels will warn against participation in the mark of the beasts system.

And another angel, a third *(of the three angels that will make announcements),* followed them saying in a loud voice, 'If anyone worships / prostates oneself before the beast and the image of the beast, and receives a mark on their forehead or upon their hand, that one will also drink of the wine of the wrath of God; having been mixed / poured out undiluted in the cup of God's wrath. That one will be tormented in the fire and brimstone, before the holy angels, and before the Lamb. And the smoke of their torment ascends forever and ever. Those who worship the beast and its image, and anyone who receives the mark of the name of the beast, have no rest day and night.'

Required here is the endurance of the saints, those keeping the commandments of God and the faith of Jesus. Revelation 14:9-12 translated

In addition to living an eternal torment with burning sulfur in the presence of the holy angels and the Lamb / Jesus Christ, and no respite or relief, those who participate in the mark of the beasts system will also be the recipients of the plagues that will be dispensed with the pouring out of the bowls of God Most High's wrath / seven last plagues.

About three and a half years after the mark of the beasts system will be initiated, after the events associated with the sounding of the sixth trumpet / woe #2 — part 2 has been completed with the death, resurrection and ascension of the two witnesses; the sounding of the seventh trumpet / woe #3, the pouring out of the seven bowls of God Most High's wrath / seven last plagues events will begin.

During the finale for the era of the time of Jacob's Trouble, and the pouring out of the first bowl of God Most High's wrath / first last plague, John the Revelator documented:

<u>First bowl: sores upon those registered in the mark of the beasts system</u>

The first (angel) departed and poured out his bowl into the earth. And injurious and evil sores came upon the humanity that have the mark of the beasts and upon those worshiping his image. Revelation 16:2 translated

The first bowl / first last plague was designated to afflict <u>only</u> the people who received the mark of the beasts and who worshiped the idol / image of the beast of the sea.

Those not marked with the seal of God Most High (previous to the future abomination of desolation event - Revelation 9:1-6) and those who received the mark of the beasts (after the future abomination of desolation event) will most probably be the same group of people. With the sounding of the fifth trumpet / woe #1, earlier in the era of the time of Jacob's Trouble, the inhabitants of the earth, not sealed by God will have received the five months of sores from the stings received from the scorpion locusts that will come from the Abyss (Revelation 9:1-6).

So, with the pouring out of the first bowl of God Most High's wrath / first last plague, those who participated the mark of the beasts system will be the recipients of their second plague of ugly and painful sores.

During the plagues of Egypt recorded in Exodus 7-11, God Most High would make a point to distinguish the people of Israel from the people of Egypt; the people who belonged to the God of Israel, from the people who worshiped the gods of Egypt.

During the era of the time of Jacob's Trouble, God Most High will again differentiate who will be the recipients of the plagues, from who will not be affected by the plagues.

Just to reiterate the eternal experience designated for those who will participate in the mark of the beasts system, the revelation provided to John the Revelator of those who were resurrected, echoed the exclusion of those who received the mark of the beast from experiencing resurrection.

I saw thrones on which were seated those who had been given authority to judge. Then I saw the souls of those who had been beheaded because of their testimony about Jesus and the word of God. They were those who did not worship the beast nor the image of him. And they did not take the mark of the beasts on their forehead or on their hands. They lived and reigned with Christ a thousand years. Revelation 20:4 translated

Those who will receive the mark of the beasts, must plan on experiencing a second death. Their first death will be their physical death when their physical body ceases to operate. The second death will be total separation from God Most High and total separation from eternal life in the kingdom of heaven. The second death will come at the end of the Thousand Years Reign of Jesus Christ, after the resurrection of all of humanity who were not raised during the return of Jesus Christ, in order for every individual human being to participate in the Great Day of Judgment. The Great Day of Judgment will take place after the Thousand Years Reign of Jesus Christ.

The requirement of the willingness of the recipient, to receive the mark of the beasts – Revelation 14:9-12, 20:4-5

God Most High made it clear that offerings to God Most High should be from a joyful, cheerful heart and with the prompting that originates from one's own heart. Offerings to God Most High were not to be received out of the giver's sense of obligation or as a price to be paid to appease God Most High or given under compulsion. This concept was even recorded in the Law given to Moses (Exodus 25:2, 35:21, Deuteronomy 15:10). God Most High has always been clear that the relationship between God Most High and God's people including both the people of Israel and the followers of the Lamb / Jesus Christ, is a heart to heart relationship and not a compulsory relationship or financial transaction.

Psalm 51:16-17 said, 'You (God) do not delight in sacrifice, or I would bring it. You do not take pleasure in burnt offerings.'

'My sacrifice, O God, is a broken spirit; a broken and contrite heart you, God, will not despise.'

But within religions that are not the authentic faith system established by God Most High, religious leaders have adopted the concept that compulsory worship unites people to covenant the people to the governance of its divinely appointed rulers.

In religions that are not God Most High's authentic faith system, religious leaders use religion as a means for obtaining personal power, prestige, and wealth. And the kings of the earth have discovered that because religious leaders employ compulsory means in the practice of religion, that the kings of nations should also employ compulsory means in exercising their governance.

In this world, there are 'giver' relationships and 'taker' relationships. God Most High is a giver that seeks to enter into giver relationships. 'For God so loved the world that God <u>gave</u> God's one and only Son....,' the greatest treasure that God Most High had to give (John 3:16f).

So when a religious organization, whether it is a 'Christian' organization or a baal / mystery / mythology religious organization, or any other kind of religious organization; places a price on worship or a price for finding favor with their god(s), or has established a price list for the forgiveness of sins, or seeks to be the authority that determines one's eternal destination, or presents itself as having established the requirements for entrance into heaven, or seeks to determine one's station once entrance into heaven has been obtained; that organization no longer represents God Most High. That organization has become a 'taker' organization and the best that organization has to offer, is a 'taker' relationship model.

Relationships made up of people intent upon 'giving,' work. Relationships made up of people intent upon 'taking' will eventually expire when there is nothing left to be taken.

Jesus Christ displayed disappointment during Passover, when the Jewish religious leaders had turned the temple sacrifice into a money making operation. Three of the gospel writers recorded the incident (Matthew 21:12, Mark 11:15, John 2:15). Jesus overturned the tables of the money changers, made a whip out of cords and drove all of them from the temple courts, along with the sheep, cattle, and doves that they brought. Jesus also scattered their coins, removing their profit for the day.

God Most High envisioned a body of Christ / church that was dedicated to God Most High with loyalty and devotion of their hearts, not out of what they could pay or out of their guilty consciences, as an attempt to appease God with their material belongings. And God Most High did not accept offerings and sacrifices made under compulsion or duress.

But the great prostitute / baal / mystery / mythology religion, either hidden covertly under the name of Christianity or under the names of other religions, consistently substituted the object of loyalty and devotion that was supposed to be God Most High a giving God, with a new loyalty and devotion focused upon appeasement of the religious leaders who have convinced humanity that they control access to all gods.

One of the dynamics that will make the worship of the idol / image of the beast of the sea so abhorrent to God Most High, will be the compulsory aspect of that worship.

And yet, John the Revelator documented that even though the two beasts of Revelation 13 will require all inhabitants of the earth to worship tie idol / image of the beast of the sea, and will control the global economy through the mark of the beasts system, both the worship of the idol / image of the beast and participation in the mark of the beasts system will be voluntary. And because ultimately participation will be voluntary, when a person makes the choice to participate, they have sealed their eternal relationship with the red dragon / serpent / Satan, Inc. and the kingdom of Satan, Inc. / kingdom of man. (Revelation 14:9-11, 19:20, 20:4)

One of the truths that the biblical record stressed was that receiving the mark of the beasts will be a voluntary act, even though the beast of the earth 'causes all the small and the great, and the rich and the poor, and the free and the servants, that it should give them a mark on their right hand or on their forehead,' Revelation 13:16 translated

The nature of the kingdom of heaven is that God the Father, God the Son / messiah / the Lamb / Jesus Christ, and God the Holy Spirit, do not force themselves or the kingdom of heaven, upon any individual. The God of the kingdom of heaven will not force anyone who does not want to, to live an everlasting life with the God of the kingdom of heaven. Concerning the individual human being, the God of the kingdom of heaven is determined to follow the rules of chivalry and not to trespass where the God of heaven is not personally invited.

The same kind of 'rules of the game' have been imposed upon the red dragon / serpent / Satan, Inc. Even though the inhabitants of the earth will be 'forced' to participate, the inhabitants of the earth will also have the option to opt out.

The first evidence that there will be a way to opt out of the mark of the beasts system was documented with the *third angel that will provide warning to humanity. There would be no need to provide a warning, if action could not be taken to avoid the impending disaster.*

Prior to the future abomination of desolation event, there will be three angels who will issue three warnings. The third angel's warning will specifically address the mark of the beasts system.

And another angel, a third, followed them saying in a loud voice, 'If anyone worships / prostates oneself before the beast and the image of the beast, and receives a mark on their forehead or upon their hand, that one will also drink of the wine of the wrath of God; having been mixed / poured out undiluted in the cup of God's wrath. That one will be tormented in the fire and brimstone, before the holy angels, and before the Lamb. And the smoke of their torment ascends forever and ever. Those who worship the beast and its image, and anyone who receives the mark of the name of the beast, have no rest day and night.'

Required here is the endurance of the saints, those keeping the commandments of God and the faith of Jesus. Revelation 14:9-12 translated

Another documentation that participation in the mark of the beasts system will be made by individual choice, was in the vision provided to John the Revelator of the resurrection of God's holy people.

When messiah / the Lamb / Jesus Christ returns and defeats the enemies of God Most High and of the kingdom of heaven, Jesus Christ will fully establish the kingdom of heaven on earth. John the Revelator described the vision he received of the full establishment of the kingdom of heaven on earth:

I saw thrones on which were seated those who had been given authority to judge. Then I saw the souls of those who had been beheaded because of their testimony about Jesus and the word of God. They were those who did not worship the beast nor the image of him. And they did not take the mark of the beasts on their forehead or on their hands. They lived and reigned with Christ a thousand years. Revelation 20:4 translated

There will be tremendous pressure to become connected to the mark of the beasts system. Many will be beheaded just because they reject being connected to the mark of the beasts system. But choosing to receive the

mark of the beasts, will be an irrevocable transaction of the individual's human soul.

And those that refuse to worship the beast or its image, and who do not receive the mark of the beasts, will retain their human autonomy instilled within each human being by God the Creator. They will be eligible for resurrection into perfected and everlasting life.

The ultimate reward for rejecting the mark of the beasts and its system – Revelation 20:4-6

In the revelation that the resurrected and ascended Jesus Christ provided to John the Revelator, John saw the vision of the Thousand Years Reign of Jesus Christ.

I saw thrones on which were seated those who had been given authority to judge. And I saw the souls of those who had been beheaded because of their testimony for Jesus and because of the word of God. They had not worshiped the beast of the sea / false prophet / beast from the Abyss / eighth king beast or his image and had not received his mark in their foreheads or their hands. They came to life and reigned with Christ a thousand years. (The rest of the dead did not come to life until the thousand years were ended.) This is the first resurrection. Blessed and holy are those who have part in the first resurrection. The second death has no power over them, but they will be priests of God and of Christ and will reign with Christ for a thousand years. Revelation 20:4-6

To receive a position in the kingdom of heaven, and to reign with Jesus Christ during his Thousand Years Reign, and to be a priest; one must totally reject receiving the mark of the beasts and refrain from worshiping the beast or the image of the beast, even if it means being beheaded because of one's testimony for Jesus Christ.

The fragility of the mark of the beasts system

While the two beasts of Revelation 13 will present their mark of the beasts system as the only thing that will endure into eternity, and the only true offer of everlasting existence, in reality the mark of the beasts system will be fragile and will be broken.

Surrounding the mark of the beasts system will be trickery, delusion, and illusionary miraculous signs for the purpose of convincing people to become converts to kingdom of Satan, Inc / kingdom of man. The biblical record made it clear that those who receive the mark of the beasts and participate in the mark of the beasts system, will be those who have been mesmerized by the two beasts of Revelation 13.

The beast of the sea will appear to be undefeatable in war. The beast of the earth will hypnotize and captivate the minds of the inhabitants of the earth to join in the new lawless culture of the world. Together the two beasts of Revelation 13 will create an undeniable craving within the inhabitants of the earth, to be part of the new prestigious class of people. The inhabitants of the earth will support the elite and elect ruling class, in pursuit of being the recipients of the promise that the elite and elect ruling class 'love and care about them,' unlike God Most High who has established laws that confine individuals.

But possibly the most important marketing point will be the promise that the mark of the beasts system will provide humanity with a form of everlasting life. And the two beasts of Revelation 13 will quickly point out that for six thousand years, humanity has experienced death, with only a promise from the God of the kingdom of heaven that God's people will be resurrected, and that promise has not yet been fulfilled. Even God's chosen people, the people of Israel believe that Jesus' disciples stole his crucified body.

The fake healing that the beast of the sea will experience, will be the proof that the two beasts of Revelation 13 are the only ones who can provide an everlasting existence, within the virtual reality of the mark of the beasts system.

But Jesus Christ provided John the Revelator with an understanding of the fragility of the mark of the beasts system.

In Revelation 13, John the Revelator documented that the supernatural power and authority of the two beasts will last for only a forty two month term (Revelation 13:5, 13:12).

Revelation 11:1-14 documented the failure that the beast of the sea / beast from the Abyss will experience as the assassinated two witnesses sent by God Most High, are resurrected and ascend into heaven.

Revelation 17 documented the frustration of the beast of the sea / beast from the Abyss / eighth king beast that will motivate him to turn his attention to commissioning the ten horns / ten kings to wage war against the Lamb / Jesus Christ.

But it was the record of Revelation 19, that documented that the two beasts, who will have claimed to hold the power over everlasting life, will themselves be defeated, captured, and imprisoned in the lake of fire. The two undefeatable beasts, will indeed be themselves defeated. And when they are defeated, all their false promises will be defeated with them.

And I saw the beast, and the kings of the earth, and their armies having been gathered together to make war with the one sitting on the horse with his army. The beast was captured, and with him the false prophet. The beast was the one having performed the signs on behalf of the false prophet, by which the beast deceived those having received the mark of the beasts and those worshiping the image of the beast.

The two were cast into the lake of fire burning with brimstone. And the rest were killed with the sword of the one sitting on the horse having gone forth from out of his mouth. And all the birds were filled with their flesh. Revelation 19:19-21 translated

During the era of the time of Jacob's Trouble, initially the two beasts of Revelation 13, will act in tandem. They will effectively act as partners that will lift each other up in their rise to assuming power and authority. Only during the finale for the era of the time of Jacob's Trouble will the two men become jealous of each other's power and then both will eventually work against each other, fulfilling Jesus' words, 'Every kingdom divided against itself will be ruined, and every city or household divided against itself will not stand.' Matthew 12:25 (Mark 3:25, Luke 11:17).

The shattering of the nation of Israel's covenant peace treaty agreement – Daniel 9:24-27

The beast of the sea that will act as the head of the global religious community, will have come from a long history of antisemitism. But it will be the beast of the earth who will be the party that will be most responsible for the breaking of Israel's seven year covenant peace treaty agreement.

The Old Testament / Tanakh prophet Daniel (fl. 605 to 530 BC) - prophet of Judah, received the prophecy of seventy 'sevens' / 'weeks.' Each 'seven' represented seven years. In the middle of the sixty ninth seven, the promised and prophesied messiah was 'cut off / killed. Then a gap of time (almost two thousand years) followed before the seventieth 'seven' which was also designated as seven years, would be realized.

Jeremiah (fl. 626 to 585 BC) - prophet of Judah, referenced Daniel's seventieth 'seven' as the era of the time of Jacob's Trouble.

Seventy weeks are determined for your people, for your holy city, to finish the transgression – to make an end of sins, and to make reconciliation for iniquity and to bring in everlasting righteousness; and to seal up vision and prophecy, and to anoint the Most Holy. Daniel 9:24 translated

After the sixty two weeks, messiah will be cut off, and will have nothing.

The people of the prince / ruler who is to come, will destroy the city and the sanctuary.

And the end of it shall come with a flood. War will continue until the end and desolations are determined.

<u>The prince / ruler will confirm a covenant with many, for one 'seven' / 'week.' But in the middle of the 'seven' / 'week,' the prince / ruler will bring an end to the sacrifice and offering</u>. On the wing (of the temple), the prince / ruler will establish abominations that will cause desolation, even until the consumption which has been determined is poured out on the desolate / the one who destroys. Daniel 9:26-27 translated

It was Daniel who documented that during the seventieth 'seven' that the nation of Israel would establish a covenant with many.

September 15, 2020, the Abraham Accords were signed. It was a covenant between the nation of Israel and other nations. The date of its signing also served to document that the conclusion of the era of the time of Jacob's Trouble, would take place seven years after the establishment of this covenant peace treaty agreement.

While many have interpreted Daniel's statement to mean that the ruler who is to come / beast of the earth will establish this covenant, what Daniel actually stated was that the ruler who is to come will confirm this covenant, which did not indicate that he would absolutely be active in establishing the covenant.

What was most important in Daniel's message was the fact that in the middle of the seven years, the ruler who is to come will shatter the covenant peace treaty agreement with the future abomination of desolation event. Three and a half years following the establishment of the Abraham Accords, would be sometime around the middle of March 2024. It will be the future abomination of desolation event that provide the final confirmation of these dates.

The beast of the sea / false prophet / beast from the Abyss / eighth king beast's traditional foundation for antisemitism

In order to hold authority over the temple mount to be able to set up the idol / image of the beast of the sea on the temple mount, the beast of the earth will actually need to be a Jewish leader (Daniel 9:27, 11:31, 11:45, Revelation 13:14).

The beast of the sea / false prophet / beast from the Abyss / eighth king beast will be a Gentile, and need to share his supernatural power and authority with the beast of the earth, even though the beast of the sea will be antisemitic.

The Gentile beast of the sea / false prophet / beast from the Abyss / eighth king beast will act as the head of the global religious community. The global religious community, will include Christian denominations and other religions, under its umbrella. While the Roman Catholic Church will serve as the foundation for the global religious community, all groups that join under the umbrella of the global religious community will agree, and in essence accept and adopt as their own, the historical tenets of the Roman Catholic Church including its abuses throughout history. More importantly, all groups that snuggle under the umbrella of the global religious community will embrace the antisemitism that was fostered and fermented within the Roman Catholic Church since its formation (381 AD).

Urban II (fl. 1088 to 1099) inspired the first Crusade in 1096. The crusades served as a revenue producing initiative. But every offensive war needs a villain to attack. For Urban II, the people of Israel became the small and almost defenseless target. The Crusade leader, Godfrey of Bouillon sought to avenge the blood of Jesus through the annihilation of the Jews. Urban II labeled the Jews as 'an accursed race, utterly alienated from God.' In exchange for destroying the people of Israel, Urban II offered full forgiveness of sins. The biblical message has two problems with Urban II's theology; first those who curse Abram / Abraham and his descendants will be cursed because all peoples on earth will be blessed through Abram / Abraham (Genesis 12:3), and second only God Most High or Jesus Christ can forgive sins, not the pope (Matthew 6:15, 9:2-6, 26:28, Mark 2:2-10, 11:25, Luke 5:20-24, 7:48-49, 11:4, Acts 2:38, 5:31, 10:43, Ephesians 1:7, 1 John 1:9).

In 1205, Innocent III (fl. 1198 to 1216) portrayed the people of Israel as consigned to perpetual servitude.

In 1311, the Council of Vienna forbade sexual relationships between Christians and Jews.

In 1434, the Council of Basel confined the people of Israel to residing in ghettos and forced them to wear a distinguishing badge.

Even the Protestant Reformers like Martin Luther, taught antisemitic views.

In 1555, Paul IV (fl. 1555 to 1559) relegated the people of Israel to slaves and rag merchants. Marriages between Catholics and Jews was punishable by death. Only one synagogue per city was allowed with all other synagogues being destroyed.

Pius VII (fl. 1800 to 1823), Leo XII (fl. 1823 to 1829), Pius VIII (fl. 1829 to 1830), and Gregory XVI (fl. 1831 to 1846) treated the people of Israel as lepers without rights.

In 1873, Pius IX (fl. 1846 to 1878) addressed the Roman Curia and branded all Jews as money lusting enemies of Christ and Christianity.

In 1882, the Jesuit journal, *Civilta Cattolica* claimed that Judaism required crucifying Christian children and using their blood in ceremonies, a totally untrue claim.

When Theodore Herzl (1860 to 1904) approached Pius X (fl. 1903 to 1914) in 1904 requesting support for the Zionist movement and the establishment of a homeland for the people of Israel, Herzl was met with Pius X's response of, 'We cannot prevent the Jews from going to Jerusalem, but we could never sanction it. As head of the Church, I cannot recognize the Jewish people.'

Adolph Hitler could not have created a national hatred of Jews in Germany which led to the Holocaust, without the centuries of church inspired antisemitism.

When Adolph Hitler was approached by Vatican representatives on April 26, 1933, Hitler's response was that for one thousand five hundred years, the Roman Catholic Church had regarded Jews as parasites to be killed and that he intended to provide a 'final solution to the Jewish problem.' This would be the annihilation of the very people that birthed Jesus Christ and who provided Judaism which was the foundation for Christianity and all Christian churches.

Cardinal Eugenio Pacelli, before he became Pope Pius XII, had provided money to Hitler out of the Vatican treasury in order to aid Hitler in starting the Nazi Party.

The Second Vatican Council, in 1965, affirmed the centuries of the Roman Catholic Church's stance that God Most High had abandoned the covenant that God Most High made with the people of Israel and replaced the Church as the new people of God. The Holy City, the City of God, the Eternal City, is now Rome, not Jerusalem. Only in 1994, did the Roman Catholic Church finally recognize Israel as a nation, forty six years after Israel became a nation in 1948.

It will be odd for the antisemitic Gentile beast of the sea to share power and authority with the Jewish beast of the earth, in attempting to establish their global governance. But the Jewish beast of the earth will bridge some of the gap in their relationship through visually sharing the Jewish temple with the Gentile beast of the sea, constructing the image of the beast of the sea for the purpose of worship, and possibly taking part in the pseudo healing of the beast of the sea's injury. John the Revelator documented that at the beginning of their relationship, the two beasts of Revelation 13 will have a symbiotic type of relationship, with each depending on the other for elevation in position and for support. The two beasts will share a common goal of attempting to destroy the people of Israel (Revelation 12, 13)

When their shared forty two months of power and authority are completed, the two witnesses will be assassinated at the temple, by the Gentile beast of the sea / false prophet / beast from the Abyss / eighth king beast (Revelation 11:1-14, 17:8), of course with the permission and blessing of the beast of the earth who will hold control over the temple mount.

In the work of the two beasts of Revelation 13, the dynamic of the beast of the sea's antisemitism will finally impact their ability to be united, and to accomplish their mission. John the Revelator portrayed the relationship of the two beasts around the end of the second half of the era of the time of Jacob's Trouble, as having distance between them in their relationship (Revelation 17).

But when the two beasts of Revelation 13 will decide to renew their relationship once again, the two beasts will both contribute in the pursuit of war against the Lamb / Jesus Christ. The conclusion of this final battle of this age will see the two beasts defeated by the Lamb / Jesus Christ, and incarcerated in the fiery lake (Revelation 16:13, 17, 19:19-20).

The Character of God is Unchanging and God's Promises Are Forever (Not Just for Sometimes)

There are those who believe that during the era of the time of Jacob's Trouble, God will somehow suspend God's character. In their deluded thinking, God will have such mercy on the followers of the Lamb / Jesus Christ that God will not force them to endure the tribulations of the era of the time of Jacob's Trouble and will rapture them out, give them an escape to the clouds to somehow live in the clouds or in heaven, for up to seven years until Jesus Christ returns for the battle of Armageddon. Rapture theology is filled with theological contradictions.

The followers of the Lamb / Jesus Christ and the church have had a responsibility throughout the last two thousand years to tell people of the kingdom of heaven and of Jesus Christ as the reigning monarch of the fully established kingdom of heaven. That responsibility continues during the era of the time of Jacob's Trouble more than at any other time in history. If the followers of the Lamb / Jesus Christ are not present during the era of the time of Jacob's Trouble, then who will there be to tell people who are not yet followers of the Lamb / Jesus Christ, about who God Most High is and what God Most High is doing?

God Most High did not spare Noah from his responsibility to preach to the antediluvian / preflood world. It must have been difficult for Noah and his family to preach for one hundred twenty years before the deluge / flood, without significant results. Noah's message was 'repent or God Most High will destroy...' Knowing that all the world around Noah was going to change through the deluge / flood and would never be the same again, had to weigh heavily upon the eight of them. During the time they were building the ark, they were required to prepare every timber, place every nail, and collect every provision, with the knowledge that God Most High was going to act, and with the knowledge that the masses of people would not heed God Most High's message, and with the knowledge that the eight of them would need to fully experience the deluge / flood as God Most High transitioned them into the new and promised postdiluvian / postflood world. Noah and his family were the only eight in the world of approximately eight billion people, who believed. Surely, God Most High could have easily 'raptured' out eight people...

But God Most High did not 'rapture' this party of eight because God Most High had a plan for Noah and his family that required them to participate in the ark and deluge / flood experience. Noah and his family were God

Most High's provision for carrying the story of God Most High's mighty acts into our postdiluvian / postflood world.

    God Most High's instruction to Moses at the time of the exodus out of Egypt, was that the people of Israel were to tell their children and their children's children about God Most High's mighty acts. If God Most High would have not caused the people of Israel to experience the exodus out of Egypt, complete with experiencing the ten plagues and passing through the Red Sea, then the people of Israel would not have had anything to tell to their children and to their children's children about God Most High's mighty acts. The people of Israel would not have had their heritage that forged them into a nation with a national identity that jettisoned them into giving birth to messiah.

    Before Jesus went to his crucifixion, Jesus prayed, 'My Father, if it is possible, may this cup be taken from me. Yet not as I will, but as you will.' Matthew 26:39 God Most High did not spare Jesus Christ from the experience of the crucifixion and death. If God Most High had spared Jesus Christ from the experience of crucifixion and death, then there would not have been the resurrection of Jesus Christ as the firstfruits from death for all of us 'second fruits.'

    God Most High is not going to spare the followers of the Lamb / Jesus Christ from their responsibility to teach to a hostile world, even during the era of the time of Jacob's Trouble.

    We who live during this era of the time of Jacob's Trouble have a job to do. First, we must provide education to a hostile world concerning God Most High's solution to hostility. After the return of messiah / the Lamb / Jesus Christ and the defeat of God Most High's enemies has been accomplished, we will be responsible for telling of God's mighty acts throughout the Thousand Years Reign of Jesus Christ. We cannot fulfill our responsibilities to tell of God's mighty acts if we are not present to witness them.

    What the followers of the Lamb / Jesus Christ have as an ally is God Most High. God Most High is even larger than God Most High's plan. God Most High's plan is not larger than God Most High. And God Most High's plan and God Most High's character do not take a holiday. God Most High will not be resting until *after* the era of the time of Jacob's Trouble has been completed. God Most High was, is, and always will be consistent throughout time. God Most High is ready to pour out God Most High's strength and power upon the followers of the Lamb / Jesus Christ so that all will truly know the depth of God Most High.

While the weapons of the kingdom of Satan, Inc. / kingdom of man will be magic, delusion, domination, destruction, etc., God Most High's weapon that cannot be defeated is love. When the channel of love between a person and God Most High is active and flowing, there can be nothing that can sever that channel; not magic, not delusion, not domination, not destruction, etc. Our love may dwindle to a trickle. But God Most High's love will only flow as a monsoon. For God so loved the world that God sent us God's one and only begotten Son, so that whoever believes in him will / shall / is insured to have, eternal life with the author of all love.

God Most High will not be defeated by a mere detail like physical death. God Most High will definitely not be defeated by two men in the midst of eight billion, who mistakenly develop a god complex. And God Most High will not forget even a single follower of the Lamb / Jesus Christ. The God of the kingdom of heaven has carefully recorded the name of every believer in messiah (BC) and follower of the Lamb (AD) in the book of life.

God Most High has a counterplan to the plan of the red dragon / serpent / Satan, Inc. And that plan requires your participation.

> To the chief musician, a psalm of Daivd.
> In you Lord, I put my trust.
> Let me never be ashamed, ever.
> Deliver me in your righteousness.
> Bow down your ear to me.
> Come quickly to deliver me.
> Be my rock of refuge,
> A fortress of defense to save me.
> For you are my rock and my fortress.

Therefore, for the sake of your name,
Lead me and guide me.
Pull me out of the net which they have secretly laid for me.
For you are my strength.
Into your hand I commit my spirit.
You have redeemed me, Lord God of truth.
I have hated those who esteem useless idols.
But I trust in the Lord.
I will be glad and rejoice in your mercy,
For you have considered my trouble.
You have known my soul in adversities.
And you have not surrendered me into the hand of the enemy.
You have set my feet in a spacious place.
Have mercy on me, O Lord, for I am in trouble.
My eye wastes away with grief,
Yes, my soul and my body.
For my life is spent with grief,
And my years with sighing.
My strength fails because of my iniquity,
And my bones waste away.
I am scorned among all my enemies,
But especially among my neighbors,
And I am repulsive to my acquaintances.
Those who see me outside, flee from me.
I am forgotten like a dead man, out of mind.
I am like a broken vessel.
For I hear the slander of many.
Fear is on every side.
While they take counsel together against me,
They scheme to take away my life.
But I trust in you Lord.
I say, 'You are my God.'
My times are in your hand.
Deliver me from the hand of my enemies,
And from those who persecute me.
Make your face sine upon your servant.
Save me for your mercies' sake.
Lord, do not let me be ashamed, for I have called upon you.
Let the wicked be ashamed.
Let them be silent in the grave.
Let the lying lips be silenced,
Which proudly and contemptuously speak against the
        righteous, audacious things.
Oh, how great is your goodness,
Which you have laid up for those who fear you,
Which you have prepared for those who trust in you,
In the presence of generations of humanity.
You will hide them in the secret place of your presence,

From the plots of humanity.
You will keep them concealed in your shelter, from contentious
    tongues.
Blessed be the Lord.
For the Lord has shown the Lord's marvelous kindness to me
    in a strong city.
For in my haste, I said, 'I am cut off from before your eyes.'
Nevertheless, you heard the voice of my pleas when I cried out
    to you.
Love the Lord, all you his holy ones.
For the Lord preserves the faithful, and fully repays the
    arrogant person.
Be of good courage, and God will strengthen your heart,
All who hope in the Lord. Psalm 31:1-24 translated

You are my hiding place.
You will protect me from trouble and surround me with songs of
    deliverance. Psalm 32:7

For the word of the Lord is right and true.
The Lord is faithful in all that the Lord does.
The Lord loves righteousness and justice.
The earth is full of the unfailing love of the Lord. Psalm 33:4-5

I will extol the Lord at all times; the praise of the Lord will
    always be on my lips.
My soul will boast in the Lord; let the afflicted hear and rejoice.
Glorify the Lord with me; let us exalt the name of the Lord
    together.
I sought the Lord, and the Lord answered me; the Lord
    delivered me from all my fears.
Those who look to the Lord are radiant; their faces are never
    covered with shame. Psalm 34:1-5
The angel of the Lord encamps around those who fear the Lord
    and the Lord delivers them.
Taste and see that the Lord is good; blessed is the one who
    takes refuge in the Lord.
Fear the Lord, you holy ones of the Lord, for those who fear the
    Lord lack nothing.
The lions may grow weak and hungry, but those who seek the
    Lord lack no good thing. Psalm 34:7-10

The righteous cry out, and the Lord hears them; the Lord
    delivers them from all their troubles.
The Lord is close to the brokenhearted and saves those who
    are crushed in spirit.
A righteous person may have many troubles, but the Lord
    delivers the righteous one from them all; the Lord

protects all the bones of the righteous person, not one of them will be broken. Psalm 34:17-20

Evil will slay the wicked; the foes of the righteous will be condemned.
The Lord redeems the servants of the Lord; no one will be condemned who takes refuge in the Lord. Psalm 34:21-22

I was young and now I am old, yet I have never seen the righteous forsaken or their children begging for bread. They are always generous and lend freely; their children will be blessed. Psalm 37:25-26
For the Lord loves the just and will not forsake the Lord's faithful ones. Psalm 37:28

Come and see the works of the Lord, the desolations the Lord has brought on the earth.
The Lord makes wars cease to the ends of the earth.
The Lord breaks the bow and shatters the spear.
The Lord burns the shields with fire.
'Be still and know that I am God.
I will be exalted among the nations.
I will be exalted in the earth.' Psalm 46:8-10

Cast your care on the Lord and the Lord will sustain you; the Lord will never let the righteous fail.
But you, O God, will bring down the wicked into the pit of corruption; bloodthirsty and deceitful people will not live out half their days.
But as for me, I trust in you. Psalm 55:22-23

Have mercy on me, O God, have mercy on me, for in you my soul takes refuge. I will take refuge in the shadow of your wings until the disaster has passed. I cry out to God Most High, to God, who fulfills God's purpose for me. God sends from heaven and saves me, rebuking those who hotly pursue me; God sends God's love and God's faithfulness. Psalm 57:1-3

Give us aid against the enemy, for the help of humans is worthless. With God we will gain the victory, and God will trample down our enemies. Psalm 60:11-12

In you Lord, I put my trust. Let me never be put to shame, ever.
Deliver me in your righteousness, and cause me to escape. Incline your ear to me and save me.
Be my strong refuge, where I may continuously go. You have given the commandment to save me, for you are my rock and my fortress.

My God, deliver me out of the hand of the wicked, out of the hand of the unrighteous and cruel humanity. For you are my hope, Lord God. You are my trust from my youth. By You, I have been I have been sustained from birth. You took me out of my mother's womb. My praise will be continually of you.

I have become a curiosity to many. But you are my strong refuge.

Let my mouth be filled with your praise, and with your glory all day.

Do not cast me off in the time of old age. Do not forsake me when my strength fails. For my enemies speak against me. And those who lie in wait for my life, take counsel together, saying, 'God has forsaken him. Pursue and take him, for there is none to deliver him.'

God, do not be far from me. My God, hurry to help me. Let them be confounded and consumed, who are adversaries of my life. Let them be covered with reproach and dishonor who seek to hurt me.

But I will hope continually. I will praise you more and more. In all manner, yet will I praise you.

My mouth will tell of your righteousness, and your salvation all day, for I do not know their limits.

I will go in the strength of the Lord God. I will make mention of your righteousness, of yours only.

God, you have taught me from my youth. And to this day, I declare your wondrous works.

And when I am old and have gray hair, God, do not forsake me; until I declare your strength to this generation and your power to everyone who is to come. Psalm 71:1-18 translated

For the chief musician of David, a psalm
Lord, you have searched me and known me.

You know my sitting down and my rising up. You understand my thought from afar.

You understand my path an my lying down. You are acquainted with all my ways.

Before I speak a word, behold, Lord, you know it already.

You have hemmed me in, behind and before me. You laid your hand upon me.

Such knowledge is too wonderful for me, far too high for me to reach.

Where can I go from your Spirit? Or where can I flee from your presence?

If I ascend into heave, there you are. And if I make my bed in hell, behold you are there.

If I take the wings of the morning, and dwell in the uttermost parts of the sea, even there your hand will lead me and your right hand will hold me.

And if I say, 'Surely the darkness will hide me and the light become night around me,' even the darkness will not be dark to you.

The night will shine like the day, for darkness and light are both alike to you.

For you formed my innermost parts. You covered me in my mother's womb.

I will praise you, for I am fearfully and wonderfully made. Marvelous are your works. And my soul knows that very well.

My bones were not hidden from you when I was made in secret, intricately woven in the depths of the earth. Your eyes saw me before I was formed. And in your book, your plan for all my days was written, before any of my days existed.

How precious are your thoughts to me, O God! How great is the sum of them! If I would count them, they would be more in number than the sand. When I awake, I am still with you.

Oh that you would kill the wicked, O God! Away from me, you who are bloodthirsty.

For they speak against you, wickedly. Your enemies take your name in vain.

Lord, I hate them who hate you, and loathe those who rise up against you.

With perfect hatred, I hate them. I count them my enemies.

Search me God, and know my heart. Try me and know my anxious thoughts. See if there is any wicked way in me, and lead me in the way everlasting. Psalm 139:1-24 translated

The Lord delights in those who fear the Lord, who put their hope in the Lord's unfailing love. Psalm 147:11

There are so many more promises that God Most High has made to us. It is God Most High who is the faithful party in this cosmic battle. And it is God Most High who faithfully will lead the followers of the Lamb / Jesus Christ who will experience this time of cosmic challenge.

The biblical record was written and kept for this very hour, the hour of preparation for the return of Jesus Christ and the hour of the full establishment of the kingdom of heaven on earth. In order to understand more of God Most High's activity that will work to counter the plans of the red dragon / serpent / Satan, Inc. and their representatives, refer to the rest of the biblical record.

Also remember to be recording God Most High's activity surrounding you. God Most High's new mighty acts will be what you will be able to tell to the next generations.

The Miracles Performed Through the Followers of the Lamb / Jesus Christ

The biblical record documented that the era of the time of Jacob's Trouble will be the most challenging era of all of human history, even more challenging than the experience of the deluge / flood.

'For then there will be great tribulation, such unequaled from the beginning of the world until now, and never to be equaled again.' Matthew 24:21 translated

But the God who can merely speak and have a world appear, is also the God who even the wind and the sea obey.

God Most High did not leave Jesus unattended nor powerless. The God of the kingdom of heaven provided Jesus Christ with protection when Jesus needed it, and all that Jesus Christ needed to be successful in achieving his mission.

God Most High has also given the followers of the Lamb / Jesus Christ responsibilities to fulfill. And God Most High will give the followers of the Lamb / Jesus Christ all the power and equipment that they need to successfully complete their missions.

This has been the consistent biblical message documenting six thousand years of human history. There was nothing in the biblical record that indicated that God Most High's record of bringing salvation will change.

God Most High equipped Enoch. God Most High equipped Noah. God Most High equipped Shem. God Most High equipped Abraham, Tamar, Joseph, Moses, Joshua, Rahab, Deborah, Gideon, Naomi and Ruth, David, Elijah, Jeremiah, Ezekiel, Mary, Jesus, Peter, James, the apostles and the disciples of Jesus Christ, and John the Revelator. The biblical record was a continual list of people that God Most High equipped to do great and mighty things. God Most High will also equip the followers of the Lamb / Jesus Christ and prepare them for this adventure.

Toward the end of Jesus Christ's ministry, Jesus said, 'Truly I tell you, whoever believes in me will do the works I have been doing, and they will do even greater things than these, because I am going to the Father. And I will do whatever you ask in my name, so that the Father may be glorified in the Son. You may ask me for anything in my name, and I will do it.' John 14:12-14

This promise that Jesus proclaimed, has yet to be fulfilled. Jesus fed multitudes, healed the sick, drove out demons, raised Lazarus from the dead after three days of occupying the tomb, prophesied, etc. The apostles did many of these things, but not in a greater way than Jesus had done them. This promise is yet to be fulfilled. It will be during the era of the time of Jacob's Trouble that the world will observe the fulfillment of this promise. And it will be the modern day followers of the Lamb / Jesus Christ that God Most High will utilize in fulfilling this promise.

Hidden within the biblical record, there were many promises recorded, especially promises concerning the followers of the Lamb / Jesus Christ. Each one must be fulfilled.

Jesus' instructions to the disciples as he sent them out to do ministry: 'As you go, preach this message: The kingdom of heaven is near. Heal the sick, raise the dead, cleanse those who have leprosy, drive out demons. Freely you have received, freely give. Matthew 10:7-8

Jesus' instructions to the disciples as he sent them out to do ministry: 'Be on your guard against people; they will hand you over to the local councils and flog you in their synagogues. On my account you will be brought before governors and kings as witnesses to them and to the Gentiles. But when they arrest you, do not worry about what to say or how to say it. At that time, you will be given what to say, for it will not be you speaking, but the Spirit of your Father speaking through you.' Matthew 10:17-20

Jesus replied, 'I tell you the truth, if you have faith and do not doubt, not only can you do what was done to the fig tree, but also you can say to this mountain, 'Go, throw yourself into the sea,' and it will be done. If you believe, you will receive whatever you ask for in prayer.' Matthew 21:21-22

'Have faith in God,' Jesus answered. 'I tell you the truth, if anyone says to this mountain, 'Go, throw yourself into the sea,' and does not doubt in their heart but believes that what they say will happen, it will be done for them. Therefore, I tell you, whatever you ask for in prayer, believe that you have received it, and it will be yours. And when you stand praying, if you hold anything against anyone, forgive them, so that your Father in heaven may forgive you your sins.' Mark 11:22-26

Jesus said to them, 'Go into all the world and preach the good news to all creation. Whoever believes and is baptized will be saved, but whoever does not believe will be condemned. And these signs will accompany those who believe: In my name they will drive out demons; they will speak in new tongues; they will pick up snakes with their hands; and when they drink deadly poison, it will not hurt them at all; they will place their hands on sick people, and they will get well.' Mark 16:15-18

Jesus replied, 'I saw Satan fall like lightning from heaven. I have given you authority to trample on snakes and scorpions and to overcome all the power of the enemy; nothing will harm you.' Luke 10:18-19

Then *(after the ascension of Jesus Christ into heaven)* the disciples went out and preached everywhere, and the Lord worked with them and confirmed his word by the signs that accompanied it. Mark 16:20

It is a reasonable expectation for the followers of the Lamb / Jesus Christ of this age, to be able to have signs that accompany their message.

Now there was a man of the Pharisees named Nicodemus, a member of the Jewish ruling council. He came to Jesus at night and said, 'Rabi, we know you are a teacher who has come from God. For no one could perform the miraculous signs you are doing if God were not with them.' John 3:1-2

Jesus did many other miraculous signs in the presence of his disciples, which are not recorded in this book. John 20:30

Jesus did many other things as well. If every one of them were written down, I suppose that even the whole world would not have room for the books that would be written. John 21:25

Greater things than what Jesus did

Jesus said: **'I tell you the truth, anyone who has faith in me will do what I have been doing. They will do even greater things than these** because I am going to the Father. And I will do whatever you ask in my name, so that the Son may bring glory to the Father. You may ask me for anything in my name, and I will do it.' John 14:12-14

The same John that is John the Revelator, wrote the gospel of John and recorded this truth.

Jesus Christ's promise is that the followers of the Lamb / Jesus Christ, will do even greater things than Jesus Christ did, when the request is made in Jesus Christ's name. This prophecy has yet to be fulfilled in its entirety.

2 Kings 2:1-18 documented Elijah being taken into heaven. The mantle of Elijah fell upon Elisha who was granted twice the amount of Holy Spirit power on him than Elijah was given. But it will be Elijah who returns to be a witness on the temple mount, not Elisha. It is plausible that while the two witnesses will be sent to the people of Israel to again tell them the message that Jesus Christ is the promised and prophesied messiah, there will be many around the world who will be demonstrating the power of God Most High with an almost equal effectiveness.

Elijah – Elisha was just one example of one of the strategies of God Most High. It seems that this strategy in the midst of spiritual conflict, consists of convincing the red dragon / serpent / Satan, Inc. that the power of God Most High that was exhibited through the conflicts that Elijah faced, came back with an even greater level of activity in the second round (Elisha with double the power).

This strategy of increasing power through subsequent encounters, was demonstrated in the interaction of Moses with Pharaoh beginning with the demonstration of the snakes, the ten plagues, and the greatest demonstration of three million people crossing the sea on dry ground with the subsequent drowning of Pharaoh's military.

The promise to the followers of the Lamb / Jesus Christ that will be living during the era of the time of Jacob's Trouble was that they will experience an era of repeating those miracles / mighty acts of God Most High. Every time that God Most High comes back with mighty acts, the most recent mighty acts outshine the previous mighty acts.

Just as the Israelites were surprised and amazed at God's activity with Pharaoh and just as Ahab and Jezebel were surprised, amazed and angered with God's activity through Elijah, the era of the time of Jacob's Trouble will *cause surprise and amazement for those who oppose God's holy people and the kingdom of heaven.*

In the culture of the early apostolic church: Everyone was filled with awe, and many wonders and miraculous signs were done by the apostles. Acts 2:43

The many wonders and miraculous signs were that were accomplished by the apostles, was not disclosed in the biblical record. If they would have been greater acts than what Jesus had performed, we would have been recorded.

The power of the Holy Spirit poured out in these days

Jesus said: 'When the Spirit of truth comes, the Spirit will guide you into all truth. The Spirit of truth will not speak on his own; the Spirit of truth will speak only what the Spirit of truth hears, and the Spirit of truth will tell you what is yet to come.' John 16:13

Jesus said: 'In that day you will no longer ask me anything. I tell you the truth, my Father will give you whatever you ask in my name… Ask and you will receive, and your joy will be complete.' John 16:23-24

The Lord declared: 'And it will come to pass afterward, that I will pour out my Spirit on all flesh – Your son and your daughters shall prophesy. Your old men will dream dreams. Your young men will see visions.'

'And also on my servants, both men and women, <u>in those days will I pour out my Spirit</u>.'

'And I will show wonders in the heavens and in the earth, blood and fire and pillars of smoke.'

'The sun shall be turned into darkness, and the moon into blood, before the coming of the great and awesome day of the Lord.' Joel 2:28-32 translated *(Joel was a prophet of Judah (fl. ~800 to 700 BC))*

'In the last days, God says, I will pour out my Spirit on all people. Your sons and daughters will prophesy, your young men will see visions, and your old men will dream dreams. Even on my servants, both men and women, I will pour out my Spirit in those days, and they will prophesy. I will show wonders in the heaven above and signs on the earth below, blood and fire and billows of smoke. The sun will be turned to darkness and the moon to blood before the coming of the great and glorious Day of the Lord. And everyone who calls on the name of the Lord will be saved.' Acts 2:17-21 *(On the Day of*

Pentecost immediately following the resurrection of Jesus Christ, 30 AD)

There were so many pieces of the prophecy of Joel and the prophecy of Peter recorded in Acts, that have yet to be experienced.

The full pouring out of God Most High's Spirit has certainly not been realized. On the day of Pentecost following the resurrection of Jesus Christ, the world received a taste of the flavor of what that will look like. Some of this prophecy will not be completed until Jesus Christ actually returns. But in the time in between, during the era of the time of Jacob's Trouble, the pouring out of the Holy Spirit will be a drastic contrast to what the world experiences now. It will begin with the Holy Spirit being poured out dramatically on the followers of the Lamb / Jesus Christ.

Sons and daughters will prophesy. Having women prophesy will be in conflict with the kingdom of Satan, Inc. / kingdom of man, where in Genesis 3:15 God Most High infused hatred between the kingdom of Satan, Inc. and women. Yes, sexism was an invention of God Most High and will be a descriptive marker for those who will appear in sheep's clothing on behalf of God Most High, but inwardly will be ravenous wolves. Women are vital to the kingdom of heaven. The kingdom of Satan, Inc. / kingdom of man will characteristically consider women to be evil; and this will be an indicator that will work to disclose which kingdom a person has pledged allegiance to, the kingdom of heaven or the kingdom of man.

Old men will dream dreams. Young men will have visions. This is a reversal of what is natural. Usually, it is the young men who dream for their future with their future ahead of them for fulfilling the dreams. Usually, it is the wiser elderly who receive the visions because they have the life experience to understand the visions they receive. But during this era of the time of Jacob's Trouble, old men will have the necessity and opportunity to dream dreams; and young men will have the wisdom to receive visions.

While Peter repeated Joel's prophecy after the crucifixion, death, resurrection and ascension of Jesus Christ on the Day of Pentecost, Joel's prophecy clearly was set to be fulfilled in the context of the era when the sun will be turned to darkness, the moon will turn to blood, etc. Joel's prophecy will be for those who live during the era of the time of Jacob's Trouble. Which means that the followers of the Lamb / Jesus Christ will need to be present for Joel and Peter's prophecy to be fulfilled.

A God who can transcend lifetimes in such a way to communicate a message, can surely accomplish whatever that God has planned to do.

Now to each person the manifestation of the Spirit is given for the common good. To one there is given through the spirit the message of wisdom, to another the message of knowledge by means of the same Spirit, to another faith by the same Spirit, to another gifts of healing by that one Spirit, to another miraculous powers, to another prophecy, to another distinguishing between spirits, to another speaking in different kinds of tongues, and to still another the interpretation of tongues. All these are the work of one and the same Spirit, and the Spirit gives to each one, just as the Spirit determines. 1 Corinthians 12:7-11

The Gifts of the Spirit will be more important during the era of the time of Jacob's Trouble than at any previous point in human history.

Follow the way of love and eagerly desire spiritual gifts, especially the gift of prophecy. ...
Everyone who prophesies speaks to people for their strengthening, encouragement and comfort. 1 Corinthians 14:1, 3

God also testified to the message of Jesus Christ by signs, wonders and various miracles, and gifts of the Holy Spirit distributed according to the will of the Holy Spirit. Hebrews 2:4

Signs, wonders, various miracles, and the gifts of the Holy Spirit will mark, will define, will empower the message of Jesus Christ through the followers of the Lamb / Jesus Christ because testifying to the message of Jesus Christ is a priority for God Most High.

Further instruction on how to better access the power of the God of the kingdom of heaven

In the presence of God and of Christ Jesus, who will judge the living and the dead, and in view of his appearing and his kingdom, I give you this charge:

Preach the Word. Be prepared in season and out of season. Correct, rebuke and encourage – with great patience and careful instruction.

For the time will come when people will not put up with sound doctrine. Instead, to suit their own desires, they will gather around them a great number of teachers to say what their itching ears want to hear. They will turn their ears away from the truth and turn aside to myths.

But you, keep your head in all situations, endure hardship, do the work of an evangelist, discharge all the duties of your ministry. 2 Timothy 4:1-5

There was no time limit applied to this instruction. This instruction to discharge the duties of ministry does not end when the message is 'out of season.'

Is any one of you in trouble? They should pray. Is anyone happy? Let them sing songs of praise. Is any one of you sick? They should call the leaders of the followers of God to pray over them and anoint them with oil in the name of the Lord. And the prayer offered in faith will make the sick person well; the Lord will raise him up. If they have sinned, they will be forgiven. Therefore, confess your sins and pray for each other so that you may be healed. The prayer of a righteous person is powerful and effective. James 5:13-17

In order to have God Most High in right relationship with us so that miracles and healing can work, we must be in right relationship with God Most High.

The Lord Almighty said: 'Therefore, the Lord said, 'This people draw near me with their mouths and with their lips to honor me, but their hearts are far removed from me, and their fear toward me is taught as the commandment produced by men.'

'Look therefore, I will again do a marvelous work among this people.'

'Among this people, I will do a marvelous and wonderous work.'

'For the wisdom of their wise men will perish. And the understanding of their intelligent men will be hidden.' Isaiah 29:13-14 translated

Possibly the greatest miracle of all that will take place during the era of the time of Jacob's Trouble will be the transformation of the hearts of the people of Israel. The people of Israel, and many of the Gentiles who may have a

modicum of faith in messiah / Jesus Christ, currently go through the motions of honoring God Most High.

The two witnesses will arrive with sackcloth for clothes. It will be a demonstration by God Most High of the message that clothes do not make the man. It is God's Holy Spirit within the man that makes the man.

The era of the time of Jacob's Trouble will be rife with torment, devastation, change at a level that the world has never known before and never will experience again. But in the midst of all of this, God Most High will provide wonder upon wonder because at the core of everything that God Most High does, God Most High is intent upon winning back the hearts of the people of Israel. This was the core of the covenant that God Most High made with Abraham and Sarah. This never-ending love of God Most High was the most overriding characteristic of God Most High, and it was the characteristic that is obfuscated by evil. As evil is peeled back, this unfathomable love of God Most High will be all that is revealed.

The most astonishing time in all human history to be alive in, will be during the era of the time of Jacob's Trouble. All previous work that God Most High has done, will pale in comparison to the astounding wonders of wonders that God Most High has planned for the benefit of the people of Israel and for the followers of the Lamb / Jesus Christ.

www.ingramcontent.com/pod-product-compliance
Lightning Source LLC
Chambersburg PA
CBHW071956150426
43194CB00008B/898